POWER AND NEGOTIATION IN ORGANIZATIONS

Readings, Cases, and Exercises

Edited by:

Steven C. Currall
Rice University

Deanna Geddes
Temple University

Stuart M. Schmidt
Temple University

Arthur Hochner
Temple University

KENDALL/HUNT PUBLISHING COMPANY
4050 Westmark Drive   Dubuque, Iowa 52002

Contents

3 Negotiation: Assessment of the Parties   161

A. Self Assessment

B. Assessing Others

C. Cultural Factors in Assessing Others

4 Negotiation Agenda and Strategy   237

A. The Negotiation Agenda: Priorities and Objectives

B.   Adversarial versus Cooperative Negotiation Strategies

5 Getting What You Want: Using Negotiation Tactics   329

A.   Influence Tactics

B.   Ethical Issues Relating to Negotiation Tactics

6 Communication Issues in Negotiation 401

7 Third Party Intervention: Mediation 435

Preface

In teaching undergraduate and graduate courses on power and negotiation, we needed to make these abstract concepts more concrete and personally relevant. To do this, we have assembled a collection of readings, cases, and exercises that offer a practical perspective with regard to power and negotiation. Our emphasis is on basic principles of power and negotiation that operate across organizational settings. That is, the book is not restricted to, for example, collective bargaining or buyer-seller negotiations. The book can be used in undergraduate or graduate courses in management, psychology, sociology, industrial relations, communication, political science, or education.

The readings, cases, and exercises are designed to teach students both analytical skills and behavioral skills. Analytical skills give insight into the causes of organizational conflict, sources of power in organizations, and social psychological factors that influence negotiator behavior. Behavioral skills are necessary to successfully negotiate and be influential. Career achievement in today's organizations is increasingly tied to these behavioral skills. Moreover, employees with strong negotiation skills facilitate organizational effectiveness, efficiency, and productivity.

How is this book different from others of its kind? The main difference is that our approach does not deal exclusively with negotiation. Instead, our approach has been to set the stage for understanding negotiation by beginning with a fundamental question: "What properties of relationships in organizations make negotiation central in day-to-day organizational life?" Thus, as a prelude to the nuts-and-bolts of how to be an effective negotiator, the book's readings give emphasis to interdependence, power, and conflict as the properties of relationships in organizations that make negotiation skills indispensable. This focus provides a broad context from which students may better understand the necessity of developing negotiation skills.

Of the three relational issues (i.e., interdependence, power, and conflict), the greatest number of readings deal with power. Power, the capacity to change another's behavior or attitudes despite their resistance, and its related issue, politics, are facts of organizational life. This truism reflects our theoretical focus that stems from a political model of organizations.[1] Bacharach and Lawler (1982) state that:

> Organizations are neither the rational, harmonious entities celebrated in managerial theory nor the arenas of apocalyptic class conflict projected by Marxists. Rather, it may be argued, a more suitable notion lies somewhere between those two—a concept of organizations as politically negotiated orders. Adopting this view we can observe organizational actors in their daily transactions perpetually bargaining, repeatedly forming and reforming coalitions, and constantly availing themselves of influence tactics (p. 1).

The political model of organizations argues that negotiation is a central component of relationships in work settings.[2] Negotiation is "a process of potentially opportunistic interaction by which two or more parties, with some apparent conflict, seek to do better through jointly decided action than they could otherwise."[3] Intensive negotiation training offered by employers and the rise of negotiation courses in preeminent American business schools evince that, due to the political nature of organizational life, negotiation skills are seen as a necessity by both practitioners and academics alike.

---

1   Cyert, R.M. & March, J.G. (1963). *A behavioral theory of the firm.* Englewood Cliffs, NJ: Prentice-Hall. Bacharach, S.B. & Lawler, E.J. (1982). *Power and politics in organizations: The social psychology of conflict, coalitions and bargaining.* San Francisco: Jossey-Bass.
2   Kochan, T.A. & Verma, A. (1983). *Negotiations in organizations: Blending industrial relations and organizational behavior approaches.* In M. Bazerman and R. Lewicki (Eds.) *Negotiating in organizations.* Beverly Hills: Sage. Lax, D. & Sebinius, J. (1986). *The manager as negotiator.* New York: Free Press.
3   Lax & Sebinius (1986) p. 11.

Each separate reading has corresponding study questions that help students focus on the reading's central points. In addition to readings, each section of the book contains cases or exercises designed to bring to life the concepts discussed in the readings. Instructor's materials containing teaching notes on cases and exercises are provided under separate cover.

The book is divided into eight related sections. Section 1 lays the groundwork for the rest of the book by introducing the concepts of power, politics, and negotiation. Section 2 overviews three properties of relationships within organizations, namely, interdependence, power, and conflict.

The sequence of material for the remainder of the book follows an order one might use if preparing for actual negotiations. Section 3 begins the focus on how to be an effective negotiator. Readings on self assessment in Section 3-A give students insight into factors influencing their own behavior. Extending the "assessment" theme, Section 3-B discusses how judgments are made about the other negotiator, and Section 3-C expands this topic by including material on how cross-cultural factors impinge on judgments of one's opponent. Because of the prevailing frequency of international business negotiations, cross-cultural factors are especially important.

Section 4 addresses negotiation agenda and strategy. Section 4-A explains how one prepares an agenda and how priorities and objectives are set. Section 4-B discusses the formation of negotiation strategies. Strategies are distinguished as primarily adversarial or cooperative, although most real negotiations are a mix of the two. The terms "adversarial" and "cooperative" are broad umbrella concepts akin to distributive and integrative bargaining as used in the literature on collective Bargaining.[4]

Section 5-A concerns using negotiation tactics. Here, an influence perspective on negotiation is introduced along with a range of tactics from flattery to humor. Section 5-B addresses ethics, a critical and increasingly challenging issue with respect to the choice of negotiation tactics.

Section 6 covers communication issues, including how cross-cultural factors affect communication in negotiations. The final section, Section 7, focuses on how third party interventions, such as mediation, facilitate agreements and unblock impasses.

Finally, we want to acknowledge the invaluable help of several individuals. We are grateful to colleagues who shared their ideas and materials with us: Max Bazerman (Northwestern University), Jeanne Brett (Northwestern University), Peter Cappelli (University of Pennsylvania), Lewis Brown Griggs (Griggs Productions), David Kipnis (Temple University), and Roy J. Lewicki (Ohio State University). Our research assistants, Andrea Brooks, Frank Linnehan, and Anita Verghese provided first-rate help with the background research for the book. During the preparation for this book Steve Currall was supported by the National Center for the Educational Quality of the Workforce.

---

4   Walton, R. E. & McKersie, R. B. (1965). *A behavioral theory of labor negotiations: An analysis of a social interaction system.* New York: McGraw-Hill.

SECTION 1

Introduction to Power and Negotiation in Organizations

This section sets the stage for the book by suggesting that much of day-to-day work in organizations depends on social relations, that people use a variety of political behaviors in their social relations, and that negotiating to resolve conflict in social relations is a central feature of a manager's job.

In **"Organizational Life: There is More to Work Than Working,"** Schmidt maintains that the "mechanistic" view of organizations, held by many technical professionals, is unsatisfactory because it neglects the importance of social relations at work. Schmidt argues that members of organizations must use influence tactics and relationship-building, combined with technical competence, to achieve organizational objectives and to develop successful careers.

Farrell and Peterson, in **"Patterns of Political Behaviors in Organizations,"** describe the political behaviors individuals engage in as (1) being directed toward individuals within the organization or outside the organization (i.e., internal-external), (2) being directed toward individuals above or at the same level in the organizational hierarchy (i.e., vertical-lateral), or (3) being ethically acceptable or unacceptable (i.e., legitimate-illegitimate).

In highlighting the importance of conflict resolution and negotiating skills for managers, Lax and Sebenius (**"The Manager as Negotiator"**) set out the critical components of negotiations. They provide a brief case study illustrating the utility of being a good negotiator. Lax and Sebenius argue that, whether managers are dealing with superiors or subordinates, they must use negotiating skills to achieve their goals.

Never trained in negotiation, Williams (**"How I Learned to Stop Worrying and Love Negotiating"**) says when she started negotiating, her strategy was backwards. That is, she prepared for negotiations by focusing first on her goals and alternatives. Now, she claims that an approach which ingnores the needs and feelings of the other side is extremely risky and ultimately can destroy valuable business alliances. Her definition of negotiation? "A business relationship in action."

* * *

1

Organizational Life: There Is More to Work Than Working

Stuart M. Schmidt
**Human Resource Administration
School of Business and Management
Temple University**

Technical professionals who solely follow a rational model may neglect social relations at work. These relations are important for achieving objectives. Ambitious employees use a variety of tactics for influencing others. A successful career depends on building relationships and using organizational politics in addition to technical competence.

John Danforth, industrial engineer:

For five years I kept my nose to the grindstone . . . My supervisors agreed that my performance was excellent . . . I hardly ever went out for lunch . . . I usually stayed late finishing projects while others were off having a beer . . . I often came in on Saturdays to work while most of my coworkers played golf . . . Where did all this work get me? I have not moved up in five years while many of those I started with have been promoted . . . Promotions are political around here.

John Danforth, like most technical professionals, used a rational model of his firm to guide his behavior. More often than not, operation research (OR) professionals are rationally oriented. They value logical systems and are comfortable abiding by organizational rules. Their training and their personalities suit them to structured settings. Applying the rational model to organizational life, they believe that to do well and get ahead they should produce results and excel at problem solving. They are concerned first and foremost with their work.

Adherents of rational models usually use a mechanistic metaphor to describe organizational life. They see an organization as an engine, using such expressions as "running smoothly" . . . "they mesh well" . . . "build a head of steam" . . . "well-balanced" . . . "well oiled." They picture organizational life as inanimate and mechanical. In their minds, effective employees are well-tooled parts assembled to function in concert as a smoothly running engine. This mechanistic metaphor has no place for the emotions, attitudes, needs, or conflicts of human beings [Morgan 1986]. If anything, human emotions, needs, and wants are seen as undesirable intrusions in the work place. At best social relations are considered transitory aberrations. Such human deviations are discredited and avoided.

Technical professionals who hold this mechanistic view consider socializing at work inappropriate. They regard personal banter and relationships as nonproductive. They communicate through logical arguments backed by facts, figures, and data. People who adhere to a mechanistic view of organizational life believe that excellent performance will be recognized and rewarded. Since rules are formally articulated, they think it reasonable to expect those who follow the rules to be rewarded. They do not engage in socializing or self-promotion, because hard work will win the day. But will it?

An alternative to the rational, mechanistic view of organizational life is a political perspective [Morgan 1986]. Typically the term political has pejorative connotations. We associate sleazy and disputable activities with the word political. The popular belief is that decent, hardworking, competent people need not stoop to being political. Indeed, many believe that people with any decency flee from political situations.

However, sociologists use the term political without negative connotations. A person with a political perspective recognizes that organizations consist of people who have different perceptions, needs, abilities, objectives, preferences, and power. Furthermore, their interests may legitimately conflict with one another. Those with a political perspective try to describe organizational life as it is rather than as some would like it to be. As long as organizations are designed and staffed by people, they will have human characteristics, for better or for worse. March and Simon [1958] pointed out that human decision makers operate from rather limited information bases, process information inefficiently, and may perceive and interpret the same information very differently from one another. This means that decision making will be, at best, only subjectively rational and subject to human emotions, selective perception, and human frailties.

Going back to John Danforth's situation, promotions may go to those seen as amiable team players rather than to the hardest workers. The criteria for promotion may have been quite different from what Danforth imagined. While he may have been fulfilling his job description as an industrial engineer, Danforth may not have been behaving in a manner appropriate for a supervisory position. As we go up organizational hierarchies, the work requires more social skills and fewer technical skills. By focusing exclusively on his work, and not socializing, Danforth insured that no one knew him and that no one observed his ability to get along with others. He may have been seen as a hermit who was unable to function with others.

Did John Danforth have to play politics to get ahead? That depends on how we understand organizational politics. Politics can be thought of as nonrational tactics designed to influence others, especially those at higher levels, to promote or maintain one's vital interests. These tactics usually include ingratiation, bargaining, and the formation of coalitions [Kipnis, Schmidt, and Wilkinson 1980]. Almost every strategy except using logic, facts, figures, and data usually is considered nonrational. Even friendliness can be viewed with suspicion or contempt by those who hold the rational, mechanistic view.

Researchers find that approximately 60 percent of those asked reported that organizational politics occur quite frequently in their organizations [Gandz and Murray 1980]. Politics pervade organizational life.

People play politics in most organizations, more often at middle and upper levels than at lower levels. Gandz and Murray [1980] found over 90 percent of those asked reported that

playing politics was more frequent at the middle and upper levels than at lower levels.

People play politics more frequently in some functional areas than in others and among staff positions more than among line positions. Researchers discovered that politics were most prevalent in marketing, sales, manufacturing, and personnel departments [Madison et al. 1980]. They were least prevalent in accounting, finance, and production [Madison et al. 1980].

Even across functions, managers report a higher level of playing politics in certain organizational situations than in others. Two studies found the highest reported incidence of politics in situations where resources were being allocated: reorganizations, personnel changes, budget allocations, and so forth.

Thus, even though people play politics in most organizations, they do so more frequently in certain functional areas and situations than in others, typically in departments and situations that have few standard operating procedures or rules and during periods of organizational change.

Organizational politics is virtually inherent in organizational life. Playing politics is a normal part of functioning in an organization, not an aberration. Playing politics is a multistage process that encompasses the situation, one's objectives, the other players, and their actions.

Organizational politics begin with aspiring, motivated people who want to either obtain more resources and status or defend what they have. They may want a promotion or a share of the department's budget. Ambitious people who are seeking to get ahead are most eager to play politics, to be successful either in their own interest or in the interest of their organizational unit. They have objectives and goals to achieve; needs to fulfill. Ambitious people are a necessary but not sufficient precondition to politics being played.

Burned out, alienated employees who are not ambitious seldom play politics. They tend to be docile, compliant people who are not trying to promote their own interests or those of their organizations.

Staffing an organization with unambitious people minimizes the probability of organizational politics but insures organizational stagnation. Docile, compliant employees, while easy to manage, are not innovators, nor do they generate organizational energy.

People's objectives in playing politics are not necessarily self-serving, like obtaining a raise. Ambitious employees may play politics to benefit their work groups or departments as well as themselves. Many managers are friendly and form coalitions with people at higher organizational levels to obtain resources for their work units. Others may engage in horse trading to get work done. Their objectives are in the organizational interest. True, some may be merely seeking narrow personal benefits, such as more pay or less work. Still others may participate in politics to demonstrate that they are team players and, hence, worthy of promotion. In all cases, ambitious employees play politics to accomplish their objectives.

What situations foster people playing politics? Research indicates that departments and situations marked by few standard operating procedures are marked by political behavior [Allen and Porter 1983]. Such departments and situations lack information about how to pursue objectives or about the efficacy of rational tactics. The resulting uncertainty about organizational processes and outcomes encourages political behavior. An example of such a situation is a company reorganization, an infrequent occurrence with profound consequences for the employees affected, about which they suffer a great deal of uncertainty.

Uncertainty is disconcerting. We try to reduce or avoid it, especially when our vital interests are threatened. We want to know the rules for action. In organizational settings, ambitious employees rely on predictability in objectives. They want an organizationally sanctioned way to accomplish their goals. However in the absence of standard operating procedures, people expand their range of tactics for influencing others. They don't just write logical memos and wait for their good performance to be noticed. They hedge their bets.

Employees try to get their way with decision makers by using a wide range of tactics. Typically they try to create a favorable impression with the boss or form coalitions. Achieving success, for example, getting promoted, often depends on more than objectively measured performance. Promotions are usually based on fitting-in with the administrative team. Adequate technical performance may be a necessary condition, but it is not sufficient. John Danforth's coworkers actively sought out their boss and tried to create a good impression. They wanted to be seen as team players in tune with the boss. To accomplish this, they had to make themselves known. They socialized with the boss. Sometimes merely creating an opportunity for getting acquainted is enough to create a good impression.

Other times, employees have to work more actively to create a favorable impression. They may try to make themselves appear more similar to the boss by wearing clothes similar to hers or his. They may talk about topics of interest to the boss and espouse similar ideas [Jones 1964]. Social psychologists have found that such ingratiating tactics are pervasive in social relations and are often quite effective, though not without costs [Kipnis and Schmidt 1988]. People tend to think well of those whom they see as similar to themselves. They may, however, suspect the motives or competence of someone who relies too heavily on friendliness.

People need to create a good impression before their logical arguments and data are taken seriously. An excellent example of the use of friendliness combined with reason is exhibited by the typical lawyer in a jury trial. First lawyers sell themselves to juries by being friendly and sympathetic. After establishing their credibility, they present their logical arguments and evidence. Effective lawyers know that reason alone is not persuasive. The same tactic works in our organizations.

Unfortunately, many OR professionals neglect or are oblivious to social relations that can influence others, and they pay the price of dissatisfying careers. They rely on a limited repertoire of tactics, mainly reason, believing that anything else is unsavory and inappropriate. Instead of acting according to the rules of an organization created, staffed, and managed by people, OR professionals are often trapped in illusions of how organizations ought to function.

Learning to play politics is important for OR professionals in industry. They are usually in staff positions, and these positions typically entail high levels of politics. They also institute changes that affect others in their organizations. Those affected often offer stiff resistance. To be effective in their complex jobs and really influence others, OR professionals must use a wide range of tactics that go beyond mere reason. They must move beyond the mechanistic view of organizations and learn to establish effective social relationships in getting the job done. •

References

Allen, Robert W. and Porter, Lyman W. 1983, *Organizational Influence Processes,* Scott, Foresman and Company, Glenview, Illinois.

Gandz, Jeffrey and Murray, Victor V. 1980, "The experience of workplace politics," *Academy of Management Journal,* Vol. 23, No. 2, pp. 237–251.

Jones, Edward E. 1964, *Ingratiation,* Appelton-Century/Crofts, Division of Prentice Hall, Englewood Cliffs, New Jersey.

Kipnis, David and Schmidt, Stuart M. 1988, "Upward influence styles: Relationship with performance evaluation, salary, and stress," *Administrative Science Quarterly*, Vol. 33, No. 4, pp. 528–542.

Kipnis, David; Schmidt, Stuart M.; and Wilkinson, Jan 1980, "Intraorganizational influence tactics: Explorations in getting one's way," *Journal of Applied Psychology*, Vol. 65, No. 4, pp. 440–452.

Madison, Dan L.; Allen, Robert W.; Porter, Lyman W.; Renwick, Patricia A.; and Mayes, Bronston T. 1980, "Organizational politics: An exploration of managers' perceptions," *Human Relations,* Vol. 33, No. 2, pp. 79–100.

March, James G. and Simon, Herbert A. 1958, *Organizations,* John Wiley and Sons, New York.

Morgan, Gareth 1986, *Images of Organization*, Sage Publications, Inc., Newbury Park, California.

*   *   *

Study Questions

1. What is meant "there is more to work than working?" and how does this counter assumptions of rational/mechanistic models of the organization?

2. What are organizational politics, according to Schmidt?

3. What conditions (within the workplace) increase the frequency of politicking?

Patterns of Political Behavior in Organizations

Dan Farrell
James C. Petersen
Western Michigan University

This paper suggests that despite the current renaissance of interest in organizational power and politics, organization theory neglects individual political behavior within organizations. The need for a concern for individual political behavior is explored, and three key dimensions of political behavior are suggested: internal-external, vertical-lateral, and legitimate-illegitimate. A typology based on these dimensions is proposed, and predictions about the different types of political behavior are offered.

Now that organizational scholars have discovered and explored the environment, the new growth stock appears to be organizational politics. A host of recent works (Bacharach & Lawler, 1980; Gandz & Murray, 1980; Mayes & Allen, 1977; Pfeffer, 1978, 1981; Tushman, 1977) have attempted to remedy the neglect of power and politics that scholars such as Mowday (1978) and Madison, Allen, Porter, Renwick, & Mayes (1980) have seen as characteristic of the organizational literature. Despite this upsurge of attention to politics, some aspects of political phenomena continue to be neglected in the organizational literature. This paper argues for the theoretical importance of individual political behavior, proposes three key dimensions of political behavior, and suggests a typology derived from these dimensions. Also, variables useful for predicting the form of individual political actions are suggested.

The current wave of literature on organizational power and politics may be viewed best as a "rediscovery" of politics in organizations. Issues of power and politics within organizations were central to classic organizational writers such as Weber and Michels. The development of scientific management and human relations schools, with their managerial perspectives, diverted attention to motivation and productivity. Only rarely did organizational scholars return to the issues of power and politics—for example, March (1962), and Mechanic (1962)—until the renaissance of such literature in the late 1970s.

It is difficult to account for the timing of this rediscovery. The authors do not share a single paradigm and many of the papers are, in fact, largely descriptive rather than explicitly theoretical. It is suspected, however, that among the factors behind the revival of interest in organizational power and politics is the penetration of organizations by employees socialized into politics during the protests of the 1960s. Further, political behavior in organizations recently has been highlighted against a societal background of decreasing trust in authority and by an increase in journalistic revelations of wrongdoing. Within the scholarly literature there has been an increase in Marxist and conflict theories of organizations (see the special issue of *Sociological Quarterly*, Winter, 1977). Pfeffer, for example, has observed that the dominant managerial perspective within organizational studies has neglected "one of the most important issues and activities—the conflict in preferences among organizational participants and the resulting contest over the organization" (1978, p. 29). Also, the various attacks—for example, March and Olsen (1976) and Weick (1979)—on the goal approach and the general rational model of organizations may have made political models of organizations seem more relevant.

The new wave of interest in organizational politics and organizational power is composed of several distinct types of work. First, a number of authors (Butler, Hickson, Wilson, & Axelson, 1977–78; Mayes & Allen, 1977; Tushman, 1977) have simply urged that organizations be viewed as political arenas or have provided a conceptual framework to permit such an approach. These calls for political analysis of organizations are an essential starting point. Dachler and Wilpert (1978), although not explicitly concerned with politics, provided a conceptual framework for participation in organizations. The implications of participation for democratization and the diffusion of decision making suggest that this might also be seen as a call for political analysis.

Second, the theme of power in organizations is receiving substantial attention. Although organizational theorists generally have treated power as distinct from organizational politics, the two concepts are linked theoretically and empirically. Madison et al. reported that among their sample of managers "the successful practice of organizational politics is perceived to lead to a higher level of power, and once a high level of power is attained, there is more opportunity to engage in political behavior" (1980, p. 94). Contemporary writers, in returning to the Weberian interests of power and authority, are focusing on bases of power (Salancik & Pfeffer, 1974), loci of power (Madison et al., 1980), influence processes (Mowday, 1978), and the measurement of power. Power typically is explained by linking it to environmental uncertainty and resource control. A limitation of this literature is that it provides only a partial view, focusing on either the upward or downward flow of power. The organizational literature on power would benefit from Gamson's (1968) widely acclaimed synthesis of the social control and influence literatures on power. Incorporating Gamson's work would ensure that future discussions of power would be more comprehensive and would permit greater integration of structure, authority, power, and politics.

Among the recent works on organizational politics, actual studies of political behavior are, in fact, quite rare. There are, however, studies of attributions of politicization and perceived organizational politics (Gandz & Murray, 1980; Madison et al., 1980). There also are studies of group behavior, especially interorganizational power relations for example, Salancik and Pfeffer (1974)—and coalitions— for example, Bacharach and Lawler (1980). Work on political behavior by individuals is scarce although recent research on the filing of grievances (Dalton & Todor, 1979; Muchinsky & Maassarani 1980) provides a good example.

The relative neglect of individual political behavior in the current wave of interest in organizational research seems strange. Dominant American values stress individualism and American social science typically reflects this with a heavy stress on individual behavior. Furthermore, several early articles on organizational politics (Burns, 1962; Mechanic, 1962; Strauss, 1963) dealt with political actions by individual organizational members. But these early leads have not been followed with much vigor. It is believed that the neglect of individual political behavior has three principle sources: (1) failure to distinguish required job behavior from discretionary political behavior, (2) failure to distinguish calculated from accidental political behavior, and (3) failure to distinguish clearly between macro and micro levels of analysis. Political behavior has been described as providing the "nonrational influence on decision making" (Miles, 1980, p. 154) and as existing as a "backstage" activity (Burns, 1962, p. 260). However, current definitions of organizational politics that focus on the exercise of power (Miles, 1980), the manipulation of influence (Madison et al., 1980), or the mobilization of resources in competition (Burns, 1962) do not clearly distinguish political behaviors from those actions required while filling organizational positions. The present authors agree with Mayes and Allen that "a suitable definition of organization politics must allow exclusion of routine job performance from consideration" (1977, p. 674). Porter, Allen, and Angle (1981) also exclude behaviors that are required or expected from their discussion of organizational politics, treating political behavior as discretionary. The present authors believe that political behavior resides in informal structures and relates to the promotion of self and group interests rather than being part of those formal roles regulated by organizational norms and goals. Further, examinations of political behaviors in organizations should focus on intended or overt actions by members while recognizing that unintended actions or even personal idiosyncracies may have political consequences. Friendships and romantic associations occasionally may have indirect consequences for organizational politics, but they should not be a first focus of attention. Finally, existing analyses of organizational politics blur the distinction among different units of analysis by talking about the power of individuals, units, and interorganizational networks in the same discussion. By combining macro and micro levels of analysis at the initial stage of discussion, organizational scholars fail to consider the critical issues of the distinctiveness or similarity of correlates of politics for each level of analysis as well as the linkages between different levels.

Individual Political Behavior

In order to focus attention on individuals, it is suggested that the term political behavior be reserved for political activities by individual organization members. Political behavior in organizations may be defined as those activities that are not required as part of one's organizational role but that influence, or attempt to influence, the distribution of advantages and disadvantages within the organization. This definition draws on Froman's (1962) resource conceptualization of politics. It provides a definition of individual political behavior general enough to encompass such diverse examples of organizational politics as whistleblowing, filing of grievances, using symbolic protest gestures, spreading rumors, leaking information to the media, and filing lawsuits.

These political behaviors within organizations, although widely recognized by organization members, have not been integrated into organizational theory. Development of an organizational analogue to political participation in societies promises to have important implications for theory development. A brilliant example of an organizational analogy drawn from another social unit is Albert Hirschman's (1970) seminal work, *Exit, Voice and Loyalty: Responses to Decline in Firms, Organizations, and States*. Political scientists and political sociologists have long recognized that one of the most basic political acts is the "personalized contact" (Verba, Nie, & Kim, 1971) in search of either a social or an individualized outcome. Hirschman (1970) referred to this type of interest articulation as "voice" and demonstrated that it could be applied with equal utility in various social groups. In a recent exposition, Kolarska and Aldrich (1980) refined voice by distinguishing between indirect and direct voice. Direct voice refers to appeals to authorities within the focal organization; indirect voice refers to appeals to outside authorities or agents. In subtle ways voting is an essential part of many organizations. Zaleznik (1970) argues that the flow of capital

funds and subordinate enthusiasm for manager's projects constitute referenda. Further, the process of leadership selection and control of authority in business and other organizations can resemble, under some conditions, the campaign and election procedures of other political communities (Lipset, Trow, & Coleman, 1956). When problems arise with internal processes, proxy fights and boardroom showdowns often are the organizational counterparts to recalls and ethics committee investigations. The incorporation of these and similar groups of behaviors not only supplements the rational model but also links organizational theory to a rich empirical tradition.

Patterns of Political Behavior

Given the great variety of political behavior within organizations and the substantial amount of work remaining to be done in mapping its diversity, it is premature to propose an exhaustive set of dimensions of political behavior. Instead, proposed here is the consideration of three key dimensions of political behavior that are clearly useful in classifying political activities in organizations: the internal-external dimension, the vertical-lateral dimension, and the legitimate-illegitimate dimension. These dimensions represent distinct continuua along which political activities may be ordered. They reflect tactical choices that organizational members make in seeking resources or mobilizing available resources to influence the distribution of advantages and disadvantages within the organization.

The internal-external dimension of political behavior is concerned with the focus of resources sought by those engaging in political behavior in organizations. In cases such as whistleblowing, lawsuits, leaking information to the media, or forming alliances with persons outside the focal organization, organization members attempt to expand the resources available for mobilization by going outside the boundaries of the organization and attempting to involve "outsiders." Internal political behaviors, on the other hand, employ resources already within the organization, as in the exchange of favors, trading agreements, reprisals, obstructionism, symbolic protest gestures, "touching bases," forming alliances with other organization members and, in coercive organizations, riots and mutinies. It seems likely that organizational members may progress from internal to external activities as they come to believe that success is possible only if resources outside the organization can be mobilized. As Kolarska and Aldrich note, however, appeals to outside authorities or interest groups (indirect voice) may be resorted to for a variety of reasons:

People may use indirect voice after direct voice fails, when they are afraid of using direct voice, when they do not believe in the effectiveness of direct voice or when they do not know how to use direct voice (1980, p. 44).

It is contended here that external political behavior will be attempted more often by lower participants in organizations or by those with lower levels of power because they are most likely to expect defeat if conflicts are resolved without introducing outside resources. As Weinstein has observed, whistleblowing may be seen as "attempts to change a bureaucracy by those who work within the organization but do not have any authority" (1979, p. 2).

Hierarchy is a dominant feature of most organizations and the vertical-lateral dimension of political behavior recognizes the difference between influence processes relating superiors to subordinates and those relating equals. Such political activities as complaining to a supervisor, bypassing the chain of command, apple polishing, and mentor-protege activities are best seen as vertical political behavior. Mechanic's (1962) discussion of sources of power of lower organizational participants points out that implicit trading agreements often develop between physicians and ward attendants in situations in which attendants relieve the M.D.s of many obligations and duties in return for increased power over patients.

Lateral political behaviors have received less systematic attention but would include exchange of favors, offering help, coalition organizing, and talking to an occupational peer outside the organization. Some examples also can be found in the leadership literature under discussion of lateral relations (Hunt & Osborn, 1981; Osborn & Hunt, 1974; Sayles, 1964).

These "exchanges" between a leader and those at or near his own organizational level, outside his own chain of command, are quite

often important but often neglected. While we call this aspect of leadership "lateral relations," perhaps a more common term is "politics." Regardless of the label used, these exchanges can build discretion by providing a more consistent flow of varied resources, reducing uncertainty and/or increasing independence or autonomy (Hunt & Osborn, 1980, p. 57).

Dalton's (1959) classic study of managers recognized the importance of discretionary lateral political behaviors. Employees of the Milo Company were quickly socialized regarding the importance of Masonic and Yacht Club memberships When executives are appraised for promotion, political skills are considered in addition to formal competence because of the need to "utilize and aid necessary cliques, and control dangerous ones" (Dalton, 1959, p. 181). In his discussion of lateral relations among purchasing agents, Strauss observed that "to some extent agents operate on the principle of reward your friends, punish your enemies," and are involved in a network of exchange of favors—and sometimes even reprisals (1963, p. 174). Lateral political actions may occur at all levels of organizations although it seems likely that those at lower levels, lacking substantial resources, may be highly motivated to increase their power by joining forces with peers. In large pyramidal organizations, middle level management would seem to have the most opportunities to engage in vertical political behaviors.

The final dimension, legitimate-illegitimate, acknowledges that in organizations, as in states, distinctions are made between normal everyday politics and extreme political behavior that violates the "rules of the game." Though unofficial and unauthorized, organizational politics is widely recognized as a reality by organizational participants, especially those who like to feel they are "playing hardball." The rules of the game that develop in organizations typically rule out certain kinds of actions as too dangerous or threatening to the organizations. Kolarska and Aldrich report, for example, that research in Poland "uncovered the existence of a set of moral norms regulating interorganizational exchange. One norm concerned the impropriety of using forms of voice such as lawsuits, press leaks, and appeals to supervising organizations (indirect voice)"

(1980, p. 52). Such norms, of course, change and evolve, and one would hardly expect a young executive to respond to a symbolic office protest with quite the horror of the stereotypical gray flannel-suited manager. Political behaviors widely accepted as legitimate would certainly include exchanging favors, "touching bases," forming coalitions, and seeking sponsors at upper levels. Less legitimate behaviors would include whistleblowing, revolutionary coalitions, threats, and sabotage. During the Vietnam War, another illegitimate activity received considerable publicity—the killing of officers in military units ("fragging"). Legitimate politics typically is expected to be engaged in by those at upper levels of organizations and by those who are strongly committed to the organization. Illegitimate political behavior is likely to be action taken by alienated members and by those who feel they have little to lose.

A Typology of Political Behavior

A cross-tabulation of the three dimensions of political behavior (internal-external, vertical-lateral, and legitimate-illegitimate) permits the development of a multidimensional typology of political behavior in organizations. Cross-classifying these three dichotomized dimensions yields an 8-celled collocation. Despite the renewed interest in organizational power and politics, no other system has emerged that explored the variety and interrelationships of these behaviors. The need to provide institutionalized typology offered by Mayes and Allen (1977) organized organizational politics relative to normal job behaviors, but it did not deal with specific political behaviors. The examples provided in Figure 1 are not exhaustive of all political actions in organizations, but they include those forms of political behavior that have received scholarly and journalistic attention. In addition, the three dimensions are sufficiently general to make the typology inclusive of all forms of organizational political behavior.

It is contended that the four types of political behavior included in the "legitimate" category include the vast majority of all organizational political actions. Cell I behaviors, which are normal internal political behaviors, would, it seems, be most frequent in organizations with large differences in rewards, in tall organizations, and in those in which participation in

decisions is limited. Under such conditions obstructionism is a common tactic by which lower participants resist organizational policies and decisions through inaction or excessive adherence to rules. Lateral political behaviors, such as those described in Cell II, can be expected to increase under loose supervision, if there is more equal positional power, and in nonline-and-staff organizations (Cleland, 1967).

Figure 1: A Typology of Political Behavior in Organizations

LEGITIMATE		ILLEGITIMATE	
Vertical	Lateral	Vertical	Lateral
I	II	V	VI
Direct voice	Coalition forming	Sabotage	Threats
Complain to supervisor	Exchanging favors	Symbolic protests	
Bypassing chain of command	Reprisals	Mutinies	
Obstruction-ism		Riots	
III	IV	VII	VIII
Lawsuits	Talk with counterpart from another organization	Whistle-blowing	Organizational duplicity
	Outside professional activity		Defections

External-vertical behaviors such as lawsuits or indirect voice (Cell III) generally occur in areas in which the legitimacy of conflict is well established. The growth of work related regulatory agencies such as N.L.R.B., E.E.O.C., and O.S.H.A. is an indication of increasing social recognition of the means for resolving recurring disputes. Through occupational and informal contacts with those outside the focal organization (Cell IV), organizational members frequently gain access to information and other power resources.

Such contacts, though not required, are accepted behavior for higher participants.

Unlike legitimate political behaviors, illegitimate actions pose the very real risk of loss of membership or extreme sanctions. Mutinies and riots are the most dramatic examples of vertical-internal illegitimate behavior (Cell V). Related but frequently overlooked are symbolic protests by organizational members. Unorthodox dress, button wearing, and "blue flu" may be miniature forms of organizational revolt. A form of illegitimate behavior that, in contrast, has attracted great journalistic attention is whistleblowing (Cell VII). This action, which also has been called "internal muckraking" (Peters & Branch, 1972), occurs when organizational members go public and release to the media details of organizational misconduct, neglect, or irresponsibility that jeopardize the public interest. Organizational defections (Cell VIII) occur when executives move to a competitor or begin their own firms, abandoning loyalty to the first firm. In cases of organizational duplicity, however, there is dual membership and uncertain loyalties. A classic example is the dedicated journalist who dons "bunny ears" to write a good story.

Predicting Types of Political Behavior

Empirical studies of the process by which individuals select the types of political behavior in which they engage have not been conducted. An exchange framework, however, permits certain predictions about such choices. An exchange approach is especially appropriate to the study of political behavior because exchange theory emphasizes the person-organization relationship and also stresses the distribution of scarce resources (advantages and disadvantages). The use of four abstract concepts allows one to describe, from the perspective of the organizational actor, the context of the political exchange. Furthermore, these four abstract variables permit the incorporation of a substantial amount of previous research.

Investments

Investments encompass those resources that organizational participants commit to a relationship in the expectation of increased future benefit (Farrell & Rusbult, 1981). Typically, workers become invested in a firm as they acquire nonportable training, friendship, and seniority. These "side-bets" as Becker (1960) calls them, decrease an individual's propensity to leave an organization by increasing the cost of exit. The present authors believe that investments also lessen the likelihood of an individual engaging in illegitimate political behavior because such behavior places the investments at risk and there exist expectations of better outcomes in the future. Those with low investments, on the other hand, have little to lose by illegitimate political behavior. In some cases investments can be induced. Kolarska and Aldrich cite the action of authorities who attempt "to socialize the dissidents into the special organizational knowledge of the inner professional circle" (1980, p. 51).

Investments may have other effects in directing political behavior. Vertical behavior may be increased, Mechanic (1962) argues, because investments in specialized skills and knowledge produce dependence; in this manner upper level participants lose power to technical staff. The likelihood of internal or external political behavior also can be shaped by the extent of investments. When investments are high and portable as in professions or what Thompson (1967) calls "late-ceiling" occupations, employees seek advantage by going outside the organization. In early-ceiling occupations, however, individuals "seek leverage in the negotiation process through collective action" (Thompson, 1967, p. 113).

Alternatives

Alternatives are readily available opportunities to obtain rewards from other associations. The quality of an individual's alternatives is improved when there is a favorable labor market, when the person has acquired scarce skills or knowledge, and when the individual makes an extensive search for alternatives. In some organizations, however, alternatives may not exist or may be extremely limited. Prisons virtually eliminate alternatives for specified periods of time, as do most military units, especially ships at sea. Employees in isolated company towns may be captives of their employer. In general, poor alternatives prevent members from leaving the organization and thus increase the likelihood of internal protest.

Hirschman has argued that "the voice option is the only way in which dissatisfied customers or members can react whenever the exit option is unavailable" (1970, p. 33).

As alternatives are unrealized associations, subjective perceptions play a key role in the absence of objective data. Classic organizational cosmopolitans frequently exercise disproportionate influence within the focal organization because it is difficult for other members to assess precisely the magnitude of external power bases. Another perceptual distortion occurs when alternatives are limited: "a lack of alternatives raises people's perceived investments in an organization and increases the potential payoff of voice" (Kolarska & Aldrich, 1980, p. 53). Even perceived increases in investments should result in more structured low-risk political behaviors.

When the available alternatives are very different types of associations offering nonparallel sets of rewards, as when an individual exchanges corporate membership for the risks and challenge of independent entrepreneurship (Perrucci, Anderson, Schendel, & Trachtman, 1980; Wright, 1980); illegitimate external behaviors may become more likely.

So far only a few journalistic and legal studies have been reported that describe cases of individuals in business firms and government agencies who regarded the public interest as overriding the interest of the organization they served and decided to "blow the whistle"—to inform public or legal authorities that their organization was involved in corrupt, socially harmful, or illegal activity. . . . While there were unique features in every case, the whistle-blowers seem to have had in common a strong sense of professional standards, a high level of personal self-esteem, and social support from a spouse or close friend, which enabled them to overcome both subtle pressures from respective organizations to remain "team players" and unsubtle threats of blacklisting, social ostracism, and dismissal (Janis & Mann, 1977, p. 273).

Trust

Trust refers to the perceived necessity for influence (Gamson, 1968). When lower participants hold high levels of trust, they express the belief that authorities will produce desired outcomes without the participants taking any action. Those with low trust, however, hold no

expectation of receiving such desired outcomes. The trust concept, prominent in discussions of society and the state (Gamson, 1971; Miller, 1974), also can be applied to political behavior within organizations. The salience of politics is associated with the level of trust of organizational members: "If there is an extraordinarily high degree of trust, such as participants assuming that each is acting in each other's interests, then there need be little concern with issues of control and governance" (Pfeffer, 1978, p. 38). Trust is very closely related to perceptions of organizational dependability (Alutto & Belasco, 1972; Buchanan, 1974; Spencer & Steers, 1980).

In addition to helping predict the overall level of political behavior, trust helps dictate the form of such behavior. High levels of trust should be associated with the exercise of legitimate political behavior because to do otherwise is to risk backlash from authorities expected to produce desired outcomes. In contrast, those with low levels of trust experience few restraints to extreme actions. Thus Gamson observes that an appeal to the disaffected that they are hurting their cause by illegitimate behaviors will fall on deaf ears: "to point out to poor negroes in urban ghettos that riots are resented is a rather irrelevant communication to a group which feels there is little likelihood of obtaining favorable actions from authorities in the absence of such riots" (1968, p. 169). Beyond suppressing the level of political behavior in general and inhibiting illegitimate actions in particular, high trust should reduce vertical political behaviors. To the extent that trust is directed at higher authorities, there is little reason for those who already expect desired outcomes to expend resources in attempting vertical influence. Lack of leader control over some advantages, zero-sum conditions, or organizational retrenchment may produce lateral political behaviors even in high trust environments.

Efficacy

Efficacy is generally treated as the perceived ability to influence (Gamson, 1968). Thus it refers not to the need to engage in political behavior, but rather to the expectation that one's political actions will yield desired outcomes and thus be worth the costs of action.

Those who perceive their efficacy within the organization to be low will, in the long run, engage in little political behavior. It may be that new organizational members (or those who have changed units within the organization) and those who experience low levels of efficacy will respond by intensified efforts to gain political influence. Unless such actions result in increased levels of perceived ability to influence, however, the level of political behavior would be expected to decline as members come to define their actions as futile.

External political behaviors frequently are pursued when it is impossible to engage in internal political behavior or when there is little expectation of success through internal actions (Kolarska & Aldrich, 1980). Individuals with low internal efficacy may go outside the organization either to seek additional resources or simply to leave the organization. Hirschman observed that "the decision whether to exit will often be taken in light of the prospects for the effective use of voice" (1970, p. 37). In his view, exit may serve as a "last resort after voice has failed." In addition to shaping the internal-external flow of political activity, efficacy affects the selection of legitimate or illegitimate forms of political behaviors. It is believed that those organizational members with high levels of efficacy will tend to engage in legitimate political behaviors as they have a vested interest in maintaining the organization and thus they will play within the rules and avoid threatening the organization.

Implications

In calling for a focus on individual political behavior in organizations, a supplement to the rational model of organizations is suggested. Those organizational theories that draw on the rational model, although they provide a useful simplification of organizational reality, inevitably explain only a portion of the behavior that occurs. Organizational life involves contradictions because it encompasses two organizational realities: the rational and the political (Miles, 1980). Although these two realities may involve contradictions, they frequently complement one another. Burns has observed that "members of a corporation are at one and the same time cooperators in a common enterprise and rivals for the material and intangible rewards of successful competition with each other" (1962, p. 258).

Identifying the internal-external, vertical-lateral, and legitimate-illegitimate dimensions of political behavior provides added insight to the current understanding of organizational behavior, and it offers options for future research. It now appears that research in the rational traditions seems to focus almost exclusively on internal legitimate political behaviors. As the typology presented here indicates however, this hardly exhausts the range of political activity that may occur in organizations. The handful of existing studies that have looked at such phenomena as whistleblowing (Parmerlee, Near, & Jensen, 1980; Perrucci et al., 1980), organizational dissent (Stanley, 1981), and organizational protest (Lipset, 1971), now may be more clearly related to the full range of political behavior in organizations. Illegitimate political behaviors, though uncommon, provide a rich site for future research. Not only are they of interest in themselves, but they provide insight into organizational norms and values.

The integration of a focus on political behavior in organizations with the rational model can enrich the understanding of such key organizational problems as effectiveness. The rational view always has assumed that efficient means-ends chains are the route to organizational effectiveness. The present authors believe that successful management of political activity in organizations is equally necessary for producing organizational effectiveness. In some instances, political activity is a precondition of rational administrative behavior. Bargaining has been shown to maintain organizational structure (Burns, 1962), and successful coalition formation within the executive structure, Zaleznik (1970) argues, helps avoid paralysis in decision making. Political tactics also may serve as a direct managerial tool, as in Mowday's (1978) finding that selective filtering of information and exchanging favors were associated with high effectiveness among elementary school principals. In light of such findings, to attempt to explain organizational effectiveness without incorporating political variables is to guarantee no more than partial success. •

References

Alutto, J. A., & Belasco, J. A. A typology for participation in organizational decision making. *Administrative Science Quarterly,* 1972, 17, 117–125.

Bacharach, S. B., & Lawler, E. J. *Power and politics in organizations.* San Francisco: Jossey-Bass Publishing, 1980.

Becker, H. S. Notes on the concept of commitment. *American Journal of Sociology,* 1960, 66, 32–40.

Buchanan, B. Building organizational commitment: The socialization of managers in work organizations. *Administrative Science Quarterly,* 1974, 19, 533–546.

Burns, T. Micropolitics: Mechanisms of organizational change. *Administrative Science Quarterly,* 1962, 6, 257–281.

Butler, R. J., Hickson, D., Wilson, D. C., & Axelson, R. Organizational power, politicking and paralysis. *Organization and Administrative Science,* 1977–78, 8 (4), 45–49.

Cleland, D. I. Understanding project authority. *Business Horizons,* 1967, 10 (1), 63–70.

Dachler, H. P., & Wilpert, B. Conceptual dimensions and boundaries of participation in organizations: A critical evaluation. *Administrative Science Quarterly,* 1978, 23, 1–39.

Dalton, M. *Men who manage.* New York: Wiley, 1959.

Dalton, D., & Todor, W. D. Manifest needs of stewards: Propensity to file a grievance. *Journal of Applied Psychology,* 1979, 64, 654–659.

Farrell, D. J., & Rusbult, C. E. Exchange variables as predictors of job satisfaction, job commitment, and turnover: The effects of rewards, costs, alternatives, and investments. *Organizational Behavior and Human Performance,* 1981, 28, 78–95.

Froman, L. A. *People and politics.* Englewood Cliffs, NJ: Prentice Hall, 1962.

Gamson, W. A. *Power and discontent.* Homewood, IL.: Dorsey, 1968.

Gamson, W. A. Political trust and its ramifications. In G. Abcarian & J. Soule (Eds.), *Social psychology and political behavior.* Columbus, Ohio: Merrill, 1971, 40–55.

Gandz, J., & Murray V. V. The experience of workplace politics. *Academy of Management Journal,* 1980, 23, 237–251.

Hirschman, A. O. *Exit, voice and loyalty: Responses to decline in firms, organizations, and states.* Cambridge, Mass.: Harvard University Press, 1970.

Hunt, J. G., & Osborn, R. N. A multiple-influence approach to leadership for managers. In P. Hersey & J. Stinson (Eds.), *Perspectives in leadership effectiveness.* Athens, Ohio: Ohio University Press, 1980, 47–62.

Hunt, J. G., & Osborn, R. N. Towards a macro-oriented model of leadership: An odyssey. In J. G. Hunt, H. Sekaran, & C. A. Schriesheim (Eds.), *Leadership: Beyond establishment views.* Carbondale, IL: Southern Illinois University Press, 1981, 196–221.

Janis, I. L., & Mann, L. *Decision making.* New York: Free Press, 1977.

Kolarska, L., & Aldrich, H. Exit, voice, and silence: Consumers' and managers' responses to organizational decline. *Organization Studies,* 1980, 1, 41–58.

Lipset, S. M. *Rebellion in the university.* Boston: Little, Brown & Co., 1971.

Lipset, S. M., Trow, M., & Coleman, J. *Union democracy.* Glencoe, IL: The Free Press, 1956.

Madison, D. L., Allen, R. W., Porter, L. W, Renwick, P. A., & Mayes, B. T. Organizational politics: An exploration of managers perceptions. *Human Relations,* 1980, 33, 79–100.

March, J. G. The business firm as a political coalition. *Journal of Politics,* 1962, 24, 662–678.

March, J. G., & Olsen, J. P. *Ambiguity and choice in organizations.* Bergen, Norway: Universitetsforlaget, 1976.

Martin, N. H., & Sims, J. H. Power tactics. In D. A. Klog, I. M. Rubin, & J. M. McIntyre (Eds.) *Organizational psychology.* 2nd ed. Englewood Cliffs, N. J.: Prentice-Hall, 1974.

Mayes, B. T., & Allen, R. W. Toward a definition of organizational politics. *Academy of Management Review,* 1977, 2, 672–678.

Mechanic, D. Sources of power of lower participants in complex organizations. *Administrative Science Quarterly* 1962, 7, 349–364.

Miles, R. H. *Macro organizational behavior.* Santa Monica, Cal.: Goodyear Publishing, 1980.

Miller, A. H. Political issues and trust in government. *American Political Science Review,* 1974, 68, 951–972.

Mowday, R. T. The exercise of upward influence in organizations. *Administrative Science Quarterly,* 1978, 23, 137–156.

Muchinsky, P. M., & Maassarani, M. A. Work environment effects on public sector grievances. *Personnel Psychology,* 1980, 33, 403–414.

Osborn, R. N., & Hunt, J. G. Environment and organizational effectiveness. *Administrative Science Quarterly,* 1974, 19, 231–246.

Parmerlee, M. A., Near, J. P., & Jensen, T. C. Correlates of whistle blowers' perceptions of organizational reprisal. Working paper, Indiana University, 1980.

Perrucci, R., Anderson, R. M., Schendel, D. E., & Trachtman, L. E. Whistle-blowing: Professionals' resistance to organizational authority. *Social Problems,* 1980, 28, 149–164.

Peters, C., & Branch, T. *Blowing the whistle.* New York: Praeger, 1972.

Pfeffer, J. The micropolitics of organizations. In M. Meyer & Associates (Eds.), *Environments and organizations.* San Francisco: Jossey-Bass, 1978, 29–50.

Pfeffer, J. *Power in organizations.* Boston, Mass.: Pitman Publishing, 1981.

Porter, L. W., Allen, R. W., & Angle, H. L. The politics of upward influence in organizations. In L. L. Cummings & B. M. Staw (Eds.), *Research in organizational behavior* (Vol. 3). Greenwich, Conn.: JAI Press, 1981.

Salancik, G. R., & Pfeffer, J. The cases and uses of power in organizational decision making: The case of a university. *Administrative Science Quarterly,* 1974, 19, 453–73.

Sayles, L. R. *Managerial behavior.* New York: McGraw-Hill, 1964.

Spencer, D. G., & Steers, R. M. The influence of personal factors and perceived work experiences on employee turnover and absenteeism. *Academy of Management Journal,* 1980, 23, 567–572.

Stanley, J. E. Dissent in organizations. *Academy of Management Review,* 1981, 6, 13–19.

Strauss, G. Tactics of lateral relationship: The purchasing agent. *Administrative Science Quarterly,* 1963, 1, 161–185.

Thompson, J. D. *Organizations in action.* New York: McGraw-Hill, 1967.

Tushman, M. L. A political approach to organizations: A review and rationale. *Academy of Management Review,* 1977, 2, 206–216.

Verba, S., Nie, N. H., & Kim, J. O. *The modes of democratic participation: A cross-national comparison.* Beverly Hills, Cal.: Sage Publications, 1971.

Weick, K. E. *The social psychology of organizing.* 2nd. Reading, Mass.: Addison-Wesley Publishing Co., 1979.

Weinstein, D. *Bureaucratic opposition.* New York: Pergamon Press, 1979.

Wright, J. P. *On a clear day you can see General Motors: John Z. DeLorean's look inside the automotive giant.* Ossing, New York: Carolina House, 1980.

Zaleznik, A. Power and politics in organizational life. *Harvard Business Review,* 1970, 48 (3), 47–60.

* * *

Dan Farrell is Assistant Professor of Management at Western Michigan University. **James C. Petersen** is Associate Professor of Sociology and Associate Director of the Center for Social Research at Western Michigan University.

The authors wish to thank Jean Ramsey, John Rizzo, and Linda Rouse for their comments on an earlier draft of the paper.

Study Questions

1. List factors contributing to the "rediscovery" of organizational power and politics.

2. How are power and politics connected?

3. How do the authors define and characterize "political behavior"?

4. Explain the three key dimensions of political behavior and be able to identify examples from the resulting typology.

5. How can exchange theory help us predict the types of political behavior initiated by organizational members?

6. Understand how investments, alternatives, trust, and efficacy may promote certain types of political behavior.

The Manager as Negotiator

David A. Lax
James K. Sebenius

Negotiating is a way of life for managers, whether renting office space, coaxing a scarce part from another division, building support for a new marketing plan, or working out next year's budget. In these situations and thousands like them, some interests conflict. People disagree. And they negotiate to find a form of joint action that seems better to each than the alternatives.

Despite its importance, the negotiation process is often misunderstood and badly carried out. Inferior agreements result, if not endless bickering, needless deadlock, or spiraling conflict. In this book, we diagnose the causes of these problems, show how they infect negotiations, and point the way to superior outcomes.

Virtually everyone accepts the importance of bargaining to sell a building, resolve a toxic waste dispute, acquire a small exploration company, or handle like situations. Yet negotiation goes well beyond such encounters and their most familiar images: smoke-filled rooms, firm proposals, urgent calls to headquarters, midnight deadlines, and binding contracts. Though far less recognized, much the same process is involved when managers deal with their superiors, boards of directors, even legislators. Managers negotiate with those whom they cannot command but whose cooperation is vital, including peers and others outside the chain of command or beyond the organization itself. Managers even negotiate with subordinates who often have their own interests, understandings, sources of support, and areas of discretion.

In a static world, agreements once made generally endure. Yet change calls on organizations to adapt. And rapid changes call for new arrangements to be envisioned, negotiated, and renegotiated among those who know the situation best and will have to work with the results.

Certainly negotiation is a useful skill for important occasions, but it also lies at the core of the manager's job. Managers negotiate not only to win contracts, but also to guide enterprises in the face of change. Our task in this book is to show why this is so and how it can be done better.

Thus we develop a special logic for negotiators, useful inside the organization and out. It is an ambitious agenda, one that we now introduce by describing a manager's continuing efforts to settle a lawsuit. Once we discuss the dilemma that trapped Les Winston in his negotiation with an "outside" party, we focus back "inside" the organization. There, the negotiations that occupy managers' lives run up against versions of the same dilemma.

Les Winston's Dilemma

Metallurgist Les Winston was sharing a drink with his old friend Tom, a noted analyst of negotiations. Les described his ongoing ordeal trying to settle a suit brought against him by the Ammetal Corp., his former employer. If Ammetal won in court, Les's two-year-old company would be forced down from its high-flying course into bankruptcy. And their latest settlement demand—for half of his firm's revenues during the next ten years—seemed ruinous. Concerned, Tom pressed for details.

Les had joined Ammetal just after graduate school and had happily worked in their labs and testing facilities for the next nine years. Happily, that is, until he had a strong hunch that a new process might reduce production costs for an important specialty alloy, whose market Ammetal now dominated. While his boss had not forbidden him to work on this process, he had given Les no resources for it and had loaded him down with other tasks. Still, Les had devoted all his spare time to following up his hunch at home. Soon he was convinced that he had solved the problem and excitedly showed his results to his boss—who again seemed unimpressed, dismissing Les's work as "inconclusive." In fact he urged Les to forget the whole thing since, in his judgment, the only improvement worth making required a radically different process that no one, including Les, thought had better than a one-in-thirty chance of ever working.

That did it. Though Les really liked his colleagues and most of his job at Ammetal, especially the research, he quit to start his own business, scraping together capital from relatives and borrowing heavily from one large backer. Eighteen months later, the modest plant that he had adapted for his process had more orders than it could handle. Best of all, Les was absolutely certain that he had just cracked the secret of the radically different process, which could, with several months of development, slash current production costs by more than half. Though he currently enjoyed about a 20 percent cost advantage over Ammetal, this new knowledge should eventually permit him to push his former employer completely out of the market.

So he was stunned to read an announcement one morning that Ammetal planned to build a large plant that obviously would use the process currently in place in his plant. (It was nearly impossible to protect such processes by patent; secrecy was the only hope.) Les was further dismayed that same day to learn that Ammetal had filed suit to enjoin *him* from further using his process. They alleged that he had violated his employment contract with them, improperly using results from his work in the Ammetal labs. When his lawyer examined his old contract and gave him only a fifty-fifty chance of a successful defense, Les's spirits sagged. It did not cheer him at all that his lawyer argued—and had also heard informally from an old partner who worked in Ammetal's legal department—that the other side could expect no more than even odds of winning a case like this.

Five months into this discouraging episode, Les had decided that some form of negotiated settlement could protect him against the chance of losing the case, avoid further legal costs, lessen his anxiety, and free him to spend his time helping his business to grow. He had initially offered Ammetal a 3 percent royalty for the next three years, and had gradually raised

his offer to 15 percent during the next five years. (This was about equal to the highest royalty rate in the industry for an analogous, but friendly, licensing agreement.) But Ammetal was miles away, insisting at first on 60 percent indefinitely, and now, on a "rock-bottom final" demand of 50 percent for the next decade. There they had deadlocked, with the trial only a week hence.

With an air of resignation, Les finished his recitation and said to Tom, "So, that is how we stand, and all I can see is doing my damndest to increase the odds of winning that suit. Otherwise, . . ." His voice trailed off as he rolled his eyes back and sliced across his neck with his forefinger. "Except, of course, that I'll eventually recover, pick up the pieces, put together a new organization, and blow them out of the water when I get the new process going. It might even be fun, watching them write off their big new plant, which will suddenly become obsolete. But what a price for revenge!"

Tom registered all this, then leaned forward and asked Les to describe what he would really like to come out of it. A bit taken aback, Les thought and replied, slowly, "Well, I would really like to be left alone to continue with the current process, until the new one is perfected. That, however, will take some months and I'd need to raise a lot of money. Actually, Tom," he continued meditatively, "it may sound a little strange after all Ammetal has done, but I would most enjoy working on this new process with my good friends in the lab there—and not have to worry about all the financing and logistics and administrative headaches of running my own show. Ammetal's manufacturing and distribution networks are first class once they've got a good product. Of course, I don't want to give up the money, quite a fortune really, that would come from doing it myself. Also, freedom feels very good, especially after dealings with that jerk of a boss."

"So why not propose a joint venture?" Tom queried.

"In fact," Les replied, "I suggested just that to Albert Laxel [a social acquaintance and senior VP at Ammetal]. I ran across him playing tennis last weekend and told him how sick I was of this whole miserable thing, how I wished they would just drop the suit and forget their new plant, which they'd end up regretting anyway. I finished by tossing out the idea of jointly commercializing my new process—on the right terms, of course. He seemed sympathetic, especially about my old R&D boss, who's been on everyone's nerves for a while, who championed their newly announced alloy venture—and who undoubtedly instigated the suit against me.

"Still, Albert dismissed my idea out of hand, saying something about how this episode must be taking a real toll on me. Otherwise, why would I make such an obvious bluff about discovering the new process—which no one could take seriously, especially given my current fix, and how remote everyone, including me, had judged the odds of its working.

"The only way to convince Ammetal, would be to actually show them the new work—which there's a snowball's chance in hell of my doing now, just so they could steal it, too. The irony of all this," Les continued, "is that we would both be better off if they didn't sink a ton of money into a useless plant and if I could do only what I want with the new process—with no extraneous business stuff—and yet still profit handsomely from it."

Tom thought for a moment, and then intoned professorially, "Well, Les, maybe it wouldn't be so hard to persuade them that you have the new process and that they should think again." With Les's full attention now, Tom continued, "Why not drop your current position and better their demand for 50 percent of your revenues? Why not just offer them a 60 percent royalty on your current operation? Or really shock them by offering even more?"

Les slowly put down his drink, figuring that Tom could not possibly have been listening. "Tom, that's crazy. It wouldn't convince them of anything about my new discovery—low or high, a royalty settlement has nothing to do with it. And why on earth would I give up my only card, the even chance I have of winning the suit? If I win, they know I'll stay in the industry, and that they can't go ahead with their plans. Even if I only had my current process, two plants would lead to an oversupply situation. It's a very lucrative market, but the volume is not that great. That's why they've got to knock me out through the courts. I've heard of

demanding unconditional surrender but never *offering* it."

"Les, I understand. But that's the whole point. The 60 percent royalty would indeed burn your bridges with your current operation. But the only way you could possibly make such an offer is to be *sure* that the new process worked. Unless you were suicidally inclined or nuts, you would not set up a situation in which the only route left for you—commercializing the new process—was a dead end. So, with a little thought, Ammetal's got to realize you're telling the truth and that they shouldn't plan to build a new plant. Of course, as you enter the final round of negotiations, you should bring in an agreement to that effect for them to sign, *but* that agreement should *also* commit them to a joint venture, where you get a very big piece of the action, once," Tom looked sly, "once they offer you your old boss's job. After all, he's been the bad guy in this from the start."

*   *   *

Les Winston had been caught in a simple version of a central dilemma of bargaining. Devising a joint venture to benefit both parties depended on his actually having the new process. Yet directly sharing this information would open him to gross exploitation. If Les did not really have the process and yet bluffed that he did, Ammetal would be deterred from going ahead with their plans—if they believed him. Knowing this, they would suspect any such statement from him. Les had to find a way to make his assertion credible without becoming vulnerable in doing so.

Tom's analysis suggested the means safely to untangle a self-serving bluff from a truthful signal: a seeming concession that committed Les to an action that would make sense only if he actually had the process. And this illustrates one small piece of a much broader problem with which we will grapple throughout this book: negotiators must manage the inescapable tension between cooperative moves to create value for all and competitive moves to claim value for each.

Again and again, we will find this central tension, whether in this relatively simple negotiation "outside" Les's firm or in more complex and subtle negotiations "inside" organizations—in which building trust and relationships as well as repeated dealings figure much more prominently than they did in the end game between Les and Ammetal.

Key Elements of Negotiation

Virtually everyone would concur that Les "bargained" or "negotiated" to settle the suit. (We use these two terms interchangeably.[1]) Shortly after he had rejoined Ammetal as head of the new venture, Les said, understandably, that he was relieved to have "negotiation" behind him so he "could get on with his job." By "his job," he meant working out with the CEO next year's capital budget and just how many employees would be assigned to his new project. Les meant getting the engineering and production people committed to completing the design rapidly and convincing the sales force to promote the now-cheaper alloy aggressively, even though it was only one of many products they handled. He meant talking to the accounting department to reduce some of the overhead they were allocating to his project and to modify a transfer price they had proposed for semi-finished metal he would need from another division. Not to mention working out the allocation of tasks among his project team or new arrangements with his slightly edgy former peers at the R&D lab, whose boss he had replaced. To us, these aspects of his job centrally involve negotiation.

Like Les, many people have much too limited a view of the negotiation process, thinking mainly of explicit, well-acknowledged examples such as merger contests or collective bargaining. Yet its key elements occur far more widely in and out of management. Consider interdependence, some perceived conflict, opportunistic potential, and the possibility of agreement—four of the most important such elements of negotiation:

Interdependence. When Joseph depends on Laura, he cannot achieve the results he wants as cheaply, as well, or at all without her help (if only by her not interfering). Usually, dependence among people in organizations is mutual. While the reasons for a subordinate's reliance on a boss are often obvious, superiors generally

depend on subordinates as well. Reasons for this include valuable, hard-to-replace skills, specialized information, or relationships with other critical players. Think, for example, of the many ways that the chief executive depends on her long-time personal secretary. Or how the shop floor supervisor relies on the one technician who can fix a key, cranky machine. Or how a sales manager needs the field knowledge of his sales force. (In turn, of course, the sales people depend on his support at headquarters and with the production and delivery people.)

Mutual dependence implies limits to how much one party can do alone, or at what cost, or how desirably. Joint action may be preferable for everyone. This possibility makes interdependence a key element that defines negotiating situations.

Obviously, those who run public organizations' must cope with complex interdependencies, often by negotiation. Think of a public manager's dealings with political superiors, other governmental units, media contacts, interest groups, legislative overseers and staffs, not to mention the civil servants and others who can help or impede the agency's work. While people in private firms have always depended on one another, however, many factors have combined in recent years to increase their interdependencies. It is worth touching on a few reasons for this.[2]

Ten or twenty years ago, it was quite common for a manager to deal with a single product or service in a specific geographic area, and for the firm to concentrate mainly on that line of business. But the processes of making and distributing products or performing services are often more complex than they used to be, from the science and engineering involved to the logistics and new information technologies. These factors increase reliance on those with specialized skills.

Further, firms are often much larger than before, more diversified in products and markets, and increasingly international. More and more parts interrelate, depend on each other, and need to be harmonized. Businesses have traditionally had two-way dependencies with other parties such as customers, suppliers, banks, and unions. Yet an increased number of such parties have strong interests in the behavior of business and can greatly affect its success. Significant examples include organized consumer, community, and environmental groups and government regulators, along with the popular and business media.

Interdependence, therefore, is a fact of life for managers. And when dependent, the "powerful" and "weak" alike must take others into account when considering possible actions. The ability of one person to further his or her objectives depends, at least in part, on the choices or decisions that the others will make. The reliance of the parties—superiors and subordinates alike—on each other for the possibility of realizing joint gain, preserving working relationships, or minimally, avoiding interference, leads to some margin of liberty or irreducible discretion for each.[3] And negotiation can influence how this discretion is exercised.

Some Perceived Conflict. If neither of two parties can make a pie alone, their dependence by itself need not imply bargaining; there must be potential conflict over dividing the pie, or at least, different preferences over how to make it. A manufacturer's determination of how many small service vehicles to turn out in the fall illustrates a standard kind of conflict that produces negotiations inside the firm: the production department wants long, predictable runs of uniform models; sales wants fast turnaround, custom design, quick delivery, and deep parts inventories; the financial types want advance planning and minimal stocks.

Or consider the three-year-old firm that can now afford to hire one more senior scientist for its R&D unit. Should this person's field be advanced materials, where two key board members and the CEO—also a respected scientist—think the best new opportunity lies, or numerical controls, where the remarkably successful R&D head believes they need more depth? This process can involve much more than working out the "objectively best" choice; apart from their genuinely different beliefs about the right field, suppose that the CEO had his way on the last scientist they hired—who worked out splendidly. Yet the R&D chief is weighing an offer at a competitor's firm and is known to want more autonomy for his unit. With reasons, preferences, and stakes in apparent conflict,

some negotiation between these mutually dependent executives is virtually certain.[4]

That this process could end with the CEO making a forceful "final" decision in no way takes away from the observation that they are negotiating. In fact, the CEO's command is equivalent to a take-it-or-leave-it offer in more familiar kinds of bargaining—and it could be taken or left. If the CEO were in a "strong" position, the odds are that his order would stick. If not, the process might continue. Incidentally, an ultimatum from the R&D chief could also be understood as a similar "move" in his negotiation with the CEO.

Increased interdependence of diverse people virtually guarantees the potential for conflict. The interests and perceptions of people in different organizational units—associated with different products, services, markets, programs, and functions—naturally become identified with their units. And this is even more true for third parties and those in other organizations entirely. In the words of the old saying, "Where you stand depends on where you sit."[5]

With an increasingly heterogeneous workforce, especially in terms of sex, ethnic background and age, perspectives will further diverge. More educated and professional workers come to expect and value their autonomy. All these factors exacerbate the potential conflicts that have always been present in organizations. The widely noted decline in people's acceptance of formal authority often leads them to express such conflicts more openly than before. And the general slowdown in world growth has intensified resource conflicts both for public and private organizations.

Some people resist the fact that conflict pervades organizations, judging it to be unhealthy or threatening.[6] Recognizing conflicting interests can seem to legitimate differences in interest when a myth of pure shared interests might be more congenial to smooth management. Real conflicts will sometimes be diagnosed as "failures to communicate" or "personality problems." When similar problems repeatedly surface as different people pass through the same position, the diagnoses of "personality" or "communications" difficulties should be suspect. Uncomfortable as it may be to some, conflict is a fact of life in organizations. (Destructively handling it, however, need not be.)

Opportunistic Interaction.[7] Beyond dependence and conflict, the potential for each side to engage in opportunistic interaction—less than fully open motives and methods, self-interested maneuvers—is associated with bargaining situations. When two or more people try to influence each others' decisions through negotiation, they usually guard some information, move to stake out favorable positions, seek to mold perceptions and aspirations, and the like. This need not take the form of overt "gamesmanship"; the facade may be highly cooperative or submissive to authority. All that is required is that people care about their own interests, some of which conflict with others', and pursue them by seeking to influence decisions, not cooperating fully, turning situations to their advantage, or even resisting outright.

Without any strategic maneuvering of this sort, with no subtle or blatant jockeying for advantage, the interaction might best be called pure "problem solving." Without interaction, merely clashes of interest, "war" may be a better description than "negotiation."[8]

The Possibility of Agreement. When interdependence, conflict, and the potential for opportunism are present, people can negotiate to arrive at a joint decision that is better than their unilateral alternatives. Their goal is to find out whether an agreement is advantageous. Agreements can take many forms, most familiarly, a contract, a treaty, a memo confirming the choice. But agreements can be much more subtle: a nod, a word of affirmation, silent adjustment to the terms informally worked out, or other forms of tacit accord. And quite often, agreements do not formally bind the parties, or not for long. Revision of contracts and understandings are almost as common as the negotiation that led to them in the first place.

*　　*　　*

Inspecting a management situation and finding these four elements should strongly suggest the possibility of negotiation. More precisely, *we characterize negotiation as a process of potentially opportunistic interaction by which* *two or more parties, with some apparent conflict, seek to do better through jointly decided action than they could otherwise.* The special logic we develop in later chapters is tailored to this kind of process, which is widespread in and around organizations.[9]

Negotiation is Central to the Manager's Job

Familiar negotiations readily display interdependence, conflict, and opportunistic interaction. So do many other management activities where some form of "agreement" is sought. In this section, we pick apart common dealings with subordinates, superiors, and those outside of the chain of command to see where these telltale factors are present—and thus, where negotiation analysis can be profitable.

Dealing Outside the Chain of Command: Indirect Management

Managers often find that their formal authority falls far short of their responsibilities and their success is dependent on the actions of others outside the chain of command. Though people in this predicament may yearn for more control, there is often no practical way to follow the textbook advance to match authority with responsibility. "Indirect management" is the name we give to this increasingly important phenomenon of concentrated responsibility but shared authority and resources. It calls for a very different approach from traditional line management.

Consider the job of a typical product manager in a firm such as General Foods.[10] To ensure that nothing falls between the cracks and that all efforts are productively coordinated, this person has direct profit responsibility for a particular product line. However, she must depend on many others over whom she has little or no formal authority. The product may be manufactured in an entirely separate firm; advertising is carried out in a different division; the sales force is in another chain of command; and the distributors are likewise independent. To make matters worse, these other people deal with many individual products and lines.

So, without being a nuisance, how can the product manager ensure that a promotional campaign comes off as planned, that manufacturing overhead is fairly allocated to her line, that snags in one part of the chain do not paralyze efforts down the line? Handling these kinds of lateral relationships requires ongoing and often subtle forms of negotiation, with emphasis on building relationships, trust, and a sense of mutual obligation among the parties. This manager needs to work out and constantly renegotiate a chain of "agreements" that ultimately result in better sales.

Public managers have traditionally confronted indirect management situations. Take the case of Tom Sullivan, a regional official of Health, Education and Welfare (HEW). One day Sullivan received a directive from then-HEW Secretary Caspar Weinberger in Washington. In effect, Sullivan was ordered to expedite the inspections for fire safety of nursing homes in Massachusetts, where many of these homes were old, many-storied, made of wood, and scandalously underinspected. Federal funds supported many of these homes and could have been withdrawn absent inspection and fire-code compliance. But this would have "thrown many old people on the streets," given the acute shortage of any such facilities. Though several state agencies had to coordinate and actually carry out the inspections, Sullivan had no formal power over any of them. Further, the Massachusetts legislature was reluctant to approve money for additional inspectors required to meet the deadlines.

Sullivan was facing a classic indirect management situation. Long experience had taught him that a "hard approach," adverse publicity and withholding funds, would almost surely boomerang, with the feds taking intense press and congressional heat for being highhanded and insensitive. So he would have to arrange a "deal" across government boundaries that would cause these inspections to be carried out. For example, he might secure compliance in return for modifying federal standards to apply more directly to Massachusetts's situation as well as offering federal personnel and money. Such aid might, incidentally, further state goals apart from the inspections. Sullivan could also appeal to shared interests in protecting old people from fire while holding the (undesirable and non-too-credible) shutdown option as an alternative. If successful, he would have crafted a series of understandings to get the inspections underway, arrived at through an overt and covert process of persuasion, inducement, and threat.

Indirect management is common when a firm procures an item or when a government official seeks to produce or procure a good or service through the actions of regional, state, local, or even private entities. More generally, it occurs with respect to those outside the chain of command—peers, parallel organizational units, or other organizations—whose cooperation is needed.[11] In all such cases, the "usual" internal management tools and control systems are mainly out of reach. Nevertheless, the manager who has to produce indirectly is often strictly accountable for the results. With shared authority and resources but concentrated responsibility, in short, in an age of indirect management, effective negotiation with the other sharers is often the key to success.

Dealing With Subordinates

Though less noticed than they deserve, indirect management situations represent the "easy" case for showing the importance of negotiation to the job of a manager. Once these situations are recognized, negotiation seems as inevitable as it is in collective bargaining or out-of-court settlements. The "hard" case, though, would seem to involve subordinates and others over whom one has direct authority.

For example, when a colleague of ours once wrote about the manager's "external" functions, his choice of words clearly suggested the importance of negotiation ("dealing with external units," "dealing with independent organizations," "dealing with the press and public.")[12] Yet, when describing the management of "internal" operations, his language revealingly implied a much more unilateral function, where command, control, and systems hold sway ("organizing and staffing" in which "the manager establishes structure," "directing personnel and the personnel system," and "controlling performance"). So isn't it true that the possibilities of command and control inside the organization relegate negotiation to a peripheral role?

Commands. Though many managers instinctively recognize the extent to which they negotiate with subordinates, others subscribe to a powerful belief in the omnipotence of authority—what might be called the "British sea captain" view: "Do it or be flogged! Refuse again and be keel hauled!" If barking out orders were the essence of management, why bother discussing negotiation at all?

A good reason is the frequent ineffectiveness of command, even at the highest levels. Richard Neustadt, former White House aide and student of the American Presidency, published a widely influential analysis of presidential power. The most important ingredient, he argued, is not the President's ability to command, but instead his skill, will, and tenacity as a bargainer within and outside the Executive branch. In a famous passage on the limits of presidential orders, Neustadt referred to his former boss, Harry Truman:

In the early summer of 1952, before the heat of the campaign, President Truman used to contemplate the problems of the General-become-President should Eisenhower win the forthcoming election. "He'll sit here" Truman would remark (tapping his desk for emphasis), "and he'll say, 'Do this! Do that' and nothing will happen. . . . Poor Ike" . . . Eisenhower evidently found it so.[13]

While a manager's unquestioned right to fire a subordinate plays a role in negotiations, it may not yield desired results. Consider the example of Felix, the young protege of Allen, the managing partner of a financial consulting firm. Over the last year, Felix violated normal procedures, including using employees from competing projects under dubious pretenses, to generate considerable business in a new area. The executive committee decided that the firm should not pursue this area any further and after brutal discussions with Allen, Felix resigned from the firm for "personal reasons." What was the role of negotiation here?

Allen feared that Felix, if fired, would take much business and many of the firm's brightest young people with him; in turn, Felix liked the security and camaraderie of the firm. To avoid this undesirable outcome, the pair negotiated intensely but unsuccessfully to find a mutually acceptable path for Felix back to the firm's traditional areas. If such a mutually acceptable path did in fact exist, executing the "else" of Allen's "do this or else" ultimatum represented a failure of negotiation. Of course, agreement is by no means always preferable to what is possible by going separate ways.

In short, even where formal authority for the final say is clearly lodged, much direct managerial action still involves negotiation. Initial proposals to do this or that elicit contrary preferences, arguments for reformulation, and mutual adjustment, but often also convergence to final agreed action. Think of organizing a sales campaign, working out who will have which responsibilities for an upcoming client meeting or interagency session, or the deliberations over a new facility's timing and location.

Interdependence, conflict, the existence of an irreducible degree of discretion and autonomy throughout organizations, the difficulties and costs of monitoring and enforcing orders, as well as the decentralized and far-flung presence of information needed even to formulate many commands have all led many organizational analysts to rank command as but one—albeit important—among numerous means for influencing others.[14]

We do not mean to imply that sensible superiors do not tell workers what to do, or that command is generally an inefficient management tool. The real question is not "negotiation versus authority." A subordinate often goes along with an order because doing so is part of a larger bargain with the superior. For example, in return for other considerations, Joe may give Janet the right to direct him within the limits of an overarching agreement. Yet both the content of the commands and the limits themselves are often subject to tacit renegotiation.

More importantly, a serious direct order functions exactly the same as a take-it-or-leave-it offer in conventional negotiation: one party stakes a great deal of credibility on a "final" proposal, intending the other to accept it or forget any agreement. Of course, the final offer, just like a command, may succeed or fail. It is more likely to work (1) the more appealing it is in substance to the person on the receiving end, (2) the worse that person's other alternatives to going along, (3) the less it is taken as an affront, and (4) the more credible its "finality." Thus our later analysis of final offers in conventional negotiation will strongly bear on the effective use of command and authority in management.[15]

In sum, three main reasons lead us to look at negotiation even where commands are a possible way of dealing with subordinates. First, management by edict can be ineffective, especially where interdependence is high. Second, even where useful, commands make up only a fraction of the manager's world. And, third, the formal exercise of authority itself is part and parcel of a larger negotiation.

Management Systems. Beyond personal interactions with subordinates, managers devote much attention to an array of traditional administrative tools. These usually include systems to affect budgets, information, compensation, personnel, and the organization's structure.

Early managerial theories sought strategies to design and structure organizations for efficiency with respect to particular goals. Such early views and their later descendants conceived of organizations as rationally seeking to maximize specified values. In these conceptions, management consists of detailing a set of objectives, assigning responsibilities and performance standards, appropriately arranging incentives and sanctions, monitoring performance, and making internal adjustments to enhance the attainment of goals.[16] The first such theories saw organizations almost as physical mechanisms; subsequent versions saw more complicated "systems" to be controlled.[17] But central to such systems views is the potent, if inadequate, image of management as equivalent to "command and control," which we discussed in the last section.

Direct management systems try to set the rules for organizational interaction. Typically, however, they do not even pretend to eliminate the discretion that inevitably flows from the interdependence of the people in the organization. And considerable bargaining accompanies their design, implementation, and use.

Consider a situation that we will analyze in detail in Chapter Eight. A few years ago, a major chemical corporation, like many other companies and units of government, adopted a "zero-base" budgeting system. In our example, Chris Hubbard, the manager of one of the larger divisions, has just emerged from an unprecedented stormy meeting of his department heads who have been trying to arrive at overall budget rankings. Hubbard wants the final rankings to reflect his overall divisional strategy, but also to strengthen this new budget process and to enhance a sense of cooperation and teamwork. He would prefer the department heads to agree on a budget allocation rather than to impose one on them. But, how ever the result is reached, it will constitute the division head's opening "position" at the corporate budget meeting that will decide on overall allocation of financial resources.

How close does Hubbard come to managing by pure "system engineering?" Not very. In effect, he is negotiating for a preferred outcome—on the budget, on how the new process is used, and on teamwork. As he seeks closure, Hubbard has many bargaining tools at his disposal: possibilities of exchange, options to alter material and psychological incentives, potential to link or separate other issues, techniques of persuasion, occasions to make shared interests salient, and potential to influence the very terms of discussion. In fact Hubbard's role as a negotiator closely resembles that of a mediator, but one with a strong interest in the content of any "agreement." It also comes close to that of an arbitrator who has the means of shaping or even imposing a settlement if the participants cannot.

With skill, Hubbard may be able to convert a situation that his subordinates perceive as "zero-sum"—where one's budget seems to come only at the expense of another's—into a more cooperative quest for the best divisional strategy for all. He is also engaged in tacit negotiation with his subordinates over the precedent of how seriously and constructively they will take this new budget process. But the interdependence, conflict, and possibilities for opportunism make a wide range of outcomes entirely possible.

More generally, studies of the actual workings of information, policy development, and budgeting systems reveal something far from the antiseptic, efficient image of internal command and control. After detailed observation, Joseph Bower concluded:

Perhaps the most striking process of resource allocation as described in this study, is the extent to which it is more complex than managers seem to believe . . . The systems created to control the process sometimes seemed irrelevant to the task. They were based on the fallacious premise that top management made important choices in the finance committee when it approved capital investment proposals. In contrast, we have found capital investment to be a process of study, bargaining, persuasion, and choice spread over many levels of the organization and over long periods of time.[18]

In sum, conflict, dependence, and possibilities of opportunistic maneuvering again reveal bargaining to be an important part of the manager's inside job. Of course, to emphasize the bargaining is not to reduce the organization to a bucket crawling with crabs, each seeking to clamber onto the back of others. Rather, organizational structure and systems often strongly affect internal negotiations. By the same token, however, these systems are themselves the subject and results of negotiation.

The Cooperative Approach. Many people instinctively reject the idea of the manager as commander or systems engineer and look toward a more cooperative view.[19] During the 1930s, this orientation produced the human relations movement.[20] From the 1950s through the early 1970s, this approach produced studies of leadership[21] and participative management,[22] along with methods of organizational development and change that stressed building interpersonal trust, openness, communications, and other strategies that assumed a natural congruence between the goals of individuals and organizations.[23] The most recent version of this school takes cues from Japanese management and centers around the concept of "organizational culture"[24] and efforts to change behavior in a manner that is consistent with the values and philosophies of the top executives in the organization.

In evaluating this tradition, it is crucial to realize that all these approaches rest on the assumption that, at bottom, "organizations are homogeneous units."[25] Even though common values are important, these conceptions are incomplete since they tend to ignore or downplay widespread clashes of interest and perception in and around organizations. Along with varying degrees of autonomy and abilities to resist orders, recognition of conflict leads straight back to the key role of bargaining.[26]

Beyond Pure Command, Systems, and Cooperation. If reliance on command ignores interdependence and discretion and if a pure cooperative approach is blind to conflict, what view takes account of these important aspects of management?[27]

Along with many others,[28] we find it useful to look at organizations as arenas in which people with some different interests negotiate for status, effect on decisions, and relative advantage in the allocation of scarce resources. Thus a boss's formal position in the hierarchy is important but only one of many factors that affect the outcomes of this continuing contest. Others include specialized knowledge, a reputation for expertise, control of resources or information, alternatives available to the parties, and the ability to mobilize external support. Thus, how things turn out may only weakly relate to the preferences of who is "in command."

People converge to decisions by visible and hidden bargaining. This process does not require that the parties agree on common goals, nor does it necessarily require that everyone concur in the outcome. It only requires that they adjust their behavior mutually if they have an interest in preserving a working relationship as a means of allocating resources and making joint decisions. By implication, management consists of influencing—by a host of means not limited to direct orders, systems manipulation, or appeals to common goals—a complex series of bargained decisions that reflect the preferences, interpretations, and resources of subordinates.[29]

To some, the very idea of negotiation signals weakness. Indeed, the manager who negotiates allows others' interests to affect the outcome. As we see it, though, this is not "weak"; negotiation makes sense only when agreement promises joint improvement—for superior as well as subordinate—over what is possible by unilaterally imposed penalties, brute force, or other noncooperative options. And the boss's "final offer" (command) can certainly be very tough. We would not replace the visionary leader with the indecisive manager who cajoles and pleads. In our view, strong negotiation buoys leadership and vice versa.

Dealing with Superiors

If our premise is right, that superiors inevitably negotiate with subordinates, then the reverse must also be true. Of course, a boss depends on those who work for him to perform needed tasks as well as for knowledge and expertise. And subordinates whose perceptions and interests may differ depend on their boss for resources, information, and backing. Hence, the ingredients for negotiation "up." (Of course, "subordinates" themselves are often middle managers.) Even entrepreneurs, who may have little apparent need for any dealings with "superiors," must often negotiate with potential financial backers over amounts of resources, sharing of rewards and risk, and the control others will exercise.

The importance of this kind of negotiation is especially obvious in public settings. Consider the case of attorney Irene Malik, recently appointed head of the Toxic Waste Division (TWD) of her state's Environmental Protection Department. The legislature created the TWD to oversee a new toxic waste cleanup law. Now Malik must chart a course through ill-defined legal and political terrain. Though the law provides formal authority, its wording allows a broad range of interpretations. For guidance, support, and resources, Malik must rely on her superiors in the Environmental Protection Department, the budget office, the governor, as well as the state legislature's finance and environmental committees. Little is more important to her mission than obtaining what she needs from these entities, yet each of them seems to tug in a different direction. In turn, of course, these "superior" bodies look to her for producing various results. Malik must carefully tend to these ongoing, linked negotiations if she is to succeed.

Even setting the strategy for a firm like General Motors or Volkswagen—an activity normally thought to be the sole prerogative of the firm—requires that top management negotiate with a variety of parties, including the board members who can grant necessary authority. In a provocative paper, Malcolm Salter argued that firms in politically salient industries like automobiles implicitly negotiate their strategies with state and federal political leaders, environmental, health, and safety officials, and in some instances with unions, key institutional shareholders, and other "stakeholders."[30] And, when top management fears a takeover, the opinions of large shareholders and influential directors about the firm's direction typically have greater sway.

Managers at all levels have goals. Perhaps these come from personal visions, long experience, the workings of sophisticated analytic processes, readings of legislative intent, or consideration of historical precedent. But to go forward, the manager typically must deal with direct superiors and, perhaps, a variety of other "superior" bodies. Beyond formal authority, these groups can help with financial capital, personnel allocations, charters, licenses, information, positive publicity, quiet or visible backing, or, at least, agreements not to attack. Of course, each of these groups wants its purposes furthered. The manager offers the potential for this to happen. Hence their interdependence.

Yet the match of goals between the manager and these other entities is often imperfect. The necessary authority and resources are contested; the manager wants more with fewer strings while superiors prefer to give less with more strings. Also to be worked out—tacitly or explicitly—are a set of expectations, a measurement system, and unspoken set of "good conduct" provisions, as well as the eventualities under which the various understandings may be revised or revoked.

Generally, there is a considerable range of accommodation within which all sides would prefer to continue the relationship rather than pursue their ends elsewhere. In short, their mutual dependence implies a zone of possible agreement. Within this zone, there is conflict and maneuvering. The joint desirability of convergence to some point induces negotiation. Though critical, this kind of negotiation with superiors has traditionally received scant attention from students of management.

*   *   *

The picture that emerges from this discussion is of a manager constantly at the nexus of two evolving networks of agreement, constantly building, maintaining, and modifying them. One set of agreements concerns goals, authority, resources, and expectations; the other involves actual production. At a minimum, these two should be consistent; ideally, they will strongly reinforce each other.

Resistance to the Role of Negotiation

The last section illustrated the key role of negotiation in dealings outside the chain of command ("indirect management"), as well as with subordinates and superiors. Indeed, negotiation—even over whether to negotiate explicitly—is inescapable in most managers' job. Though this seems evident to many, some people remain skeptical. Impressions that "real" management is mainly the exercise of unilateral control and authority seem as resistant as cockroaches.

Such resistance can come from too narrow a conception of negotiation: it is simply incongruous to imagine IBM's sleek headquarters as a bazaar teeming with white-collared hagglers. As this chapter has illustrated, we use "negotiation" much more expansively. It may be acknowledged and explicit or unacknowledged and tacit. The basis for agreement may be a conventional quid pro quo or it may include actions that further identical interests but that do not involve a material or psychic exchange. Along with more "standard" gambits are actions intended to persuade; to alter the issues, parties, alternative to agreement, and evoked interests; as well as to learn and to transform perceptions of the situation. An agreement, if one results, may range in form from a legal document to an implicit understanding. Such a result may effectively and permanently bind the parties or it may be fragile and renegotiable. Public and private managers find themselves in all kinds of situations that require this process and closely related activities that are amenable to similar analysis (mediation, arbitration, changing the game, influencing decisions at some remove). The "manager as negotiator" is a shorthand reference to this complex of roles,[31] not a claim that managers must constantly sit across tables from subordinates and others patiently trading proposals.

Some people unconsciously resist the idea of managerial negotiation since overt recognition of the widespread bargaining in organizations can strain systems of status and hierarchy.[32] It can also legitimate the actual differences in the participants' goals. Thus, problems that really involve bargaining will often be organizationally defined as problems whose solution can be found technically or through more careful analysis in terms that mask the actual conflict.

Moreover, some standard images of good management leave little room for "inside" bargaining. To recognize its existence is inevitably to recognize some indeterminacy of outcomes as well as mutual dependence and conflict. Certainly, some tough managers will argue, effective command, control, or careful manipulation of subordinate routines should drive out these pathologies. And, the successful shaper of organizational culture achieves consensus on values, norms, and purposes; not conflict, opportunistically employed discretion, and unpredictability. Because the existence of bargaining seems to imply a failure of management when viewed through such common lenses, some may miss the existence and even virtues of manager-negotiators.

"Negotiation Abounds." Manager to Academic: "So What?"

At this point, one might be tempted to say "Yes, Virginia, there is important negotiation in organizations." Since many studies seem to stop at the triumphant discovery that this indeed is the case,[33] one might next be tempted to say, not impolitely, "so what?"[34]

This skeptical reaction has merit. Most academic studies tend toward careful, analytic description. And though bargaining has been widely studied outside organizations, with a few exceptions,[35] systematic prescriptive approaches have remained underdeveloped.

Unfortunately, most popular negotiation handbooks are little better, falling mainly into two categories. First are those promising to show "How to get yours and most of theirs too" (e.g., arrive only by stretch limousine or helicopter; make your chair slightly higher than theirs; have them face a painfully bright light;

start dealing with the real issues at midnight when they have a dawn plane). Other handbooks seek converts to the "win-win" religion and seem to assume that "meaningful communication" can unfailingly convert implacable enemies into one big happy family. And everywhere are the negotiation fortune cookies, containing solemn messages that tend to be obvious, useless, or wrong: "Timing is of the essence. It's all psychology. Be creative. Always keep communication lines open. Seek power. Use it shrewdly. Get the real facts."

A deeper and more useful approach to negotiation is needed. It must encompass more than parties formally exchanging offers to fashion a quid pro quo. It must allow for the subtlety of interests in shared purposes and intense concern with process as well as more tangible stakes. It must incorporate a shifting mix of cooperative and competitive elements. It must admit moves to change the "game" itself. It should be systematic and adapted to managerial considerations.

We approach this task in the spirit of decision analysis, highlighting negotiation characteristics capable of generalization across varied managerial situations. We seek to develop advice for a particular person without assuming strict rationality of all participants.[36] The principles we set forth in the next several chapters apply most directly to negotiations aimed at reaching contracts or formal understandings. As we proceed, we will hint at more subtle applications that we treat directly later.

Our task, then, is to develop a special logic of negotiation, helpful both to practitioners and students of the process. We have designed this logic to be hospitable, not closed. Lessons from other approaches and from experience should only enhance its value.[37] •

Footnotes

[1]Some authors treat "negotiation" as including the full range of interaction among the parties and consider "bargaining" to be a narrower process, taking place in the frame of negotiation. Others adopt the reverse usage. For a sample discussion of who calls which what, see Gulliver (1979: 69–73). As will become clear in the ensuing chapters however, distinctions between "wider" and "narrower" tend to blur badly until one rigorously defines a negotiation's "configuration" and classifies actions with respect to it—at which point any bargaining-negotiation distinction is a minor implication rather than a helpful category. (See Chapter Nine.) Given this, plus the wide variation in usage, we see no special advantage in distinguishing the terms.

[2]For a concise discussion of how these and other factors are changing private managerial life, see Kotter (1985: 16–30) and also Kochan and Bazerman (1986).

[3]Elmore (1978); Lipsky (1980); Crozier and Friedberg (1980).

[4]If, here or elsewhere, the parties have no conflict—interests and beliefs are identical—their search for the best joint action might more aptly be called pure "problem solving."

[5]See March and Simon (1958) on subgoal identification.

[6]It is important to distinguish between situations in which different parties have interests or perceptions that conflict and a common use of the term "conflict," which connotes a dysfunctional expression of conflicting interests. See March and Simon (1958) for an example of this usage. We argue that managers in an organization will more than likely have interests or perceptions that conflict but that this need not be expressed in a destructive manner. We will generally use the term "conflict" to imply that interests or perceptions conflict—more technically, that the Pareto-frontier in subjective expected utilities has more than one point—and not only that the interaction is being poorly handled. It is interesting to note that March and Simon's discussion of problem-solving, persuasion, bargaining, and politics in organizations is contained in a chapter on conflict, by which they refer only to unproductive behaviors that differ from the "normal" functioning of the firm. Our focus is on bargaining as a pervasive part of a firm's normal functioning.

[7]Rather than "opportunistic" we would prefer to use the term "strategic" in the game-theoretic sense, meaning that each party seeks advantage by taking the other's actions and plans into account in deciding what to do, expecting the other to do likewise. Yet the many other uses of "strategic" continually produced confusion among readers of early drafts. Thus, we settled on the less satisfactory "opportunistic," with its connotations of self-interested, self-conscious maneuver.

[8]If the objects of certain managerial actions are located farther and farther away, the amount of opportunistic interaction among the parties may decrease. Face-to-face encounters shade into analogous but more unilateral attempts to influence the decisions of others who do not reciprocate. Never-

theless, some of the same considerations prevalent in direct, personal negotiations may be of considerable utility when a manager is engaged in such related processes of "decision influence."

[9]Later we will discuss some of the implications of this view of negotiation. But several things are worth brief note: (1) the process is not limited to "trades" but can aim to realize a shared interest—whether a tangible outcome that all parties want or an identical vision; (2) the elements of negotiation need not be fixed, that is, the parties, issues, interests, alternatives to agreement, beliefs, rules, and so on may change; (3) managers engage in a number of closely related processes (mediation, arbitration, persuasion, influencing decisions at some distance, etc.) that can be approached using much the same logic as we will develop for more "pure" negotiation.

[10]This description draws heavily on Kotter (1985: 71).

[11]For discussions of indirect management in a public context, see, e.g., Mosher (1980); Salomon (1981); Moore (1982); or Sebenius (1982). Kotter's (1985) treatment of lateral relationships has much the same flavor. Also see the literature on policy implementation, e.g., Pressman and Wildavsky (1973); Derthick 1975); Hargrove (1975); van Meter and van Horm (1975); Elmore and Williams (1976); Bardach (1977); Ingram (1977); Weinberg (1977); Rein and Rahinovitz (1978); Lipsky (1980); Sabatier and Mazmanian (1980).

[12]Allison (1979).

[13]Neustadt (1980: 9).

[14]Dahl and Lindblom (1963); McGregor (1960).

[15]In Chapter Fourteen, we will look more closely at the intimate relations among negotiation, command, and authority.

[16]For a summary of this view, see Elmore (1978: 191).

[17]Landau and Stout (1979: 148) observe how commonly and intensely held is this systems view that "to manage is to control." With respect to the "management control system (MCS)," they note that it has so pervaded the discipline of applied management science as to:

have become its central preoccupation. In its literature, now vast in proportion, the term itself (MCS) has been used to cover and to commend a variety of formulas—PPB, PERT, CPM, MBO, Command and Control, and all manner of information systems. That these have not as a group produced striking successes, that many of them show a sustained record of failure, has not served to diminish either the expected utility or the normative appeal of the concept. Enthusiasm remains high, efforts to secure foolproof management control systems continue un-

abated, promising to perpetuate what must now appear as an unending cycle of vaunted introduction and veiled discard.

[18]Bower (1970: 320-1). Similarly, instead of finding a rational maximizing process as postulated by economic explanations, Wildavsky (1984) described an essentially political process over budget formulation in the public sector. Recent work on both public and private processes of strategy and policy formation reveals analogous situations (Porter, 1980; Bourgeois and Brodwin, 1982).

[19]This discussion follows Thomas Kochan and Anil Verma (1983: 15–17) extremely closely.

[20]Mayo (1933)

[21]Fleischman et al. (1955).

[22]Likert (1961, 1967)

[23]Argyris (1964); Schein (1969); and Beckhard (1969).

[24]Ouchi (1981)

[25]Kochan and Verma (1983: 16). They continue that all these approaches assume "that strategies for changing or controlling behavior in a way that is consistent with a single value system are functional for individuals, organizations, and society as a whole." Kochan and Verma (1983: 16–17).

[26]March and Simon (1958) noted that the usual economic theory of the private firm simply assumes away differences in goals and perceptions within organizations. Dissatisfied with this premise and conventional theories of organization, Cyert and March (1963) elaborated a theory of the business firm as a collection of bargaining coalitions. They argued that the nominal goals of the organization are vague and unhelpful as guides to overall decision making. Instead, constant conflict among subunits based on their particular organizational interests offers a far more accurate image of decision making. See also Strauss (1978); Bacharach and Lawler (1981); Pfeffer (1981); Huntington (1961); Snyder, Buck, and Sapin (1962).

[27]The following two paragraphs closely follow Elmore's very nice synthesis of this line of argument (1978: 217–218).

[28]Footnote 26 cites a few of the many studies that have documented the widespread presence of bargaining, especially in private settings. In arguing for the utility of a similar interpretation in the public sector, Allison (1971) noted that "the decisions and actions of governments are . . . political resultants . . . in the sense that what happens is not chosen as a solution to a problem, but rather results from compromises, conflict, and confusion of officials with diverse interests and unequal influence." In his review of well over one hundred detailed case studies, Herbert Kaufman (1958: 55) wrote ". . . the case studies . . . point up the intricate process of negotia-

tion, mutual accommodation, and reconciliation of competing values from which policy decisions emerge and reveal administration as process and as politics . . . These same elements appear in *virtually every case* regardless of the level of government, the substantive programs, the administrative echelons, and the periods described." (Emphasis supplied.)

[29]Obviously, management is more than negotiation. When a manager employs an analytic process to, say, conceptualize a strategy for the firm or agency, or figure out what consumers or clients really want, we do not consider negotiation to be taking place. Similarly, accounting for resources, designing and installing new technologies, fulfilling certain legal requirements, acting in a figurehead or symbolic capacity, engaging in certain public relations or advertising campaigns, gathering competitor intelligence in a library or from some outside sources, or going through the mechanics of hiring and firing need not he understood as negotiation. Likewise, it is not normally helpful to classify actions completely decided by voting, adjudication, or dictatorship as bargaining. Of course, negotiation may go on "in the shadow" of and be heavily affected by these other activities.

[30]Salter (1984).

[31]We might have chosen what some analysts would have seen as more accurate terms that were less evocative and less clearly tied to the kind of prescription that we develop for negotiators. But somehow, the leading rivals—"manager as interactive decision maker," "manager as participant in mixed-motive, mutual influence processes," or "manager as partisan mutual adjuster"—made our choice easy.

[32]March and Simon (1958: 119–121) incisively make this argument.

[33]See, e.g., Bacharach and Lawler (1980); Bazerman and Lewicki (1983); or, the flood of manuscripts that arrives when one starts a new journal on negotiation.

[34]Or more precisely and politely, as Kochan and Verma say (1983: 15–16):
Yet, much of this conceptual discussion has been heard before. The framework for studying organizations as political systems, and the discussion of conflict, power, and negotiations, is insightful and refreshing, but all of these works are still focused at the level of paradigm development and articulation. None of them take us far down the conceptual ladder to suggest strategies for organizational design and principles for guiding organizational activity that can be used by individuals interested in influencing or changing organizations or the behavior of individuals within them.

[35]Most notably, Raiffa (1982). We do not intend to dismiss the considerable value of descriptive work. But, along with Kochan and Verma's (1983) remark in footnote 34, we hope to avoid the continued rediscovery that there is negotiation in organizations; instead, we especially welcome descriptive work in areas that will aid prescription. See Raiffa's (1982) discussion of "asymmetrically prescriptive/descriptive research."

[36]In Howard Raiffa's terminology, we take an "asymmetrically prescriptive" approach.

[37]Other approaches are quite valuable. Notable studies have been insightfully done in particular disciplines such as collective bargaining (e.g., Walton and McKersie, 1965; Kochan, 1980) and diplomacy (Ikle, 1964; Zartman and Berman, 1982) or for special positions like the presidency (Neustadt, 1980) or bureaucratic decision making (Allison, 1971). Historians describe many past diplomatic encounters; the memoirs of such figures as Talleyrand, Bismarck, and Kissinger provide a great deal of insight. Anthropologists analyze negotiation and conflict resolution in terms of culture, myth, ritual, symbol, kinship relations, and the like (Nader and Todd, 1978; Gulliver, 1979). Social psychologists conduct laboratory experiments to establish behavioral propositions (Rubin and Brown, 1975; Pruitt, 1981). Game theorists and mathematical economists impose strict conceptions of rationality and investigate the behavior of fully rational individual actors in well-structured, circumscribed situations (Luce and Raiffa, 1957; Roth, 1979). And others have blazed brilliant paths taking game theory as a starting point but without its self-imposed, exceedingly restrictive assumptions (Schelling, 1960, 1966; Raiffa, 1982).

*　　*　　*

Study Questions

1. With whom do managers negotiate?

2. Why is negotiation considered "the core of the manager's job?"

3. Define and explain the role of negotiation's four key elements. (Know the resultant definition of negotiation).

4. What factors have contributed to an increased potential for organizational conflict?

5. How are indirect management and negotiation connected?

6. Even when "commands" are appropriate, why might a manager think twice about using this approach with subordinates?

7. What are some of the problems inherent in the "cooperative" assumptions of the Human Relations movement?

How I Learned To Stop Worrying And Love Negotiating

Marjory Williams

I never planned to go into business, much less to own and operate one. In fact, I studied Shakespeare. I taught Shakespeare at the Chinese University of Hong Kong and taught Faulkner in Bombay. But through a variety of odd circumstances, I dropped Macbeth to go first into real estate, then into the rag trade. I found that one was as dramatic as the other—Shakespeare, real estate, retail.

That surprised me. I had never understood from the outside how exciting business can be—the strategizing, the risk taking, the untidy surprises, the successes. And to my mind, there is no place where all of these things come into play as fully as when I sit down at the negotiating table, be it with my banker, my vendors, or one of my landlords. The fun of negotiating is that it's alive.

The art of negotiation has not come naturally to me. It's taken a while to realize that the process improves with patience—by no means my long suit. And the truth is, I started out backwards. I prepared for each round by focusing on my goals and alternatives first, and then on the people I was negotiating with. My reasoning went something like this: who has ever won the Olympics without knowing where the finish line is? Who has ever won a chess tournament without assessing alternative moves and outcomes?

But this strategy doesn't always work, as I found out 10 or 12 years ago, during my first job as a buyer for a large department store. I'd been there only a short time when my boss laid out my assignment: "Marjory, the department is overstocked, and the markdowns are way too high. One of the major problems is such-and-such a vendor. On this New York City trip, go tell him the inventory levels are too high, the goods aren't performing, we need to send back 25% of our inventory, and we need $8,000 to help cover our markdowns."

No sooner had I shaken hands with the vendor in his Manhattan showroom than I told him precisely that. It was my first experience with the boom-zero effect. He was insulted and angry. Who was I, brand new in this area, to say his products weren't good? And who was I to make demands of him? Ignoring his needs, not to mention his feelings, I scored a fat zero.

Still, I couldn't go back to Minneapolis empty-handed, and over the next three or four weeks we arrived at a compromise. But it was clear to me that I had reached an acceptable solution by the sheer force of the store's buying power and by my will and determination. By guts, not skill. By force, not finesse. I had won financial concessions but not a strong relationship. And I'm in a business where ongoing relations with vendors is key.

More important than the financial results, I brought out of that experience the awareness that one ignores the feelings of the other side at one's own risk. Determination and goal setting are good complements to people skills, but not good substitutes.

Some people think of negotiating as a game, which is certainly the way I first looked at it, with my Olympics-and-chess mind-set. And the analogy has a lot of appeal. The idea is that each party is out to pursue his or her own interest and to win, which makes each wary of the other. It's assumed that it takes certain skills to play well and succeed, and that, above all, a sportsmanlike attitude is appropriate.

Now while all these points are true, I believe that negotiating is not a game. It's a business relationship in action. And nothing can kill a negotiation more quickly and more completely than a me-against-you attitude. While the "gotcha" approach may work in a single transaction, it is hardly likely to produce a successful, ongoing business relationship. Over time, both partners have to win. Otherwise, the loser will drop out.

Certainly all of us have negotiated with folks who, emotionally, just don't have all their ducks in a row. At the extreme are those with the Agent 007 complex: they believe the world is full of guile, jeopardy, and illusion, but that they will prevail, because they are ready and able to go for the kill. They believe any overtures and any efforts at mutual problem solving are a game of deceit, that they can't win unless you lose.

It's with just such people that being a chief executive officer really comes in handy. As often as possible, I choose to deal with these would-be negotiators by dealing them out. Who's in a better position than a CEO to select which resources to use and which not to use? Surely there's another bank, another accounting firm, another vendor, another site. Why negotiate at all with 007s? Better to walk.

Maybe you've had the experience, as I have, of one of these dropping uninvited into your business life. Meet "Alfred," the new president of your number-one vendor, Agent 007. You can't ignore him without jeopardizing your business. Here I just keep it smooth, take the grief, and start developing new vendors so I can scale this one down, down, down.

Aside from the 007s of the world, I've found that most businesspeople respond favorably to looking for mutually beneficial solutions. There's a catch, though. "Mutually beneficial" means not only that they have to benefit from the deal, but also that they have to perceive that they are benefiting. The perception factor is so strong that sometimes I've had to put in much more effort than seems necessary to get the other side to see the benefits. Here's an example.

Not so long ago, I was very happy with my bank, but not at all happy with the terms of my line of credit. I sat down with the bankers, laid out the reasons why my company was a good account, and asked for a better rate and other improvements in the terms of the credit line. They explained their position, listened to me, and said they would get back to me. When they did, the news wasn't good.

I was annoyed. I knew the account was a money-maker for them, and safe. So what was keeping the bankers from satisfying a good customer? Apparently, they did not perceive that they would benefit. Did they want to lose this account? No, the problem was that they didn't feel there was any substantial risk that they would lose my company's business. Therefore, to charge me less interest would be giving up something for nothing.

As it happens, they were wrong. They had a very good chance of losing our account since my research had shown we were overpaying. But they were right—switching banks was not my preference. I sat down with them again and said, "I don't want to change banks. Let's come up with terms we can both be satisfied with." No. They still didn't see anything to be gained by satisfying my request.

The choice now was to accept overpaying or to look for a new bank. After I had invested hours in talking with various banks, my bankers suddenly realized that, indeed, I was going to leave. Finally, they saw the benefit to them of improving the rate and terms, which they promptly did. They won me back and I won my terms.

While negotiations weave in and out of my business life, they are not my main activity. Occasionally, though, I work with people—a leasing agent for a regional mall, say, or for a retail specialty center—whose primary job is to negotiate. Some of them have phenomenal skills. The thing that strikes me about the great negotiators is that they are outstanding problem solvers. And they are persuasive. Now, when I work with these experts, I focus strongly on my own goals, so that I am not swept into a situation that is bad for my company. I can easily think of times when I have let my guard down too much, and the reason I can remember those times is that I am still living with the results.

One incident involved the developer of an upscale shopping center in Minneapolis, who had targeted our company as a prospective lead tenant. Since this center would have no major department-store anchors, the developer had to land some strong specialty stores and restaurants, known within the local retail community, in order to attract other local stores.

The leasing agent came to talk to me. I listened and said, "The project sounds great, and I wish you success, but it doesn't fit our plans." I wasn't negotiating—I simply had no interest. My location plan called for six stores in the area, and SHE Inc. had five stores up and running, with space for the sixth already leased. I had no intention of opening a seventh store at that time in the Twin Cities.

Soon afterward, the leasing agent brought me back a proposal, which I, of course, rejected. Since I didn't want the location, I didn't negotiate at all, and he left with very little information. Somewhat to my surprise, he drafted a second proposal, which I again refused. Then I didn't hear anything. As 8 to 10 weeks went by, I assumed that the book was closed.

But no, he was simply waiting. If I had been bluffing, his tactic would have flushed me out. I would have been thinking, "Whoops, I had better renew contact." Since I virtually never bluff, however, and wasn't bluffing here, he lost a lot of ground by his delay. When he came back after a couple of months, with no more tenants signed up than before, I thought, "They really must be having a hard time getting lead tenants. Clearly, they are hurting." If I didn't want to go in before, I certainly wasn't going to budge now when the success of the project was so clearly in doubt. If the agent had started out at minus 10, now he was at minus 100.

But budge me he did, by taking me unawares. "Look," he said, "we want you in. If you go in, a lot of others will follow. Surely there must be terms under which it is in your interest to be in our center. Tell me what those terms are."

I was unprepared for this approach. It attacked me at my Achilles' heel: I am susceptible to reasonableness. How could I maintain that there were no terms under which signing on would make sense? Besides, he had appealed to my pride.

So I talked to him. But here was the catch: being susceptible to reasonableness, I couldn't get myself to suggest a package that was totally unreasonable from the landlord's point of view. So I did half the negotiating for the developers by ruling out from the start any outrageous requests. And, since I was involved in saying what would satisfy our needs, how could I reject the proposal?

I was hooked and they pulled me in. Not only that, they successfully negotiated their minimum rent up through the term of the lease, because otherwise how were they going to make money with the terms so favorable to me? Reasonable, right?

Of course, to look on the bright side, I did learn a lot. And there were advantages to working with such skillful people—they put together an excellent specialty center. •

Marjory Williams is founder and chief executive of SHE Inc./Laura Caspari Ltd. affiliated retail chains with 19 stores nationwide and annual sales of $5 million. She was recently named Entrepreneur of the Year by both the governor of Minnesota and the Minnesota chapter of the National Association of Women Business Owners.

Study Question

1. In negotiation, what does "mutually beneficial" mean pragmatically?

CASE: Jerry and Dave

John P. Kotter

1

A few years ago I encountered a rather dramatic example of how differences in the focus of early career efforts can lead to major differences in outcome. The people involved, let's call them Jerry and Dave, were classmates in our MBA program.

Jerry was a bright, ambitious young MBA student. In many ways, he was typical of the people in his class. During the spring of his second year in the MBA program, he interviewed for thirty different jobs in twenty companies from nine different industries. This process eventually landed him five attractive job offers. He accepted one as a manager of a small-staff department in a large manufacturing firm. He felt this was the best offer because it sounded "like the most exciting opportunity," and because it paid the most money.

Jerry began work with great enthusiasm. He spent most of his time the first month on the job learning his department's activities and identifying its problems. In this, he was able to apply successfully his education and his intelligence. Within sixty days Jerry felt he had clearly diagnosed the group's strengths and weaknesses. Shortly thereafter he finished designing a plan of action for improving the department's performance.

Three months after starting work, Jerry announced a basic reorganization of his department, fired one of his employees, and requested permission from his boss to add one new lower-level position. He immediately received word that his boss wanted to talk to him about these plans. The subsequent discussion was a difficult one; his boss expressed concern over his plans and asked a long list of tough questions, some of which Jerry was unprepared for. As a result of the meeting, Jerry was asked to delay making any changes until his boss could study his plans more carefully. When Jerry had to announce to his employees that the changes would not be implemented immediately, his credibility with his people, which had been slowly growing up to that point, began to deteriorate.

Within the next four weeks, new problems began to emerge in the department. Jerry pointed to these problems as evidence that his changes were very much needed. But his boss was unimpressed. Instead, his boss interpreted the problems as evidence that Jerry was having difficulty with "basic" aspects of management. His boss felt that Jerry should master these "basics" before undertaking a more sophisticated reorganization of the department. Jerry disagreed and found discussing all this with his boss very frustrating. He was convinced it was important to take action quickly. But his boss continued to delay all major actions.

In his sixth month, Jerry received a scathing memo from another department manager, with a copy to his and Jerry's boss, complaining about some of the work Jerry's subordinates had recently completed. This created a minor crisis, and the series of meetings that followed absorbed much of Jerry's time for the next eight weeks. Jerry felt the memo overstated the problem and that it was sent to his boss for "political" reasons. Nevertheless, his boss took the criticisms very seriously; he saw them as more evidence that Jerry was still not mastering the basics. The "fact-finding" efforts which took place after this incident further strained relationships between Jerry and his subordinates. And morale in his department collapsed.

In his eighth month, two of his subordinates sent an anonymous complaint to Jerry's boss regarding the management of the department. This letter set in motion another series of meetings that absorbed much of Jerry's time for the next two months. By the twelfth month the situation had degenerated even further. Everyone seemed to be fighting with Jerry or with each other. By then, Jerry fully realized he was in a hopeless position ("I have trouble even getting a letter typed around here"), so he began looking for a new job in another company.

Jerry's sad early career experience stands in vivid contrast to Dave's. Dave was like Jerry in many ways, and he ended up in a very similar job. But he went about the entire process of getting that job and getting started in that job in an entirely different way.

Dave spent a considerable amount of time during the fall of his second year assessing both himself and the various types of job possibilities he knew would be available during the spring. He thought long and hard about what he really valued, what kind of people he liked and disliked, what kind of situations he tended to thrive in or have difficulty in. He also did as much research as was practical on various industries, companies, and types of entry-level jobs. By January, he had made a number of decisions regarding how he was going to focus his job search. He stood by these decisions during February and March despite a multitude of distractions that would have broadened his search. In doing so, he interviewed for twelve jobs in ten firms in three different industries, and eventually got four good job offers. After some more soul searching, he selected the one that seemed best to fit his goals, values, talents, and prior experience.

Before starting his job, Dave spent time doing some homework on his new department. In this effort he learned many things, including the chief complaint voiced by those working in the department ("not enough office space") and the most visible weakness in the department's performance ("poor planning resulting in people becoming overwhelmed with work three or four times a year"). He also took some time to develop his relationship with the company's president, who had briefly interviewed him during the recruiting process. In his final discussion with the president before starting work, he brought up what he thought were the legitimate complaints about office space and received a commitment that the department's space would be increased by about thirty percent.

Because Dave had made an impression on the president even before starting work, the president stopped by to see Dave for a few minutes during his first week on the job. Dave's new subordinates were in awe: no one could remember the president ever coming into the department before. Dave also made the announcement about the increase in office space. His employees were elated.

In his first two months on the job, Dave concentrated on developing good relations with his subordinates, his boss, and others in other departments that he needed to depend on. For example, he sat down with each of his new subordinates and discussed their jobs; by reaching consensus regarding responsibility and authority, he created a sense of obligation in them to focus on important responsibilities and to defer to Dave's authority in certain key areas. He also devoted his attention to finding an easy way to make some progress on the planning and scheduling problem faced by the department. And he eventually did find a way. By applying some simple tools learned in graduate school in conjunction with his prior knowledge of the industry (he had worked in this industry for two years before going to graduate school), he was able to schedule work assignments so as to reduce the next peak work period significantly. Implementing the new schedule was easy, because Dave avoided changes that could have upset people.

During his tenth week, the annual "end of August chaos" didn't happen. There was still an increase in work and a decrease in the department's ability to respond quickly, but the normal peak with its associated problems disappeared. The improvement was very visible to Dave's subordinates, to other departments, and to upper management. All were impressed. As a result of this and other victories, in less than four months on the job Dave established such a strong position that he was able to convince his boss that he needed two extra staff positions, above and beyond the budget. And he was able to get most of his subordinates to respond more systematically (and effectively) to their work.

Dave's fifth through twelfth months on the job progressed in a similar way. He continued to build good relationships with those around him. He continued to receive more resources to help him do his job. Each month he took on more difficult problems, but only after he felt he had the power to solve them. In his fifth and sixth months he developed and implemented new information and control systems. In the seventh and eighth months he reorganized the department. In his ninth month, he confronted a few personnel problems that he had been aware of since joining the firm. Two of his people simply were not performing their jobs satisfactorily. He fired one of them and got the other transferred into a more appropriate job in another department. As a result, by his tenth month, Dave had a department that was a model for others. And at the end of his first year on the job—in extreme contrast with Jerry—Dave was very successfully managing the complex milieu around him and was already starting to make a difference in his firm. He was already emerging as a young leader.

It is tempting to explain away the contrasting situations of Jerry and Dave by employing either the concept of luck (i.e., Dave was lucky and Jerry was not) or some vague notion of ability (i.e., Dave is a good manager, Jerry is not). Neither is convincing. Attributing the difference in outcomes to luck assumes no causal patterns exist that can explain those differences; in this and similar cases such a causal pattern does exist. Attributing the differences to ability requires an identification of the specific attributes involved, and that is difficult. On the surface, Jerry and Dave were very similar in intellect, social presence, general business knowledge, etc. •

Study Questions

1. To what degree do the different experiences of Jerry and Dave reflect their different abilities to play organizational politics?

2. How does this case illustrate the importance of the role of negotiation in management?

3. Based on Jerry's and Dave's experiences, what advice would you give new managers to help them enhance their effectiveness and their career growth?

SECTION 2

Relationships in Organizations

The ways in which we interact with each other to meet our diverse needs are the subject of endless fascination in literature, art, business, and everyday life. In this section we present some perspectives on the contexts, motivations, resources, and problems involved in the use of power and the conflicts that arise from clashing needs.

A. *Interdependence.* The two readings in this sub-section demonstrate a key principle—that power can be best understood in the context of human interrelationships, rather than as simply a trait or quality individuals possess.

In **"The Interdependence of Persons,"** Raven and Rubin show the "complex ways in which we are interdependent with others," i.e., how we need others to get what we want. Their examples range from everyday interactions between family members to the fascinating, though abstract, *Prisoner's Dilemma.* By giving us a list of factors which affect competitive as well as cooperative behaviors, Raven and Rubin give us tools to understand how we relate to others.

Paradoxically, power is based on giving, say Bacharach and Lawler (**"Power Dependence and Power Paradoxes in Bargaining"**). Their framework defines one's power as the dependence of others on the benefits one can provide. Thus, the amount of power we have hinges on how much others need us, and this perspective enables fresh insights into the intricacies of power struggles.

B. *Relational Power and Authority.* While we may agree that our power is a matter of others' dependence on us, we have yet to discuss the sources of that dependency. Each of the readings in this sub-section focuses on the needs met through the exercise of power and the specific contexts that block or strengthen its use.

Why do humans strive for power, asks Kipnis (**"Motivation for Power"**). Is such striving the sign of sickness, or is desire for power a part of the normal, healthy personality? Kipnis draws from classic political theory, psychoanalytic theory, and psychology to provide a multi-faceted answer. Not only is it important to have self-knowledge, but we need to know what motivates others, so we can effectively deal with power.

In their classic piece, **"The Bases of Social Power,"** French and Raven identified five types of resources that individuals and groups bring to the power relationship: reward, coercion, legitimacy, reference, and expertise. These resources, however, exist within interdependent relationships. Power resources must be psychologically recognized and accepted by those we wish to influence and must satisfy their perceived needs.

Where do people get power resources? Within organizations, key roles confer power bases, as Salancik and Pfeffer see it (**"Who Gets Power—And How They Hold On to It: A Strategic-Contingency Model of Power"**). But the power of jobs is not simply prescribed in the organizational chart. Power comes from control of the key resources the organization needs to survive and prosper.

The difficulties of achieving clear awareness of the sources of our own power is demonstrated by Kipnis in **"The View From the Top."** Using insights gained from the study of how we attribute causality to the effects we see, Kipnis shows how holding a power position changes and distorts our vision. Are others doing what we want because we command and control them, or are they acting through their own wills and abilities? What you see depends on where you stand.

Many business periodicals have commented on one of the key effects of the restructured, recession-weary economy of the late 1980s and early 1990s—i.e., the declining loyalties of corporations to employees and vice versa. Thomas Atchison (**"The Employment Relationship:**

Untied or Re-tied?"), examines the radically changing culture of employee relations. Is it possible under the changing power dynamics between employers and employees to have cooperative interdependency? Atchison shows us the obstacles to this goal as well as the directions we must explore to achieve it.

C. Conflict. Interdependent relationships and struggles for power typically involve conflict, which may be resolved through discussion or may get out of control and become disruptive. While traditional management notions considered conflict as negative, unacceptable, and something that must be squelched, we now recognize that conflict cannot be eliminated but must be managed. The articles in this sub-section provide some questions to ask as well as specific procedures to use to manage conflict productively.

Leonard Greenhalgh ("**Managing Conflict**") draws our attention to seven fundamental dimensions of conflict that we can use to "understand the [conflict] situation as it is seen by the key actors involved." Awareness of these dimensions encourages us to ask questions that will reveal the underlying dynamics of conflicts and will enable us to manage them with minimal disruption.

If conflict is inevitable, what should we do when it comes our way? With a most pragmatic approach, Danny Ertel ("**How to Design a Conflict Management Procedure That Fits Your Dispute**") identifies desirable attributes of effective methods. The all-too-common choice of formal legal action, i.e., traditional litigation, is contrasted with the growing trend towards alternative dispute resolution (ADR). Ertel's methods can be used to draft policies and procedures adapted to particular organizations' needs.

The system which we develop to control, manage, and resolve disputes should be designed to enhance peoples' abilities and skills to understand their disputes and to have several channels for settlement, argue Kolb and Silbey ("**Enhancing the Capacity of Organizations to Deal With Disputes**"). Dispute resolution systems help families, organizations, communities, and nations deal with these problems systematically and continuously, not just on a one-shot basis. In fact, the more we express disputes, the authors posit, the better we can function.

Blake, Shepard and Mouton focus in large part on the ways that groups set up expectations for those performing roles that serve group members' needs, particularly the role of group representative ("**Foundations and Dynamics of Intergroup Behavior**"). Groups tend to enforce internal cohesion and conformity. Those who represent them to other groups must not only be loyal to group goals, values and norms, but they must seek agreement with their counterparts. These dictates complicate the process of conflict resolution between group representatives.

* * *

The Interdependence of Persons

**Bertram H. Raven
Jeffrey Z. Rubin**

Interdependence During An Uneventful Day

In the course of a single, not especially eventful day in the lives of most of us, we are expected and required to make an extraordinary number of judgments that pertain to the complex ways in which we are interdependent with others. Here, for example, is a sequence of events that happened one day in the life of a professor of social psychology.

Beginning in the late morning, at the conclusion of my weekly graduate seminar on social psychology, the students and I are discussing plans for our next meeting. We agree to spend our next session critiquing a body of social psychological research and decide that, in order to have a really fruitful discussion, each person will read the same set of experimental papers. I have most of the articles the students are to read, but many of them are too long to duplicate. As a consequence, the students must decide on some sharing arrangement. Phone numbers are exchanged, and an elaborate plan is established for coordinating the reading. Since there are five students in the seminar and five articles to be reviewed, each student will read a different article on the first day and then, round-robin fashion, pass the article along to someone else. In this way, each student will be able to study each of the papers by the following meeting.

After the seminar, I join several other faculty members and students for lunch at a local restaurant. Midway through our meal, we overhear four businessmen at the next table each insisting that today he must pay the check. Soon, however, it becomes clear that none of them really wants to pick up the tab; the bill is lying in the middle of the table, and any one of them could easily pick it up if he really wanted to. Why, then, this elaborate ritual? And what strategy is each using to make his offer seem honest—while not getting stuck with the bill?

Later in the day I have a brief meeting with the department chairman. After our other business has been completed, I decide to broach the subject of my salary for next year. With as much delicacy as I can muster, I inquire about the possibility of a raise. His response is surprisingly disarming. He points out, first of all, that he considers me worthy of a raise, and that he will do his very best to help me. But, he cautions, I must remember that his hands are tied. The university administration has allotted him only a fixed amount of money for departmental salaries, which he must distribute as he sees fit. Thus, if I get the raise that I deserve, someone else will not. I experience pangs of guilt at the thought that one or more of my equally competent and deserving colleagues may suffer because of my avarice. After a moment or two, I suggest that we solve the problem by encouraging the administration to allocate a larger sum of money to our department, thereby allowing all who deserve raises to receive them. The chairman assures me that he will try his hardest.

That evening, my wife and I set about the task of preparing dinner. Following our usual division of labor, I fix the salad while she prepares the meat and salad dressing. After dinner, I wash the dishes and empty the garbage, while she waters the plants. Since it is Friday, and thus the end of a workweek, we decide to go out for the evening. But where? During the course of our conversation, the following dialogue takes place:

Me: Why don't we go to a movie?
My wife: That's fine with me. Or we could go to a play.
Me: It sounds like you'd rather see a play.
My wife: That would be nice—but a movie is fine also. I'm easy.
Me: Me too.

(Silence)

Me: So how are we going to decide?
My wife: What movie did you want to see?
Me: *Cries and Whispers.*
My wife: It may be difficult to get seats.
Me: That's true. What play did you want to see?
My wife: *Don Juan in Hell.*
Me: It'll probably be just as difficult to get seats for that as for the movie.

(Silence)

Me: So how are we going to decide?
My wife: What would you like to do?
Me: I'd like to go to a movie—but only if you'd like to also.
My wife: *Cries and Whispers* is fine.
Me: Okay. But do you really want to go—or are you just saying that because you know I want to go and are being nice?
My wife: *Cries and Whispers* is fine. (Pause) Look, why don't you stop fooling around and decide. I made the decision last time.
Me (thinking to myself): She says she's willing to go to the movie, but I suspect she really wants to see the play. She's saying the movie is okay because she knows my preference and wants to please me. But her impatience with my ambivalence suggests that she isn't as "easy" about what we're going to do as she's letting on. I think I'll give her a pleasant surprise.
Me: Okay. Let's go to the play. We'll see the movie another time.

And so it goes—one example of interdependence following another. But now, let us examine this scenario of events, the details of which vary from person to person, and from day to day. In what ways are the events recounted here similar? In what ways do they differ? And, most important, what are the consequences of these similarities and differences for the ways in which people behave with one another?

The Problem of Coordination

The individual actors in our drama of an uneventful day were busily, and characteristically, engaged in a process that we shall call *coordination*: they were each trying to phase their preferences, intentions, and/or expectations with those of others. It is by means of coordination that people transform their interdependent relationships into behavioral reality. Coordination, in other words, is interdependence made visible.

People are often fully aware of the coordination process in which they engage. For example, I knew perfectly well that my wife preferred a play to a movie and plant-watering and dishwashing. At other times, however, people are only dimly aware of their interdependence or have no awareness at all. Thus, while speaking to another person, we may adjust the tone of our voice and our articulation so that we will be understood by, but not annoy, him. If he is socially sensitive, he will adjust his own speech in turn. And all this may take place without either person being consciously aware of it.

In order to study the coordination process that emerges when neither person is aware of his interdependence with another, three psychologists conducted a rather interesting experimental study of a "minimal social situation." . . . Two subjects were placed in separate rooms, but neither was told of the other's existence. Each subject was presented with two buttons; although he was not informed of the purpose of the buttons, he was told that he could press them in any manner or order that he wanted. He was further informed that he would receive points on a counter in front of him, but that he might also receive a shock through an electrode that was attached to him. He was instructed to try to get as many points as possible and to avoid shocks. Unknown to the subjects, one of Subject A's buttons was wired to give a point to Subject B and the other was wired to shock Subject B. B's buttons were similarly wired to Subject A. Note that neither subject could reward or shock himself, but only the other.

You might think that in a situation such as this, complete and utter chaos would result. To the contrary, the experimenters found that the number of shocks received by both subjects steadily decreased, while the number of points obtained increased. Thus, despite the subjects' ignorance of their interdependent relationship (not to mention their ignorance of one another's existence), they still learned to help, rather than hurt, each other. But how could this happen? It appears that, over time, each subject learns to adopt the identical, simple strategic rule—"win-stay, lose-change." That is, each person tends to repeat (stay with) his last response after receiving a positive outcome (a point), but he tends to change it after getting a negative one (a shock). For example, if Subject A receives a point and B receives a shock, then we might expect A (who "won") to repeat his last response and B (who "lost") to change. Now both A and B would get a shock. If they both changed their response, then they would both get points. And, since they have both "won" now, both might be expected to repeat their last response—and continue to win.

In many relationships people are unaware of their interdependence. The central implication of the "minimal social situation" research is that in any relationship where people are uncertain about which of several courses of action to pursue, they may adopt the strategic "win-stay, lose-change" rule. But note the inherent conservatism of this rule: If things are going well, it says, continue doing whatever you have been doing ("you must be doing something right"), but if things are not going well, change ("you have little to lose—and possibly much to gain"). By adhering to this rule, we learn to persist in behavior for which we are rewarded (by ourselves, but even more so by others) and to change behavior for which we are punished (or at least not rewarded).

Now that we have seen how coordination may occur even when people are ignorant of one another's existence, let us look at the more frequent case in which people do know about their interdependence. In analyzing this situation and the various strategies that result, it may be useful to distinguish among three types of coordination problems: those in which people's interests are either *convergent* (common), *divergent* (different), or both *convergent and divergent*.

Convergent Interest Coordination

Try to solve the following problem: . . . You and a total stranger, whom you have never met and with whom you cannot communicate, are seated in separate rooms. On a table in front of each of you is a pencil and a piece of paper. Your task is to write down a sum of money. If you and the stranger both name the same amount, you can each have as much as you have named. But, if you and the other person write down a different amount, neither of you will win anything.

Guessing What the Other Person Will Do. Okay, what amount did you indicate? $1? $5? $1 million? Next, ask yourself how you went about trying to solve this problem. Perhaps you said something like this to yourself: "Since I know nothing at all about this other person, why not assume that he is just like me? I will figure out the amount of money I want to write down, and then assume that he will do exactly the same thing." Or perhaps you reasoned as follows: "I cannot really assume that the other person is just like me (I'm probably a bit smarter), but I'll try to guess what he (an average person) might put down and then give the same answer myself." Or perhaps, if you were especially clever, you thought to yourself: "In order to decide what amount to put down, I will first have to figure out how much the other person thinks I'm going to write down—which will be the amount he will then specify to match my choice—which will be the amount I will put down to match his guess about my choice." And so on, perhaps endlessly, this cycle of interpersonal perspectives might continue, each person making his choice dependent upon his guess about the other's guess about his guess about the other's guess. . . .

Picking a Prominent Solution. Obviously, in attempting to solve a problem like this, each person must try his best to coordinate his preferences, intentions, and expectations with those of the other. In this particular problem, each person knows only that the other person is in exactly the same interdependent relationship as he—and that the other is aware that he knows this. Given this limited information about one another, perhaps the wisest course of each to take would be to seek out a "solution" that is somehow prominent. . . . Thus, $1 is a more prominent solution than $0.73. Heads is more prominent than tails in the flip of a coin, and so forth. Of course, if you knew anything at all about the other person, this would greatly increase your chances of finding a prominent solution. If, for example, you thought he was a student, you might guess that he would write a relatively small amount of money—$1, $10, or $100 perhaps, but certainly not $1,000. On the other hand, if you were a millionaire playing with Howard Hughes in a game conducted by Aristotle Onassis, $1,000 or even $1 million might emerge as a more prominent solution.

Using Additional Information about the Other Person. What we have done so far is to take the "minimal social situation" and modify it by letting each of our two people know that there is another with whom he is interdependent in a particular kind of way. Let us now further enrich and complicate this situation by systematically introducing new information about the other person. The following example is based upon a study conducted by Arlene F. Frank and Jeffrey Z. Rubin. . . . Suppose that you and the stranger are once again seated in separate rooms without any means of communication. On the table in front of each of you is a pencil and a piece of paper, on which six circles have been drawn in a horizontal row. The circles are of equal size and are spaced evenly apart. Your task is to put a check mark in one of the six circles. If both of you check the same circle, you will each win some identical (but hypothetical) sum of money. But if you and the other person check different circles, neither of you will win anything. Let us suppose that you are a native-born American who reads from left to right; therefore (other things being equal) you have a natural preference for the extreme left circle.

If I were to tell you that the stranger was also an American, you might readily assume that he had the same left preference and thus check off the extreme left circle. But suppose I informed you that the stranger came from a Middle Eastern country (where words are written from right to left). Then you could assume that he would have a preference for the extreme right circle and simply pick that one. Fine! But wait a minute. Does he know that you are an American? If so, he might expect you to choose the left, and so he would do likewise—despite his own inclinations—in order to coordinate with you. Then you would both lose, although each had been trying to accede to the other's inclinations.

To go one step further, suppose that before making your choice, I told you your partner's preference and to him yours (and informed you of this). Now your partner knows that you prefer the extreme left circle, but he does not know that you are aware of his preference for the extreme right. What would you do? Probably you would stick with your initial preference. After all, if he knows your preference (and you are aware of this), but he does not know that you are aware of his preference, it will probably be incumbent upon him to change his preference to match yours. However, if each of you knows not only the other's preference, but also that the other person is aware that you know, you would both be in a quandary again about what to choose.

Knowing the Other Too Well May Hinder Coordination. In sum, perfect knowledge about the other (and his knowledge about you) may not facilitate a coordinated solution; to the contrary, it may hinder progress. Recall the example of my wife and I trying to decide how to spend Friday evening. She wanted to see a play, while I wanted to see a movie, and we were each aware of the other's preference. Given this state of knowledge, as well as our shared desire to spend the evening together, it was difficult to make a decision. If only my wife had not known that I wanted to see a movie, yet had known that I was aware of her desire to see a play (or vice versa), we might have easily settled on a course of action and been relatively satisfied. The one who was ignorant of the other's choice would "stay," while the one who knew would "change." However, we each knew the other's choice and were aware that we both wanted to do whatever the other preferred. It was extremely important for us to please each other. Therefore, how could I know that when my wife said that seeing a movie was fine with her, she really meant it? Perhaps she only said it in order to please me. If only I had been ignorant of her desire to please me, I could have accepted her offer to go to the movie at face value and been pleased with our solution. And if only I had not been so intent on trying to please her, I might not have invested so much energy in trying to determine what she "really" wanted to do. But such is life!

People are forever trying to "get inside one another's heads"—to take the other person's perspective in order to coordinate behavior. A humorous aspect of such role-taking is presented in the Jewish folklore of Eastern Europe as, for example, in the tragicomic stories of the ghetto community of Chelm. One of the "wise men of Chelm," while visiting the big city, wrote home to his wife:

Please send me your slippers. I say send me your slippers because I really want my slippers. But if I had written 'Please send me my slippers' then you would have read 'my slippers' and you would have sent me your slippers. But I do not want your slippers, I want my slippers. And this is why I write and ask you to please send me your slippers.

Divergent Interest Coordination

The Aalsmeer Flower Auction. For study of coordination of divergent interests in a natural setting, one would be hard-pressed to find a more colorful example than a Dutch flower auction. In the small town of Aalsmeer, the preparation begins at night, as barges arrayed with the most amazing concentration of color and fragrance float down the canals into the village. Early the next morning, the buyers assemble in a large sales room, each with an assigned and numbered seat that is equipped with a signal button. The flowers are wheeled in before the buyers in huge lots. As each lot number and a description of the flowers is announced, the auctioneer sets in motion a large clock-like meter, which starts ticking down the price of the flowers: "100 guilders, 95, 90, 85." Suddenly the meter stops, and the result flashes on a board: Buyer number 16 has pressed his button to stop the clock at 85 guilders, and so the lot is now his. The next lot is then brought forth, and the auction continues. The whole proceeding takes place rather quickly so that a large number of flowers can be shipped off early in the morning for sale to the public.

Imagine that you are a merchant bidding for flowers at the Aalsmeer auction. A cart full of especially attractive flowers has just been wheeled in. You would like to buy this lot, since you know that the sale of these flowers will bring you a handsome profit, and you suspect that the other bidders feel very much as you do. The meter begins ticking down the price of the flowers. How long should you wait before stopping the clock? The longer you wait, the

while the meter lowers the purchase price of the lot, the greater will be your potential profit when the flowers are sold at retail later in the day. However, the longer you wait, the greater will be the chance that another bidder will stop the meter and buy the flowers instead. What you need to do, therefore, is to try to stop the meter just a few guilders ahead of anyone else. However, other buyers may be watching you, trying to figure out when you will make your bid, so that they can bid just a moment earlier. You may decide to stage something of an act— pretending to have no real interest in a given lot of flowers—until you are ready to make your move. But perhaps other buyers seem disinterested also—and perhaps they are also play-acting for your benefit.

Of course, the buyers at the Aalsmeer flower auction may not always engage in this sort of strategic reasoning and behavior. They probably meet each other on a daily or weekly basis, know each other quite well, and know what each is likely to bid; therefore, they may not try to disguise their intentions by bluffing. Moreover, since the buyers are aware that many lots of flowers are to be auctioned off, they may believe that even if they don't get a particularly desirable lot, they can probably get another one that is almost as good at a reasonably good price; therefore, they may not bother to try to figure out what the other buyers are going to bid. Trying to outfox others at an auction may be more likely to occur when the bidders know little or nothing about one another and when they are vying for a single, highly coveted item such as a rare stamp, an unusual antique, or any unique acquisition.

Comparing Convergent and Divergent Interest Coordination. Let us now examine some of the points of similarity and difference between problems of convergent and divergent interest coordination. Both require the use of complex chains of interpersonal reasoning that are fundamentally alike. In trying to decide how to act, one must first try to take into account the other's expected behavior, his expectations of your behavior, and so forth. Then each must correctly coordinate his own behavior with his guess about the other's. Convergent and divergent problems differ, however, in the purposes for which these guesses are made. In the former, interpersonal information is used in order to reach a solution that is mutually beneficial; if you make a mistake, everybody loses. In the latter, information is used for the purpose of obtaining a competitive advantage; if you make a mistake, you lose!

To successfully outwit the other bidders at an auction, one must first figure out what the highest other bid is likely to be and then bid just more than that oneself. If your judgment is incorrect, you stand to lose in one of two ways: either you fail to get the object you seek (if you bid too little) or you end up paying more for it than you really had to (if you bid too much).

As the democratic primaries were drawing to a close in the late spring of 1972, four Democratic senators—McGovern, Muskie, Humphrey, and Jackson—were still in contention. Senator McGovern was building up a commanding lead, and it appeared increasingly probable that he would have the support of a majority of the delegates by convention time. Among his rivals, there appear to have been two prominent goals: to win the nomination or, failing that, to obtain a position of prestige and influence within the party. Think about the dilemma facing Senator Muskie during the late California primary: At what strategic point should he concede and throw his support to McGovern? To do so too early would mean giving up any chance of winning the nomination as well as any possible bargaining power with McGovern. To do so too late would mean that all or most of the other candidates would have already done so; McGovern's candidacy would be assured and Muskie's endorsement would have little value and gain him little bargaining power.

Finally, recall the example of the four businessmen "fighting" over the luncheon check. In trying to decide how many times to offer to pick up the tab, so that he does it one time less than the next guy, each man must first make a shrewd guess about the probable behavior of the other three. Up to this point, it can be seen that the problem is somewhat similar to that which confronts the participants in a convergent coordination task: each wants to have an accurate understanding of the other. However, each person's guess about the other's probable behavior is then used not for mutual, but for

individual, advantage. Each businessman, in effect, said to himself: "In order to solve this problem I must estimate how many times each of my colleagues (none of whom really wants to pay the bill) will offer to pay. Then I will try to coordinate my actions with theirs so that I avoid two possible mistakes: the Scylla of offering to pick up the tab *too often*, in which case I'll get stuck, and the Charybdis of *not offering often enough—in* which case I may be seen as cheap by the others. So I should offer to pay exactly one time less than the man whom I believe will make the greatest number of offers."

In some instances it is neither knowledge alone or ignorance alone, but the coupling of one person's knowledge with the other person's ignorance that makes convergent interest coordination problems relatively easy to solve. My ignorance of your preference, coupled with your knowledge of my preference (and your awareness of my ignorance) can result in a mutually beneficial, coordinated solution: I stick with my preference, while you change your choice accordingly. He who is ignorant "stays," while he who knows "changes." Does this "ignorance-stay, knowledge-change" rule apply to divergent coordination? The answer is no, for the following reason: If our interests are divergent, and I am ignorant of your preference while you know mine, you would surely win and I would surely lose. You would be able to exploit your knowledge and my ignorance to your competitive advantage. Similarly, in order to be able to outwit you, I would have to begin with some knowledge (or at least a good guess) about your preference.

Of course, one person could *pretend* to be ignorant of the other's preference, in order to gain a strategic advantage in the relationship. Suppose you and another driver are approaching an unmarked intersection at right angles, each apparently wanting to cross first. How might you manage to prevail in this conflict of interest? One possibility would be for you to adopt a strategy of staring straight ahead into space, thereby communicating your total unawareness of his desire to cross the intersection first—and even your ignorance of his very existence. Assuming that he has good eyesight and can see that you "don't see him" (which is untrue, of course, but hopefully he doesn't know that), your "unawareness," coupled with his knowledge of this, compels him to cede the right of way. What you have done, in Thomas Schelling's . . . language, has been to "bind" (irrevocably commit) yourself to a course of action, thereby shifting the locus of control over a possible collision from your shoulders to his. Note, however, that if the other driver even suspects that you are only pretending, he is far less likely to yield.

Mixed-Motive Relationships: Coordinating Convergent and Divergent Interests

Although many relationships exist in which the parties' interests are either purely convergent or divergent, the most common interdependent situations are those that contain both convergent and divergent interests. These situations are called "mixed-motive" since the parties are motivated both to cooperate and to compete.

Many relationships that appear, at first glance, to be examples of pure divergent interests are, in fact, mixed-motive relationships— they contain convergent interests as well. The two drivers racing to be the first to cross the intersection appear to be in a purely competitive relationship. Yet, although they want to beat each other, they also share a common interest in getting across the intersection safely and thus avoiding a collision. Similarly, in the event described earlier, my colleagues and I appeared to have purely divergent interests with respect to our salaries (the larger my raise, the smaller theirs would be, the chairman argued). Our interest would also be convergent to the extent that we might collectively urge the administration to increase the departmental budget, or to the extent that we might use one professor's raise to try to extract raises for the others.

Minimizing Divergence through Redefinition. Under some circumstances, a relationship that is characterized by divergent interests can be redefined as a convergent one. Consider the behavior of two boys in a badminton game, as observed so sensitively by the psychologist, Max Wertheimer. The 12-year-old boy (we'll call him Johnny) was obviously much more

skilled than the 10-year-old (Billy), and was defeating him in game after game. Billy finally threw down his racket and said that he would not play anymore. Johnny was puzzled and a bit angry. He had enjoyed the game and especially the winning. Billy had enjoyed playing at first, but he did not like being beaten over and over again. Johnny tried to persuade Billy to continue the game, for without Billy he could not play and, thus, could not win. Suddenly he thought of a solution: "I have an idea—let us now play this way: Let's see how long we can keep the bird going between us, and count how many times it goes back and forth without falling. What score could we make? Do you think we could make it 10 or 20?" Billy agreed readily, and so they played the game that way. Billy enjoyed it more, of course, and so did Johnny— for apparently he realized that beating the younger boy at a game at which Billy was unskilled was not really such a rewarding experience. In fact, what had happened was that both boys had redefined a divergent interest situation as a convergent one.

In many respects our interaction with others day in and day out can be viewed as a game in which we have both convergent and divergent interests. Social exchange theory is a way of analyzing interpersonal attraction and rejection. Let us see how this theory applies to mixed-motive relationships.

Social Exchange Theory

The social exchange approach in social psychology originated in economic analysis and game theory. Although it has been presented in various forms, our approach is the one proposed by John Thibaut and Harold Kelley. Thibaut and Kelley began by examining the limited social interaction of two people and later extended their analysis to more complex interaction in larger groups. The social exchange relationship is often represented in matrix form, as in Exhibit 1, which depicts the exchange relationship between a husband and a wife on a Sunday afternoon. Each has five possible activities in which he or she may engage. Clearly, they have both divergent and convergent interests. The satisfaction or dissatisfaction that each receives is a function of the combination of what they both do. (The wife's

Exhibit 1: SOCIAL EXCHANGE RELATIONSHIP

Husband's Possible Activities	Wife's Possible Activities									
	Go to Museum		Read Sunday Newspaper		Go Bicycling		Visit Aunt Suzie		Write Article	
Go to Museum	-5	+10	-8	-2	-8	+4	-8	+4	-8	+5
Read Sunday Newspaper	+4	-4	+3	+6	+4	-3	+4	+4	+4	+7
Go Bicycling	+7	-5	+7	-5	+5	+8	+3	+4	+7	+5
Visit Aunt Suzie	-5	-5	-5	-5	-5	-5	-2	+9	-5	+5
Play Squash	+10	-5	+10	+1	+10	-5	+10	+4	+10	+5

A social exchange analysis of a husband's and wife's activities on a Sunday afternoon. In each box, the value in the nonshaded box represents the wife's costs or rewards, and the value in the shaded box represents the husband's. The wife prefers most of all to go to the museum with her husband, while he prefers most of all to play squash—regardless of what she does.

costs and rewards are above the diagonals, and the husband's are below.) Note that the wife would most enjoy going with her husband to the museum (+10). The husband would not like to go to the museum at all (-5), but, if he does go, he would rather go with his wife than alone (the other cells in that row show -8). What does the husband want to do? He really wants to play squash (+10); furthermore, he wants to play no matter what his wife does (the other cells in that row also show +10). Although the wife's first choice is to go to the museum with her husband, she would rather do anything with him than by herself. But playing squash is not available as an alternative to her (since she doesn't even belong to the squash club), so, in all likelihood, the husband will spend the afternoon playing squash and the wife will do some more work on an article she is writing—the most attractive activity in that row (+5).

Social exchange theory provides a useful conceptual scheme for analyzing a variety of social interaction phenomena. A matrix analysis is, of course, not without its limitations. For example, it is often difficult to determine the values that should be assigned to the cells; moreover, only a few activities can be included in a simple matrix. Obviously, we did not deal with the possibility of the husband nagging his wife or of being inconsiderate to her at a later time if she refused to let him play squash. Nevertheless, analyzing social interaction in terms of mutual rewards and costs has proved to be very useful.

The Prisoner's Dilemma Game: A Paradigm for Mixed-Motive Problem-Solving

Let us now apply the exchange analysis of costs and rewards to a research problem that has captured the imagination of large numbers of social psychologists—the Prisoner's Dilemma. Imagine that you and an incommunicado stranger are seated in separate rooms. In front of each of you are two buttons, one black and the other red. Your task is simply to push one of these buttons. Depending upon the choices made by both you and the other person, you will each win or lose an amount of money, as follows: If you both push black, you will each win $1, if you both push red, you will each lose $1, and if one pushes red while the other pushes black, the one who pressed the red button will win $2 while the one who pressed the black button will lose $2. The amounts of money you and the other person can win or lose, depending upon your combined choices, are summarized in Exhibit 2.

When confronted with this problem, many people are inclined to choose red, perhaps reasoning as follows: "Since I don't know anything about the other person, I don't know whether he would be more likely to choose red or black. What I should do, therefore, is to figure out what choice to make if he pushes black and what to do if he chooses red. Let's see. If he pushes his black button, I can make more by choosing red ($2) than by choosing black (only $1); therefore, I should push my red button. If, on the other hand, he pushes his red button, I'm going to lose regardless of what I choose—but I will lose less by choosing red (-$1) than by choosing black (-$2); therefore, I should push my red button in this case as well. In other words, regardless of what the other person does, I should choose red because I stand both to make the most (if he presses black) and lose the least (if he presses red)."

Sound logic, indeed! The only problem is that the other person may have reasoned in exactly the same way—in which case, you will each choose red and lose $1, whereas you could have each chosen black and won $1!

This particular situation is called the "Prisoner's Dilemma" game, because of the example originally used by R. Duncan Luce and Howard Raiffa to illustrate this type of coordination problem. In their example, which is not too far afield from some real-life situations, two burglary suspects are apprehended together by the police. Since the evidence is not sufficient to convict either one, the police interrogators devise a clever stratagem. One of the suspects is isolated in a room and told: "Look. We know we don't have the evidence to convict you, but we are questioning your partner. We will make it worth his while to squeal on you, and we believe he will. If so, you will get four years for burglary and he'll get off scot-free. But you can make it a bit easier on

yourself by telling on your partner; you will then get a reduced sentence for turning state's evidence—only 18 months. If your partner doesn't tell on you, we will still get you on a vagrancy charge, which will keep you in jail for six months. And even then, it would be worth your while to squeal on him, for then we would let you free." The prisoner correctly guesses that his partner has been told the same thing. The payoff matrix is presented in Exhibit 3.

Of course, the possibility that you both end up in the reduced sentence cell of the matrix in the Prisoner's Dilemma, as well as in the—$1 cell of the black-red game, is due in part to your inability to communicate and work out a convergent arrangement. Communication is obviously important. (In the badminton game, if Billy and Johnny had become so angry that they could not speak to one another, Johnny could never have conveyed his plan for a convergent relationship). It should be stressed, though, that communication is meaningless without mutual trust. If the two prisoners had met and were suspicious of each other, then a mutual agreement to remain silent still might not be honored when they were separated again. Each might suspect that the other was using him to get free. When there is communication without trust, we try all sorts of stratagems to mislead the other person.

Consider for example, the old parable about the two competing merchants (call them A and B) who meet at the train station one day. A turns to B and inquires where he is going, to which B replies "To Minsk." After some thought, A retorts: "You say you are going to Minsk in order to make me think that you are going to Pinsk, but I know you are really going to Minsk. Do you think you can fool me?" Notice that A has a choice in this situation. He has the option of trusting B and simply accepting his reply ("to Minsk") at face value. But, instead of this, he appears to proceed from the assumption that B is untrustworthy and out to fool him. Paradoxically, through this double-think process, A ends up by accepting B's statement as fact after all. Question: By what path of reasoning could B best outwit A?

A participant in a mixed-motive relationship has a choice not unlike that confronting A. He can view the relationship as one of convergent

Exhibit 3
Prisoner's Dilemma

Choices of Prisoner 1	Choices of Prisoner 2			
	Remain Silent		Squeal on Partner	
Remain Silent	Jailed for Vagrancy -6	Jailed for Vagrancy -6	Full sentence for burglary -48	Set free 0
Squeal on Partner	Set free 0	Full sentence for burglary -48	Reduced sentence for burglary -18	Reduced sentence for burglary -10

Here are the jail sentences for each of two burglars, depending upon whether each remains silent or testifies against his partner.

interests, in which case he should behave cooperatively (while expecting the other person to do the same). Or he can view the relationship as one of divergent interests, in which case he should attempt to outwit and exploit the other person. Whether he decides to view the relationship as one of convergence or divergence depends upon both how much he trusts the other person to behave cooperatively and how much he can be trusted to behave cooperatively himself. Two hostile nations that can decide either to limit their arms production to an agreed upon level or to compete with each other for military superiority are in very much this sort of situation.

Factors That Affect Cooperation and Competition in the Prisoner's Dilemma

Mixed-motive games, particularly the Prisoner's Dilemma, have given rise to hundreds of experiments in the past decade—largely, we suspect, because of the intrinsic interest, importance and prevalence of relationships that contain a mixture of cooperative and competitive motives. Let us now look at a few of the factors that affect the degree of cooperation.

1. **Number of Interactions.** As you might expect, when pairs of strangers are asked to play the black-red version of the Prisoner's Dilemma game just once, they tend to act less

cooperatively than when they play the game repeatedly. Why? Because when playing just once, each person knows that he cannot be held accountable for his future behavior and is therefore more willing to attempt to exploit the other (by choosing red). Both players thus tend to choose red, and both lose.

Exhibit 2: BLACK-RED PROBLEM

You Choose	The Other Person Chooses			
	Black		Red	
Black	+$1.00	+$1.00	-$2.00	+$2.00
Red	+$2.00	-$2.00	-$1.00	-$1.00

The number in the shaded box is the amount of money you can win or lose by choosing black or red. The number in the non-shaded box is the amount of money your partner can win or lose by choosing black or red.

When the Prisoner's Dilemma game is played over a series of turns, and both players are told the other's choice at the end of each turn, there is more likely to be cooperation, although it may eventually deteriorate. In general, social psychologists have observed a pattern of choice behavior in games with multiple turns like the hypothetical one depicted in Exhibit 4.

Assuming that neither Person A nor Person B begins with prior information about the other or how to act toward him, our two players might start by choosing black on their first turn. In this way, each shows that he is willing to trust the other and to be trustworthy himself; the result is a set of outcomes (+1, +1) that is mutually and equally beneficial. Once A and B have established this kind of cooperative relationship, they typically maintain it for quite some time. After a while, however, one person, A (turn 4 in our diagram), may decide to defect. The reasons for this defection are not completely clear. Perhaps A decided that B was an "idiot" who could be exploited readily and indefinitely; perhaps A simply became more greedy, rivalrous, or even just plain bored with so much cooperation. In any event, he defects, while poor B (totally unaware of A's decision) once again gives a trusting and cooperative response. As a result, A succeeds in exploiting B. On the following turn (5), things typically deteriorate further. A, in effect, says to himself: "It worked once. Why shouldn't it work again? And anyway, if B gets angry, he will surely choose red to protect himself. So I should choose red in either case." B, on the other hand, probably thinks: "That dirty, rotten S.O.B.! I can't afford to trust him anymore. I've got to choose red to protect myself against further exploitation." So both choose red, and both lose. For the next several turns, this mutually competitive pattern will probably continue, A hoping that B will slip back into a trusting black choice, and B remaining totally committed to defending himself against A's aggression. After a while, however, as the pair continues this costly, destructive course, losing money on every turn, one person (typically the one who defected in the first place) tries to return the relationship to its earlier, more prosperous state. Perhaps A thinks to himself: ""Wow, did I make a mess of things! If it weren't for me and my errant ways, we'd still be riding the high road to mutual fortune. I've got to show B that I want to change. I will choose black." B, however, knows nothing of A's plan to reform, and so he continues to choose what he feels he must in order to protect

himself—namely, red. The result (turn 8) is that A loses, while B inadvertently exploits A and wins. Now A may say to himself: "Things are hopeless. It's just not going to work. I've made an irreconcilable enemy of B. He's going to continue to defend himself. Therefore, I've got to defend myself as well. I'll choose red." B, meanwhile, is thinking: "Wow! A has finally seen the light. I'll choose black and everything will be okay again." So A chooses red, while B chooses black (turn 9) and the pair miscoordinates once again. And so, in this Kafkaesque way, A and B may continue—one person making a cooperative overture while the other behaves competitively (or defensively). Eventually what often happens is that the pair slips back into a pattern of mutually competitive, costly behavior (turn 10), locks into this pattern, and remains there.

Exhibit 4
Hypothetical Choices
in the Prisoner's Dilemma Game
(black-red version)

Turn	Person A		Person B	
	Choice	Outcome	Choice	Outcome
1	Black	+1	Black	+1
2	Black	+1	Black	+1
3	Black	+1	Black	+1
4	Red	+2	Black	-2
5	Red	-1	Red	-1
6	Red	-1	Red	-1
7	Red	-1	Red	-1
8	Black	-2	Red	+2
9	Red	+2	Black	-2
10	Red	-1	Red	-1

The two players typically begin the game cooperatively (black-black). Eventually, one person (A) defects, and then both compete and miscoordinate to their mutual disadvantage.

Gloomy? Indeed it is! However, some pairs eventually manage to find a way out of this impasse. This happens when one person chooses black not once but at least twice consecutively, thereby indicating his willingness to trust the other and conveying his conviction that cooperation represents the only reasonable course of action. Such persistent attempts at cooperation by one person, especially after the pair has pursued a mutually destructive course of action, typically enable the pair to restore a cooperative relationship. And once restored, cooperation tends to continue.

2. **Initial Orientation to the Situation.** By varying the introduction to the Prisoner's Dilemma game, experimenters have elicited vastly different behaviors on the part of the two participants. When the players are told that they are in a competitive game and that their goal is to try to get a higher score than their partner (and that he will be doing the same thing), the participants almost invariably end up in the red-red square. However, when the situation is presented as a cooperative game, in which each player is supposed to try to help the other beat the bank and to get the banker to pay out as much as possible, the players generally finish in the black-black square. And finally, when the game is presented as an individualistic endeavor, in which each player is supposed to try to get the highest score for himself (without regard for the other's winnings or losses), there is greater variability in behavior. However, the players typically end up in the red-red cell (with both of them losing) more often than in the black-black cell.

3. **Personality Predispositions.** Individual differences in personality are especially inclined to affect behavior in the Prisoner's Dilemma game when the players begin with an individualistic orientation. A person who is inherently suspicious of others, distrusting, or malicious is especially apt to make a red response. He expects his partner to be untrustworthy, and so he chooses competitively, causing his partner to do likewise; therefore, his own expectations are confirmed as a self-fulfilling prophecy. If both partners are open and trusting, however, a black-black response is much more probable.

4. **Communication.** As we have mentioned, communication may help to reduce competition, so that the players can redefine the situation as a cooperative one. An explicit cooperative communication (for example, "I would like you to choose black. I intend to choose black. But if you continue to choose red, then I shall choose red also") will probably elicit a cooperative response. But once distrust and hostility have been initiated, they are extremely difficult to change.

5. **Partner's Strategy.** When the Prisoner's Dilemma game is played for a series of turns (as depicted in Exhibit 4), each choice becomes a form of communication. A black response is perceived as an intention to be cooperative; a red response is viewed as an intention to be competitive. A series of black responses may elicit cooperative responses in return, so that the more favorable black-black cell pattern is established. However, there is one danger. Sometimes a succession of cooperative responses is perceived as a danger. Sometimes a succession of cooperative responses is perceived as a sign of ignorance or naivete, and so it invites exploitation. There is evidence that a more realistic strategy for eliciting cooperation from one's partner requires some form of matching—after one's partner chooses black once or twice, one should begin to reciprocate by choosing the same color as he did on the preceding turn. If your partner chooses red, retaliate with red on the next trial to show that you mean business. Turning the other cheek is often not the best strategy.

6. **Cultural Factors and Cooperation.** Cultural norms can influence a person's cooperative or competitive orientation in a manner that is very similar to one's personality predisposition. As the cultural anthropologist Margaret Mead demonstrated many years ago, some cultures encourage a cooperative, trusting orientation toward people, while others foster competition, distrust, and hostility. •

Study Questions

1. Define coordination. Explain the three types of coordination problems.

2. What is the typical rule people adopt when uncertain about which course of action they should follow?

3. Compare and contrast convergent and divergent interest coordination.

4. What is a mixed-motive relationship?

5. Explain the social exchange theory game, Prisoner's Dilemma.

6. What factors influence whether the Prisoner's Dilemma game orients toward cooperation or competition?

Power Dependence and Power Paradoxes in Bargaining

Samuel B. Bacharach
Edward J. Lawler

In an earlier work (Bacharach and Lawler, 1981), we proposed a dependence approach to the bargaining process. Building on some of the earlier ideas in power-dependence theory (Emerson, 1972), we outlined a general theory of bargaining power, the central idea of which is that the bargaining power of a party— whether an individual, organization, or nation— is based on the dependence of others on that party. For example, the power of the United States over Japan is determined by the dependence of Japan on the United States for valued benefits; similarly, the power of Japan in its relationship with the U.S. is a function of the dependence of the U.S. on Japan for valued benefits. Within the dependence framework, the bargaining power of each party is determined by the OTHER'S dependence on them, not its own dependence on the other.

Dependence varies according to: (1) the commitment to (i.e., value or importance of) the benefits at stake in the relationship; and, (2) the availability of the benefits from other parties. The theory assumes that there is an existing two-way flow of benefit in the relationship (i.e., an "exchange"), and that dimensions of dependence apply to such benefits. Thus, the dependence of Japan on the U.S. would be based on two conditions: how important the benefits provided by the United States are to Japan (i.e., the "commitment" to the benefits in the terms of the theory); and (2) the availability of these benefits from other nations. Soybean sales to Japan would increase the power of the U.S. to a degree that soybeans are of considerable importance to Japan and not readily available (in sufficient quantities, at least) from alternative nations.

Beginning with these simple notions, we have made a series of modifications in the theory. First, we treat dependence (and, hence, bargaining power) as nonzero-sum in character. That is, our framework allows for the possibility that both parties in a continuing relationship will increase their bargaining power, and rejects the assumption that an increase in one party's power necessarily decreases the other's power. Over time, the bargaining power of both parties may also change in the same direction (increase or decrease). Therefore, the total power in the relationship is not constant; it can vary. Second, our framework stresses the tactical aspects of the bargaining process. That is, our purpose is to develop a framework for understanding how parties translate structural or environmental conditions into tactical action and how this tactical action affects the power relationship in the long run. The tactics of primary concern to us are those that modify the power dependent relationship.

The central ideas of dependence theory are obviously not new. In one form or another, they are a common part of public debate on foreign policy. They can also be found in the social psychology (Rubin and Brown, 1975; Pruitt, 1981) and collective bargaining (Chamberlain, 1955; Walton and McKersie, 1965) literatures and can be traced to elementary economics and operant psychology.

What this article (and our larger program of work) is designed to demonstrate is that these very simple ideas represent a particularly suitable starting point for understanding the power struggle between parties who regularly engage in negotiation. Specifically, in this article we show that the approach contains certain paradoxes regarding the acquisition and use of power in an ongoing bargaining relationship. The dependence framework treats the ongoing relationship as a power struggle in which each party tries to maneuver itself into a favorable power position.

A key problem for parties in bargaining is to weigh both the short-term and long-term effects of tactics used in current negotiations. The paradoxes we identify essentially indicate

Samuel Bacharach and Edward Lawler, "Power Dependence and Power Paradoxes," in *Negotiation Journal*, April 1986. Reprinted by permission of Plenum Publishing Corporation. All rights reserved.

that tactics with short-term, immediate benefits (producing concessions on a particular issue) often reduce their users' power in the long term. Because of this, winning in the short run may be associated with losing in the long run.

Paradox 1: Power is Based on Giving

The obvious implication of dependence theory is that to gain power you must make the other party dependent on you. This is accomplished by providing benefits to the other (i.e., by giving the other something that he or she values). For example, on the most basic level, the power of the United States over a third-world country is contingent on what benefits the U.S. provides the third-world country and vice versa; the power of management over labor is determined by what management provides the workers and vice versa. Both actors, of course, want to use the benefits they provide to the other to extract more benefits in return; that is, they want to give the other things they themselves don't value (but which the other highly values) and receive in return outcomes that they highly value.

From the theoretical standpoint, maximization of power means that a party must increase the difference between what it provides the other and that the other can get from alternate outcome sources.

To illustrate this concept using a labor-management context, let's simplify the dependence relationship and assume that there are four basic flows of benefit: (1) the benefit to labor from management (label this "L"); (2) the benefit to management from labor (label this "M"); (3) the prospective benefit to labor from alternative sources (Lalt) and (4) the prospective benefit to management from alternative sources (Malt). The dependence of labor on management is a function of the difference between the benefit received from management and that which can be acquired from alternative outcome sources (L-Lalt); similarly, the dependence of management on labor is a function of the difference between the benefit from the union and its workers versus alternative outcome sources (M-Malt).

If power is based on giving, each party in a bargaining relationship has an incentive in the long run to provide benefit significantly above the prospective benefit from the alternative sources. Thus, the maximization of labor's power implies a maximization of the difference between what labor provides management (M) and what management can get elsewhere (Malt).

There are actually two ways to maximize the other party's dependence (and hence one's own power): provide benefits to the other party, or obstruct the flow of benefits that party can get from alternative sources. The provision of benefits is the most critical because it is clearly under the control of the actor. Cutting off the opponent from alternatives can be time-consuming and costly. In the long run, this tactic is adopted by all actors in a conflict. Unions and management vie for control over the supply of employees and sometimes develop relationships of a formal or informal nature with organizations that offer alternative outcome sources to their immediate adversaries; likewise, nations vie for access to and influence over third-world nations. Despite the potential to use tactics that produce "real" changes in the other party's alternative outcome sources, "giving benefits" appears to be the most readily available tactic for manipulating the dependence of an opponent.

The central implication of this first paradox is that there are conditions in which "losing" in the short run will increase the power an actor can wield in future encounters—assuming that losing involves the provision of more benefits to the opponent and an increase in the difference between the benefits provided and those available from alternative sources.

In this sense, accepting a poor agreement in particular negotiations may not suggest weakness in the next set of negotiations and beyond. For example, one might argue that the wage concessions by unions in recent years could enhance their power in the future (all other things being equal).

Capitulation can be a strategic move involving the acceptance of short-term losses to reap longer-term benefits by enhancing the opponent's dependence on the capitulator.

Paradox 2: To Use Power Is to Lose It

The flip side of giving, of course, is coercion, which may entail either an increase in benefits taken or a decrease in benefits given to the other party. An actor has the capacity to withdraw benefits (or, at least, make the provision of those benefits more costly). As frequently suggested in the literature on power (e.g., French and Raven, 1959), the provision of benefits implies a threat of losing those benefits.

However, if giving is the foundation of dependence and power, then there are serious limitations to the degree that one actor can coerce the other—not in the short run, but in the long run. A union that extracts large wage increases over time may motivate management to reduce labor costs via layoffs, mechanization, etc.; a nation that increases the costs of trade to its trading partners encourages those nations to seek similar or substitute commodities elsewhere. While these observations are obvious, the implications for the dynamics of power are not necessarily so obvious: By using power to achieve short-term goals, a party often undermines its ability to extract substantial concessions in future negotiations.

The impact of the two forms of coercion—a reduction of benefits provided to the other and an increase in the benefits taken from the other—can be clarified with the simplified formulation used in the last section. The coercive capability of labor is the equivalent of management's dependence on labor (i.e., M-Malt); and, conversely, the coercive capability of management is essentially the dependence of the union on management (L-Lalt). The use of coercion by labor involves either a reduction in M (the benefits provided to management) or an increase in L (the benefits taken from management). Both involve a reduction in the benefit the other party receives from the relationship.

Using this conceptualization, consider the impact of the use of coercion—via the withdrawal of benefits or an increase in "taking"—on the power relationship. First, if labor reduces the benefits to management (M) in contract negotiations, then labor's power decreases because the dependence of management on the union declines (i.e., the difference between M and Malt). Second, if labor increases the amount of benefit taken from management, there is an increase in labor's dependence on management and, hence, an increase in

management's power. Both methods of coercion actually undermine the power position of labor over time (assuming, of course, that the alternative outcome sources are constant). Thus, the dependence framework suggests that coercion that persists over time will decrease the power of the coercer; in other words, to use power is to lose it.

The most extreme scenario is that labor reduces M to the point that it is equal to or less than Malt. This would destroy the relationship between management and labor because labor can use coercion only to the extent that the benefit to management exceeds the prospective benefit from alternative outcome sources. A union that extracts benefits from management that also result in plant closings and massive layoffs may have failed to consider the long-term implications of coercive tactics used in particular contract negotiations. By the same token, an organization subject to substantial losses due to theft, damaged products, absenteeism, and turnover may have misperceived the consequences of forcing a poor agreement on workers in previous negotiations. The development and maintenance of harmonious relations may require high mutual dependence that is perceived as such by both parties.

Our analysis of the paradox "to use power is to lose it" warrants a caveat. While this is a defensible theoretical implication of dependence theory, it is not an inevitable consequence of using power. First, the term "use of power" in this context refers to coercive action (i.e., reducing the other's benefits or increasing the benefits taken from the other). Second, in order for use to lead to a deterioration of the user's power position, we must assume that there is no change in the prospective benefits from alternative parties. Third, environmental changes (e.g, in government regulations, the economy, etc.) may counteract the impact of power on a party's future power position. Despite these qualifications, however, dependence theory provides a cogent explanation for the counterproductive consequences of coercion over time in a power relationship.

Paradox 3: Tactical Manipulation of the Power Relationship May Have Integrative Rather than Disintegrative Effects on the Bargaining Relationship

Efforts to change a power relationship are often met with hostility—or at least this is thought to be the case. Tactics designed to change the power relationship are tantamount to an effort to modify the terms on which an existing relationship rests. Thus it is not surprising that such actions are often thought to have a negative or disintegrative effect on the relationship. The dependence framework, however, suggests that such tactical action—even though based on competitive, self-interested goals—will often have an integrative or harmonizing effect on the bargaining relationship over time.

Using the dependence framework, there are two broad types of tactical options available for actors who want to modify the power relationship: (1) tactics that increase the opponent's dependence: and (2) tactics that decrease the party's dependence. Each category can subsume a wide variety of specific actions, but the relative emphasis each party places on categories is most important to our discussion.

In its relationship with Japan, for instance, the U.S. might place primary emphasis on increasing Japan's dependence on the U.S. or on decreasing its own dependence on Japan. The choice made or emphasis adopted by the U.S., in conjunction with the choice of Japan, will determine the long-term effects of the tactical action on the power relationship. Specifically, the conjoint emphasis of parties determines whether the power struggle over time will have integrative or disintegrative effects on the bargaining relationship.

When a party engages in action that falls into one of these categories, opposing parties respond with tactical action that also fits into one of the two categories. Two types of responses are possible: blockage and matching (Bacharach and Lawler, 1981).

A blockage tactic attempts to forestall or prevent the action taken by the opponent. If successful, blockage tactics maintain the existing power relationship. A matching tactic reciprocates the tactical action of the actor which, in terms of dependence theory, means that the tactic falls into the same broad category adopted by the actor. For example, a union adopting tactics that increase management's dependence on the union might be confronted with management actions that reciprocate by increasing the union's dependence on the organization. The key to understanding the integrative and disintegrative consequences of a power struggle is to be found in the nature of the tactical-countertactical patterns.

TABLE 1
IMPACT OF TACTICAL PATTERNS ON MUTUAL DEPENDENCE OVER TIME

PARTY B	PARTY A	
	Decrease Own Dependence	Increase Other's Dependence
Decrease Own Dependence	MATCHING (over time, a reduction in mutual dependence)	BLOCKAGE (over time, no change in mutual dependence)
Increase Other's Dependence	BLOCKAGE (over time, no change in mutual dependence)	MATCHING (over time, an increase in mutual dependence)

The nature of the tactic-countertactic patterns and the effect of these patterns on the power relationship is presented abstractly in Table 1. If Party A increases B's dependence and Party B responds with action that decreases its dependence (to a comparable degree), there is no change in the mutual dependence or total power in the relationship. If Party A decreases its dependence on Party B and Party B matches this action—that is, B also reduces its dependence—there is a decrease in the mutual dependence. Finally, if Party A increases Party B's dependence on A and Party B matches this action by increasing A's dependence on B, then there is an increase in the mutual dependence between the actors. These effects of tactical patterns on mutual dependence, of course, assume that both parties are equally effective at producing the changes. Different degrees of tactic success would produce shifts not only in the mutual dependence (i.e., "total power") within the relationship, but also in the relative power position.

It should be clear from Table 1 that the dominant tactical patterns will determine the level of mutual dependence in the relationship over time. If both actors stress increases in the other's dependence, mutual dependence will grow as will the potential for a more cooperative, integrative negotiation relationship. If labor and management stress efforts to decrease their own dependence on the other, then mutual dependence should decline over time, along with the ease of reaching agreements in negotiations. Thus, some tactical action designed to achieve an advantage can actually lay the foundation for conflict resolution in future negotiations.

In summary, the dependence framework conceptualizes an ongoing, longer-term bargaining relationship as a power struggle. Power struggles are activated and maintained by parties' attempts to alter the existing power relationship. In most any conflict, efforts to change the power relationship are likely, and any such effort will be met with counteraction of some sort (Bacharach and Lawler, 1980: Chapter 7). The major thrust of dependence theory is that the continual manipulation and maneuvering for position that characterizes a power struggle need not have a negative or disintegrative effect on the bargaining relationship. Certain tactic-countertactic patterns will increase harmony in the relationship, even if they are motivated solely by self-interest.

Paradox 4: An Inferior Power Position Can Provide a Tactical Advantage

Recall from our earlier discussion that dependence theory identifies two determinants of dependence: (1) the availability of alternative parties from whom the outcomes at stake might be obtained, and (2) the "commitment" of a party to the benefits at stake, defined as the importance of or value attributed to the benefits. This paradox deals only with the commitment dimension.

The commitment dimension of dependence has contradictory implications for power and

tactical action. Clearly, the theory stipulates that a party highly committed to the benefits at issue will have less power capabilities than a party with a lower level of commitment (Bacharach and Lawler, 1976, 1981). High commitment means that one party controls benefits of substantial value or importance to the other.

The paradox is that high levels of commitment may also lead a party to expend more tactical effort to manipulate the other and, thereby, acquire the highly valued outcomes (Lawler and Bacharach, 1976; Bacharach and Lawler, 1981). A party with low power on the commitment dimension has every reason to push strongly in the bargaining; and, an opponent with lower commitment might be more inclined to yield to a party with higher commitment on the benefit issue. Thus, a party with high power in these terms may yield more than predicted by the power position.

There appear to be two motives underlying the willingness of the higher power actor to yield under such circumstances. First, there is strong pressure by the party with lower power for outcomes not highly valued by the party with higher expectation (tacit or otherwise), so that the lower power actor will yield on other issues that are more important to the higher power actor (i.e., a tradeoff); secondly, by yielding, the higher power party may convey an image of benevolence that improves the long-term relationship—and also future power position. Overall, where parties have dissimilar commitments to the outcomes of the issue, the party with less power in these terms should be successful (all other things equal) because yielding by the party with more power is a low cost act that may produce long-term benefit.

There is empirical support for the tactical-effort implications of commitment that suggests that the alternatives and commitment dimensions represent qualitatively distinct bases for power (Bacharach and Lawler, 1981: Chapter 3). While high power in terms of the alternatives available is clearly an advantage (and one that shows in the tactical success of the actors), high power in terms of commitment to the benefits is not inevitably an advantage. This paradox suggests the fallacy of assuming a perfect correspondence between the power relationship, tactical action, and bargaining outcomes and also the importance of placing the short-term aspects of bargaining in the context of the ongoing power struggle.

Conclusion

In most international and labor-management contexts, bargaining occurs between actors who have a continuing relationship that transcends the bargaining at a given point in time. While it is well known that the expectation of future interaction affects the bargaining process (Rubin and Brown, 1975; Pruitt, 1981), little effort has been made to link the bargaining process in particular negotiations to the larger power relationship within which parties deal with each other.

Our perspective assumes that parties in continuing relationships will engage in relatively persistent efforts to enhance their own power or reduce the other's. Successful acquisition of a favorable power position at one point in time does not assure its continuation, however; in fact, such a gain motivates the other party to devote even greater effort to modifying the power relationship. The nature of the power relationship is likely to fluctuate over time because of such tactical maneuvering.

Dependence theory can be used to analyze the larger power struggle within which specific negotiations tend to occur. The paradoxes discussed in this article suggest that tactical action within specific negotiations can have unintended effects on the power relationship: A union that makes substantial concessions at one point in time increases management's dependence on the union; a union that adopts coercive tactics over time may in the process gradually erode its power base by making alternative outcome sources (e.g., subcontracting) more viable for management; if both union and management stress tactical efforts to increase the other's dependence, then mutual dependence will rise over time and, all other things being equal, relations should become more harmonious. It is the fact that dependence theory raises such issues and provides general answers that makes it a useful framework for analyzing the tactical processes of bargaining.

The dependence framework offers a multidimensional conceptualization of power rather than a unidimensional one. It traces power to basic propositions about interdependence found in psychology, sociology and economics; it proposes a variable-sum rather than a zero-sum treatment of power, which is critical to an understanding of power relationships that change over time; and, it adopts a tactical approach to bargaining. Overall, the dependence framework suggests a more dynamic analysis of power relationships, one that incorporates both the short and long-term effects of tactical action. •

References

Bacharach, S.B. and Lawler, E.J. "The Perception of Power." *Social Forces* 55 (1976): 123–134.

— *Power and Politics in Organizations: The Social Psychology of Conflict, Coalitions and Bargaining.* San Francisco: Jossey-Bass, 1980.

— *Bargaining: Power, Tactics and Outcomes.* San Francisco: Jossey-Bass, 1981.

Chamberlain, N.W. A *General Theory of Economic Process.* New York: Harper and Row, 1955.

Emerson, R.M. "Exchange Theory, Part II: Exchange Relations, Exchange Networks, and Groups as Exchange Systems." In *Sociological Theories in Progress*, vol. 2, ed. J. Berger, M. Zelditch, and B. Anderson. Boston: Houghton-Mifflin, 1972.

French, J.R., Jr., and Raven, B.H. "The Bases of Social Power." In *Studies in Social Power,* ed. D. Cartwright. Ann Arbor: University of Michigan Press, 1959.

Lawler, E.J. and Bacharach, S.B. "Outcome Alternatives and Value as Criteria for Multistrategy Evaluations." *Journal of Personality and Social Psychology* 34 (1976): 885–894.

Pruitt, D.G. *Negotiation Behavior.* New York: Academic Press, 1981.

Rubin, J.Z. and Brown, B.R. *The Social Psychology of Bargaining and Negotiations.* New York: Academic Press, 1975.

Schelling, T. C. *The Strategy of Conflict.* New York: Oxford University Press, 1960.

Walton, R.E. and McKersie, R.B. *A Behavioral Theory of Labor Negotiations.* New York: McGraw Hill, 1965.

Young, O.R., ed., *Bargaining: Formal Theories of Negotiation.* Chicago: University of Illinois Press, 1975.

*   *   *

Samuel Bacharach is Professor of Organizational Behavior at the New York State School of Industrial and Labor Relations, Cornell University, Ithaca, New York.

Edward J. Lawler is Professor and Chairman of the Department of Sociology, the University of Iowa.

Note

The order of authorship in this article does not reflect differential contributions. The authors are grateful to Dr. Sharon Conley and Dr. Bruce Cooper for comments on this article.

Study Questions

1. According to power-dependence theory, what is the source of a party's bargaining power?

2. Dependence will vary according to what two factors?

3. What does it mean that dependence (bargaining power) is "nonzero-sum?"

4. How can individuals maximize another's dependence on them?

5. Understand the central implications of each paradox noted in the article.

6. Identify two forms of coercion.

7. What are the two types of tactical options for modifying the power relationship, the two types of responses to these actions, and the possible outcomes of these interactions?

8. What does high (vs. low) commitment mean in a power relationship?

9. How is power from alternatives different than power from commitment?

CASE: Jerry Cutler

John P. Kotter

A typical example of this problem is seen in the case of a young man who was a programmer for one of the firms located in northern California's Silicon Valley. His name was Jerry Cutler, and he was about thirty-five years old at the time of this episode. Jerry had been with his employer for four years, and although he had never completed college, he was a well-respected and well-paid technical specialist in his firm.

Jerry's interest in the medical applications of the type of equipment his company produced first developed in 1978 when his mother-in-law was hospitalized for nearly six months. During that half-year period, he and his wife visited the hospital two or three times each week. What started as short and casual conversations between Jerry and assorted nurses and doctors eventually turned into serious and exciting explorations about important medical needs and emerging technology that could possibly meet those needs at a fraction of the cost of current methods.

Because of these conversations, in the fall of 1978, Jerry told both his boss and his boss's boss he would like to meet with them about an important matter. At that meeting, he reported recent events at the hospital and then showed them rough specifications he had developed for a new piece of medical equipment. The device was essentially a clever modification of one of the company's existing products, a product which was not then used for medical applications.

Jerry's bosses were impressed. They liked both the concept and Jerry's obvious enthusiasm. As a result, about a week later, they gave Jerry permission to allocate up to one half of his time for the following two months to work with the appropriate people in engineering, marketing, and manufacturing in order to develop a prototype of the product and a financial forecast of its economic viability.

Jerry began working on his project with more excitement than he had felt in years. And at first, all went exceptionally well. He was able to get a number of other people in the firm interested in the potential product. Furthermore, the initial market research suggested that a very lucrative market might exist, one in which there was no comparable product.

But after a good start, Jerry began to run into problems. At first the problems were small, but nevertheless annoying and time consuming. For example, the payroll department in accounting returned his expense report, which asked that a neighborhood high school student be paid fifty dollars for spending a total of twelve hours helping Jerry do some metalworking in Jerry's basement shop. Payroll said, "Company policy requires that such requests be approved *in advance* by someone at least at level 7 in the firm." Jerry spent nearly half a day arguing with people in accounting, but to no avail. Eventually he had to get his boss, who was more than a little annoyed, to intervene in his behalf.

The problems began to get more serious starting a month after the project began. One of the managers within the main engineering department called Jerry on a Tuesday afternoon and told him that the engineer who was working on his project was spending "far too much time" on it. He was told that they had "other priorities and deadlines, and I'm sorry, but I just cannot spare him anymore." Another more junior engineer was assigned to help Jerry, but only for a maximum of five hours a week. Jerry complained that the loss of continuity, experience, and hours would really hurt the project. The engineering manager said he was sorry, but that he could do nothing about it.

Jerry complained immediately to his boss, who retorted in a somewhat angry way that Jerry also was spending too much time on the project. Jerry's other responsibilities were being neglected, he said. Jerry left that meeting predictably upset.

The situation got even worse the next day. A telephone call at about 10:30 A.M. informed Jerry that the person in manufacturing who was supposed to be estimating production costs for the new machine was in New York, dealing with a small crisis in a plant. The caller was not sure when this person would return, or how much progress he had made on Jerry's project. Jerry thought about going to his boss for help, but realized that was probably not a good idea.

The next and most damaging incident came three days later. At four o'clock that afternoon Jerry's boss informed him that someone in marketing had redone the market potential analysis based on new data from the sales department. The new forecast projected a market about one fifth the size of the original forecast. Based on this new information, Jerry's boss told him they would have to stop investing time in the project. Other priorities were more important. "Sorry."

Jerry was furious. After investing so much time and energy in the project, he was intellectually convinced of its importance and was emotionally committed to it. Could the company be this stupid, he wondered? Do I really want to work for a company that is this stupid?

At 4:45 P.M. Jerry resigned and went home. His boss called him two or three times the next day, but Jerry refused to take the calls. It took him a week to get over his rage. It took another six weeks to get a new job.

Shortly after he started his new job, Jerry received a call from an old friend who still worked for his previous employer in a programming job. His friend related to him a story that was circulating among some of the people there. The story went like this: An executive in the sales department learned of Jerry's project about three weeks before the project was terminated. According to the story, he instantly disliked the idea, basically because selling the machine would require a knowledge of hospitals and medical purchasing practices that his sales force did not have. So—again according to the story—he got one of his people to develop some very pessimistic numbers about market potential which he sent to a marketing executive, who was also a good friend, along with a note asking, "Why are we wasting research on this project?" •

Study Questions

Boss, Marketing, engineering, payroll, etc.

1. Upon whom was Jerry Cutler interdependent to complete his work?

2. Discuss how Jerry Cutler's failure to understand convergent interdependence and divergent interdependence led to his downfall.
   page 43   *page 45*

3. Did the power struggles Jerry Cutler had with the engineering and marketing departments have to be "zero-sum" conflicts?

Motivation for Power

David Kipnis

The problem of man's strivings for power as Veroff and Veroff (1972) have written has held a perpetual and pervasive fascination for students of the human race. We are continually perplexed by the vigor of this motivation as it seeks expression in myriads of encounters and transactions. We are troubled at the ease with which forces striving for power seem to overcome so easily the forces striving for community, harmony and love. Despite the centrality of this issue, and its intrinsic interest, less has been said in psychology about the origins and consequences of power motivations than has been said about, say, the origins of the motive to achieve or to affiliate or to avoid anxiety. It may well be that this omission stems from the fact, as Rollo May (1972) hints, that striving for power is in fact striving for self-assertion, self-development and growth and that there is very little to be said about power motives, per se, except in the context of discussion of striving for competence. From this view perhaps one can argue that human beings need power as they need air to breathe and that there are no real mysteries to be solved in this area.

The previous chapters provided the reader with various reasons why powerholders might be motivated to use influence or to restrain themselves from using it. Basically these reasons were concerned with motivations that arise out of the situation in which the individual finds himself, such as his role expectations, or the existence of threats to his own safety, and so on. The purpose of this chapter is to examine the more enduring aspects of human strivings for power. The reader should not be surprised to learn that explanations for power motivation overlap and even at times are contradictory. Power has many faces, some ugly, some bland, and some that are considered admirable by all (McClelland, 1969). According to which face the particular theorist chooses, the reasons for striving for power will be viewed approvingly or disapprovingly—as manifestations of man's inborn urge to overcome odds and create new works, or as a sick manifestation of childhood traumas that seek expression years afterward.

Power Striving as Neurotic Behavior—Sick People Seek Power

McClelland (1969) has made the observation that persons tend to derive great satisfaction in being told that they have high drives to achieve, or to affiliate, but experience guilt if they are told they have a high drive to achieve power. These emotions occur because of the many negative meanings associated with power motives in our culture. To be told that you are highly motivated for power tends to mean, in the everyday view, that you are a sadistic person who derives great enjoyment from controlling the fate of others. Indeed several psychoanalytic theories see power strivings as representing sick, neurotic behavior. The sickness is based upon the fact that the individual seeks power not as a means for achieving goals that require the services of others but simply as a means of controlling others. By controlling others, various psychological needs of which the person is not aware may be satisfied.

Neo-Freudians were among the first to be concerned with the question of power strivings as a manifestation of neuroses. In particular, psychoanalysts such as Alfred Adler, Karen Horney, and Eric Fromm have seen a direct link between the early social development of the child and subsequent strivings for power. In the psychoanalytic view the initial goals of persons with high needs for power are to use this power as a defense against feelings of low esteem and worthlessness. Neurotic strivings for power, as Horney notes, are born of anxiety, hatred, and feelings of inferiority. The normal person's striving for power is born of strength, the neurotic's of weakness.

While the psychoanalytic school has been in agreement in identifying the early socialization process with subsequent adult power strivings, there has been less agreement concerning the specific causes for such strivings to arise in the first place. In Adler's view (1956), power strivings arise out of childhood feelings of weakness. Adler points out that, from the point of view of nature, humans alone are inferior organisms. They are weak and defenseless. These feelings of inferiority and insecurity serve as basic motivational forces that goad people to discover better ways of adapting to their world. At the positive pole, this pressure to survive leads to the development of speech, intelligence, and communal activities. At the negative pole, it lends to strivings for superiority and dominance over others.

Children are particularly vulnerable to feelings of helplessness and dependency. If this general helplessness is balanced by rejecting or brutal parents, or if the child suffers from some physical disability, then in Adler's view the world tends to be seen by the child as enemy country. In fact Adler says that children with physical disability become particularly involved in a struggle for existence that strangles their social feelings. Instead of adjusting to their fellows, they are preoccupied with themselves, their survival, and with the impressions they make on others. One mode of adjustment is for the child to overcompensate for his weakness by striving for superiority. Through this exaggerated compensatory mechanism he attempts to reduce his feelings of inferiority and loss of self-esteem. Here, then, the process of character development begins in the child's attempts to better his chances for survival.

As an adult, this neurotic striving for power manifests itself in continual attempts to prove one's own superiority by outdoing and controlling others. When the world is viewed as the enemy, Adler states, there is a good deal of hostility associated with attempts to outdo and control. The power-striving individual tends to experience satisfaction rather than sorrow and pity if he finds that his actions have caused target persons to suffer.

This early description of the origin of power strivings was correct as far as it went, but it did not cover all the dynamic forces with which the helpless child must cope. Much more than compensatory strivings over physical weaknesses may be involved in the adult's neurotic striving for power. The incompleteness of the statement was one of the reasons for Karen Horney's

(1950) more explicit considerations of the meaning of early childhood feelings of rage and hostility in the development of adult behavior. Once again we begin with the defenseless child. Only, in Horney's view, it is not physical disability which serves as the overwhelming threat but the absence of parental love and protection. Her assumption was that the child who does not receive unconditional love and affection develops feelings of anger and hostility which cannot be openly expressed for fear of further antagonizing his parents. Thus the child is faced with the "double bind" of being angry and yet being afraid of being abandoned. Unable to cope with this kind of conflict, the child experiences deep fears and anxieties. And it is the child's efforts to reduce these noxious feelings that produce neurotic life-styles, including the striving for power.

In Horney's thinking, power is sought when the person's anxiety is coupled with the belief that the world is out to take advantage of the person. Here the strivings for power can serve two purposes. First, to be powerful is an assurance against the nagging fears of being helpless and abandoned. No longer does the person have to beg for help—rather, it is up to him to decide whether to help others. Rather than seek advice, which is a form of weakness, he gives advice. Other manifestations of this seeking to appear strong and dominant, according to Horney, are the neurotic person's incessant attempts to make others admire and love him for his beauty, or his intelligence, or his force of character. In short, by one means or another, he seeks to be the master and so bolster his self-esteem and repress the suspicion that he is not worthy.

A second purpose that is served by these neurotic forms of power striving is to allow the adult to express repressed hostility. Hostility takes the form of attempting to dominate others through insults and sharp criticisms. Horney has observed in her clinical practice that, when a patient's conscious motives were to dominate and control others, the patient had continued difficulties in maintaining affectionate relations with others. This is because the goal of power over others leads to a rejection of equality. Loving relations become especially difficult to maintain, unless the person finds a partner who actively enjoys the submissive role.

In practice, the neurotic strivings for power are seen in the person's incessant demands that others obey him, that he receive a greater share than others, and that others restrain from criticizing him. These strivings can be detected in the unhappiness of others who are required to bear the brunt of the neurotic power-striving person's anger, manipulations, and unconscious cruelties.

In the next chapter I will suggest that similar outcomes may occur in interpersonal relations through the continued exercise of power that is not resisted. However, the distinction between the metamorphic effects of power described in the next chapter and those effects described by Horney is that in the second instance the powerholder unconsciously seeks dominance and devaluation of others as a means of reducing feelings of basic anxiety and helplessness. Rather than being a consequence of exercising power, dominance and belittlement of others are the very reasons why power is sought by such neurotic persons in the first place.

Political Power and Childhood Deprivations

If we accept the idea that one origin of striving for power is in childhood deprivations, then it is possible to ask how such strivings manifest themselves in adult behavior. A particularly informative illustration can be found in the studies of political leaders by Harold Lasswell. Since this research is consistent with the idea of a continuity between early childhood experiences and subsequent power-seeking in adults, we will examine one of Lasswell's studies (Rogow and Lasswell 1963) in some detail.

The basic question asked by Lasswell is how political power is used and abused once it has been gained. Further, he asks whether there is a relation between the ego needs of political leaders and the tendency to abuse the power of elected office. To provide answers, Rogow and Lasswell analyzed the careers of thirty elected political leaders who in various ways had been involved in political scandal. Of interest was Lasswell's finding that early material poverty as well as psychological poverty, could produce an adult character structure obsessed with

power-seeking. That is, a politician's misuse of power associated with his office could be traced to early childhood deprivations of either a psychological or material kind.

Lasswell divided the thirty politicians into two types according to their early childhood experiences. The first type was called the "game politician." These officeholders tended to come from wealthy families in which they, as children, were either weak or fragile or had fathers who were strict disciplinarians. The image presented here is of children made to feel helpless and unloved by reason of either physical disabilities or tyrannical parents. Striving for political power, then, was seen as a means of compensating for low self-esteem. These politicians saw politics as a "game" that allowed them the self-expression and self-realization they had been denied as children.

Power was sought by game politicians as a means of obtaining prestige, adulation, and a sense of importance. However, game politicians showed no inclination to make money from illicit use of their power. While corruption surrounded their tenure in office, this corruption was tolerated not for personal gain but to win friends by being a party to deals which involved buying and selling political favors. Game politicians regarded the uses and abuses of money in politics as legitimate so long as they promoted the financial interests of their friends. What they received in return was the flattery and admiration of their special friends—ego needs that had been denied them as children.

A second type of politician was labeled by Rogow and Lasswell as the "gain politician." Generally these persons came from poor, migrant families that struggled continuously for money and food. However, these families did provide the child with love and emotional security. As adults, gain politicians fought their way to power in their neighborhoods, using physical force if necessary, until finally they controlled a local political machine. Rather than prestige, the dominant motive of gain politicians was to make money for themselves and their families. To this end they engaged in payoffs, deals, and provided inside information to the highest bidders. Unlike the game politicians, they cared little for what others thought of them so long as it did not interfere with their moneymaking.

Rogow and Lasswell in summarizing their findings offered the following observations concerning the importance of early childhood experience for the motivations of these politicians.

1. Severe early deprivation may encourage the striving for power and the use of it in corrupt forms as a means of controlling one's environment.

2. The nature of the early deprivation affects the purposes for which power is employed.

3. If deprivation mainly affects the need for love and ego needs, power will be used in corrupt forms for self-aggrandizement.

4. If the early deprivation mainly affects welfare values, power will be used in corrupt forms for material advantages.

Power Striving as a Substitute for Affection

Some people experience strong pleasure in being able to control the fate of others. Haroutunian (1949) has described the pleasure of exercising power as follows:

To lord it over others is a means of security, freedom, goods, and so on. But it is also a good in itself. A good which can overwhelm every other good dictated by reason and conscience alike. It is strangely gratifying to make people come and go at our bidding, to overrule their minds and their wills, to take away their power, and virtually annihilate them . . . There is a soul fulfillment in mastery over human beings. There is no pleasure quite like it, and for its sake men have risked every good and done every conceivable evil. It is well to remember these facts and take them seriously. [p. 9]

This enjoyment seems particularly important to people identified in the psychological literature as high in need for dominance (Watson 1972) or as Machiavellians (Christie and Geis 1970). The question to be considered here is whether those who enjoy exercising power for its own sake are in fact the same persons identified by Adler and by Horney as suffering from early childhood deprivations, or is "something more" involved? Several writers suggest that "something more" is in fact involved and that childhood experiences are not enough to

account for the subsequent enjoyment of manipulating the lives of others.

This "something more" involves the simple truth that human beings are unable to live in isolation from their fellows. Not only do we need others as a means of evaluating ourselves, in the manner suggested by George Herbert Mead and by Charles Cooley, but also we need others to provide us with emotional support. Human beings alone, deprived of friendship, social relations and love, yet always aware of their own mortality, may seek power in order to gain by force the love and esteem from others that they cannot obtain freely.

As a result of this need to make contact with one's fellow humans, the striving for mastery over others for the sake of mastery itself may paradoxically originate in man's fear of being estranged from his fellows (Haroutunian 1949).

In its more modest forms this need may be expressed in using the power to reward (as was suggested in Chapter 4) as a means of binding the affection of indifferent target persons. At its extreme this motive expresses itself in such sentiments as the sadistic desire to kill and torment others and in this perverted way, paradoxically to express one's linkages with others (Fromm 1959).

Thus another source goading human beings to seek power over others originates in feelings of aloneness and emotional emptiness rather than in childhood experiences. The awful chaos that threatens a person who has no emotional ties, who is the perpetual stranger, can be warded off by forcing others, through power, to give that person the love he craves. Further, the very act of forcing others tends to be seen as an affirmation of one's existence. It is no accident that the principal character in Albert Camus's *The Stranger* resorts to senseless violence as a means of affirming his emotional existence, after having remained for a long period emotionally isolated from others. Here and in other works such as his *Caligula* Camus recognized the link between aloneness and subsequent explosions of sadism and violence. Through these acts of domination one affirms one's own existence and one's emotional ties to others. An important derivation from this view of power striving, which we may now examine, is that any arrangement of society that isolates human beings from each other will encourage the development of power motives whose goal is the domination of others.

The extensive writings of Eric Fromm perhaps best express the interdependency between societal arrangements and man's strivings for mastery over others. Human beings have a basic need to receive love, comfort, and companionship, Fromm argues, and it is how these basic wants are met that determines the structure of motives. From a historical perspective Fromm sees man's relations with others as having been drastically altered by the advent of the industrial revolution and the growth of capitalism. In earlier times the individual was "locked" into relations with his primary family from birth to death. The primary ties of family and work provided each person with a sure sense of personal identity and emotional support. The advent of capitalism forced man from these static primary ties. Man's position in society was no longer predestined by birth and family name. Yet paradoxically this very freedom carried with it an enormous price. Now each person by his own efforts had to establish loving relations with others. No longer were these needs to be automatically satisfied by the structure of society.

To make an emotional connection with someone else is difficult to achieve in a modern society in which the emphasis is on "doing better" than others, in which the enormous concentrations of wealth and technology leave each individual with a profound sense of insignificance and lack of control, and in which the concentrations of people in large cities increase each person's sense of isolation from his neighbor. What then? How is the person to satisfy this basic need of relations with others? How is the person to escape from the unbearable position of aloneness and powerlessness?

One solution, among several examined by Fromm, is to force others to provide one with companionship. This solution may be expressed in sadistic behavior, in which the person desires to have absolute and unrestricted power over others. As Fromm says, the individual's feelings of strength are rooted in the fact that he is master of someone else, and this realization may satisfy his desire to commune with others. The pleasure in his complete domination over another person springs paradoxically from the individual's inability to bear aloneness. One can see a striking parallel between Fromm's views of the consequences of social isolation and Zimbardo's description of the consequences of deindividuation. In both instances isolation of self increases the urge to dominate and control others.

Men isolated from their fellows by the norms, customs, and arrangements of society may develop enormous cravings for power as the best means to establish relations with others. They hope to do with power what they have been unable to accomplish with love. And in part they are correct. I have already pointed out that people will flock around a person with power, flatter him, offer him love and admiration, deference and respect, which he so badly wants.

The problem with this solution is that the more power one seeks and obtains, the more one tends, paradoxically, to isolate oneself from others. The powerholder frequently suspects that the respect and admiration he is given is not for his own self but is given in recognition of the power he controls. As a result he may find himself holding in contempt those persons who surround him, considering them as lackeys or worse. The affection received from such persons, rather than satisfying his basic need for love, may in fact make the craving more unbearable. Thus in one sense power may increase suspicion and distrust of others, the very opposite of the original hopes of the person striving for power. Rather than decrease the "abhorrent void within," to use Kenneth B. Clark's (1971) phrase, the isolation of power may increase it, forcing the person, in anger over his failure to make the desired contacts with others, to ever greater attempts to dominate them.

All People Seek Power

So far the reasons offered for striving for power have been entirely negative. In terms of the description of the power act offered in Chapter 2, the individual's motives for wanting to exercise control are concerned with domination for its own sake. McClelland (1969) has suggested that there is another face of power that is not concerned with these dark motives. This face of power focuses on the beneficial reasons why power motives may arise, reasons in which there is no intent to harm or psychologically diminish the other person.

The intent, rather, is to have the means to control one's world. From this perspective survival is seen as the basic motive underlying universal strivings for power. The sociologist Robert A. Nisbet (1970) writes in this regard that control is the conscious or unconscious aim of all human behavior; and that every element of the individual's socialization process is designed to help the individual acquire control over the environment.

People seek power, then, to survive and to control their worlds. This section will examine the origins of this explanation of power motivation. The reader will see that the explanation for a universal tendency to strive for power centers around the fact that human beings seek not only to survive, but to maximize their own outcomes, and in so doing come into conflict with fellow human beings likewise so engaged. As a result power is sought not for its own sake but for aid in the competitive struggle with others. If this conclusion is valid, it further suggests that strivings for power do not originate in an instinctive desire to control and dominate others, as has been suggested by Freud, but as Hobbes suggests, in a pervasive tendency in mankind to satisfy one's appetites. Out of this need comes the pursuit of power.

An interesting derivation of this view is that the more the developing individual is socialized to achieve, to strive, to maintain the uniqueness of his identity, the more likely it is that he will, as an adult, pursue power. In this connection Skinner has argued, in his book *Beyond Freedom and Dignity* (1971), that a society that stresses the importance of self-realization rather than communal goals is bound in the final analysis to force its members into power strivings, since uniqueness tends to be defined in terms of "doing better" than others.

Rollo May (1972), in discussing human growth, also reflects this view: "Power is essential for all living things. To survive, man must use his powers and confront opposing forces at every point in his struggle" (p. 1). To survive, to grow, to create, all persons must

pursue power, since without it these positive goals cannot be achieved. In fact May argues that persons who deliberately avoid using power, glorifying in what they consider their own innocence, tend to be the best candidates for mental illness. Such innocence, May contends, manifests itself eventually in depression and self-hatred as the person's own psychological growth is thwarted by his unwillingness to exert influence and in this way to affirm his own worth.

The point of May's argument is, of course, that all persons seek and use power for instrumental reasons rather than because they enjoy controlling others. To deny the importance of power, May argues, is to commit oneself to continued helplessness. Yet one may ask, why should this be? Given the multitude of technological advances that have made the distribution of food, shelter and clothing widespread, why is it necessary for humans to evoke their resources and force others to carry out some act? Seemingly, if there is enough for all, enlightened self-interest would suggest that a reliance on "innocence," in May's term, is surely better than a reliance on power. Furthermore, if there is abundance, why doesn't the motive to strive for power wither away in mankind?

Thomas Hobbes in the seventeenth century, writing in *Leviathan*, explained the universal striving of man for power as the logical result of self-interest. Human beings, according to Hobbes, are motivated by appetites, some inborn but most learned from experience. These appetites are incessant and continually change. Most important, appetites steer man's behavior because, as Hobbes states, "Men desire 'felicity'— that is men desire continual success in satisfying their appetites." Thus in terms of human behavior Hobbes gives us the image of human beings seeking to satisfy a never-ending stream of wants and desires. When one appetite is satisfied, new ones press for "felicity."

Of course the problem is how man shall satisfy these neverceasing appetites. To answer this question Hobbes turned his attention to an analysis of power. According to Hobbes, "the power of man is his present means to obtain some future apparent good." That is, man satisfies his appetites and achieves "felicity" through his access to power. Power in Hobbes usage, appears to be equivalent to our definition of the control of resources. Power resides in those resources that are needed or feared by others because they are in short supply. Thus power is seen by Hobbes as the extent to which one person's means exceeds those of his fellows:

The value or worth of a man is as of all other things, his price, that is to say, so much as would be given for the use of his power; and therefore is not absolute, *but a thing dependent on the need and judgment of another.* An able conductor of soldiers is of great price in time of war, ongoing and imminent, but in Peace not so. A learned and uncorrupt judge is much worth in time of peace, but not so much in war. And as in other things, so in man, not the seller, but the buyer determines the price. For let a man (as most men do,) rate themselves as the highest value they can; yet their true value is no more than it is esteemed by others. [Pp. 151–52; emphasis added]

In other words Hobbes is telling us that the judgment by others of our skills, abilities, and possessions determines the power we possess. In the 1950s, when there were relatively few engineers to service an expanding American economy, engineers held great prestige and power. They could force employers to provide them with large salaries and benefits, by threatening to withhold their services. By the early 1970s, however, many persons had become engineers and consequently the bargaining power of engineers with employers was practically nil. In short, resources can be invoked to achieve intended effects so long as there is a buyer, to use Hobbes's terms. Intelligence provides no special advantage to the individual, when all are equally gifted and bright. Similarly, beauty is no longer a base of power when all are beautiful and money loses its special advantage for purchasing goods and services when everyone is equally rich.

What determines an individual's potential power? The answer supplied by Hobbes has a particularly modern ring and covers both personal resources (natural power, in Hobbes's terms) and resources originating from society and institutions. Here is a brief excerpt from *Leviathan* which lists some of the many bases of power that can be used to provide satisfaction of man's incessant appetites.

Natural Power is the eminence of the facilities of body or mind: extraordinary strength, form, eloquence, and mobility. To have friends is power, for they are strength united. Also riches joined with liberality is power; because it procures friends and servants. Reputation of power is power; because it attracts with it the adherence of those that need protection. Also what quality soever maketh a man beloved or feared of many; or the reputation of such quality is power because it is a means to have the assistance and services of many. [p. 150]

The timelessness of Hobbes's definition of power is shown in a recent discussion in the *New York Times Magazine* (October 7, 1973) on the reason why the American Bar Association can have a major effect on state legislatures, "Its greatest source of power, and the way it is exercised," explained a staff member, "comes from the standing of the lawyers in the community and the state bar association. They are the pillars of the community. They know their Congressmen and Senators personally." In short, the lawyer's "reputation of power is power," as Hobbes said. Power, then, is ultimately whatever gives the person access to the "pooled energy of many" (Mott 1970), so that the powerholder can cause others to carry out acts that will bring him "felicity."

Hobbes's system of assumptions leads to the inevitable conclusion that all persons must continuously strive for power, without ceasing. The reason for this may be traced in propositional form as follows: (1) human beings are driven by a never-ending stream of appetites that must be satisfied; (2) the possession of power is the means by which these appetites are satisfied; (3) power always resides in the possession of commodities or resources that are in short supply; (4) because power resides in those commodities that are in short supply, all persons must continually strive for power if they are to satisfy their wants. If everybody possesses a resource in equal amounts it is no longer in scarce supply and hence cannot be used to satisfy one's appetites; thus one must continually scramble for new resources to keep ahead of others striving for scarce resources; (5) an inevitable byproduct of this power striving is that human beings are forced into conflict with each other in order to obtain effective bases of power. Hobbes states most eloquently these sobering conclusions:

So that in the first place I put for a general inclination of all mankind, a perpetual and restless desire of Power after power, that ceaseth only in death. And the cause of this is not always that a man hopes for a more intensive delight than he has attained already, or that he cannot be content with a moderate power, but because he cannot assure the power and means to live well which he has present without the acquisition of more.

Thus every one is necessarily pulled into a competitive struggle for resources, or at least to resist the efforts of others to command their resources (Macpherson 1968). Since by definition there can never be enough scarce resources, and all persons have the same wish for happiness, they must necessarily struggle with each other in order to gain power to secure for themselves the future. In answer to our question then as to why technology cannot reduce power strivings, Hobbes would answer that needs are incessant and continually changing. Technology cannot keep up with the continual stream of "appetites" that humans invent and for which they need power to find "felicity." One might conclude from Hobbes's analysis that, to avoid the continual chase after power, one must give up one's appetites, since more power leads to more appetites, which require more power, and so on—a never-ending circle.

We have given this attention to Hobbes's views because they serve as the basis for most modern-day conceptions of the idea that power strivings may be a universal phenomenon, not one limited to the psychologically sick person. However, the basic goal of Hobbes's writings was not to provide a psychological analysis of power strivings but to give a political justification of the need for a strong monarchical system. As a result, Hobbes's ideas are at best a combination of psychological observations of man's nature (all persons are driven by appetites) combined with an economic analysis of the problem attendant on the fact that resources become less valuable as they become more common.

Various modern psychologists have adopted aspects of the Hobbesian analysis, although with less emphasis on the pessimistic aspects of power strivings that pertain to the continual struggle to obtain more than one's fellows. For instance, Tedeschi and his colleagues (Tedeschi, Schlenker, and Bonoma 1971) have assumed a universal drive for power in proposing an alternate explanation to dissonance theory.

Basically, the explanation of Tedeschi et al. originates in the finding that the dissonance effect is most likely to occur when people believe that their behaviors are engaged in freely and are not under the experimenter's control. Tedeschi et al. ask why perceived freedom should have this effect. The answer proposed by these writers is that all persons are concerned with the impression they make on others. That is, consistency of words and deeds enhances the individual's own credibility and *enables him to be more successful in influencing others*. For a person to state, for instance that he likes apples on one day and that he hates apples on the next would cause others to be uncertain as to what statements by the person to believe. Hence the impression they have of him might be less favorable. It is this state of affairs that each person wishes to avoid, since everyone intuitively realizes that people trust others who act rationally. If we are distrusted, our goal of exercising power and influence is blocked.

The motive to avoid doing contradictory things, in Tedeschi et al.'s view, can be seen as not arising from an internal experience of psychological tension, as proposed by dissonance theory, but from a calculated desire by the individual to be in the best position to exert influence and power, by presenting a public stance of rationality and consistency. While Tedeschi et al. do not explicitly propose that all persons seek power, their related hypothesis that all persons seek to maintain a consistent public image so as to influence others is clearly in the Hobbesian tradition.

Effectiveness and Power Motivation

Hobbes in his discussion of human appetites makes no distinction between the drives of individuals to secure wealth and material possessions and the drive to obtain self-knowledge and self-worth. Many psychologists, however, view the individual in terms of his strivings to become a mature adult. Less attention is paid to his attempts to gain material wealth. As could be expected, there appears to be a definite relation between the development of power motives and the striving for psychological growth and effectiveness. May, in *Power and Innocence* (1972), explicitly traces this relation. "Man's basic psychological reason for living," he states, "is to affirm himself, to struggle for self-esteem, to say I am, to do this in the face of nature's magnificent indifference." To do this all people must seek power, if only because, without power to command attention, the individual is basically helpless to realize these goals.

May's view of power strivings as a necessary correlate of attempts to achieve psychological well-being is a valuable addition to the literature on this subject. This is because he provides a view of power motives as a potentially positive rather than negative force in life. He stresses the idea that the reasons for seeking power do not have to center around the goal of dominating and exploiting others but can spring from the assertion of one's own individuality. Of course what is missing from May's writings is a consideration of what may happen when all people simultaneously strive to assert their own individuality. In what ways will they come into conflict with each other?

A Hobbesian analysis of such strivings for maturity suggests inevitable conflict as all strive to assert their will against the indifference of nature and human beings. On the other hand, such conflict may promote the attempts by mature persons to learn how to compromise and to turn competition into cooperation.

Some People Seek Power

So far this chapter has contained little empirical data that pertain to individual differences in power striving. Perhaps the strongest contribution to the empirical literature on individual and group differences is based upon the analysis of power imagery in stories, speeches, and fantasy (Veroff and Veroff 1972; Winter 1973). This research is based on the assumption that the greater the amount of power imagery in the verbal and written expressions of people, the greater their need to control and exercise influence.

Before we can examine the research on power imagery, it is necessary to point out that there are two methods of measuring power imagery in use, each yielding very different findings. The first measure, developed by Veroff (1957), can be labeled *fear of* and measures a person's desire to be free from the control of others. This motive is most likely to be aroused when freedom of choice is threatened. The second measure, developed by Winter (1973), involves a positive attraction to the use of power. This second measure closely approximates everyday ideas about "power cravings," in that persons with high scores on Winter's measure are described as deriving satisfaction from influencing other persons.

Through the use of these two measures, an impressive variety of empirical relations have been uncovered concerning how power motives are expressed in day-to-day life. With reference to the *fear of power* measure, the findings indicate, as I mentioned, that this motive is most likely to be aroused when self-assertion is threatened. Veroff and Veroff (1972) report that high *fear of power* scores have been found more often, for instance, among black respondents than among white respondents, among educated women more than among educated men—in general among status groups concerned with overcoming their own weaknesses.

These findings can be interpreted as meaning that, when persons are without power, when their goals of achieving psychological growth or material well-being have been blocked, then their conscious motive structure will center around thoughts of power. To have power under these circumstances will allow the individual, at a minimum, as Veroff and Veroff suggest, to be free from the control of others. These empirical findings are consistent with the idea of Alfred Adler that power motives arise as compensations for physical or psychological weaknesses and threats.

Using the Winter measure of power needs, the findings appear more complex for persons who hold high motives to influence others. Basically, however, such persons have been found by Winter to be attracted to situations and things that enhance the possibility of exercising power. Winter has reported that persons scoring high on his measure of need for power tended to buy prestige objects that would cause envy in others, were attracted to occupations where they could exercise influence (teaching, sales), were more likely to run for political office, tried to dominate others in group discussions, and at times drank too much as a means of fantasizing about power. This is, in many ways, a not very attractive portrait of an individual's single-minded pursuit of power. While Winter does not provide us with the early developmental history on those who scored high on his measure or power motive, the picture that is presented appears consistent with the description of neurotic power-seekers provided by Alfred Adler, Karen Horney, and Eric Fromm.

The research of Winter has so far not been concerned with an analysis of the process by which power is exercised, nor does it tell us what persons with a high need for power think of themselves or others as a result of continually seeking to exercise power.

Suppose, for example, that persons with high scores on the Winter measure of power striving were given access to a range of means of influence (expert power, reward power, coercive power, and so on). If these power bases could be freely used to influence targets without costs to these persons, would those with high power-needs enjoy themselves? Would they be more adept at selecting the appropriate influence mode to overcome various kinds of target resistances than persons with low power-needs?

Some answers to these questions are suggested by turning to the results of studies that have employed the Machiavellian scale developed by two psychologists, Richard Christe and Florence Geis (1970). This scale was specifically constructed to measure the tendency of some persons to take advantage of other persons. While a full description of the scale and its uses is beyond the scope of this book, it suffices to point out that Winter's description of persons with high need for power and the description of persons scoring high on the Machiavellian scale appear to overlap considerably. Thus it seems reasonable to extrapolate the findings from the latter area of research to the former. Studies of persons classified as Machiavellian personalities have found that

when they were placed in positions of influence over peers (but given no formal means of influence) they invented a variety of verbal influence modes to use with their targets and enjoyed the chance to fool and deceive others. Further, those with high Machiavellian scores were found to be more exploitive in situations involving the opportunity to gain resources at another's expense. Studies by Banks (1974) and by Berger (1973) have also found that high scorers on the Machiavellian scale were less credible in their use of power and more adept in its use. Thus the available data point to the conclusion that persons who enjoy exercising control over people use different power tactics than those who do not enjoy exercising such influence.

One further point concerning Winter's measure of power motivation. There is still, I believe, a good deal to be learned about what happens when "power-driven" persons are in situations that allow a full range of power to be exercised. The research described above only indirectly touches on the potential explosiveness of such combinations. Studies of the presence of power imagery in the speeches of American presidents (Winter 1973), for instance, suggest that conflict may be an inevitable outcome of this combination. This is because the demands of leaders with strong power motives are never-ending when they have access to unlimited resources. Conflict arises because sooner or later these demands produce stronger and stronger resistances among target persons or target nations.

So far we have speculated about how persons scoring high on the Winter measure of power motivation would actually use different means of influence. Similar speculation can be raised concerning the Veroff measure of fear of power. The most likely answer is that persons with high fear of power needs would be attracted to the use of threats and punishments as the preferred power tactic. This suggestion is made because many of the characteristics associated with persons with high fear-of-power scores (that is, persons deprived of material or psychological resources) appear similar to those of persons discussed in Chapter 6 who stated that they lacked self-confidence or who believed that they were not in control of their own behavior. It would appear that what links these variously described individuals are low expectations of successful influence and the associated belief that only strong means of influence will cause others to comply.

Summary

The general conclusion to be drawn from this chapter is that all forces that reduce the individual's feelings of competence, or that serve to promote new wants and aspirations, increase the individual's motives to gain power. Feelings of weakness in any form, as Veroff and Veroff note (1972) are associated with high power motivations. We have attempted to distinguish in this chapter when such feelings of weakness attract the individual to seek power for its own sake and when such feelings do not establish a bond between power and the desire to control and dominate. It has been suggested that if these feelings of weakness originate from psychological traumas of early childhood or from present alienation from others, then the goal of power motives is most likely to be to dominate and control others for the sake of the control itself. If the feelings of weakness originate from a need to obtain commodities, or to further goals of growth and maturity, then it appears that the goal of power motives will not include the dream of manipulation of others as an end in itself. Rather power will be used as a means of obtaining services or objects that are controlled by other people. Once these services or objects have been obtained, the power-holder's concern with the exercise of influence tends to cease. •

Study Questions

1. Discuss the different perspectives regarding individuals' quest for power. In particular, contrast the "unhealthy" with "healthy" explanations for this drive/need.

2. Which perspective(s) seem particularly relevant to the issue of negotiation?

The Bases of Social Power

John R. P. French, Jr.
Bertram Raven

Most social theories conceive of power as involving a communication relationship. With their authority hierarchies, opportunities for political action, and communicatively rich relationships, work organizations are therefore natural sites for the study of power. But power is a complicated subject that requires a good descriptive foundation for further thought.

In an oft-cited article that we have abridged here, French and Raven define power as the ability to influence an individual's psychological field, including behavior, opinions, attitudes, goals, needs, and values. The article is best known for its identification of five sources of power: referent, expert, reward, coercive, and legitimate. French and Raven delineate the general circumstances when it is appropriate to use each source of power and describe how using power may have consequences for the person who holds the power.

The processes of power are pervasive, complex, and often disguised in our society. Accordingly one finds in political science, in sociology, and in social psychology a variety of distinctions among different types of social power or among qualitatively different processes of social influence (1, 7, 14, 20, 21, 24, 25, 29, 32). Our main purpose is to identify the major types of power and to define them systematically so that we may compare them according to the changes which they produce and the other effects which accompany the use of power.

Our theory of social influence and power is limited to influence on the person, P, produced by a social agent, O, where O can be either another person, a role, a norm, a group, or a part of a group. We do not consider social influence exerted on a group.

The Bases of Power

By the basis of power we mean the relationship between O and P which is the source of that power. It is rare that we can say with certainty that a given empirical case of power is limited to one source.

Normally, the relation between O and P will be characterized by several qualitatively different variables which are bases of power (25). Although there are undoubtedly many possible bases of power which may be distinguished, we shall here define five which seem especially common and important. These five bases of O's power are: (a) reward power, based on P's perception that O has the ability to mediate rewards for him; (b) coercive power, based on P's perception that O has the ability to mediate punishments for him; (c) legitimate power, based on the perception by P that O has a legitimate right to prescribe behavior for him; (d) referent power, based on P's identification with O; (e) expert power, based on the perception that O has some special knowledge or expertness.

Reward Power

Reward power is defined as power whose basis is the ability to reward. The strength of the reward power of O/P increases with the magnitude of the rewards which P perceives that O can mediate for him. Reward power depends on O's ability to administer positive valences and to remove or decrease negative valences. The strength of reward power also depends upon the probability that O can mediate the reward, as perceived by P. A common example of reward power is the addition of a piece-work rate in the factory as an incentive to increase production.

The new state of the system induced by a promise of reward (for example, the factory worker's increased level of production) will be highly dependent on O. Since O mediates the reward, he controls the probability that P will receive it. Thus P's new rate of production will be dependent on his subjective probability that O will reward him for conformity minus his subjective probability that O will reward him even if he returns to his old level. Both probabilities will be greatly affected by the level of observability of P's behavior. Incidentally, a piece rate often seems to have more effect on production than a merit rating system because it yields a higher probability of reward for conformity and a much lower probability of reward for nonconformity.

The utilization of actual rewards (instead of promises) by O will tend over time to increase the attraction of P toward O and therefore the referent power of O over P. As we shall note later, such referent power will permit O to induce changes which are relatively independent. Neither rewards nor promises will arouse resistance in P, provided P considers it legitimate for O to offer rewards.

The range of reward power is specific to those regions toward within which O can reward P for conforming. The use of rewards to change systems within the range of reward power tends to increase reward power by increasing the probability attached to future promises. However, unsuccessful attempts to exert reward power outside the range of power would tend to decrease the power; for example, if O offers to reward P for performing an impossible act, this will reduce for P the probability of receiving future rewards promised by O.

Coercive Power

Coercive power is similar to reward power in that it also involves O's ability to manipulate the attainment of valences. Coercive power of O/P stems from the expectation on the part of P that he will be punished by O if he fails to conform to the influence attempt. Thus negative valences will exist in given regions of P's life space, corresponding to the threatened punishment by O. The strength of coercive power depends on the magnitude of the negative valence of the threatened punishment multiplied by the perceived probability that P can avoid the punishment by conformity, i.e., the probability of punishment for nonconformity minus the probability of punishment for conformity (11). Just as an offer of a piece-rate bonus in a factory can serve as a basis for reward power, so the ability to fire a worker if he falls below a given level of production will result in coercive power.

Coercive power leads to dependent change also, and the degree of dependence varies with the level of observability of P's conformity. An excellent illustration of coercive power leading to dependent change is provided by a clothes presser in a factory observed by Coch and French (3). As her efficiency rating climbed above average for the group the other workers began to "scapegoat" her. That the resulting plateau in her production was not independent of the group was evident once she was removed from the presence of the other workers. Her production immediately climbed to new heights.*

At times, there is some difficulty in distinguishing between reward power and coercive power. Is the withholding of a reward really equivalent to a punishment? Is the withdrawal of punishment equivalent to a reward? The answer must be a psychological one—it depends upon the situation as it exists for P. But ordinarily we would answer these questions in the affirmative; for P, receiving a reward is a positive valence as is the relief of suffering. There is some evidence (5) that conformity to group norms in order to gain acceptance (reward power) should be distinguished from conformity as a means of forestalling rejection (coercive power).

The distinction between these two types of power is important because the dynamics are different. The concept of "sanctions" sometimes lumps the two together despite their opposite effects. While reward power may eventually result in an independent system, the effects of coercive power will continue to be dependent. Reward power will tend to increase the attraction of P toward O; coercive power will decrease this attraction (11, 12). The valence of the region of behavior will become more negative, acquiring some negative valence from the threatened punishment. The negative valence of punishment would also spread to other regions of the life space. Lewin (23) has pointed out this distinction between the effects of rewards and punishment. In the case of threatened punishment, there will be a resultant force on P to leave the field entirely. Thus, to achieve conformity, O must not only place a strong negative valence in certain regions through threat of punishment, but O must also introduce restraining forces, or other strong valences, so as to prevent P from withdrawing completely from O's range of coercive power. Otherwise the probability of receiving the punishment, if P does not conform, will be too low to be effective.

Legitimate Power

Legitimate power is probably the most complex of those treated here, embodying notions from the structural sociologist, the group-norm and role oriented social psychologist, and the clinical psychologist.

There has been considerable investigation and speculation about socially prescribed behavior, particularly that which is specific to a given role or position. Linton (24) distinguishes group norms according to whether they are universals for everyone in the culture, alternatives (the individual having a choice as to whether or not to accept them), or specialties (specific to given positions). Whether we speak of internalized norms, role prescriptions and expectations (27), or internalized pressures (15), the fact remains that each individual sees certain regions toward which he should locomote, some regions toward which he should not locomote, and some regions toward which he may locomote if they are generally attractive for him. This applies to specific behaviors in which he may, should, or should not engage; it applies to certain attitudes or beliefs which he may, should, or should not hold. The feeling of "oughtness" may be an internalization from his parents, from his teachers, from his religion, or may have been logically developed from some idiosyncratic system of ethics. He will speak of such behaviors with expressions like "should," "ought to," or "has a right to." In many cases, the original source of the requirement is not recalled.

Legitimate power of O/P is here defined as that power which stems from internalized values in P which dictate that O has a legitimate right to influence P and that P has an obligation to accept this influence. We note that legitimate power is very similar to the notion of legitimacy of authority which has long been explored by sociologists, particularly by Weber (32), and more recently by Goldhammer and Shils (14). However, legitimate power is not always a role relation: P may accept an induction from O simply because he had previously promised to help O and he values his word too much to break the promise. In all cases, the notion of legitimacy involves some sort of code or standard, accepted by the individual, by virtue of which the external agent can assert his power. We shall attempt to describe a few of these values here.

Bases for Legitimate Power. Cultural values constitute one common basis for the legitimate power of one individual over another. O has characteristics which are specified by the culture as giving him the right to prescribe behavior for P, who may not have these characteristics. These bases, which Weber (32) has called the authority of the "eternal yesterday," include such things as age, intelligence, caste, and physical characteristics. In some cultures, the aged are granted the right to prescribe behavior for others in practically all behavior areas. In most cultures, there are certain areas of behavior in which a person of one sex is granted the right to prescribe behavior for the other sex.

Acceptance of the social structure is another basis for legitimate power. If P accepts as right the social structure of his group, organization, or society, especially the social structure involving a hierarchy of authority, P will accept the legitimate authority of O, who occupies a superior office in the hierarchy. Thus legitimate power in a formal organization is largely a relationship between offices rather than between persons. And the acceptance of an office as right is a basis for legitimate power—a judge has a right to levy fines, a foreman should assign work, a priest is justified in prescribing religious beliefs, and it is the management's prerogative to make certain decisions (10). However, legitimate power also involves the perceived right of the person to hold the office.

Designation by a legitimizing agent is a third basis for legitimate power. An influencer O may be seen as legitimate in prescribing behavior for P, because he has been granted such power by a legitimizing agent whom P accepts. Thus a department head may accept the authority of his vice-president in a certain area because that authority has been specifically delegated by the president. An election is perhaps the most common example of a group's serving to legitimize the authority of one individual or office for other individuals in the group. The success of such legitimizing depends upon the acceptance of the legitimizing agent and procedure. In this case it depends ultimately on certain democratic values concerning election procedures. The election process is one of legitimizing a person's right to an office which already has a legitimate range of power associated with it.

Range of Legitimate Power of O/P. The areas in which legitimate power may be exercised are generally specified along with the designation of that power. A job description, for example, usually specifies supervisory activities and also designates the person to whom the Job-holder is responsible for the duties described. Some bases for legitimate authority carry with them a very broad range. Culturally derived bases for legitimate power are often especially broad. It is not uncommon to find cultures in which a member of a given caste can legitimately prescribe behavior for all members of lower castes in practically all regions. More common, however, are instances of legitimate power where the range is specifically and narrowly prescribed. A sergeant in the army is given a specific set of regions within which he can legitimately prescribe behavior for his men.

The attempted use of legitimate power which is outside of the range of legitimate power will decrease the legitimate power of the authority figure. Such use of power which is not legitimate will also decrease the attractiveness of O (11, 12, 28).

Legitimate Power and Influence. The new state of the system which results from legitimate power usually has high dependence on O though it may become independent. Here, however, the degree of dependence is not related to the level of observability. Since legitimate power is based on P's values, the source of the forces induced by O include both these internal values and O. O's induction serves to activate the values and to relate them to the system which is influenced, but thereafter the new state of the system may become directly dependent on the values with no mediation by O.

Accordingly this new state will be relatively stable and consistent across varying environmental situations since P's values are more stable than his psychological environment.

We have used the term legitimate not only as a basis for the power of an agent, but also to describe the general behaviors of a person. Thus, the individual P may also consider the legitimacy of the attempts to use other types of power by O. In certain cases, P will consider that O has a legitimate right to threaten punishment for nonconformity; in other cases, such use of coercion would not be seen as legitimate. P might change in response to coercive power of O, but it will make a considerable difference in his attitude and conformity if O is not seen as having a legitimate right to use such coercion. In such cases, the attraction of P for O will be particularly diminished, and the influence attempt will arouse more resistance (11). Similarly the utilization of reward power may vary in legitimacy; the word "bribe," for example, denotes an illegitimate reward.

Referent Power

The referent power of O/P has its basis in the identification of P with O. By identification, we mean a feeling of oneness of P with O, or a desire for such an identity. If O is a person toward whom P is highly attracted, P will have a desire to become closely associated with O. If O is an attractive group, P will have a feeling of membership or a desire to join. If P is already closely associated with O he will want to maintain this relationship (31). P's identification with O can be established or maintained if P behaves, believes, and perceives as O does. Accordingly O has the ability to influence P, even though P may be unaware of this referent power. A verbalization of such power by P might be, "I am like O, and therefore I shall behave or believe as O does," or "I want to be like O, and I will be more like O if I behave or believe as O does." The stronger the identification of P with O the greater the referent power of O/P.

Similar types of power have already been investigated under a number of different formulations. Festinger (6) points out that in an ambiguous situation the individual seeks some sort of "social reality" and may adopt the cognitive structure of the individual or group with which he identifies. In such a case, the lack of clear structure may be threatening to the individual and the agreement of his beliefs with those of a reference group will both satisfy his need for structure and give him added security through increased identification with his group (16, 19).

We must try to distinguish between referent power and other types of power which might be operative at the same time. If a member is attracted to a group and he conforms to its norms only because he fears ridicule or expulsion from the group for nonconformity, we would call this coercive power. On the other hand if he conforms in order to obtain praise for conformity, it is a case of reward power. The basic criterion for distinguishing referent power from both coercive and reward power is the mediation of the punishment and the reward by O: to the extent that O mediates the sanctions (i.e., has means control over P) we are dealing with coercive and reward power; but to the extent that P avoids discomfort or gains satisfaction by conformity based on identification, regardless of O's responses, we are dealing with referent power. Conformity with majority opinion is sometimes based on a respect for the collective wisdom of the group, in which case it is expert power. It is important to distinguish these phenomena, all grouped together elsewhere as "pressures toward uniformity," since the type of change which occurs will be different for different bases of power.

The concepts of "reference group" (30) and "prestige suggestion" may be treated as instances of referent power. In this case, O, the prestigeful person or group, is valued by P; because P desires to be associated or identified with O, he will assume attitudes or beliefs held by O. Similarly a negative reference group which O dislikes and evaluates negatively may exert negative influence on P as a result of negative referent power.

It has been demonstrated that the power which we designate as referent power is especially great when P is attracted to O (2, 6, 8, 9, 13, 21, 25). In our terms, this would mean that the greater the attraction, the greater the identification, and consequently the greater the referent power. In some cases, attraction or prestige may have a specific basis, and the range of referent power will be limited accordingly: a group of campers may have great referent power over a member regarding campcraft, but considerably less effect on other regions (25). However, we hypothesize that the greater the attraction of P toward O, the broader the range of referent power of O/P.

The new state of a system produced by referent power may be dependent on or independent of O; but the degree of dependence is not affected by the level of observability to O (7, 21). In fact, P is often not consciously aware of the referent power which O exerts over him. There is probably a tendency for some of these dependent changes to become independent of O quite rapidly.

Expert Power

The strength of the expert power of O/P varies with the extent of the knowledge or perception which P attributes to O within a given area. Probably P evaluates O's expertness in relation to his own knowledge as well as against an absolute standard. In any case expert power results in primary social influence on P's cognitive structure and probably not on other types of systems. Of course changes in the cognitive structure can change the direction of forces and hence of locomotion, but such a change of behavior is secondary social influence. Expert power has been demonstrated experimentally (9, 26). Accepting an attorney's advice in legal matters is a common example of expert influence; but there are many instances based on much less knowledge, such as the acceptance by a stranger of directions given by a native villager.

Expert power, where O need not be a member of P's group, is called "information power" by Deutsch and Gerard (4). This type of expert power must be distinguished from influence based on the content of communication as described by Hovland et al. (17, 18, 21, 22). The influence of the content of a communication upon an opinion is presumably a secondary influence produced after the primary influence (i.e., the acceptance of the information). Since power is here defined in terms of the primary changes, the influence of the content on a related opinion is not a case of expert power as we have defined it, but the initial acceptance of the validity of the content does seem to be based on expert power or referent power. In other cases, however, so-called facts may be accepted as self-evident because they fit into P's cognitive structure; if this impersonal acceptance of the truth of the fact is independent of the more-or-less enduring relationship between O and P, then P's acceptance of the fact is not an actualization of expert power. Thus we distinguish between expert power based on the credibility of O and informational influence which is based on characteristics of the stimulus such as the logic of the argument or the "self-evident facts."

Wherever expert influence occurs it seems to be necessary both for P to think that O knows and for P to trust that O is telling the truth (rather than trying to deceive him).

Expert power will produce a new cognitive structure which is initially relatively dependent on O, but informational influence will produce a more independent structure. The former is likely to become more independent with the passage of time. In both cases the degree of dependence on O is not affected by the level of observability.

The "sleeper effect" (18, 22) is an interesting case of a change in the degree of dependence of an opinion on O. An unreliable O (who probably had negative referent power but some positive expert power) presented "facts" which were accepted by the subjects and which would normally produce secondary influence on the opinions and beliefs. However, the negative referent power aroused resistance and resulted in negative social influence on their beliefs (i.e., set up a force in the direction opposite to the influence attempt), so that there was little change in the subjects' opinions. With the passage of time, however, the subjects tended to forget the identity of the negative communicator faster than they forgot the contents of his communications, so there was a weakening of the negative referent influence and a consequent delayed positive change in the subjects' beliefs in the direction of the influence attempt ("sleeper effect"). Later, when the identity of the negative communicator was experimentally

reinstated, these resisting forces were reinstated, and there was another negative change in belief in a direction opposite to the influence attempt (22).

The range of expert power, we assume, is more delimited than that of referent power. Not only is it restricted to cognitive systems but the expert is seen as having superior knowledge or ability in very specific areas, and his power will be limited to these areas, though some "halo effect" might occur. Recently, some of our renowned physical scientists have found quite painfully that their expert power in physical sciences does not extend to regions involving international politics. Indeed, there is some evidence that the attempted exertion of expert power outside of the range of expert power will reduce that expert power. An undermining of confidence seems to take place.

Summary

We have distinguished five types of power: referent power, expert power, reward power, coercive power, and legitimate power. These distinctions led to the following hypotheses.

1. For all five types, the stronger the basis of power the greater the power.

2. For any type of power the size of the range may vary greatly, but in general referent power will have the broadest range.

3. Any attempt to utilize power outside the range of power will tend to reduce the power.

4. A new state of a system produced by reward power or coercive power will be highly dependent on O, and the more observable P's conformity the more dependent the state. For the other three types of power, the new state is usually dependent, at least in the beginning, but in any case the level of observability has no effect on the degree of dependence.

5. Coercion results in decreased attraction of P toward O and high resistance; reward power results in increased attraction and low resistance.

6. The more legitimate the coercion the less it will produce resistance and decreased attraction. •

References

Asch, S. E. *Social psychology.* New York: Prentice-Hall, 1952.

Back, K. Influence through social communication *Journal of Abnormal and Social Psychology,* 1951, 46, 9–23.

Coch, L., & French, J. R. P., Jr. Overcoming resistance to change. *Human Relations,* 1948, 1, 512–532.

Deutsch, M., & Gerard, H. A study of normative and informational influences upon individual judgment. *Journal of Abnormal and Social Psychology,* 1955, 51, 629–36.

Dittes, J., & Kelley, H. Effects of different conditions of acceptance upon conformity to group norms. *Journal of Abnormal and Social Psychology,* 1956, 53, 629–636.

Festinger, L. Informal social communication. *Psychological Review,* 1950, 57, 271–282.

Festinger, L. An analysis of complaint behavior. In M. Sherif & M. O. Wilson (Eds.), Group relations at the crossroads. New York: Harper, 1953. Pp. 232–256.

Festinger, L., Schachter, S., & Back, K. *Social pressures in informal groups.* New York: Harper, 1950, Chap. 5.

Festinger, L., et al. The influence process in the presence of extreme deviates. *Human Relations,* 1952, 5, 327–346.

French, J. R. P., Jr., Israel, J., & As, D. *Arbeidernes-medvirkning i industribedriften: En eksperimentell undersokelse.* Oslo, Norway: Institute for Social Research, 1957.

French, J. R. P., Jr., Morrison, H. W., & Levinger, G. Coercive power and forces affecting conformity. *Journal of Abnormal and Social Psychology,* 1960, 61, 93–101.

Raven, B., & French, J. R. P., Jr. Legitimate power, coercive power, and observability in social influence. *Sociometry,* 1958, 21, 83–97.

Gerard, H. The anchorage of opinions in face-to-face groups. *Human Relations,* 1954, 7, 313–325.

Goldhammer, H., & Shils, E. Types of power and status. *American Journal of Sociology,* 1939, ff, 171–178.

Herbst, P. Analysis and measurement of a situation. *Human Relations,* 1953, 2, 113–140.

Hochbaum. G. Self-confidence and reaction group pressures. *American Sociological Review* 1954, 19, 678–687.

Hovland, G., Lumsdaine, A., & Sheffield, F. *Experiments on mass communication.* Princeton, N.J. Princeton Univ. Press, 1949.

Hovland, C., & Weiss, W. The influence of credibility on communication effectiveness. *Opinion Quarterly,* 1951, 15, 635–650

Jackson, I., & Saltzstein. H. The effect of person-group relationships on conformity processes. *Journal of Abnormal and Social Psychology,* 1958, 57, 17–24.

Jahoda, M. Psychological issues in civil liberties. *The American Psychologist,* 1956, 11, 234–240.

Kelman, H. Three processes of acceptance of social influence: Compliance, identification, and internalization. Paper read at the meetings of the American Psychological Association, August, 1956.

Kelman, H., & Hovland, C. Reinstatement of the communicator in delayed measurement of opinion change. *Journal of Abnormal and Social Psychology,* 1953, 48, 327–335.

Lewin, K. *Dynamic theory of personality.* New York: McGraw-Hill, 1935. Pp. 114–170.

Linton, R. *The cultural background of personality.* New York: Appleton-Century-Crofts, 1945.

Lippitt, R., et al. The dynamics of power. *Human Relations,* 1952, 5, 37–64.

Moore, H. The comparative influence of majority and expert opinion. *American Journal of Psychology,* 1921, 32, 16–20.

Newcomb, T. *Social psychology.* New York: Dryden, 1950.

Raven, B., & French, J. Group support, legitimate power, and social influence. *Journal of Personality,* 1958, 26, 400 409.

Russell, B. *Power: A new social analysis.* New York: Norton, 1938.

Swanson, G., Newcomb, T., & Hartley, E. *Readings in social psychology.* New York: Holt, 1952.

Torrance, E., & Mason, R. Instructor effort to influence: An experimental evaluation of six approaches. Paper presented at USAF-NRC Symposium on Personnel, Training, and Human Engineering. Washington, D.C., 1956.

Weber, M. *The theory of social and economic organization.* Oxford: Oxford Univ. Press, 1947.

*   *   *

*Though the primary influence of coercive power is dependent, it often produces secondary changes in the life space of the prisoner, but these dependent changes can lead to identification with the aggressor and hence to secondary changes in ideology which are independent.

Study Questions

1. Define the five sources of power.

2. How does the "range of power" vary for each power base?

3. What happens when individuals attempt to utilize this power outside its range?

4. What are the typical "effects" in using each power base?

Who Gets Power—And How They Hold on to It: A Strategic-Contingency Model of Power

Gerald R. Salancik
Jeffrey Pfeffer

Power is held by many people to be a dirty word or, as Warren Bennis has said, "It is the organization's last dirty secret."

This article will argue that traditional "political" power, far from being a dirty business, is, in its most naked form, one of the few mechanisms available for aligning an organization with its own reality. However, institutionalized forms of power—what we prefer to call the cleaner forms of power: authority, legitimization, centralized control, regulations, and the more modern "management information systems"—tend to buffer the organization from reality and obscure the demands of its environment. Most great states and institutions declined, not because they played politics, but because they failed to accommodate to the political realities they faced. Political processes, rather than being mechanisms for unfair and unjust allocations and appointments, tend toward the realistic resolution of conflicts among interests. And power, while it eludes definition, is easy enough to recognize by its consequences—the ability of those who possess power to bring about the outcomes they desire.

The model of power we advance is an elaboration of what has been called strategic-contingency theory, a view that sees power as something that accrues to organizational subunits (individuals, departments) that cope with critical organizational problems. Power is used by subunits, indeed, used by all who have it, to enhance their own survival through control of scarce critical resources, through the placement of allies in key positions, and through the definition of organizational problems and policies. Because of the processes by which power develops and is used, organizations become both more aligned and more misaligned with their environments. This contradiction is the most interesting aspect of organizational power and one that makes administration one of the most precarious of occupations.

What is Organizational Power?

You can walk into most organizations and ask without fear of being misunderstood, "Which are the powerful groups of people in this organization?" Although many organizational informants may be unwilling to tell you, it is unlikely they will be unable to tell you. Most people do not require explicit definitions to know what power is.

Power is simply the ability to get things done the way one wants them to be done. For a manager who wants an increased budget to launch a project that he thinks is important, his power is measured by his ability to get that budget. For an executive vice president who wants to be chairman, his power is evidenced by his advancement toward his goal.

People in organizations not only know what you are talking about when you ask who is influential but they are likely to agree with one another to an amazing extent. Recently, we had a chance to observe this in a regional office of an insurance company. The office had 21 department managers: we asked 10 of these managers to rank all 21 according to the influence each one had in the organization. Despite the fact that ranking 21 things is a difficult task, the managers sat down and began arranging the names of their colleagues and themselves in a column. Only one person bothered to ask, "What do you mean by influence?" When told "power," he responded, "Oh," and went on. We compared the rankings of all ten managers and found virtually no disagreement among them in the managers ranked among the top five or the bottom five. Differences in the rankings came from department heads claiming more influence for themselves than their colleagues attributed to them.

Such agreement on those who have influence, and those who do not, was not unique to this insurance company. So far we have studied over 20 very different organizations—universities, research firms, factories, banks, retailers, to name a few. In each one we found individuals able to rate themselves and their peers on a scale of influence or power. We have done this both for specific decisions and for general impact on organizational policies. Their agreement was unusually high, which suggests that distributions of influence exist well enough in everyone's mind to be referred to with ease—and we assume with accuracy.

Where Does Organizational Power Come From?

Earlier we stated that power helps organizations become aligned with their realities. This hopeful prospect follows from what we have dubbed the strategic-contingencies theory of organizational power. Briefly, those subunits most able to cope with the organization's critical problems and uncertainties acquire power. In its simplest form, the strategic-contingencies theory implies that when an organization faces a number of lawsuits that threaten its existence, the legal department will gain power and influence over organizational decisions. Somehow other organizational interest groups will recognize its critical importance and confer upon it a status and power never before enjoyed. This influence may extend beyond handling legal matters and into decisions about product design, advertising production, and so on. Such extensions undoubtedly would be accompanied by appropriate, or acceptable, verbal justifications. In time, the head of the legal department may become the head of the corporation, just as in times past the vice-president for marketing had become the president when market shares were a worrisome problem and, before him, the chief engineer, who had made the production line run as smooth as silk.

Stated in this way, the strategic-contingencies theory of power paints an appealing picture of power. To the extent that power is determined by the critical uncertainties and problems facing the organization and, in turn, influences decisions in the organization, the organization is aligned with the realities it faces. In short,

power facilitates the organization's adaptation to its environment—or its problems.

We can cite many illustrations of how influence derives from a subunit's ability to deal with critical contingencies. Michael Crozier described a French cigarette factory in which the maintenance engineers had a considerable say in the plant-wide operation. After some probing he discovered that the group possessed the solution to one of the major problems faced by the company, that of trouble-shooting the elaborate, expensive, and irrascible automated machines that kept breaking down and dumbfounding everyone else. It was the one problem that the plant manager could in no way control.

The production workers, while troublesome from time to time, created no insurmountable problems; the manager could reasonably predict their absenteeism or replace them when necessary. Production scheduling was something he could deal with since, by watching inventories and sales, the demand for cigarettes was known long in advance. Changes in demand could be accommodated by slowing down or speeding up the line. Supplies of tobacco and paper were also easily dealt with through stockpiles and advance orders.

The one thing that management could never control nor accommodate to, however, was the seemingly happenstance breakdowns. And the foremen couldn't instruct the workers what to do when emergencies developed since the maintenance department kept its records of problems and solutions locked up in a cabinet or in its members' heads. The breakdowns were, in truth, a critical source of uncertainty for the organization, and the maintenance engineers were the only ones who could cope with the problem.

The engineers' strategic role in coping with breakdowns afforded them a considerable say on plant decisions. Schedules and production quotas were set in consultation with them. And the plant manager, while formally their boss, accepted their decisions about personnel in their operation. His submission was to his credit, for without their cooperation he would have had an even more difficult time in running the plant.

Ignoring Critical Consequences

In this cigarette factory, sharing influence with the maintenance workers reflected the plant manager's awareness of the critical contingencies. However, when organizational members are not aware of the critical contingencies they face, and do not share influence accordingly, the failure to do so can create havoc. In one case, an insurance company's regional office was having problems with the performance of one of its departments, the coding department. From the outside, the department looked like a disaster area. The clerks who worked in it were somewhat dissatisfied; their supervisor paid little attention to them, and they resented the hard work. Several other departments were critical of this manager, claiming that she was inconsistent in meeting deadlines. The person most critical was the claims manager. He resented having to wait for work that was handled by her department, claiming that it held up his claims adjusters. Having heard the rumors about dissatisfaction among her subordinates, he attributed the situation to poor supervision. He was second in command in the office and therefore took up the issue with her immediate boss, the head of administrative services. They consulted with the personnel manager, and the three of them concluded that the manager needed leadership training to improve her relations with her subordinates. The coding manager objected, saying it was a waste of time, but agreed to go ahead with the training and also agreed to give more priority to the claims department's work. Within a week after the training, the results showed that her workers were happier but that the performance of her department had decreased, save for the people serving the claims department.

About this time, we began, quite independently, a study of influence in this organization. We asked the administrative services director to draw up flow charts of how the work of one department moved onto the next department. In the course of the interview, we noticed that the coding department began or interceded in the work flow of most of the other departments and casually mentioned to him, "The coding manager must be very influential." He said "No, not really. Why would you think so?" Before we could reply, he recounted the story

of her leadership training and the fact that things were worse. We then told him that it seemed obvious that the coding department would be influential from the fact that all the other departments depended on it. It was also clear why productivity had fallen. The coding manager took the training seriously and began spending more time raising her workers' spirits than she did worrying about the problems of all the departments that depended on her. Giving priority to the claims area only exaggerated the problem, for their work was getting done at the expense of the work of the other departments. Eventually the company hired a few more clerks to relieve the pressure in the coding department and performance returned to a more satisfactory level.

Originally we got involved with this insurance company to examine how the influence of each manager evolved from his or her department's handling of critical organizational contingencies. We reasoned that one of the most important contingencies faced by an profit-making organizations was that of generating income. Thus we expected managers would be influential to the extent to which they contributed to this function. Such was the case. The underwriting managers, who wrote the policies that committed the premiums, were the most influential; the claims managers, who kept a lid on the funds flowing out, were a close second. Least influential were the managers of functions unrelated to revenue, such as mailroom and payroll managers. And contrary to what the administrative services manager believed, the third most powerful department head (out of 21) was the woman in charge of the coding function, which consisted of rating, recording, and keeping track of the codes of all policy applications and contracts. Her peers attributed more influence to her than could have been inferred from her place on the organization chart. And it was not surprising, since they all depended on her department. The coding department's records, their accuracy, and the speed with which they could be retrieved, affected virtually every other operating department in the insurance office. The underwriters depended on them in getting the contracts straight; the typing department depended on them in preparing the formal contract document; the claims department depended on them in adjusting claims; and accounting depended on them for billing. Unfortunately, the "bosses" were not aware of these dependencies, for unlike the cigarette factory, there were no massive breakdowns that made them obvious, while the coding manager, who was a hard-working but quiet person, did little to announce her importance.

The cases of this plant and office illustrate nicely a basic point about the source of power in organizations. The basis for power in an organization derives from the ability of a person or subunit to take or not take actions that are desired by others. The coding manager was seen as influential by those who depended on her department, but not by the people at the top. The engineers were influential because of their role in keeping the plant operating. The two cases differ in these respects: The coding supervisor's source of power was not as widely recognized as that of the maintenance engineers, and she did not use her source of power to influence decisions; the maintenance engineers did. Whether power is used to influence anything is a separate issue. We should not confuse this issue with the fact that power derives from a social situation in which one person has a capacity to do something and another person does not but wants it done.

Power Sharing in Organizations

Power is shared in organizations; and it is shared out of necessity more than out of concern for principles of organizational development or participatory democracy. Power is shared because no one person controls all the desired activities in the organization. While the factory owner may hire people to operate his noisy machines, once hired they have some control over the use of the machinery. And thus they have power over him in the same way he has power over them. Who has more power over whom is a mooter point than that of recognizing the inherent nature of organizing as a sharing of power.

Let's expand on the concept that power derives from the activities desired in an organization. A major way of managing influence in organizations is through the designation of activities. In a bank we studied, we saw this

principle in action. This bank was planning to install a computer system for routine audit evaluation. The bank, rather progressive-minded, was concerned that the change would have adverse effects on employees and therefore surveyed their attitudes.

The principal opposition to the new system came, interestingly, not from the employees who performed the routine credit checks, some of whom would be relocated because of the change, but from the manager of the credit department. His reason was quite simple. The manager's primary function was to give official approval to the applications, catch any employee mistakes before giving approval, and arbitrate any difficulties the clerks had in deciding what to do. As a consequence of his role, others in the organization, including his superiors, subordinates, and colleagues, attributed considerable importance to him. He, in turn, for example, could point to the low proportion of credit approvals, compared with other financial institutions, that resulted in bad debts. Now, to his mind, a wretched machine threatened to transfer his role to a computer programmer, a man who knew nothing of finance and who, in addition, had ten years less seniority. The credit manager eventually quit for a position at a smaller firm with lower pay, but one in which he would have more influence than his redefined job would have left him with.

Because power derives from activities rather than individuals, an individual's or subgroup's power is never absolute and derives ultimately from the context of the situation. The amount of power an individual has at any one time depends not only on the activities he or she controls, but also on the existence of other persons or means by which the activities can be achieved and on those who determine what ends are desired and, hence, on what activities are desired and critical for the organization. One's own power always depends on other people for these two reasons. Other people, or groups or organizations, can determine the definition of what is a critical contingency for the organization and can also undercut the uniqueness of the individual's personal contribution to the critical contingencies of the organization.

Perhaps one can best appreciate how situationally dependent power is by examining how it is distributed. In most societies, power organizes around scarce and critical resources. Rarely does power organize around abundant resources. In the United States, a person doesn't become powerful because he or she can drive a car. There are simply too many others who can drive with equal facility. In certain villages in Mexico, on the other hand, a person with a car is accredited with enormous social status and plays a key role in the community. In addition to scarcity, power is also limited by the need for one's capacities in a social system. While a racer's ability to drive a car around a 90 degree turn at 80 mph may be sparsely distributed in a society, it is not likely to lend the driver much power in the society. The ability simply does not play a central role in the activities of the society.

The fact that power revolves around scarce and critical activities, of course, makes the control and organization of those activities a major battleground in struggles for power. Even relatively abundant or trivial resources can become the bases for power if one can organize and control their allocation and the definition of what is critical. Many occupational and professional groups attempt to do just this in modern economies. Lawyers organize themselves into associations, regulate the entrance requirements for novitiates, and then get laws passed specifying situations that require the services of an attorney. Workers had little power in the conduct of industrial affairs until they organized themselves into closed and controlled systems. In recent years, women and blacks have tried to define themselves as important and critical to the social system, using law to reify their status.

In organizations there are obviously opportunities for defining certain activities as more critical than others. Indeed, the growth of managerial thinking to include defining organizational objectives and goals has done much to foster these opportunities. One sure way to liquidate the power of groups in the organization is to define the need for their services out of existence. David Halberstam presents a description of how just such a thing happened to the group of correspondents that evolved around Edward R. Murrow, the brilliant journalist, interviewer, and war correspondent of CBS News. A close friend of CBS chairman and controlling stockholder William S. Paley, Murrow, and the news department he directed, were endowed with freedom to do what they felt was right. He used it to create some of the best documentaries and commentaries ever seen on television. Unfortunately, television became too large, too powerful, and too suspect in the eyes of the federal government that licensed it. It thus became, or at least the top executives believed it had become, too dangerous to have in-depth, probing commentary on the news. Crisp, dry, uneditorializing headliners were considered safer. Murrow was out and Walter Cronkite was in.

The power to define what is critical in an organization is no small power. Moreover, it is the key to understanding why organizations are either aligned with their environments or misaligned. If an organization defines certain activities as critical when in fact they are not critical, given the flow of resources coming into the organization, it is not likely to survive, at least in its present form.

Most organizations manage to evolve a distribution of power and influence that is aligned with the critical realities they face in the environment. The environment, in turn, incudes both the internal environment, the shifting situational contexts in which particular decisions get made, and the external environment that it can hope to influence but is unlikely to control.

The Critical Contingencies

The critical contingencies facing most organizations derive from the environmental context within which they operate. This determines the available needed resources and thus determines the problems to be dealt with. That power organizes around handling these problems suggests an important mechanism by which organizations keep in tune with their external environments. The strategic-contingencies model implies that subunits that contribute to the critical resources of the organization will gain influence in the organization. Their influence presumably is then used to bend the organization's activities to the contingencies that determine its resources. This idea may strike one as obvious. But its obviousness in no way diminishes its importance. Indeed, despite its obviousness, it escapes the notice of many organizational analysts and managers, who all too frequently think of the organization in terms of a descending pyramid, in which all the departments in one tier hold equal power and status. This presumption denies the reality that departments differ in the contributions they are believed to make to the overall organization's resources, as well as to the fact that some are more equal than others.

Because of the importance of this idea to organizational effectiveness, we decided to examine it carefully in a large midwestern university. A university offers an excellent site for studying power. It is composed of departments with nominally equal power and is administered by a central executive structure much like other bureaucracies. However, at the same time it is a situation in which the departments have clearly defined identities and face diverse external environments. Each department has its own bodies of knowledge, its own institutions, its own sources of prestige and resources. Because the departments operate in different external environments, they are likely to contribute differentially to the resources of the overall organization. Thus a physics department with close ties to NASA may contribute substantially to the funds of the university; and a history department with a renowned historian in residence may contribute to the intellectual credibility or prestige of the whole university. Such variations permit one to examine how these various contributions lead to obtaining power within the university.

We analyzed the influence of 29 university departments throughout an 18 month period in their history. Our chief interest was to determine whether departments that brought more critical resources to the university would be more powerful than departments that contributed fewer or less critical resources.

To identify the critical resources each department contributed, the heads of all departments were interviewed about the importance of seven different resources to the university's success. The seven included undergraduate students (the factor determining size of the state allocations by the university), national prestige, administrative expertise, and so on. The most critical resource was found to be contract and grant monies received by a department's faculty for research or consulting services. At this university, contracts and grants contributed somewhat less than 50 percent of the overall budget, with the remainder primarily coming from state appropriations. The importance attributed to contract and grant monies, and the rather minor importance of undergraduate students, is not surprising for this particular university. The university was a major center for graduate education; many of its departments ranked in the top ten of their respective fields. Grant and contract monies were the primary source of discretionary funding available for maintaining these programs of graduate education, and hence for maintaining the university's prestige. The prestige of the university itself was critical both in recruiting able students and attracting top-notch faculty.

From university records it was determined what relative contributions each of the 29 departments made to the various needs of the university (national prestige, outside grants, teaching). Thus, for instance, one department may have contributed to the university by teaching 7 percent of the instructional units, bringing in 2 percent of the outside contracts and grants, and having a national ranking of 20. Another department, on the other hand, may have taught one percent of the instructional units, contributed 12 percent to the grants, and be ranked the third best department in its field within the country.

The question was: Do these different contributions determine the relative power of the departments within the university? Power was measured in several ways; but regardless of how measured, the answer was "Yes." Those three resources together accounted for about 70 percent of the variance in subunit power in the university.

But the most important predictor of departmental power was the department's contribution to the contracts and grants of the university. Sixty percent of the variance in power was due to this one factor, suggesting that the power of departments derived primarily from the dollars they provided for graduate education, the activity believed to be the most important for the organization.

The Impact of Organizational Power on Decision Making

The measure of power we used in studying this university was an analysis of the responses of the department heads we interviewed. While such perceptions of power might be of interest in their own right, they contribute little to our understanding of how the distribution of power might serve to align an organization with its critical realities. For this we must look to how power actually influences the decisions and policies of organizations.

While it is perhaps not absolutely valid, we can generally gauge the relative importance of a department of an organization by the size of the budget allocated to it relative to other departments. Clearly it is of importance to the administrators of those departments whether they are squeezed in a budget crunch or are given more funds to strike out after new opportunities. And it should also be clear that when those decisions are made and one department can go ahead and try new approaches while another must cut back on the old, then the deployment of the resources of the organization in meeting its problems is most directly affected.

Thus our study of the university led us to ask the following question: Does power lead to influence in the organization? To answer this question, we found it useful first to ask another one, namely: Why should department heads try to influence organizational decisions to favor their own departments to the exclusion of other departments? While this second question may seem a bit naive to anyone who has witnessed the political realities of organizations, we posed it in a context of research on organizations that sees power as an illegitimate threat to the neater rational authority of modern bureaucracies. In this context, decisions are not believed to be made because of the dirty business of politics but because of the overall goals and purposes of the organization. In a university, one reasonable basis for decision making is the teaching workload of departments and the demands that follow from that workload. We would expect, therefore, that departments with heavy student demands for courses would be able to obtain funds for teaching. Another reasonable basis for decision making is quality. We would expect, for that reason, that departments with esteemed reputations would be able to obtain funds both because their quality suggests they might use such funds effectively and because such funds would allow them to maintain their quality. A rational model of bureaucracy intimates, then, that the organizational decisions taken would favor those who perform the stated purposes of the organization—teaching undergraduates and training professional and scientific talent—well.

The problem with rational models of decision making, however, is that what is rational to one person may strike another as irrational. For most departments, resources are a question of survival. While teaching undergraduates may seem to be a major goal for some members of the university, developing knowledge may seem so to others; and to still others, advising governments and other institutions about policies may seem to be the crucial business. Everyone has his own idea of the proper priorities in a just world. Thus goals rather than being clearly defined and universally agreed upon are blurred and contested throughout the organization. If such is the case, then the decisions taken on behalf of the organization as a whole are likely to reflect the goals of those who prevail in political contests, namely, those with power in the organization.

Will organizational decisions always reflect the distribution of power in the organization? Probably not. Using power for influence requires a certain expenditure of effort, time, and resources. Prudent and judicious persons are not likely to use their power needlessly or wastefully. And it is likely that power will be used to influence organizational decisions primarily under circumstances that both require and favor its use. We have examined three conditions that are likely to affect the use of power in organizations: scarcity, criticality, and uncertainty. The first suggests that subunits will try to exert influence when the resources of the organization are scarce. If there is an abundance of resources, then a particular department or a particular individual has little need to attempt influence. With little effort, he can get all he wants anyway.

The second condition, criticality, suggests that a subunit will attempt to influence decisions to obtain resources that are critical to its own survival and activities. Criticality implies that one would not waste effort, or risk being labeled obstinate, by fighting over trivial decisions affecting one's operations.

An office manager would probably balk less about a threatened cutback in copying machine usage than about a reduction in typing staff. An advertising department head would probably worry less about losing his lettering artist than his illustrator. Criticality is difficult to define because what is critical depends on people's beliefs about what is critical. Such beliefs may or may not be based on experience and knowledge and may or may not be agreed upon by all. Scarcity, for instance, may itself affect conceptions of criticality. When slack resources drop off, cutbacks have to be made—those "hard decisions," as congressmen and resplendent administrators like to call them. Managers then find themselves scrapping projects they once held dear.

The third condition that we believe affects the use of power is uncertainty: When individuals do not agree about what the organization should do or how to do it, power and other social processes will affect decisions. The reason for this is simply that, if there are no clear cut criteria available for resolving conflicts of interest, then the only means for resolution is some form of social process, including power, status, social ties, or some arbitrary process like flipping a coin or drawing straws. Under conditions of uncertainty, the powerful manager can argue his case on any grounds and usually win it. Since there is no real consensus, other contestants are not likely to develop counterarguments or amass sufficient opposition. Moreover, because of his power and their need for access to the resources he controls, they are more likely to defer to his arguments.

Although the evidence is slight, we have found that power will influence the allocations of scarce and critical resources. In the analysis of power in the university, for instance, one of the most critical resources needed by departments is the general budget. First granted by the state legislature, the general budget is later allocated to individual departments by the university administration in response to requests from the department heads. Our analysis of the factors that contribute to a department getting more or less of this budget indicated that subunit power was the major predictor, overriding such factors as student demand for courses, national reputations of departments, or even the size of a department's faculty. Moreover, other research has shown that when the general budget has been cut back or held below previous uninflated levels, leading to monies becoming more scarce, budget allocations mirror departmental powers even more closely.

Student enrollment and faculty size, of course, do themselves relate to budget allocations, as we would expect since they determine a department's need for resources, or at least offer visible testimony of needs. But departments are not always able to get what they need by the mere fact of needing them. In one analysis it was found that high-power departments were able to obtain budget without regard to their teaching loads and, in some cases, actually in inverse relation to their teaching loads. In contrast, low-power departments could get increases in budget only when they could justify the increases by a recent growth in teaching load, and then only when it was far in excess of norms for other departments.

General budget is only one form of resource that is allocated to departments. There are others such as special grants for student fellowships or faculty research. These are critical to departments because they affect the ability to attract other resources, such as outstanding faculty or students. We examined how power influenced the allocations of four resources department heads had described as critical and scarce.

When the four resources were arrayed from the most to the least critical and scarce, we found that departmental power best predicted the allocations of the most critical and scarce resources. In other words, the analysis of how power influences organizational allocations leads to this conclusion: Those subunits most likely to survive in times of strife are those that are more critical to the organization. Their importance to the organization gives them power to influence resource allocations that enhance their own survival.

How External Environment Impacts Executive Selection

Power not only influences the survival of key groups in an organization, it also influences the selection of individuals to key leadership positions, and by such a process further aligns the organization with its environmental context.

We can illustrate this with a different study of the selection and tenure of chief administrators in 57 hospitals in Illinois. We assumed that since the critical problems facing the organization would enhance the power of certain groups at the expense of others, then the leaders to emerge should be those most relevant to the context of the hospitals. To assess this we asked each chief administrator about his professional background and how long he had been in office. The replies were then related to the hospitals' funding, ownership, and competitive conditions for patients and staff.

One aspect of a hospital's context is the source of its budget. Some hospitals, for instance, are not much like other businesses. They sell bed space, patient care, and treatment services. They charge fees sufficient both to cover their costs and to provide capital for expansion. The main source of both their operating and capital funds is patient billings. Increasingly, patient billings are paid for, not by patients, but by private insurance companies. Insurers like Blue Cross dominate and represent a potent interest group outside a hospital's control but critical to its income. The insurance companies, in order to limit their own costs, attempt to hold down the fees allowable to hospitals, which they do effectively from their positions on state rate boards. The squeeze on hospitals that results from fees increasing slowly while costs climb rapidly more and more demands the talents of cost accountants or people trained in the technical expertise of hospital administration.

By contrast, other hospitals operate more like social service institutions, either as government healthcare units (Bellevue Hospital in New York City and Cook County Hospital in Chicago, for example) or as charitable institu-

tions. These hospitals obtain a large proportion of their operating and capital funds, not from privately insured patients, but from government subsidies or private donations. Such institutions rather than requiring the talents of a technically efficient administrator are likely to require the savvy of someone who is well integrated into the social and political power structure of the community.

Not surprisingly, the characteristics of administrators predictably reflect the funding context of the hospitals with which they are associated. Those hospitals with larger proportions of their budget obtained from private insurance companies were most likely to have administrators with backgrounds in accounting and least likely to have administrators whose professions were business or medicine. In contrast, those hospitals with larger proportions of their budget derived from private donations and local governments were most likely to have administrators with business or professional backgrounds and least likely to have accountants. The same held for formal training in hospital management. Professional hospital administrators could easily be found in hospitals drawing their incomes from private insurance and rarely in hospitals dependent on donations or legislative appropriations.

As with the selection of administrators, the context of organizations has also been found to affect the removal of executives. The environment, as a source of organizational problems, can make it more or less difficult for executives to demonstrate their value to the organization. In the hospitals we studied, long-term administrators came from hospitals with few problems. They enjoyed amicable and stable relations with their local business and social communities and suffered little competition for funding and staff. The small city hospital director who attended civic and Elks meetings while running the only hospital within a 100-mile radius, for example, had little difficulty holding on to his job. Turnover was highest in hospitals with the most problems, a phenomenon similar to that observed in a study of industrial organizations in which turnover was highest among executives in industries with competitive environments and unstable market conditions. The interesting thing is that instability characterized the industries rather than the individual firms in them. The troublesome conditions in the individual firms were attributed, or rather misattributed, to the executives themselves.

It takes more than problems, however, to terminate a manager's leadership. The problems themselves must be relevant and critical. This is clear from the way in which an administrator's tenure is affected by the status of the hospital's operating budget. Naively we might assume that all administrators would need to show a surplus. Not necessarily so. Again, we must distinguish between those hospitals that depend on private donations for funds and those that do not. Whether an endowed budget shows a surplus or deficit is less important than the hospital's relations with benefactors. On the other hand, with a budget dependent on patient billing, a surplus is almost essential; monies for new equipment or expansion must be drawn from it, and without them quality care becomes more difficult and patients scarcer. An administrator's tenure reflected just these considerations. For those hospitals dependent upon private donations, the length of an administrator's term depended not at all on the status of the operating budget but was fairly predictable from the hospital's relations with the business community. On the other hand, in hospitals dependent on the operating budget for capital financing, the greater the deficit the shorter was the tenure of the hospital's principal administrators.

Changing Contingencies and Eroding Power Bases

The critical contingencies facing the organization may change. When they do, it is reasonable to expect that the power of individuals and subgroups will change in turn. At times the shift can be swift and shattering, as it was recently for powerholders in New York City. A few years ago it was believed that David Rockefeller was one of the ten most powerful people in the city, as tallied by *New York* magazine, which annually sniffs out power for the delectation of its readers. But that was before it was revealed that the city was in financial trouble, before Rockefeller's Chase Manhattan Bank lost some of its own financial luster, and before brother Nelson lost some of his political influence in Washington. Obviously David Rockefeller was no longer as well positioned to help bail the city out. Another loser was an attorney with considerable personal connections to the political and religious leaders of the city. His talents were no longer in much demand. The persons with more influence were the bankers and union pension fund executors who fed money to the city; community leaders who represent blacks and Spanish-Americans, in contrast, witnessed the erosion of their power bases.

One implication of the idea that power shifts with changes in organizational environments is that the dominant coalition will tend to be that group that is most appropriate for the organization's environment, as also will the leaders of an organization. One can observe this historically in the top executives of industrial firms in the United States. Up until the early 1950s, many top corporations were headed by former production line managers or engineers who gained prominence because of their abilities to cope with the problems of production. Their success, however, only spelled their demise. As production became routinized and mechanized, the problem of most firms became one of selling all those goods they so efficiently produced. Marketing executives were more frequently found in corporate boardrooms. Success outdid itself again, for keeping markets and production steady and stable requires the kind of control that can only come from acquiring competitors and suppliers or the invention of more and more appealing products—ventures that typically require enormous amounts of capital. During the 1960s, financial executives assumed the seats of power. And they, too, will give way to others. Edging over the horizon are legal experts, as regulation and antitrust suits are becoming more and more frequent in the 1970s, suits that had their beginnings in the success of the expansion generated by prior executives. The more distant future, which is likely to be dominated by multinational corporations, may see former secretaries of state and their minions increasingly serving as corporate figureheads.

The Nonadaptive Consequences of Adaptation

From what we have said thus far about power aligning the organization with its own realties, an intelligent person might react with a resounding ho-hum, for it all seems too obvious: Those with the ability to get the job done are given the job to do.

However, there are two aspects of power that make it more useful for understanding organizations and their effectiveness. First, the "job" to be done has a way of expanding itself until it becomes less and less clear what the job is. Napoleon began by doing a job for France in war with Austria and ended up Emperor, convincing many that only he could keep the peace. Hitler began by promising an end to Germany's troubling postwar depression and ended up convincing more people than is comfortable to remember that he was destined to be the savior of the world. In short, power is a capacity for influence that extends far beyond the original bases that created it. Second, power tends to take on institutionalized forms that enable it to endure well beyond its usefulness to an organization.

There is an important contradiction in what we have observed about organizational power. On the one hand we have said that power derives from the contingencies facing an organization and that when those contingencies change so do the bases for power. On the other hand we have asserted that subunits will tend to use their power to influence organizational decisions in their own favor, particularly when their own survival is threatened by the scarcity of critical resources. The first statement implies that an organization will tend to be aligned with its environment since power will tend to bring to key positions those with capabilities relevant to the context. The second implies that those in power will not give up their positions so easily; they will pursue policies that guarantee their continued domination. In short, change and stability operate through the same mechanism, and as a result, the organization will never be completely in phase with its environment or its needs.

The study of hospital administrators illustrates how leadership can be out of phase with reality. We argued that privately funded hospitals needed trained technical administrators more so than did hospitals funded by donations. The need as we perceived it was matched in most hospitals, but by no means in all. Some organizations did not conform with our predictions. These deviations imply that some administrators were able to maintain their positions independent of their suitability for those positions. By dividing administrators into those with long and short terms of office, one finds that the characteristics of longer-termed administrators were virtually unrelated to the hospital's context. The shorter-termed chiefs on the other hand had characteristics more appropriate for the hospital's problems. For a hospital to have a recently appointed head implies that the previous administrator had been unable to endure by institutionalizing himself.

One obvious feature of hospitals that allowed some administrators to enjoy a long tenure was a hospital's ownership. Administrators were less entrenched when their hospitals were affiliated with and dependent upon larger organizations, such as governments or churches. Private hospitals offered more secure positions for administrators. Like private corporations, they tend to have more diffused ownership, leaving the administrator unopposed as he institutionalizes his reign. Thus he endures, sometimes at the expense of the performance of the organization. Other research has demonstrated that corporations with diffuse ownership have poorer earnings than those in which the control of the manager is checked by a dominant shareholder. Firms that overload their boardrooms with more insiders than are appropriate for their context have also been found to be less profitable.

A word of caution is required about our judgment of "appropriateness." When we argue some capabilities are more appropriate for one context than another, we do so from the perspective of an outsider and on the basis of reasonable assumptions as to the problems the organization will face and the capabilities they will need. The fact that we have been able to predict the distribution of influence and the characteristics of leaders suggests that our reasoning is not incorrect. However, we do not think that all organizations follow the same pattern. The fact that we have not been able to predict outcomes with 100 percent accuracy indicates they do not.

Mistaking Critical Contingencies

One thing that allows subunits to retain their power is their ability to name their functions as critical to the organization when they may not be. Consider again our discussion of power in the university. One might wonder why the most critical tasks were defined as graduate education and scholarly research, the effect of which was to lend power to those who brought in grants and contracts. Why not something else? The reason is that the more powerful departments argued for those criteria and won their case, partly because they were more powerful.

In another analysis of this university, we found that all departments advocate self-serving criteria for budget allocation. Thus a department with large undergraduate enrollments argued that enrollments should determine budget allocations, a department with a strong national reputation saw prestige as the most reasonable basis for distributing funds, and so on. We further found that advocating such self-serving criteria actually benefited a department's budget allotments but, also, it paid off more for departments that were already powerful.

Organizational needs are consistent with a current distribution of power also because of a human tendency to categorize problems in familiar ways. An accountant sees problems with organizational perfomance as cost accountancy problems or inventory flow problems. A sales manager sees them as problems with markets, promotional stategies, or just unaggressive salespeople. But what is the truth? Since it does not automatically announce itself, it is likely that those with prior credibility, or those with power, will be favored as the enlightened. This bias, while not intentionally self-serving, further concentrates power among those who already possess it, independent of changes in the organization's context.

Institutionalizing Power

A third reason for expecting organizational contingencies to be defined in familiar ways is that the current holders of power can structure the organization in ways that institutionalize themselves. By institutionalization we mean the establishment of relatively permanent structures and policies that favor the influence of a particular subunit. While in power, a dominant coalition has the ability to institute constitutions, rules, procedures, and information systems that limit the potential power of others while continuing their own.

The key to institutionalizing power always is to create a device that legitimates one's own authority and diminishes the legitimacy of others. When the "Divine Right of Kings" was envisioned centuries ago it was to provide an unquestionable foundation for the supremacy of royal authority. There is generally a need to root the exercise of authority in some higher power. Modern leaders are no less affected by this need. Richard Nixon, with the aid of John Dean, reified the concept of executive privilege, which meant in effect that what the President wished not to be discussed need not be discussed.

In its simpler form, institutionalization is achieved by designating positions or roles for organizational activities. The creation of a new post legitimizes a function and forces organization members to orient to it. By designating how this new post relates to older, more established posts, moreover, one can structure an organization to enhance the importance of the function in the organization. Equally, one can diminish the importance of traditional functions. This is what happened in the end with the insurance company we mentioned that was having trouble with its coding department. As the situation unfolded, the claims director continued to feel dissatisfied about the dependency of his functions on the coding manager. Thus he instituted a reorganization that resulted in two coding departments. In so doing, of course, he placed activities that affected his department under his direct control, presumably to make the operation more effective. Similarly, consumer-product firms enhance the power of marketing by setting up a coordinating role to interface production and marketing functions and then appoint a marketing manager to fill the role.

The structures created by dominant powers sooner or later become fixed and unquestioned features of the organization. Eventually, this can be devastating. It is said that the battle of Jena in 1806 was lost by Frederick the Great, who died in 1786. Though the great Prussian leader had no direct hand in the disaster, his imprint on the army was so thorough, so embedded in its skeletal underpinnings, that the organization was inappropriate for others to lead in different times.

Another important source of institutionalized power lies in the ability to structure information systems. Setting up committees to investigate particular organizational issues and having them report only to particular individuals or groups, facilitates their awareness of problems by members of those groups while limiting the awareness of problems by members of other groups. Obviously, those who have information are in a better position to interpret the problems of an organization, regardless of how realistically they may, in fact, do so.

Still another way to institutionalize power is to distribute rewards and resources. The dominant group may quiet competing interest groups with small favors and rewards. The credit for this artful form of co-optation belongs to Louis XIV. To avoid usurpation of his power by the nobles of France and the Fronde that had so troubled his father's reign, he built the palace at Versailles to occupy them with hunting and gossip. Awed, the courtiers basked in the reflected glories of the "Sun King" and the overwhelming setting he had created for his court.

At this point, we have not systematically studied the institutionalization of power. But we suspect it is an important condition that mediates between the environment of the organization and the capabilities of the organization for dealing with that environment. The more institutionalized power is within an organization, the more likely an organization will be out of phase with the realities it faces. President Richard Nixon's structuring of his White House is one of the better documented illustrations. If we go back to newspaper and magazine descriptions of how he organized his office from the beginning in 1968, most of what occurred subsequently follows almost as an afterthought. Decisions flowed through virtually only the small White House staff; rewards, small presidential favors of recognition, and perquisites were distributed by this staff to the loyal; and information from the outside world—the press, Congress, the people on the streets—was filtered by the staff and passed along only if initialed "bh." Thus it was not surprising that when Nixon met war protestors in the early dawn, the only thing he could think to talk about was the latest football game, so insulated had he become from their grief and anger.

One of the more interesting implications of institutionalized power is that executive turnover among the executives who have structured the organization is likely to be a rare event that occurs only under the most pressing crisis. If a dominant coalition is able to structure the organization and interpret the meaning of ambiguous events like declining sales and profits or lawsuits, then the "real" problems to emerge will easily be incorporated into traditional molds of thinking and acting. If opposition is designed out of the organization, the interpretations will go unquestioned. Conditions will remain stable until a crisis develops, so overwhelming and visible that even the most adroit rhetorician would be silenced.

Implications for the Management of Power in Organizations

While we could derive numerous implications from this discussion of power, our selection would have to depend largely on whether one wanted to increase one's power, decrease the power of others, or merely maintain one's position. More important, the real implications depend on the particulars of an organizational situation. To understand power in an organization one must begin by looking outside it—into the environment—for those groups that mediate the organization's outcomes but are not themselves within its control.

Instead of ending with homilies, we will end with a reversal of where we began. Power, rather than being the dirty business it is often made out to be, is probably one of the few mechanisms for reality testing in organizations. And the cleaner forms of power, the institutional forms, rather than having the virtues they are often credited with, can lead the organization to become out of touch. The real trick to managing power in organizations is to ensure somehow that leaders cannot be unaware of the realities of their environments and cannot avoid changing to deal with those realities. That, however, would be like designing "the self-liquidating organization," an unlikely event since anyone capable of designing such an instrument would be obviously in control of the liquidations.

Management would do well to devote more attention to determining the critical contingencies of their environments. For if you conclude, as we do, that the environment sets most of the structure influencing organizational outcomes and problems, and that power derives from the organization's activities that deal with those contingencies, then it is the environment that needs managing, not power. The first step is to construct an accurate model of the environment, a process that is quite difficult for most organizations. We have recently started a project to aid administrators in systematically understanding their environments. From this experience, we have learned that the most critical blockage to perceiving an organization's reality accurately is a failure to incorporate those with the relevant expertise into the process. Most organizations have the requisite experts on hand but they are positioned so that they can be comfortably ignored.

One conclusion you can, and probably should, derive from our discussion is that power—because of the way it develops and the way it is used—will always result in the organization suboptimizing its performance. However, to this grim absolute, we add a comforting caveat: If any criteria other than power were the basis for determining an organization's decisions, the results would be even worse. •

_____

Study Questions

1. According to strategic-contingency theory, how does organizational power accumulate? That is, what will define an organizations' dominant coalition/leader?

2. What is the relationship between power and organizational adaptation?

3. What is the eventual problem with "in place" dominant organizational members?

4. What common strategy do groups use to guarantee their continued domination?

5. Explain how three conditions in the organizational setting affect the use of power in the decision-making process.

6. Why is power shared in organization?

7. Explain the statement, "power organizes around scarce and critical resources."

The View from the Top: Successful Use of Power Corrupts How We See Those We Control

David Kipnis

No one wants to be powerless. Psychologist Rollo May observed that people who are unwilling or unable to use power condemn themselves to lives of frustration. Many psychologists advocate and teach ways to empower such people, to increase their control over life, to make them more assertive.

Yet, while the absence of power often creates problems, so may its presence. Writers and social philosophers have noted since the time of Sophocles that the control of power produces strong psychological changes. Power-holders start to exploit those they control; they become puffed up with their own importance; their moral values become self-serving. Power thus changes people's view of themselves and of others. The person dominated becomes, to use philosopher Martin Buber's terms, an "it," a subject, instead of a "thou," an individual. This is true whether the power-holders are men or women who dominate their spouses, executives who run business organizations or political leaders who rule countries. I call these changes in the power-holder "metamorphic effects of power."

To understand how such effects occur, my colleagues and I have studied a number of dimensions of power, including the strength of the tactics people use to get their way. There are basically three types: "soft tactics"—being nice, flattering, pleading; "rational tactics"—explaining, discussing, compromising; and "strong tactics" (the kind favored by most power-holders)—ordering, threatening, getting angry.

My research suggests that the use of strong tactics triggers the following events: First, their success strengthens the power-holder's belief that he or she controls the other person. The powerholder demands, the other obeys. As

an example, suppose a husband says to his wife, "I'm having the boss here for dinner on Friday, and it better be special." If his wife goes along with his wishes, knowing that he'll be an ogre if she refuses or if the souffle falls, the husband will conclude, reasonably enough, that his demands forced his wife to obey. This is particularly true if the same tactics succeed time after time.

The dynamics are much different if the husband says: "Please, honey, do me a favor, I really need your help to get that promotion," and his wife agrees. Then the husband's most reasonable conclusion is that his wife thought the matter over and decided to comply. Her action was a matter of choice, her choice, rather than coercion by an outside force.

The difference in perception is important because the successful use of strong tactics has a second effect—devaluation of the person being influenced. My colleagues and I have found in several different studies (see below) that people evaluate others less favorably when they see them as controlled by forces outside themselves. Specifically, if we make people do what we want, we attribute their behavior, no matter how good it is, to our orders rather than to their abilities and motivations. Hence we fail to give them full credit for what they accomplish.

Metamorphic effects, then, arise from the successful use of strong influence tactics. If these tactics produce compliance, the power-holder's views of others are changed for the worse. To the extent that power-holders (husbands or wives, politicians or executives) believe that they control another person's behavior, that other person is likely to be devalued. This sets the stage for subsequent exploitation of the less powerful.

To show how these observations apply in day-to-day relations, my colleagues and I gathered information from dating and married couples and from managers supervising the work of others. We used both field interviews and laboratory simulations of work situations.

In research with 195 couples (76 married and 119 dating), we asked all partners individually to describe the influence tactics they used to get their way, the extent to which they controlled power in the relationship and their affectionate feelings toward their partners.

We learned how often each person used strong and controlling tactics, rational tactics and weak tactics. To determine who held the power in each relationship, we asked who made the final decisions about important issues such as how and where to spend money, their sex lives, their lifestyle and their friendships. From their responses we classified some people as controlling decision-making power ("I have the final say"), others as sharing it ("We decide together") and still others as having no power over important decisions ("My partner has the final say"). Since we found no important differences in these factors between married and dating couples, our conclusions apply to both groups.

Not surprisingly, we found that most companions who used strong tactics to influence their partners also said that they shared decision-making, while men and women who used weak tactics admitted that their partners had the power. Next, we examined how the power balance influenced the degree of affection between partners. After all, it is possible that having a compliant and obedient partner promotes harmony and affection. What we found was just the opposite. People who unilaterally controlled decision-making had a less satisfactory relationship than those who shared power.

The dominant partners (usually men) also described their companions in less flattering terms in regard to intelligence, success or skill than did partners who shared power. These less-flattering evaluations make sense, since in such relationships the submissive partner is not allowed to display competence by planning or making decisions. Dominant partners also expressed less love and affection for their partners and were generally unhappier with the relationship.

These findings illustrate the general principle that dominance and power are negatively associated with feelings of affection. Even sexual relations, frequently associated with power and dominance, were evaluated as far less satisfactory by those who unilaterally controlled power than by those who shared it.

While these facts about power are hardly surprising, few people seem to apply them in their daily lives. Because getting one's way, controlling others and asserting one's power provide immediate and potent gratification, few people stop to think about the emotional risks of such behavior. And even if it is noticed, the loss of affection can easily be blamed on the increasing stupidity and incompetence of the submissive partner.

Power, then, has its price in domestic relations. But what are its effects in the work place? To answer this question, researchers Stuart Schmidt, Karl Price, Chris Stitt and I conducted a recent experiment in which we controlled how much power leaders had over employees and examined how this variation in power affected the leaders' subsequent evaluations of their employees.

We appointed 200 business students to act as managers of small work groups and instructed them to manage in one of two ways: Authoritarian leaders were told to assert complete control over all decisions concerning how the work (assembling model cars) was to be done. Democratic leaders were instructed to allow their employees to share in decisions about work.

We found, as expected, that authoritarian leaders retained control by using strong tactics such as direct orders and threats, while the democratic leaders shared power by reasoning and explaining to get people to do the work. Such variations in control, of course, occur naturally in actual business settings. But our experiment, in which we knew precisely which individuals managed which way, enabled us to see how these different methods shaped the leaders' subsequent evaluations of their employees.

The study revealed that while employees working for both types of leaders did equally good work, they were evaluated in ways that varied considerably and consistently: Authoritarian leaders routinely complained that their employees were not motivated to work hard. They also evaluated their employees' work less favorably than democratic leaders did. That is, the authoritarians rated their workers as less suitable for promotion and downplayed their skills and talents.

These differences make sense if we accept the idea that people who control the behavior of others do not give them credit for the work they do. Since the authoritarian leaders told employees what to do and exactly how to do it, they did not attribute any subsequent good work to employees' skills and talents.

The metamorphic effects of power are not limited to the use of strong verbal tactics in face-to-face relations. For better or worse, society has developed many ways to control behavior that do not depend upon personal confrontations. The following vignettes illustrate what can happen to social relations when technological innovation makes work routine.

At a Party:

Guest: "My God, this cake is delicious. You're a wonderful cook."
Host: "Well, to tell the truth, I used a cake mix. You know, add water and bake, wonderful stuff."
Guest: "Oh, I'm so glad to hear it. I was getting jealous, you have so many talents as it is."

In The Office:

First Executive: "Hey, the secretaries are doing terrific work. For the last week my letters and reports have been perfect."
Second Executive: "Forget the secretaries. Still the same hacks. We just added word processors with automatic dictionaries. They don't even have to know how to spell now. Just type in the words, press the button and out comes perfect copy, margins and all."

As the above vignettes imply, people are valued to the extent that bosses and others attribute successful performance to the person's own skills and talents. When technology destroys the link between personal competence and performance, it, rather than the individual involved, is given credit for the performance. The issue of who is responsible for performance becomes particularly important at work. Social philosophers from Karl Marx to contemporary writers such as labor theorist Harry Braverman have called the routinization of work a power strategy of management designed to shift control away from employees. An employee's bargaining position is more powerful when work requires the use of scarce skills and talents. When management reduces the skill component through technological changes, the balance of power shifts away from labor. Skilled mechanics are valued far more than assembly-line workers.

How do these shifts in power affect managers' relations with their employees? Two points apply here. First, metamorphic effects occur when individuals don't seem to be in control of their behavior. Second, routinization of work creates the impression that the machine rather than the individual is in charge. With these points in mind, I recently examined how routinization affects managers' evaluations in two different work settings.

First, I asked 129 managers of men and women doing routinized and nonroutinized work to evaluate their employees' performance in terms of whether the employees required close supervision, accepted responsibility for their work and took pride in doing high quality work.

In addition, I conducted experiments in which each of 62 college students, appointed as managers, supervised two other students doing either routinized or nonroutinized work. The work required students to make airplane models using LEGO bricks. In the routinized condition, workers snapped blocks together to make subunits of the model, then placed them on a conveyor belt. The model was constructed by other workers who sequentially snapped together larger and larger units. In the nonroutinized situation each worker was told to build a complete model and given blueprints.

Each manager was told that examination of the models showed that one of his workers was doing poor work while the other was doing well. This manipulation enabled us to see how the managers of people doing routine or nonroutine work differed in their explanations for workers' supposedly good or bad performance, something we could do only by inference in the field studies.

The results were remarkably consistent. In both the field and laboratory settings, how the workers were evaluated by their managers depended on the degree of routinization. The more routine the work, the less favorable were the managers' evaluations of the employees.

More specifically, employees doing routine work were seen as requiring close supervision and taking little responsibility for their work.

In fact, the only time employees doing routine work in either setting were viewed as responsible for their work was when it was not satisfactory. In these cases, the managers believed that poor work was deliberately caused by the workers. They described the employees as lazy, having poor attitudes and lacking motivation. Such hostile judgments made psychological sense, whatever their objective truth. If work has been so simplified that a child can do it, then the obvious explanation for mistakes is operator malice or laziness.

Managers of employees doing nonroutine work, on the other hand, usually attributed poor performance to difficulty of the work, equipment failures or the fact that the employees needed more training. Seldom did they say that the poor work was deliberate.

The exercise of strong control over people, then, whether through face-to-face encounters or indirectly through environmental alterations that lessen free choice, worsens relationships between power-holders and those they control. Routinization of work enmeshes individuals in a system in which they are given little credit for acceptable performance, yet are routinely blamed for poor performance. In terms of the metamorphic model of power, the loss of control experienced by employees is reflected in lower performance evaluations and hostile judgments from their managers.

Many social scientists and business experts recognize the problems that routinization creates for employees. Suggested solutions have included enlarging and enriching work and increasing worker participation in the decision-making process. Both solutions serve to increase employee power in relation to managers and counter the undervaluing that occurs as technological improvements lessen worker influence.

These solutions, however, are frequently resisted because of the important economic gains achieved by routinization. Indeed, such gains have spurred the social sciences to develop comparable techniques. These techniques, ranging from contingency leadership training to behavior modification, serve to make human behavior more predictable and controllable for advertisers, supervisors, therapists and politicians—anyone who wants to influence others.

Such attempts to reduce behavioral uncertainty, unfortunately, often involve reducing the amount of control and free choice available to those being influenced. To the extent that these techniques are effective, I expect increased disruptions in social relations between managers and employees. This will happen not necessarily because employees will resent being influenced, but because the manager will attribute employee compliance and work effectiveness to their techniques rather than to the employees' efforts and abilities. These attributions of control will contribute to a steady process of denigration and disruption of relationships. ●

David Kipnis is chairman of the psychology department at Temple University.

Study Questions

1. Explain the metamorphosis in individuals that arises from the successful use of strong influence tactics.

2. Give an example of each basic (soft, rational, strong) type of influence tactic.

3. What specific consequences follow strong tactics with regard to powerholders' beliefs about their target?

4. In personal relationships, what is the connection between decision-making control and relationship satisfaction?

5. What is the relationship between affection and dominance?

6. How did authoritarian (vs. democratic) leaders evaluate employees? What can account for these perceptions?

7. How can technology and the "routinization of work" contribute to the devaluation of employees?

8. During the Lego airplane experiment, when were "routinized" employees seen as responsible for their behavior?

The Employment Relationship: Un-tied or Re-tied?

Thomas J. Atchison

Employment relationships in the United States are under attack. As American companies attempt to become internationally competitive, many people see a new cooperative employment relationship being created. However, given the recent business environment during the past ten years—lay offs, wage and benefit reductions, and harder work—a cooperative relationship seems unlikely.

This article starts by presenting divergent views on the definition of cooperation, how viewing the organization as family is dysfunctional, the Human Resource Department's role, and the question of unequal power between management and the employee.

Several new employment relationships are starting to appear. Three types are examined here: core, contractual, and flexible. These new relationships, particularly the core one, reflect the changing nature of work and the work force in America. If we are to move to a cooperative relationship, these changes in employment relationships are going to require changes in managerial attitudes and behavior.

"Employees are running so scared that there is a whole culture that says don't make waves, don't take risks—just at the time we need innovation."[1]

This executive's statement reflects employees' fear and anxiety about their jobs today. It also highlights three concerns about changes occurring in the employment relationship.

The first concern is that the nature of the employment relationship has changed considerably. "Companies want fewer obligations to their employees, not more," said one economist in a recent *Time* article.[2] The way that employees are responding to these changes is the second concern. The title of the *Time* article,

"Where Has the Gung-Ho Gone?" effectively sums up the motivational problem which is being created. It shows how this motivational problem is negatively affecting productivity. The timing for employee malaise is terrible. This is the third concern. Competitiveness, which has spawned the movement for lean and mean organizations, will only occur if employees are more productive, not less.

This is not the first time that the employment relationship has undergone radical change. Entrepreneurs, at the beginning of the Industrial Revolution, sought to free themselves from the responsibilities of being the master in the master-serf relationship established in the Middle Ages.[3] After decades of labor strife, a labor-capital accord was finally reached in the 1930s. Labor relinquished claims over the control of production thereby granting management broad powers to operate organizations without interference. This included the ability to adjust the size of the work force to meet economic conditions. In return, wage increases were to keep up with the increasing growth of the economy. In addition, rules governing procedural justice, such as job classification, movement of employees between jobs, and how wages were to be set were established.[4] Both labor and management agreed to this arrangement because they wished to prevent further government intrusion into the employment relationship.

In 1980, this accord came apart. External pressures, such as foreign competition and deregulation, led management to believe that employment conditions must change if American industry was to be competitive.[5]

What is emerging out of the current situation? One view is that a new employment relationship emphasizing cooperative rather than adversarial relations between management and employees is coming about and will be the answer to America's productivity crisis.[6] This new cooperative relationship is patterned after the Japanese style.[7] While seemingly new, philosophically it is like Frederick W. Taylor's idea that management and labor should "take their eyes off the division of the surplus as the

Reprinted from *Academy of Management Executive*, (No. 5, 1991), by permission of Academy of Management Publications, Ohio Northern University. All rights reserved.)

all important matter, and together turn their attention towards increasing the size of the surplus . . ."[8] Such cooperation did not occur in the 1920s; will it happen today?

Cooperation at What Cost?

Cooperation assumes two parties working together to achieve a desired end. Much of what has occurred in the past ten years does not fit this model. Massive layoffs at all organizational levels, wage reductions in most union contracts, takeovers and mergers destroying jobs as well as pensions systems have been all too common. Job classifications have been changed and white collar employee layoffs have reduced their job security. These actions, more typical of an adversarial relationship than a cooperative one, make management look like it's taking unilateral action to the detriment of its employees.

The following allegory illustrates employee confusion about talk of cooperation in the employment relationship. In this example, the employment relationship is replaced with the marriage relationship:

Suppose as the two of you come in the door from work your spouse says to you:

"Sit down I want to talk to you. Our relationship has got to change. The reasons for this are partly you and partly outside pressures. You have been asking for too much and giving too little. At the same time we are facing a deteriorating financial condition so there is not as much for us to share. I have given this a great deal of thought and here are the changes that must take place.

"I need more from you. I want you to be more cooperative and involved with our relationship. You need to look around the house and see what needs to be done and do it. Then we should sit down more often and decide on what things need to be done and how. We are not going to be able to afford help so you need to devote more time and do more around here. All this means you must be more flexible and take on a wider variety of responsibilities around the house.

"You are going to have to cut back on the amount of money you use each week. I have had to borrow a large amount of money to keep this house going and at the same time have needed money for maintaining other activities so there is less for you. There is an up side to this however. First, you will be on an incentive system that will give you a share of any

savings in expenses that we can make by sitting down together and working through ideas to save costs. Second, since you are doing a wider variety of tasks around the house and experiencing more responsibility you should find this to be intrinsically satisfying.

"This is not all. We cannot afford to put any more money into the savings account we established for retirement. But I did find that, with the increase in the value of our investments, the account has gained more value than we planned so I didn't think you would mind if I used that money for other purposes.

"Oh! By the way. I have been working on a deal with some other people. It is possible that in the near future that I will be offered an opportunity that involves me moving on and leaving you with a new partner. I realize that this might seem tough on you but it is the best thing for me and I know you can survive the change.

"Last, I am concerned that our relationship is not productive enough to survive. If I find that it is not in the next six months you will find your bags packed and outside the front door when you come home some evening."

This is not a new cooperative relationship at all but a coerced one which one party has imposed upon the other. True cooperation will require management to change its attitudes toward the capabilities of employees to make decisions and be involved with the operation of the company. The tone in this allegory is autocratic, where one person makes all the family decisions. It is to this view of the organization as family that I now turn.

One Big Happy Family?

In the recent movie "Roger and Me" the narrator is talking to a public relations official who is leaning out of a plant window. He questions her about a pending layoff and she replies that this is a "family business." The image of company as family is popular and, given the ideas of cooperation discussed above, it seems to be becoming more popular. The smaller size of organizations today also fosters this view of the organization.

But such metaphors, intentionally or not, convey the characteristics of the image on to the object.[9] While the image of business as a family may be comforting to many business executives, like all metaphors, it focuses on some aspects of reality while ignoring others.

In this case, when the metaphor is more closely examined it suggests some unattractive comparisons for both management and the employee.

In the organization as family metaphor the manager is the parent and the employee is the child. Decision making is placed on management and employees are dependent on their managers. While management may find this a comfortable arrangement, it is not what is needed to create a climate of cooperation. A more enlightened view may be that of an older family, where the children are grown and independent or in the extreme where the children are grown and caring for the elder parent. But this image would be discomforting to managers. It suggests that employees would strive for independence from the employer or even seek to make the employer dependent upon them.

An image of organizations as family may make more sense in the Japanese culture.[10] The concept of family is collective. It encourages loyalty from the employee and protection by and from the employer. The push towards ridding the organization of low performers and downsizing in general is antithetical to the idea of family. Families turning out or leaving behind children are illustrations of the most extreme negative circumstances in literature and history.

The parental role in this "organization as family" metaphor focuses on the child's achievement and performance. But what of the parents' nurturing role? It is absent. Including the nurturing role refocuses the metaphor on a different and more affective employment relationship. For instance, focus may shift to caring, listening, and developing employee self esteem.[11]

Is there a place in organizations where this more nurturing, caring, and protective role is fostered? Is this a major function of the Human Resource Department?

The Human Resource Department: Ombudsman or Strategist?

Fairness is a major concern in any relationship. The management literature calls this organizational justice and it has three aspects: distributive, procedural, and corrective. All three have been damaged by changes to the employment relationship in the past ten years.

Distributive justice, which is the allocation of revenues, has experienced a shift. Employees are receiving a smaller share of the organizational income pie, even as that pie has grown. Leveraging, with its consequent burden of huge interest payments, has taken a larger proportion. Large increases in executive salaries, while not a major portion of the total pie, have increased pay differences between the top and bottom of the organization. This has created a negative impression with employees.[12] Finally, the upsurge in the stock market during the 1980s significantly increased stockholders' wealth. Wages have not risen proportionately thereby violating employees feelings of distributive justice.

Procedural justice involves establishing rules for how to divide the pie and corrective justice has to do with correcting mistakes. These two have also been changed to the detriment of the employee recently. With unions, procedural and corrective justice were accomplished by collective bargaining and contract administration. Today, as fewer employees are union members, fewer have their rights protected.

In *The Transformation of American Industrial Relationships,* the authors (Kochan, Katz, and McKersie) see the rise of a strong and enlightened human resource department within the organization as the replacement for unions.[13] The strength of this modern human resource department emanates from a strategic focus which contributes to the organization's overall strategy. This focus is necessary if human resources are to be considered truly important.[14] The way this often gets interpreted, however, is disturbing. The human resource administrator is to "contribute to the bottom line" and show the result of human resource activities in financial terms. While there are places where this is appropriate, such as with cost containment of benefits, in general good human resource management is better stated in terms of productivity than profits. Human resource management best fits with organizational strategy when the strategist's role is perceived to represent the organization's stakeholders rather than the stockholders.[15]

These events have long-term consequences to organizational strategies. Changes in employee attitudes are one documented consequence. Employees become more cynical.[16] Employees who once gave their commitment and energy to the organization vow that they will never be fooled again. Such employees are hard to gain cooperation from or to motivate for higher productivity.

If the human resource department is to effectively replace unions, the strategic model may not be the best approach. Viewing the human resource executive as an ombudsman may be a more apt model. An ombudsman is a person who knows the system and can protect the individual from the excesses of that system.[17] This, however, places the human resource executive back in a role perceived as not central to accomplishing organizational goals.

In pursuing a more competitive strategy, management has taken many unilateral actions during the past decade which have proved to be detrimental to employees. Neither unions nor an enlightened human resource department have been able to soften the negative impact on employees. Is management to be allowed the latitude to continue to make these decisions unfettered, or will its power be curtailed?

Where is the Countervailing Power?

The concept of countervailing power is central in American political science and extends to most other aspects of our society as well. No single decisionmaker or decision making body is to have total power. Galbraith in *American Capitalism* extended this idea into the economic sphere with a tripartite relationship among management, labor unions, and the government where a rise in the power of one leads to a rise in the power of at least one of the other two.[18] But with the weakened power of unions, the relationship is out of balance. A redress of the power balance could come from three sources: employees, government, or resurgent unions.

Employees

Employees must be able to influence the terms of a new relationship. It is the only long term solution that will be acceptable to employees and society. In fact, employees are soon likely to possess more power in determining their work relationships. The labor market, which for the last twenty years has experienced a surplus of employees due to the baby boom, is drying up as the baby bust generation moves into the work force. Predictions indicate that there will be a shortage of employees in most skilled and professional areas.[19] A surplus of employees will occur only in unskilled areas where demand is falling and the labor pool is poorly educated. Thus, there will be a valued group of employees with more power and another group that is less valued with reduced power. This split in the work force is being reflected in society and creates a "have-not" class which could threaten the stability of our social and political structures.[20]

Women will represent the majority of new entrants into the work force during the next ten years. Obtaining their commitment and involvement will require substantial changes in human resource policies. One major area that must be addressed is the work-family conflict. Organizations need to revise policies to provide more flexibility in employment; time and place of work, career paths, and benefit options, for example.

New forms of communication and the computer enable organizations to adapt and be more flexible on hours and work locations. But even more important is the attitudinal change that balances the organization's needs with the employee's home life. The separation of work and family which began with the industrial revolution may be reversing.[21]

The highly educated, including women, will definitely impact organizations, not because they are organizing to do so, but rather as a result of organizations attempting to recruit them and adopting policies to maintain an adequate labor force. It is here that the enlightened human resource department can have a significant impact by introducing sophisticated personnel planning systems to complement the organization's other planning systems.

Government

Recently, government has been steadily increasing its role in defining conditions of the employment relationship, both through legislation and the courts.

Legislation regarding the employment relationship has moved from a reliance on collective labor law which encouraged collective bargaining to individual labor law which provides specific protection to all employees.[22]

The most dramatic change in individual labor law has come from the re-definition of the at-will principle of employment. This doctrine has allowed employers to dismiss any employee for any reason whatsoever. The United States is the last of the industrialized countries not to have replaced this doctrine with an unjustified discharge law, one that restricts employers to firing employees only for cause. Even so, the impact of the at-will principle has been steadily eroding as select employee groups have been protected from arbitrary discharge. The Civil Rights Act is a case in point. In addition, courts have begun to develop exceptions to the at-will principle for violations of public policy, implied contract, and bad faith. Clearly we are close to replacing the at-will principle in the United States with a doctrine of justifiable discharge.

As the move for a new civil rights bill and family leave benefits indicate, there is a continuing push for new labor legislation. The long-term results of this intrusion by law are clear and should be disturbing to the business executive; the demands of employees through elected union representatives are being replaced by legislation and court decisions. These constraints are more unilateral, leaving the manager less room for negotiating reasonable change.

Unlike collective labor law, which established the system for determining the details of the employment relationship, these individual labor laws focus on specific perceived problems without defining any overall employment policy. The result is a mass of overlapping laws and regulations that requires an expert to understand.

Dealing with these pressures is another major challenge for the human resource department. It becomes the organizational watchdog responsible for "keeping the organization legal." It is a necessary but not necessarily desirable role.

Resurgent Unions?

Collective bargaining is the alternative to individual bargaining or government control. But the prospect of unions being a powerful force in re-defining the employment relationship is not good. Union membership and power has been steadily declining for the past twenty years. The movement from a manufacturing to a service economy which led to this decline is not likely to change.

Unions would have to attract large numbers of white collar employees in the service industries in order to grow. A high level of dissatisfaction and powerlessness would have to exist in these employees for this to happen.[23] Preventing these conditions is exactly what Kochan, Katz, and McKersie see as the human resource department's contribution.

Why have unions stood by passively as management has made drastic changes in the employment relationship during the last ten years? Increased global competition and an emerging world economy may be part of the answer. The United States must become more competitive and changes and hardships are perceived as the cost that union members must pay for their role in the problem. However, as a 1987 *Los Angeles Times* Labor Day editorial stated, management must beware that it does not use this feeling on the public's part as a way to exploit its employees.[24]

Further, Kochan, Katz, and McKersie explain that with the rising power of management, a latent dislike for unions has emerged, resulting in a resurgence of anti-unionism.[25] Is this attitudinal change only restricted to the union? Or is it the organization's attempt to create a stable situation by turning employees into a compliant resource? This kind of thinking, however, is not conducive to cooperation. Compliance and cooperation are not the same thing. Trust, built on mutual respect, is the major building block for cooperation between management and the employee. In the labor accord forged in the 1930s both sides gained and paid for some advantage. A new accommodation is needed if American industry is to survive. Employees must be empowered to control their work and influence the operation of the organization.

The New Employment Relationships

Despite the concerns expressed here, the outlines of some new employment relationships are already clear. Changes in American industry and the workforce are creating not one but a number of new employment relationships. C. Handy in *The Age of Unreason* expresses this best by observing that organizations today can be pictured as a shamrock with three leaves, each representing a different group of employees with a different employment relationship. These groups he calls the core, contractor, and flexible.[26]

The Core Group

The labor accord of the 1930s began to unravel because of changes in U.S. work patterns. A redefined employment relationship for the organization's core group of employees is being built upon these changes. A discussion follows of the major characteristics needed to establish a new employment relationship with the employees that perform the organization's base operations—the core group.

1. *The Nature of the New Work.* The employment relationship of the 1930s encouraged job simplification. The life cycle of products today, competition, and new technology all combine to require greater employee skills. Technology has made the work environment more complex and requires employees to change the way they perform their jobs. Flexibility is now a major requirement. Employees must be able and willing to do different tasks every day.

How do we obtain this flexibility and willingness to change? One way is to provide jobs that allow the employee to exercise more discretion on the job—to be empowered. In a way, empowerment is an updated version of an old idea—participative management.[27] How is it different? First is a focus on work. The new work requires decision making, flexibility, and higher skill levels. Second, the work group as opposed to the individual is key. Self-managing work teams are held accountable for producing a product and making all the necessary production decisions.[28]

The idea of empowerment reverses a trend that began with the Industrial Revolution. It was strongly influenced by scientific management which put managers in charge of determining what was to be produced and how production was to be accomplished. F.W. Taylor, in *Principles of Scientific Management,* suggests that planning the work should be completely separate from doing the work which characterizes this trend.[29] Reversing this way of thinking will not be easy because doing so jeopardizes traditional power relationships.

Suggesting the use of company work groups changes the metaphor from family to team. Employees cooperate within their team to accomplish a goal. Teamwork also suggests a new role for the supervisor—that of coach. The supervisor focuses on teaching and learning instead of authority and command.

2. *Employee Training.* Empowerment requires that employees possess skills at three levels: reading and computation, job knowledge, and interpersonal skills. Finding employees who have all these qualities is becoming difficult. Part of the problem is that there is a shortage of young employees entering the workforce. School systems are struggling to educate today's diverse student population. The result is a work force which is deficient in language and computational skills.

The most positive change American business could make is to increase employee training. To build on the strength of our diverse work culture, companies must provide educational opportunities for language competence, work skills, and company work ethic standards. The evidence suggests that such training pays off. For example, Motorola and Corning have extensive training programs which complement work reorganization. These programs have been successful in making the companies more competitive.[30]

Linking jobs to specific educational requirements is another step companies can take. Unlike countries like Germany, that have a strong apprenticeship tradition, organizations in the United States have not required either particular levels or types of education to obtain specific jobs. Given the changing job requirements, organizations would do well to establish a clear "line of sight" between the completion of courses and degrees and employability. Countries that have made this connection have a lower unemployment rate and higher productivity among young employees.[31]

3. *Work Continuity.* Job security is the number one concern of employees today. The downsizing of American industry has affected all types of employees, including executives and professionals. Finding new jobs has been difficult and finding jobs at the same level of work has been even harder.

If American industry is going to engage in empowerment and training, then job security is a necessity. Organizations lose an enormous investment in human resources when downsizing. The more training invested in the employee, the greater the loss of human capital. Costs associated with downsizing are large and planned cost savings almost never achieved. Remaining employees feel guilty and fear that they will be next.[32] The atmosphere that job insecurity produces is detrimental to employees' mental health and decreases productivity in the organization.[33]

4. *Flexibility in Work Arrangements.* Organizations are slowly changing policies to increase workplace flexibility—when, how much and where people work. Workplace flexibility is often suggested as a female issue. It should be viewed, however, as a changing society issue. Women need to work for economic reasons and organizations need the skills represented by the best educated segment of our society. Since the U.S. family structure is being altered, the issue shifts to families, in which case all of us are affected.[34]

Flexibility and responsiveness to family life is congruent with empowerment. Organizations need to offer employees choices so that they can balance their professional and personal life. Management must trust employees to use good judgment in arriving at mutually acceptable work patterns.

5. *Work Rewards.* Compensation practices changed little in the United States for more than fifty years. Emphasis was placed on internal equity and external competitiveness. The past ten years, has seen a trend toward relating pay to performance and making it variable with the fortunes of the company. Some portion of the employee's pay is "put at risk" to give the organization flexibility and to focus employee attention on the organization's success. This trend has encouraged interest in incentive plans, particularly those that are oriented to organizational success, such as gainsharing.

Contractors and Flexible Employees

The five conditions just discussed define the employment relationship for a core group of employees. In the past decade, the downsizing of American industry and technology changes has considerably reduced the size of the core group.

Two other groups fill out the shamrock organization and create very different employment relationships.

Contractors are the first of the two. These people may be former core employees brought back as consultants, independent professionals who perform work for a group of organizations, or employees of organizations who provide specific services. The employment relationship for this group is defined in a contract and usually in terms of specified outcomes for a set price. The positive side of this relationship is that work can be expanded and contracted by the organization easily. A negative aspect is that in expansionary times a low supply of these people may leave the organization without sufficient human resources.

The flexible work force, or temporary and part-time employees is the third leaf of the shamrock. This group is often viewed as being disposable. Organizations often fail to treat these employees as important assets. Handy pointed out that "treated as casual labor, such people respond casually."[35] Most organizations, however, depend on this group when the production level is anything more than the minimum.

Many people prefer to be in this flexible group. They do not wish to work the long hours or make the commitment required of the core group. This, however, does not mean that they should not be treated equitably. The cornerstone of this employment relationship from the organization's standpoint is the ability to adjust the workforce at will. The employee's focus is on time, the job, and being rewarded fairly. This group should not be expected to express commitment to the organization. Rewards systems should focus on competitive pay and short-term bonuses for good work.

Conclusion

That these new employment relationships require new employee behavior and attitudes is clear but the change also affects managers. The new employment relationship requires that employees be self-reliant and active in defining their future. Gone is the paternalism of yesterday. Each party in the employment relationship must focus on defining their needs and taking responsibility for meeting them.[36]

Treating employees as adults, empowering them, and creating true cooperative relationships are all part of a new dynamic employment relationship. Achieving this new relationship is difficult for managers. Two recent articles in the *Harvard Business Review* identified some principles that worked for two executives. Ricard Semler, who heads a manufacturing company in Brazil, was guided by three principles when turning the company around to a profitable position. Workforce democracy, profit sharing, and free access to information are three interrelated principles to Semler. Workforce democracy, or treating people like adults, led to employees making corporate decisions, determining their own flexible work arrangements, and browsing through the company's books.

Ralph Stayer heads up a family business called Jacksonville Sausage. He also found that the company needed to be turned around if it was to survive. Stayer was concerned that people did not seem to care about the company or their own job performance. What he began to realize after a few false starts was that he had to give up his hold over the decisions made in the company and thereby his authority. The line workers have now taken over quality control, personnel functions, scheduling, budgeting, and capital improvement. Stayer believes that he has now worked himself out of a job and the organization is doing just fine.[37]

Growth and productivity will come when the employees share in the rewards and take responsibility for increasing productivity. Employee empowerment must not be limited to work methods but must also include the broader set of rules that defines the procedural justice pattern within the organization, as well as strategic policy decisions. Without this, the employees' perception of cooperation will be too narrow. The purpose of empowerment must go beyond "giving employees the feeling of participation" to a true sharing of power in the organization. As also seen in the previous examples, empowerment threatens traditional management power. Empowerment is not just listening to employees but allowing them to make decisions about their work and the organization's operations.

If the appropriate metaphor for the organization is the team, then the appropriate metaphor for the manager is the coach. This focuses the manager on motivating employees through training and getting the best out of them, not by commanding them. Such an approach requires managers to respect their employees and perceive that they are competent adults who can be depended on to do their work. •

Footnotes

[1]J. Castro, "Where Did the Gung-Ho Go?" *Time,* September 11, 1989, 52–56.

[2]"The Password is 'Flexible,'" *Business Week* September 25, 1989, 154.

[3]R. Bendix, *Work and Authority in Industry,* (New York: Harper and Row, 1956).

[4]See for instance: S. Bowles, and H. Gintis, "The Labor-Capital Accord" in F. Hearn, *The Transformation of Industrial Organization,* (Belmont, CA: Wadsworth Publishing. 1988). 75–84 and P. Osterman, Employment Futures, (New York: Oxford University Press. 1988).

[5]Osterman, Ibid.

[6]See for example: E.E. Lawler, *High Involvement Management,* (San Francisco: Jossey-Bass, 1988) and T.J. Peters, and R.H. Waterman, *In Search of Excellence,* (New York: Harper and Row, 1982).

[7]C.J. Grayson, and C. O'Dell, *The Two Minute Warning,* New York: The Free Press, 1988).

[8]F.W. Taylor, *Principles of Scientific Management,* (New York: Harper and Row, 1912), 29–30.

[9]G. Morgan, *Images of Organization,* (Beverly Hills, CA: Sage Publications, 1986).

[10]G. Hofstede, "Cultural Dimensions in Management and Planning," *Asia Pacific Journal of Management*, Jan. 1984, 81–99

[11]P.C. Lunneborg, *Women Changing Work,* (New York: Bergin and Garvey, 1990).

[12]"Is the Boss Getting Paid Too Much," *Business Week,* May 1, 1989, 46–52.

[13]T.A. Kochan, H.C Katz, and R.B. McKersie, *The Transformation of American Industrial Relations, (New* York: Basic Books, 1986).

[14]R.S. Schuler, "Repositioning the Human Resource Function: Transformation or Demise?" *Academy of Management Executive,* August, 1990, 49–60.

[15]I. Mitroff, *Stakeholders of the Organizational Mind,* (San Francisco: Jossey-Bass Publishers, 1983).

[16]D.L. Kanter, and P.H. Mirvis, *The Cynical Americans,* (San Francisco: Jossey-Bass. 1989).

[17]M. Waxman, "Reactive and Proactive Resolution of Employee Responsibilities and Rights Staff Issues Via the Ombudsman Concept," in C.A.B. Osigweh, Ed., *Managing Employee Rights and Responsibilities.* (New York: Quorum Books, 1989), 161–174.

[18]J.K. Galbraith, *American Capitalism,* (Boston: Houghton Mifflin Co., 1962).

[19]M.M. Greller, and D.M. Nee, *From Baby Boom to Baby Bust,* (Reading, Mass: Addison-Wesley Publishing, 1989).

[20]"Where the Jobs Are is Where the Skills Aren't," *Business Week,* Sept. 19, 1988, 104–108.

[21]F.S. Rogers, and C. Rogers, "Business and the Facts of Family Life," *Harvard Business Review,* November–December 1989, 121–131.

[22]K.L. Sovereign, *Personnel Law,* 2nd. Ed., (Englewood Cliffs, New Jersey: Prentice-Hall, 1989).

[23]J.M. Brett, "Why Employees Want Unions," *Organizational Dynamics,* Spring 1980, 47–59.

[24]"Looking at Labor and Business," *Los Angeles Times,* September 7, 1987, II, 6.

[25]Kochan et al., Op Cit.

[26]C. Handy, *The Age of Unreason.* (Boston: Harvard Business School Press, 1989).

[27]Lawler, *High Involvement Management.* Op Cit.

[28]See for example, M.A. Frohman, "Human Resource Management and the Bottom Line: Evidence of the Connection," *Human Resource Management,* 1984, 315–34.

[29]F.W. Taylor, *Scientific Management,* Op Cit.

[30]W. Wiggenhorn, "Motorola U.: When Training Becomes an Education," *Harvard Business Review,* July–August 1990, 71–83 and J. Hoerr. "Sharpening Minds for a Competitive *Edge,"* *Business Week,* Dec. 17, 1990, 72–8.

[31]Hoerr, Ibid.

[32]J.F. Bolt. "Job Security: Its Time has Come," *Harvard Business Review,* November–December 1983.

[33]J. Hartley, D. Jacobsen, B. Klandermans, and T. Van Vuuren, *Job Insecurity,* (Newbury Park, CA: Sage Publications, 1991).

[34]Rodgers. Op Cit.

[35]Handy, Op Cit 100.

[36]K.P. DeMeuse, and W.W. Tornow, "The Tie that Binds Has Become Very, Very Frayed," *Human Resource Planning,* 1990, no. 3, 203–213.

[37]R. Stayer. "How I Learned to Let My Workers Lead." *Harvard Business Review*, November–December 1990, 66–83 and R. Semler, "Managing Without Managers," *Harvard Business Review,* September–October 1989, 76–84.

*   *   *

Thomas J. Atchison is a professor of management at San Diego State University. He teaches courses in human resource management with an emphasis on compensation administration. He is the co-author of two books and more than a dozen articles in journals such as *Personnel Psychology* and *Industrial Relations*. He has been active in the Academy of Management, Industrial Relations Research Association, Human Resource Planning Society, and the American Compensation Association. His current research interests are in the changing work relationship, the effects of innovative compensation programs on employees, and strategic alternatives in staffing.

Study Questions

1. Explain the labor-capital accord reached in the 1930s.

2. How did the 1980s affect this accord?

3. Why is the organization-as-family analogy problematic for organizational functioning?

4. Define the three aspects of organizational justice.

5. What has happened in the past 10 years to reduce justice for employees?

6. When does human resource management best fit organizational strategy?

7. Explain the concept of countervailing power.

8. What types of employees are most likely to redress the unbalanced power among management, government, and labor?

9. Define and explain the differences between the at-will principle and unjustified discharge laws.

10. Why is legislation more problematic for management union demands, and what is the ultimate concern of individual labor laws?

11. How can the HR department affect each of the "countervailing" powers?

12. How have job requirements changed (since the 30s) and how can this potentially enhance employee power?

13. What changes in the workplace can help establish a productive employee relationship with the organization's "core group?"

14. What skills are necessary for employees to be empowered in today's companies?

15. Who are contractors, how is their relationship specified, and what are the advantages and disadvantages of this new employee relationship?

16. What is the relationship situation with temporary/flexible employees?

17. From the employee perspective, how will growth and prosperity come to the organization?

CASE: Sporting Goods Store

G. Yukl

Bill Thompson is the new manager of a retail sporting goods store that is part of a national chain. Bill, who is 23 years old, has been working for the company since he finished college three years ago. Before his promotion, he was the assistant manager for two years at another store in the chain. Last week, he was briefly introduced to the daytime employees by his boss, the regional manager. The profit performance of his new store is below average for its location, and Bill is looking forward to the challenge of improving profits. When he was an assistant manager, he was given mostly minor administrative duties and paperwork, so this will be his first opportunity to show he can be an effective manager.

The base salaries of the fifteen employees who work in Bill's store are set by the regional office, but appraisal ratings by the store manager influence the size of an employee's annual merit raise. These recommendations must be justified to the regional manager, especially if they are not consistent with individual and department sales. Bill can suspend or fire employees with the approval of his boss, but in practice it is difficult to do so unless there is a strong case. The basic store layout and most prices are set by the headquarters office. However, store performance can be affected to a limited extent by the store manager. One way is to keep cost of staff low by making sure they are working efficiently and not taking excessive sick days. Another way is to insure that employees are providing a high level of customer service so that customers will return to make other purchases rather than going to a different store next time. Customer service depends on knowing the products well, being polite, providing prompt service, and making sure that inventories of popular goods are maintained so that customers can find what they want. Pay is low for this type of retail selling job, turnover is high, and it takes a few months for a new employee to learn the merchandise well enough to be helpful to customers. Thus, it is also desirable to keep effective employees satisfied enough to stay with the company.

Although it is only his first week on the job, Bill believes that he has already discovered some of the problems at this store. The ski department is potentially the highest profit department in the store, but its sales are only about average for the stores in this region. He noticed that service in the ski department appears to be very slow. There has been a line of customers waiting to be served on several occasions, and he has overheard some grumbling about how long it takes to get served. One customer said he was leaving to go to another store that didn't make him "wait all day to have the privilege of spending hundreds of dollars on ski equipment." Upon close examination, Bill observed that Sally Jorgenson, the department manager, spends a lot of time socializing with her three sales people and with customers, including friends who drop in to visit and talk about ski conditions, resorts, fashions, equipment, racing, and so forth. On a couple of occasions, Bill saw customers waiting while she was talking to friends. Bill, who doesn't ski, cannot understand what they find so interesting to talk about or, for that matter, why anybody in their right mind would want to spend a small fortune and risk permanent injury to hurtle down a mountain in blizzard conditions, and then stand in long lines and ride up a freezing chairlift just to do it all over again. •

From *Leadership in Organizations*, Prentice-Hall, 1994. Copyright © 1994 by G. Yukl. Reprinted by permission.

Study Questions

1. How much of each type of power does Bill have now (e.g., amount, a lot)? Explain your answer in the space provided.

   a. Legitimate Power

   b. Reward Power

   c. Coercive Power

   d. Expert Power

   e. Referent Power

2. How useful are each of the following influence tactics in this situation? Explain your answer in the space provided.

   a. Legitimate Tactics

   b. Pressure Tactics

   c. Exchange Tactics

   d. Rational Persuasion

   e. Inspiration Appeals

   f. Personal Appeals and Ingratiation

   g. Coalition

   h. Consultation

3. Which combination of tactics is likely to be most effective?

CASE: Behind Revolt at GM, Lawyer Ira Millstein Helped Call the Shots

Joseph B. White
Paul Ingrassia
Staff Reporters of *The Wall Street Journal*

Power Play at Secret Meeting

On Saturday, March 28, the outside directors of General Motors Corp. summoned Chairman Robert C. Stempel to a secret meeting near O'Hare Airport in Chicago. They told Mr. Stempel he wasn't moving fast enough to cure GM's ills, and then dictated their terms.

They wanted Mr. Stempel to dump two senior executives, including his longtime friend, GM President Lloyd E. Reuss. The outsiders also wanted Mr. Stempel to step down as chairman of GM's executive committee in favor of someone from their ranks, John G. Smale.

For Mr. Stempel, the meeting was a painful rebuke: He became the first GM chief executive in more than 70 years to lose control of his board. For another man in the room, New York attorney Ira M. Millstein, the meeting was a sweet and spectacular triumph in his quest to reform the way companies are run.

For if Mr. Smale was the leader of GM's board-room revolt, Mr. Millstein, the chief counsel to GM's outside directors for more than five years, was its ideologist. "In their permissive and passive stances, most boards are likely not to appraise the performance of CEO's critically enough ... and to wait too long to respond to ongoing political, social and economic change," Mr. Millstein and a colleague wrote in 1988.

Few philosophers in the arena of corporate governance ever get a chance to translate their theories into practice. Mr. Millstein, however, has just done it with the largest industrial corporation in the world, which means his theories are reverberating in board rooms everywhere.

And Mr. Millstein, who has never been a GM employee or director, has done it all behind the scenes, without attracting so much as a footnote of public attention. The spotlight has been focused instead on GM's newly assertive outside directors, notably Mr. Smale, the retired chairman of Procter & Gamble Co. But, declares one GM executive angry with last week's turn of events, "Millstein is the snake in the grass on this."

Avid Audience

Not that Mr. Millstein is exactly unknown. He's a high-profile New York lawyer whose career had included teaching at Columbia University and negotiating the recent Drexel Burnham Lambert bankruptcy settlement.

But starting in 1985, Mr. Millstein has developed an increasingly close relationship with GM's outside directors. He has served as GM board's counselor, hand-holder and chief adviser on corporate governance. The gregarious New York City native found fertile ground for his views as GM's once-sleepy board began to wrestle with its role in the historic decline of America's pre-eminent corporation.

Mr. Millstein, age 65, delved deeply during the 1980s into the esoteric topic of how companies are run. He is the author or co-author of two books, and dozens of academic papers and speeches on the subject. He helped to establish, and is chairman of, the board of advisers to the Institutional Investor Project at Columbia University, a think tank for study of the role of big pension funds in corporate affairs. For many years, Mr. Millstein was an adviser on corporate governance to the Business Roundtable, the business lobbying group.

His message: Directors should be far more independent of the entrenched managements of corporations, and should exert far greater influence than in the past. "New times may require new board processes," he said in a speech at Harvard's Kennedy School of Government last year. The goal, he added, is to rebuild America's competitiveness.

Shaking the Executive Suite

Mr. Millstein declined to be interviewed for this article, as did GM directors. But others familiar with the board's deliberations, and with Mr. Millstein's role, provide a road map to a climactic meeting in Dallas on April 6 when GM's directors made history.

The stage was set a week beforehand, when the outside directors—with Mr. Millstein at their side—confronted Mr. Stempel in Chicago. Mr. Reuss, who had presided over losses totalling $11.68 billion in GM's North American operations over the past two years, had to go. The directors also targeted Robert T. O'Connell, GM's chief financial officer.

A shaken Mr. Stempel returned to Detroit to figure out how to salvage some role in the company for Messrs. Reuss and O'Connell. On April 6, GM announced that its stunning shake-up was "unanimously approved by the board of directors, upon recommendation by the chairman." That statement was technically correct. But Mr. Stempel, left with little choice, had merely recommended what his board told him it wanted.

Here's how GM's board-room revolt, inspired by Mr. Millstein, evolved over several years:

Making Friends

In 1985, Ira Millstein was a well-regarded corporate lawyer and a partner in the New York law firm of Weil, Gotshal and Manges, which has its offices in the GM building in midtown Manhattan. Among other things, he was representing the French Pasteur Institute in litigation with the National Institutes of Health over which of the two organizations had first identified the AIDS virus. He had also established credentials as a corporate philosopher in a 1981 book, "The Limits of Corporate Power."

GM, however, had a more mundane matter for which it wanted Mr. Millstein's counsel. The auto maker was in the process of issuing a new class of common stock in connection with its $5 billion acquisition of Hughes Aircraft Co. The new common, called GMH, represented a dividend interest in the performance of the GM unit that included Hughes. The GMH shares were thus similar to the GME shares GM had issued to finance the purchase of Electronic Data Systems Corp. in 1984.

These so-called "alphabet stocks" essentially allowed then-GM Chairman Roger B. Smith to generate new money from investors to finance acquisitions. But they also created a potential problem: GM directors worried that holders of so-called "classic" GM common could attack the company for slighting them in favor of holders of the alphabet stocks.

GM's general counsel at the time, Elmer Johnson, told the board it needed independent advice. It's not uncommon in corporate America for boards to retain outside counsel, particularly in times of difficulty. GM has done it off and on for years. Now, at the suggestion of Mr. Johnson, himself an avid student of corporate governance, the board hired Mr. Millstein.

Mr. Millstein's introduction to the GM board came just as the giant auto maker's fortunes were teetering. In less than two years, beginning in 1984, Mr. Smith had transformed the stodgy auto giant, completely recasting its corporate hierarchy. GM was no longer just America's No. 1 car maker. It was the nation's No. 1 computer services company, through EDS, and one of the nation's largest defense contractors, through Hughes.

But underneath all these mega-moves, GM's costs were soaring, and its quality plunging. What's more, Chairman Smith was beginning his blood feud with GM director H. Ross Perot, the Texas billionaire from whom he had purchased EDS. After weeks of negotiations, GM agreed to pay Mr. Perot $700 million for his stock, in return for his departure from the board.

Getting Advice

On Nov. 30, 1986, jittery GM directors met to approve the deal. They knew that no matter what they did, they were likely to face lawsuits from angry shareholders. They knew they needed a lawyer. They turned to Mr. Millstein.

Mr. Millstein led the GM board through carefully orchestrated deliberations that lasted some six hours. His performance sowed the seeds of what was to come.

For indeed, GM's outside directors did get sued over the Perot buy-out. And once again, they turned to Mr. Millstein. He spent hours during the months following the buy-out accompanying the directors to depositions, often having lunch with them between sessions or dinner afterward. He developed close relationships with such directors as Mr. Smale, Thomas H. Wyman, the former CBS chairman who himself was ousted in a board-room coup, and Anne L. Armstrong, a prominent Texan and former ambassador to England.

All the while, GM's fortunes were spiraling downward. In 1987, the company's share of U.S. car sales plunged to 36.3%, down nearly 10 percentage points from earlier in the decade. Mr. Smith and GM's board were coming under withering attack from big shareholders for the Perot buy-out and the company's disappointing performance. Mr. Perot, himself, derided the GM directors as "pet rocks."

A Better Idea

Against this background, Mr. Millstein in April 1987 delivered a speech to a group of big institutional investors. Investors, Mr. Millstein said, are wasting their time nitpicking corporations over such issues as anti-takeover defenses and proxy voting rules. If a company isn't performing, he said, go after the board of directors.

The message struck a nerve with some big investors, notably officials of Calpers, the $41 billion California Public Employee's Retirement System which holds a block of GM shares. "We said, 'That makes sense,'" recalls Richard Koppes, Calpers general counsel.

Mr. Millstein, in speeches and essays, began to expand on his ideas about the proper roles of big investors and outside directors. The huge pension funds, he argued, had to act as "responsible owners," not just short-term players in a company's stock. That meant they should put pressure on directors—their representatives—when a company isn't performing.

Directors, in turn, had to become bolder. Mr. Millstein joined a growing chorus in favor of separating leadership of the board from the position of chief executive officer. He said independent directors should meet regularly, without management, to discuss whether the chief executive measured up to the board's goals.

That hadn't happened at GM in modern memory. Mr. Millstein went further and said directors shouldn't hesitate to dismiss a chief executive who didn't perform.

The Board Stirs

Mr. Millstein, of course, also had other irons in the fire during the 1988 to 1992 period. He represented Drexel as it tottered into bankruptcy and AMR Corp., the parent of American Airlines, in an antitrust action. He served on a task force appointed by New York Gov. Mario Cuomo to study pension-fund investments.

But back at GM, the directors were stirring. Messrs. Smale and Wyman and Mrs. Armstrong, along with other outside directors, began to worry that GM's continuing malaise would start to damage their personal reputations, according to people close to the board.

In mid-1988, the outside directors jolted Chairman Smith by refusing to support his plan to put three more GM executives on the board. It was the first time Mr. Smith had been rebuffed in such a direct way. It was also a move straight out of the Millstein playbook: Mr. Millstein had been advocating that boards reduce the number of insiders.

Also, two new outside directors joined the board. One was hotel magnate J. Willard Marriott Jr., who joined in 1989, and the other Ann D. McLaughlin, former U.S. Secretary of Labor and now a visiting fellow at the Urban Institute, in 1990. Both were willing to speak their minds.

Mr. Marriott, GM insiders say, began demanding detailed information about GM's ailing North American operations. His questions encouraged Mr. Smale, who for several years had been asking why GM was earning less money than Ford Motor Co., a company just two-thirds as large. Mr. Wyman and J.P. Morgan & Co. Chairman Dennis Weatherstone—both of whom joined the board in the mid-1980s—also liked the board's new assertiveness.

In early 1990, it was time to select a successor to Chairman Smith. The obvious choice was Mr. Stempel, GM's president and chief operating officer since 1987. A reformer and conciliator instead of a revolutionary, Mr. Stempel would be the first non-finance man to head GM in more than 30 years.

But a test of wills developed over who would succeed Mr. Stempel as No. 2. Mr. Stempel wanted Mr. Reuss, a fellow engineer. The two men had worked together closely during their 32 years at GM. And after Mr. Stempel had beaten Mr. Reuss for the presidency in 1987, Mr. Reuss had displayed tireless effort in running GM's North American vehicle operations, and in showing loyalty to Mr. Stempel.

The board balked. GM's North American operations, which Mr. Reuss was running, were losing money. The board's candidate for president was John F. "Jack" Smith Jr. (no relation to Roger Smith), who had made GM's European operations hugely profitable.

Finally the board caved in and made Mr. Reuss president, but signaled its reservations by refusing to name him chief operating officer. (Jack Smith became vice chairman for international operations.) The board was sending a message, but Mr. Stempel didn't seem to get it.

Mr. Stempel took over as chairman on Aug. 1, 1990. The next day, Iraq invaded Kuwait, and the U.S. economy plunged into a recession. GM began a "kamikaze dive," as Mr. Stempel would describe it later. GM took a $2.1 billion write-off in the third quarter of 1990 to close excess plants; its losses started to mount at a staggering rate. So did the board's impatience.

Between June 1990 and September 1991, GM rolled up five straight quarterly losses totaling $5.8 billion. Late last year, the company's outside directors began stepping up their discussions with Mr. Millstein, as did big institutional investors, such as the California Pension Fund.

Mr. Millstein became both go-between and catalyst. He assured big investors that the board was asserting itself. And he told outside directors that the investment community wanted prompt action.

Catching Up

At a board meeting on Dec. 9, Mr. Stempel said GM was working on a plan to close more factories, dismiss thousands of employees and take another huge write-off. He said the specif-

ics weren't yet in place, but he would bring the board more details at its January meeting.

It was a huge mistake. Wall Street wanted a clear signal that GM would act promptly and decisively to stop its hemorrhaging, but Mr. Stempel was taking a deliberate tack. Securities analysts and institutional investors aired their complaints to reporters, and the company's stock dropped to a four-year low.

So on Dec. 18, Mr. Stempel hastily convened a press conference at GM headquarters. There he dropped the bombshell that GM would close 21 more plants and shed 74,000 jobs by the mid-1990s. Internally, Mr. Stempel began telling subordinates GM must strive to break even in 1992.

To outside directors, Mr. Stempel's abrupt decision to accelerate the announcement was jarring. And the goal of breaking even just didn't sit well. They wanted the world's largest auto maker to set its sights on getting profitable, no matter what it took.

In January 1992, GM's board held its regular monthly meeting in Detroit. But Mr. Stempel was in Tokyo, reluctantly accompanying President Bush on his trade mission. The outside directors used his absence to meet privately with Mr. Millstein, a once-unthinkable act, and key board members flew back to New York with Mr. Millstein on a GM plane. Word of the huddle spread among GM executives.

The Coup

Out in California, Calpers was taking to heart Mr. Millstein's theories. The fund had written a letter to GM's board in 1990, expressing concern about the company's performance. In 1991, Calpers officials had met with Mr. Stempel to reiterate their dismay. By early this year, the fund was about to demand another meeting. But Calpers officials began getting signals from Mr. Millstein to hold off. Something was about to happen, he hinted.

Mr. Smale, at the board's behest, had begun conducting private interviews with GM's top 20 or so executives. He wanted to know what the hangups to progress were, and who was causing them. He took names, GM executives say.

In their meetings with Mr. Millstein earlier this year, outside directors focused their views.

Mr. Stempel hadn't moved fast enough last year for a company in crisis. They had completely lost confidence in Mr. Reuss, who had devised "26 strategies" for a North American turnaround that weren't producing results. And Mr. O'Connell, at least in the minds of directors, was too linked to former GM Chairman Smith, his one-time mentor.

Mr. Stempel, meanwhile, was busy damping suggestions that an executive shake-up was in the works. "Lloyd's my man," he told reporters on Feb. 24, in response to speculation that Mr. Reuss might be dumped. On March 11, in a newspaper interview, he added: "You've just got to have the patience to stay with me."

Running Out of Time

But the board's patience was nearly spent. And GM's directors were about to witness a dramatic—though entirely coincidental—example of board-room assertiveness at Chrysler Corp.: On March 16, Chrysler's board had a special Saturday meeting in New York. They rebuffed Chairman Lee A. Iacocca's bid to stay on the job beyond his retirement date at the end of this year. Chrysler's board chose Robert J. Eaton, the highly regarded head of GM Europe, to succeed Mr. Iacocca.

Two weeks later, on March 28, GM's outside directors held their own Saturday session, in Chicago, to stand up to their chairman. With Mr. Millstein at their side, they dictated to Mr. Stempel much of the script for the events nine days later.

On Sunday afternoon, April 5, the directors flew into Dallas, home of the EDS computer-service subsidiary for their regular monthly meeting the next day. First, though, the outside directors met among themselves, with Messrs. Stempel and Millstein present. (Roger Smith, the retired GM chairman who remains on the board, wasn't invited.) At that gathering, Mr. Stempel agreed to replace Mr. Reuss as president with Jack Smith, who was already a board member. Mr. Smith also would get the title of chief operating officer, previously denied to Mr. Reuss.

But left unresolved were some key issues: Mr. Reuss's new position, and whether Mr. O'Connell would be removed as chief financial officer.

The Decision Is Made

Later, the outside directors held another private session at which Mr. Stempel addressed those issues. The final details were hashed out the next morning. All that remained was the formal vote of the full board after lunch.

Mr. Reuss, 55, was demoted to executive vice president. His duties would include a grab-bag of operations, ranging from the Saturn subsidiary to electric cars. He also was removed from GM's board, as was executive Vice President F. Alan Smith, who wasn't highly regarded by the board. The moves reduced the number of active GM executives on the board to just three of 15: Mr. Stempel, Jack Smith and Robert J. Schultz, vice chairman.

Mr. O'Connell, 53, previously an executive vice president, was demoted to senior vice president. He will take charge of General Motors Acceptance Corp., GM's big finance subsidiary.

Mr. O'Connell was replaced as chief financial officer by William E. Hoglund, 57, whose appointment was a resurrection of sorts. A GM blue-blood whose father and brother both were company vice presidents, Mr. Hoglund had long been on cool terms with Mr. Stempel. Previously in charge of components operations, he was the only one of GM's top six officers who didn't report directly to the chairman.

As for Mr. Smale, age 64, his role as chairman of the executive committee looks remarkably like that of lead director, as described in Mr. Millstein's writings.

The Aftermath

GM announced all its moves last Monday barely 15 minutes after the board meeting broke up. The next night, April 7, Messrs. Reuss and O'Connell attended an Engineering Society of Detroit dinner at which Mr. Reuss was being honored. Even their detractors gave both men credit for making a graceful public appearance.

Mr. Reuss, besieged by reporters, said he was "disappointed but not humiliated," and pledged to stay at GM. Mr. O'Connell, for his part, quipped "27 down, 11 to go," referring to his years of service at the company, and his years until retirement.

Roger Smith, GM's former chairman, reacted stoically to the revolt by the board he had once run with an iron hand. Mr. Smith told friends that the board "just got impatient," and acted just as the company's fortunes were about to improve. Had the directors held off six months, he added, they might not have acted at all.

As for Mr. Stempel, there's widespread skepticism in the business community that he can remain an effective chairman after having his wings clipped so publicly. Last Wednesday, two days after the shake-up, Mr. Smale issued a statement saying Mr. Stempel has the board's full confidence. Directors have confided to friends that they really do hope he can make it.

"Bob's heart is in the right place," one outside director said nearly a year ago, "but bold moves aren't in his nature. He needs to be prodded. That's where the board comes in."

Mr. Millstein, for his part, was exhilarated at what happened. A friend who called him the next day found him "almost giddy" with excitement.

For finally, his ideas had come in from the cold. "We know of no case where an American corporation has been made less competitive over the long run because its board of directors was playing too active a role," he and a colleague once wrote. "We know of many whose competitiveness has deteriorated, at least in part, because boards have been too passive, and did not challenge management to see what was coming and to act before the crisis occurred." •

Study Questions

1. Your assignment is to analyze the power struggle at GM between the board of directors and top management. It is necessary to use the technical language of power, influence and negotiation in the analysis. The report should be no more than two to five double spaced manuscript pages.

SMR Forum: Managing Conflict

Leonard Greenhalgh

While conflict is not necessarily "bad," or something that should be squelched (it is inherent in organizational life), it can impair relationships among people who need to interact effectively. Therefore, conflict needs to be managed. The author synthesizes much of the diverse writing on conflict management and presents a useful model that can help people diagnose a conflict situation and thus plan tactics for managing it. [SMR Ed.]

Managers or change agents spend a substantial proportion of their time and energy dealing with conflict situations. Such efforts are necessary because any type of change in an organization tends to generate conflict. More specifically, conflict arises because change disrupts the existing balance of resources and power, thereby straining relations between the people involved. Since adversarial relations may impede the process of making adaptive changes in the organization, higher-level managers may have to intervene in order to implement important strategies. Their effectiveness in managing the conflict depends on how well they understand the underlying dynamics of the conflict—which may be very different from its expression—and whether they can identify the crucial tactical points for intervention.

Conflict Management

Conflict is managed when it does not substantially interfere with the ongoing functional (as opposed to personal) relationships between the parties involved. For instance, two executives may agree to disagree on a number of issues and yet be jointly committed to the course of action they have settled on. There may even be some residual hard feelings—perhaps it is too much to expect to manage feelings in addition to relationships—but as long as any resentment is at a fairly low level and does not substantially interfere with other aspects of their professional relationship, the conflict could be considered to have been managed successfully.

Conflict is not an objective, tangible phenomenon; rather, it exists in the minds of the people who are party to it. Only its manifestations, such as brooding, arguing, or fighting, are objectively real. To manage conflict, therefore, one needs to empathize, that is, to understand the situation as it is seen by the key actors involved. An important element of conflict management is persuasion, which may well involve getting participants to rethink their current views so their perspective on the situation will facilitate reconciliation rather than divisiveness.

Influencing key actors' conceptions of the conflict situation can be a powerful lever in making conflicts manageable. This approach can be used by a third party intervening in the conflict or, even more usefully, by the participants themselves. But using this perceptual lever alone will not always be sufficient. The context in which the conflict occurs, the history of the relationship between the parties, and the time available will have to be taken into account if such an approach is to be tailored to the situation. Furthermore, the conflict may prove to be simply unmanageable: one or both parties may wish to prolong the conflict or they may have reached emotional states that make constructive interaction impossible; or, perhaps the two executives may agree to disagree on a conflict is "the tip of the iceberg" and resolving it would have no significant impact on a deeply rooted antagonistic relationship.

Table 1 presents seven perceptual dimensions that form a useful diagnostic model that shows what to look for in a conflict situation and pinpoints the dimensions needing high-priority attention. The model can thus be used to illuminate a way to make the conflict more manageable. The point here is that conflict becomes more negotiable between parties when a minimum number of dimensions are perceived to be at the "difficult-to-resolve" pole and a maximum number to be at the "easy-to-resolve" pole.

The objective is to shift a viewpoint from the difficult-to-resolve pole to the easy-to-resolve one. At times, antagonists will deliberately resist "being more reasonable" because they see tactical advantages in taking a hard line. Nevertheless, there are strong benefits for trying to shift perspectives; these benefits should become apparent as we consider each of the dimensions in the model.

Issues in Question

People view issues on a continuum from being a matter of principle to a question of division. For example, one organization needed to change its channel of distribution. The company had sold door-to-door since its founding, but the labor market was drying up and the sales force was becoming increasingly understaffed. Two factions of executives sprung up: the supporters were open to the needed change; the resisters argued that management made a commitment to the remaining sales force and, as a matter of principle, could not violate the current sales representatives' right to be the exclusive channel of distribution.

Raising principles makes conflict difficult to resolve because by definition one cannot come to a reasonable compromise; one either upholds a principle or sacrifices one's integrity. For some issues, particularly those involving ethical imperatives, such a dichotomous view may be justified. Often, however, matters of principle are raised for the purpose of solidifying a bargaining stance. Yet, this tactic may work against the party using it since it tends to invite an impasse. Once matters of principle are raised, the parties try to argue convincingly that the other's point of view is wrong. At best, this approach wastes time and saps the energy of the parties involved. A useful intervention at this point may be to have the parties acknowledge that they understand each other's view but still believe in their own, equally legitimate point of view. This acknowledgment alone often makes the parties more ready to move ahead from arguing to problem solving.

At the other extreme are divisible issues where neither side has to give in completely; the outcome may more or less favor both par-

ties. In the door-to-door selling example, a more constructive discussion would have ensued had the parties been able to focus on the economic commitment the company had to its sales force, rather than on the moral commitment. As it was, the factions remained deadlocked until the company had suffered irrevocable losses in market share, which served no one's interests. Divisible issues in this case might have involved how much of the product line would be sold through alternative channels of distribution, the extent of exclusive territory, or how much income protection the company was willing to offer its sales force.

Size of Stakes

The greater the perceived value of what may be lost, the harder it is to manage a conflict. This point is illustrated when managers fight against acquisition attempts. If managers think their jobs are in jeopardy, they subjectively perceive the stakes as being high and are likely to fight tooth and nail against the acquisition. Contracts providing for continued economic security, so-called golden parachutes, reduce the size of the stakes for those potentially affected. Putting aside the question of whether such contracts are justifiable when viewed from other perspectives, they do tend to make acquisition conflicts more manageable.

In many cases the perceived size of the stakes can be reduced by persuasion rather than by taking concrete action. People tend to become emotionally involved in conflicts and as a result magnify the importance of what is really at stake. Their "egos" get caught up in the winning/losing aspect of the conflict, and subjective values become inflated.

A good antidote is to postpone the settlement until the parties become less emotional. During this cooling-off period they can reevaluate the issues at stake, thereby restoring some objectivity to their assessments. If time does not permit a cooling off, an attempt to reassess the demands and reduce the other party's expectations may be possible: "There's no way we can give you 100 percent of what you want, so let's be realistic about what you can live with." This approach is really an attempt to induce an attitude change. In effect, the person is being persuaded to entertain the thought, "If I can get by

Table 1: CONFLICT DIAGNOSTIC MODEL

Viewpoint Continuum		
Dimension	Difficult to Resolve	Easy to Resolve
Issue in Question	Matter of Principle	Divisible Issue
Size of Stakes	Large	Small
Interdependence of Parties	Zero Sum	Positive Sum
Continuity of Interaction	Single Transaction	Long-term Relationship
Structure of the Parties	Amorphous or Fractionalized, with Weak Leadership	Cohesive, with Strong Leadership
Involvement of Third Parties	No Neutral Third Party Available	Trusted, Powerful, Prestigious, and Neutral
Perceived Progress of the Conflict	Unbalanced: One Party Feeling the More Harmed	Parties Having Done Equal Harm to Each Other

with less than 100 percent of what I was asking for, then what is at stake must not be of paramount importance to me."

A special case of the high-stakes/low-stakes question is the issue of precedents. If a particular settlement sets a precedent, the stakes are seen as being higher because future conflicts will tend to be settled in terms of the current settlement. In other words, giving ground in the immediate situation is seen as giving ground for all time. This problem surfaces in settling grievances. Thus, an effective way to manage such a conflict is to emphasize the uniqueness of the situation to downplay possible precedents that could be set. Similarly, the perceived consequences of organizational changes for individuals can often be softened by explicitly downplaying the future consequences: employees are sometimes assured that the change is being made "on an experimental basis" and will later be reevaluated. The effect is to reduce the perceived risk in accepting the proposed change.

Interdependence of the Parties

The parties to a conflict can view themselves on a continuum from having "zero-sum" to "positive-sum" interdependence. Zero-sum interdependence is the perception that if one party gains in an interaction, it is at the expense of the other party. In the positive-sum case, both parties come out ahead by means of a settlement. A zero-sum relationship makes conflict difficult to resolve because it focuses attention narrowly on personal gain rather than on mutual gain through collaboration or problem solving.

Consider the example of conflict over the allocation of limited budget funds among sales and production when a new product line is introduced. The sales group fights for a large allocation to promote the product in order to build market share. The production group fights for a large allocation to provide the plant and equipment necessary to turn out high volume at high-quality levels. The funds available have a fixed ceiling, so that a gain for sales appears to be a loss for production and vice versa. From a zero-sum perspective, it makes sense to fight for the marginal dollar rather than agree on a compromise.

A positive-sum view of the same situation removes some of the urgency to win a larger share of the spoils at the outset. Attention is more usefully focused on how one party's allocation in fact helps the other. Early promotion allocations to achieve high sales volume, if successful, lead to high production volume. This, in turn, generates revenue that can be invested in the desired improvements to plant and equipment. Similarly, initial allocations to improve plant and equipment can make a high-quality product readily available to the sales group, and the demand for a high-quality product will foster sales.

The potential for mutual benefit is often overlooked in the scramble for scarce resources. However, if both parties can be persuaded to consider how they can both benefit from a situation, they are more likely to approach the conflict over scarce resources with more cooperative predispositions. The focus shifts from whether one party is getting a fair share of the available resources to what is the optimum initial allocation that will jointly serve the mutual long-run interests of both sales and production.

Continuity of Interaction

The continuity-of-interaction dimension concerns the time horizon over which the parties see themselves dealing with each other. If they visualize a long-term interaction—a continuous relationship—the present transaction takes on minor significance, and the conflict within that transaction tends to be easy to resolve. If, on the other hand, the transaction is viewed as a one-shot deal—an episodic relationship—the parties will have little incentive to accommodate each other, and the conflict will be difficult to resolve.

This difference in perspective is seen by contrasting how lawyers and managers approach a contract dispute. Lawyers are trained to perceive the situation as a single episode: the parties go to court, and the lawyers make the best possible case for their party in an attempt to achieve the best possible outcome. This is a "no-holds-barred" interaction in which the past and future interaction between the parties tends

to be viewed as irrelevant. Thus the conflict between the parties is not really resolved; rather, an outcome is imposed by the judge.

In contrast, managers are likely to be more accommodating when the discussion of a contract is viewed as one interaction within a longer-term relationship that has both a history and a future. In such a situation, a manager is unlikely to resort to no-holds-barred tactics because he or she will have to face the other party again regarding future deals. Furthermore, a continuous relationship permits the bankrolling of favors: "We helped you out on that last problem; it's your turn to work with us on this one."

Here, it is easy, and even cordial, to remind the other party that a continuous relationship exists. This tactic works well because episodic situations are rare in real-world business transactions. For instance, people with substantial business experience know that a transaction is usually not completed when a contract is signed. No contract can be comprehensive enough to provide unambiguously for all possible contingencies. Thus trust and goodwill remain important long after the contract is signed. The street-fighting tactics that may seem advantageous in the context of an episodic orientation are likely to be very costly to the person who must later seek accommodation with the bruised and resentful other party.

Structure of the Parties

Conflict is easier to resolve when a party has a strong leader who can unify his or her constituency to accept and implement the agreement. If the leadership is weak, rebellious subgroups who may not feel obliged to go along with the overall agreement that has been reached are likely to rise up, thereby making conflict difficult to resolve.

For example, people who deal with unions know that a strong leadership tends to be better than a weak one, especially when organizational change needs to be accomplished. A strongly led union may drive a hard bargain, but once an agreement is reached the deal is honored by union members. If a weakly led union is involved, the agreement may be undermined by factions within the union who may not like some of the details. The result may well be chronic resistance to change or even wildcat strikes. To bring peace among such factions, management may have to make further concessions that may be costly. To avoid this, managers may find themselves in a paradoxical position of needing to boost the power of union leaders.

Similar actions may be warranted when there is no union. Groups of employees often band together as informal coalitions to protect their interests in times of change. Instead of fighting or alienating a group, managers who wish to bring about change may benefit from considering ways to formalize the coalition, such as by appointing its opinion leader to a task force or steering committee. This tactic may be equivalent to cooptation, yet there is likely to be a net benefit to both the coalition and management. The coalition benefits because it is given a formal channel in which the opinion leader's viewpoint is expressed; management benefits because the spokesperson presents the conflict in a manageable form, which is much better than passive resistance or subtle sabotage.

Involvement of Third Parties

People tend to become emotionally involved in conflicts. Such involvement can have several effects: perceptions may become distorted, nonrational thought processes and arguments may arise, and unreasonable stances, impaired communication, and personal attacks may result. These effects make the conflict difficult to resolve.

The presence of a third party, even if the third party is not actively involved in the dialogue, can constrain such effects. People usually feel obliged to appear reasonable and responsible because they care more about how the neutral party is evaluating them than by how the opponent is. The more prestigious, powerful, trusted, and neutral the third party, the greater is the desire to exercise emotional restraint.

While managers often have to mediate conflicts among lower-level employees, they are rarely seen as being neutral. Therefore, consultants and change agents often end up serving a mediator role, either by design or default. This role can take several forms, ranging from an umpire supervising communication to a messenger between parties for whom face-to-face communication has become too strained. Mediation essentially involves keeping the parties interacting in a reasonable and constructive manner. Typically, however, most managers are reluctant to enlist an outsider who is a professional mediator or arbitrator, for it is very hard for them to admit openly that they are entangled in a serious conflict, much less one they cannot handle themselves.

When managers remain involved in settling disputes, they usually take a stronger role than mediators: they become arbitrators rather than mediators. As arbitrators, they arrive at a conflict-resolving judgment after hearing each party's case. In most business conflicts, mediation is preferable because the parties are helped to come to an agreement in which they have some psychological investment. Arbitration tends to be more of a judicial process in which the parties make the best possible case to support their position: this tends to further polarize rather than reconcile differences.

Managers can benefit from a third-party presence, however, without involving dispute-resolution professionals per se. For example, they can introduce a consultant into the situation, with an explicit mission that is not conflict intervention. The mere presence of this neutral witness will likely constrain the disputants' use of destructive tactics.

Alternatively, if the managers find that they themselves are party to a conflict, they can make the conflict more public and produce the same constraining effect that a third party would. They also can arrange for the presence of relatively uninvolved individuals during interactions; even having a secretary keep minutes of such interactions encourages rational behavior. If the content of the discussion cannot be disclosed to lower-level employees, a higher-level manager can be invited to sit in on the discussion, thereby discouraging dysfunctional personal attacks and unreasonable stances. To the extent that managers can be trusted to be evenhanded, a third-party approach can facilitate conflict management. Encouraging accommodation usually is preferable to imposing a solution that may only produce resentment of one of the parties.

Progress of the Conflict

It is difficult to manage conflict when the parties are not ready to achieve a reconciliation. Thus it is important to know whether the parties believe that the conflict is escalating. The following example illustrates this point.

During a product strategy meeting, a marketing vice-president carelessly implied that the R&D group tended to overdesign products. The remark was intended to be a humorous stereotyping of the R&D function, but it was interpreted by the R&D vice-president as an attempt to pass on to his group the blame for an uncompetitive product. Later in the meeting, the R&D vice-president took advantage of an opportunity to point out that the marketing vice-president lacked the technical expertise to understand a design limitation. The marketing vice-president perceived this rejoinder as ridicule and therefore as an act of hostility. The R&D vice-president, who believed he had evened the score, was quite surprised to be denounced subsequently by the marketing vice-president, who in turn thought he was evening the score for the uncalled-for barb. These events soon led to a memo war, backbiting, and then to pressure on various employees to take sides.

The important point here is that from the first rejoinder neither party wished to escalate the conflict; each wished merely to even the score. Nonetheless, conflict resolution would have been very difficult to accomplish during this escalation phase because people do not like to disengage when they think they still "owe one" to the other party. Since an even score is subjectively defined, however, the parties need to be convinced that the overall score is approximately equal and that everyone has already suffered enough.

Developing Conflict Management Skills

Strategic decision making usually is portrayed as a unilateral process. Decision makers have some vision of where the organization needs to be headed, and they decide on the nature and timing of specific actions to achieve tangible goals. This portrayal, however, does not take into account the conflict inherent in the decision-making process; most strategic decisions are negotiated solutions to conflicts among people whose interests are affected by such decisions. Even in the uncommon case of a unilateral decision, the decision maker has to deal with the conflict that arises when he or she moves to implement the decision.

In the presence of conflict at the decision-making or decision-implementing stage, managers must focus on generating an agreement rather than a decision. A decision without agreement makes the strategic direction difficult to implement. By contrast, an agreement on a strategic direction doesn't require an explicit decision. In this context, conflict management is the process of removing cognitive barriers to agreement. Note that agreement does not imply that the conflict has "gone away." The people involved still have interests that are somewhat incompatible. Agreement implies that these people have become committed to a course of action that serves some of their interests.

People make agreements that are less than ideal from the standpoint of serving their interests when they lack the power to force others to fully comply with their wishes. On the other hand, if a manager has total power over those whose interests are affected by the outcome of a strategic decision, the manager may not care whether or not others agree, because total power implies total compliance. There are few situations in real life in which managers have influence that even approaches total power, however, and power solutions are at best unstable since most people react negatively to powerlessness per se. Thus it makes more sense to seek agreements than to seek power. Furthermore, because conflict management involves weakening or removing barriers to agreements, managers must be able to diagnose successfully such barriers. The model summarized in Table 1 identifies the primary cognitive barriers to agreement.

Competence in understanding the barriers to an agreement can be easily honed by making a pastime of conflict diagnosis. The model helps to focus attention on specific aspects of the situation that may pose obstacles to successful conflict management. This pastime transforms accounts of conflicts—from sources ranging from a spouse's response to "how was your day?" to the evening news—into a challenge in which the objective is to try to pinpoint the obstacles to agreement and to predict the success of proposed interventions. Focusing on the underlying dynamics of the conflict makes it more likely that conflict management will tend toward resolution rather than the more familiar response of suppression. Although the conflict itself—that is the source—will remain alive, at best its expression will be postponed until some later occasion; at worst, it will take a less obvious and usually less manageable form.

Knowledge of and practice in using the model is only a starting point for managers and change agents. Their development as professionals requires that conflict management become an integral part of their use of power. Power is a most basic facet of organizational life, yet inevitably it generates conflict because it constricts the autonomy of those who re-spond to it. Anticipating precisely how the use of power will create a conflict relationship provides an enormous advantage in the ability to achieve the desired levels of control with minimal dysfunctional side effects. •

Leonard Greenhalgh is Associate Professor at the Amos Tuck School of Business Administration, Dartmouth College. Dr. Greenhalgh holds the BS degree in biology and the M.B.A. degree from the University of Rhode Island, and the Ph.D. degree in organizational behavior from Cornell University. His current research and teaching interests center on the processes of power, negotiation, and conflict resolution. Dr. Greenhalgh has been working with the National Institute for Dispute Resolution in a nationwide program to develop courses and executive programs in this subject area.

Study Questions

1. What tends to generate conflict in the organizations?

2. How can you tell if conflict has been "managed?"

3. What is conflict, in comparison to its manifestations?

4. What roles do empathy and persuasion play in managing conflict, and what factors other than these should managers consider when attempting conflict management?

5. Understand Table 1, and be able to list at least one strategy for each dimension that will shift the target's perceptions toward "easy to resolve" orientations.

6. Why is "principle" so problematic in conflict management?

7. Explain the particular problems of precedents with regard to size of stakes.

8. What is the problem of the zero-sum orientation with regard to perceived gains?

9. Contrast how a manager and a lawyer would approach a conflict management "episode."

10. Why would management typically prefer to deal with strong union leadership?

11. Why is mediation preferable than arbitration in resolving conflicts in the organization?

How to Design a Conflict Management Procedure That Fits Your Dispute

Danny Ertel
Conflict Management, Inc.
Harvard Negotiation Project

Litigation, arbitration, mediation, mini-trial—choosing from the menu of dispute resolution processes can be difficult. Ertel argues that, instead of choosing from available options, managers should consider building their own. Each dispute has its own history and characteristics that will dictate the most appropriate resolution process and settlement. In this article, he elaborates a series of steps for developing this process. By thoroughly understanding the nature of the conflict, managers can prescribe remedies and lead their organizations toward a solution of mutual gain.

In ancient Greece, a tale was told of a roadside inn where a traveler might find lodging for the night, and although the traveler might be tall, short, fat, or thin, the inn's bed fit all just the same. The innkeeper, of course, was Procrustes, a giant who tied travelers to the bedstead and either stretched them or chopped their legs to make them fit. Many business disputes seem to be approached this way today: no matter how diverse the parties, issues, or stakes, litigation is the answer. And even those managers or counsel who, unlike Procrustes' guests, perceive a choice among several available "beds"—litigation, arbitration, or even minitrials—rarely make further attempts to tailor the dispute resolution process to the conflict at hand. Instead they allow the parties to be realigned, the issues reframed, or the stakes redefined.

Managers must deal with a broad range of conflicts, many of which involve parties external to the organization: valuable business partners, threatening competitors, or inquisitive regulators. But scorched-earth litigation fol-

lowed by an on-the-courthouse-steps settlement is clearly not the answer to every dispute. Dealing with a competitor turned potential alliance partner whose third-level subsidiary may be infringing on a patent calls for a different approach than does responding to a "professional plaintiff" who has filed a frivolous shareholder derivative suit. Both of these may be different still from how one might want to manage the plausible antitrust claim of a disgruntled distributor.

Sensing the need for a better approach to process selection, both in-house and outside counsel have begun, with the help of academics and specialized professionals, to serve up a choice between traditional litigation and ADR—alternative dispute resolution. But that either-or choice is hardly confidence inspiring: expensive and disruptive litigation on the one hand, and an enigmatic acronym on the other.

Those who do opt for ADR face another vexing choice: should we go into arbitration, mediation, or a mini-trial? The standard, if somewhat unfair, criticisms of each process are well known: "arbitrators split the baby in half"; "mediators never resolve really difficult cases"; "there is more 'trial' than 'mini' in mini-trials." At the other end of the spectrum, ADR partisans indiscriminately and somewhat disingenuously extol the virtues of all ADR processes as uniformly cheaper, faster, and more confidential than the litigation strawman. The choice among the two or three most commercially established ADR mechanisms often feels like the choice offered at a "new and improved" Procrustean Inn: not one, but three beds, accompanied by the familiar promise of "an exacting fit."

Of course, not every dispute requires a custom-designed process any more than every ancient traveler required stretching or hacking. But misdirected attempts to fit the problem to the process exact high tolls in both human and economic terms: wasted time and money, damaged morale, lost opportunity, and unwanted publicity, to name a few. Effective dispute management requires more informed decision making, based on a careful analysis of the con-

---

flict and of the means available to resolve it. The manager responsible for the conflict, whether the disputant or a superior, should probably make these decisions and subsequently design and implement the appropriate process, with the advice and support of legal counsel. This essay, then, is directed at such individuals or teams—the conflict managers.

If no single dispute resolution process can effectively, fairly, and efficiently address all concerns raised by the rich universe of external business disputes, what the conflict managers need is a consistent analytical framework. Instead of refining questionnaires or checklists for choosing between litigation and ADR, and instead of sorting through the benefits and drawbacks of standard litigation alternatives, thoughtful managers should change the question. They should ask not *which* process should we use (suggesting a choice among discrete options), but how can we resolve *this* conflict? They should try to understand the dispute and determine whether designing a more well-suited resolution process is cost effective. Borrowing problem-solving tools from engineering and medicine, conflict managers should attempt to understand what about the conflict has prevented its being quickly and effectively resolved. Only then will they be well equipped to make an informed decision about how to proceed, and if appropriate, to devise a process

capable of resolving the conflict.

In this essay, I propose a methodology to allow managers and their counsel to consider systematically either particular conflicts or categories of disputes and then to devise, refine, and implement appropriate procedures for dealing with them.[1] The method, structured as a set of inquiries that the disputants may attempt to answer independently or jointly, starts by positing a standard against which one might measure success. It is a vision of what a good conflict resolution process should look like. The conflict managers can then consider existing difficulties or symptoms against the backdrop of that clear objective. Next they can then try to formulate a diagnosis based on their real-world understanding of business disputes and try to prescribe some general approaches or strategies. Finally, they can specify procedures and an implementation plan. At each step of the way, the conflict managers can rely on the articulated measure of success to instruct their analysis and evaluate their prescriptions. Figure 1 offers a schematic view of the process.[2]

This methodology should prove useful at different levels. Industry groups or professional associations, for example, might devise and publish model procedures for broad classes of disputes. Indeed, the Center for Public Resources, Inc., a New York-based coalition of general counsel, private practitioners, judges,

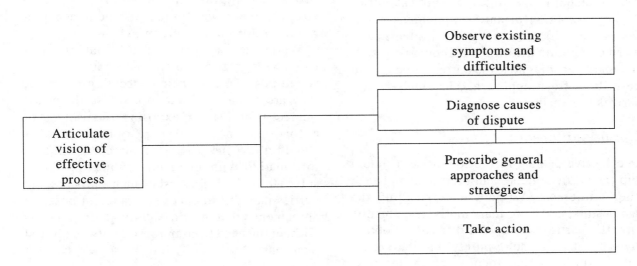

Figure 1   Overview of Methodology

and academics has adopted this methodology for designing alternatives to certain types of securities litigation. Parties entering a long-term business relationship such as a strategic alliance have used it to draft sophisticated dispute resolution protocols in anticipation of potential disputes. Ultimately, if disputants either lack or are dissatisfied with available model procedures, they can use this approach to negotiate an appropriate process.

Attributes of an Effective Conflict Management Process

Mechanisms for resolving conflict always incorporate some implicit tradeoffs, such as between accuracy and cost, creativity and enforceability, speed and thoroughness. Different conflicts, parties, and relationships require different choices. For example, a disagreement among joint venture partners may call for a highly confidential, forward-looking process that focuses primarily on preventing similar incidents in the future, whereas a dispute with product end users might require litigation to finality, so as to establish a firm precedent. Establishing consensus among disputants early on with respect to the attributes of a good process will facilitate discussion of the design.

I propose the following interest-oriented process for managing business disputes, based in part on the body of theory being developed at the Harvard Negotiation Project.[3] This seven-element framework is a set of categories for organizing information and ideas about process and for analyzing the tradeoffs between competing priorities. It should help conflict managers diagnose the current process and prescribe a fresh approach. The sidebar summarizes the attributes.

Clarifies Interests

An effective dispute resolution process should help the parties understand their own and each other's interests. Without understanding the basic wants, needs, or fears motivating the dispute, the parties will find it difficult to obtain anything but zero-sum, purely distributive results. A process that focuses on the parties' stated *positions* or demands will inevitably leave the parties feeling somewhat dissatisfied

with both the process and the outcome. A bluffing contest, however entertaining it may be for buying a used car, cannot be the best way to resolve complex, multi-issue disputes.

While positions may be in conflict, underlying interests need not be. There may be room for dovetailing those interests in such a way that both parties can gain, or at least find themselves distributing a great deal more value than they initially thought was at stake. For example, an engineer who had developed an innovative stamping tool was preparing to retire. He demanded a 3 percent royalty from his former employer for its use. The company, after carefully analyzing the value added to the production process by the tool, and on the advice of its accountants and investment bankers, extended a firm offer of 1.5 percent. After months of haggling, they were no closer.

With some work, a facilitator learned that the engineer had sought 3 percent as a means of insuring himself should he be held personally liable for a young shop worker sustaining injuries from the high-speed stamping tool. After further discussions, the facilitator discovered that the company could bring the engineer under its corporate liability policy, at nominal cost to the company. The company had never offered to do so because it did not understand the interest underlying the engineer's bargaining position. The engineer, upon learning that his retirement could be protected against the unlikely but catastrophic event, was quite satisfied to accept a royalty of around 1 percent.

While most experienced negotiators intuitively recognize the difference between their stated position and their underlying interests, they are often reluctant to disclose their real interests for fear of exposing themselves to extortion. An effective resolution process should allow the parties to share this kind of information without unduly subjecting themselves to such a risk. Absent such a process, the parties may fail to uncover a range of possible agreements that would satisfy their interests without the need to compromise between initial positions.

Attributes of an Effective Conflict Resolution Process

1. Clarifies Interests
- by encouraging the parties to explore the interests underlying their respective bargaining positions
- by facilitating the exploration of common and nonconflicting interests
- by communicating each party's interests to the other without unduly exposing anyone to extortion on the basis of such interests

2. Builds a Good Working Relationship
- by enabling the parties to deal effectively with their differences in the current dispute
- by fostering the type of relationship the parties would have wanted to have but for the present dispute
- by making it easier for the parties to deal with each other next time

3. Generates Good Options
- by spurring the parties to brainstorm many options before evaluating them and choosing among them
- by encouraging the parties to devise ways to create value for mutual gain

4. Is Perceived as Legitimate
- by not being seen to cause the parties to forfeit legal or other rights disproportionately (i.e., the process should not be seen as itself tilting the balance of power)
- by not being perceived as contrary to the public interest
- by instilling in the parties a sense that the solutions it produces will be fair and equitable

5. Is Cognizant of the Parties' Procedural Alternatives
- by allowing both sides to develop realistic assessments of their own and the other side's procedural and substantive alternatives
- by being more attractive to the parties along whatever axis is most important to them (e.g., costs, time, degree of disclosure, nature of outcomes, and quality of compliance)

6. Improves Communication
- by encouraging the questioning and testing of underlying assumptions
- by facilitating the understanding and discussion of partisan perceptions
- by establishing effective two-way communication between decision makers

7. Leads to Wise Commitments
- by enabling the parties to devise commitments that are realistic, operational, and compliance-prone
- by positioning the parties with efficient recourse to litigation in the event they fail to reach agreement or in the event of non-compliance

Builds a Good Working Relationship

The parties to a conflict have some sort of relationship, if only for the purposes of the dispute. And whatever that relationship is, it could probably be better. A good working relationship should enable them to deal effectively and efficiently with the disagreements, large and small, that inevitably arise in any complex interaction between institutions.

A well-designed dispute resolution process should serve two relationship functions. First, it should fill in where the working relationship is breaking down, facilitating the parties' ability to resolve the problem on its merits, as they might have been able to do but for the current breakdown. That might mean, for example, that the process would include mechanisms that temporarily replace the parties' need to trust each other by guaranteeing performance in some easily enforceable manner, or that it would specify use of a third party to help set aside personality issues.

Second, an effective process should also help the parties work purposely toward the kind of relationship they want to have. It may be that the parties want to have no relationship at all and the process should facilitate closure. But if they want a long-term, cooperative relationship in which each feels consulted and accepted, they should probably not follow a purely retrospective process designed to allocate blame.

Both relationship functions add up to the same thing: the process should leave the parties at least slightly better able to deal with each other next time, whenever that happens to be. That need not mean the corporate equivalent of a long-term love affair, but parties who would find it mutually beneficial to work together should not be prevented from doing so because their dispute resolution process has made it even harder for them to speak to each other.

Generates Good Options

Most managers would prefer to choose the best course of action from among several options than from a list of one. The more options on the table (within limits, of course), the greater the likelihood of discovering a productive path. What may seem like a foolish or risky approach at first glance may, after reconsideration and refinement by others, develop into a mutually profitable one. An effective dispute resolution process should spur the parties, perhaps with external support or advice, to generate a list of such options before evaluating and choosing among them.

To the extent possible, the process should also orient the parties toward designing options that create value, rather than merely distribute it. By making mutual gain the expressed goal, the options generated are likely to be more creative and value generating.

Is Perceived as Legitimate

Costly and inefficient as it may be, litigation does incorporate certain norms and rules that society believes are essential to the social order. For example, some liability standards and burdens of proof have been tilted in favor of one party or the other in support of legislative policy goals. For an "alternate" process to succeed, the parties must believe it will produce a good solution without requiring them to give up substantial rights they would have had in litigation. An alternate process that seemed to shift the balance of power dramatically would most likely meet resistance from at least one party—including possibly their refusal to participate in the process, or failure to comply fully with any result. Similarly, an alternate process that negated advantages conferred by the legislature on certain classes of parties might well come under powerful criticism as being contrary to the public interest.[4]

No one likes being taken advantage of. A desirable dispute resolution process should instill in the parties a sense that the solution is fair and equitable and was arrived at in a principled fashion. If the new process requires voluntary participation by the disputants, neither the procedures nor the solutions they produce may be perceived as partisan or arbitrary.

Is Cognizant of the Parties' Procedural Alternatives

Notwithstanding prior commitments to arbitration, mediation, or some other process, few conflicts arise that cannot at some point and in some form lead to litigation. Given that state of affairs, a good process permits the parties to assess realistically their own and their counterpart's litigation alternative. In order to be effective, the process must appear, along whatever axis the parties consider most important, to be preferable to litigation. If cost is of principal concern, the new process should be less expensive than litigation; if confidentiality is at issue, it should afford the parties greater control over disclosure; if a long-term relationship is at stake, then perhaps the process should produce forward-looking solutions rather than allocate blame. Ultimately what this means is that the process should generate solutions that are more efficient and satisfying for each side than what they expect litigation could produce. For instance, in a consent-based process the parties might well agree to take more constructive steps than anything a court could order them to do.

Improves Communication

Many a dispute escalates because one side misunderstands what the other has said or done. If such misunderstandings are common enough among trusted business partners, they are legion among adversaries and especially their zealous advocates. In the middle of litigation, a simple request for information can be perceived as an attempt to blackmail or coerce, an innocent joke can be taken as an insult, and an attempt to reschedule a meeting as an example of bad faith. Why do we inevitably see the others' actions in the worst possible light and expect them to give us the benefit of the doubt? Part of the reason is that we all operate on the basis of many unstated assumptions. One common assumption about adversaries is that they want what we want and that if something is good for them, it must be bad for us. Regardless of whether those assumptions have merit in any given case, acting on them without articulating and testing them is simply unwise. A good dispute resolution process should help the parties articulate and examine their assumptions before they act on them.

Similarly, a great many of us tend to see the facts in the way most favorable to our own side. Once we make up our mind about something, we tend systematically to filter out inconsistent data and to gather as much supporting evidence as possible. It is an inclination well worth resisting, and a good dispute resolution process should facilitate a discussion of those partisan perceptions and how they might be biasing each side's assessment of the situation. One partner in a large national law firm periodically instructs his young associates to begin research on a particular side of a case without telling them they have actually been engaged to represent the opposite side. When they report back to him with their preliminary research (which is usually quite favorable), he tells them, "Remember this well, because this is how strong our opponents think their case is; now prepare our case in response."

Understanding someone's concerns need not make us agree with them; it should, however, help us persuade them that they do not have to meet their needs at our expense. Good communication between decision makers is essential to effective conflict management. If an executive cannot make herself understood, how can she influence anyone? And if she does not understand her counterpart, how can she craft a persuasive proposition? A good process for resolving disputes should establish and maintain effective communication channels.

Leads to Wise Commitments

A good process should enable the disputants to craft wise commitments after they have carefully considered all the relevant information and a number of possible options, and after they have determined that their alternatives away from the table are not as good as what they can obtain through a negotiated agreement. Only then will they be able to craft a commitment that is realistic, operational, and compliance-prone. To minimize the risk that one party will use the process as an expensive dilatory tactic, an effective process should also position the disputants with efficient recourse to litigation or some other self-help alternative in the event they fail to reach agreement or one party fails to comply with its obligations.

*   *   *

Having identified the attributes of the dispute resolution procedure, the conflict manager can begin examining the problem at hand—whether it is an ongoing or an anticipated dispute or class of disputes—and to craft procedures for dealing with it. The design process should be structured and systematic: observe the existing difficulties or symptoms, diagnose their possible causes, and then prescribe general approaches to dealing with them. Finally, make an informed decision about what specific actions to pursue. Figure 2 illustrates this methodology.

Observe Symptoms and Difficulties

Before a doctor attempts a diagnosis, she gathers information. She asks the patient to describe his symptoms, to explain in some detail what has brought him into her office in search of a remedy. Good managers, before launching into conflict resolution, should try to understand the conflict as well as possible. Before they can put something right, they must identify what is wrong; in doing so, they should consider both the nature of the dispute and the traditional means of resolving it.

Although categorizing complex business conflicts is no easier than describing everything that can be physically or psychologically wrong with a human being, conflicts do have some characteristics in common that may instruct the resolution design. The methodology described here poses a series of inquiries concerning the parties and the issues. No single answer to a question will determine conclusively the "best" process to follow; each response will, however, help to identify concerns that should somehow be acknowledged.

The Nature of the Dispute

The questions that follow are designed to help conflict managers gather and structure information.[5] They should also challenge conflict managers to question their assumptions about their own interests, the other side's intentions, the likely perceptions of third parties, and so forth.

Parties. How many parties are there? Are they individuals or institutions? How sophisticated (financially and legally) are they? Is either party a "repeat player" with respect to this type of conflict, or is this likely to be a one-shot experience for both?

By knowing something about the number and relative sophistication and experience of the disputants, the conflict manager can better design a process that addresses each of their interests. Large institutional entities with experienced in-house or outside counsel, for example, may be less likely to require a process that provides education and reality testing than would individuals who have never litigated previously or who may be ill equipped to evaluate complex settlement proposals.

Stakes. Do the parties agree about what is at stake? Is this a dispute over money? If so, is the conflict over a fixed sum, or will a subjective determination of the amount be required? Is this a dispute about assigning blame for past conduct, or is the primary goal to define permissible future conduct? Is publicity a major concern for either party? Does this dispute pri-

---

Figure 2: Designing the Process

What is the problem?

Observe Symptoms and Difficulties

- What is the nature of the dispute (parties, stakes, linkage, and speed)?
- Would litigation accomplish the objectives (stages, costs, and benefits)?

Why has it not been settled?

Diagnose Causes

- What are the parties' underlying interests?
- What is the state of the parties' working relationship?
- How are options generated and considered?
- Is the process legitimate?
- Do both parties understand the risks of not settling?
- How are the parties communicating?
- What kind of agreement do the parties expect to reach?

How can we overcome these difficulties?

Prescribe Approaches

- How can we overcome these impediments to settlement?
- Can the parties' differences be exploited?
- How can the parties cooperate?

What do we do next?

Take Action

- How should the process interact with litigation?
- What kind of outcome should we produce?
- Would participation of a neutral party help?
- How formal should the process be?
- Who should bear which costs?

---

marily concern the relative competitive posture of the parties? Is this merely "strategic" litigation, with no substantive goal other than to delay or distract?

Understanding what is at stake requires more than reading the prayer for relief in a civil complaint. Without developing a clear sense of the disputants' underlying interests, it will be difficult, if not impossible, to design a procedure that allows each to feel confident that his or her interests can and will be addressed.

Linkage. How is the resolution of this conflict tied to other pending or contemplated disputes between the parties or with others? What collateral consequences will either adjudication or settlement have for one or both parties?

The collateral consequences, whether real or imagined, of resolving a particular dispute are often at least as important as the issue at hand. In designing a procedure, care must be taken to consider whether one or both parties would want the results exported to other disputes, or whether confidentiality of the outcome and avoidance of setting a precedent is the key to resolving the conflict.

Speed. Is speedy resolution important to either party? Would either benefit from delay? Why? Is it simply a matter of the stakeholder enjoying the time value of the money or are other factors at play?

Speed is often one of the first items on the list of ADR advantages. But is it always a good thing? Although over-crowded dockets generally cause some of the delay associated with litigation, litigants are themselves responsible for substantial delay. Conflict managers must consider the relevance of the passing of time to one or both disputants, whether to allow tempers to cool, fiscal years or reporting periods to close, or key personnel to turn over. These can be as important, in some cases, as the time value of money or the urge to bring unpleasant situations to a prompt conclusion.

The Litigation Path

Conflict managers must generally face the reality that litigation is readily available to the disputants. In order to craft a better process for managing a particular dispute or class of disputes, they should become familiar with the traditional litigation process and learn from litigation's flaws and virtues.

Stages. What are the various stages through which the litigation must go? What is the intended purpose of each? In practice, what happens at each stage? How much time typically passes between each phase? At what points are these suits typically settled, if at all?

Dispute resolution procedures need not be wholly divorced from litigation, nor need they be a complete substitute. The judicial process offers the most effective means of dealing with some issues. Alternative procedures may actually complement litigation, for example, by streamlining discovery and reducing the number of disputed questions of law or fact. By developing an understanding of the various stages of the traditional litigation path, parties can better design a process tailored to their needs.

Costs and Benefits. How expensive is litigation in expended fees and lost productivity? How are expenses incurred over the dispute's life (front-weighted, evenly distributed, end-weighted)? Are the costs evenly borne by the parties? Aside from the actual court award, what other benefits does either party expect from litigation (public vindication, blame-shifting, fulfilling fiduciary duty in attempting to recover funds)? Do the costs have proportional impact or significance to the parties?

Litigation, like any other product or service a manager buys, delivers some value. It may produce a favorable outcome, but even it if does not, it at least provides some finality and generally delivers a credible and legitimate result. At a minimum it often succeeds in shifting responsibility for the outcome from the line executive to the legal department. The key question, however, is at what cost does it accomplish these objectives? Is this a product worth buying, or could the same interests be met for less? The decision to litigate is a business decision. A manager charged with that decision must consider the alternatives and compare how litigation fares with other means of meeting personal and institutional interests.

Diagnose Causes

Depending on how one defines ADR, the term may well encompass ordinary negotiation between the parties in the course of preparing to litigate. In that sense, there is nothing new, different, or unusual about it—90 percent to 95 percent of all civil lawsuits are settled. The key to designing a procedure that will help disputants make better decisions about whether and how to settle, and to generate more attractive choices in the majority of cases, is to focus on what has kept the parties from resolving their conflict until now. Having developed a picture of the conflict, the conflict manager should now ask, "Why haven't the parties settled yet?"

The range of possible answers to this question is very broad. Any given conflict will generally have multiple barriers to settlement. One or more impediments to resolution may leap out as obvious; others may be more subtle, yet nonetheless significant. The framework for an effective process may serve as an analytical guide to sort through and organize these diagnoses. By comparing the current process with the target process, the conflict manager can generate ideas for remedying the deficiencies.

Interests vs. Positions

Have negotiations to date focused on demands and concessions? Are the parties being forthcoming about their underlying interests? If pressed, could each party answer the following questions in a manner to which the other would agree: "What do your counterparts really hope to accomplish in this dispute?" and "For what purpose?"

One exceedingly common cause of breakdowns in negotiations is that both parties get locked into extreme positions from which neither can easily make concessions. One telltale sign is a pattern of negotiating along single, highly quantifiable variables, such as money. A process that encourages such negotiation exacerbates the zero-sum mentality that generally accompanies bitter disputes. For example, as long as the engineer and the manufacturing company were locked into a positional haggle over the royalty percentage, they could make no progress without one side or the other feeling that it had backed down.

Relationship Problems

What relationship did the parties have prior to the dispute? Are they likely to have future dealings? Has one party threatened to terminate the business relationship unless the other gives in?

Another possible cause for the negotiation breakdown could be the parties' working relationship. All too often, personality problems keep the parties from discussing the problem's merits. Sometimes personal trust has broken down so far that the parties cannot even agree to disagree, for fear that the other is trying to pull a fast one. In diagnosing why the dispute has not yet been resolved, it might be useful to know whether the real problem has become the people involved.

Limited Generation of Options

Who has introduced the options that have been considered so far? Does one party typically take the lead in presenting proposals, or do the parties share the burden? Are the parties reluctant to put the first offer on the table? Do time constraints operate differently on them? Do cost constraints affect the settlement (e.g., might it be easier to settle a suit in a particular fiscal year or under another project's budget)?

Another consequence of negotiation on the basis of positions rather than interests is a relative poverty of good options to choose from. If the negotiators perceive their preparation as girding themselves for battle, and their proposals as starting positions to be defended but eventually modified, they will more likely than not craft proposals that are highly favorable to their own side, expecting to make some concessions later. As both sides do this, blithely ignoring their counterpart's interests and constraints as "their problem," no one is devoting any energy to inventing mutually advantageous options that might bring added value to the table.

Fear of Arbitrary, Illegitimate Outcomes

Do the negotiators have critical constituencies to which they must report their handling of the dispute? Do those constituents expect their agents to follow certain rituals? Are there readily available standards, within the industry or otherwise, that cover how disputes such as this one are settled?

One reason a party refuses to settle a dispute may have more to do with the dispute resolution process than with the settlement's content. If the process feels arbitrary or coercive, the party may devalue an outcome that it might otherwise have accepted. In baseball, for example, players and owners both accept an arbitrator's award that coincides with their counterpart's final offer more readily than they do if that same salary figure is proposed by the other side in a blustering "take it or leave it" fashion. Similarly, a party may reject an attractive offer if the terms seem unrelated to any external standards or somehow conjured up out of thin air. Without some supporting rationale, the party might well wonder whether through more strategic negotiating it could do better. A party's inability to explain the logic of a particular settlement to its constituents may well stand in the way of a profitable resolution.

Overestimation of the Litigation Alternative

Do the negotiators have access to an objective assessment of the dispute, whether internally or outside their institution? Have they done any systematic analysis of the litigation risk? How carefully have they thought through the nonmonetary consequences of not settling?

Sometimes the principal impediment to settlement stems from one or both parties' limited understanding of their procedural alternatives. A failure to grasp the true costs and benefits of litigation can keep one or both parties from settling a case that should never have been litigated. An interesting example arose in an intellectual property dispute. Two parties that shared a profitable market sued and countersued each other over a number of aggressive trade practices, challenging the validity of one's right to exclude the other from certain market segments or from certain applications of the intellectual property. Only after careful analysis did they realize that if *either* prevailed in court on its principal theories, they would open the market to a host of new competitors, to the detriment of both. Without that understanding, however, there had been little room

for settlement: each viewed its chances of prevailing at trial optimistically enough that no settlement offer or counter-offer that either could reasonably propose was likely to be acceptable to the other.

Poor Communication

What channels do the decision makers use to communicate? Do they always go through lawyers or other agents or do they sometimes communicate directly? How does each party perceive the other's motives? Do the parties disagree on the facts or on the inferences to be drawn therefrom?

If the parties have very different pictures of the conflict and consequently have drawn very different conclusions as to how to resolve it, it may be impossible for them to reach an agreement. A debtor and a creditor may look at the distribution of proceeds from asset liquidation in the same way the pessimist and the optimist observe the proverbial glass of water: one perceives the glass as half empty, posing the problem of how to refill it, while the other perceives it as half full, presenting an opportunity to distribute its contents between the parties.

Differing perceptions may be formed a number of ways—an individual's psychological makeup or a career of working on an emotionally charged issue. Or perhaps each side has access to only part of the information necessary to understand the situation and its context. Depending on the primary reasons for the differing perceptions, the conflict managers might devise procedures for gathering information, testing the objectivity of the parties' perceptions, or facilitating their discussion of such perceptions. To get past the unproductive clash of perceptions, each party must be helped to understand how the other sees it, without feeling that to understand that perspective means it has also to agree with it.

Unclear Commitments

Assuming some agreement could be reached, would it require a one-time act, such as a cash payment, or would compliance involve an ongoing commitment to a more complicated program? What issues must a settlement address?

Who would have to cooperate in order to make the agreement operational?

If the parties have not considered or discussed with each other what the outline of an agreement would look like, they may develop very different ideas. The more different these images are, the more difficult it will be for them to arrive at a workable resolution. If one views the problem as an imminently bursting dam in need of an immediate stop-gap solution, while the other thinks the dispute is really about the long-term management of a complex navigation and irrigation system, they will be working toward radically different objectives and each will have a tough time understanding the other. Unless the process can help them clarify the nature and scope of the final commitment, they will probably escalate the conflict in an effort to impose a solution. The international diplomacy analogue makes the front pages all too often: in most armed conflicts, the opponents eventually talk about whether and how to cease hostilities. Unless those operational terms are clearly understood by both sides, one side may find its efforts to work toward an interim cease fire frustrated by the other's perception of the demand as a permanent cessation and full demobilization. Consequently, both sides increase combat, to "remind" the other side of how bad things can be in the absence of an agreement.

Prescribe Approaches

Now the conflict managers are better prepared to devise a process that can overcome, or at least mitigate, the effect of the impediments described above. They can systematically review their particular diagnoses and devise general approaches to build a process that approximates their view of effective dispute resolution. A few illustrations should help capture the flavor of the task.

Overcome Impediments

If the parties are locked into a positional bargaining battle in which substantial concessions seem unlikely, mechanisms to clarify their interests, as distinguished from their positions, may be of value. The classic object of single-variable positional bargaining is money, but underlying a demand for a particular sum are usually other interests that could perhaps be satisfied some other way. An outside facilitator may be able to solicit this kind of information confidentially. When a highly leveraged entrepreneur was attempting to sell one of his magazine properties, his bottom-line asking price was $400,000. No amount of haggling could get him to move, even though no buyer had offered more than $325,000, and independent appraisals had estimated the property's fair market value as somewhere between $280,000 and $325,000. Only after extensive prodding by an outside facilitator did he admit that his problem was not that he needed $400,000, or that he thought the magazine was worth that much. Rather, he felt constrained by a financing clause that treated any write down of more than $100,000 on any asset as a condition of default. Since all of his financing had cross-default provisions, he could not possibly accept less than $400,000 for a property he had initially purchased at $500,000. Once they understood that, the parties, in consultation with their lawyers and accountants, devised a creative financing scheme that would not trigger a default, but that nonetheless represented real cost to the purchasers of about $310,000.

If both sides are much too willing to take their chances in court, a helpful prescription might afford them a confidential way to develop a realistic assessment of their litigation prospects. The decision-tree and risk-analysis tools long familiar to business decision makers are now being used with some success in analyzing litigation decisions.[6] Such an analysis, carried out independently and confidentially for each side by an outside expert, might inject a useful dose of reality into the process.

If partisan perceptions arising from a disparity in the parties' experience and access to information are impeding communication, the conflict managers may want to devise an information-sharing process that enables one party to "catch up." If neither party has sufficient information, perhaps a joint or neutral fact-finding process would help. If one side is concerned that the terms of an agreement will be disclosed, the conflict managers might incorporate into the process some means of managing the flow of information about the agreement.

Sometimes, the greatest impediment to settling a dispute comes from the way in which the conflict has been framed, which in turn constrains the types of options the parties consider. To the extent that the parties view the problem as principally involving the distribution of something—money, liability, kudos, or blame—they will conclude that more for one necessarily means less for the other and will proceed to address the problem on that basis. While it is not always possible to settle a dispute by "enlarging the pie," experience teaches that truly adversarial disputants can always produce a result that leaves less for both, a "negative sum." Some conflicts, because of the parties' needs and resource constraints, may never be settled unless someone attempts to generate mutual gains. The small trade magazine that grievously but wholly unintentionally libels the fast-rising entrepreneur may simply not have the ability to make him whole through cash compensation. If he insists on a lump sum payment equivalent to what he might expect to be awarded in court, he may well end up with an unenforceable judgment against a bankrupt company. But a cover story on his visionary leadership in an emerging industry might net him valuable exposure and the publisher an interesting article, made richer and more credible by the subject's full cooperation.

One of the conflict managers' goals, and potentially their greatest contribution, is identifying opportunities for turning the dispute into a positive-sum game. By orienting the parties toward joint problem solving instead of adversarial posturing, and by facilitating communication and information exchange, a well-designed process can help the parties resolve their dispute more profitably for both sides. Two rich sources of value-enhancing potential are the parties' differences and their ability to cooperate.[7]

Exploit Differences

Do the parties place different values on possible outcomes or on different goods and services? Do they face different tax or other incentives? Do they have different concerns about publicity? Do the parties have different expec-

tations about contingent events, different attitudes toward risk? Do they have different preferences about the resolution's timing or the performance of the settlement?

One school of thought suggests that the best way to resolve a dispute is to minimize the parties' differences. The more alike the two disputants seem, the more likely they are to reach some accommodation. While that may sometimes be true, it is not always possible to accomplish. Some parties may just have too diverse a set of interests and expectations to be homogenized. Besides, many differences are valuable and worth preserving. Many a business alliance is struck not because the parties are similar, but precisely because the parties have different strengths or perspectives that they believe make for a good fit. A good process for managing conflict should facilitate the way the parties deal with their differences rather than paper over them.

Facilitate Cooperation

Is cooperation between the parties a desirable and efficient manner of resolving the problem? Are economies of scale possible? Do the parties have shared interests in some substantive outcome, public good, or public perception of their handling of the dispute? Can one side take steps to benefit the other significantly at minimal cost to itself?

Cooperation with the enemy is usually the last thing disputants consider. Yet it is precisely because that whole class of solutions is so often overlooked that it should be systematically considered in almost every dispute. Sometimes the best way to resolve a problem about past performance is jointly to devise a better mechanism for encouraging, facilitating, and monitoring future performance. Perhaps the prior OEM agreement was not fulfilled because it would have worked better as a full-fledged joint venture. In most business conflicts, there is usually some way that one side could confer substantial value on the other at comparatively low cost, if only in business referrals or good public relations, or more tangibly in at-cost supply contracts or third-party guarantees. The failure to systematically consider those options costs money.

In many business conflicts there are also activities that both sides would agree constitute a good use of resources and from which both would derive at least indirect benefit; they should consider committing part of what is at stake in the conflict to some such mutually beneficial activity instead of squandering more resources in fighting over how to allocate the nominal stakes between them.

Take Action

The analysis thus far has proceeded through the classic problem-solving stages. The first step defined a desired outcome—an effective process for managing business disputes. Second, the conflict managers were encouraged to make observations of the conflict, as yet unresolved by traditional means. The third step encouraged them to diagnose the causes for the parties' failure to settle the case thus far. Fourth, based on these diagnoses, they were to prescribe some general approaches for dealing with the identified problems. Now is the time to take action. What should the conflict managers do next? How do they go from scratchpad to an action plan for resolving this conflict?

Making Process Choices

Designing a custom dispute resolution process requires making some specific decisions about types of mechanisms to use and how they might fit together. These decisions will vary significantly from one case to another.

The Interaction with Litigation. If the process replaces traditional litigation, should it aim primarily at facilitating settlement, or would some sort of partial or streamlined adjudication be preferable? How should the alternative procedures interact with the traditional litigation track? Should litigation be temporarily stayed? Should judicial approval of the alternative procedures be sought in advance?

Sometimes the only way to apply sufficient pressure on the parties to reach a productive settlement is to keep litigation going full steam ahead while someone else tries to settle the case on a "second track." Indeed, this is one way to make the parties more comfortable with trying a new approach; they don't have to surrender any perceived advantage in court. Al-

though such an approach does seem to require committing additional resources to the conflict, it may still pay off handsomely in the efficiency and quality of the outcome. If the "second track" succeeds, the savings from early termination of the "litigation track" alone will easily outweigh the additional expenditures.[8] Other times, in order for an innovative dispute resolution procedure to have a real chance of success, the parties must agree to a temporary cease-fire on the legal battlefield, to enable the negotiators to explore a problem-solving approach and exchange information safely.

Expected Product. Should the outcome be binding on the parties, or merely advisory? What will be gained or lost in the flexibility of the process, the seriousness with which parties participate, or their willingness to accept the process at all?

The procedures should help the parties craft a solution that meets their interests, feels legitimate, and is preferable to their best alternative away from the table. Such procedures need not impose an outcome on any party; indeed, by definition any such solution will enjoy the support and consent of every party. Yet some nonbinding procedures may lend themselves to bad faith manipulation and may be used solely for delay and intelligence-gathering. For such situations, dispute resolution procedures can be designed to generate a resolution to which all parties will be bound, even if none would have advocated it.

Participation by a Neutral. Would a neutral party be of some help? In what capacity? Should a neutral facilitate communication between the parties, evaluate their positions, generate settlement proposals, or ascertain facts? Each of these involves different degrees of intrusion into the process by a stranger to the conflict.

The intervention of a neutral is often charged with tension and anxiety. Some will worry about how the neutral will perceive them and their position and will seek the neutral's approval. Some will worry that outsiders will see the use of a neutral as an admission that they cannot solve their own problems; they will either try to conceal the request for intervention or show public disdain for the neutral's efforts. Often such public posturing becomes a self-fulfilling prophecy and the neutral, stripped of credibility and trust, cannot help but fail. Before seeking intervention, try to visualize the neutral's role. What procedural deficiencies might the neutral address? Is there some other way of addressing them effectively?

Many of the tasks neutrals undertake actually require only someone who does not have a vested interest in the resolution of the conflict, rather than a wholly nonpartisan stranger. In many contexts it is possible and desirable to overcome barriers to settlement by using "internal neutrals," that is, individuals within one or both organizations who are not directly involved in the dispute and whose primary interest is in helping manage the conflict. So-called "wise men" procedures, whereby senior executives within two organizations are designated as process resources to help jointly resolve, for example, a dispute between line managers, are worth considering for any complex, long-term business relationship.

Formality. How formal or informal a process seems best suited to the parties and the dispute? Should rules be specified concerning the stages of the process or their timing? What rules of discovery, if any, should be incorporated? How should the presentation of evidence and testimony (whether to each other or to a neutral) proceed? Should there be avenues of review?

At the risk of turning the design process into a legislative drafting exercise, it is important that the conflict managers think carefully through the operational aspects of the process and the consultative and verification mechanisms that will be necessary to resolve the inevitable procedural disputes. Not only must they think about what process would best help the parties resolve their substantive conflict, but they must consider how to deal with disputes about the process itself. During the discovery phase of traditional litigation, for example, counsel are expected to work out their differences, but if they are unable to do so, they may seek a ruling from the judge, magistrate, or special master presiding over that aspect of the case. While that is not to say that one should adopt an adversarial litigious process to re-

solve disputes about the process, it does mean that these mechanisms require careful attention, and that the participation of legal counsel may be especially useful.

Costs. Who should bear the cost of a failure to reach agreement under the new process? In the event the parties reach an agreement, how should costs be allocated among them?

Much has been written about the importance of cost incentives in dispute resolution, both for counsel and their clients.[9] The parties can decide whether they will cover their own costs or allocate costs some other way. Although there may not be an easily identifiable winner in the sense there is in litigation, it may be worth considering whether those responsible for making the parties incur additional costs should bear them. Some dispute resolution mechanisms in litigation, for example, place the burden on the party declining a good faith settlement offer to "do better" by forcing them to bear the risk (in the form of a redistribution of litigation costs) of failing to do so.

Getting Started

As noted earlier, the method described in this essay can be applied by professional organizations to draft model procedures for classes of disputes, or by parties to a business venture who want to draft dispute resolution protocols for future conflicts between them, or by a manager facing a problem that has not been resolved earlier in the process. Whichever the case, conflict managers should make use of as much information as is available.

Although once a conflict arises it may be more difficult to establish the kind of joint problem-solving relationship that might have been available earlier, more facts may be known at that time, and these should permit the parties to devise a process better suited to the specific dispute than to a hypothetical conflict. Mutual consent will generally be required to undertake anything but traditional litigation. The parties will have to negotiate procedures and details, and such negotiations may provide an opportunity for the parties to begin to cooperate.

The analysis described here should enable managers facing an escalating conflict to do several things: first, they should be able to decide whether it is worthwhile to structure a custom dispute resolution process and to discuss the option clearly and systematically with legal counsel; second, even if the conflict managers choose not to negotiate about the process, by having diagnosed the existing problem they should be better prepared to think about how to settle it on the merits; and third, if they decide to approach their counterparts to discuss the possibility of a better process, they will be prepared for negotiating over it.

To initiate such negotiation, managers might try to schedule a meeting with their counterparts to explore conflict management procedure, making it clear that the substance of the dispute is not on the agenda for that meeting. Accompanying the invitation to such a meeting might be a draft of what an effective process should be able to accomplish (rather than what it should look like), along the lines of the attributes described in the sidebar, and an invitation to revise the draft. A list of attributes of a good dispute resolution process is sufficiently removed from the substance of the conflict that the managers may well be able to approach the problem of designing appropriate procedures much the way they might handle a less adversarial problem-solving session: whatever their respective views of the dispute itself, they have a shared interest in using a process that is tailored to the problem, and that might be less painful than letting Procrustes help them into one of those "one size fits all" beds. •

Footnotes

[1] Based on their experience with labor-management disputes in the coal industry, Ury et al. have come up with a useful and somewhat different checklist of steps that should be included in systems for managing recurring conflicts within an organization. See: W. Ury, J. Brett, and S. Goldberg, *Getting Disputes Resolved* (San Francisco: Jossey-Bass, 1988).

[2] This diagnostic approach to designing a dispute resolution process is based in part on the Circle Chart described in: R. Fisher and W. Ury, *Getting to Yes* (Boston: Houghton 1981), pp. 68–71.

[3] The seven elements of the framework have been described in different forms in a variety of published and unpublished papers. The use of this framework for designing alternatives to litigation is, to my knowledge, original to this essay. For a brief definition, see: R. Fisher, "Negotiating Inside Out," *Negotiation Journal* 5 (1989): 33–41.

[4] O. M. Fiss, "Against Settlement," *Yale Law Journal* 93 (1984): 1073–1090.

[5] These inquiries have evolved from a related set of considerations outlined in S. Goldberg, E. Green, and F. Sander, *Dispute Resolution* (Boston: Little, Brown & Co., 1985), pp. 545–548; H. Raiffa, *The Art and Science of Negotiation* (Cambridge, Massachusetts: Belknap Press, 1982), pp. 14–19; and other works that attempt to identify the "ADR potential" of a dispute or to produce a classification scheme for disputes.

[6] Raiffa (1982); M. Raker, "The Application of Decision Analysis and Computer Modeling to the Settlement of Complex Litigation" (Cambridge, Massachusetts: ILP Symposium, MIT, 1987).

[7] D. Lax and J. Sebenius, *The Manager as Negotiator* (New York: The Free Press, 1986), pp. 88–116.

[8] R. Fisher, "He Who Pays the Piper," *Harvard Business Review,* March–April 1985, pp. 150–159; P. Mode and D. Siemer, "The Litigation Partner and the Settlement Partner," *Litigation,* Summer 1986, pp. 33–35.

[9] S. Shavell, "Suit, Settlement, and Trial: A Theoretical Analysis under Alternative Methods for the Allocation of Legal Costs," *Journal of Legal Studies* II (1982): 55–81; J.C. Coffee, Jr., "Undemanding the Plaintiff's Attorney: The Implications of Economic Theory for Private Enforcement of Law through Class and Derivative Actions," *Columbia Law Review* 86 (1986): 669–727.

* * *

Danny Ertel is a negotiation consultant at Conflict Management, Inc., in Cambridge, Massachusetts, and an Associate of the Harvard Negotiation Project. He is also special lecturer at the University of Toronto Faculty of Law and co-author of the forthcoming *Beyond Arbitration: Designing Alternatives to Securities Litigation* (Butterworth Legal Publishers).

Study Questions

1. How is Procrustes' approach to tired travelers related to traditional views of handling disputes?

2. What is ADR?

3. Identify the attributes of an effective conflict resolution process.

4. Why should disputants go beyond positions to parties' interests?

5. What two relationship functions are served in a well-designed dispute resolution process?

6. How do you know if you have a "wise" commitment?

7. What is involved in observing dispute symptoms?

8. Explain the designing process in dispute resolution.

9. What is the key to designing ADR procedures as alternatives to litigation?

Enhancing the Capacity of Organizations to Deal with Disputes

Deborah M. Kolb
Susan S. Silbey

Conflict is a dirty word in organizations. Managers invest considerable time and money on programs and policies that either contain conflict or that work to convert difference into consensus. The general aim is to make organizational functioning smooth and noncontentious.

To accomplish these tasks, corporations purchase from an expanding market a wide array of services designed to clean up the clutter of human conflict littering organizations. Among the current titles of such offerings are "dealing with diversity," "win-win negotiations," "interpersonal peacemaking," "mediation skills for managers," and "structuring for collaboration." The newest entry in the catalogue of conflict management services is dispute systems design.

Dispute systems design is an extension of alternative dispute resolution processes such as mediation and other forms of assisted negotiation into the instructional and programmatic realm. It is an intervention to help clients— families, organizations, communities, nations— deal systematically with a continuing stream of disputes rather than a single episode. The design of a dispute system is based on a diagnosis of the state of disputing in an organization or relationship, with an eye toward reducing the costs of conflict and enhancing the benefits to those involved. Costs are reduced and benefits realized by expanding the range of alternatives available while emphasizing interest-based dispute resolution methods rather than processes that rely primarily on rights (arbitration, litigation) or coercive power (war, strikes). (See Ury, Brett, Goldberg, 1988; cf. Silbey and Sarat, 1988.)

Dispute systems designers promise in-house, cost-efficient service, and consumer satisfaction for resolving conflicts. Promoters make it sound like dispute systems do it all. But does dispute systems design prevent conflict in organizations?

There are two primary issues to consider in discussing this question. The first concerns the concept of prevention and what it implies about the way organizations work. We want to suggest that the very notion of prevention is inconsistent with contemporary conceptions of effective process in organizations. A more useful way to view the issue is to consider, not prevention, but enhanced capacity. The second issue relates to the ways in which dispute systems designed by expert outsiders indirectly enhance or constrain the ability of members at all levels of hierarchy to deal with disputes and differences in more open and productive ways.

The Problem With Prevention

What does it mean to have a dispute design system that prevents conflict? As systems designers discuss it, prevention implies that the frequency of disputes in an organization is reduced, in part, because a dispute system encourages people to deal with the underlying or deeply rooted causes of conflict. There are several problems with this conception, however.

Dysfunctional. First, it assumes that conflict is somehow detrimental to organizational functioning. Clearly, administrators and others in charge of organizations bemoan the existence and imputed inefficiency of conflict in their institutions and seek means of silencing it. But even observers who take a broader view that conflict is functional, mobilizes innovation, promotes flexibility and adaption, and builds group cohesion (Coser, 1956; Bacharach and Lawler, 1981) nonetheless end up providing support for this perspective. Debates about the functions or dysfunctions of social conflict seem to reinforce the perception that the presence of conflict is evidence of organizational malfunctioning (Weick, 1979).

In contrast with these analyses of the positive and negative functions of conflict, recent scholarship on conflict in organizations is based on a different premise (Bacharach and Lawler, 1980; Kolb and Bartunek, forthcoming; Pfeffer and Salancik, 1978). Contemporary organization theory and research is marked by a shift away from consensual and rationalized models of organization process and toward ones that emphasize power and political struggle. Instead of viewing conflict as either detrimental to or facilitative of organizational functioning, this recent research defines conflict as the essence of organization. Conflict is central to what an organization is and contributes to its durability. Indeed, Pondy (1986) notes that the oldest organizations in the world, four parliaments and sixty-two universities, are ones that have conflict and diversity at their very foundations. To prevent conflict by dealing with its causes is incompatible with this view of organizations.

What is a Cause of Conflict? Secondly, claims to prevent conflict by dealing with root causes confuse what we mean by *cause*. Conflict is foundational in organizations because it is built into the very structure and modes of operating. For instance, we know that when you create different departments and divisions in order to work more efficiently, conflict often arises between departments over matters such as scheduling and responsibility. It has also been observed that when a new layer of management is created in order to organize and rationalize work, others in the organization simultaneously lose some autonomy and control. Sometimes two or more groups in an organization, formerly separate with independent and different modes of operating, have to work closely in an integrated fashion to bring out a new product. Division of labor, delegation of authority, the requirements for task interdependence, and more immediate issues such as sharing a common resource pool, all cause conflict in organizations.

These causes are not usually obvious: the reason is that conflict in organizations is typically embedded in the ongoing events and activities of members, and specific conflict episodes are not easily disentangled from other forms of interaction. What is a cause and, in-

deed, what is in dispute will be understood in different ways depending upon who gets involved, the interests they have to serve and protect, and the kinds of outcomes envisioned (Burroway, 1979). Ask the manager of an organization about the working relationship between two professionals, then ask the professionals, then ask the support staff. The stories each tells about that relationship—and particularly about conflict in that relationship—will be different, as will the attribution of cause.

Diagnosing cause is also complicated by conflict "splitting" in organizations—that is, when conflict splits off and moves around an organization and gets expressed in locations quite different from its point of origin (Smith, 1989). For example, two male senior managers who act outwardly in a congenial and collaborative manner ship their disputes with each other to two female subordinates elsewhere in the organization. The women develop reputations as contentious and difficult to work with. Feeling that this relationship is having a detrimental effect on the organization, the senior managers hire a consultant to help "fix the women," that is to help them work out their difficulties (Smith and Berg, 1987). Over a period of several months, the consultants begin to trace the problem back to the senior managers who were not consciously aware of their own dispute.

There is also a consistent finding in the literature that those engaged in conflict tend to experience it in personal and immediate terms, and to attribute cause to the personality or behavior of the other—the "unreasonable" boss, the uncooperative subordinate in sales, the ambitious colleague, the generic "difficult" person (Pettigrew, 1973; Kolb, 1989a). Determining whether the person is the problem or whether it is the particular situation or the encompassing systemic structure, will always be both a methodological and theoretical judgment that has a major impact on the kinds of causal diagnoses a dispute system designer might make.

Too Many Disputes? A third problem with the "dispute-systems-design-decreases-conflict" concept is that designers, in their desire to reduce the frequency of conflict, suggest that a major problem in organizations is that there are just too many disputes. This judgment is challenged by numerous studies which suggest that most conflicts in organizations, as well as other settings such as families, communities, and informal groups, never get publicly expressed as disputes. When probed, people reveal all sorts of grievances, complaints, and differences that could be—but rarely are—voiced. Sometimes people fear retribution or loss of social acceptance, others avoid entrapment in complex processes; others believe that they lack sufficient resources to pursue their grievance; while yet others see complaining and confrontation as evidence of moral laxity or lack of independence (e.g., Miller and Sarat, 1980–81; Merry and Silbey, 1984; Bumiller, 1987; Greenhouse, 1986; Goodman, 1986). For example, in a study of professional accounting firms, Morrill (forthcoming) reports that 73% of conflict episodes among partners are never expressed directly. Avoidance and toleration are the modal forms of conflict management rather than confrontation and negotiation. The consequences of avoidance are serious. Not only does the organization lose opportunities for innovation and change, but suppressed conflict also generates resistance to organizational goals.

In summary, we suggest that the notion of prevention is problematic because it is based on assumptions that conflict is dysfunctional for organizations; that its causes are accessible to objective diagnosis and remedy; and that there are too many disputes in an organization rather than too few. Recent scholarship challenges all of these assumptions. Further, prevention in the service of organizational agendas (lower costs and greater tranquility) inevitably leads to the preservation of the status quo to the detriment of those who may be disempowered or disadvantaged by current arrangements (See Martin, forthcoming).

However, there is another way to think about dealing with the clutter of conflict in organization, and that is in terms of *enhancing capacity* for the expression of differences.

Enhancing Capacity

Dispute system designers seek to improve the handling of conflict by directly addressing the organizational barriers that interfere with low cost, interest-based resolution of persistent disputes. This approach tends to focus on proximate or presenting causes of conflict. If one accepts the notion that organizations are patterned systems of conflict, it is clear that the capacity of dispute systems designers to reduce the frequency of conflict by attending to underlying causes is severely limited.

Nonetheless, there may be other ways that dispute systems designers, like the wide range of currently available management consultants and interventionists, might have an impact on the capacity of an organization and its members to deal with conflict. Rather than directly prevent disputes (which we have argued is mistaken) they may indirectly reduce the frequency of disputes that are processed through *formal* systems. There are three ways that this might occur.

Alter Understandings of Conflict and Its Causes. Disputes can be read in many ways. One indirect effect of a dispute-focused intervention may be that new, and more complicated, ways of understanding conflict, its causes and possible outcomes, become possible. For example, when members of an organization view their disputes as ones based on personal differences, they are often reluctant to voice problems and work toward accommodating difference. A dispute interventionist working on this organization may enlarge members' understanding of causality (i.e., that conflict is in the structure and roles of the organization rather than within particular personalities).

Another example of the enlarged understanding that can develop is the case of a vice-president in an aero-space company, who insisted that the two people charged with planning and operations on a special project just could not get along with each other because their personalities were incompatible. After several reorganizations had failed to resolve matters, expert intervention helped the aero-space vice president to see that the problem was not in the personnel but in the organization's structure and goals. The existing arrangement of tasks and responsibilities continually had put the two managers at odds with each other while the vice president had failed to establish or assist in setting priorities for balancing long and short-term milestones.

Similarly, people experience bias as an individual problem. Racist remarks and sexist treatment is typically viewed as the conscious or unconscious mistreatment by particular persons rather than a product of the culture within which the incident occurred (Silbey, 1989). Thus, a woman manager speaks of her sexist boss who refuses to allow her the visibility to attract clients necessary for her success. She complains through an ombudsman's office and, by exploring the problem, she and the ombudsman come to see the problem differently. They then recast the problem in terms of the institutional culture that legitimates what appears to be individual actions. Changing this situation will require much more than dealing with the particular supervisor.

When dispute systems designers enlarge people's understandings of the causes of conflict, new outcomes are possible. Broader understanding may also produce greater tolerance for conflict. A culture of tolerance can lead to effective changes in informal arrangements as people feel able to communicate openly. Organizational creativity may also be enhanced as people are empowered to confront those in positions of authority. Studies of organizations in which the capacity for the expression of conflict is high suggest that these cultures, which value difference and diversity, channel these differences into productive and imaginative, task-related endeavors (Kunda, forthcoming).

Enhanced capacity can result in significant structural change as well. When members' understandings about their disputes shift from isolated individual episodes to ones that question the entire system, the possibilities for emancipatory changes in organizations become possible.

Encourage Spillovers from the Formal Dispute System. When interventionists describe themselves as dispute systems designers, they typically emphasize deliberate and segregated mechanisms for monitoring, handling, and resolving conflicts. If conflict is the essence of organization, however, disputes should not be pigeonholed into specialized procedures. Acknowledging and embracing the intransigence of conflict, dispute interventionists and management consultants should attend to the informal, diffuse, routine interactions that may re-

sult from experiences with formalized procedures. There are two primary ways this may occur:

First, experience in the legitimate expression of differences, collaborative and cooperative problem solving, as well as interest-based forms of management (learned in the context of a formal disputing system) can spill over into other aspects of organizational life and impact earlier stages in a disputing process. Thus personnel who participate in dispute resolution procedures generally become more adept at dealing with their differences not only at the negotiating table but within the content and experience of the dispute.

For example, in a dispute over who should get overtime, a machine operator with recent experience in mediation observed that the current practice of assigning overtime failed to take account of the family responsibilities of the women on the line, and so decided to use this mediation experience to engage her supervisor in a discussion of these assignments. For this kind of interaction to occur, however, employees must be able to express diverse interests and supervisors need to be tolerant of employees who challenge their decisions and authority. Those expressions of interest and challenge are not perceived as welcome nor legitimate if they are segregated and isolated in specialized procedures. Legitimacy and tolerance require taking the conflict out of the closet.

Secondly, dispute capacity can be enhanced as experience in a dispute system is generalized and members come to see the consequences of their actions in new ways. In grievance mediation, for example, there is a practice in some organizations to invite an audience of managerial and union personnel to participate alongside the parties immediately involved in the grievance. This broad participation often encourages the immediate parties to the grievance to see their actions from the variety of perspectives presented in the process, an insight that may lead to new models of conflict management on the shop floor (Kolb, 1989b). In this way, conflict escalation—here defined as movement into specialized procedures—may be contained.

Learning from Dispute Data. Dispute processing mechanisms in organizations cover a wide range of formal procedures and informal processes (Ewing, 1989). These include grievance procedures, peer review boards, ombuds offices, speak outs, open-doors, electronic bulletin boards, etc. The complaints that funnel through these systems are most often individual—that is, they are initiated by members based on a specific experience.

However, taken as a whole, these complaints provide data that can be analyzed to diagnose organizational well-being and to identify sources of stress. If dispute processing data is to become a source of insight about organizational effectiveness, however, expressions of grievance, conflict, and difference must be solicited, respected, and prized rather than suppressed, contained, or prevented.

These data may be the basis for both narrow and broad-based change agendas in organizations. In one organization, for example, continual complaints about the provision of certain insurance benefits led to a change in procedures that eliminated this particular problem. In another organization, several complaints from women about their limited career options led to a wide-ranging analysis and subsequent intervention to effect changes in the organizational culture (Kolb, 1989a). Similarly, in yet another organization, persistent complaints by minority members about subtle forms of exclusion led to an in-depth analysis of the institutional culture and, ultimately, to the commitment of resources to effect significant change (Silbey, 1989).

For these kinds of action to occur, those charged with overseeing a dispute system need to encourage expressions of conflict and pay attention to patterns among individual cases, aggregating issues where appropriate. This would require that they define their roles as change agents and not simply dispute resolvers and preventers.

Barriers to Increased Capacity

It is clear that dispute systems designers can have both direct and indirect impacts on the capacity of organizations to deal with conflict. However, it is also well to consider the ways in which such systems designers may interfere with some of the naturally occurring ways that conflicts are handled in organizations.

Disputes arise in the context of relationships and within a structure of everyday activities. While some differences may be publicly aired, field research on conflict processes in organizations suggests that the vast majority occur out of sight (Kolb and Bartunek, forthcoming).

Some people in organizations emerge as mediators or peacemakers working behind-the-scenes to empower members in confronting disagreement and orchestrating the airing and resolution of disputes (Kolb, 1989a). Peacemakers are sought out by their organizational colleagues for their position, their skills, the relationships they have with others, and often, their gender (cf. Merry, 1982). In conducting a peacemaking process, the locus of the dispute and the intervention are closely entwined. There is also an emphasis on preserving and enhancing relationships (Putnam, 1990).

Dispute systems design may work against these less public approaches. The danger is that conflicts are channeled into a system, often centralized and rationalized, that is removed from the work settings in which the conflicts occur. Dispute processing comes to be seen as something external to routine interactions, the province of experts or outsiders, rather than an integral part of the organization's structure and culture. People need to bring problems to the expert system rather than problem solving indigenously. What we know about expert-designed systems is that, over time, they create a dependency among users, simplify and categorizes people and problems, routinize solutions, and mask power by claiming to be neutral (Silbey and Sarat, 1988). Ironically, while informal dispute resolution takes place with little or no fanfare, the expert systems seem to require constant "selling" and negotiation to attract users and to implement solutions (see Ury, Brett, and Goldberg, 1988, Chapter 6).

Conclusion

Conflict is a pervasive fact of organizational life. Enhancing members' capacities to understand their disputes in new ways, to feel free to express differences and know they will be heard, and to have multiple channels available makes for more humane and, perhaps, more productive organizations. While unlikely to reduce the frequency of disputes in organizations, dispute systems, if broadly construed, can contribute directly and indirectly to this end.

In designing these systems, however, we need to attend to the informal, behind-the-scenes, interstitial and nourishing forms of disputing. These interactions are often unnoticed and devalued in organizations. However, from a fuller appreciation of informal and formal modes of conflict management comes the potential for enhancing the capacity of organizations to deal with differences and diversity and the interplay between them. This—not prevention—is the real service which dispute interventionists can offer. •

References

Bacharach, S. and Lawler, J. (1980). *Power and politics in organizations.* San Francisco: Jossey-Bass.

Bumiller, K. (1987). *The civil rights society.* Baltimore: John Hopkins University Press; "Victims in the Shadow of the Law," Signs, 12:421.

Burroway, M. (1979). *Manufacturing consent.* Chicago: University of Chicago Press.

Coser, L. (1956). *The functions of social conflict.* New York: Free Press.

Ewing, D. (1989). *Justice on the job: Resolving grievances in the nonunion workplace.* Cambridge, Mass.: Harvard Business School Press.

Goodman, L. H. (with Sanborne, J.). (1986). "The legal needs of the poor in New Jersey: A preliminary report." Submitted to the Legal Services Program of New Jersey, National Social Science and Law Center, Washington, DC.

Greenhouse C. (1986). Praying for justice. Ithaca: Cornell University Press.

Kolb, D. M. (1989a). "Labor mediators, managers, and ombudsmen: Roles mediators play in different contexts." In *Mediation research,* edited by K. Kressel and D. Pruitt. San Francisco: Jossey-Bass.

—. (1989b). "How existing procedures shape alternatives: The case of grievance mediation." *Journal of Dispute Resolution* (1989): 59–87.

Kolb, D. M. and Bartunek, J. (forthcoming). *Disputing behind the scenes: New perspectives on conflict in organizations.* Newbury Park, Calif.: Sage.

Kunda, G. (forthcoming). *Engineering culture: Culture and control in a high-tech organization.* Philadelphia: Temple University Press.

Martin, J. (forthcoming). "Deconstructing organizational taboos: The suppression of gender conflict in organizations." *Organization Science.*

Merry, S. E. (1982). "The social organization of mediation in nonindustrial societies: Implications for informal community justice in America." In *The politics of informal justice* (vol. 2), edited by R. Abel. New York: Academic Press.

Merry, S. E. and Silbey, S. S. (1984). "What do plaintiffs want: Reexamining the concept of dispute." *Justice System Journal* 9: 151–179.

Miller, R. and Sarat, A. (1980–1981). "Grievances, claims, and disputes: Assessing the adversary culture." *Law and Society Review* 24: 1–9.

Morrill, C. (forthcoming). "Little conflicts: The dialectic of order and change in professional relations." *In Disputing behind the scenes,* edited by D. Kolb and J. Bartunek. Newbury Park, Calif.: Sage.

Pettigrew, A. (1973). *The politics of organizational decision-making.* London: Tavistock.

Pfeffer, J. and Salancik, G. (1978). *The external control of organizations.* New York: Harper and Row.

Putnam, L. (1990). "Feminist theories, dispute processes, and organizational communication." Paper presented at Arizona State University Conference on Organizational Communication: Perspectives for the 90s.

Pondy, L. (1986). "Reflections on organizational conflict." Paper presented at the 25th Academy of Management Meeting, Chicago, IL.

Silbey, S. (1989). *Report of the Task Force on Racism at Wellesley College.* Wellesley, Mass.: Wellesley College.

Silbey, S. and Sarat, A. (1988). "Dispute processing in law and legal scholarship: From institutional critiques to the reconstruction of the juridical subject." *Denver University Law Review* 66:437–499.

Smith, K. (1989). "The movement of conflict in organizations: The joint dynamics of splitting and triangulation." *Administrative Science Quarterly* 34:1–21.

Smith, K.K. and Berg, D. N. (1987). *Paradoxes of group life.* San Francisco: Jossey-Bass.

Ury, W. L., Brett, J. M., and Goldberg, S. B. (1988). *Getting disputes resolved.* San Francisco: Jossey-Bass.

Weick, K. (1979). *The social psychology of organizing.* Reading, Mass.: Addison Wesley.

*   *   *

Deborah M. Kolb is Professor of Management at the Simmons College Graduate School of Management and Associate Director of the Program on Negotiation at Harvard Law School. **Susan S. Silbey** is Associate Professor and Chair of the Department of Sociology at Wellesley College.

Study Questions

1. Define dispute systems design.

2. What are the problematic assumptions associated with conflict prevention?

3. An enhanced understanding of the causes of conflict can produce what favorable outcomes?

4. What broad-based benefits can come about through individual opportunities to dispute?

5. Why should overseers of dispute systems define their roles as change agents?

6. Why should system designers be particularly aware of informal, unexpressed, and behind-the-scenes forms of disputing and resolution?

Foundations and Dynamics of Intergroup Behavior

R. R. Blake
S. Shepard
J.S. Mouton

This paper deals with achieving effective coordination between units of an organization, such as management and union, sales and operations, staff and line, headquarters and field.

The behavior of two members of a corporation in relation to each other is determined by three or more sets of forces.

The first of these is formal job description- the kinds of responsibilities each brings to the situation. That is, each routinely behaves according to the requirements of his role within the corporation. Secondly, their behavior is determined by their backgrounds of training and experience. A case in point is a foreman who has risen from the ranks, discussing an issue with a graduate engineer. The third factor which determines their behavior is the role they feel themselves to be in as representatives of a particular group in the corporation. For example, in a discussion between the Vice President of sales and the Vice President of manufacturing, each may be representing a viewpoint arrived at and held with conviction by himself and other members of his group.

Behavior at the Interpersonal Level

When a man speaks as a group representative, his behavior is to some extent dictated by the fact that he is a member of that group. In contrast, when a man speaks from the framework of his job responsibilities, he speaks only for himself. In the latter case, disagreement between the parties is a *personal* matter.

Factors Influencing Supervisory-Subordinate Relations Where Disagreement is a Personal matter

Industrial organizations usually have a number of mechanisms for resolving interpersonal disagreements. For example, when a subordinate disagrees with a supervisor on a job-related issue, the supervisor can resolve the difference in several different ways. The supervisor may decide to resolve the matter himself, he may turn it over to his subordinate; or he may "table" the matter. Alternatively, the supervisor may seek a third position to which they both can agree. In any event, the procedure for resolving the conflict and the ultimate decision lies with the supervisor.

Resolving Interpersonal Conflict Between Peers

In most respects, a similar situation exists where individuals are peers rather than supervisor and subordinate. They may be unable to satisfactorily resolve their differences through argumentation. Finally, when each is unable to influence the other and an impasse is reached, they can take the matter to a common supervisor. The supervisor can then dispose of the matter through his higher authority. However, the complexity of a conflict situation increases greatly when the disagreeing parties are representatives of different groups, as will be discussed shortly.

The point of these illustrations is to show that where individuals are acting in their own behalf, or simply within their job responsibilities, they normally are able to resolve their differences with relative ease. Resolution may be accomplished through argumentation, by administrative action, or by the introduction of additional facts.

Factors Influencing the Resolution of a Dispute When Disagreement is an Intergroup Matter

Though superficially similar to the two-person relationship examples, significant differences appear when a person's interactions with another are dictated by his membership in or leadership of a group. Under these conditions, the individual is not free in the same sense as the person who acts independently out of job description or rank alone. Now the person's behavior is determined by many additional factors.[1]

The Dynamics of Group Interplay in Resolution of Disputes

In situations where an individual is interacting with another and both are representatives of groups, additional forces, quite complex, come into play. Acting as an individual, a man is free to change his mind on the basis of new evidence. But as a group representative, if he changes his thinking or position from that of his group's and capitulates to an outside point of view, *he is likely to be perceived by them as a traitor.*[2] On the other hand, if as a representative, he is able to persuade a representative of the other group to capitulate to his point of view, *his group receives him as a hero.* In other words, when a man is acting as a representative of one group in disagreement with another, the problem is no longer a personal affair. It is an *intergroup* problem. And as such, it can become a significant factor in accounting for his actions—as we will see.

Group Responsibilities of Individual Members

Often, men are quite aware that they have responsibilities as group representatives as well as individual job responsibilities. But formal organizational practices and attitudes often prevent this awareness from being discussed or from being openly considered.

As an example, consider the situation where the Vice President of sales speaks with the Vice President of operations. Formal organizational theory commonly assumes that each man speaks for himself, out of the background of his individual job and responsibilities. In practice, however, each may be keenly aware that he is representing the goals, values and convictions of his own group, and furthermore, when he speaks for them, he also speaks for himself. When problems between sales and operations seem difficult to resolve, it is not, as a rule, a sign of rigidity, incompetence, or personality conflict.[3] Rather, it is more likely, to be a product of the complex task of seeking resolutions which will not violate the attitudes, values, and interests of the many other persons that each represents.

Incompatible Group Norms, Goals and Values

Just as formal organizational theory, as written, recognizes only that the individual speaks for himself out of his job responsibilities, similarly it may fail to recognize other facts of organizational life. Formal organization theory assumes that the goals, norms and procedures of different functional groups in the organization are, by definition, similar, complementary or identical. The Vice President of sales and the Vice President of manufacturing are aware that their groups are similar and thus complement each other. However, they are also aware of wide differences and disparities in the viewpoints and goals that may exist between the groups they represent. As mentioned, if the interactions of these men were based entirely on job description, and a disagreement were to arise, there would be adequate organizational mechanisms for dealing with it. Similarly, if men only dealt with one another out of clearly agreed-upon concepts of organization purpose and procedures, there would be little room for disagreement and dispute.

There is increasing recognition, however, that neither of these circumstances accurately describes many situations in modern industrial life. This recognition has led to an acknowledgment that men, in fact, are group representatives within the framework of an organization. In turn, it has led to an awareness and appreciation of how an individual acting as a member, or as a leader, of a group, is confronted with a host of additional problems.[4] These problems must be dealt with in terms of their genuine complexities if unity of organizational purpose is to be achieved.

The roots of these complex problems which group representatives face are characteristic of groups and of individuals. As will be seen, group membership is complicated further by the characteristics of intergroup relations. After looking briefly at these characteristics of groups, we will turn our attention to the dynamics of intergroup relations.

The Structure and Process of Groups in Isolation

There are a number of ways of describing the characteristics of groups-in-isolation which we should consider prior to dealing with industrial intergroup relations.[5,6]

Regulations of the Interdependent Behavior Of Members of Groups-in-Isolation

Fundamentally, a group consists of a number of individuals bound to each other in some stage or degree of interdependence or shared "stake." Their problem is to guarantee the survival of the group in order to attain some purpose or goal. Taking for granted that the group's goals are clearly understood by its members, the interdependence among individuals, then, must be regulated to insure partial or entire achievement of these goals.

The Emergence of Group Structure, Leadership and Normative Rules

The need to regulate interdependence leads to three further properties of groups. When these properties emerge in group life they become additional forces which influence individual behavior. Let us look at each of these.

1. *Group Structure.* A differentiation of individual roles often is needed to accomplish group objectives. Differentiation inevitably results in some individuals who have varying degrees of power to influence the actions of others. The result is that some group members carry greater weight than others in determining the direction of group action, its norms, values and attitudes.

2. *Leadership.* When the power system among members of an informal group is crystallized, it is common to speak of that individual with the most power as the leader. In some groups, he is boss, or supervisor; other members are subordinates. The leader is looked to by the members for guidance and direction. The power and influence of the leader varies according to his ability to aid the group in achieving its goals.[7] Where the leader is appointed by a more powerful group rather than being selected by his own group, the above generalizations must be qualified. For instance, if the goals of the sub-ordinate group clash with those of the group by which he is appointed, he will be received not as leader, but as a representative of a different group.

3. *Normal Rules Guiding Group Behavior.* Along with the emerging set of power relations is the evolution of a normal set of "rules of the game," which specifies the conditions of interaction between group members. In other words, varying degrees of familiarity, influence, interaction and other relationships between members are sanctioned by the group according to an individual's role and position in the group hierarchy. Deviations from the rules and procedures by a member can lead to subtle but potent pressures by his fellow members to insure that the deviant "swings back into line." Such pressures act quite differently on each person as a function of his status and personality, but they do act.

Identification with One's Group

The preceding three characteristics of group formation and operation—goals, leadership and norms—lead to varying degrees of identification with one's group. When feelings of identification are strong, the group is said to have high morale; it is highly cohesive.[8] The opposite is true when feelings of identification with group goals are low. Under circumstances of unacceptable power distribution or inappropriate norms, for example, the result is feelings of low morale, demoralization, low cohesion or possibly alienation. The greater the sense of identification a member has with his group, the greater are the pressures on him to follow, at times blindly, the direction and will of the group position.[9,10]

These are all common properties of organized groups. A representative of a group, whether leader or member, is compelled to acknowledge in some way these group properties as he comes in contact with members of other groups whose interests support or violate those of his own. For a representative to agree to actions which other members feel are contrary to group goals can result in his being seen to have acted in a betraying way, or in poor faith. On the other hand, acting effectively against opposition and in support of group purpose and goals, and consistent with internal norms and values, insures retention or enhancement of his status.[11]

The Relationship of the Organization Framework to Individual and Group Relations

The internal properties of a group are only one of the significant matters involved in understanding and managing intergroup relations. When the actions of individuals and groups are viewed within the framework of a complex organization, we can identify additional determinants of behavior.[12]

A Framework of Interdependent Organizational Subgroups

Consider the following circumstance in a large and complex organization: the total membership of the organization is subdivided into many smaller groups. Each subgroup has its own leadership and its own rules and regulations. Each has its own goals which may or may not be in accord with overall organizational goals.[13] Each operates with its own degree of cohesion which varies with feelings of failure or accomplishment.[14] In an organization, these groups are interdependent with one another. They may be interdependent in performing a complex task requiring coordination of effort, in geographical proximity, or in terms of the reward system of the organization. Differences among them immediately become apparent to members.

Comparison between groups. Perception of differences between groups leads spontaneously to a comparison and to a "we-they" orientation.[5] Attention quickly focuses on similarities and differences. Furthermore, these spontaneous comparisons are intensified by the tendency of higher levels of authority to evaluate and reward by group comparison. For example,

group incentive plans, awarding of plaques or other symbols of organization success to the highest selling group, the group with the highest safety record, and so forth, all tend to highlight group differences.[15] Thus, in a sense, "winning" and "losing" groups are held up for all to see. The organization's rationale is that a spirit of competition is a "healthy" motivating force for achieving organizational ends.[16,17]

On the other hand, these comparisons sometimes lead to the discovery of common values and mutually supportive opportunities which can result in greater intergroup cohesion. When this happens, it is possible to achieve an intergroup atmosphere that can lead to effective problem solving and cooperation. Feelings of shared responsibility may then lead to identification with overall organizational goals, and to heightened recognition of similarities with resulting reduction of differences and tensions between them.[18]

Pitfalls of comparisons across groups. There is no assurance, however, that comparisons between groups inevitably lead to favorable outcomes. Instead, in the process of comparison, groups may discover discrepancies in treatment and privileges,[19] points of view, objectives, values, and so on. Then a different process unfolds. Comparisons tend to become invidious.[5] Differences are spotlighted and come to the focus of attention. Distortions in perception occur which favor the ingroup and deprecate the outgroup.[20,21,22] Each group finds in the other's performances an obstacle to attaining some or all of its own goals. When this situation extends beyond some critical point, each group may view the other as a threat to its own survival. At this point, disagreements are seen as permanent and inevitable, and the only possible resolution seems to lie in defeat of the other group in order to gain one's own objectives. Then all of the tools of common power struggles are brought into play.[23]

The manner in which representatives of groups interact, then, is colored by the background and history of agreements or disagreements of the groups they represent. The forces involved are powerful. The individual group's representative does not act only in terms of his job description or his specific background or training. Nor does he act solely within the context of his position within the group. Rather, he must be governed to some extent, depending on circumstances, by pre-existing relationships between the group he represents and the opposing group or representative of it that he is addressing.

Evaluated in terms of the forces acting in intergroup life, effective management of intergroup relations is a dimension of management that requires more analysis, more theory, and more skills than has been traditional in industrial life. To gain the necessary perspective, managers must focus not only on effective methods of resolving intergroup differences, but also on dysfunctional methods which lead to undesirable and disruptive side effects. Many dysfunctional methods for resolving conflicts have become common. These common practices have become embedded in the traditions of groups and organizations and must be understood to avoid their unthoughtful repetition.

Three Basic Assumptions Toward Intergroup Disagreement

Three basic assumptions or attitudes toward intergroup disagreements and its management can be identified.

1. *Disagreement is Inevitable and Permanent.* One identifiable basic assumption is that disagreement is inevitable and permanent. When A and B disagree, the assumption is that the disagreement must be resolved in favor of *A* or in favor of *B*, one way or the other. Under this assumption there seems to be no other alternative. If two points of view are seen to be mutually exclusive, and if neither party is prepared to capitulate, then any of three major mechanisms of resolution may be used:

A. *Win-lose* power struggle to the point of capitulation by one group.

B. Resolution through a *third-party* decision.

C. Agreement *not* to determine the outcome, namely, *fate* arbitration.

2. *Conflict Can Be Avoided Since Interdependence Between Groups is Unnecessary.* A second orientation to intergroup relations rests on the assumption that while intergroup disagreement is not inevitable, neither is inter-

group agreement possible. If these assumptions can be made, then interdependence is not necessary. Hence, when points of conflict arise between groups, they can be resolved by reducing the interdependence between parties. This reduction of interdependence may be achieved in three ways.

A. One group withdrawing from the scene of action.

B. Maintaining, or substituting *indifference* when it appears there is a conflict of interest.

C. *Isolating* the parties from each other; or the parties isolating themselves.

All of these (A, B, and C) share in common the maintenance of independence, rather than any attempt to achieve interdependence.

3. *Agreement and Maintaining Interdependence is Possible.* The third orientation to intergroup disagreement is that agreement is possible and that a means of resolving it must found. Resolving conflict in this way is achieved by smoothing over the conflict while retaining interdependence. For example, visible though trivial reference may be made to overall organizational goals to which both parties are in some degree committed. Then attention is shifted away from real issues with surface harmony maintained. Alternatively, agreement may be achieved by bargaining, trading, or compromising. In a general sense, this is splitting the difference that separates the parties while at the same time retaining their interdependence. Finally, an effort may be made to resolve the disagreement by a genuine problem-solving approach. Here the effort is not devoted to determining who is right and who is wrong. Nor is it devoted to yielding something to gain something. Rather, a genuine effort is made to discover a creative resolution of fundamental points of difference.

As mentioned earlier, each of these three orientations is related to another dimension which determines the specific approach to be used in managing disagreement. This dimension might be pictured as extending from a *passive* attitude or low stakes to an *active* orientation involving high stakes.

Framework for Viewing Intergroup Conflict

Figure 1 pictures the possibilities within each of the three major orientations just described. These orientations (three vertical columns in Figure 1) are:

1. Conflict inevitable. Agreement impossible.
2. Conflict not inevitable, yet agreement not possible.
3. Agreement possible in spite of conflict.

At the bottom of each orientation is the method of resolution likely to be used where stakes in the outcome are low. The middle shows mechanisms employed where stakes in the outcome are moderate, and the upper end shows mechanisms likely to be adopted where stakes in the outcome of the conflict are high.

All the approaches in the left-hand orientation (column) presume a condition of win-lose between the contesting parties. Fate strategies come into force when stakes in the outcome are low, arbitration when the stakes are moderate, and win-lose power struggles when the stakes are high.

The right-hand vertical column of the graph reflects three opposite approaches to resolving disagreement. These approaches assume that though disagreement is present, agreement can be found. The most passive orientation here is identified as "smoothing over." This approach involves such well-known cultural phenomena as efforts to achieve intergroup cohesion and co-existence without really solving problems. The assumption is that somehow or another, peaceful co-existence will arise and that people will act in accordance with it.

The more active agreement contains the element of splitting differences. This is a more positive (active) approach than smoothing over differences, but it leaves much to be desired for it often produces only temporary resolution.

In the upper right-hand corner is the orientation of problem solving. This position identifies the circumstances under which the contesting parties search out the rationale of their agreements as well as the bases of their disagreements. It also identifies the causes for reservations and doubts of both parties. Here, the parties work toward the circumstances which will eliminate reservations. This climate affords the opportunity to actively explore means for achieving true agreement on issues without 'smoothing over' or compromising differences.

The middle column which utilizes such methods as withdrawal, isolation and indifference or ignorance is discussed in complete detail in Chapter 6.

Figure 1
The Three Basic Assumptions Toward Intergroup Disagreements And Their management

	Conflict Inevitable Agreement Impossible	Conflict Not Inevitable, Yet Agreement Not Possible	Although There is Conflict, Agreement Is Possible	
Active				High Stakes
	Win-Lose Power Struggle	Withdrawal	Problem-Solving	
	Third-Party Judgment	Isolation	Splitting the Difference (Compromise, Bargaining, etc.)	Moderate Stakes
Passive	Fate	Indifference or Ignorance	Peaceful Coexistence ("Smoothing Over")	Low Stakes

Summary

The behavior of organization members in relation to each other is, at the least, determined by one of three sets of forces:

1. Job responsibilities.
2. Social backgrounds represented in such considerations as training and experience.
3. The set of complex forces acting on them by virtue of their active memberships in different groups.

This chapter has been concerned primarily with the third set of forces.

As a group member, whether leader or member, *an individual is a representative of his group* whenever he interacts with others in different groups, provided the groups are in some way interdependent. As a representative, a group member's opinions and attitudes are shaped by the goals, norms and values he shares with others of his group. Normal rules of conduct and the expectations of others in his group do not allow him to act independently of his group's interests when areas of disagreement arise between his group and another.

Large organizations are composed of many small groups. Because of the size, complexity and nature of present-day organizations, group comparisons, particularly of an invidious character, are bound to occur. Under such circumstances, differences, rather than similarities and commonness of purpose, are highlighted, with conflict the inevitable result. The result is that organizational needs for interdependence and cooperation among groups are not met as well as they might have been, had managerial personnel applied greater understanding to intergroup relations.

Three basic orientations to intergroup disagreement, in combination with these different degrees of 'stake in the outcome,' and their accompanying approaches for achieving resolution were outlined. •

Footnotes

[1]Sheppard, H. L. "Approaches to conflict in American Industrial Sociology," *Brit. J. Sociol.,* 5, 1954, 324–341.

[2]Blake, R. R. "Psychology and the Crisis Of Statesmanship." *Amer. Psychologist,* 14, 1959, 87–94. Blake, R. R. and Mouton, J. S., *Group Dynamics—Key to Decision Making.* Houston: Gulf Publishing Co., 1961, 87.

[3]Faris, R. E. L. "Interaction Levels and Intergroup Relations." In M. Sherif, (Ed.) *Intergroup Relations and Leadership.* John Wiley and Sons, Inc., 1962, 24–45.

[4]Stogdill, R. M. Intragroup-Intergroup Theory and Research. In M. Sherif (ed.), *Intergroup Relations and Leadership.* New York: John Wiley and Sons, Inc., 1962, 48–65.

[5]Sherif, M. and Sherif C. *Outline of Social Psychology* (revised). New York: Harper & Bros., 1956.

[6]Cartwright, D. and Zander, A. *Group Dynamics: Research and Theory,* (2nd edition). Evanston, Illinois: Row, Peterson & Co., 1960.

[7]Hamblin, R. L., Miller, K. and Wiggins, J. A. "Group Morale and Competence of the Leader," *Sociometry, 24,* (3), 1961, 295–311.

[8]Sherif, M. and Sherif, C. W. *Outline of Social Psychology (revised), op cit.*

[9]Cartwright, D. and Zander, A. *Group Dynamics: Research and Theory,* (1st edition). Evanston, Ill. Row, Peterson & Co., 1953.

[10]Gerard, H. B. "The Anchorage of Opinion in Face to Face Groups," *Human Relat.,* 7, 1954, 313–325; and Kelley, H. H. and Volkart, E. H., "The Resistance to Change of Group Anchored Attitudes," *Amer. Sociol. Rev,* 17, 1952, 453–465.

[11]Pryer, M.W., Flint, A.W., and Bass, B.M. "Group Effectiveness and Consistency of Leadership," *Sociometry,* 25, (4), 1962, 391; and Sherif, M. and Sherif, C.W. *Outline of Social Psychology* (revised), op. cit.

[12]Arensberg, C. H. "Behavior and Organization: Industrial Studies." In J. H. Rohrer and M. Sherif (eds.) *Social Psychology at the Crossroads* New York: Harper & Bros., 1951.

[13]Cooper, H.C. "Perception of Subgroup Power and Intensity of Affiliation with a Large Organization." *Amer. Sociol Rev.,* 26, (2) 1961, 272–274.

[14]Wolman, B. B. "Impact of Failure on Group Cohesiveness," *J. Soc. Psychology,* 51, 1960, 409–418.

[15]Sherif, M. and Sherif, C. W. *Outline of Social Psychology revised), op. cit.*

[16]Sayles, L. R. "The Impact of Incentives on Intergroup Relations: Management and Union Problem," *Personnel,* 28, 1982, 483–490.

[17]Spriegel, W. R. and Lansburgh, R. H. *Industrial Management* (5th edition). New York: John Wiley, 1955; and Strauss, G. and Sayles, L. R. *Personnel* Englewood Cliffs, N. J.: Prentice-Hall, 1960.

[18]Sherif. M. "Superordinate Goals in the Reduction of Intergroup Conflict," *Amer. J. Sociol.*, 43, 1958, 394–356.

[19]Strauss, G. "Group Dynamics and Intergroup Relations." In W. F. White (ed.), *Money and Motivation.* New York: Harper & Bros., 1955, 90–96.

[20]Sherif, M. and Sherif, C. W. *Outline of Social Psychology* (revised), op. cit.

[21]Cohen, A. R. "Upward Communication in Experimentally Created Hierarchies," *Human Relat.,* 11, 1958, 41–53; Kelley, H. H. "Communication in Experimentally Created Hierarchies," *Human Relat., 4, 1951,* 39–56; and Thibaut, J. "An Experimental Study of the Cohesiveness of Under-Privileged Groups," *Human Relat.,* 3, 1950, 251–278.

[22]Blake, R. R. and Mouton, J. S. "Comprehension of Own and Outgroup Position Under Intergroup Competition, *J. Confl. Resolul.,* 5, (3 1961, 304–310.

* * *

Study Questions

1. What three forces come into play when two organizational members interact?

2. Explain dispute resolution at the *personal* level. What's involved? How accomplished?

3. Why does group membership complicate individuals' efforts to resolve disputes?

4. How do the issues associated with the three properties of groups affect a group's functioning and cohesion?

5. What is the relationship among group identification, morale, cohesion and representing the group?

6. In what ways can groups in the same organization be different?

7. What influences how group representatives interact?

8. Explain the three basic orientations one can have toward intergroup disagreement.

9. What is "fate arbitration?"

10. Explain the main ideas of Figure 1.

CASE: Torando Electronics

G. Yukl

The prototype project development department of Torando Electronics Company played an essential role in the development of the product lines sold by the firm. The department consisted of 12 engineers and 35 technicians who worked on the first floor of the plant. Each project usually had at least two engineers and five technicians working together under the direction of a project supervisor.

When each project was started, the engineers submitted a written work order, and the department manager would assign the technicians to work with the engineers. Upon completion of each project, a quality control assessor would inspect the work. The engineers were recognized by the top management of the company as having the expertise to submit top-quality work orders, and in only a few instances were their requests rejected. The engineers were college graduates and were paid on a salary basis.

Most of the 35 technicians had previously worked as assembly workers at Torando, and they knew plant operations very well. They were paid on an hourly basis, and most of their pay raises were based primarily on seniority. The majority of technicians worked the day shift, although some had to work the other two shifts. Seniority was used to schedule the shift workers.

The technicians interacted with each other off the job, either through activities such as softball, bowling, card games, or professional football parties on the weekends during the season. The technicians ate lunch and took coffee breaks together.

The engineers rarely, if ever, spent any off-the-job time with the technicians. They had an engineering office where they took coffee breaks and often met after work to schedule some activity for the evening.

Rudy Garcia, the new department manager, was concerned about the strained relationship that existed between the technicians and engineers. He noticed the engineers complaining about the slowness and poor quality of work being done by the technicians. These complaints were occurring regularly. It was also obvious to Rudy that the productivity of the department was extremely low compared to similar departments in other plants of the company.

Because of the perceived problems in the department, Rudy started to investigate the relationship between the engineers and technicians. For two weeks he talked to a number of the technicians and most of the engineers to learn more about the interaction between the two groups. He found that the technicians believed that the engineers requested work orders for projects that were poorly developed. The technicians also believed that their suggestions on how to accomplish projects were never followed.

Rudy discovered that the engineers believed that they were part of the management team and needed control over the technicians. The engineers believed that the technicians were feared by management because they were unionized. In addition, the engineers thought that the technicians were "dragging their feet" and passively resisting any suggestions or recommendations initiated by the engineers.

After his preliminary investigation of the situation, Rudy concluded that immediate action had to be taken. He wanted to be fair but firm in his efforts to minimize or resolve the friction. •

Study Questions

1. What conditions contributed to the conflict between engineers and technicians? Consider each of the following conditions:

    Competition for Resources

    Task Interdependence

    Jurisdictional Ambiguity

    Status Struggles

    Communication Barriers

2. What actions could Rudy take to improve relations between the engineers and technicians? Consider each of the following types of intervention:

    Mediation

    Process Analysis

    Organizational Changes

Exercise—Intergroup Competition and Negotiations

Red 1

Arthur Hochner

A. Purposes
1. To experience group processes.
2. To experience intergroup negotiations.
3. To explore interpersonal and intergroup trust.

B. Activities
1. Form an even number of groups of about 5 people each.
2. Groups will be paired as Red and Blue teams.
3. Five rounds of decisions.

C. Rules
1. Groups are *not* to communicate with each other, verbally or nonverbally, except when told to do so.
2. Groups will write their decisions on a slip of paper and hand it to the instructor when time is up.
3. Group representatives will receive their instructions from their groups and will report back to their groups before the group makes its decision on rounds 3, 4, and 5.
4. Groups will try to gain positive points.

D. Exercise Instructions
For 5 rounds, the Red team will choose between A or B and the Blue team will choose between X or Y. The points each team receives in a round is determined by the pattern made by the choices of both teams, according to the schedule below.

BLUE TEAM (upper right hand corner of boxes)

		X	Y
RED TEAM (lower left hand corner of boxes)	A	+3 / +3	+6 / −6
	B	−6 / +6	−3 / −3

RESULTS

ROUND	MINUTES	RED'S CHOICE	BLUE'S CHOICE	RED POINTS	BLUE POINTS
1	3				
2	3				
3*	3 (reps) 3 (team)				
4**	3 (reps) 5 (team)				
5**	3 (reps) 5 (team)				

* —All points are doubled for this round.
** —All points are tripled for this round.

Study Questions

For each group

1. What happened and why?

2. What was the group's structure, i.e., who led, who followed, who initiated, who represented the group? Did different people take on these different roles at different times?

3. How did the group make its decisions, i.e., consensus, majority rule, dictatorship, other?

4. Did over time the group become more or lose conspiratorial, more or less cohesive, more or less argumentative, more or less serious or humorous, etc.?

5. Did the group's strategy change?

6. Were friendly, hostile, or neutral thoughts about the other group expressed during the group's discussions?

7. How did the group treat its representative, both before negotiations and afterward?

For general discussion:

8. What kinds of conflict and cooperation do groups in the workplace experience with each other?

9. How could better intergroup cooperation be achieved?

10. How does or doesn't this situation apply to the interactions among peers, subordinates, and managers within the workplace?

SECTION 3

Negotiation: Assessment of the Parties

This section emphasizes the importance of examining and understanding participants in the negotiation relationship. The first few articles reassert the value in maintaining positive relations before, during, and after the negotiation encounter. The bulk of the section, however, focuses on various individual factors that impact perceptions and actions of negotiators in this relationship.

Gilkey and Greenhalgh ("**The Role of Personality in Successful Negotiating**") explore personality's role in shaping the negotiating process. Personality traits are seen as stable and enduring characteristics of individuals. Negotiators who are self-aware can adjust their bargaining strategies in light of their own personality traits. This article, through case example, connects the concepts of personality and negotiating outcomes, and highlights various assessments available to negotiators who see the value in self-examination.

Through examples of prejudice and stereotypes on a global scale, Breslin ("**Breaking Away from Subtle Biases**") considers personal prejudices and biases that may create an "us versus them" mentality in the negotiating process. His article asks readers to acknowledge the fact that we are likely guilty of adopting stereotypes that cause us to view an opponent *as* the problem rather than seeing them as colleagues who can work with us to *solve* the problem.

In Christie's "**The Machiavellis Among Us**," the personality trait labeled "Machiavellianism" is considered. Christie discusses how the Mach IV questionnaire scale was created to assess the degree individuals believe others are manipulable. Research incorporating Mach IV is discussed with a focus on behavioral implications for high versus low Machs.

Bazerman's "**Negotiator Cognition**" is an extension of his classic 1983 article on negotiator judgment. Here, he counters prescriptive principles aimed at the "rational" negotiator with a complementary approach detailing how systematic deviations from rational judgments impact negotiation effectiveness. Examining issues such as framing, mythical fixed pie, escalation of conflict, and overconfidence helps us appreciate the cognitive information processing of negotiators.

Neale and Bazerman elaborate on the role of "framing" in their article "**Negotiating Rationally**." Frames are cognitive biases that can restrict information search and analysis and thus reduce the effectiveness with which people negotiate agreements. They explain how managers use and guard against various frames that impact efforts to resolve disputes.

The process of opponent analysis is detailed in "**Getting to Know Them**" by Geddes. She argues that the degree to which individuals engage in (1) information gathering, (2) sense making, and (3) expectation setting with regard to an opponent affects the efficacy of personal bargaining strategy as well as the eventual negotiated outcome. A model of the opponent analysis process, and a table highlighting specific communicative behaviors reflective of each phase are included in the article.

Finally, whether one chooses to be a "hard" or "soft" bargainer, Copeland and Griggs ("**How to Win in Foreign Negotiations**") provide 19 specific rules to increase effectiveness in international negotiations. Because it is unlikely negotiators from different countries share frames of reference, Copeland and Griggs argue that negotiation becomes more a "game" of perspective than skill. Specifically, they propose that international negotiation has "less to do with overcoming an adversary than with creating a new picture of reality that is acceptable from two different points of view.

* * *

The Role of Personality In Successful Negotiating

Roderick W. Gilkey
Leonard Greenhalgh

Anyone who has negotiated with people who are stubborn, short-tempered, shy, Machiavellian, or risk-averse will attest to how important negotiators' personalities can be in determining how negotiations unfold. These traits are a small sample of the wide range of personality factors that can make negotiations productive or unproductive. Traits are stable and enduring characteristics of individuals that predispose negotiators to react to situations in particular ways. Negotiators who are aware of their own traits can adjust the strategies and tactics their personalities induce them to adopt; negotiators who are keen observers of others' personality characteristics know what to expect and can make strategic adjustments in dealing with others. Thus every negotiator should be a student of how individuals differ from each other and how such differences affect negotiating behavior.

Despite the importance of this topic, almost no comprehensive attention has been given to how personality affects negotiation (a notable exception is Rubin and Brown, 1975). This neglect is occurring at a time when there is a welcome, sudden growth in the number of books and articles about negotiation. Most of this emerging literature focuses on either the decision making of negotiators (e.g., Raiffa, 1982) or the approaches and tactics negotiators use (e.g., Walton and McKersie, 1965; Fisher and Ury, 1982; Lewicki and Litterer; 1985). Personality, which is more difficult to study, tends not to receive the attention it deserves.

Before looking more specifically at how personalities affect negotiations and what can be done to develop negotiators' self-understanding and awareness of others, it is useful to pause and consider what, exactly, is meant by the term "personality."

Personality concerns patterns in individuals' behavior that reappear in various situations. Personality *traits* are labels that summarize those patterns. For example, "conservatism" is an example of a trait that reappears in such diverse areas as political views, style of dress, childrearing practices, and negotiated business decisions. Similarly, an "aggressive" person is likely to be aggressive on dates, behind the wheel of a car, in business meetings, at sports activities, as well as in conflict situations. Such patterns exist because traits are *predispositions* to respond in characteristic ways: situations simply trigger what "comes naturally" to each individual.

Conflict situations trigger the participants' characteristic styles of dealing with conflict (see, e.g., Thomas, 1975). To illustrate the importance of personality in conflict situations, consider how different personality types might approach the negotiation of a divorce settlement. If the husband tends to be highly *competitive,* he is likely to define the situation as one in which he must win as much as possible in the settlement. If the wife tends to be highly *accommodating,* she might submit to his exploitive demands and not strive to preserve her own interests. She might even let his lawyer handle the whole thing.

Consider instead the case in which both parties are *compromisers.* They would be likely to seek outcomes that split the difference between his interests and her interests. The result might be a solution that is not optimal for either party. Suppose, for example, that the couple had a breeding pair of championship Siamese cats. A simple middle-of-the-road settlement would be that the wife take one cat and the husband take the other; but, since the value of the cats is in their being a breeding pair, both husband and wife would lose some value in this settlement. If instead of being compromisers, the couple both tended to be *collaborators,* they would search for solutions to the problem that would benefit them both. Perhaps one party could keep the breeding pair and the other could keep all the kittens in the next litter.

Even worse than the situation in which both parties are compromisers is the situation in which both parties are conflict *avoiders*. Here the couple may let the marriage drag on after it should have been ended. This may place the children in a situation that is worse than living with one or the other divorced parent.

These enduring personality traits may well have evolved before the individuals reached grade school. The traits are likely to have developed as a result of the individuals' relationships with their parents and siblings. For example, if children find that they usually get their way by being intransigent, then intransigence will have been reinforced and is likely to emerge when the individual is involved in a disagreement. If ingratiation or passive-aggressiveness works better, then those traits will endure instead. Other children will learn to compromise or to stand up and fight for what they want, or perhaps to smooth out conflicts whenever these arise between their siblings or even their parents. These early lessons often are the foundation for adults' negotiating styles.

It is therefore important for negotiators to learn to recognize their own tendencies and make adjustments in their negotiating behavior if these tendencies prove to be more of an impediment than a help. Likewise, capable and alert negotiators should be able to identify accurately such tendencies in those with whom they negotiate—and again, compensate as necessary. Thus, personality assessment and feedback, along with individualized development of compensatory mechanisms, should be an important component of programs to develop negotiators.

The Tuck Personality Assessment And Feedback Program

A course in power and negotiation has been under development for many years at The Amos Tuck School of Business Administration at Dartmouth College. Four years ago, with the addition of a clinical psychologist to the faculty, it became possible to explore in depth the influence of personality on negotiating behavior and to determine how negotiators can build on their strengths and compensate for their weaknesses.

The course is designed to develop students' abilities to negotiate and does so primarily through the use of simulations based on actual business negotiations. The students write a comprehensive analysis of their performance in each negotiation as a part of a continuous journal. The instructors provide confidential feedback on each entry. In addition, selected simulations are videotaped and further feedback is given.

Specific feedback concerning students' personality traits and how these affect negotiating performance is provided as a result of a personality appraisal program. The program is conducted by a clinical psychologist and is highly confidential. Although participation in this aspect of the course is voluntary, all of the 64 students in the course take advantage of this opportunity.

Data are gathered by means of an in-depth personality assessment, and a summary of the results is presented to each student. This information becomes the basis for an ongoing working relationship between the individual students and the course instructors. Once students know their basic predispositions, they become keen observers of how their personality affects their performance in negotiations and the instructors help them build on their strengths and either compensate for or hold in check the traits that get in their way.

The comprehensive assessment program provides an in-depth profile of each individual. The clinician needs this information to fully understand the basic psychodynamic features of each individual, particularly central conflicts and ego defenses. To achieve this depth, participants spend two hours of their own time filling out test batteries, another two hours doing group-administered projective tests, and at least one more hour in a face-to-face meeting with the clinician. The set of tests used is explained in Appendix I; further information can be obtained by contacting the authors.

Some of the results are fed back to students in written form, but the major vehicle for feedback is interaction with the clinician. In many cases the students initiate a series of follow-up meetings in which there is extended exploration of the issues addressed in the initial feedback session. The agenda for such discussions is set by the individual students, usually as a part of a general effort to change particular aspects of their negotiating style. The findings from the personality assessment provide a focus for the discussions that follow, in which the student supplements his or her self-observations with the results of the tests. In this way, the objective of the program is to facilitate self-improvement rather than change students' behavior.

The emphasis of these sessions is on trying to help students identify their own particular strengths as managers who need to be effective in achieving negotiated agreements, and to refine their approaches to fully capitalize on these strengths. Liabilities are addressed as "areas to work on," and the discussions focus only on those conflicts and defenses that are close to the individual's consciousness—in other words, there is no attempt to engage in in-depth psychotherapy.

In those few instances where there is clear evidence of serious pathology, the scope and depth of the feedback is carefully limited so as not to disrupt the individual's already fragile psychological defenses. Of course, students have in some cases used the personality assessment experience as an opportunity to explore some of their general psychological adjustment difficulties. These cases demonstrate the necessity for only the most experienced and well-trained clinicians to be involved in such efforts.

Personality Profiles of Negotiators: Some Examples

The examples presented earlier were oversimplified in that we discussed only one personality attribute, such as conflict-avoidance. In practice, the personality assessment process is quite comprehensive and yields a complex profile of each individual. In this section, we present three such profiles to illustrate how personality can affect performance in negotiations.

The case examples chosen illustrate some of the diversity in the personalities we have encountered. Of course, participants in the program spanned the range from those having personality characteristics that were virtually debilitating in negotiation to those who were well-adjusted to interpersonal interactions. For the individuals who were well-adjusted, much

of the assessment and feedback process involved sensitizing them to realize how others might have different personalities that would predispose them to react in different ways. Additional attention was given to helping these high-functioning negotiators experiment with and refine their negotiating styles—for example, by going over their videotapes—to make sure these individuals were capitalizing on their strengths. The three cases presented next depict individuals whose personalities were posing some disadvantages in negotiations.

Case Example: Paul

Like most students who come to the Tuck School, Paul had considerable previous work experience. He had been a product manager for the marketing division of a consumer goods company, where he was described as a solid performer. However, his employer believed that Paul had not fully realized his leadership potential, and Paul agreed with this assessment. He was friendly with members of his product management team, had demonstrated sound decision-making skills, and had the capacity to generate good marketing concepts. However, he had not "made things happen": his good ideas were often overlooked, even though he was respected by everyone.

In the negotiation course, Paul quickly emerged as an articulate and often forceful mediator. However, it was not long before his impact on others began to diminish, and Paul sensed that his peers no longer gave him or his ideas the consideration they once had. He also noticed a similarity between the way his classmates responded to him and the way his former co-workers responded to him.

Data from the testing program showed that Paul was a bright, energetic young man with strong affiliative needs and a high degree of interpersonal sensitivity (for example, both his Interpersonal Orientation and Empathic Concern scores were high). While he was capable of being very focused and decisive, his apprehension about hurting or alienating others led him to withdraw from interpersonal conflict situations. His anxiety about displaying his aggression led him to quickly give in whenever it became clear to him that he was not going to achieve his objectives immediately. Consequently, he began to feel rather powerless in situations where he should have been quite capable of influencing important outcomes. Despite his general effectiveness, Paul's high score on external locus of control evidenced his experience of losing control when his anxiety level was high.

Consistent with these tendencies, Paul's highest score on the Thomas-Killman Conflict Mode Instrument was Competing (that is, forcefully pursuing his interests in a directive manner). His second highest score, however, was being Accommodating, reflecting his tendency to sacrifice his own interests in favor of the other person's. He scored low on Collaborating and Compromising—traits that measure an individual's tendency to participate in give-and-take bargaining to resolve differences.

As a result of the feedback program, Paul became more aware of these features of his personality and the effect they had on his negotiating performance, and he began to alter his style. He began to demonstrate more patience when his point of view was not immediately accepted, and learned to persist quietly rather than give way to the other party. This tolerance allowed him to participate in a collaborative process of negotiating so that his ideas began to receive more consideration and were more frequently adopted.

At times, Paul complained that his negotiating sessions had become "more of a hassle than before." But, he also observed, "I know at the same time that more of my ideas are being used and implemented, especially in a group situation." This, of course, is an important managerial lesson: It always seems more expedient for a manager to make decisions without consulting those affected by them; however, decisions are easier to implement if the others are drawn into the decision process, and thereby become committed to making the agreed-upon course of action successful.

While Paul's discomfort in bargaining situations was noticeable, he had learned to discipline himself so that he would continue to engage himself in the process, and he became more consistently effective. He was able to build on his ability to establish rapport with others and engage them in mutually productive exchanges. These relationship-building abilities, which had always been present, had been underutilized particularly when Paul was called upon to exert his leadership in more formal or stressful circumstances. Paul was, therefore, a good example of someone who learned to mobilize existing strengths and overcome limitations of his negotiating style.

Case Example: Bruce

As an "idea man" in an advertising agency, Bruce had advanced very rapidly because of his creative and innovative ideas. He had worked with a small group of people with whom he had been closely associated for a number of years. "We all liked each other—we understood each other, we thought the same way, and so we didn't have to explain ourselves to each other," he noted. Bruce had returned to school for an MBA degree so that he might more easily move into a general management position in marketing.

While he was successful in the creative, collaborative environment of the ad agency, Bruce's style did not appear to serve him well in other settings. He was characterized as being a "flighty" individual who jumped to conclusions and was unable to explain the logic of his position. At worst, he was described as being a "flake" whose impressionistic approach to problem solving left others confused and frustrated. Bruce was very aware that if he was to achieve his next career goal, he would have to change his interpersonal style, and he had enrolled in the negotiating course to help achieve this change.

The personality assessment revealed that Bruce was a very intuitive individual who made full use of his rich inner resources. His Rorschach responses were highly elaborated and creative. He took great pleasure in the process of arriving at original responses to the ink blots; however, he seemed to be unaware of the difficulties he was causing the clinician who was trying to record his numerous responses. This insensitivity to others was consistent with his low scores on Interpersonal Orientation and on the Collaboration index of the Thomas-Killman Conflict Mode Instrument.

In contrast, Bruce was measured as having a high tolerance of ambiguity which was consistent with his general relaxed and creative style.

Though Bruce reported that he had been interpersonally attuned in the environment of the ad agency, in general he appeared to be more absorbed by his inner life than by the presence of those around him. Despite these tendencies toward introversion, Bruce was very concerned about his impact on others and the difficulty he was having "constructively connecting with other people to get things done."

When the results of the personality assessment and the observations cited above were shared with him over the course of a number of discussions, Bruce began to work on changing his approach to negotiating. He quickly recognized, for example, that he was going to have to spend more time preparing for his negotiating sessions so that he could clearly spell out the logic of his position for others. He also learned to elaborate his points to increase the clarity of the way he expressed himself and thereby enhance his general credibility. He worked hard to listen better to others, so that he could gain a clearer understanding of their positions and reasoning.

Bruce's efforts to alter his style were largely successful. Based on the journal entries of his fellow students, it was clear that he was able to gain a great deal of credibility. People began to recognize Bruce's ability to provide new insights in problem-solving situations as he learned to explain his ideas in a more focused, detailed manner. His ability to contribute also increased as he made efforts to gain more information and ideas from others by actively probing and listening.

Bruce reported greater satisfaction and pleasure in his negotiations as he saw himself as a more collaborative participant. Though he still reported being concerned about losing some of his creative ability by "over-planning" and "over-involving myself in too much group stuff," Bruce recognized that this was a necessary risk if he was going to make the transition from being an idea man to a manager. While it is too soon to know whether Bruce will succeed in his career objective, he did make definite progress as a negotiator and greatly enhanced his prospects for managerial success.

Case Example: Wendy

Working as a commodities trader, Wendy had distinguished herself as an intense, competitive and effective trader. She elected to pursue an MBA degree to expand her career options. In the negotiation course, she quickly emerged as a hard bargainer who was tough, resourceful, and determined to be a "winner." One of her male peers described her in a journal entry as "an attractive lady, but I wouldn't want to meet her in a dark alley." During the initial phases of the course, she clung to her win/lose approach to negotiating. However, her competitiveness often led her to become combative and abrasive, and her peers soon brought these tendencies to her attention. The impetus for change thus came from other people; she found it painful to be criticized by those whom she liked and respected.

The personality tests yielded data that were generally consistent with Wendy's self-assessment, but some had the benefit of being quite specific in pointing out her exact strengths and weaknesses as a negotiator. Her responses on the Thematic Apperception Test (TAT) exhibited a high need for power. She had apparently learned how to satisfy this need, according to her high score on Internal Locus of Control: that is, she had discovered how to become generally successful at making things happen the way she wanted them to turn out. Her forceful style was diagnosed in her scores on the Thomas-Killman Conflict Mode Instrument. Her tendency was to ruthlessly pursue her own interests, as evidenced by her high score on Competing and low scores on Compromising and Avoiding. Consistent with this urge to dominate others was her high score on the Masculinity scale of the Bem Sex Role Inventory.

There were, however, tendencies that counterbalanced these more Competitive and Authoritarian traits. For example, she received a relatively high score on Interpersonal Orientation and similarly high scores on Empathetic Concern and Perspective-Taking Ability.

With her customary energy and intensity, Wendy worked hard to alter her perspective and behavior in dealing with others. She made lists of objectives for herself which included both attitudinal changes ("try to be more receptive and open, think about mutual opportunities for gain and joint solutions"), and behavioral ones ("don't interrupt, ask more questions, take more time"). She was critical of her efforts and impatient with herself, and needed occasional support and encouragement so that she created realistic expectations about how soon she could expect to change things for herself. Her capacity for self-observation was excellent, and she was able to note that she would fall back into "the old style" when she felt pressured or fatigued. This self-monitoring ability helped her to continue to alter and refine her negotiating style. She finally emerged with a much more cooperative style for dealing with conflict. While she was jokingly able to say that her desire to "always get my way" was still at the core of her personality, she succeeded in altering her tactics for dealing with others, a change that was obvious both to herself and to her fellow students.

Learning from Personality Assessment

Personality assessment can be a valuable teaching tool in expanding negotiators' awareness of the way they think and act. In addition to mobilizing their capacities for self-awareness, negotiators also learn to benefit from the feedback of peers and clinically-trained observers. In addition, as they become more aware of their particular assets, they can make more explicit and effective use of them. Such self-awareness can often create the desire for change as the students become aware of alternative approaches to dealing with conflict that can allow them to use their individual strengths more fully.

The program has evolved beyond its developmental phase and is now being used in executive programs that specialize in negotiation. Because the executive programs run for only three to five days, the personality assessment component is condensed. Selected tests and measures that can be self-administered are mailed out to the executives in advance of the seminar (particularly the Bem Sex Role Inventory, the Perspective-Taking Ability and Empathic Concern scales, the Interpersonal Orientation Scale, the Conflict Mode Instrument, and the psychological history questionnaire). Pro-

jective tests (Rorschach and Thematic Apperception Test) are administered in a group session during the early part of the program. Following this, one-hour private feedback sessions are scheduled. These highly interactive discussions focus on the identification of key strengths that are fundamental in negotiation and on the exploration of abilities that the individual may be underutilizing (for example, the capacity for empathy and collaboration can easily be overlooked as a key strength to be used in negotiation).

Individual feedback is also provided during a videotaped negotiation session in which pairs of negotiators are taped doing one of the negotiations, and then provided with an appraisal of their performance. In addition, a certain amount of unscheduled time is built into these programs to allow for informal private exchanges between executives and the clinician. When combined with the simulated negotiations and group debriefing sessions, participants are provided with multiple opportunities to learn more about their personality and its effects on their negotiating style. Because executives are more experienced in handling organizational conflicts and therefore are much more aware of their dominant approaches, the learning process seems more efficient and the discussions much richer. Personality assessment and feedback has therefore been a well-received addition to executive programs on negotiation.

Our experience suggests that some knowledge of the underlying dynamics of personality (such as the individual's motives, needs, and fears) is necessary to produce lasting change in an individual's negotiating style. This does not mean probing into their core conflicts or interpreting major ego defenses; rather, it means providing a supportive, confidential environment so students can engage in self-exploration. In that environment, those dynamics that are closest to consciousness and most amenable to change can emerge and be freely discussed. While the permanence of any change effort can never be taken for granted, it seems probable that some of the major changes in perspective and attitude toward negotiation are likely to be enduring.

For example, we had an opportunity to work with Wendy one year after graduation, when she returned to the Tuck School for a visit. Her behavior displayed a significant change from what we had encountered at the beginning of the assessment and feedback process. Instead of the tough, competitive demeanor that predominated during her early days in the MBA program, we were impressed with the warmth and personableness that was showing through. She was receptive and accommodating and conveyed a sense of interpersonal concern and sensitivity that earlier had been masked by her dominating tendencies.

Our clinical impression was that some of her tests (interpersonal orientation, perspective-taking ability, and empathetic concern) had successfully identified latent traits in Wendy's personality that were becoming manifest as she continued to evolve her approach to interacting with others. While progress is attributable to the maturing experience of a year of corporate life, it seems likely that the course and the assessment and feedback program had done much to accelerate her progress. Such progress would be accelerated because the program pinpointed aspects of her personality that might not serve her well in certain types of negotiations. Armed with this knowledge, she was given the opportunity to experiment with different approaches in simulated managerial situations in which she could get specific feedback as to how effective were her attempts to compensate for dysfunctional tendencies.

As we endeavor to understand more about the factors associated with successful negotiation, the importance of understanding the individuals involved must not be underestimated. Heretofore, the role of decision-making approaches and tactics has been given disproportionate consideration. However, a truly comprehensive understanding of how conflicts are handled through negotiation may not be possible without equal attention being given to understanding the negotiators themselves, especially their personal perspectives, motives, and aims. The Tuck Personality Assessment and Feedback Program is a step toward this objective.

Career Assessment

The addition of the Assessment and Feedback component to the negotiation course was viewed by students as a great success. They did indeed learn that what made them different as individuals made them different as negotiators. They also learned that this new knowledge was directly relevant to the job choices they were making. In fact, many of them wished they had had the information earlier in the Tuck MBA program, before they had chosen summer jobs, and certainly before they had chosen courses in the second year.

As a result of this demand, we designed a more general Career Assessment and Feedback program for entering MBA students. Ninety percent of the first-year class chose to participate. They filled out several questionnaires on their personal history and job preferences. They also took a number of personality tests to help them assess such diverse qualities as their motivation, general style of coping with pressure, interpersonal behavior, and capacity to deal with stress. After this information had been collected, a trained psychologist gave each person a clinical interview. At that time, students were given feedback from the various personality assessment instruments and had the opportunity to discuss the implications of these psychological findings as they related to job selection and performance. Students were then given recommendations to help them capitalize on their strengths and deal with their weaknesses. In some cases, follow-up programs were developed to help students improve their listening skills, their ability to make presentations, or their ability to cope with pressure.

While the short-term goal of the project was to help students make realistic and appropriate choices for summer jobs, the long-term goal was to help them gain a self-awareness that would allow them to develop and use their full potential in whatever jobs they chose after graduation. The objective was to help students gain sufficient self-understanding so they could mobilize their strengths to deal with both problems and people in their organizations; at the same time, we wanted them to be aware of their weaknesses.

The importance of being aware of weaknesses is illustrated in the case of a young manager in strategic planning who tended to lose his long-range perspective whenever he was under pressure. Why this happened to him and what he could do to overcome the problem was the central focus of his feedback interview. Such problems are often the result of subtle features of the individual's personality of which he or she is unaware. As in the case of negotiators, once people become aware of some of the unconscious causes of their problems, they are more likely to be able to handle them constructively.

Appendix I

Summary of the Tests Used in Assessment

1. *Thematic Apperception Test.* Participants study a series of pictures and comment on what images the pictures evoke for them. Such imagery reflects underlying needs. Of particular interest in the context of negotiation are the need for power (the need to feel in control of relationships and not feel dominated by others) and the need for affiliation (the extent to which the individual will sacrifice immediate gain in order to preserve and improve the relationship with others).

2. *Rorschach Test.* The clinician observes how participants respond to the classic inkblots. Responses to these ambiguous stimuli reflect how participants characteristically perform in conceptual problem-solving situations. The test is therefore obviously relevant to the problem-solving aspect of the negotiation process.

Participants' interpretations of the inkblots provide insights about whether they tend to focus on "the big picture" or on small detail. Those who rely on their intuitive sense of the whole must become aware of the dangers of overlooking vital components of a negotiated agreement. Opposite types must be wary of becoming hung up on small details of the agreement at some sacrifice to the total package.

The Rorschach test also measures creativity. People who provide novel responses are likely to be innovative in the search for clever integrative solutions; those who are not particularly creative may be well-advised to involve others in brainstorming ideas for solutions.

Finally, the Rorschach can even provide insights as to how emotions—such as anger and anxiety—evoke defenses that in turn affect problem-solving ability. For example, anxiety gives some people "tunnel vision" in which anxious negotiators fail to see the rich array of alternatives available to them. Individuals who become aware of this tendency can make a point of "thinking out loud" in the presence of colleagues, friends, or consultants, to help them overcome tunnel vision.

3. *Bem Sex-Role Inventory.* This test shows whether participants have predominantly masculine or feminine tendencies. Our own research (Greenhalgh and Gilkey, 1986) shows these tendencies to be related to fundamentally different approaches to negotiating. Masculine negotiators tend to have a short-term, winner-takes-all, dominating approach, whereas feminine negotiators tend to have a long-term, relationship-preserving, nurturing approach. It is obviously crucial for negotiators to be aware of their own tendencies and to make adaptations to others having opposite tendencies.

4. *Empathy Measures.* Two tests were used to determine the extent to which participants are attuned to the people with whom they are dealing. The first, Perspective Taking Ability, measures the cognitive dimension of empathy—the extent to which the participant takes into account the other negotiator's point of view. The second, Empathic Concern, measures the emotional dimension—the extent to which the participant identifies with the other negotiator's feelings. Because a central aspect of negotiation is responding to the other person's needs, empathic tendencies are vitally important.

5. *Interpersonal Orientation.* Less specific but closely related to the empathy measures is Interpersonal Orientation. People who score high on this dimension are interested in and reactive to other people. They tend to take others' behavior very personally. They are highly sensitive to others' cooperativeness and competitiveness, the relative power and dependencies in relationships, and the fairness of exchanges. By contrast, people who score low on this dimension tend to be unresponsive to interpersonal aspects of negotiations. They focus instead on their own gain with little concern for the other party's outcome, approach, or fair-

ness. Participants scoring on either extreme need to be counseled as to the potential hazards of their predispositions. The high scorers' tendency to take the other negotiator's behavior very personally can get in the way of a productive, ongoing relationship, whereas the insensitivity of the low scorers can impede the development of that relationship.

6. *Assertiveness.* Assertiveness is the ability to be firm in pursuing one's interests. People who score low on this dimension do not know how to insist that their interests be given adequate consideration without offending the other, and are consequently anxious and vulnerable to exploitation. This test is therefore a good diagnostic tool to identify those who need coaching in self-assertion tactics (such as avoiding the use of powerless speech, and facilitating face-saving when refusing to comply with another person's attempt to influence them).

7. *Leadership Opinion Questionnaire.* This test measures two orientations in a leader's relationship to others that are applicable to understanding negotiators' relationships to others. Someone whose focus is on "structure" gives attention to the task at hand, concentrating on the content of the negotiation; someone whose focus is on "consideration" gives attention to the relationship, concentrating on the process of the negotiation. It is important to know whether a negotiator has a tendency to focus on one at the expense of the other. An ideal negotiator is, perhaps, one who can give both dimensions equal emphasis.

8. *Locus of Control.* This test measures whether participants generally believe that their actions give them some control over what happens in their lives, (internals) or believe that luck or other forces determine their fate (externals). As a measure of the general feeling of power versus powerlessness, one would expect an effect on people's attitudes toward negotiation. For example, internals might be likely to initiate solutions, to persist in pursuing their interests, and to display self-confidence and a positive outlook in negotiations. At the extreme, however, internals can be overly controlling and abrasive. They can even become overwhelmed with the burden of negotiations: Because they believe so strongly in their own efficacy, extreme internals feel singularly responsible for

outcomes, and as a result, are unable to delegate responsibility to other members of the negotiating team. Others become discouraged at their lack of involvement and the extreme internals become frenzied because the entire burden rests on their shoulders. By contrast, extreme externals would be likely to react to others' initiatives, give in easily, and have a fatalistic outlook in negotiations. At the extreme, externals can be helpless and apathetic, and avoid conflict.

9. *Conflict Resolution Mode.* This self-appraisal measure provides an assessment of a person's approach to conflict on five different dimensions: Competing, Collaborating, Compromising, Accommodating, and Avoiding. The five separate scores can be used to create a profile that can help participants identify their dominant approaches to dealing with conflict and consider which particular modes they might be overutilizing or underutilizing. •

References

Fisher, R. and Ury, W.L. *Getting to YES: Negotiating Agreement Without Giving In.* Boston: Houghton Mifflin, 1981.

Greenhalgh, L. and Gilkey, R.W. "Our Game, Your Rules: Developing Effective Negotiating Approaches." In *Not as Far as You Think: The Realities of Working Women,* edited by L. Moore. Lexington, Mass.: Lexington Books, 1986.

Lewicki, R.L. and Litterer, J.L. *Negotiation.* Homewood, IL.: Irwin, 1982.

Raiffa, H. *The Art and Science of Negotiation.* Cambridge, Mass.: Harvard University Press, 1982.

Rubin, J.Z. and Brown, B.R. *The Social Psychology of Bargaining and Negotiation.* New York: Academic Press, 1975.

Thomas, K. "Conflict and Conflict Management." In *The Handbook of Industrial and Organizational Psychology,* edited by M.D. Dunnette. Chicago: Rand McNally, 1975.

Walton, R.E. and McKersie, R.B. *A Behavioral Theory of Labor Negotiations.* New York McGraw-Hill, 1965.

*　　*　　*

Roderick Gilkey is Associate Professor of Management at the School of Business Administration, Emory University, Atlanta, Georgia. He is co-author of the forthcoming book on mergers and acquisitions, *Joining Forces.*

Leonard Greenhalgh is Associate Professor at the Amos Tuck School of Business Administration, Dartmouth College. He is co-author of "The Effects of Negotiator Preferences, Situational Power, and Negotiator Personality on Outcomes of Business Negotiations" in the *Academy of Management Journal,* Vol. 28 (1985) 9–33.

Study Questions

1. What is the advantage (in negotiation) of self-awareness with regard to certain personality traits?

2. Briefly describe negotiation-relevant "personality" tests that are available to the would-be negotiator (see appendix).

Breaking Away From Subtle Biases

J. William Breslin

"I have a bias which leads me to believe in the essential goodness of my fellow man, which leads me to believe that no problem of human relations is ever unsolvable."
—*Ralph Bunche*

[From remarks made at a May 9, 1949, testimonial in honor of Mr. Bunche, held in New York City and sponsored by the American Association for the United Nations.]

Few people would question the wisdom of the particular kind of bias advocated by Ralph Bunche, whose determined humanism was one of the hallmarks of a life of accomplishment. Some might carp that there are individuals, nations, and organizations which are *not* essentially good, and that any attempt at interaction with them is fruitless. That would miss the point of Bunche's eloquent advice, for it assumes failure even before any kind of human interaction is attempted. If one has complete contempt for the other side, denying them any shred of humanity, then there really isn't much point in even attempting communication. The optimist—and the practical negotiator—rejects that stance, recognizing that solutions to conflict begin with talking, an acknowledgment of the common humanity we all share. That simple nonprejudicial act, which is surely not easy to achieve in all circumstances, is a prerequisite for negotiation to occur.

In addition to dealing with our perceptions about others, negotiators must also be concerned about the prejudices others have for or against us when they come to the table. For example, any Iranian-American negotiating relationship in 1989 is certainly colored by the very public fear and loathing the governments of both nations have displayed toward one another in recent years. Millions of Iranians view the United States as the "Great Satan," while Americans perceive Iran as a bloodthirsty outlaw nation. Each nation has occasionally succeeded in humiliating the other on the world stage, and such insults are difficult both to forgive and forget. Thus, any sort of dealings between Americans and Iranians are likely to be strongly influenced by the excess baggage of prejudice each side currently bears for the other. The same could be said for a couple in the throes of a bitter divorce or for the main actors in a strife-filled labor and management negotiation.

Past histories of anger and dissension result in clearcut "us vs. them" and "them vs. us" prejudices that are generally easy to identify in a negotiating relationship. Because this form of prejudice is a known factor in a relationship, dealing with it is relatively simple. However, there are other, more subtle forms of bias that often cloud negotiations, potentially posing an even greater threat to the chances of a good settlement than those caused by "upfront" prejudice. One such type of prejudice was explored during an exercise at the 1988 Salzburg (Austria) Seminar on the theory and practice of the international negotiation process. The exercise, although it was only a small component of the curriculum for the full two-week session in Salzburg, provided a dramatic jumping-off point for a discussion of the unconscious biases negotiators bring with them to the table.

Briefly, the fifty Salzburg Fellows were divided into small groups of roughly similar (in some cases, *very* roughly similar) national and/or ethnic backgrounds. Since the number of Fellows was limited and time likewise was in short supply, some decisions on group formation were arbitrary—e.g., a Sudanese and a Ugandan composed a group representing all Sub-Saharan nations; an American of Chinese descent, a Thai, a Malaysian, and a Singapore national represented "Asians."

Perceptions

The small groups were then asked to meet for about fifteen minutes and develop a list of several stereotypic characteristics that people from other nations and cultures have about them. The lists would not be a description of legitimate differences in national negotiation styles; rather, they were to be an assessment of how others perceived them simply because they belonged to that particular grouping. In most cases, the assumptions included negative characteristics. Following is a sampling of the lists of stereotypes drawn up by the various groups:

Austrians: Friendly, sloppy, conservative, stubborn, culture-loving.

Mediterraneans: Warm-hearted, "Latin lovers," emotional, tendency toward procrastination, not punctual, disorganized, individualists, good businesspeople.

Sub-Saharan Africans: Mediocre and second-rate, emotional, irrational, easy-going and lazy, possessing more physical abilities than mental.

Central Americans: Idealistic, impractical, disorganized, unprepared, stubborn in arguments, flowery in style.

British: Old-fashioned, arrogant, reserved, eccentric, self-deprecating, fair, "generally British, really."

Irish: Fast-talking, good for a laugh but not reliable, simple but shrewd, quarrelsome and argumentative, good "social grease" (though not with each other) but not to be taken seriously.

Levantine (Lebanon, Syria, and Palestine): Violent—they're all terrorists; racist, aggressive, indecisive, irrational and temperamental; emotional, impulsive, and romantic; traditional and backward, illiterate, and primitive in social relations; hospitable "to the point of insanity" and naive.

Americans: Arrogant, impatient, direct and blunt, naive, generous, friendly and tolerant; self-critical; individualistic; risk-takers; idealistic; materialistic; domineering and aggressive.

Asians: Reserved, not verbose; careful; less open than others; mandate is limited by a hierarchical seniority system; conflict-avoiding; stress importance of personal relationships; shrewd and alert.

Israelis: Tough, single-minded, and well-connected; clever; self-righteous; cunning; ostracized; paranoid.

Germans: Disciplined and hardworking; rigid; well-organized but fanatic at times; keen to learn others' opinions of them; dominating and imposing; adhere to principles; stubborn.

Dutch: Reliable, thorough, and direct; too serious; inflexible; not very creative; tolerant.

A Fact of Life

When the "Sub-Saharan African" group reported that the stereotypic perception of their group was as "mediocre and second-rate . . . easygoing and lazy," there were several gasps from the other Salzburg Fellows. "That is definitely *not* the case," one of the Fellows remarked a bit angrily. "We are all internationalists here—there's no place for that kind of prejudice in international relations."

At the Salzburg Seminar, that is certainly true. However, the exercise—which was not intended as a scientific study of perceived biases—did effectively make the point that negotiators believe such biases do exist in some negotiating forums. Whether we like it or not, prejudicial stereotyping, on the basis of national origin, gender, occupation, or some other characteristic, is a fact of life. So too is the perception of such prejudice, an assumption most negotiators bring with them to the table. Such an assumption itself is a form of bias— "They won't listen to me because of what I represent." That perception is likewise damaging, and can be self-defeating as well.

In the discussion that followed the exercise, several practical suggestions were made to help negotiators break away from prejudicial stereotyping. Much of the advice centered on focusing always on the individual, not the group he or she may represent by virtue of ethnic background, race, or gender. It was pointed out that differences within particular groups are often far greater than differences between groups; thus, an individual may or may not exhibit behavior that fulfills the perceived stereotype of his or her group. Increased, productive conflict among different groups was another means suggested to combat stereotyping. If representatives of various groups learn more about one another, assumptions—particularly negative ones—will have less of an influence.

Perhaps the most valuable advice given was to urge individuals to be aware of the fact that they may be guilty of stereotyping or victimized by it. Stereotyping is often done unconsciously, and becomes an ingrained, unnoticed practice. Such biases are particularly deadly because they predispose a negotiator to view people as the problem, not as colleagues who work together to resolve a problem. •

Notes

1. The Salzburg Seminar is an independent, nonprofit educational organization that annually offers a series of seminars on topics of world significance at the Schloss Leopoldskron in Salzburg, Austria. Fellows invited to participate in these seminars are generally midcareer professionals who are already prominent or display promise in their respective fields.

"Negotiation Theory and Practice: Political Differences" took place May 22–June 4, 1989, in Salzburg with a faculty that included Jeffrey Z. Rubin of Tufts University, chair, Victor Kremenyuk of the Institute of USA and Canada Studies, Moscow; Roger Fisher and Bruce M. Patton of Harvard Law School; Louis Sohn of the University of Georgia; Pauline Neville-Jones, Britain's economic minister in Bonn, Federal Republic of Germany; and Howard

Raiffa of the Harvard Business School. Fifty diplomats, educators, and business executives participated as Fellows in this seminar, which was the first in a three-year sequence of negotiation studies that is jointly being sponsored by the Program on Negotiation at Harvard Law School and the Salzburg Seminars. Howard Raiffa is serving as chair of the 1989 seminar, focused on international business disputes, and Lawrence Susskind of the Massachusetts Institute of Technology is serving as chair of the 1990 seminar, focused on the negotiation of international environmental conflicts.

A report on the 1988 Salzburg Seminar, entitled "Negotiation Theory and Practice: Political Differences" is available as Working Paper no. 89-3 of the Program on Negotiation at Harvard Law School. To obtain a copy, contact the Clearinghouse of the Program on Negotiation, 513 Pound Hall, Harvard Law School, Cambridge, Mass. 02138.

* * *

J. William Breslin is Director of Publications for the Program on Negotiation at Harvard Law School.

Study Questions

1. What was the purpose of the stereotype lists conducted by fifty Salzburg Fellows?

2. List three practical suggestions to help negotiators break away from prejudicial stereotyping.

The Machiavellis Among Us

Richard Christie

Because this is to be asserted in general of men, that they are ungrateful, fickle, false, cowardly, covetous, and as long as you succeed they are yours entirely; they will offer you their blood, property, life and children when the need is far distant; but when it approaches they turn against you . . . and men have less scruple in offending one who is beloved than one who is feared. For love is preserved by the link of obligation which, owing to the baseness of men, is broken at every opportunity for their advantage; but fear preserves you by the dread of punishment which never fails.

The Prince (XVII)
Niccolo di Bernardo Machiavelli

The use of guile and deceit to influence and control others is a popular theme in myth and folklore throughout history. Political theorists in all ages and countries have been fascinated by the topic even in cultures as remote as those of ancient China and India. For example, the Arthasastra of Kautilya gives rulers very detailed advice on espionage: who should be kept under surveillance, what roles spies should take, how they should be paid, how to verify the accuracy of their reports, how to keep from being stabbed while one is busy in the harem and so on. He even discussed the use of classmates as spies—more than two millennia before the FBI.

Kautilya's advice to rulers suggests that India in 300 B.C. would have made Machiavelli's Florence in the 1500s look like a kindergarten. Yet it is Machiavelli we remember for his cynical view of man and the way in which man should be manipulated. This may be unfair, and in fact eminent historians are in violent disagreement about Machiavelli's writings. Mattingly Garrett, an American, has argued convincingly that *The Prince* was written as political satire. G. P. Gooch, an Englishman, felt that Machiavelli was unfair to mankind because

he saw a limited portion of the vast field of experience. And the German Friedrich Meinecke thought that Machiavelli rose to the highest ethics in advocating that a prince behave unlawfully cruelly and shamefully for the sake of the state.

Thinkers

My interest in Machiavellianism began some 15 years ago when I was puzzling over the nature of individuals who are effective in manipulating others. At the time I was at the Center for Advanced Study in the Behavioral Sciences (Stanford) for a year with nothing to do but think great thoughts. To relieve anxiety over this ominous responsibility my fellow thinkers and I formed work groups on various topics. Some six of us met to discuss the psychology of leaders—manipulators—having discovered that most of the literature was on followers—the manipulated.

Our early conversations led to four hunches about the perfect manipulator:

1. He is not basically concerned with morality in the conventional sense.
2. He is basically cool and detached with other people. Once a person becomes emotionally involved with another person it is difficult to treat him as an object.
3. He is more concerned with means than ends, thus more interested in conning others than in what he is conning them for. Good manipulators therefore come in all ideological colors.
4. He is not pathologically disturbed nor would he have clinical symptoms of neurosis or psychosis. The manipulator must be able to function successfully in the real world and thus must have an undistorted view of reality. If anything, he would be overrational in dealing with others.

Scale

To get some ideas for a test that could identify this ideal type we examined the writings of power theorists throughout history. Viewed in this broad perspective Machiavelli is not unique. He differs from other power theorists in being explicit in the assumptions he made about human nature. Most political theorists or philosophers base their prescriptions on implicit assumptions; namely that man is basically weak and gullible and a rational man takes advantage of the foibles of others. Machiavelli's essays in *The Prince* and the *Discourses* each illustrated a particular point.

This explicitness enabled us to construct a scale. Some of the items we chose for it came directly from his essays with slight updating such as: *Most men forget more easily the death of their father than the loss of their property.* Some comments we reversed to avoid wholesale agreement or disagreement; for example, his reflection on man's cowardice became *Most men are brave.* Finally, we invented some new statements that we felt Machiavelli would have approved, such as *Barnum was right when he said there's a sucker born every minute.*

Camouflage

After pretesting, revising and eliminating some of our original 71 statements, we ended up with 20 items: 10 worded in a pro-Machiavelli direction and 10 in an anti-Machiavelli direction. This balanced scale, our fourth variation on the theme, was dubbed Mach IV.

However, many persons are reluctant to agree unequivocally with Machiavellian statements even if they believe in them because in our culture agreement with Machiavellianism has low social desirability. Thus we constructed another form of the scale (Mach V) to minimize this effect, using the same 20 items.

This done we began studies that attempted to relate the Mach scales to other pencil-and-paper tests, and to identify the kinds of persons most likely to agree with Machiavelli's precepts. We found:

1. Males are generally more Machiavellian than females.
2. High Machs do *not* do better than Low Machs on measures of intelligence or ability.
3. High Machs though they are detached from others are not pathologically so, at least as measured by the Minnesota Multiphasic Personality Inventory psychopath scale or Lykken's sociopath scale.
4. Machiavellianism is not related to authoritarianism although superficially it seems that it should be. We decided that there is a basic philosophical difference between these two orientations: the moralistic authoritarian says, "People are no damn good *but they should be*;" the Machiavellian says, "People are no damn good *so why not take advantage of them*?"
5. High Machs are more likely to be in professions that primarily control and manipulate people. Lawyers, psychiatrists, and behavioral scientists, for example (including social psychologists), are more Machiavellian than accountants, surgeons, and natural scientists.
6. Machiavellianism is not related to a respondent's occupational status or education, marital status, birth order, his father's socioeconomic position, or most other demographic characteristics. We base these conclusions on results from a representative national sample of adults from another study of thousands of college students, and findings from a variety of nonstudent samples by other investigators.
7. On a societal level, industrialization and urbanization apparently contribute to the emergence of Machiavellianism. Survey studies have shown that High Machs are likely to come from urban rather than rural backgrounds. In addition, young adults have higher Mach scores than older adults, perhaps because they grew up in a period of transition toward a cosmopolitan society.

Global

In fact, studies in the United States and in other cultures indicate that increased cosmopolitanism is creating a generation of Machiavellis—worldwide. Armando de Miguel gave a Spanish version of Mach V to 15 groups of Spanish students from nine provinces and found that scores were highly related to the degree of industrialization of the provinces these students were from. Lois Oksenberg translated Mach IV into Mandarian Chinese and gave it to high school students in Hong Kong. She found that those attending a westernized school, where the language of instruction was English and where the curriculum followed the British system, scored higher on Machiavellianism than students attending a traditional (Confucian) Chinese high school.

A Machiavellianism score, of course, represents only the degree to which a person believes that people in general are manipulable. He does not necessarily claim that *he* would, or does, manipulate. However, we inferred that agreement

A Test: Are you Machiavellian?

	Disagree		Neutral	Agree	
	A Lot	A Little		A Little	A Lot
1. The best way to handle people is to tell them what they want to hear.	1	2	3	4	5
2. When you ask someone to do something for you, it is best to give the real reasons for wanting it rather than giving reasons which might carry more weight.	1	2	3	4	5
3. Anyone who completely trusts anyone else is asking for trouble.	1	2	3	4	5
4. It is hard to get ahead without cutting corners here and there.	1	2	3	4	5
5. It is safest to assume that all people have a vicious streak and it will come out when they are given a chance.	1	2	3	4	5
6. One should take action only when sure it is morally right.	1	2	3	4	5
7. Most people are basically good and kind.	1	2	3	4	5
8. There is no excuse for lying to someone else.	1	2	3	4	5
9. Most men forget more easily the death of their father than the loss of their property.	1	2	3	4	5
10. Generally speaking, men won't work hard unless they're forced to do.	1	2	3	4	5

Check the point on the scale that most closely represents your attitude. To find your Mach score, add the numbers you have checked on questions 1, 3, 4, 5, 9, and 10. For the other four questions, reverse the numbers you checked—5 becomes 1, 4 is 2, 2 is 4, 1 is 5. Total your 10 numbers. This is your score. The National Opinion Research Center, which used this short form of the scale in a random sample of American adults, found that the national average is 25.

with such cynical views of human nature might go along with the emotional detachment and amoral attitude for successful deception.

Cheaters

Ralph Exline and his colleagues constructed a devious experiment that piqued our curiosity. Exline used a confederate—who posed as another subject—to induce individual subjects to cheat on a test. The experimenter then returned for a post-test interview, during which the eye movements of the subjects were recorded. The experimenter first expressed surprise at the subjects' unusually good performances on the test, then became suspicious, and finally accused the subjects of cheating. In this stressful confrontation, subjects who had scored high on Mach IV resisted confessing. They also looked the experimenter in the eye significantly longer while denying that they had cheated than low-scoring subjects did.

Money

This defensive maneuver appeared to be consistent with what we might expect from a good manipulator and it suggested that there were behavioral correlates of Machiavellian attitudes. Would High Machs behave just as predictably when they had the opportunity for aggressive rather than defensive manipulation?

To find out, Florence Geis and I did an experiment we came to call the $10 game. Three subjects—with high, middle, and low scores on the Mach scales—took seats around a table. We placed 10 $1 bills on the table with the following simple instructions: any *two* of the players could divide the money between themselves in any fashion—five and five, six and four, eight and two, etc. The game would end when two of the subjects came to a final decision, with the crucial stipulation that no agreement could be made to cut the third person in after the session. Theoretically this is an endless game: the excluded person can always break any tentative agreements by offering one of the other two a better deal. And on and on the game goes.

When we started we had no notion how long the subjects would sit, dividing and redividing the dollars. It turned out that the game, far from being endless, varied in duration from 15 seconds to 15 minutes. The High Mach was in the winning combination in every group. Overall, High Machs won significantly more money than would be expected by chance. In this case, their winning was due to their persistence and the reluctance of the Low Machs to hassle over money.

Miss Rheingold

High Machs impressed us as being much more curious about the nature of our experiments than Low Machs did. They asked more questions about the ground rules and in general seemed to case the experimental situation with an eye to taking maximum advantage of it. We began to wonder: were they more attuned to subtle cues in the environment?

Virginia Boehm and I attempted to answer this question in our Miss Rheingold experiment. Perhaps you remember the Miss Rheingold contest. For over 20 years the Liebmann Breweries annually selected six young ladies to vie for the honor of being used in promotional advertising the following year. Before the contest was ended, some 20 million votes per year were being cast.

We decided to use these pictures in our experiment partly on the basis of a grocery clerk's remark that he could always pick the winner.

This seemed highly unlikely; the brewery selected fresh-faced, wholesome types who might have been the proverbial girl next door, and it was hard to tell one from another. For this reason, the pictures appeared to be a good way of testing whether High Machs were more perceptive of subtle cues. If so, they should learn more quickly than Low Machs to identify winners.

So we obtained color photographs of the contestants for the preceding 20 years, and made slides of the six girls for each year. We presented the slides in chronological order, and after each exposure, respondents guessed the winner and runner-up. We gave them feedback about the identities of the winners after they made their choices.

To our surprise, there was no difference between High Machs and Low Machs in learning to identify the winners. All respondents chose the winner with greater-than-chance accuracy on the first block of 10 trials, and made a much greater number of correct choices on the second block of 10.

Parameters

Why did degree of Machiavellianism make a difference in the $10 game but not in the Miss Rheingold contest? Florence Geis and I have since analyzed some 50 laboratory studies and have found three parameters that determine whether Machiavellianism is salient. High Machs make out better when three crucial conditions are met:

1. When the laboratory interaction is face-to-face with another person.
2. When there is latitude for improvisation; that is the subject has a chance to respond freely and is not restricted to pushing buttons or taking tests.
3. When the situation permits the arousal of emotions; that is, where the experiment has serious consequences. Playing for money rather than say points is an example.

Of the 50 Machiavelli experiments that we tabulated, High Machs were more likely to "win"—that is, get more money or points, con someone else, or otherwise perform successfully—when—all three of these conditions are met. They did not win when the conditions were absent.

It became clear why High Machs won consistently in the $10 game but not the Miss Rheingold contest. In the latter case, there was no interaction since all subjects responded to pictures. There was no latitude for improvisation since the choice was limited to one of six pictures per year. There was no competition with other subjects and no reward, except self-satisfaction for improving one's guesses. And the stimuli were likely to arouse much emotional involvement since the young ladies were characterized by a bland homogenized wholesomeness. The money game, however, met all three conditions.

Cool

Other experimental studies have shown that the High Machiavellian is extremely resistant to social influence, although he can be persuaded by rational arguments; he appraises a situation logically and cognitively rather than emotionally; and he tends to initiate and control the structure of the situation when possible. The cool syndrome is his trademark.

The Low Machiavellian by contrast is the perfect soft touch. He is susceptible to social influence he empathizes with others and he tends to accept the existing definitions of the situation. Far from being cool, he is warm and gets caught up in ongoing human interaction.

Geis and I have the impression that the High Machiavellian is an effective manipulator *not* because he reads the other person and takes advantage of his weakness, but because his insensitivity to the other person permits him to bully his way through in pursuit of coolly rational goals. The Low Mach's empathic ability prevents him from being detached enough to take advantage of the other.

Geis and I concluded that Machiavellianism shows up as an interaction between some enduring interpersonal orientation and specified kinds of situations. We then began to wonder about the genesis of such a manipulative style—how soon it appears in children and how it is acquired.

Susan Nachamie ingeniously constructed a Kiddie-Mach scale—modified Mach IV items—for use with elementary-school children, and gave it to a ghetto-school's sixth-graders (mostly of Chinese, black and Puerto

	Number of Parameters Present			
High Machs win	0	1	2	3
High Mach don't win	0	5	7	13
	11	8	5	1

Total: 50 studies

Rican parentage). The children played a dice game that provided immediate payoffs in M&M candies. The game matrix was asymmetric, so that successful bluffing and challenging were rewarded disproportionately. Children with High Mach scores won significantly more M&Ms than those with low scores.

Crackers

Dorothea Braginsky administered a modified version of the scale to fifth grade children in two small Northeastern cities. Those scoring high and low on the test were chosen as subjects, and the middle scorers were used as targets. Braginsky was introduced as a home economist working for a large bakery that was testing a new health cracker—actually a cracker soaked in quinine. After each child had fully savored the bitterness he rated the cracker's flavor on a graphic rating scale and was then given water and chocolate to help kill the taste. (A few children who said they liked the cracker were not used in the rest of the study.)

Braginsky told the children that although they did not like the cracker, it had been found that sometimes if people ate enough crackers they developed a fondness for them. She offered the children a chance to help her by asking each to persuade another student (the Middle-Mach target) to eat as many crackers as possible. For this help, she said, she would give the child one nickel for every cracker he could persuade the target to eat.

Needless to say, the High-Mach children talked the targets into eating over twice as many crackers as the Low Machs did. Interestingly there were no sex differences in scores or persuasive ability.

Parents

Machiavellianism apparently does exist in nascent form in preadolescence. Do the children acquire this orientation by modeling themselves after their manipulative parents?

Braginsky obtained Mach-IV and -V scores on the parents of some two-thirds of the children. To her surprise, she found that consistently Low Mach parents had children who were significantly higher on her version of the Kiddie-Mach scale. The children who were more successful in pushing noxious crackers came from Low-Mach parents. This finding seemed to contradict much current research in developmental psychology—and theory that emphasizes the importance of identification with adults (usually parents). How do we account for this?

An infant sends out many signals, from coos to cries, to bring his needs to the attention of a responsible adult, most often the mother. Some of these behaviors are successful, others are not; and those that are rewarded with the mother's attention are more quickly learned. Mothers, of course, vary in their degree of Machiavellianism; some are more manipulable than others: We would therefore predict that the small children of Low-Mach mothers are able to get away with a greater variety of manipulative actions than children of High-Mach mothers.

A preliminary check on these speculations has been started by Dora Dien in Japan. She related Machiavellianism scores of a group of mothers to the amount of cheating done by their nursery-school children. Children of Low-Mach mothers did cheat considerably more when they were alone in the laboratory situation. This study is currently being replicated in the United States.

Wrangle

It is remarkable to me that the Mach tests seem simple enough and the meaning universal enough to be readily translated into other languages. In 16th-century Italian, modern English, Mandarin Chinese, or Spanish, Machiavelli's concept of human nature still serves to locate individuals along a continuum of agreement to disagreement with his precepts. Whether his advice to rulers was valid or not, I am not qualified to say. I am content to let historians and politicians wrangle about their interpretation of Machiavelli, secure in my appraisal that he was a most astute observer of man. •

Study Questions

1. What seven generalizations were found with regard to individuals who agree with Machiavellian precepts?

2. How are authoritarians and Machiavellians different?

3. What does the Mach score actually represent?

4. What international findings have emerged with regard to Mach scores and country or education systems?

5. List the three conditions crucial for High Machs to make out better than others.

6. Contrast the typical characteristics of High versus Low Machs.

7. Why do Low Mach parents fairly often have High Mach children?

CASE: Why the Mega-Merger Collapsed: Strong Wills And a Big Culture Gap

Dennis Kneale, Johnnie L. Roberts and Leslie Cauley
Wall Street Journal staff reporters

Mr. Malone's 23 Questions

The final unraveling of Bell Atlantic Corp.'s breathtaking bid to acquire cable titan Tele-Communications Inc. began with Bell Atlantic Chairman Raymond W. Smith poised in front of a television set on Tuesday morning. He was watching C-SPAN.

On-screen, the Federal Communications Commission had just imposed a new 7% reduction in cable subscription rates. Mr. Smith, watching from Bell Atlantic offices in Arlington, Va., shrugged, left the room—and set a numbers-crunching team to work to come up with a new and lower price to offer for TCI.

The next day, in a law office in New York, Mr. Smith and three lieutenants faced off against TCI Chief Executive John C. Malone and four other TCI men, who were braced to resist. By midafternoon, the deal was dead.

And so went one of the largest flame-outs in the history of corporate mergers. Ultimately, the sharply divergent cultures of Bell Atlantic and TCI—and the stubborn convictions of their respective chief executives—worked against the would-be partners in trying to fashion a final deal. The gap proved too difficult to bridge as the deal got snagged on Bell Atlantic's sliding stock price and on concerns over TCI's future cash flow.

In the wake of the collapse, the industry's hellbent rush to wire up America has lost the two champions that were ready to spend the most money, the most quickly, to serve up new interactive services—some $15 billion to $20 billion over five years. Bell Atlantic and TCI now are adrift and separated, despite their avowed belief that they simply couldn't enter the multimedia future without one another's help.

And a future that had envisioned titanic combinations of phone companies and cable giants may get rewritten, creating what one TCI adviser calls "a new paradigm." Instead of gobbling up entire companies, rivals may seek smaller-scale partnerships and technology-sharing pacts along the lines of U S West Inc.'s 25% stake in Time Warner Inc.'s entertainment business. Larger deals won't disappear altogether, but the frenzy to do them will almost certainly abate.

Yet Bell Atlantic's Mr. Smith, for one, had dismissed milder approaches as inefficient and less likely to work when he mounted the TCI deal four months ago.

Laying Blame

Publicly, both companies managed to blame the FCC and Washington—Bell Atlantic in polite tones, TCI in blunter, blistering criticism—for their own failure to complete what could have been a far-reaching deal. Messrs. Smith and Malone say that the parting was friendly, that they admire and like one another, and that they look forward to pursuing joint ventures together, albeit nothing approaching their original hopes.

Both companies are trying to keep their gaze focused on the future. The phone giant, with its prodigious $5 billion in annual cash flow, says it will proceed with plans to deliver home shopping, movies on demand and other interactive services to 1.2 million homes by the end of next year, and to eight million homes by the year 2000. It also wants to pursue programming ventures with TCI's Liberty Media, which owns stakes in cable channels including CNN and TNT; it may, it says, seek separate partners in various markets rather than one grand ally.

And at TCI, potential new deals are expected to be a pressing topic at a board meeting today. Mr. Malone has already intensified his pursuit of a Hollywood studio. One prospect: Sony Corp., which is peddling at least part of its cash-draining entertainment operations, which include the Columbia Pictures and TriStar studios. Mr. Malone has also approached the MCA unit of Matsushita Electric Industrial. "We're already on to the next deal," says one TCI man.

In a conference call yesterday, a buoyant Mr. Malone raised the prospect that TCI might join with an existing partner, QVC Inc. chief Barry Diller, in pursuit of a new deal, now that QVC has lost its fight for Paramount Communications Inc. Added Mr. Malone: "We'll come out of this bigger and better and stronger than ever."

Despite those rosy outlooks, some outsiders ask how two power players could let what some people see as a short-term blip derail such boldly ambitious plans to shape the interactive future.

The business world had been stunned by the notion that Bell Atlantic, a staid and heavily regulated product of the sclerotic Bell System, could dare to acquire TCI, paragon of the bare-knuckle, freewheeling world of cable entrepreneurs.

Mr. Smith had prided himself on his efforts to free his company from the cautious and conservative ways of the past. But old ways die hard. When the two CEOs took the podium Oct. 13 to announce their pairing, Mr. Malone couldn't resist citing Bell Atlantic's "stuck-in-the-mud conservatism" and his hope of transforming it into "a more outspoken, more entrepreneurial enterprise."

According to a person in the TCI camp, Mr. Malone had continuing concerns about the differences in corporate culture. He even drew up a list of 23 questions articulating his concerns. Did Bell Atlantic have the backbone to break its tradition of paying annual dividends? Did it have the stomach for high-growth ventures? Was it committed to leading the way into the interactive era, or was it just giving lip service to the idea?

After the deal was announced, Mr. Malone dispatched aides to grill senior Bell Atlantic executives, who were also asked to name the five most effective top managers and explain why.

The survey was hardly encouraging, according to one person familiar with the exercise. In many instances, according to this person, Bell Atlantic executives could name no more than three highly-effective managers. The bottom-line assessment: Change wouldn't come early, or easy.

The Bickering Begins

The culture clash became evident soon after the deal was announced. The agreement at first blush seemed startlingly simple, even elegant. Bell Atlantic would issue new nondividend shares to pay $1.8 billion for most TCI cable systems, which reach into one-quarter of the nation's 60 million cable homes. Later, the Baby Bell would pay more stock, worth upward of $4 billion, to acquire Liberty Media's enviable stable of cable channel stakes. Bell Atlantic would assume the two cable firms' combined debt of almost $10 billion.

But the dickering started within days of the deal's debut. "There was tension over pricing almost from the start," says one person in the TCI camp.

Mr. Malone, known for renegotiating even after terms have been reached, began pushing for new terms almost immediately, as Bell Atlantic stock slid.

The stock had surged to a high of $67.625 the day after the TCI deal was unveiled, well above the $54 level Bell Atlantic had guaranteed to TCI. But the shares started slipping a day later and dropped below the $60 mark by Dec. 31, never to rebound. (Yesterday, Bell Atlantic shares rose $1.75 to close at $54.50 in composite trading on the New York Stock Exchange, while TCI shares dropped $1.875 in Nasdaq trading to $22.375.)

The slippage made it all the more difficult to put a hard value on the new nondividend shares that Bell Atlantic would use to pay for TCI. The shares would probably trade below the price of regular Bell Atlantic stock, since they would lack the $2.68-a-year dividend—but TCI and Bell Atlantic couldn't agree on just how much lower.

TCI argued the new shares would trade at a deep discount, and therefore Bell Atlantic should have to pay out even more than the 220 million shares it had already pledged for the cable systems. But Bell Atlantic wasn't eager to flood the market with still more shares; it already expected the initial phase of the deal to dilute its earnings per share by upward of 35% for a few years. Draining earnings even more might anger institutional investors and other shareholders, and invite unkind scrutiny from consumer advocates and federal and state regulators.

Shrugging Off Critics

The rough-hewn frontiersmen at TCI were unaccustomed to losing any sleep over such sensitivities, after years of seeing their company vilified in Washington as a monopolist and corporate heavy. Entrepreneurs who had build TCI through brassy tactics and with a prescient eye on the future, Mr. Malone and TCI founder Robert Magness embraced the long-term view and an abiding belief that they could build value.

The TCI men, therefore, were less than entirely sympathetic when their new partners at Bell Atlantic began worrying about the cable company's cloudy near-term outlook for cash flow. Wall Street had some concerns, too. TCI's stock price dropped 26% from the time the Bell Atlantic deal was announced to the day it was scuttled; while that was partly due to Bell Atlantic's own slide, the TCI drop was even sharper than the 21% decline in Bell Atlantic shares.

By the time of the final confrontation this week, the two sides had renegotiated the deal three times. Always, Bell Atlantic's first concern in evaluating each package was how it would play among its various constituencies in Washington, on the state level and on Wall Street.

Bell Atlantic loathed the idea of paying too high a price for TCI in a milieu of uncertainty in Washington over how much cash cable systems would be allowed to generate. TCI had a contrary concern: Should Malone & Co. sell out at a lower price than they deserved during that same short-term period of uncertainty?

Still, the two partners were able to arrive at their fourth and, they hoped, final accord on Monday of this week. Through a complex array of formulas that spanned 50 pages, they agreed that Bell Atlantic would pay about 0.6 share of new nondividend stock for each share of the combined TCI-Liberty, down from an indicated ratio of .65 initially.

That would total 372 million shares of new stock—for everything. At the $53-a-share rate that Bell Atlantic's regular stock had closed at last Friday, that would total $19.7 billion, plus the assumption of $9.6 billion in debt. Put another way, and including debt, the entire price would come in at about $2,000 per TCI cable subscriber, down from $2,350 originally, one knowledgeable executive says.

"We had gotten pretty close," says Lawrence T. Babbio Jr., one of Bell Atlantic's chief negotiators and the chairman of its international businesses. But the two sides left open the opportunity to negotiate further after the FCC decision came out the next day, he says. (The TCI camp disagrees, saying they thought the price was firm and that Bell Atlantic had pledged to absorb any impact of an FCC ruling).

On Tuesday, Mr. Smith and his Bell Atlantic team watched the FCC proceedings live on TV. He had hoped the FCC would only freeze cable rates rather than impose a new cut. When he saw the 7% reduction imposed, "I knew it was going to put us in a difficult situation," he said in an interview yesterday.

Even TCI executives projected the new rate cut would reduce their company's cash flow—by 15%, or about $144 million a year. That might seem less than devastating given that the combined companies would have had annual revenue of $17 billion and cash flow of $6 billion. But the lower rate would have reduced the combined companies' ability to raise new capital by at least $900 million a year, at a time when they were planning to spend billions on the elusive information highway.

Bell Atlantic executives were further spooked by other elements of the FCC action, such as linking future cable-rate increases to inflation and creating new levels of oversight that hadn't existed before. "This was not going to be just a one-time reduction in rates," says Bell Atlantic's Mr. Babbio.

Mr. Malone had put in a call to Mr. Smith immediately after the FCC action appeared on C-SPAN; when they finally talked hours later, the two agreed to meet the next day in New York. Neither said so, but they both knew the deal was on shaky ground.

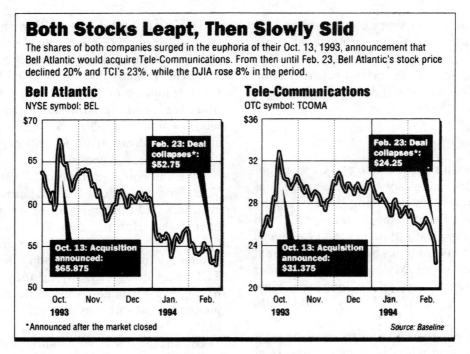

Both Stocks Leapt, Then Slowly Slid

The shares of both companies surged in the euphoria of their Oct. 13, 1993, announcement that Bell Atlantic would acquire Tele-Communications. From then until Feb. 23, Bell Atlantic's stock price declined 20% and TCI's 23%, while the DJIA rose 8% in the period.

Bell Atlantic
NYSE symbol: BEL

Feb. 23: Deal collapses*: $52.75

Oct. 13: Acquisition announced: $65.875

Oct. Nov. Dec. Jan. Feb.
1993 1994

*Announced after the market closed

Tele-Communications
OTC symbol: TCOMA

Feb. 23: Deal collapses*: $24.25

Oct. 13: Acquisition announced: $31.375

Oct. Nov. Dec. Jan. Feb.
1993 1994

Source: Baseline

At this point the two sides diverge in their account of events, and the disagreements raise questions about their repeated claims that they have split amicably.

Mr. Smith's version: The Malone team arrived at the meeting—held at the offices of Bell Atlantic's legal advisers, Skadden, Arps, Slate, Meagher & Flom—and Mr. Malone soon launched into a discourse on why the deal now wouldn't work. Mr. Malone told the Bell Atlantic executives, "You wouldn't be in your right mind if you accepted the current (terms)" that the companies had set on Monday, Mr. Smith says. But, he says, Mr. Malone added that "I cannot budge a nickel."

Mr. Smith says that—still thinking he could salvage the deal—he countered with other ways they might be able to work the numbers. He says he gave up when Mr. Malone's lawyer pulled out an already-prepared press release announcing the deal's collapse.

"At that point, it was pretty clear that John was serious," Mr. Smith says.

The TCI version of events is that it was Mr. Smith who opened with a litany of reasons why the deal in its current version wouldn't work. Mr. Malone took the floor only after becoming convinced that Bell Atlantic was refusing to stick to the previous day's agreement, his supporters say.

As for the press release, one person on the TCI side says it hadn't been drafted for the Wednesday meeting—it was written weeks earlier, when TCI executives thought the deal was in danger of collapsing as the parties missed the first of three deadlines.

"Everyone, in essence, had blessed the deal," says the high-level member of the TCI camp. But "when the FCC announcement came out, [Bell Atlantic executives] were frightened out of their minds."

Mr. Malone was almost as pointed in a conference call with the news media yesterday. He softened some of his previous criticism of the FCC action and said the bottom line on why the deal didn't go through was that Mr. Smith was "unwilling to go forward with a price that was on the table three days ago. We are unwilling to see any reduction in the price."

And the TCI chief executive said his company isn't typically rattled by measures the FCC takes—unlike some of the "Chicken Littles" out there. Mr. Malone further took a shot at the seven Baby Bells as a group: Washington may view TCI as a monopolist, he said, "but these guys have been monopolists for 120 years." •

Study Questions

1. How do the personalities of Malone and Smith affect the cultures (personalities) of TCI and Bell Atlantic respectively?

2. What other factors may affect the cultures (personalities) of TCI and Bell Atlantic?

3. What role did organizational culture (personality) play in the dissolution of the attempted merger of TCI and Bell Atlantic?

4. How could the roles of personality have worked in favor of a TCI and Bell Atlantic merger?

Negotiator Cognition

M. Bazerman

The decision analytic approach to negotiation tells us that it is rational for two parties to strike an agreement whenever a positive bargaining zone exists. Why, then, do actors in such two-party negotiations frequently fail to settle? The decision analytic approach also asserts that our agreements should be fully integrative. Why, then, do most negotiation settlements result in outcomes that are not pareto-efficient?

This chapter explores the ways in which the competitive dynamics of negotiations place cognitive limitations on our abilities to be rational negotiators. Drawing from our earlier discussions of individual limits to rationality and additional research in negotiations, we will explore five key issues that affect our reasoning as negotiators (also referred to as negotiator cognitions): (1) the mythical fixed pie of negotiation, (2) the framing of negotiator judgment, (3) the nonrational escalation of conflict, (4) negotiator overconfidence, and (5) the tendency to ignore the cognitions of others. In the following chapter, each section clarifies how negotiator decision making often differs from a prescriptive analysis of negotiator behavior and discusses how we as negotiators can better respond to these deviations.

Issue 1: The Mythical Fixed Pie of Negotiations

As stated in Chapter 6, integrative agreements are nonobvious solutions to conflict that yield higher joint benefit than purely distributive agreements. However, negotiators often fail to reach the integrative solutions (recall the case of the sisters who fought over the orange). Why is this? Perhaps it is because of the **fixed pie assumption** which represents a fundamental bias in human judgment. That is, negotiators have a systematic intuitive bias that distorts their behavior. When negotiating over an issue, they assume that their interests necessarily and *directly* conflict with the other party's interests.

The fundamental assumption of a fixed pie seems to be rooted in social norms that lead us to interpret most competitive situations as win-lose. This win-lose orientation is manifested in our society in athletic competition, admission to academic programs, corporate promotion systems, and so on. Individuals tend to generalize from these objective win-lose situations and create similar expectations for other situations that are not necessarily win-lose. Faced with a mixed-motive situation requiring both cooperation and competition, it is the competitive aspect that becomes salient, resulting in a win-lose orientation and a distributive approach to bargaining. This, in turn, results in the development of a strategy for obtaining the largest possible share of the perceived fixed pie. Such a focus inhibits the creative problem solving necessary for the development of integrative solutions.

In reality, most conflicts are not purely distributive problems, because most conflicts have more than one issue at stake, with the parties placing different values on the different issues. Once this condition exists, the conflict is objectively no longer a fixed pie. Consider a Friday evening on which you and your spouse are going to dinner and a movie. Unfortunately, you prefer different restaurants and different movies. It is easy to adopt a distributive attitude toward each event to be negotiated. In contrast, if you do not assume a fixed pie, you may find out that you care more about the restaurant selection and your spouse cares more about the movie choice. Similarly, purchasing goods is often treated as a distributive problem. Often, however, a retailer is suddenly willing to reduce the purchase price if payment is made in cash (no receipt, and so on), while you care only about price.

The tendency of negotiators to initially approach bargaining with a mythical fixed pie perception has been documented by Bazerman, Magliozzi, and Neale (1985). Their simulation allowed individuals, acting as buyers and sellers, to complete transactions on a three-issue, integrative bargaining problem. The goal was to complete as many transactions with as many opponents as possible in a fixed amount of time, while maximizing total individual profit. The profit available to sellers and buyers for various levels of the three issues on a per transaction basis is shown in Tables 1a and 1b. Note that buyers achieve their highest profit levels and sellers their lowest profits at the A levels of delivery, discount, and financing; whereas sellers achieve their highest profits and buyers their lowest profits at the I levels. A negotiated transaction consisted of the two parties agreeing to one of the nine levels for each of the three issues. As can be observed, a simple compromise solution of E-E-E results in a $4,000 profit to each side. However, if the parties are able to reach the fully integrative solution of A-E-1 (by trading issues), then each receives a profit of $5,200.

The mythical fixed pie bias argues that negotiators will approach this competitive context with a fixed pie assumption and only relax this assumption when provided with evidence to the contrary. This hypothesis was supported by the results. Figure 1 plots the average of buyer and seller profit of all agreements (sample size equals 942 transactions) reached in each five-minute segment of the market (aggregated across six runs of the market simulation). The diagonal line in this figure shows the joint profits to the two parties if they make simple compromises (for example, E-E-E). The curved line shows the pareto-efficient frontier available to the negotiators. (Recall from Chapter 6 that the pareto-efficient frontier is defined as the set of agreements for which there is no point that would simultaneously improve the outcomes to either or both parties.) This figure shows that negotiators start the free-market simulation by obtaining agreements that would be predicted by a mythical fixed pie hypothesis (that is, the transactions approach the distributive point of $4,000, $4,000). As the negotiators gain experience, however, the myth is disproved, and far greater integrative behavior is observed (the transactions approach the fully integrative point of $5,200, $5,200).

The pervasiveness of the fixed pie perception, as well as the importance of integrative

bargaining, can be seen in the housing market. When interest rates rose dramatically to between 12 percent and 17 percent in 1979, 1980, and 1981, the housing market came to a halt. Sellers continued to expect the value of their property to increase. However, buyers could not afford the monthly payments on houses they aspired to own, due to the drastically higher interest rates. Viewing the problem as a distributive one, buyers could not afford the prices that sellers were demanding. This fixed pie assumption (which was prevalent throughout the industry) led to the conclusion that transactions would not occur until seller reservation points decreased, buyer reservation points increased, interest rates came down, or all three. However, once the industry began to view real estate transactions integratively, some relief was provided. Specifically, sellers cared a great deal about price—partly to justify their past investment. Buyers cared about finding some way to afford a house they aspired to own—perhaps their first house. The integrative solutions were the wide variety of creative financing developments (such as seller financing) of the early 1980s, which allowed sellers an artificially high price in exchange for favorable financing assistance to the buyer. Creative financing integrated the interests of buyers and sellers, rescuing an entire industry from our common fixed pie assumptions.

The mythical fixed pie is also partially responsible for the decline in the U.S. manufacturing sector over the last 20 years. Since management and unions were accustomed to viewing their negotiations as fixed-sum, they never stopped to realize the real loss that might accrue if they failed to reach more integrative agreements. After enough companies went under and enough employees lost their jobs, the two sides realized that worker participation, employee ownership, and flexible work rules were strategies that could make both sides better off. Unfortunately, a crisis from which we may never recover was necessary to get management and union leaders to break their fixed pie assumptions.

The foregoing arguments suggest that while fixed pies do exist, most resolutions depend on finding favorable tradeoffs between negotiators—tradeoffs which necessitate eliminating

Table 1 Buyer and Seller Schedules for Positively and Negatively Framed Negotiations

Table 1a Seller Net Profit Schedule

	Delivery Time		Discount Terms		Financing Terms
A	$ 000	A	$ 000	A	$ 000
B	200	B	300	B	500
C	400	C	600	C	1,000
D	600	D	900	D	1,500
E	800	E	1,200	E	2,000
F	1,000	F	1,500	F	2,500
G	1,200	G	1,800	G	3,000
H	1,400	H	2,100	H	3,500
I	1,600	I	2,400	I	4,000

Table 1b Buyer Net Profit Schedule

	Delivery Time		Discount Terms		Financing Terms
A	$4,000	A	$2,400	A	$1,600
B	3,500	B	2,100	B	1,400
C	3,000	C	1,800	C	1,200
D	2,500	D	1,500	D	1,000
E	2,000	E	1,200	E	800
F	1,500	F	900	F	600
G	1,000	G	600	G	400
H	500	H	300	H	200
I	000	I	000	I	000

Table 1c Seller Expense Schedule (Gross Profit = $8,000)

	Delivery Time		Discount Terms		Financing Terms
A	$-1,600	A	$-2,400	A	$-4,000
B	-1,400	B	-2,100	B	-3,500
C	-1,200	C	-1,800	C	-3,000
D	-1,000	D	-1,500	D	-2,500
E	-800	E	-1,200	E	-2,000
F	-600	F	-900	F	-1,500
G	-400	G	-600	G	-1,000
H	-200	H	-300	H	-500
I	000	I	000	I	000

Table 1d Buyer Expense Schedule (Gross Profit = $8,000)

	Delivery Time		Discount Terms		Financing Terms
A	$000	A	$000	A	$000
B	-500	B	-300	B	-200
C	-1,000	C	-600	C	-400
D	-1,500	D	-900	D	-600
E	-2,000	E	-1,200	E	-800
F	-2,500	F	-1,500	F	-1,000
G	-3,000	G	-1,800	G	-1,200
H	-3,500	H	-2,100	H	-1,400
I	-4,000	I	-2,400	I	-1,600

Source: Bazerman, Magliozzi, and Neale (1985)

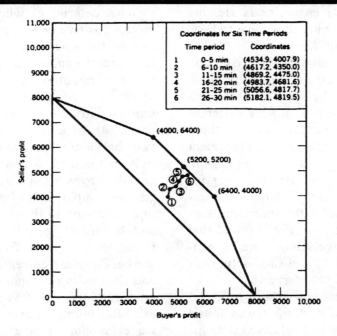

our intuitive fixed pie assumptions. Chapter 5 argues that individuals are often limited in finding creative solutions by the false assumptions that they make. The fixed pie perception is a fundamentally false assumption that hinders finding creative, integrative solutions. A fundamental task in training negotiators lies in identifying and eliminating this false assumption and institutionalizing the creative process of integrative bargaining.

Issue 2: The Framing of Negotiator Judgment

Consider the following two scenarios:

You are a wholesaler of refrigerators. Corporate policy does not allow any flexibility in pricing. However, flexibility does exist in terms of expenses that you can incur (shipping, financing terms, and so on), which have a direct effect on the profitability of the transaction. These expenses can all be expensed in dollar-value terms. You are negotiating a $10,000 sale. The buyer wants you to pay $2,000 in expenses. You want to pay less expenses. When you negotiate the transaction, do you try to minimize your expenses (reduce these losses from $2,000) or maximize net price (or price less expenses—that is, do you increase the net price from $8,000)?

You bought your house in 1983 for $60,000. You currently have the house on the market for $109,900, with a real target of $100,000 (your estimation of the true market value). An offer comes in for $90,000. Does this offer represent a $30,000 gain in comparison with the original purchase price or a $10,000 loss in comparison with your current target?

The answer to the question posed in each scenario is "both." Each is an "Is the cup half full or half empty?" situation. From a rational perspective, and based on our intuition, the difference in the two points of view is irrelevant. However, as described in Chapter 3, Kahneman and Tversky (1979, 1982; Tversky and Kahneman, 1981) have demonstrated that important differences exist in the ways in which individuals respond to questions framed in terms of losses versus gains. This difference is critical to describing negotiator behavior.

To exemplify the importance of "framing" to negotiation, consider the following labor-management situation: The union claims they need a raise to $12 an hour and that anything less represents a loss given current inflation. Management argues that they cannot pay more than $10 an hour and that anything more imposes an unacceptable expense. What if each side had the choice of settling for $11 an hour (a certain settlement) or going to binding arbitration (a risky settlement)? Since each side is viewing the conflict in terms of what they have to lose, following Tversky and Kahneman's (1981) findings, each side is predicted to be risk seeking and unwilling to take the certain settlement. Changing the frame of the situation to a positive one, however, results in a very different predicted outcome. If the union views anything above $10 an hour as a gain, and management views anything under $12 an hour as a gain, then risk aversion will dominate, and a negotiated settlement will be likely. Using an example conceptually similar to the foregoing scenario, Neale and Bazerman (1985) found that negotiators with positive frames are significantly more concessionary and successful than their negatively framed counterparts.

In the study by Bazerman, Magliozzi, and Neale (1985) described earlier, it was found that the frame of buyers and sellers systematically affected their negotiation behavior. Negotiators were led to view transactions in terms of either (1) net profit (gains) or (2) expenses (losses) away from the gross profit of the transactions. The net profit (gain) payoff tables were shown in Tables 1a and 1b. To create a negatively framed, or "losses," condition, these tables were converted into "expenses" that the subject would incur—that would be taken away from the $8,000 gross profit received for each completed transaction. This transformation is shown in Tables 1c and 1d. Since net profit is defined to be equal to gross profit minus expenses, Table 1a and 1b are objectively equivalent to Tables 1c and 1d. For example, the seller's profit for A-E-1 is $5,200, the sum of $0 + $1,200 + $4,000 (Table 1a). In Table 1c, this same transaction would result in expenses of $2,800, the sum of $1,600 + $1,200 + 0. When $2 800 is subtracted from the $8,000 gross profit, the same net $5,200 is received. While both frames of the schedule yield the same objective profit result, positively (gain) framed negotiators experienced the risk aversion necessary to have an incentive to compromise. This incentive to compromise led negotiators with a positive frame to (1) complete a larger number of transactions and (2) obtain greater overall profitability than negotiators with a negative frame.

What determines whether a negotiator will have a positive or negative frame? The answer lies in the selection of a perceptual anchor. Consider the anchors available to a union negotiator in negotiating a wage: (1) last year's wage; (2) management's initial offer, (3) the union's estimate of management's reservation point, (4) the union's reservation point, or (5) your bargaining position which has been publicly announced to your constituency. As the anchor moves from 1 to 5, what is a modest *gain* in comparison to last year's wage is a loss in comparison to the publicly specified goals, and the union negotiator moves from a positive frame to a negative frame. For example, for workers who are currently making $10 an hour and demanding an increase of $2 an hour, a proposed increase of $1 an hour can be viewed as a $1 an hour gain in comparison to last year's wage (anchor 1) or a loss of $1 an hour in comparison to the goals of the union's constituency (anchor 5). In order to avoid the adverse effects of framing, negotiators should always be aware of their frames and examine alternative frames.

A curious, consistent, and robust finding is that buyers tend to outperform sellers in symmetric negotiation experiments (cf. Bazerman et al., 1985; Neale, Huber, and Northcraft, 1987). Given the artificial context of the experiment and the symmetry of the design, there is no logical reason that buyers would do better than sellers. However, Neale and colleagues (1987) found that sellers think about the transaction in terms of gaining resources (how much do I gain by selling the commodity?), whereas buyers view transaction in terms of loss (how much do I have to give up?). As a result, buyers tend to be risk seeking and sellers tend to be risk averse. When a risk-averse party meets with a risks taking party, the risk-seeking party is more willing to risk the agreement by holding out longer, and the risk-averse party must make the additional concession to close the agreement. The critical issue is that there are naturally occurring frames in life. One that has been identified is the differing frames that are created by the buying and selling roles.

It is easy to see that the frames of negotiators can result in the difference between an important agreement and impasse. Both sides in negotiations typically talk in terms of a certain wage or price that they must get—setting a high reference point against which gains and losses are measured. If this occurs, any compromise below (or above) that reference point represents a loss. This perceived "loss" leads negotiators to adopt a negative frame to all compromise proposals, exhibit risk-seeking attitudes, and be less likely to reach settlement.

In addition, framing has important implications for the tactics that negotiators use. The framing effect suggests that in order to induce concessionary behavior in an opponent, a negotiator should always create anchors that lead the opposition to a positive frame and negotiate in terms of what the other side has to gain. In addition, the negotiator should make it clear to the opposition that the opponent is in a risky situation where a sure gain is possible.

Finally, the impact of framing has important implications for mediators. To the extent that the goal is compromise, a mediator should strive to have both parties view the negotiation in a positive frame. This is tricky, however, since the anchor that will lead to a positive frame for one negotiator is likely to lead to a negative frame for the other negotiator. This suggests that when mediators meet with each party separately, they need to present different anchors to create risk aversion in each party. Again, if mediators are to affect the frame, they also want to emphasize the realistic risk of the situation, thus creating uncertainty and leading both sides to prefer a sure settlement.

Issue 3: The Nonrational Escalation of Conflict

Consider the following situation:

It is 1981 PATCO (the Professional Air Traffic Controllers Organization) decides to strike to obtain a set of concessions from the U.S. government. It is willing to "invest" in a temporary loss of pay during the strike in order to obtain concessions. No government concessions result or appear to be forthcoming. PATCO is faced with the option of backing off and returning to work under the former arrangement or increasing their commitment to the strike to try to force the concessions it desires.

In this example, PATCO has committed resources to a course of action. PATCO is then faced with escalating that commitment or backing out of the conflict. This example illustrates the concept of escalation (from Chapter 4) in a competitive situation. The escalation literature predicts that PATCO is far more likely to persist in its course of action than a rational analysis would have dictated—which, in fact, it did.

It is easy to see the process of the nonrational escalation of commitment unfold in a wide variety of actual situations. The negotiation process commonly leads both sides to initially make extreme demands. The escalation literature predicts that if negotiators become committed to these initial public statements, they will nonrationally adopt a nonconcessionary stance. To the extent that negotiators believe that they "have too much invested to quit," inappropriate stubbornness is likely. Further, if both sides incur losses as a result of a lack of agreement (as is the case in a strike), their commitment to their positions is likely to increase, and their willingness to change to a different course of action (that is, compromise) is likely to decrease. For example, it could be argued that in the Malvinas/Falklands conflict, once Argentina had suffered the initial loss of life, it had the information necessary to rationally pursue a negotiated settlement. The escalation literature, in contrast, accurately predicts that the loss of life (a significant commitment to a course of action) would lead Argentina to a further escalation of its commitment not to compromise on the return of the Malvinas to Britain. More recently, the decision of the "hard-liners" in China to fire on the students in the spring of 1989 can be explained in terms of the nonrational escalation of commitment. Virtually all analysts agree that this decision was irrational from any political analysis. However, the "hard-liners" had made public commitments to stop the student protests. When nothing else worked, they escalated their commitment, killed many people, and weakened their political standing within the international community.

One important result from the escalation literature is that the public announcement of one's position increases one's tendency to escalate nonrationally (Staw, 1981). Once the general public (or one's constituency) is aware of the commitment, one is far less likely to retreat from his/her previously announced position. This suggests that escalation can be reduced if negotiators and third parties avoid the formation of firmly set public positions. However, implementation of this recommendation is contradictory to everything known about how negotiators (such as labor leaders, political leaders, representatives of management) behave when they represent constituencies. A firmly set public position is typically perceived as necessary to build constituency support and allegiance. Thus it may be that what is best for the constituency is not necessarily what the constituency rewards.

An understanding of escalation can also be very helpful to a negotiator in anticipating the behavior of an opponent. When will the other party really hold out, and when will it give in? The escalation literature predicts that the other side will hold out when they have "too much invested" in their position to quit. This suggests that there are systematic clues to indicate when you can threaten an opponent and win versus when such threats are likely to simply escalate commitment to prior positions. Strategically, this suggests that a negotiator should avoid inducing any statements or behaviors from an opponent that will create the perception of having too much invested to quit.

Issue 4: Negotiator Overconfidence

Consider the following scenario:

You are an advisor to a major-league baseball player. In baseball, a system exists for resolving compensation conflicts that calls for a player and a team owner who do not agree to submit final offers to an arbitrator. Using final-offer arbitration, the arbitrator must accept one position or the other, not a compromise. Thus, the challenge for each side is to come just a little closer to the arbitrator's perception of the appropriate compensation package than the opposition. In this case, your best intuitive estimate of the final offer that the team owner will submit is a package worth $200,000 per year. You believe that an appropriate wage is $400,000 per year but estimate the arbitrator's opinion to be $300,000 per year. What final offer do you propose?

This scenario sets up a common cognitive trap for negotiators. As we learned in Chapter 2, individuals are systematically overconfident

that their judgments are correct. Thus, they are likely to be overconfident in estimating the position of a neutral third party and in estimating the likelihood that the third party will accept their position. In the baseball example, if the arbitrator's true assessment of the appropriate wage is $250,000, and you believe it to be $300,000, you are likely to submit an inappropriately high offer and overestimate the likelihood that the offer will be accepted. Consequently, the overconfidence bias is likely to lead the advisor to believe that less compromise is necessary than a more objective analysis would suggest.

Farber (1981) discusses the problem of negotiator overconfidence in terms of negotiators' divergent expectations. That is, each side is optimistic that the neutral third party will adjudicate in its favor. Consider the situation in which (1) the union is demanding $8.75 an hour; (2) management is offering $8.25 an hour; and (3) the "appropriate" wage is $8.50 an hour. Farber suggests that the union will typically expect the neutral third party to adjudicate at a wage somewhat over $8.50, while management will expect a wage somewhat under $8.50. Given these divergent expectation, neither side is willing to compromise at $8.50. Both sides will incur the costs of impasse and aggregately do no better through the use of a third party. In the baseball scenario, if one side had a more objective assessment of the opponent's offer and the position of the arbitrator, it could use this information strategically to its advantage in final-offer arbitration.

Research demonstrates that negotiators tend to be overconfident that their positions will prevail if they do not "give in." Neale and Bazerman (1983; Bazerman and Neale, 1982) show that negotiators in final-offer arbitration consistently overestimate the probability that their final offer will be accepted. In laboratory studies in which there was only a 50 percent chance of all final offers being accepted, the average subject estimated that there was a much higher probability that his or her offer would be accepted. In terms of Walton and McKersie's bargaining zone, overconfidence may inhibit a variety of settlements, despite the existence of a positive bargaining zone. If we consider a final offer as a judgment as to how much compromise is necessary to win the arbitration, it is easy to argue that when negotiators are overconfident that a particular position will be accepted, their reservation point becomes more extreme, and their incentive to compromise is reduced. If a more accurate assessment is made, the negotiator is likely to be more uncertain and uncomfortable about the probability of success and is more likely to accept a compromise. Based on the biasing impact of this overconfidence, Neale and Bazerman (1985) found "appropriately" confident negotiators to exhibit more concessionary behavior and to be more successful than overly confident negotiators.

Training negotiators to recognize the cognitive patterns of overconfidence should include the realization that overconfidence is most likely to occur when a party's knowledge is limited. As we learned in Chapter 2, most of us follow the intuitive cognitive rule "When in doubt, be overconfident." This suggests that negotiators should seek objective assessments of worth from a *neutral* party, realizing that this neutral assessment is likely to be systematically closer to the other party's position than the negotiator might have intuitively predicted.

Issue 5: Ignoring the Cognitions of Others

Imagine that you are in a foreign country. You meet a merchant who is selling a very attractive gem. Although you have purchased a few gems in your life, you are far from an expert. After some discussion, you make the merchant an offer that you believe, but that you are not certain, is on the low side. He quickly accepts, and the transaction is completed. How do you feel? Most people would feel uneasy with the purchase after the quick acceptance. This feeling is known as the "winner's curse." Yet why would you voluntarily make an offer that you would not want accepted? Now consider the problem in Exercise 1.

The "Acquiring a Company" exercise is conceptually similar to the gem-merchant problem. In the "Acquiring a Company" exercise, one firm (the acquirer) is considering making an offer to buy out another firm (the target). However, the acquirer is uncertain about the ultimate value of the target firm. It knows only

---

Exercise 1 Acquiring a Company

In the following exercise you will represent Company A (the acquirer), which is currently considering acquiring Company T (the target) by means of a tender offer. You plan to tender in cash for 100% of Company T's shares but are unsure how high a price to offer. The main complication is this: the value of Company T depends directly on the outcome of a major oil exploration project it is currently undertaking. Indeed, the very viability of Company T depends on the exploration outcome. If the project fails, the company under current management will be worth nothing—$0/share. But if the project succeeds, the value of the company under current management could be as high as $100/share. All share values between $0 and $100 are considered equally likely. By all estimates, the company will be worth considerably more in the hands of Company A than under current management. In fact, whatever the ultimate value under current management, the company **will be worth fifty percent more under the management of A than under Company T.** If the project fails, the company is worth $0/share under either management. If the exploration project generates a $50/share value under current management, the value under Company A is $75/share. Similarly, a $100/share value under Company T implies a $150/share value under Company A, and so on.

The board of directors of Company A has asked you to determine the price they should offer for Company T's shares. This offer must be made *now, before* the outcome of the drilling project is known. From all indications, Company T would be happy to be acquired by Company A, *provided it is at a profitable price.* Moreover, Company T wishes to avoid, at all cost, the potential of a takeover bid by any other firm. You expect Company T to delay a decision on your bid until the results of the project are in, then accept or reject your offer before the news of the drilling results reaches the press. Thus, *you (Company A) will not know the results of the exploration project when submitting your price offer, but Company T will know the results when deciding whether or not to accept your offer. In addition, Company T is expected to accept any offer by Company A that is greater than the (per share) value of the company under current management.*

As the representative of Company A, you are deliberating over price offers in the range of $0/share (this is tantamount to making no offer at all) to $150/share. What price offer per share would you tender for Company T's stock?

My Tender Price is: $ _____ per share.

Source: from Samuelson and Baserman (1985)

Figure 2
The distribution of price offers

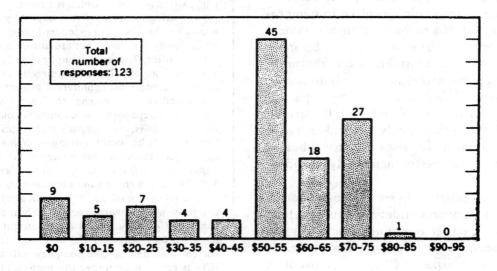

that its value under current management is between $0 and $100, with all values equally likely. Since the firm is expected to be worth 50 percent more under the acquirer's management than under the current ownership, it appears to make sense for a transaction to take place. While the acquirer does not know the actual value of the firm, the target knows its current worth exactly. What price should the acquirer offer for the target?

The problem is analytically quite simple (as will be demonstrated shortly), yet intuitively quite perplexing. The responses of 123 MBA students from Boston University are shown in Figure 2. The table shows the dominant response was between $50 and $75. How is this $50-to-$75 decision reached? One common, but wrong, explanation is that "on average, the firm will be worth $50 to the target and $75 to the acquirer; consequently, a transaction in this range will, on average, be profitable to both parties." Now consider the logical process that a rational response would generate in deciding whether to make an offer of $60 per share:

If I offer $60 per share, the offer will be accepted 60 percent of the time—whenever the firm is worth between $0 and $60 to the target. Since all values are equally likely between $0 and $60 the firm will,

on average, be worth $30 per share to the target when the target accepts a $60 per share offer, and will be worth $45 per share to the acquirer, resulting in a loss of $15 per share ($45 to $60). Consequently, a $60 per share offer is unwise.

It is easy to see that the same kind of reasoning applies to *any* positive offer. On the average, the acquirer obtains a company worth 25 percent less than the price it pays when its offer is accepted. If the acquirer offers $X and the target accepts, the current value of the company is worth anywhere between $0 and $X. As the problem is formulated, any value in that range is equally likely, and the expected value of the offer is therefore equal to $X/2. Since the company is worth 50 percent more to the acquirer, the acquirer's expected value is 1.5($X/2) = 0.75($X)—only 75 percent of its offer price. Thus, for any value of $X, the best the acquirer can do is not to make an offer ($0 per share). The paradox of the situation is that even though in all circumstances the firm is worth more to the acquirer than to the target, any offer above $0 leads to a negative expected return to the acquirer. *The source of this paradox lies in the high likelihood that the target will accept the acquirer's offer when the firm is least valuable to the acquirer—that is, when it is a "lemon"* (Akerlof, 1970).

The answer to this problem is so counterintuitive that only 9 of 123 subjects correctly offered $0 per share. Recent replications with Massachusetts Institute of Technology master's students in management have produced similar results. Finally, even subjects who were paid according to their performance exhibit the same pattern of responses as depicted in Figure 2 (Bazerman and Carroll, 1987).

Most individuals have the analytical ability to follow the logic that the optimal offer is $0 per share. Yet without assistance, most individuals make a positive offer. Thus, individuals systematically exclude information from their decision-making processes that they have the ability to include. They fail to realize that their expected return is *conditional* on an acceptance by the other party, and that an acceptance is most likely to occur when it is least desirable to the negotiator making the offer.

The famous comedian Groucho Marx understood the tendency to ignore the decisions of others. He said that he didn't want to be a member of any club that would have him as a member. Why? Their acceptance of his application told him something about their standards, and if they were so low as to accept him, he didn't want to be a member of that club! The key feature of the "winner's curse" in the bargaining context is that one side often has much better information than the other side, the party with the better information is usually the seller. Although we are all familiar with the slogan "buyer beware," our intuition seems to have difficulty putting this idea into practice when asymmetric information exists. Most people realize that when they buy a commodity they know little about, their uncertainty increases. The evidence presented here indicates that against an informed opponent, our expected return from such a transaction decreases dramatically. Practically, the evidence suggests that people undervalue the importance of getting accurate information when making important transactions. They undervalue a mechanic's unbiased evaluation of a used car, a professional inspector's assessment of a house, or an independent jeweler's assessment of a coveted gem. Thus, the knowledgeable gem merchant will accept your offer selectively, taking the offer when the gem is probably worth less than your estimate. To protect yourself, you need to develop or borrow professional expertise to balance the inequity of information. While the experimental evidence presented was highly artificial, the negative effects of the winner's curse should be considered by any negotiator dealing with a better-informed opponent.

Neale and Bazerman (1983) found that individuals who had a greater tendency to think about the perspective of others were more successful in laboratory negotiations. This focus on the perspective of the other party allowed them to better predict the opponent's goals, expectations, and reservation points. While taking the perspective of the other party is important, most individuals lack sufficient perspective-taking ability (Bazerman and Neale, 1983; Davis, 1981; Bernstein and Davis, 1982). Overall, *negotiators tend to act as if their opponent was a fairly inactive party to the negotiation and systematically ignore valuable information that is available.* Bazerman and Neale (1982) suggest that training mechanisms should be developed to increase the perspective-taking ability of negotiators. This is consistent with the literature on negotiator role reversal, which suggests that having each bargainer verbalize the viewpoint of the other increases the likelihood of a negotiated resolution (see Pruitt, 1981). Thus, increasing the tendency of negotiators to take their opponents' perspective should be the mediator's central focus.

This tendency to ignore the perspective of others can be seen in the escalation bias described in Chapter 4. Why do bidders get involved in Shubik's dollar-auction exercise? Because they see the potential for profit early in the auction and then fail to take the perspective of what the auction will look like to other bidders. *The central message of this section is obvious: Consider the decisions of the other party before you commit to a course of action as a negotiator.* This piece of advice is counterintuitive; most individuals falsely act as if the opponent is a passive party to the negotiation.

Integration

From Chapter 6, we learned how to think rationally when approaching two-party decision-making contexts. In this chapter, we explore why it is not always easy for us, or for our opponents, to act rationally in these situations. Drawing upon the biases in individual decision making introduced in Chapters 2 through 5, we see that we experience similar biases in two party decision-making contexts. First, we too readily assume a fixed pie mentality in negotiations. Second, our ability to assess possible settlement options is impacted by the framing of those options. Framing dramatically affects not only how we view decisions as the focal negotiator, but also whether or not a settlement is likely to be reached by the parties or not. Third, we find that it is important to recognize our own, as well as our opponents' tendencies to nonrationally escalate commitment, espe-cially after public statements have been made. Fourth, our tendency toward overconfidence inappropriately impacts on our ability to assess the reasonableness of our positions. Finally, and probably most important, we tend to ignore the cognitions of others when assessing negotiation situations. All of these biases can lead to foolish behaviors and unwise settlements in two-party decision making. Yet, like the behaviors outlined in earlier chapters, we are often not aware of these biases. To become more successful negotiators in multiparty decision-making contexts, we need to understand the analytical concepts introduced in Chapter 6, while becoming more aware of the cognitive barriers that inhibit us and our opponents in applying these concepts. In the next chapter, the material from these chapters is extended to more complex multiparty situations. •

Study Questions

1. What are the problems (including consequences) of the fixed pie assumption?

2. What is the relationship between risk-seeking/risk-aversion and framing negotiations as either positive (gains) or negative (losses)? How does this affect an agreement? concessions? How are buyers' and sellers' frames unique?

3. What can negotiators do with regard to framing to avoid potentially adverse effects?

4. What is nonrational escalation of commitment?

5. What's the problem with public commitments/threats?

6. How can overconfidence hinder negotiations?

7. What is the relationship between perspective taking and success in negotiation? What is a consistent finding with role reversal and settlements?

Negotiating Rationally: The Power and Impact of the Negotiator's Frame

Margaret A. Neale

Max H. Bazerman

In the last ten years, negotiation has moved from the industrial relations arena to the forefront of managerial interest. As the nature and structure of managerial challenges evolve, negotiation skills become necessary. Considerable research has been conducted to determine how negotiators either fail to reach agreements that are in their best interest or leave them worse off.

The focus of this article is to consider how managers could negotiate more rationally—that is reach agreements that maximize the negotiator's interests. Unfortunately, our natural tendencies in negotiation and decision making contain biases that systematically reduce our ability to reach agreements that maximize our interests. While there has been significant research directed toward identifying these cognitive biases and their impact on negotiator behavior, we explore a negotiator's predilection for framing proposals in ways that reduce information search and analysis and direct the choice of alternatives.

We suggest that the frames a manager imposes on problems or disputes are a function of the referent point by which we evaluate success or failure and gains or losses. In the context of a negotiation, there is often little objective about the choice of a particular referent point, although the point that we choose can significantly influence the attractiveness of various outcomes. We describe the impact of various frames and identify ways in which managers can guard against being unduly influenced by the frames of disputes as well as ways managers can use frames to improve the potential for resolving disputes.

Everyone negotiates. In its various forms, negotiation is a common mechanism for resolving differences and allocating resources. While many people perceive negotiation to be a specific interaction between a buyer and a seller, this process occurs with a wide variety of exchange partners, such as superiors, colleagues, spouses, children, neighbors, strangers, or even corporate entities and nations. Negotiation is a decision-making process among interdependent parties who do not share identical preferences. It is through negotiation that the parties decide what each will give and take in their relationship.

The aspect of negotiation that is most directly controllable by the negotiator is how he or she makes decisions. The parties, the issues, and the negotiation environment are often predetermined. Rather than trying to change the environment surrounding the negotiation or the parties or issues in the dispute, we believe that the greatest opportunity to improve negotiator performance lies in the negotiator's ability to make effective use of the information available about the issues in dispute as well as the likely behavior of an opponent to reach more rational agreements and make more rational decisions within the context of negotiation.

The goal of our research has been to help negotiators think rationally. This is important, not because rationality is some end-state we should strive to achieve, but rather because by negotiating rationally, we will improve the likelihood that we will reach better agreements as well as know which opportunities or deals we are better off avoiding.

To this end, we offer advice on how a negotiator should make decisions. However, to follow this advice for analyzing negotiations rationally, a negotiator must understand the psychological forces that limit a negotiator's effectiveness. In addition, rational decisions require that we have an optimal way of evaluating the behavior of the opponent. This requires a psychological perspective for anticipating the likely decisions and subsequent behavior of the other party. Information such as this can not only create a framework that predicts how a negotiator structures problems,

Reprinted from *Academy of Management Executive*, (No. 6, 1992), by permission of Academy of Management Publications, Ohio Northern University. All rights reserved.

processes information, frames the situation, and evaluates alternatives but also identifies the limitations of his or her ability to follow rational advice.

Rationality refers to making the decision that maximizes the negotiator's interests. Since negotiation is a decision-making process that involves other people that do not have the same desires or preferences, the goal of a negotiation is not simply reaching an agreement. The goal of negotiations is to reach a good agreement. In some cases, no agreement is better than reaching an agreement that is not in the negotiator's best interests. When negotiated agreements are based on biased decisions, the chances of getting the best possible outcome are significantly reduced and the probabilities of reaching an agreement when an impasse would have left the negotiator relatively better off are significantly enhanced.

A central theme of our work is that our natural decision and negotiation processes contain biases that prevent us from acting rationally and getting as much as we can out of a negotiation. These biases are pervasive, destroying the opportunities available in competitive contexts, and preventing us from negotiating rationally. During the last ten or so years, the work that we and our colleagues have done suggests that negotiators make the following common cognitive mistakes: (1) Negotiators tend to be overly affected by the frame, or form of presentation, of information in a negotiation; (2) Negotiators tend to nonrationally escalate commitment to a previously selected course of action when it is no longer the most reasonable alternative; (3) Negotiators tend to assume that their gain must come at the expense of the other party and thereby miss opportunities for mutually beneficial trade-offs between the parties; (4) Negotiator judgments tend to be anchored upon irrelevant information—such as, an initial offer; (5) Negotiators tend to rely on readily available information; (6) Negotiators tend to fail to consider information that is available by focusing on the opponent's perspective; and (7) Negotiators tend to be overconfident concerning the likelihood of attaining outcomes that favor the individual(s) involved.

Describing the impact of each of these biases on negotiator behavior is obviously beyond the scope of this article. What we will attempt to do, however, is to focus on one particular and important cognitive bias, framing, and consider the impact of this bias on the process and outcome of negotiation. The manner in which negotiators frame the options available in a dispute can have a significant impact on their willingness to reach an agreement as well as the value of that agreement. In this article, we will identify factors that influence the choice of frame in a negotiation.

The Framing of Negotiations

Consider the following situation adapted from Russo and Shoemaker:[1]

You are in a store about to buy a new watch which costs $70. As you wait for the sales clerk, a friend of yours comes by and remarks that she has seen an identical watch on sale in another store two blocks away for $40. You know that the service and reliability of the other store are just as good as this one. Will you travel two blocks to save $30?

Now consider this similar situation:

You are in a store about to buy a new video camera that costs $800. As you wait for the sales clerk, a friend of yours comes by and remarks that she has seen an identical camera on sale in another store two blocks away for $770. You know that the service and reliability of the other store are just as good as this one. Will you travel two blocks to save the $30?

In the first scenario, Russo and Shoemaker report that about ninety percent of the managers presented this problem reported that they would travel the two blocks. However, in the second scenario, only about fifty percent of the managers would make the trip. What is the difference between the two situations that makes the $30 so attractive in the first scenario and considerably less attractive in the second scenario? One difference is that a $30 discount on a $70 watch represents a very good deal; the $30 discount on an $800 video camera is not such a good deal. In evaluating our willingness to walk two blocks, we frame the options in terms of the percentage discount. However, the correct comparison is not whether a percentage discount is sufficiently motivating, but whether the savings obtained is greater than the expected value of the additional time we would have to invest to realize those savings. So, if a

$30 savings were sufficient to justify walking two blocks for the watch, an opportunity to save $30 on the video camera should also be worth an equivalent investment of time.

Richard Thaler illustrated the influence of frames when he presented the following two versions of another problem to participants of an executive development program:[2]

You are lying on the beach on a hot day. All you have to drink is ice water. For the last hour you have been thinking about how much you would enjoy a nice cold bottle of your favorite brand of beer. A companion gets up to make a phone call and offers to bring back a beer from the only nearby place where beer is sold: a fancy resort hotel. She says that the beer might be expensive and asks how much you are willing to pay for the beer. She will buy the beer if it costs as much as or less than the price you state. But if it costs more than the price you state, she will not buy it. You trust your friend and there is no possibility of bargaining with the bartender. What price do you tell your friend you are willing to pay?

Now consider this version of the same story:

You are lying on the beach on a hot day. All you have to drink is ice water. For the last hour you have been thinking about how much you would enjoy a nice cold bottle of your favorite brand of beer. A companion gets up to make a phone call and offers to bring back a beer from the only nearby place where beer is sold: a small, run-down grocery store. She says that the beer might be expensive and asks how much you are willing to pay for the beer. She will buy the beer if it costs as much as or less than the price you state. But if it costs more than the price you state, she will not buy it. You trust your friend and there is no possibility of bargaining with the store owner. What price do you tell your friend you are willing to pay?

In both versions of the story, the results are the same: you get the same beer and there is no negotiating with the seller. Also you will not be enjoying the resort's amenities since you will be drinking the beer on the beach. Recent responses of executives at a Kellogg executive training program indicated that they were willing to pay significantly more if the beer were purchased at a "fancy resort hotel" ($7.83) than if the beer were purchased at the "small, run-down grocery store" ($4.10). The difference in

price the executives were willing to pay for the same beer was based upon the frame they imposed on this transaction. Paying over $5 for a beer is an expected annoyance at a fancy resort hotel; however, paying over $5 for a beer at a rundown grocery store is an obvious "rip-off!" So, even though the same beer is purchased and we enjoy none of the benefits of the fancy resort hotel, we are willing to pay almost a dollar more because of the way in which we frame the purchase. The converse of this situation is probably familiar to many of us. Have you ever purchased an item because "it was too good of a deal to pass up," even though you had no use for it? We seem to assign a greater value to the quality of the transaction over and above the issue of what we get for what we pay.

Both of these examples emphasize the importance of the particular frames we place on problems we have to solve or decisions we have to make. Managers are constantly being exposed to many different frames, some naturally occurring and others that are purposefully proposed. An important task of managers is to identify the appropriate frame by which employees and the organization, in general, should evaluate its performance and direct its effort.

The Framing of Risky Negotiations

The way in which information is framed (in terms of either potential gains or potential losses) to the negotiator can have a significant impact on his or her preference for risk, particularly when uncertainty about future events or outcomes is involved. For example, when offered the choice between gains of equal expected value—one for certain and the other a lottery, we strongly prefer to take the certain gain. However, when we are offered the choice between potential losses of equal expected value, we clearly and consistently eschew the loss for certain and prefer the risk inherent in the lottery.

There is substantial evidence to suggest that we are not indifferent toward risky situations and we should not necessarily trust our intuitions about risk. Negotiators routinely deviate from rationality because they do not typically appreciate the transient nature of their preference for risk; nor do they take into consideration the ability of a particular decision frame to influence that preference. Influencing our attitudes toward risk through the positive or negative frames associated with the problem is the result of evaluating an alternative from a particular referent point or base line. A referent point is the basis by which we evaluate whether what we are considering is viewed as a gain or a loss. The referent point that we choose determines the frame we impose on our options and, subsequently, our willingness to accept or reject those options.

Consider the high-performing employee who is expecting a significant increase in salary this year. He frames his expectations on the past behavior of the company. As such, he is expecting a raise of approximately $5000. Because of the recession, he receives a $3500 salary increase. He immediately confronts his manager, complaining that he has been unfairly treated. He is extremely disappointed in what his surprised manager saw as an exceptional raise because the employee's referent point is $1500 higher. Had he known that the average salary increase was only $2000 (and used that as a more realistic referent point), he would have perceived the same raise quite differently and it may have had the motivating force that his manager had hoped to create.

The selection of which relevant frame influences our behavior is a function of our selection of a base line by which we evaluate potential outcomes. The choice of one referent point over another may be the result of a visible anchor, the "status quo," or our expectations. Probably one of the most common referent points is what we perceive to be in our current inventory (our status quo)—what is ours already. We then evaluate offers or options in terms of whether they make us better off (a gain) or worse off (a loss) from what (we perceive to be) our current resource state.

Interestingly, what we include in our current resource state is surprisingly easy to modify. Consider the executive vice-president of a large automobile manufacturing concern that has been hit by a number of economic difficulties because of the recession in the U.S. It appears as if she will have to close down three plants and the employee rolls will be trimmed by 6000 individuals. In exploring ways to avoid this alternative, she has identified two plans that might ameliorate the situation. If she selects the first plan,

she will be able to save 2000 jobs and one of the three plants. If she implements the second plan, there is a one-third probability that she can save all three plants and all 6000 jobs but there is a two-thirds probability that this plan will end up saving none of the plants and none of the jobs. If you were this vice president, which plan would you select (#1 or #2)?

Now consider the same options (Plan 1 or Plan 2) framed as losses: If the vice-president implements Plan 1, two of the three plants will be shut down and 4000 jobs will be lost. If she implements Plan 2, then there is a two-thirds probability of losing all three plants and all 6000 jobs but there is a one-third probability of losing no plants and no jobs. If you were presented with these two plans, which would be more attractive? Plan 1 or Plan 2?

It is obvious that from a purely economic perspective, there is no difference between the two choices. Yet, managers offered the plans framed in terms of gains select the first plan about seventy-six percent of the time. However, managers offered the choice between the plans framed in terms of losses only select the first plan about twenty-two percent of the time. When confronted with potential losses, the lottery represented by Plan 2 becomes relatively much more attractive.

An important point for managers to consider is that the way in which the problem is framed, or presented, can dramatically alter the perceived value or acceptability of alternative courses of action. In negotiation, for example, the more risk-averse course of action is to accept an offered settlement; the more risk-seeking course of action is to hold out for future, potential concessions. In translating the influence of the framing bias to negotiation, we must realize that the selection of a particular referent point or base line determines whether a negotiator will frame his or her decision as positive or negative.

Specifically, consider any recurring contract negotiation. As the representative of Company "A," the offer from Company "B" can be viewed in two ways, depending on the referent point I use. If my referent point were the current contract, Company "B's" offer can be evaluated in terms of the "gains" Company "A" can expect relative to the previous contract. However, if the referent point for Company

"A" is an initial offer on the issues under current consideration, then Company "A" is more likely to evaluate Company "B's" offers as losses to be incurred if the contract as proposed is accepted. Viewing options as losses or as gains will have considerable impact on the negotiator's willingness to accept side "B's" position—even though the same options may be offered in both cases.

Likewise, the referent points available to an individual negotiating his salary for a new position in the company include: (1) his current salary; (2) the company's initial offer; (3) the least he is willing to accept; (4) his estimate of the most the company is willing to pay; or (5) his initial salary request. As his referent moves from 1 to 5, he progresses from a positive to a negative frame in the negotiation. What is a modest gain compared to his current wage is perceived as a loss when compared to what he would like to receive. Along these same lines, employees currently making $15/hour and demanding an increase of $4/hour can view a proposed increase of $2/hour as a $2/hour gain in comparison to last year's wage (Referent 1) or as a $2/hour loss in comparison to their stated or initial proposal of $19/hour (Referent 5). Consequently, the location of the referent point is critical to whether the decision is positively or negatively framed and affects the resulting risk preference of the decision maker.

In a study of the impact of framing on collective bargaining outcomes, we used a five-issue negotiation with participants playing the roles of management or labor negotiators.[3] Each negotiator's frame was manipulated by adjusting his or her referent point. Half of the negotiators were told that any concessions they made from their initial offers represented losses to their constituencies (i.e., a negative frame). The other half were told that any agreements they were able to reach which were better than the current contract were gains to their constituencies (i.e., the positive frame). In analyzing the results of their negotiations, we found that negatively framed negotiators were less concessionary and reached fewer agreements than positively framed negotiators. In addition, negotiators who had positive frames perceived the negotiated outcomes as more fair than those who had negative frames.

In another study, we posed the following problem to negotiators:

You are a wholesaler of refrigerators. Corporate policy does not allow any flexibility in pricing. However, flexibility does exist in terms of expenses that you can incur (shipping, financing terms, etc), which have a direct effect on the profitability of the transaction. These expenses can all be viewed in dollar value terms. You are negotiating an $8, 000 sale. The buyer wants you to pay $2,000 in expenses. You want to pay less expenses. When you negotiate the exchange, do you try to minimize your expenses (reduce them from $2,000) or maximize net profit, i.e., price less expenses (increase the net profit from $6,000)?

From an objective standpoint, the choice you make to reduce expenses or maximize profit should be irrelevant. Because the choice objectively is between two identical options, selecting one or the other should have no impact on the outcome of the negotiation. What we did find, in contrast, is that the frame that buyers and sellers take into the negotiation can systematically affect their behavior.[4]

In one study, negotiators were led to view transactions in terms of either (1) net profit or (2) total expenses deducted from gross profits. These two situations were objectively identical. Managers can think about maximizing their profits (i.e., gains) or minimizing their expenses (i.e., losses). These choices are linked; if one starts from the same set of revenues, then one way to maximize profits is to minimize expenses and if one is successful at minimizing expenses, the outcome is that profit may be maximized. That is, there is an obvious relationship between profits and expenses. So, objectively, there is no reason to believe that an individual should behave differently if given the instructions to minimize expenses or to maximize profits. However, those negotiators told to maximize profit (i.e., a positive frame) were more concessionary. In addition, positively framed negotiators completed significantly more transactions than their negatively framed (those told to minimize expenses) counterparts. Because they completed more transactions, their overall profitability in the market was higher, although negatively framed negotiators completed transactions of greater mean profit.[5]

The Endowment Effect

The ease with which we can alter our referent points was illustrated in a series of studies conducted by Daniel Kahneman, Jack Knetsch, and Richard Thaler.[6] In any exchange between a buyer and a seller, the buyer must be willing to pay at least the minimum amount the seller is willing to accept for a trade to take place. In determining the worth of an object, its value to the seller may, on occasion, be determined by some objective third party such as an economic market. However, in a large number of transactions, the seller places a value on the item—a value that may include not only the market value of the item but also a component for an emotional attachment to or unique appreciation of the item. What impact might such an attachment have on the framing of the transaction?

Let's imagine that you have just received a coffee mug.[7] (In the actual demonstration, coffee mugs were placed before one third of the participants, the "sellers," in the study.) After receiving the mug, you are told that in fact you "own the object (coffee mug) in your possession. You have the option of selling it if a price, to be determined later, is acceptable to you." Next, you are given a list (See Exhibit 1) of possible selling prices, ranging from $.50 to $9.50, and are told for each of the possible prices, you should indicate whether you would (a) sell the mug and receive that amount in return, or (b) keep the object and take it home with you. What is your selling price for the mug?

Another third of the group (the "buyers") were told that they would be receiving a sum of money and they could choose to keep the money or use it to buy a mug. They were also asked to indicate their preferences between a mug and sums of money ranging from $.50 to $9.50. Finally, the last third of the participants (the "choosers") were given a questionnaire indicating that they would later be given an option of receiving either a mug or a sum of money to be determined later. They indicated their preferences between the mug and sums of money between $.50 and $9.50. All of the participants were told that their answers would not influence either the pre-determined price of the mug or the amount of money to be received in lieu of the mug.

The sellers reported a median value of $7.12 for the mug; the buyers valued the mug at $2.88; and the choosers valued the mug at $3.12. It is interesting that in this exercise, being a buyer or a chooser resulted in very similar evaluations of worth of the mug. However, owning the mug (the sellers) created a much greater sense of the mug's worth. In this case, it was approximately forty percent greater than the market (or retail) value of the mug.

The explanation for this disparity lies in the fact that different roles (buyer, seller, or chooser) created different referent points. In fact, what seems to happen in such situations is that owning something changes the nature of the owner's relationship to the commodity. Giving up that item is now perceived as a loss and in valuing the item, the owner may include a dollar value to offset his or her perceived loss. If we consider this discrepancy in the value of an item common, then the simple act of "owning" an item, however briefly, can increase one's personal attachment to an item—and typically, its perceived value. After such an attachment is formed, the cost of breaking that attachment is greater and is reflected in the higher price the sellers demand to part with their mugs as compared to the value the buyers or the choosers place on the exact same commodity. In addition, we would expect that the endowment effect intensifies to the extent that the value of the commodity of interest is ambiguous or subjective, the commodity itself is unique, or not easily substitutable in the marketplace.

Framing, Negotiator Bias, And Strategic Behavior

In the previous discussion, we described the negotiator behaviors that may arise from positive and negative frames within the context of the interaction. In this section, we identify some of the techniques for strategically manipulating framing to direct negotiator performance.

Framing has important implications for negotiator tactics. Using the framing effect to induce a negotiating opponent to concede requires that the negotiator create referents that lead the opposition to a positive frame by couching the proposal in terms of their potential gain. In addition, the negotiator should emphasize the inherent risk in the negotiation situation and the opportunity for a sure gain.

Exhibit 1. The Coffee Mug Questionnaire

For each price listed below, indicate whether you would be willing to sell the coffee mug for that price or keep the mug.

If the price is $0.50, I will sell __ I will keep the mug __.
If the price is $1.00, I will sell __ I will keep the mug __.
If the price is $1.50, I will sell __ I will keep the mug __.
If the price is $2.00, I will sell __ I will keep the mug __.
If the price is $2.50, I will sell __ I will keep the mug __.
If the price is $3.00, I will sell __ I will keep the mug __.
If the price is $3.50, I will sell __ I will keep the mug __.
If the price is $4.00, I will sell __ I will keep the mug __.
If the price is $4.50, I will sell __ I will keep the mug __.
If the price is $5.00. I will sell __ I will keep the mug __.
If the price is $5.50, I will sell __ I will keep the mug __.
If the price is $6.00. I will sell __ I will keep the mug __.
If the price is $6.50. I will sell __ I will keep the mug __.
If the price is $7.00, I will sell __ I will keep the mug __.
If the price is $7.50. I will sell __ I will keep the mug __.
If the price is $8.00. I will sell __ I will keep the mug __.
If the price is $8.50, I will sell __ I will keep the mug __.
If the price is $9.00, I will sell __ I will keep the mug __.
If the price is $9.50, I will sell __ I will keep the mug __.

As our research suggests, simply posing problems as choices among potential gains rather than choices among potential losses can significantly influence the negotiator's preferences for specific outcomes.

Framing can also have important implications for how managers choose to intervene in disputes among their peers or subordinates. Managers, of course, have a wide range of options to implement when deciding to intervene in disputes in which they are not active principals. If the manager's goal is to get the parties to reach an agreement rather than having the manager decide what the solution to the dispute will be, he or she may wish to facilitate both parties' viewing the negotiation from a positive frame. This is tricky, however, since the same referent that will lead to a positive frame for one negotiator is likely to lead to a negative frame for the other negotiator if presented simultaneously to the parties. Making use of the effects of framing may be most appropriate when a manager can meet with each side separately. He or she may present different perspectives to each party to create a positive frame (and the subsequent risk-averse behavior associated with such a frame) for parties on both sides of the dispute. Again, if the manager is to effect the frame of the problem in such a way to encourage agreement, he or she may also emphasize the possible losses inherent in continuing the dispute. Combining these two strategies may facilitate both sides' preference for the certainty of a settlement.

Being in the role of buyer or seller can be a naturally occurring frame that can influence negotiator behavior in systematic ways. Consider the curious, consistent, and robust finding in a number of studies that buyers tend to outperform sellers in market settings in which the balance of power is equal.[8] Given the artificial context of the laboratory settings and the symmetry of the design of these field and laboratory markets, there is no logical reason why buyers should do better than sellers. One explanation for this observed difference may be that when the commodity is anonymous (or completely substitutable in a market sense), sellers may think about the transaction in terms of the dollars exchanged. That is, sellers may conceptualize the process of selling as gaining resources (e.g., how many dollars do I gain by selling the commodity); whereas buyers may view transaction in terms of loss of dollars (e.g., how many dollars do I have to give up). If the dollars are the primary focus of the participants' attention, then buyers would tend to be risk seeking and sellers risk averse in the exchange. When a risk-averse party (i.e., the seller, in this example) negotiates with a risk-seeking party (i.e., the buyer), the buyer is more willing to risk the potential agreement by demanding more or being less concessionary. To reach agreement, the seller must make additional concessions to induce the buyer, because of his or her risk-seeking propensity, to accept the agreement. Thus, in situations where the relative achievements of buyers and seller can be directly compared, buyers would benefit from their negative frame (and subsequent risk-averse behavior).

The critical issue is that these naturally occurring frames such as the role demands of being a "buyer" or "seller" can easily influence the way in which the disputed issues are framed—even without the conscious intervention of one or more of the parties.

It is easy to see that the frames of negotiators can result in the difference between impasse and reaching an important agreement. Both sides in negotiations typically talk in terms of a certain wage, price, or outcome that they must get—setting a high referent point against which gains and losses are measured. If this occurs, any compromise below (or above) that point represents a loss. This perceived loss may lead negotiators to adopt a negative frame to all proposals, exhibit risk-seeking behaviors, and be less likely to reach settlement. Thus negotiators, similar to the early example involving the beach and the beer, may end up with no beer (or no agreement) because of the frame (the amount of money I will pay for a beer from a run-down grocery store) that is placed on the choices rather than an objective assessment of what the beer is worth to the individual.

In addition, framing has important implications for the tactics that negotiators use. The framing effect suggests that to induce concessionary behavior from an opponent, a negotiator should always create anchors or emphasize referents that lead the opposition to a positive frame and couch the negotiation in terms of what the other side has to gain.

In addition, the negotiator should make the inherent risk salient to the opposition while the opponent is in a risky situation. If the sure gain that is being proposed is rejected, there is no certainty about the quality of the next offer. Simultaneously, the negotiator should also not be persuaded by similar arguments from opponents. Maintaining a risk-neutral or risk-seeking perspective in evaluating an opponent's proposals may, in the worst case, reduce the probability of reaching an agreement; however, if agreements are reached, the outcomes are more likely to be of greater value to the negotiator.

An important component in creating good negotiated agreements is to avoid the pitfalls of being framed while, simultaneously, understanding the impact of positively and negatively framing your negotiating opponent. However, framing is just one of a series of cognitive biases that can have a significant negative impact on the performance of negotiators. The purpose of this article was to describe the impact of one of these cognitive biases on negotiator behavior by considering the available research on the topic and to explore ways to reduce the problems associated with framing. By increasing our understanding of the subtle ways in which these cognitive biases can reduce the effectiveness of our negotiations, managers can begin to improve not only the quality of agreements for themselves but also fashion agreements that more efficiently allocate the available resources—leaving both parties and the communities of which they are a part better off. •

Footnotes

This article is based on the book by Bazerman, M.H., & Neale, M.A. (1992). *Negotiating Rationally*. Free Press: New York.

[1]Adapted from J.E. Russo, & P.J. Schomaker, *Decision traps* (New York: Doubleday, 1989).

[2]R. Thaler, "Using Mental Accounting in a Theory of Purchasing Behavior," *Marketing Science, 4*, 1985, 12–13.

[3]M.A. Neale, & M.H. Bazerman, "The Effects of Framing and Negotiator Overconfidence," *Academy of Management Journal, 28*, 1985, 34–49.

[4]M.H. Bazerman, T. Magliozzi, & M.A. Neale, "The Acquisition of an Integrative Response in a Competitive Market Simulation," *Organizational Behavior and Human Performance, 34*, 1985, 294–313.

[5]See, for example, Bazerman, Magliozzi, & Neale (1985), op. cit.; Neale and Bazerman, (1985),

op. cit.; or M.A. Neale, & G.B. Northcraft, "Experts, Amateurs and Refrigerators: Comparing Expert and Amateur Decision Making on a Novel Task," *Organizational Behavior and Human Decision Processes,* 38, 1986, 305–317; M.A. Neale, V.L. Huber, & G.B. Northcraft, "The Framing of Negotiations: Context Versus Task Frames," *Organizational Behavior and Human Decision Processes,* 39, 1987, 228–241.

[6]D. Kahneman, J.L. Knetsch, & R. Thaler, "Experimental Tests of the Endowment Effect and Coarse Theorem," *Journal of Political Economy*, 1990.

[7]The coffee mugs were valued at approximately $5.00.

[8]Bazerman, et al., (1985), op.cit.; M.A. Neale, V.L. Huber, & G.B. Northcraft, (1987), op.cit.

* * *

Margaret A. Neale is the J.L. and Helen Kellogg Distinguished Professor of Dispute Resolution and Organizations at the J.L. Kellogg Graduate School of Management at Northwestern University. She received her Bachelor's degree in pharmacy from Northeast Louisiana University, her Masters' degrees from the Medical College of Virginia and Virginia Commonwealth University and her Ph.D. in business administration from the University of Texas. Prior to joining the faculty at Northwestern University, Professor Neale was on the faculty at the Eller Graduate School of Management of the University of Arizona. She is the author of more than forty articles and is a co-author of three books: *Organizational Behavior: The Managerial Challenge* (Dryden Press, 1990), *Cognition and Rationality in Negotiation* (Free Press, 1991), and *Negotiating Rationally* (Free Press, 1992).

Max H. Bazerman is the J. Jay Gerber Distinguished Professor of Dispute Resolution and Organizations at the J.L. Kellogg Graduate School of Management at Northwestern University. He has a B.S.E. from the Wharton School at the University of Pennsylvania and a M.S. and Ph.D. from the Graduate School of Industrial Administration at Carnegie-Mellon University. Prior to taking his position at Northwestern University, Professor Bazerman was on the faculty of the Sloan School of Management at MIT. During 1989–90, he was a fellow at the Center for Advanced Study in the Behavioral Sciences in Stanford, California. He is the author or co-author of more than seventy articles on decision making and negotiation, the co-editor of *Negotiating in Organizations and Research on Negotiations in Organizations* (Volumes 1, 2 & 3), and the author of *Judgment in Managerial Decision Making* (now in its second edition), *Cognition and Rationality in Negotiation* (with M.A. Neale), and *Negotiating Rationally* (with M.A. Neale).

Study Questions

1. What are "rational" decisions for negotiators?

2. What tends to influence the use of one reference point over another?

3. Give some examples of probable reference points for a salary negotiation. Which will tend to produce more positive or negative frames?

4. What is predictable negotiation behavior when a situation is framed as a "certain gain?" "certain loss?"

5. How are positive frames related to perceived fairness of outcome?

6. How does the "endowment effect" influence the seller's reference point/frame? What helps intensify this effect?

7. From the framing perspective, what can negotiators do to increase concessions by their opponents?

8. Managers, when acting as third parties in resolving a dispute, would be wise to talk to parties separately. Why?

Getting to Know Them: The Process of Opponent Analysis

Deanna Geddes

While preparing for an upcoming negotiation, did you ever consider how much you knew about the other party, or wonder how they would act as your opponent? If you did, you engaged in what is technically termed "opponent analysis." Opponent analysis (OA) is the process by which negotiators come to know and understand their opponent, and, in turn, anticipate their bargaining behavior. The degree to which you do this type of analysis may affect your own bargaining strategy and tactics, as well as the eventual negotiated outcome. Thus, the purpose of this article is to increase your understanding of the OA process in an effort to improve your skill as a negotiator.

The OA model, illustrated in Figure 1, consists of three phases, including information-gathering, sense-making, and expectation-setting. This model shows how individuals attempt to reduce uncertainty about their opponent by obtaining and organizing opponent-relevant information. The process involves gathering various bits of information about the opponent and then making sense of the "data base" by adding personal opinions, inferences, attributions, and judgments. This sense-making helps create an image of the opponent that reflects features considered most important or salient. With this image in mind, negotiators will generate expectations about their opponent's future moves. These expectations regarding opponent bargaining behavior influence, to a greater or lesser degree, decisions regarding the negotiator's own bargaining strategy.

Included in the model is a dual, individual/social context for OA. Simply put, individuals preparing for a one-on-one negotiation engage in mental OA as they personally acquire and process available information, and form their own image and expectations regarding the opponent. In contrast, group negotiation (vs. individual) extends OA beyond the cognitive level to the social level as group members prior to and during negotiation discuss various aspects of the opposing group. For instance, it has been shown that approximately 20–40% of all caucus interaction involves some form of OA. Thus, opponent analysis is both manifested in, and accomplished through, communication among members of a bargaining team.

Because individual OA is an "unobservable" (cognitive) process, perhaps the best way to understand opponent analysis is to look at the observable behaviors (i.e., group communication) associated with each of the three OA phases. Studies of OA have taken messages from actual caucus interactions to create a coding scheme that identifies opponent-relevant comments as serving either an information-gathering, sense-making, or expectation-setting function. The OA coding scheme along with definitions and examples is presented in Table 1 below. Examining the coding scheme should help identify some of the typical ways in which you might analyze an opponent.

To date, very little research has been done on the amount of time negotiators spend analyzing their opponents. However, preliminary studies do suggest that about one-third of all caucus deliberations involve some form of OA. It also appears that experienced negotiators engage in more OA than relatively inexperienced negotiators. In addition, "expert" negotiators engaged in opponent analysis spend the greatest proportion of their time in the sense-making phase, generating as accurate an image of their opponent as possible.

It is often the case that the more we get to know somebody, the more positively we feel toward that person. Experienced negotiators often conclude after creating an image of their opponent, that s/he is not necessarily "the enemy," but is instead an important, interested party to work with (not against) in striving for high mutual gains. Thus, it is perhaps no accident that such negotiators are much more likely to attempt cooperative, problem-solving strate-

"Getting to Know Them: The Process of Opponent Analysis," by D. Geddes. Unpublished manuscript, 1992. Reprinted by author's permission.

Figure 1: The Opponent Analysis Model

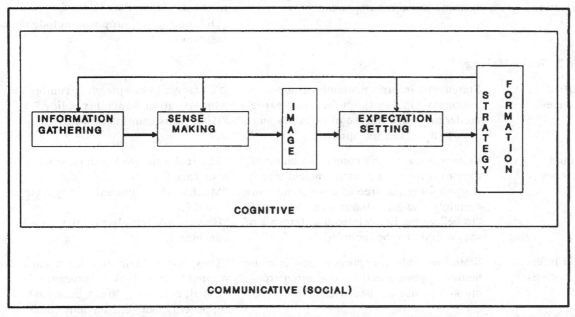

gies when engaged in reaching an agreement with their opponents. But, back to you, the more novice negotiator. How much of your negotiation planning is spent considering, discussing and/or evaluating your opponent? Whether you use a cooperative or a more com-petitive bargaining strategy, it could be that the better you know an opponent's attitudes, needs, constraints, strengths and weaknesses, the bet-ter prepared you will be to negotiate the best solutions. •

Table 1: Communication Behaviors Associated With the Opponent Analysis Process

Phase 1: Information-Gathering

Category	Description	Examples
Primary-Source Information	Statements of noninferential, verifiable information about opponent based on personal experience and including contract/settlement changes, concepts, and language.	"Well, they've come down $600 in salary." "They pay everything but $1 currently."
Secondary-Source Information	Statements of noninferential, verifiable information about opponent recalled from individuals other than self. This includes restatements.	"He said that the consultant said it is a Cadillac plan." "I heard people were saying the board should have gotten on it."

Category	Description	Examples
Requesting Information	Questions asked to obtain further information about opponent.	"What insurance company did they want to check with?" "Did their initial proposal include dental insurance?"

Phase 2: Sense-Making

Category	Description	Examples
Qualified Inferences	Statements inferring something about opponent. Opinions, not facts that express moderate to low degree of certainty and are often marked by "qualifiers".	". . . seems to be spreading rumors that the administration wants this policy." "He appears caught up in RIF."
Absolute Inferences	Statements asserting something about opponent (or their constituencies) that suggest a high degree of absoluteness or certainty and are often marked by use of "to be" verbs. Editorialized statements of fact would also be included.	"The real issue [to the opponent] is insurance." "Much of the community is against the board." "He very grudgingly said they would consider it."
Causal Inferences (Attributions)	Statements which express reason or cause behind opponent actions that often are marked by use of "because".	"They diverted our attention because we wanted them to look at insurance." "It's all because __ has a buddy who supposedly can get us a better deal."
Requesting Understanding	Questions asking another's opinion or speculation about opponent or issues relevant to opponent. Also, statements acknowledging uncertainty and/or suggesting the need for further understanding.	"Are you convinced that he is sincere?" "Is ____ really this upset?" "I think we need to have them explain their position, so we know where they're coming from.
Opponent Advocacy	Statements made in a way that reflect the opponents' own perspective. May also indicate that opponent's position is fair, accurate, and/or appropriate, and may include expressions of positive emotions, trust of opponent.	"It's not like them to blow smoke." "They've come down a lot." "They [teachers] have a strong necessity to handle RIF procedure through seniority alone."
Opponent Criticism	Statements that show a failure to understand opponent's perspective or that criticize/oppose some aspect of opponent. Also, expressions of negative emotion, lack of acceptance or trust.	"They had no clue what was going on in there." "They're being ridiculous and petty on this issue." "I just don't get what they're trying to do."
Expectations	Statements speculating on opponent's future behavior.	"They may come down to 12.4%." "My hunch is they will hold out for a while."
Expectation Confirmation	Statements indicating that earlier expectations about opponent were right.	"I thought they'd bring that up." "We did anticipate that objection."
Expectation Disconfirmation	Statements indicating that previous expectations about opponent were wrong; this includes expressing surprise.	"Yeah, I'm surprised about dental insurance." "I didn't think they would do that."

Category	Description	Examples
Expectation Disconfirmation	Statements indicating that previous expectations about opponent were wrong; this includes expressing surprise.	"Yeah, I'm surprised about dental insurance." "I didn't think they would do that."
Strategy-Expectation Links	Statements having an "if-then" form, that link expected opponent behaviors to anticipated outcomes or strategy recommendations.	"If they move more than that, we're not going to get a settlement." "If their best offer is 5 1/2%, and they're serious, let's break it off."

*   *   *

Study Questions

1. Describe the process of "opponent analysis."

2. What types of communication behaviors are typical of the three OA phases?

CASE: How Rendell emerged victorious in labor battle

Marc Duvoisin
Philadelphia Inquirer staff writer

The strategy was set early: Send a simple message, build a consensus, hold firm.

The mayor emerged from City Hall around 3:30 last Tuesday afternoon, beaming like a lottery winner. Leaders of the city's blue-collar union had just approved a tentative contract agreement with the city. A long-feared walkout by city employees had ended—after 16 hours.

Rendell was off to watch his 12-year-old son play football. On the way to his car, as he schmoozed with cops, cameramen and a few lingering pickets, he seemed not only relieved, but downright celebratory.

And who could blame him? Even as a candidate, Rendell knew he would face a confrontation with municipal unions, a fight-or-flight moment, as he tackled the city's financial crisis. A prolonged, bitter strike could have severely weakened him, undermining his larger agenda and jeopardizing his political career.

Instead, he emerged with many of the concessions he was seeking, his can-do aura intact, his trajectory still rising. This was just one contract negotiation; others lie ahead. But Rendell has made an impressive start in dealing with the kind of financial problems that have vexed mayors across the country, not to mention his predecessors in Philadelphia.

While some observers cautioned that the full cost of the settlement remains to be calculated—and others fretted over Rendell's knowledge that a tax increase might be needed—the consensus among politicians and business leaders was that he had won again and won big.

"It shows that Ed Rendell can not only talk a good game, but that he has the political wherewithal to follow through," said State Sen.

Earl M. Baker, a Chester County Republican. "It shows that the mayor is willing to lead an effort in which the city can try to pick itself up by its own bootstraps."

John P. Claypool, executive director of Greater Philadelphia First, a business group, said Rendell had managed to achieve significant savings without alienating the work force or provoking a prolonged strike that would have damaged the city's image.

"It would be tough to imagine a whole lot better outcome," he said.

"If you were keeping score," said State Sen. Chaka Fattah, a Democrat from West Philadelphia, "Rendell's doing as well as the Eagles."

The settlement was the result of a strategy that Rendell and his advisers, notably David L. Cohen, his campaign manager and later chief of staff, laid out long before he was elected. Their plan was to present a simple message, communicate it effectively, build a political consensus behind it—and then stick with it doggedly.

The message was that the city could not afford to balance its budget through steep tax increases or massive layoffs. The only solution was to "downsize the cost of government"—in large part by trimming holidays, scrapping antiquated work rules and curbing the cost of health benefits.

Rendell hammered away at this theme, month after month. At the same time, he covered his flanks politically, giving Council Members, state legislators and business leaders a voice in the development of his financial strategy.

Shared the credit

By involving others, Rendell gave them a stake in the outcome and bought protection against sniping or second-guessing when the labor standoff threatened to get ugly.

Rendell also shared credit freely with all who assisted him, storing up good will in case the settlement requires him to increase taxes or cut services. And he made effective use of television, going directly to taxpayers and un-

---

ion members with his message that "there simply isn't any money."

Eventually, Rendell succeeded in defining the terms of the debate and keeping the unions on the defensive.

"He didn't waver. That's a sign of leadership," said City Controller Jonathan A. Saidel. "If he were to have vacillated, it might have brought a long strike, because somebody might have thought there *was* money."

Rendell began preparing for the confrontation before he took office. After his landslide victory last November, his aides began gathering data on layoffs and contract concessions in the private sector and in city and state governments across the country. Rendell worked the numbers into his five-year financial plan, his bargaining proposals and his speeches.

Cost of benefits

He enlisted the nonprofit Pennsylvania Economy League, which developed independent documentation of the cost of employee benefits. On Lincoln's Birthday, then a city holiday, he held a news conference with Saidel to release a league study showing that employees enjoyed more generous benefits than their counterparts in most other cities.

The message was that times were tough all over, and that the Philadelphia unions would have to give.

Rendell also started laying the political groundwork early for a protracted battle with the unions. After his inaugural address on Jan. 5, he held a news conference with City Council President John F. Street and praised him effusively, saying that Street's views on the financial crisis were "absolutely correct."

Rendell also was willing to give Street a substantive role in shaping the administration's agenda. Administration officials briefed Street regularly on the five-year plan and sought his advice.

The approach paid dividends in the spring, when Street guided the plan to unanimous approval in Council, and again last month, when the Council president agreed to serve as a mediator in the contract talks and helped the two sides reach agreement.

Included others

Saidel, a harsh critic of Rendell's predecessor, W. Wilson Goode, was also brought on board. Findings from his office's audits were added to a long list of proposed management efficiencies in the five-year plan.

In the fall of 1990, Saidel had publicly lambasted Goode and his finance director, Betsy C. Reveal, helping to doom an effort to sell short-term notes on Wall Street. When Rendell went up against the unions, the controller was either silent or supportive.

The mayor reached out to other elected officials as well. Freshman Council members were startled—and gratified—when he called them to the podium at public appearances. Cohen, his chief aide, saw to it that calls from elected officials, on matters momentous or mundane, were promptly returned.

"Eddie has been wise from the beginning to include as many people as he could and to make people feel closer to the administration than they have in the past," said Councilman Brian J. O'Neill, a Republican. "It's so basic. If I pick up the phone and call the mayor or David Cohen, I'm going to get them. And in a short time, I'm going to get an answer. I don't feel like I'm begging."

As a result, O'Neill said, "People are willing to be a lot more helpful. People weren't out there trying to interfere [in the labor negotiations]. Interference hurts the mayor, helps the unions. There's been a cooperative environment."

Street helped here as well, exercising a strong hand in Council that discouraged freelancing by individual members.

In his hectic early weeks in office, Rendell took time to drive to Harrisburg to testify before a state Senate committee overseeing the city's financial recovery. Goode did not make such an appearance until the final year of his tenure, when he sat before the same committee to plead for the creation of an oversight board to borrow money on the city's behalf.

In July, still recuperating from surgery on an infected elbow, Rendell showed up at Veterans Stadium for a softball game with suburban legislators. He had a catheter in his chest and couldn't move his left arm much, but he played anyway.

Again, the bridge-building proved worthwhile. In September, with Philadelphia teachers preparing to go on strike, State Sen. Vincent J. Fumo and State Rep. Dwight Evans, two powerful Philadelphia Democrats, helped bring about a settlement by offering assurances that state educational subsidies would grow enough over the next few years to pay for a modest wage increase.

"More than any chief executive I've known," said Councilman James F. Kenney, "[Rendell] understands the need to have the Streets, the Fumos and the Evanses on your side rather than on your neck."

Elaborate preparation was another key to Rendell's success in the labor negotiations. Beginning in March, administration officials, bolstered by a half dozen private lawyers working for free, began laying the groundwork to implement contract cuts unilaterally if negotiations reached a stalemate.

They did far-ranging legal research and drafted Council bills and amendments to civil service rules to cut holidays and sick time, tighten rules on disability pensions and carry out the other elements of Rendell's program.

Rendell's aides also made extensive—and only semi-secret—preparations for a strike, assembling a two-inch-thick contingency plan for keeping essential services running with nonunion supervisors.

On Sept. 23, when Rendell declared an impasse and said he would implement his "last, best offer," union leaders as well as the rank and file could see he was not bluffing. He was ready to impose new terms and ride out a strike if necessary. All the machinery was in place and ready to go.

With emergency meetings of the city's Civil Service Commission and Administrative Board, and a mass mailing to employees explaining the changed working conditions, Rendell began to implement his final offer. This sparked an intensive new round of bargaining, as he hoped it would.

Of course, the labor settlement marks the start, not the end, of a long-term effort to bring the city's expenditures in line with its revenues. The contract agreement will cost more than Rendell projected in the five-year plan, so service cuts are likely and layoffs possible.

And arbitration panels that will write new contracts for police and firefighters could grant terms more expensive than the city can afford. A new law requires the panels to "accord substantial weight" to Philadelphia's financial problems and allows the city to appeal their rulings in the courts. But the provisions have never been tested before.

The significance of the abortive strike, which ended with a smiling Rendell declaring everyone a winner, was that a Philadelphia mayor had waded into the quicksand of the financial crisis and emerged with something resembling a victory.

"At this point," said Councilman O'Neill, "it's very hard to criticize him." •

Study Questions

206-208

1. Provide the Municipal Unions with an opponent analysis based on the information given in the attached article. Use ideas and terminology from the readings on opponent analysis.

2. What advice would to you give to the Municipal Unions to prepare for future negotiations with the City? Justify your suggestions based on your analysis of the City's past negotiation performance.

Exercise: Hillsborough Contract Case

Developed by Deanna Geddes
Temple University

Instructions:

You are a member of the Hillsborough school board. Carefully read the case individually first and then discuss it with the rest of the board. Your task is to prepare to meet with the teachers' union and offer a counter, "best offer" that you sincerely believe the teachers will accept so that negotiations will end this evening. The goal is a speedy settlement, but you must work within your financial budget. You should spend approximately 25 to 30 minutes identifying critical issues and discussing strategy options with your group. Then, write your best counter proposal on a separate sheet of paper. This will be submitted to the teachers' union who will review it before coming to the bargaining table.

The Case: Hillsborough School Contract

Hillsborough School District is a small midwestern education system consisting of 165 teachers, 7 schools, and 3,800 students. Teachers' contracts have been negotiated through collective bargaining for the past nine years; thus, the school board is legally obligated to bargain over salary, hours, fringe benefits, grievances, and arbitration of unresolved grievances. Because strikes are illegal, if no settlement is reached, the school district is likely to use factfinding or mediation. Nevertheless, in the past, the threat of a strike has often sped up the contract negotiation process.

The teachers' negotiation team consists of union members representing the high school, junior high, and the elementary school faculties, in addition to their professional negotiator from the state teachers' association. The school board's negotiation team consists of elected school board members, the superintendent, principals, and their hired professional negotiator (who has been employed throughout the district's bargaining history).

Both groups are engaged in full contract negotiations. Specific issues of concern this year are money-based—salary increases and insurance premiums. It is 5 o'clock in the afternoon, and there is some hope that negotiations will be over this evening. Because in the past they have been able to reach a settlement in one day, this has energized both groups. However, some members feel there is too much discrepancy between bids and have suggested that at least a week's delay might increase their settlement. Others feel "holding out" will hurt the overall (generally positive) relationship.

The first offers by each side have been proposed on the money issues. The teachers' union has requested a raise of 15% the first year and 10% the second. (Their raise last year was 8 1/2%). The Administration's first offer is 5% and 4%. There is also a possibility that the second year could be renegotiated if there is more money from the legislature next year. Both have decided they only want a two year contract if they can get a good deal. Each 1% costs the board around $23,000. The board would like to keep the *2 year* salary cost increases around $230,000 if possible. Other increased teacher-based costs such as paid sick days, substitute costs, and travel reimbursement are pretty much set at $40,000 for *this year. Their entire budget increase this year is $270,000,* but the board does not want to give this entire amount to the teachers. Instead, they would like to keep the teacher's portion of this year's increase to around *$200,000.* Budget increases for next year remain uncertain.

The cost of insurance premiums is the second money issue on the table. With increased premium costs by Healthcare Insurance Company, the school board has asked faculty to pay the increase in both life and medical premiums. Term life insurance premiums have increased to $38 (from $21 last year) per teacher. (The board currently pays $10 per teacher for term life.) The teachers' union has requested an "all but $1" payment clause, meaning the board would pay all but one dollar of this premium.

They also want the "all but $1" clause for their medical insurance premiums, which have increased an average of $200 per teacher this year. (Teachers currently got half their $1000 premiums paid by the board.) In addition, the union has added dental insurance coverage to their request. Finally, the union believes Healthcare Insurance's premiums are too high and want to open bids up to other insurance carriers within 60 days in an effort to reduce overall costs. Some rumors have begun circulating that Healthcare is giving 2-4% kickbacks to the school board.

The board is happy with Healthcare Insurance and feel the "hassle" of rebidding is not worth the possible minor reductions in premiums, but potential major reductions in benefits. School administrators currently have the "all but $1" plan with Healthcare in addition to full dental insurance. However, they gave up good raises last year to get these perks. They want teachers to pay the majority of the increases in premiums for both life and medical ("we didn't cause the rates to go up"), though no actual dollar amount was proposed. •

Study Questions

1. Explain your approach to the case, i.e., more adversarial or cooperative?

2. How much discussion was focused on information-gathering, sense-making, and expectation-setting, respectively, regarding the teachers?

3. Did any opponent criticism or opponent advocacy occur? Explain.

4. How much time was used for opponent analysis in comparison to your own strategy development?

5. What was a no-cost concession for the administration that was a critical issue for the teachers? How did your group consider this issue of alternative insurers?

6. Consider your answers to the questionnaire. What type of image of the teachers did you work from when developing a proposal you felt the teachers would accept? For instance, did you view the teachers as the "enemy" or less "reasonable" than you? Did you trust them? They you?

7. How will the teachers react to your proposal? Do you believe they will make a considerably different counterproposal? If so, what will their counterproposal be?

8. What were your feelings toward the teachers when you found out the actual settlement? How accurate was your image and expectations regarding them?

Negotiation: How to Win in Foreign Negotiations

Lennie Copeland
Lewis Griggs

A trade representative who accompanied American negotiators in South Korea noticed that in meeting after meeting, the Koreans said the same things to each new group of Americans. They seemed to have a rehearsed script and a list of stances. Finally the American was driven to ask one of the Korean negotiators about it. With a little prodding, the Korean admitted that their positions were worked out by personnel at the Korean embassy in Washington who had been studying the American negotiation style for years. The Koreans were thoroughly prepared—every word out of their mouths was uttered according to strategy.

The Americans, on the other hand, went into each negotiation expecting to "play it by ear." With scant preparation or team coordination, they stood little chance against the foreign opposition which knew so much about them and had so carefully planned for the negotiation.

*   *   *

In international business, a lot rides on the success of negotiations. The ambitions and plans of corporate planners, marketers and contractors are foiled when negotiators fail to win the required permissions, contracts or operational arrangements. And costs can be terrific when no equitable agreement is reached. The stakes in a foreign negotiation are often much higher than they would be in a comparable situation domestically because so many other aspects of the international operation may hinge on the outcome.

One U.S. Department of Commerce source estimates that for every successful American negotiation with the Japanese, there are twenty-five "failures." A consultant in the Arab world says that Americans never really win in negotiations with Arabs. A Chinese broker says Americans do so badly in negotiations in China, that by the time it is all over, American negotiators are thankful to get out with the shirts on their backs.

Everyday business involves countless negotiations, for the exporter or the diplomat, the missionary or the multinational manager, the engineer or the lawyer. Negotiating is not confined to big deals. In some countries it seems that virtually every transaction, from settling a taxi fare to buying a loaf of bread at the market, is a negotiation. The traveler who does not appreciate the local rules for give-and-take is at a serious disadvantage. Anyone doing business abroad should know how the local people bargain and when to call in a professional.

Negotiating is often described as a game, and players are seen as opponents or adversaries who accomplish their objectives in a series of moves. Skill is the winning factor. But it is not that simple in most business negotiations. Home or abroad, negotiating is not a game requiring mere skill but an art requiring forethought, imagination and strategy as well as skill. Whether bargaining for a copper pot in an Egyptian *souk* or negotiating an arms deal with a foreign government, it has less to do with overcoming an adversary than with creating a new picture of reality that is acceptable from two different points of view. If negotiating must be likened to a game, it is a game of perspective.

In every negotiation the participants have different points of view and more or less different objectives. If they did not, agreement would be automatic and negotiation unnecessary. But in international talks the negotiators are less likely to have a common frame of reference and value system; their perspectives are further apart. When arguments fail to address what is important to the other side, the resulting suspicion can bring negotiations to a halt.

International negotiations are further complicated by purely physical constraints and bureaucratic nuisances. A *New York Times* bureau chief in Beijing described the frustrations facing Americans in China: "The bloated Chinese bureaucracy has been streamlined from 98 ministries, commissions and agencies to a more manageable 52. But negotiations are still plagued by procrastination, inefficiency, nitpicking, secrecy, and internal rivalries, not to mention a hazy legal system that leaves potential investors confused about their rights."

Negotiators who have worked abroad agree: the international arena is no place for amateurs or slow learners.

Before the Negotiation

What you do before the negotiation starts is as important as what you do during the negotiation. Since Americans so often treat negotiations like games, they go into them relying on superior strength and mental or physical agility. But the traveler who counts on being able to think on his or her feet is going to find a negotiation debacle. The real art of successful negotiation is in the preparation.

Rule 1: Make sure that what you are negotiating is negotiable. A team of U.S. negotiators spent a year and a half flying back and forth to Japan negotiating a coal sale. When discussions were hopelessly stuck, one of the American members asked, "Look, if we gave you the coal *free*, what amount could you use?" Initially confused by the hypothetical question but after some explanation and supportive assurances against loss of face, the Japanese answered, "No amount." No matter what the Americans did in the negotiations, the Japanese were not going to buy their coal. They had already closed a deal with some other country and were going through the paces of negotiating with the Americans only out of politeness. Belatedly, the Americans asked themselves, "What the hell are we doing here?"

Some things are non-negotiable. Some problems cannot be resolved, some differences cannot be reconciled, and some negotiators really have little interest in reaching agreement. In some cases, the parties simply must go their separate ways. In other cases, negotiators should work on reaching a tolerable *modus vivendi,* a means for both sides to live with their differences while leaving the door open for

solutions that may come later. Circumstances do change.

When there are facts of life that cannot or will not be changed, find a way to work around them. Dick Burns, director of trading and sourcing for Levi Strauss's Eximco, says one of the mistakes he sees negotiators make in China is to argue about a schedule. The Americans have a preconceived notion of how much time is needed to manufacture a particular product; the Chinese simply will not meet the deadline even if they have agreed to it. You can save a lot of trouble if instead of negotiating a non-negotiable, you ask, "When do I have to commit our final figures for you to meet our fall production?"

Rule 2: Define what "winning" the negotiation means to you. All too many people go into a foreign negotiation with a view to getting "as much as we can get." Without a target, however, you will be shooting into the trees, and your score on "whatever we can get" will be substantially lower than what you could get when you are aiming at a clear set of objectives.

Be precise about what you want but think through a wide range of possibilities. Research findings suggest that skilled negotiators explore almost twice as many options for action than others. Think through all the variables that will affect the deal—price, quality, quantity, timing, means of delivery, warranties, costs, terms of payment, labor arrangements, inspections, and so on. "Standard business practices" vary around the world. Take nothing for granted.

Be ambitious but set a realistic walk-away. Many Americans fare badly in international negotiations because they fail to set their sights high enough—they tend to start out from a basis of what they think is fair and reasonable. They may "think big" in planning but are too embarrassed to make what might seem to be preposterous demands. In countries where haggling is the norm, such as China and the Middle East, Americans lose because their proposals start too close to the goal, without enough room for numerous concessions. Even where haggling is not customary, as in Europe and Canada, higher demands bring higher settlements. If one side opens with high demands, the other will probably reconsider its position and is likely to counter with something higher than it was planning to. The reverse happens also; by asking for too little or offering too much, you reduce your chances of a winning outcome.

When you define what "winning" means to you, also define what *not* winning means. Reaching an agreement is not necessarily winning a negotiation. At the point when an agreement no longer benefits you, you must be able to *walk away without a deal,* no matter how disappointed you are. No deal is better than a bad deal, as many companies are finding out around the world.

Rule 3: Get the facts. If you want to get what is important to you, you are going to have to understand what is important to the other side. Never assume that the foreigner wants what you want or is motivated by the same needs. You have to study the facts of the situation as well as the constraints on and the aspirations of the individual negotiators on the other side.

Before any negotiation, it is normal to have pre-negotiation meetings and information exchanges. In addition, arrange informal get-togethers. During this time, try to get inside the foreign organization. It may operate quite differently from its American counterparts. Who are the decision makers and how are decisions made? Often the decision maker is not at the negotiation table or may keep a low profile during the negotiations. What are the delivery schedules? What are the budget allocations—can you find out how much has been budgeted for your project? Where does the company want to go? What are the concerns of the decision makers? Have they had unhappy experiences doing business with Americans? How badly do they want this deal? What other commitments have been made, and on what terms? Particularly, find out what you can about members of the negotiation team—their authority to make a deal, their personal goals and their perspective on this negotiation. Find out how they think. As Tom Klitgaard of Pillsbury, Madison and Sutro says: "How they think will affect their reactions to your proposals."

Just as important as understanding the other side is understanding your own organization, management goals and negotiation parameters. Some negotiators, especially in a foreign situation, get so wrapped up in details that they lose sight of the bigger picture and reach agreements that may seem good for the deal at hand but are bad for the long-term interests of the company. You should know how important the outcome of the negotiation is to the company, and to your career. You also need to know how much rope you have to negotiate elements of a deal, such as price, time and terms. Your credibility will suffer if you have to keep checking with headquarters for each decision. If you feel you will need more time or staff support, negotiate with your superiors to get it.

Rule 4: Have a strategy for each culture and each phase. A good strategy is like a road map—it doesn't show just one road, but provides a number of routes to the same destination. If you miss the turn you wanted (and it is easy to make a wrong turn in a cross-cultural negotiation), there are a number of alternate ways to go, some more scenic, some faster, some with more roadside facilities. A good strategy allows you to make minor adjustments along your path to get to the same place. The key is flexibility. Dick Burns of Levi Strauss says that one of the biggest mistakes he sees people make abroad is rigid adherence to a "slick" strategy. You must not lose sight of the objective.

Your first strategic decision should be how to position your proposal. Americans approach a negotiation as a problem-solving exercise, hence they tend to concentrate on the problems, differences or areas of disagreement between the negotiating sides. There is evidence to suggest, however, that successful international negotiators give much more time to common ground and pay a lot of attention to areas of anticipated agreement. Instead of devoting all your energy to developing counters to the arguments you may expect, put more effort into figuring out what the other side will find appealing about your proposal.

In negotiating, as in marketing, it is important to influence how the other side perceives your proposal, particularly relative to all other competing options. You must position your proposal so that it will stand out favorably among all available alternatives. To do this well you must try to see the situation from the foreigner's point of view. Fit the proposal to local economic goals and the ambitions of the negotiating team. What are the deciding factors? What political, social or organizational pressures can be brought to bear? What does the foreigner want from you? Richard Pascale, co-author of *The Art of Japanese Management* and negotiation professor at Stanford Business School, says: "People rarely negotiate on the basis of price alone . . . The ability to create deals which benefit both parties is where the action is in international negotiations." Think about "creative packaging" for your proposals, including variations in guarantees, financial arrangements or participation of the players in the deal.

Second, decide whether to be competitive (win-lose) or cooperative (win-win). Don't always use the same style, even if you think you have developed it to perfection. Instead, determine which approach will work best in the foreign culture, given the circumstances.

There is a lot of evidence that the competitive negotiator wins better deals than the cooperative negotiator, perhaps because in de-emphasizing differences, the cooperative negotiator may give up more, while the win-lose negotiator often sets higher stakes and encourages less compromise. The Soviets, for example, are able to force us to give and give more. Says one executive working in Moscow: "The Russians never lose by putting pressure on the West; there is no win-win with the Russians." Asians, particularly the Japanese, may use cooperative styles when negotiating among themselves but can be ruthlessly competitive with outsiders. Do not assume coincidence of interest in seemingly cooperative negotiations. An appearance of cooperation and harmony should not be allowed to obscure the goals of the foreign partner.

Many Arabs are much more truly collaborative. Despite the haggling, a negotiation is not a true win-lose if you have established a relationship. If you are bargaining over an object in the market with someone you have chatted with several times in the past, you are likely to get a somewhat better price than the total stranger. The Arab often says, "For you, my friend, special deal." (It may not be a good deal, just a better deal.) Says Gary Wederspahn of Moran, Stahl & Boyer, cross-cultural consultants: "You'd better protect your flank, but when you are negotiating with the Saudi, you are, in a sense, forming a new tribe to go out against the world."

In international negotiations, a cooperative appearance is recommended; both sides must perceive a win-win. Competitive styles make sense only when power is a major element or when a one-time deal is being negotiated. Even if the competitive style is the one you choose, do not make your negotiation a contest. Never "go in for the kill." Remember, in most cross-cultural negotiations you are not just negotiating a deal but negotiating a relationship. This must color your approach whether you are at the bargaining table with a banker, landlord, supplier, employee or contractor. That does not mean be subservient—your foreign partner will not respect a loser.

Third, set your opening offer. Opening proposals are an important signal to the other side. At this early stage, foreigners are not likely to take the proposal itself seriously but will use it to size you up. The foreigner is always more interested in you than in your product or project, so make your opening bid inspire respect and trust.

The rule of thumb of professional negotiators abroad seems to be to ask for as much as you possibly can without making yourself appear imperialistic, foolish or blatantly bluffing. To make the right opening price demands, you must know two things: the cultural bargaining norms in the country, and the market realities. Not knowing these things makes you vulnerable to exploitation and loss of face, whether you are buying olives at the market or oil in the international exchange. In any country, the market realities provide ceilings and floors on the range of settlements, and it is always assumed that both sides know what the real market values are.

How much to overstate your demands depends on the country. The Chinese, Koreans, Japanese, Arabs, Israelis, Russians and others are likely to start off with an extreme position. Never express irritation—in many countries the opening bid is ritualistically extreme because the negotiator expects to back down. In China the negotiator is likely to be a professional whose only job is to negotiate. If he cannot show that he obtained "discounts," he is not doing his job. The Arab will start with an outlandish position, then retreat and claim, "See how generous I am."

Fourth, plan to control your concessions. First, make an inventory of all the concessions you might be willing to make, not just the obvious ones from your point of view but any variations that might be appealing to the other side. Think of concessions that may mean nothing to you but a lot to the foreigner—what Stanford's Richard Pascale calls "free ice in winter."

How you present your concessions can make a big difference, depending on the culture of the negotiators. Compromise and concession are not virtues everywhere. In some places an early concession might get the wheels turning, but elsewhere it might hurt your position. To the French, a thoughtful position should not be compromised unless something was wrong with the reasoning. The Mexican will not compromise, as a matter of honor, dignity and integrity. The Arab fears loss of manliness if he compromises. It's a question not of face but of control—he would rather feel he is giving out of generosity, not necessity. In Russia, "compromise" has a negative connotation; principles are supposed to be inviolable, and compromise is a matter of integrity. A negotiation is treated as a whole, without concessions. However, in the USSR and other countries where compromise is not the cultural mode, issues can be bartered, quid pro quo, without the stigma of concession.

The timing of concessions can be revealing or confusing when people from different cultures negotiate. Americans make trivial concessions right away and continue to make concessions throughout the entire course of the negotiation. We make our concessions in sequence, and the final agreement is little more than a summation of all previous agreements. Not so elsewhere. Some people don't make concessions until the end of deliberations when a total package is agreed upon. In these countries, Americans who make concessions along the way find they have "given away the store" needlessly. During the Cuban missile crisis John Kennedy stood firm against the Russians (who make concessions late), resisting the American inclination to concede early. Japa-

In Persian, the word "compromise" does not have the English meaning of a midway solution which both sides can accept, but only the negative meaning of surrendering one's principles. Also, a "mediator" is a meddler, someone who is barging in uninvited. In 1980, United Nations Secretary General Kurt Waldheim flew to Iran to deal with the hostage situation. National Iranian radio and television broadcast in Persian a comment he was said to have made upon his arrival in Tehran: "I have come as a mediator to work out a compromise." Less than an hour later, his car was being stoned by angry Iranians.

SOURCE: *Getting to Yes*, Roger Fisher and William Ury of the Harvard Negotiation Project, Penguin Books, 1983, Page 34.

---

nese negotiators are not normally able to compromise without going through the organization again.

Sincerity and consistency are important practically everywhere, and improving your offer abruptly can undermine the other side's confidence in you. The first to make a unilateral concession frequently is marked as the weaker player in the negotiation, either because the opening bid seems insincere or because the first to back down appears to need agreement more than the other side. Avoid making concessions or agreements along the way when negotiating in cultures where agreement is reached as a total package at the end of deliberations.

Rule 5: Send a winning team. Who a company sends may determine the outcome of a negotiation or whether it will be able to enter negotiations at all. In the Middle East, the top man makes the decisions and prefers to deal only with other decisionmaking executives. In Africa and some European countries such as Germany, authority generally comes with age, so the representative at the bargaining table should be at least middle-aged. In China, team members must have expertise, not just authority. When Chevron Overseas Petroleum negotiated there, the Chinese team was led by a woman who had a degree in chemical engineering and twenty-five years in oil production.

Sometimes it's better to negotiate than to make a quick decision.

In his first loan negotiation, a banker new to Japan met with seven top Japanese bankers who were seeking a substantial amount of money. After hearing their presentation, the American agreed on the spot. The seven Japanese then conferred among themselves and told the American they would get back to him in a couple of days as to whether they would accept his offer or not. The American banker learned a lesson he never forgot.

Russian negotiators are specialists in their fields, and in addition have several years in the academy of foreign trade. They are trained negotiators.

Everywhere in the world an essential ingredient of a negotiation is the creation of trust and a sense of long-term interest in the country. It does not create confidence to send a representative without much authority. Even where a deal will be hammered out by middle management, a senior manager should make opening contact. The interest of top management gives your project a sense of urgency. But keep in mind that any upper-management meetings should merely set the tone and not deal with substance. In most places the top management will not be directly involved in negotiations and you will only embarrass the other side by sending your highest people to negotiate. The novelty and prestige of doing business in China has attracted many chief executive officers there to initiate talks with the Chinese, and the Chinese have not hesitated to use these executives' general statements to their advantage when subsequently negotiating with middle managers.

Don't go alone. Foreigners will almost always have more people on a team than Americans are inclined to have. You may not be able to match them (the Japanese and Chinese will always add more people), but do try to reach some balance in authority and power. Being outnumbered is a psychological as well as practical disadvantage. You need the help of a strong team to be able to carry on all the simul-taneous activities of a negotiation: giving information, persuading, listening, thinking, preparing arguments, formulating questions and revising strategy as necessary to continue moving toward agreement. It also helps to have a number of nodding (or frowning) faces on your side to give an air of support and unity.

Always have your own interpreter. Never rely on theirs. Remember, the interpreter on the other side is working for *them*. (See Chapter 5 for rules on briefing and use of interpreters).

Exclude lawyers and accountants from the negotiating team. Few foreign negotiation teams will have attorneys at the bargaining table, although lawyers are very important behind the scenes. As a general rule, bringing a lawyer along will do great damage, arousing suspicion in some countries and contempt in others. Some foreigners snicker at us for relying on the law when we should rely instead on religion, humanity or common sense.

Foreigners who mistrust attorneys may assume from their presence that you are planning deception or that you are more interested in the fine points of a contract than the relationship. American lawyers tend to negotiate contracts when the foreigners are negotiating a relationship; lawyers concentrate on looking at words rather than the character of the business partners.

The attorney in international business plays a role that is quite different from the domestic attorney's role. The international lawyer must have a conscious appreciation of how differently business is conducted around the world, and a talent for working with these differences to accomplish legal protections and commitments while not impeding the process of business. An attorney who understands the cultural context can be a great asset.

Lawyers must be kept abreast of developments so that they can prevent later embarrassment. The final legal papers are essential, of course. You must have a trail of documents, letters of intent, or agreements to fall back on if and when a deal begins to unravel.

In some cases, use a go-between. Victor Kiam, president of Remington Products, tells the story of his first efforts to set up an organization to sell Remington shavers in Japan. He flew to Hiroshima and met with the toiletries buyer at Japan's biggest department store. Everything seemed to go well. The Japanese nodded and smiled a lot, and Kiam left after an hour thinking he had a deal. But his interpreter explained to him that actually he did not. In Japan you know you have a deal when you are told the name of the man who is going to pick up the goods that you are selling. Mr. Kiam didn't get a name. Eventually, through the intervention of a banker, the buyer agreed to meet again with Kiam, but Kiam had to go through his entire presentation again, word for word from the first hello, as though he had never met the buyer before. This way everybody could save face and the buyer could place an order.

In many places it is best never to open negotiations with a company yourself. Use someone who is known to the foreign management, such as a banker, a trading agent, a respected professor or a member of a trade association. The go-between must be equal in status to the personnel involved in the negotiations, generally at middle-management level. Often the go-between uses some neutral ground such as a hotel for the meeting. Contact, of course, must be in person.

Don't change negotiators in midstream. Much of the foreign negotiator's energy is concentrated on getting to know you. Your company goes back to zero when it brings in new faces. Moreover, by changing personnel, you will seem unreliable, confused and insincere.

Rule 6: Allow yourself plenty of time, and more.
Americans go into negotiations with an eye to the end result; our orientation is toward an outcome. Most other cultures are oriented to the process of the negotiation itself, thus they feel no sense of rush and have infinitely more patience. At the beginning of the Vietnam peace talks in Paris, Averell Harriman checked into the Ritz on a day-to-day basis. The North Vietnamese took out a two-year lease on a villa.

Experienced travelers recommend tripling the time you think a negotiation will take. With the exception of a few European cultures, most foreigners will prolong meetings, both to get to know you better and to go over details again and again until total understanding is reached. Many more people will be involved in the foreign decision-making process. Often days will

Ford Motor Company, when Lee Iacocca was running it, wanted to buy Ferrari. Some of Iacocca's top people went to see Enzo Ferrari and they came to an understanding: Ford would acquire not the race car but the production side of the company so that the Ferrari name could be used in the United States. The deal was made on handshakes between gentlemen. Soon, though, Ford's attorneys arrived in Italy with contracts, and a crew arrived to take inventory. This was normal business procedure for the Americans, but Ferrari was disgruntled—to his thinking he had an understanding with a gentleman, not with a group of attorneys and accountants—and had second thoughts. The deal fell through. In the end, Fiat stepped in and gave Ferrari the money he needed.

---

pass while authority from upper management is sought. And throughout the tedium of delays and repetition, you must maintain harmonious relations if you are to keep the negotiations alive. Chevron's Robert Armstrong says that the Chinese repeatedly told him: "Always remain flexible." Don't get mad. Try never to appear rushed. If you had set aside one day for meetings, prepare instead for three days; if it should take a week, plan on three weeks.

Never tell the other side when you are leaving. Some foreigners, if they know you are in town for ten days, will take you on tours, dinners, and continuous entertainment and meetings to keep you from talking to a competitor. As one executive says: "We've all experienced it—the jet lag, the toasts, the seven A.M. meetings. It's like brainwashing. They wear you down to malleable form." When it is about time for you to leave, they will hand you an agreement, saying, "Please sign here." Mortified to return home empty-handed after an expensive junket abroad, some travelers may sign, especially if making a straight sales deal.

When the foreign negotiators (or their personnel) ask how long you are staying, say you haven't made any plans for your return. Just in case they call your hotel to inquire about the length of your reservation (as they have been known to do), you might make reservations for an indefinite period. Your opponents are likely to proceed into negotiations, and you will be less likely to be pushed into a deal on the way to the airport. Finally, give yourself enough time so that you go into meetings rested. Henry Kissinger has stressed the importance of stamina: you must be able to persist, to hold fast while goals are ever so gradually fulfilled, and you must be able to manage stress. Be sure to schedule plenty of time for sleep and relaxation; don't engage in late-night partying before important sessions.

Beginning the Negotiating

Rule 7: Make the opening scene work for you. The practice in Hollywood is to throw away a script if it doesn't grab the reader in the first ten pages. Ten pages transforms into ten minutes on the silver screen, and average moviegoers decide whether they like the film in the first ten minutes. So the first scene has a big job to do. In international negotiations, the first scene counts too. The central characters and the thrust of your "story" are introduced. The other side's first impressions will be hard to shake. If your partners are not hooked in the beginning, it will be hard to involve them as the drama of the negotiation unfolds.

As with all international business transactions, do not expect to get straight to the point, unless you are in northern Europe. Your first negotiation meetings may seem more social than businesslike—informal gatherings where the opposite side can check you out. Do not misconstrue the casualness of these meetings. Do not behave informally at informal occasions. Be personable, not personal. And most of all, do not be careless in your remarks. Use this time to check *them* out.

In the United States this first period of "feeling out the players" is usually very brief, often no more than introductions and a few pleasantries. Elsewhere, this first phase can take a long time. Don't rush it, and try to take advantage of it yourself.

Think about the agenda. Whether you are a visitor on foreign soil or whether you are negotiating with foreigners here in America, don't just accept the agenda proposed by the other side. Read it carefully for what it contains and what it leaves out. Consider what priorities it

reveals. What will its effect be on your concession strategy—does it force your concessions too soon? If you are concerned about it, take extra time; ask for a break to study it and propose adjustments.

Watch the physical arrangements. Most people seem to agree that you have the advantage if you negotiate on your own turf, but you can use being the visitor to your advantage too: you can see their operation and how they operate within it. You can get more time, play on their obligations as hosts, and so on. Wherever the negotiation, avoid arrangements where you face the sun, and avoid noisy rooms. Be prepared for sweltering heat in summer and unheated rooms in winter.

The overture should make music. Formal negotiations typically begin with what experts call "posturing," the expected generalities and sentiments expressed to set the tone. Use the words "respect" and "mutual benefit" frequently. An air of cooperation will get the negotiations off on the right foot. Avoid any posturing statements that suggest arrogance, superiority or urgency.

Posturing is followed by a period of formal exchange of information. Presentations are made by each side, questions raised, answers sought. Alternatives may be discussed and preferences expressed. Americans are able to dispense with this stage efficiently but may become frustrated in international negotiations. The French enjoy conflict and debate, and will interrupt even the opening presentations with arguments that may or may not be relevant to the topic at hand. The Mexican always seems to be beating around the bush, suspicious and indirect, cushioning opening talks with lengthy conversation but little substance. The Soviets treat business discussions as one form of worldwide political struggle—the unsuspecting traveler can be overwhelmed by the power playing of the Russian negotiation team. Americans in China complain of being "pecked to death by a thousand Peking ducks." The Chinese ask questions that the Americans feel they have thoroughly and clearly answered, repeatedly; yet the Chinese will give only vague and ambiguous answers to the American's questions. In all cases, the only uniform rule is to persist.

The Chinese have been called technological vacuum cleaners. After about a hundred Boeing personnel compiled detailed information and over twenty Boeing people spent six weeks presenting a roomful of literature and making daily technical demonstrations to the Chinese, the Chinese said, "Thank you for your introduction." One who was present in the negotiations explains the Chinese appetite for information: "Remember, their long-term goal is to manufacture airplanes themselves, not to continue to buy from America."

Hard Bargaining

Eventually, after all the posturing, preliminary information-gathering and presentations of opening demands, negotiators move into a phase of hard bargaining. This is when the deal is hammered out, concessions may be made, and each side tries to persuade or manipulate the other side to give more. This is when your resolve will really be tested.

Rule 8: Control information. As a rule, keep your cards close to your chest. Throughout, the foreigner will want more and more information, some which may be, at least from your point of view, proprietary and confidential. Give no more information than you think is necessary for the success of your negotiations. Too many of us feel bound to answer a question as though being called upon in school. Don't do it. Field questions diplomatically. Always appear fully cooperative, but remember you can always give partial answers or answer different questions. If the information really is a proprietary secret, say so—most foreigners, even in developing countries, now understand this. Most of all, learn how to handle periods of silence. Many foreigners say that if they are silent long enough, an American will start blurting out information or lowering prices.

Be careful to guard information from the beginning of contacts with a potential negotiation opponent. Information shared casually or formally during preliminary introductions, factory tours, and dinners may come to haunt you in later negotiations. What you said in an effort toward "relationship-building" will be taken

Don't tell them everything.

An American trader participating in a trade fair in the United Arab Emirates set out looking for helium tanks and regulators to fill balloons that would decorate his booth. He found one store open, got a quote on the tanks and agreed to rent the regulators. Thankful, he told the Arab how relieved he was—the balloons were going to be a big deal at the booth and he had been unsuccessful finding anyone else who would rent him the regulators. When he arrived to pick up the equipment, the Arab told him there had been a misunderstanding—and the American had to pay a highly inflated price. This kind of thing happens all the time. The message: Never give too much information even *after* the deal has been struck.

into consideration when the other side thinks about its price. Most of us give away entirely too much information even when we ask questions. The typical American will lay out the details of what he or she wants to buy—the product, features, colors, sizes, any special markings or delivery requirements—then ask, "What will that cost if I buy ten dozen?" Worse, we might ask, "Can I have it by Christmas?" Expert negotiators such as Stanford's Richard Pascale suggest breaking down the inquiry to discrete elements so that you will get the information without tipping your hand. For example, start by asking the price of one item. Then explore the discount structure and alternative terms of payment. Discuss scheduling. Consider different features, indifferently. Then inquire about special markings, or delivery, or other variables. The more you understand about the price structure and production schedule, the better you will be able to figure out how much negotiating room you have.

"Americans, especially American men, don't ask enough questions," says a businessman from Guyana. "You always try to show how much you know, but I think we end up knowing more than you." His point: Ask your own questions, or the other side will end up with more information, and you with less. The point is not to catch your opponents off-guard (as you can arouse hostility if they are embarrassed and unprepared), but to learn as much as possible.

Rule 9: Watch your language. An American negotiator might reassuringly announce, "Well, we seem to be thinking along parallel lines," meaning "At least we seem to agree in attitude or point of view." Some foreigners might take this as less than reassuring; to many people, the same expression describes two unfortunate parties going down two separate paths that have no hope of ever meeting. Many negotiations flounder because of communication problems. The Russians and Americans had a hard time at the SALT talks because of confusion over words. When the Americans thought they had an agreement (meaning conclusive commitment), the Russians said it was an understanding (meaning an expression of mutual viewpoint or attitude). And when the Americans thought they had an understanding, the Russians said it was a procedural matter, meaning they agreed to a process for conducting the negotiation. Because words, body language and even concepts mean different things in different countries, negotiators can spend days talking **past one** another in meetings, accomplishing little more than large-scale misunderstandings. It is a good idea to agree with the opposite side on the specific meanings of certain words, including procedural terminology.

Wording is especially problematic between countries that have little experience in working together. When AMC was negotiating a joint venture to build Jeeps in China, a dispute erupted over the word "exclusivity" in the contract. The Americans wanted a guarantee that no other company in China would be given the technical documents for manufacturing Jeeps. In Chinese, "exclusivity" has negative overtones; the words "undivided heart" were substituted in the Chinese version because of their more pleasing connotations of "complete attention," a more meaningful concept among the Chinese. A Chevron attorney spent three weeks in Beijing negotiating the word "profit." It was finally struck and replaced with "remainder." At one point during negotiations one of his colleagues remarked, "To resolve this issue [in the contract] will require the wisdom of Solomon and the patience of Job." Never make that sort of comment—they wasted an hour trying to explain it.

Rule 10: Persuasion is an art. **Don't paint your argument with the wrong materials.** Artists know you can't use watercolor on an oil-paint canvas—it just won't sink in, and neither will your arguments if they do not fit into the prevailing thought and logic "fabric" of the culture. Like acrylic on oil, some of your efforts may appear to work, but eventually you will see that the message didn't stick.

Americans tend to be factual—the facts speak for themselves. And we are inductive thinkers: we amass our data and then draw conclusions, but we respond to new evidence. We worry about presenting our data clearly, with evidence documented, and are less concerned with the thought process. It is the specifics of a deal that concern us, not the principles.

What convinces an American will fall on deaf ears in many places. Other cultures are less factual but more intuitive, deductive or normative than we tend to be. In many places "evidence" is interpreted according to already established principles. The Soviets, for example, think from the general idea to the particular. Soviets deduce implications from axioms rather than the other way around. The French are philosophically analytical, believing that cold logic leads to the right conclusions. The Mexicans and Japanese are much more affective than logical in approach; emotion and drama carry more weight. The Japanese are also data collectors, and hypothetical reasoning does not convince them. Arabs are more normative; relationships and value systems are important. The Chinese focus on practicality; they deal in the concrete and particular, but they are artists in using general principles to gain an advantage in negotiation. And they are sticklers for consistency. Many an American feels that if one explanation doesn't work, perhaps another will—an approach that will backfire in Asian countries, where inconsistency may be suspect. Sometimes it is better to repeat the same explanation in different terms or even use the same words.

Thinking on the same plane is important. Americans like to think big and talk big—we like to deal with big volume, big ads, and so on.

This is inappropriate in a culture where people think in smaller, or unit, terms. Joe Garcia of Mattel says: "I've seen Americans in Spain, Germany and Hong Kong trying to negotiate their big deals, when local businessmen were worried about piece counts and profit per piece; they pick on little points. Many Americans get antsy talking about nickels and dimes and cut them off, but you have to listen to where they are coming from. Address their needs. It works."

Don't forget your concession strategy. With new information, you may need to adjust the strategy often, but wherever you are, make your concessions count. Whether you make concessions along the way or at the end of deliberations, think of them as tools in the negotiations, not required giveaways. And don't think you have to make a concession each time the other side makes one, but try to make your concessions only when the other side gives too. Don't worry about being seen as stubborn—you will be respected for your consistency. Generally it is a good idea to let the opposite side volunteer its own concessions rather than suggest them yourself.

Whenever making concessions, keep them small. Every inch should make good mileage. The other side needs to have something to chip at—giving too much too soon doesn't allow the process of negotiation. Old hands recommend accompanying each concession with sweat and tears, emphasizing the importance and generosity of the concession. One might cry, "Mr. Wong, if I gave any more, I would be out of a job! I would lose face and could never come to Taiwan again!" And throughout, keep track. Deidra Deamer, director of trading at Unison Corporation, warns: "When negotiating in China, you'd better keep the total picture in mind, or you will end up with a long tally of concessions that add up to more than you realized."

Whatever the style of your arguments, they must contain the necessary content. Many foreign governments, for example, must be convinced that a deal is consistent with their country's overall economic priorities: an import must be deemed needed for the good of the country, there being no domestic substitute available, or a project must provide for technol-ogy transfer and jobs for local laborers. Reliability may be as important as cost savings, considering the state of technology in the country. Price and quality are of concern everywhere, but other factors may be more important. Track record is usually more impressive than plans and promises. Don't waste your breath on the wrong information.

Be wary of the persuasion strategies Americans love. Many favorite American negotiation gambits can spell disaster abroad. The most outstanding approach to avoid is the "good guy-bad guy" routine. In many places the "bad guy" may generate so much hostility that negotiations will come to an end. Another American stratagem is to decompose a problem down to its smallest parts, to solve each issue separately. Many foreigners don't think this way and become suspicious when we try to force a decision on one piece without considering the whole.

New negotiation stratagems come along all the time, some of them impressive. The rule is: Whenever you learn a new technique, do not use it without questioning how appropriate it will be to the foreign culture.

Rule 11: Get in stride with the locals. Negotiations abroad are not likely to proceed the way you'd expect them to back home. Americans are uniquely linear, attacking issues sequentially, resolving one issue after another: quantity, then price. We assume we are halfway through when we are halfway down the agenda. But in many cultures, especially in the Far East, a negotiation is holistic: all issues discussed at once and no decisions made until the end. Americans tend to panic when the steps don't seem in order and when expected milestones are gone. As one expert says: "Don't fall off your horse when you lose stride. Learn to vary your pace."

Sometimes it is better for you to be active and involved; at other times you should be passive or removed. At times you will be more effective if you talk or argue your points; at other times you should be quiet or agreeable. You must be sensitive to the flow of the negotiation to know when to be flexible or determined.

Most important: Take time out. Most businesspeople don't take enough time out from negotiations to think. Whatever the local pacing, you must know when to call a caucus. Stanford's Richard Pascale insists: "Always, always, always give yourself time to think." The Vietnam peace talks were 90 percent caucus and 10 percent talks. It is vital to find ways to buy time. Like the time-out in football, the caucus is an important time for you to reconsider and prepare countermoves. Pascale suggests getting the other side to present its position before breaking for the evening, arranging to get phone calls or going to the bathroom. An interpreter or technical person can also be helpful in slowing down the negotiations. But you don't always need to be coy. It is perfectly reasonable to ask for a recess to study an issue.

Proper pacing also allows for "acceptance time," the time it takes for a new idea to sink in and become acceptable. Given enough time, people often change. Try to provide for plenty of time when you introduce new data, requirements or ideas. Unless you give time and help resolve the other side's concerns, logic will not prevail.

Rule 12: Go behind the scenes—that is where minds are changed. It is occasionally possible to see that the negotiator on the other side is blocked by some organizational, legal or policy constraint. It is often possible to move the discussion to those issues and help him resolve them, thus gaining favor and freeing up a "win" for both sides.

In some countries, particularly in the Far East, the negotiation session is less a forum for working out issues than it is a formal and public expression of what has already been worked out beforehand. It is always wise to resolve differences before a meeting. Come early to meetings so that you can chat casually, and linger again afterward. It will not be difficult to find ways to meet informally, since *houmani*—the back-door approach—is the customary procedure in so many places.

Rule 13: Give face. People who lose face can go to extremes to act out their resentment or get even behind your back. Almost every negotiation is a face-saving situation, and the successful international negotiator will carefully avoid making people uncomfortable. Be careful in your choice of words so that the other side is not offended. Grandiose presentations may seem arrogant and make the other side defensive. Always avoid criticism that might be taken personally. Many experienced international negotiators say: "The successful negotiator is the one who treats the person on the other side with respect and fair play. Do that and they will always come back and work with you."

If you must object to certain requirements or constrictions, try to deflect the blame to things outside the control of your opponent, or to "others" in the opposite side's organization. But if you need a scapegoat, be wary of treading on loyalties. In Japan you might offend people if you point blame at the government; indeed, in countries with military governments it is positively dangerous to point blame at the regime and may lead to your arrest.

Rule 14: A deadlock means neither side wins, but both may lose. No negotiator likes to deadlock, but in international negotiations, deadlock is frequently the outcome of days, weeks or months of meetings. Sometimes there is no solution and the parties must go their separate ways. But before giving up, there are a number of ways to try to get the negotiations "unstuck."

When you are stuck on a certain item, try to expose the root of the problem ("Why are we stuck here?") and make some accommodations such as minor concessions or creative repackaging of the proposal. Now would be a good time to use your go-between. He can ask discreet questions of junior employees in the company to find out what the problem is or who is resisting the deal.

You may be able to get "unstuck" by changing the deal in some way, such as by changing the timing or financial arrangements affecting cash flow or risk. Alternatively, shelve the subject temporarily and work on issues that can be resolved. Some negotiators suggest breaking a deadlock by adding to the tension level: showing anger, walking out, and postponing discussions until there is a readiness to deal with the issues. In international situations, however, these tactics should be used with extreme caution, if at all. In most countries, emotional outbursts or behavior that threatens loss of face may close the door permanently behind you.

Do not hasten to conclude that every impasse is a deadlock. In China, and in many other countries, every negotiation occurs within a complex institutional background. When progress stalls, keep in mind that the negotiators may be waiting for bureaucratic approvals. In Japan a seeming deadlock can last for weeks but is no cause for panic. Even if meetings have ceased, much can be done behind the scenes by meeting in private to rebuild the relationship and sense of interest and understanding. Throughout these trying times, always maintain harmonious relations.

Rule 15: Don't be browbeaten into a bad deal. The emphasis on harmony and cooperation in some cultures does not mean that the other side will not play tough. Often you will get ultimatums, threats, accusations and occasionally personal slights. When this happens, remember that you do not necessarily need to take abuse to win.

It is not unusual for foreign negotiators to protest loudly, "We have been your loyal allies and now you are picking on us." A U.S. trade representative describes a South Korean negotiation that began with a pathetic comparison of the rich imperialistic nation pitted against their (the Koreans') poor struggling developing economy, and ended with a condemnation of U.S. political and military position in the world. In short, they tried to make the Americans feel guilty before the negotiations even began. Infuriated, one of the Americans stood up and calmly but firmly gave it right back to them. He told them how he had fought in Korea and how many of his buddies died there. The Koreans sheepishly went into reasonable negotiations. The trade representative said, "They do play hard ball, and at the same time, the Korean Blue House controls the media, so you hear only the Korean side. They can come on like a buzz saw."

You must be able to walk away. Before the negotiation you should have defined your walkaway. When you reach that point, walk! Many international business people are lured into unprofitable agreements in hopes of future business. A bad deal, however, only sets a precedent for future bad business. You can't change your prices the next time. You don't need to take a loss to establish a relationship—don't do it. But walk away gracefully, tall and friendly, so that the other side is not too embar-

rassed to call you back. Never be bitter, or the door will be closed forever.

You must also be able to walk when you find business practices or personal conduct that is illegal or contrary to our standards. Usually there will be warnings that all is not right, and if you pay attention to these warnings there will be time to back out. The project manager of a joint venture between Triad International and a group of American agribusiness companies that were to transfer agriculture technology in the Middle East backed out just before the venture blew up. But, he says, "When the deal is big, Americans can be so dazzled that they miss the danger indicators. Everyone wanted to keep going for the big payoff. They should have paid attention to the red signals."

Don't let your walk-away limit your ability to integrate new information during negotiations and look for new solutions. The picture can change rapidly and there is always more to learn. The point is, you must be able to say no to a bad deal.

Agreements

Rule 16: Get your agreement signed before you leave. Once you are out of the country, it could take months to get a contract that you thought was agreed upon, either because of the foreigner's reluctance to deal through the mails or because other matters become more pressing when you are not there. Very likely you thought you had nailed down all the points of agreement but find that the written contract produces more unresolved issues. If more people become involved after you are gone, you may be back to zero.

Rule 17: Both sides should agree on the significance of what you are signing. The American contract formalizes a bargain and protects against either party breaking the bargain—the relationship is legal. Foreigners say Americans are bound by law, not by relationships, tradition, religion or culture. We will honor a contract to the letter, whatever circumstances later arise. But the meaning of an agreement varies around the world, making it very hard for mixed cultural groups to know precisely the significance of the documents they sign or the seriousness of a handshake.

Few Americans, Germans or British will conduct business without some form of written contract. In the Arab world a person's word may be more binding than many written agreements, and insistence on a contract may be insulting. Even so, the Arab (or other nationality) might not fulfill an "agreement" since a Westerner can mistakenly hear words of commitment when only politeness was intended. In many parts of the world, open refusal to do as another requests is rude. In some cultures, it is assumed that any agreement may be superseded or negated by a later conflicting demand, particularly by a superior or a relative. As an outsider, you will always be at a disadvantage because no foreigner will feel he owes you loyalty, and the concept of face only applies to friends, relations and colleagues.

Contracts serve different purposes around the world—often definitely un-American. A Greek sees a contract as a formal statement announcing the intention to build a business for the future; the negotiation is complete only when the work is accomplished. The Japanese treat contracts as statements of general intention, and they assume changes will be made as dictated by developments. Mexicans treat the contract as an artistic exercise of ideals and do not expect contracts to apply consistently in the real world. At the opposite extreme, a German contract cements details that contracts of other countries, even the United States, might leave to standard trade practice. Yet even there, the German Civil Code can supersede a contract, imposing duties or prohibiting items not provided for in a contract.

When the two sides of a negotiation do not define agreements or contracts in the same way, each side is likely to suspect the other of unethical or illegal practices, and future business will be jeopardized. The American who is inflexible in treatment of the contract is going to be accused of shady dealings by many foreigners. Confronted with the various points of view, you have several choices: you may choose to adopt the foreign practice and assume a contract that will be modified with circumstances, or you may try to get the foreigner to understand that you can only make the kind of agreement that is interpreted from the American point of view, i.e., abided by to the letter.

Rule 18: Be willing to give up cherished notions of the proper contract. A New York lawyer who is given a hundred-page legal brief will nonchalantly look it over on the commuter train home and breezily take issue with a few items the next day. For the U.S. attorney much of the contract is boilerplate, which can be passed over, and any deviations from boilerplate are immediately obvious.

But where contracts are short—in many places a one-page agreement is customary—the American's hundred-page contract will cause problems. Negotiations may be reduced to a continuous assault on the inevitably long and complicated American draft. The foreigner will usually insist that the document be simplified, and may not read it until it has been pared down.

Foreign organizations commonly enter negotiations either with no draft contract or with a simple standard form contract that may have been only a little revised to fit the present negotiation; they will be incomplete compared to what the Americans expect in contracts—the job will be to fatten them. Americans must come to grips with what is not in the contract and negotiate in the points that are important. Typically, you will have to write in statements about quality control and trademark protections, testing procedures, how to deal with rejects, and so on. That will not be easy. In China, for example, there is a handbook of acceptable contract terms, and if the clause is not in it, it is unlikely that the Chinese side will accept it. Foreign sellers' contracts are less detailed and stringent than their purchase contracts, so the American seller will have to meet more exacting requirements than the foreign seller. A double standard is often distinct—for example, in delivery and payment requirements. It is important to scrutinize these contracts and determine if you can live with the imbalances. As a rule, shorter is better when negotiating foreign contracts—aim for clarity and leave out all the unnecessary protections and provisions that so clutter American contracts. Use language that fosters trust rather than suspicion, as it is the relationship that will keep the business going, not the written piece of paper.

You must be willing to give up legal jargon that has no meaning, or confusing meanings, outside the United States. For example, acts that constitute force majeure vary, and if they are not defined, you may find certain things that are beyond your control not accommodated in the contract. Definition of an "act of God" may be a problem in some cultures, such as China and Russia. Always search for alternative language. Many companies have found that people who are unwilling to specify acts of God, labor unrest or strikes, will agree to "conditions beyond the control of the parties" as constituting force majeure.

Pay attention to formalities or rituals of signing agreements. Ask a knowledgeable person (even the other side) if there are any sensitivities you should be aware of. In Saudi Arabia, for example, don't send a senior executive in to sign the contract, as the Saudis may take offense when finding that they have not been dealing with senior people all along. In Korea, don't sign a contract in red ink, as it means you expect it will come to a bad end. In many countries you should leave time at the end for the banquet after signing—and you may be the host.

Beyond the Contract

Rule 19: Discussions are always preferable to court settlements. Many people around the world have become used to American insistence on detailed contracts, and many foreigners will sign them. But even then, don't count on your contract being treated as literally binding. Be ready to discuss new events, to "renegotiate" and to reach a new understanding. Handle contract violations tactfully, and you will do much better than insisting on precise adherence to the written deal.

In many countries, going to court would mean a major loss of face for all parties involved, as well as being costly and inconvenient. The foreign justice system opens up a whole new set of cultural unknowns and risks. Often a third party who is familiar with the respective sides can be a bigger help than court or arbitration.

Rule 20: Remember—without a relationship, you have no deal. Whether you have negotiated an agreement with a distributor for your product, or a supplier for your materials, or a con-

Check List for Contract Drafting:

Terms of contracts will vary depending on whether the agreement is a sales contract, technology transfer, joint venture or other transaction. Just a few of the considerations include:
1. State simply the intentions and purposes of both parties.
2. Describe the responsibilities of each party.
3. Specify which codes will apply regarding choice of law and jurisdiction.
4. Define measures of accomplishment (i.e., how you will determine that the job has been done) and methods for evaluation.
5. Agree on what standard principles of accounting will be used.
6. Make provisions (as applicable) for: delivery and terms discount structures payment and credit security dispute resolution taxes (local and foreign) force majeure controlling language notice provisions logistics expenses of personnel work permits for your personnel entry visas penalties exclusivity licenses and sublicensing rights payment of duties, and other charges warranties and guarantees insurance installation and start up quality control disclosure of information and reporting requirements safeguarding of trade secrets.
7. Translate the contract into the foreign language. Again, be careful with interpretation of meaning: use an interpreter who knows the terminology appropriate for your business.

struction contract, your foreign business depends on maintenance of good relationships. You must visit your associates repeatedly—it's a courtesy and a necessity everywhere in the world. Wherever possible, include your foreign colleagues in incentive schemes, training, translated support materials—anything to keep them working for you and with you.

Summary

In international business, a lot rides on the success of negotiations. If negotiation must be likened to a game, it is a game of perspective. What you do before negotiations is as important as what you do during negotiations.

Before the Negotiations

RULE 1: Make sure what you are negotiating is negotiable.

RULE 2: Define what "winning" means to you. Be ambitious but set a realistic walk-away.

RULE 3: Get the facts.

RULE 4: Have a strategy for each culture and phase. Position your proposal in the best light.
Decide whether the negotiation is going to be win-lose or win-win.
Decide on your opening proposal.
Plan to control your concessions.

RULE 5: Send a winning team.
Don't go alone.
Always have your own interpreter.
Exclude lawyers from the team.
Use a go-between.
Don't change negotiators in midstream.

RULE 6: Allow yourself plenty of time, and more.
Never tell the other side when you are leaving.

Beginning the Negotiations

RULE 7: Make the opening scene work for you. Think about the agenda. Watch the physical arrangements. The overture should make music.

Hard bargaining

RULE 8: Control information.

RULE 9: Watch your language.

RULE 10: Persuasion is an art. Don't paint your argument with the wrong materials.

RULE 11: Get in stride with the locals.

RULE 12: Go behind the scenes—where minds are changed.

RULE 13: Give face.

RULE 14: Deadlock means neither side wins and both may lose.

RULE 15: Don't be browbeaten into a bad deal.

RULE 16: Get your agreements signed before you leave.

Agreements

RULE 17: Both sides should agree on the significance of what you are signing.

RULE 18: Be willing to give up cherished notions of the proper contract.

Beyond the Contract

RULE 19: Discussions are preferable to court settlements.

RULE 20: Remember—without relationships, you have no deal. ●

Study Questions

1. If negotiation is a "game of perspective," why is international negotiation particularly difficult?

2. I think on my feet and play it by ear. How successful will my international negotiations be with these qualifications? Explain.

3. Are experts or novices more likely to explore multiple options in negotiations?

4. Is it true that in international negotiation, the parties normally meet for the first time across the bargaining table? Explain.

5. How is a good negotiation strategy like a road map?

6. When should international negotiators pursue a cooperative appearance? a competitive style?

7. What do you need to make a good opening bid? What does this do to your opponent?

8. How does the phrase "free ice in winter" relate to concession strategy?

9. What role should your top organizational people play in international negotiation?

10. What are the general rules about negotiating alone and bringing in lawyers in international negotiation?

11. What are some "time" issues in international negotiation?

12. What are some good rules of thumb with regard to information disclosure in international negotiation?

13. How successfully will the "good guy-bad guy" technique work in international negotiation?

14. Should you take even a "bad deal" in international negotiation? Explain.

CASE: U.S.-Japan Differences On Trade Are Reflected in the Two Negotiators

Bob Davis and Jacob M. Schlesinger
Staff Reporters of *The Wall Street Journal*

Both Sides Seek A 'Wizard'

Charlene Barshefsky's colleagues call her "Stonewall," a tribute to the U.S. official's tenacity in trade negotiations. So when Sozaburo Okamatsu, a Japanese bureaucrat, met her for talks last year, he wanted to show he was tough, too.

"If you're Mrs. Stonewall, I'm Mr. Stonewall," he told Ms. Barshefsky, who quickly told her colleagues to cut out the nicknames. "The last thing we want is for Japan to think it's all right to stonewall."

But as the two governments race the clock to try to reach a new trade agreement by Friday, that is precisely what each side is running into: a stone wall. Japanese Prime Minister Morihiro Hosokawa and President Clinton will try to sign off on a significant trade deal, based largely on the two negotiators' work. And in the run-up to the summit in Washington, the two sides still face gaping areas of disagreement, chiefly over the U.S. insistence that Japan commit to numerical goals for raising imports.

The Clinton administration, which last summer trumpeted an emerging breakthrough with Japan, still finds that it must redefine the very foundations of the U.S.-Japan trade relationship. American officials say past deals have done little to pry open Japan's closed markets, and despite early hopes, this one doesn't look much more promising. The problem, Washington complains, is intransigent career mandarins who try to talk Americans to death—such as Mr. Okamatsu.

The Japanese contend the Clintonites are wrongly, even dangerously, trying to dictate the terms of trade. The problem, Tokyo complains, is that U.S. policy is shaped by lawyers with little understanding of Japan—such as Ms. Barshefsky.

The Japanese "look at policies in their historical perspective," says Noboru Hatakeyama, a recently retired negotiator at Japan's Ministry of International Trade and Industry. "However, in the case of the U.S., almost all of their negotiators seem like they came in just yesterday."

Bureaucratic flimflam, replies Bowman Cutter, deputy director of the White House's National Economic Council. U.S. political appointees can move fast, he says, while "the pace of change is occurring much more rapidly than the senior civil servants in the Japanese ministries are able to adjust to."

The stakes are huge. Success would ease longstanding tensions, create billions of dollars in business for Americans and accelerate a much-needed restructuring of Japan's economy. A prolonged trade battle between the world's two largest economies could raise the price of imports and hobble joint ventures between U.S. and Japanese companies. Ultimately, a fight could even undermine the U.S.-Japanese political alliance while North Korea looms as a military threat and Russia's own chaos is menacing as well.

Ms. Barshefsky and Mr. Okamatsu embody the strengths and weaknesses of their countries and illustrate how the two sides are trying to reach an agreement and why they are floundering. Each makes demands that feed into the other's fears, leaving each searching for more senior officials—fixers—who will override the negotiators. In the end, the two heads of state just might break the impasse.

The negotiators couldn't differ more. He is a 56-year-old Japanese who grew up during the American Occupation and recalls eating powdered eggs distributed by GIs. She's a 43-year-old American baby boomer who quotes John Lennon to explain her negotiating style.

He is a member of Japan's government elite—a Tokyo University graduate, the son of a MITI vice minister—who spent 33 years climbing the ranks at MITI until he became vice minister for international affairs. She is the daughter of immigrants who made her mark as a high-priced trade lawyer with blue-chip clients and joined the government only last year.

He speaks so softly that he had to utter the threat of "retaliation" twice before any reporters at a news conference noticed. She is as blunt as an exclamation point.

At Ms. Barshefsky's confirmation hearings as deputy U.S. trade representative, when most nominees are deferential to the point of obsequiousness, she took on Sen. Donald Riegle. He questioned whether she was an "economic patriot" after *The Wall Street Journal* reported about her work for foreign clients. "I do not come to this job to build a reputation," she lectured the Michigan Democrat, whose own reputation was marred by his S&L lobbying. "I am here because I have a reputation."

She quickly earned a name in Japan as a brawler, arguing toe-to-toe in Tokyo last June with Mr. Hatakeyama, a MITI man widely reviled by Americans as overbearing. Mr. Cutter, whose great-great-grandfather fought in Stonewall Jackson's brigade, was so impressed that he nicknamed her after the resolute Southern general.

Then, a month later, she clashed with Mr. Okamatsu when the two countries were setting the broad outline for the framework accord. Negotiators had agreed that Japan would use "quantitative" indicators to measure the openness of its market—a critical goal from Washington's standpoint. But Ms. Barshefsky had to quash a 1 a.m. effort by Mr. Okamatsu to ease the terms, especialy as they related to quantitative measures.

A Washington Lawyer

Ms. Barshefsky honed her negotiating style at the Washington law firm Steptoe & Johnson, where she was co-head of the international law practice. She advised Boeing Co. on how to attack subsidies to its European rival, Occidental Petroleum Corp. on how to fend off complaints about its imports from Russia and a Mexican business lobby on how to assess proposals during trade talks with the U.S.

But her Japan experience was paltry—and in that respect she shares an all-too-common failing in American government: lack of institutional memory and knowledge of opponents. Before taking the trade negotiator's post, she had never visited Japan and had little recent business experience with the country. Chalmers Johnson, a Japan expert at the University of California, contends that even after the past eight months of negotiations, "Ms. Barshefsky is a lamb going to slaughter."

But she's a quick study. She came into the administration not knowing much about China, either. But she devised the administration's get-tough strategy over Chinese textile smuggling, and China agreed to concessions under threat of sanctions.

Mr. Okamatsu, by contrast, knows the U.S. well—like most Japanese trade negotiators. One of his first tasks upon joining MITI in 1960 was to try to ease trade frictions by overseeing restrictions on Japanese exports of low-priced silverware. He lived in New York for three years in the mid-1970s and has warm memories of the way he and his family were received. He has spent much of his time since then handling bilateral trade disputes in areas such as semiconductors and auto parts.

A Tokyo Bureaucrat

But Mr. Okamatsu is under fire, too, for the opposite reason that Ms. Barshefsky is. Even some of his fans say he has the common flaws of a bureaucrat—an overly conservative approach to problems and dogged loyalty to his ministry above all else. During the early 1980s, he helped lead MITI's bitter war with the telecommunications ministry over contol of information industries. Mr. Okamatsu says he was drawn to MITI because "I could make lots of important decisions, and do important jobs, from my younger days."

That kind of attitude among the nation's powerful mandarins has spawned the country's woes, many Japanese believe. "Bureaucrats are like cavities," Masao Ogura, the chairman of a major transportation company, wrote in a recent newspaper essay. "The best service to the people is to pull them out completely."

After their tussle in Tokyo, Mr. Okamatsu and Ms. Barshefsky made up. During a negotiating session in Hawaii in September, he sent flowers to her room. She gave him a pewter paperweight with an engraved eagle. He brought—what else?—a camera. Aides snapped photos of the pair on a balcony overlooking the Pacific. Even after, the U.S. negotiating team called the photos "the honeymoon shots."

But the honeymoon didn't last long. The next month, the Barshefsky team handed the Japanese a U.S. proposal calling for Japan to increase its manufacturing imports to the level of the biggest Western economies—a feat that would require at least a doubling of imports. She intentionally left blanks in the appendix, she says, so the two sides could come up with ways to measure Japan's progress. But it wasn't so easy. Instead of filling in the blanks, the two sides got into a nasty, four-month war of words over the use of quantitative measures—the very commitment the U.S. thought it had secured in July.

'Objective Criteria'

What the July accord actually called for was "objective criteria" to measure Japan's progress in opening markets. The two sides agreed to reach the first batch of agreements this Friday, covering autos and auto parts, insurance, and government procurement of medical and telecommunications equipment.

To the U.S., "objective criteria" meant specific import goals. To Japan, any numerical measures should be used only as a means of studying past performance. Mr. Okamatsu argues that rather than set specific targets in a trade agreement, the two sides can talk more about what is causing the problems. "We call this the cooperative approach," he says. "Nonsense," Ms. Barshefsky snaps. "That would analyze the past to death, with no link to future change."

Their philosophical breach reflects more than 10 years of trade tensions and mounting feelings of betrayal by both sides. To the Americans, the U.S. is trying to break the pattern in which Japan would remove one trade barrier and a new one would pop up. That's why the U.S. is turning to import goals and measurements. To the Japanese, the U.S. is rejecting free-market principles and seeking to "manage" trade between the countries.

Twice before, Mr. Okamatsu haggled over numbers with the U.S.—first, over setting a market-share target for foreign semiconductors, and later, a dollar-volume target for U.S. auto parts. In both cases, the U.S. has regularly threatened Japan with new trade sanctions if it doesn't hit the numbers, which Mr. Okamatsu said he negotiated as voluntary goals. "Lesson No. 1 and Lesson No. 2 taught me you shouldn't use numbers," he says ruefully.

Worried Observers

The pleas of Mr. Okamatsu and others won adherents in Asia, where small countries worried that the U.S. would hit them next with demands, and in Europe, where big nations worried that the U.S. would get a leg up in Japan.

The Japanese campaign against managed trade seemed audacious to U.S. officials; MITI has been, perhaps, the world's most successful manipulator of markets. Mr. Okamatsu has been involved in everything from promoting the domestic aircraft industry to launching the famous "Fifth Generation" advanced-computing project. "We have promoted some industries," he concedes. "But that was done in open-market situations."

Still, the two negotiators worked on their personal relationship, hoping that an amiable bond would help them reach a compromise. When not in a business mode, both are warm and funny. During long negotiating sessions, Ms. Barshefsky talked about her two young daughters' affection for origami and drew out Mr. Okamatsu about his family—a topic he is so shy about that some of his colleagues learned he had a daughter only when she was seen from the office window. But he endeared himself to the Barshefsky family by sending them a Japanese doll wearing a kimono. "Since your daughters must have missed you in Tokyo," he told her, "this is something to cheer them up."

The U.S. Offensive

In early December, the U.S. launched its own offensive. In talks with Mr. Okamatsu, cabinet secretaries and political power brokers, the Americans tried to explain that they weren't seeking market set-asides, as with semiconductors. Rather, they wanted Japan to open its market broadly in a verifiable way.

But the press interpreted that to mean that the U.S. was backing off on its demands, and the U.S. found itself attacked as both protectionist *and* weak.

Shortly before Christmas, the U.S. intensified its attack, explicitly casting Mr. Okamatsu and his colleagues as the villains in the drama; the goal was to draw their political bosses into the fight. Trade Representative Mickey Kantor wrote a letter to the *Nihon Keizai Shimbun*, a business newspaper, accusing Japan's bureaucrats of resisting trade liberalization "because they fear a loss of power."

Ms. Barshefsky and Mr. Okamatsu remained trapped in ritualistic negotiations, which has exasperated the hard-charging lawyer. Two weeks ago, in Washington, Mr. Okamatsu handed Ms. Barshefsky documents contending the U.S. had scored big gains in certain imports, which the U.S. deemed inflated. "I told him, 'We're not making progress; we're going to leave,'" she recalls. He threw up his hands and said, "I can't do any more."

Later, Mr. Okamatsu said, "That is her negotiating tactic." But in the end, both sides decided to re-examine the numbers rather than break off the talks.

Now, out of frustration, both sides hope to go over the negotiators' heads, in what might be called a Wizard of Oz strategy. If they could only get beyond the deadlocked negotiators, both sides think, they may find someone hidden from view—a wizard of a fixer—willing to cut a deal.

A Japanese delegation recently asked Robert Rubin, director of the National Economic Council, to come to Japan, figuring that the former Goldman, Sachs & Co. co-chairman would be more sympathetic. He declined, and Mr. Kantor, the blunt U.S. trade representative, showed up.

Making the Rounds

The U.S. search for a wizard is going just as poorly. Last week, Messrs. Kantor and Cutter made the rounds in Tokyo of the top politicians in the government coalition and even the opposition, looking for somebody to plead their case.

But with the cabinet lurching from one political crisis to another, it's not clear who can help. Meeting Mr. Kantor Thursday afternoon, Mr. Hosokawa felt he was finally ready to focus on the framework, having completed his economic package. But by Thursday night, the package had unraveled in a dispute over taxes. Mr. Hosokawa wasn't able to come up with a new plan until yesterday.

Back in Washington, Stonewall Barshefsky prepares for yet-another visit from Mr. Okamatsu, who arrived Sunday. This time, she says, she will tell him about the time her TV set conked out, just before she was due to leave for Tokyo. "Could you buy us another one in Japan," her 10-year-old asked, figuring that is where all TV sets come from. Too expensive, her mother replied, explaining how a closed Japanese market boosts prices higher than they are in Washington. Mr. Okamatsu is ready with a response: Japanese electronics companies, looking to cut the trade imbalance and raise U.S. employment, actually make lots of TVs in America.

Overall, Ms. Barshefsky's strategy is to hang tough but offer the Japanese a face-saving way out. Mr. Okamatsu gently suggests he will make sure things work out. "Our backgrounds are different," he says. "But fortunately, I have had an experience to live in the U.S. So I think I know how the American people think."

Says Stonewall Barshefsky: The Japanese will take "until the last nanosecond" before cutting a deal. •

Study Question

You are hired as a consultant to the U.S. negotiating team. What negotiating advice would you give to Ms. Barshefsky regarding her negotiations with the Japanese? Fully justify the rationale for the actions that you recommend.

pages 215-230

SECTION 4

Negotiation Agenda and Strategy

Understanding power, conflict, relationships, and the nature of negotiation is but a prelude to using them. In this section we explore the alterative strategies we can use to achieve our objectives.

To act effectively in negotiation requires a plan and its execution. The two readings in this sub-section move us to more specificity in making a realistic plan.

Gerald I. Nierenberg ("**Preparing for Negotiation**") has been nicknamed a guru of negotiations by the business press because he has taught his "Art of Negotiating" seminars to thousands of managers at many major corporations around the world. His message in this reading is simple: "*do your homework.*" That is, before you begin understand yourself and your goals, conduct research about the issues and about the other negotiating parties, and practice bargaining techniques.

The most influential recent text on negotiation, *Getting to Yes,* by Fisher, Ury and Patton, has become a best-seller because of its blend of practical idealism, which emerged from the studies and experience of participants in the Harvard Negotiation Project. The excerpt here ("**Developing your BATNA**") shows how to improve your bargaining power by developing alternatives to dependency on your opponent or to using hard-ball tactics.

A negotiator can take no action more important than doing his or her "homework." There is no substitute for proper planning prior to even scheduling the first meeting of the parties. Scott, in "**Preparing for Negotiations**," gives precise, pragmatic advice to develop strategy, tactics, and logistics.

The two contrasting "ideal types" in conflict resolution and negotiation are the adversarial approach—zero-sum, win-lose, contending—and the cooperative approach—variable-sum, win-win, collaborating.

The selection from Walton and McKersie ("**Strategies and Tactics of Distributive Bargaining**") focuses intensively on the win-lose adversarial strategies typical of labor-management conflict. It is taken from their classic book, *A Behavioral Theory of Labor Negotiations*, which presents a detailed theory about major aspects of negotiations. Few writers get so deep into the nitty-gritty aspects of the kinds of tactics negotiators use against each other at the bargaining table.

One of the most familiar settings for group conflict and negotiation is the labor-management relationship. Begin and Beal ("**Reaching Agreement: The Exchange Process**") take a systematic approach to this, looking at the types of bargaining, who participates, and the kinds of preparation that they do. Contact negotiation is a highly developed and well-defined process, but the many variables involved allow for enormous variation in how the labor-management relationship gets played out.

Legal proceedings are perhaps the epitome of the adversarial strategy. Writing for lawyers, Charles Craver ("**Negotiation techniques**") discusses the informal practices they can use to reach settlements. He emphasizes what he calls the "competitive phase" of negotiations, with the numerous tactics and tricks that practicing lawyers use. But will they lead to the cooperative stage—i.e., an agreement?

Competitive or adversarial strategies invoke the idea of winning, as if negotiations were a game. But as Greenhalgh argues ("**The case against winning in negotiations**"), even using the language of "winning" and "losing" locks us into looking at our relationships in inappropriate and dysfunctional ways.

Judith Knelman takes Greenhalgh's issue one step further by asking, "**How can I win if you don't lose?**" Her short interview with Anatol Rapoport, author of a computer program that resolves the famous *Prisoner's Dilemma* situation, reveals that the essence of relationships involves the language of "we" and of "trust."

Savage, Blair, and Sorenson in "**Consider Both Relationships and Substance When Negotiating Strategically**" suggest that one must learn which negotiating strategies are best in certain situations. They argue that traditional approaches to negotiation have underemphasized the importance of future relationships and overemphasized the importance of substantive outcomes. The authors provide a decision tree framework for choosing one's negotiation strategies.

* * *

Preparing for Negotiation

Gerard I. Nierenberg

"Thinking is more interesting than knowing, but less interesting than looking."
—*Goethe*

If you know that within one month you will find yourself across the table from your negotiating opponents, how do you prepare for this face-to-face encounter? How can you foresee the strategy of the opposite side, and how can you prepare to cope with it? The answer is not a simple one. It may be summed up, however, in a phrase reminiscent of school days: *do your homework.* There are any number of life situations for which preparation is necessary. Negotiation is one of these. For successful results it requires the most intensive type of long- and short-range preparation.

"Know Thyself"

This preparation requires, first of all, intimate knowledge of yourself.

If you can be easily goaded to anger, you are very apt to be tricked into an unfavorable settlement because of your emotional state. People in an emotional state do not want to think, and they are particularly susceptible to the power of suggestion from a clever opponent. The angry person cannot instantly change direction, even if he finds that he has just made a ridiculous blunder. The excitable person is putty in the hands of a calm, even-tempered negotiator, a negotiator who has learned how to use emotions *only* for effect.

For these reasons a long-range preparation for negotiation must begin with a form of self-evaluation. It involves an intimate examination of your sense of values, your philosophy of life; it means, in a sense, taking stock of your intellectual and emotional makeup. The question may well be raised whether an individual can accomplish this soul-searching by himself. Sometimes this can be done only with professional help. The procedure resembles the techniques of psychoanalysis. The goal, however, is not the cure of a neurosis but the ironing out of any obvious personality defect, the ferreting out of hidden bias and fixed prejudice, and the elimination, in general, of those traits and quirks of the mind that interfere with your negotiating ability. The basic precept is: *know thyself.* As Polonius advises his son, "To thine own self be true."

How do you go about examining yourself? You must have the courage to ask yourself many disturbing questions, perhaps beginning: What, in general, do you seek in life? What do you want out of your business career? What do you want from *this* particular situation? Going from the general to the specific is by no means an easy task. As Lincoln Barnett has stated: you will be trying to transcend yourself and perceive yourself in the act of perception.

Somebody has likened the self-reflective process to the endlessly repeated image that we see of ourself when seated in the barber's chair between two mirrors. Hundreds of images of our face sweep out in a curve that stretches back to infinity. Perhaps each face in the long row is some particular aspect of our character that demands an examination. If we can ask each reflected face the correct question, then they will all fuse together into one complete, healthy personality. The problem of self-evaluation becomes still more involved if we imagine seeing our image reflected from two distorting mirrors—the distortion resulting, let us say, from our personality complexes.

Other long-range training for negotiation calls for the exercise of a variety of skills. You must have the patience and accuracy of a scientist in searching the literature of past experiments. You must combine the scientific attitude with the cunning of a detective in digging up facts and figures about your opposition. You should be able to apply the current teachings of psychology to predict what the other fellow will try to do. To solve a problem it sometimes becomes necessary and important to learn many new long-range skills, an important one being the art of listening.

My father learned the art of listening at a rather early age. When he was fourteen and thought he knew everything, an old relative took him aside and said, "George, if you want to have the same knowledge at twenty-one that you have now at fourteen, then continue to talk rather than listen, because if you continue to talk, you won't know any more at twenty-one than you know now." La Rochefoucauld states this another way: "One of the reasons that we find so few persons rational and agreeable in conversation is that there is hardly a person who does not think more of what he wants to say than of his answer to what is said." The skill of listening, concentrating on what was being said, as well as what is not being said, can prove to be enormously helpful in negotiations.

After you have completed your research, you must keep an open mind and always be ready to make changes in your appraisal of the situation. It is possible that some of the facts may require modification or that your approach must be changed. Lapse of time alone often tends to call for a change in strategy. Therefore it is important to be constantly on the alert for new developments.

It has been said that one never loses until one gives up. Consider the following example. In 1935 the "Nuremberg decrees" went into effect. By 1936 all borders of Germany were sealed to the Jews. Yet sitting next to me at a closing in 1955 was a real estate investor who had managed the almost impossible feat, not only of escaping with his life, but also of taking his life savings out of Germany. The passage of time did not dim his satisfaction and pride in telling the story of this feat. The essential elements were ingenuity and guts.

It was necessary for him to trade all of his holdings at a huge discount for United States registered corporate bonds. Ingenuity enabled him to contact an agent in Switzerland, who, he hoped, would register the bonds in the United States in the name of the new Jewish purchaser. He had committed his fortune to the oral promises of others. All of this accomplished, he had to take the next step. After memorizing the precious serial numbers, with "guts" he lit a match and made a small "bond fire." Paying the necessary bribery fee, he was permitted to cross the German border "penniless." When he arrived in the United States, he went straight to the office of the register agent for the corporation that had issued the bonds. He reported the destruction of the bonds and their serial numbers, and received replacements shortly thereafter.

Do Your Homework

An important phase of short-range preparation for negotiation is research. Research should be objective; objective not in the quality of the evidence you gather but in your attitude toward such evidence. There is a positive reason for amassing information. It amasses a wealth of material in your mind so that you may take advantage of any new development in the negotiation.

You should be prepared with every possible kind of information about the people with whom you are going to negotiate. When President Kennedy was preparing to go to Vienna for his first meeting with Khrushchev, he made it a point to study all of Khrushchev's speeches and public statements. He also studied all the other material available relating to the Premier, even including his preference in breakfast food and his tastes in music. It is doubtful if such intensive research would be required in most negotiating situations, but the extreme importance of President Kennedy's conference warranted this meticulous search for every detail concerning his protagonist.

An increasing need for facts in all areas today is causing a growing furor about such ideas as a "National Data Center"—a giant computerized "dossier bank" that could pull together all the scattered statistics about any American and make them available to those who needed them.

It is a distasteful idea to many, and yet the negotiator must sometimes subordinate his personal feelings about "snooping" to the exigencies of the negotiation process.

To utilize the information you obtain from research, you must rely upon your general fund of knowledge and experience. It is essential to examine the opponent's past history, inquire into previous transactions he was connected with, and look into every business venture or deal he has consummated. Also investigate any deals he has failed to conclude successfully.

Frequently you will learn as much, or more, about people from their failures as from their successes. If you carefully analyze the reasons that a certain deal fell through or a negotiation failed, you will probably get a good understanding of how the opponent thinks, his method of operating, his psychological approach. All this will give you clues to his needs and prepare you to negotiate with him more advantageously. Consider what proposals he made, what counter-proposals he rejected and why, how flexible he was in the bargaining, how emotional was his approach.

You can obtain clues about the positions that business firms will take by studying some of their past transactions.

Sources like the following can prove helpful:

Budgets and financial plans.
Publications and reports.
Press releases.
Instructional and educational material.
Institutional advertising.
Reports of government agencies like the Securities and Exchange Commission.
Officers' speeches and public statements.
Company biographies in Moody's and Standard & Poor's.

Suppose you are studying an opponent's previous deal that involves the purchase or sale of real estate. The value of the tax stamps that were affixed to the recorded deed will tell the price at which the property was sold. Bear in mind, however, that there have been instances where an excess amount in tax stamps has purposely been used to attempt to hide the actual price of the property. Do not rely on one source. There are other agencies that will assist you in getting a fairly close idea of how much the property was sold for. Try to use more than one source for verification.

Merely by investigating a previous real estate sale, you can get an idea of what kind of man you are going to deal with. You can find out how long he held the property before he decided to sell it and how much profit he was satisfied to take. All these factors are useful in sizing up a prospective opponent. You can never know too much about the person with whom you will negotiate. In the words of Francis Bacon, in his essay *Of Negociating:*

If you would work any man, you must either know his nature and fashions, and so lead him; or his ends, and so persuade him; or his weakness and disadvantages, and so awe him; or those that have interest in him, and so govern him. In dealing with cunning persons, we must ever consider their ends, to interpret their speeches; and it is good to say little to them, and that which they least look for. In all negotiations of difficulty, a man may not look to sow and reap at once; but must prepare business, and so ripen it by degrees.

A trial lawyer's cross-examination of his adversary's expert witness should be more than a spur-of-the-moment inspiration. It must be prepared effectively. In New York State negligence cases, lawyers are required to submit the plaintiff to an examination by the defendant's doctor. No experienced attorney would let the client attend such an examination without him. When the attorney is in the doctor's office, he may have a chance to look at the doctor's library. It is advisable for him to take note of books that may have subject matter dealing with his client's injury. At the trial a most effective cross-examination, worked out in advance, can be conducted by having the doctor admit that certain books are the outstanding authority in the field, and further having the doctor admit that he possesses a copy of the book in his own library. As a result of having carefully analyzed these medical books, the prepared trial attorney will have devised a cross-examination to test any doctor's mettle as to whether he is really a qualified expert.

In examining a person's library, you can gain useful information which will add to your store of facts about him: his present and past interests, hobbies, intellectual pursuits, even the extent to which he is able to follow a subject through.

Another quite effective method of short-range preparation is to check records of previous litigation involving the prospective opponent. (These are available through litigation reports, which may be bought.) In addition to finding out if there is any recorded judgment against him, it will prove useful to know all details about any lawsuits in which he was involved. A fruitful source of information is inquiries made of the people who have litigated with your opponent. An amazing amount of useful information can be obtained from these people. They invariably contribute some facts and opinions that are not found in the ordinary record. These same methods of approach can be employed, not only to investigate the party with whom you are going to negotiate, but also to learn more about somebody you may want to enlist on your side in the negotiation.

Almost 90 per cent of the information that seems most difficult to obtain can be gotten by a direct approach. Try sitting down with your telephone and asking questions. If you are attempting to locate a person, one of the simplest methods is to call everyone in the phone book with the same last name and state that you want to locate a beneficiary under a will. With this as a reward, it is a rare instance that you would not receive full cooperation.

A wife wanted to know whether her ex-soldier husband, newly returned from World War II, was using his postal box to receive love letters from a girl friend who lived in England. When she was informed by her private detective that during the previous week her husband had not received any letters from his girl friend, the wife was not fully satisfied. After all, how could she be sure? She insisted on knowing how the detective obtained his information. He reluctantly explained his method. He merely had someone call the post office each day, explain that he was the holder of such and such a box, and ask the clerk to look and see if a very important letter expected from England had arrived. In response to the inquiry, the clerk had each day answered in the negative.

The *Dictionary of American Slang* defines the phrase "to have someone's number" as "to know the hidden truth about another's character, past, behavior, or motives. . . ." This aptly sums up what you are trying to do in your immediate preparation for negotiation. You are trying to know your opponent, you are trying to "get his number." Indeed our era could well be called the "number age." We are saddled with numbers from the day we are born until the day "our number comes up" and we die. We have a Social Security number, dozens of credit card numbers, bank account numbers, brokerage account numbers, stock certificate numbers, passport numbers, telephone numbers, house and street numbers, check numbers, and any number of other numbers. In modern society men receive more numbers than they know how to handle.

And since we all have numbers, it is easy to get information about any given individual. There are many organizations that specialize in gathering credit information and their charges are quite modest. Large corporations, especially in the retail field, spend as little as one or two dollars for a credit report on a prospective charge customer. Often a simple credit investigation will reveal a vast amount of information about the person with whom you are going to negotiate. This type of research is valuable, and one can sometimes save thousands of dollars' worth of time for a very nominal price.

In researching a situation, always examine and reexamine the rules. How can anyone understand a specific situation without knowing the rules applicable to that situation? How many people read the instructions and bulletins that go with every mechanical device they purchase or even with the medicines they buy? There is the story of the toy manufacturer who starts his assembling manual with: "When all else fails follow the instructions." This being the case, it is not surprising that people who attend an auction or a legal sale have not bothered to read the rules. Sometimes these rules are, unfortunately, learned from experience— usually a bad experience.

You may feel that you already know the rules applicable to your negotiating problem, that it is unnecessary to reexamine them. Then try a simple test. Cover the face of your wristwatch with your hand. Now think, are the numbers on the face Arabic or Roman numerals? Also, how many numerals? Uncover the face and check. Try the same test with a friend. As we go through life we look at the hands of the watch, noting their relative position, abstracting out the other details, never taking notice of the face. We do the same thing with rules. When we consider them, it is only in reference to the specific factual situation. It is therefore necessary to reconsider the rules with each new problem.

An outstanding illustration of this need to reexamine the rules was given by an associate who invited me to attend an auction of a surplus aircraft plant owned by the government. The General Service Administration had put the plant up for auction and it was, supposedly, to go to the highest bidder. Fred, my associate, and I discussed the relative value of the property and determined that we would offer $375,000 for the building and equipment. A hundred or more people had arrived at the auction before us, but Fred, by intuition, was able to look over the crowd, point out a group of three men and say, "There's our competition." He was absolutely right. Brokers and bidders in an audience behave differently. When the bidding began, we started with a bid of $100,000, and they countered with $125,000. We bid $150,000. When they had bid up to $225,000 Fred was silent and we left the auction. I was extremely puzzled; our final bid was supposed to be $375,000. But once outside, Fred explained to me that he read on the offering circular that, according to the rules of this auction, if the government did not feel that the price was high enough, they could reject it. Since we were the second highest bidder, the auctioneer would naturally contact us, tell us that the bid of $225,000 had been rejected, and ask us if we would care to make another offer. We could then counter with a higher price and at the same time ask the government for certain valuable concessions, such as taking a portion of the price in a mortgage. Within seven days this occurred just as if Fred had written the script.

Research supplies information to help anticipate the strategy of the impending negotiation. Such preparation should help answer questions like the following:

1. Are there any penalties involved in this negotiation, such as a penalty for bluffing, or a penalty for giving false information?
2. Have you recognized all of the interested parties to the negotiation?
3. Has anyone placed a time limit on the negotiation, or is there a natural time limit?
4. Who would like to maintain the *status quo* and who would like to change it?
5. What would be the cost of a stalemate?
6. In this negotiation, what will be the means of communication between the parties?
7. Can many items be introduced into the negotiation simultaneously?

By carefully exploring questions of this type, you will gain fresh insight into the strategy of the negotiation about to take place.

The Newer Methods

In addition to the traditional ways of preparing for negotiation, such as doing your homework and examining the rules, other methods have come into vogue fairly recently. These methods employ the techniques of *group drama* (the *psychodrama* and *sociodrama*), *brainstorming,* and the *conference.* At first glance such techniques may seem far removed from anything to do with negotiation. They were originated by psychologists or by the advertising fraternity. However, they are used to find the answers to problems, and in preparation for negotiation you also are seeking to solve problems. You want to know what the other fellow is going to say, what he is going to offer in response to what you say and do—in other words, what his thinking will be. The use of the group approach has proved to be a highly efficient way to get the answers to these questions. Group therapy and group methods of solving problems owe their efficacy to the power of suggestion and to the giving and getting of feedback. Solving problems through a group judgment has often proved superior to results obtained by individual judgments. This has been recognized in the advertising profession.

The method called *brainstorming* has largely superseded the ordinary conference in certain situations, such as originating a name for a new product or a slogan for a campaign. The method is essentially simple. Suppose that a problem has come up, or a new brand name is to be adopted. The usual practice would be to call a conference of the qualified executives in order to get their various opinions; then a decision would be made on the basis of what had been said. In a brainstorming session, a suitable group of people is brought together, with a secretary. The problem is presented in a clear and concise way. From this point on, the discussion and thinking aloud is permitted to move in any direction. Each person says whatever comes into his mind. No attempt is made to correct or evaluate any statements made, but the secretary takes down every word that is uttered, no matter how strange or outlandish it may seem. The entire transcript of what was said is then turned over to the top executive personnel for evaluation.

What is the theory behind this type of group meeting, and why should it produce results? It is believed that brain activity in a group becomes infectious. Ideas appear to grow by being ping-ponged back and forth. The informal atmosphere of the talk and the strong suggestive stimulus of the group thinking give a feeling of security and relieve inhibitions. Under the influence of group discussion, the individual's thinking is quickened and many fresh, original ideas are obtained that far excel those produced in a conventional conference.

Group psychotherapy, which originated with Freud, has been subjected to many refinements since its inception, and in recent years J. L. Moreno has made significant improvements in its application. Moreno uses groups of individuals to act together in a form of improvised play to solve individual problems. He calls this *psychodrama.* Psychiatrists use psychodrama to bring out hidden feelings, attitudes, frustrations, and emotions. In essence, the individual acts out different parts in the group setting.

This technique can be valuable in preparing for negotiation because it permits you to act out the entire negotiation before it takes place. At various times you can play yourself, or an adviser to your side. If you choose, you can assume the role of the other party, or his adviser. Indeed, where the circumstances warrant, it is a good idea to play every one of these roles. It helps you to see what lies before you in the coming negotiation and presents it much more vividly than if you merely talked about it. This method of selecting a definite role and acting it out with a group of other players gives you a chance to try something without the risk of failure. It permits you to bring into focus any important elements that you may have over-looked or ignored. It also permits associates to participate more fully and freely with each member of each side of the group. Furthermore, it facilitates making corrections in your preparation because it lets you put yourself in the other fellow's place. (The police use a technique of role playing when they attempt to reenact their concept of how a crime occurred.) On becoming an attorney, I was fortunate to work in the law office of Lloyd Paul Stryker, one of the outstanding trial attorneys of the day. In his book, *The Art of Advocacy,* Stryker discusses preparation for trial: "I often simulate the witness and ask one of my associates to cross-examine me and to unhorse me if he can. It is great exercise, in the performance of which I have often found that I did not do so well as I hoped. My failures and the reasons for them are then discussed, and I now ask my associate to change places with me and then I cross-examine him. From this, new ideas are developed while all the time the client is looking on and listening."

Before canonizing a saint, the Roman Catholic Church traditionally appoints a "devil's advocate," who is instructed to advance all the *negative* arguments, all the reasons why the person should *not* be canonized.

In another example, week after week during the football season coaches assign substitutes to act the role of the next opponent's star player. A substitute professional quarterback will find himself acting the role of one opponent one week, another the next.

There is an important difference between the "playacting" type of meeting and an ordinary *conference.* In brainstorming a group of people with specified knowledge, experience, and attitudes are called together. Their free and uninhibited participation in discussion can prove useful in solving a problem by group judgment. The individuals called for a conference, however, are not necessarily selected for their special knowledge or experience. A conference may be called for full discussion and fact finding. Guidance or leadership, an unimportant factor in group dramas, plays a vital part in the success of a conference. A conference is for communication, and the communication can be steered in any of three directions: upward, to solve problems; downward, to inform or instruct people; and horizontally, to coordinate or cooperate. Many useful things may emerge from a conference if open communication and a free flow of information are allowed. Certain problems are handled better by the use of the group drama technique, whereas others are dealt with more efficiently in a conference—although we can understand what Tavares Desa, Undersecretary of Public Information for the United Nations, meant when he said, "If you want to get a thing done give it to one man, if you don't want it done give it to a committee."

Group dramas give opportunities for self-analysis. A study of your own motivation and thinking often gives you clues to the probable point of view of your opponent. This gives you the chance to ask yourself exactly what you want from the forthcoming negotiation. A thorough exploration of this question will serve to clarify your thinking on acceptable solutions to the problems to be negotiated, and will also suggest possible compromises that might be made. The answers will not be in absolute terms, but will rather concern the degree of probability of the solution.

A Case History

These days, some of the most rigorous negotiation takes place within a corporation—between one department and another. No business is altogether frictionless. The executive who is trying to maximize the effectiveness of his own part of the operation sooner or later runs into conflict with other departments—and other executives who are also trying to be effective and look good in the process.

When this happens, skill at negotiations is essential to the manager. It can mean life or death for his career.

Let's take a typical case. Mantee, Inc. is a medium-sized company manufacturing a line of office equipment. The episode essentially concerns two men: Fred Jones, vice-president for engineering and design, and Lee Parker, vice-president for sales.

Mantee has begun to market a new machine, called the "500." It is not important to specify its exact function. The "500" was developed by Jones's department, which also maintains the responsibility for inspection and quality control. Parker's job is to sell the "500," along with the other products that Mantee manufactures. He is also responsible for the servicing of the equipment after it is sold.

When Jones agreed that the "500" was ready for marketing, he specified that it was not to be run at more than 1,300 units per hour. His staff was still working on modifications that could possibly double that output.

However, Jones has found out that a number of customers are running the machine at a much higher capacity. Subjected to this kind of stress, the "500" seems to have held up pretty well, but there have been some breakdowns in use.

Jones confronts Parker with this, and with other information he has learned. While Parker's salesmen are not *guaranteeing* the higher output, they also are not emphasizing that the equipment should not be run above 1,300. Parker feels that he must take full advantage of the potential of this new machine while he has an edge over competition. It isn't just a matter of selling the "500"; with the "500" as a "leader," Parker is better able to sell the whole Mantee line. Furthermore, Parker adds, breakdowns in service have not reached anything near an intolerable rate.

Parker is willing to take the responsibility, but Jones, thinking realistically, realizes that a widespread product failure would have an extremely bad effect on the company's position. It would also reflect upon Jones's reputation and certainly not enhance his career.

Mantee's president, in meaningful tones, has told Jones and Parker, "I am most anxious that you work it out between yourselves." In other words, if at all possible there is to be a negotiated settlement. A meeting has been scheduled a week hence at which the two department heads are supposed to "work it out."

Fred Jones determines that he is going to use that week to fullest advantage. But his first move is not a burst of activity. Instead, Jones sits at his desk, thinking. He contemplates himself and his relationships with the sales department.

Jones has to face the fact that these relationships have been spotty. And, he must admit, he has been partly responsible for the situation. Jones considers the sales department a necessary element of the company, but he feels superior to them. What do they know about the painstaking research and the delicate design that go into a masterpiece like the "500"? In a way it has always been a wrench to place a precision product in the hands of salesmen.

Jones faces up to this—and to other feelings. To his pride and ambition, for example. He has a personal reputation to uphold in the industry, and he does not want it to be jeopardized by a sales staff that is driving to meet quotas. Not the most admirable motivation—but there it is.

When Jones has spent adequate time reviewing himself and his own feelings, he turns his attention to his opposite number in the negotiation: Parker.

Lee Parker is a "nice guy." A hearty, outgoing type, he likes people to like him. Nevertheless he is a shrewd sales manager and a good handler of men. And he is ambitious. Jones has seen the other man in action enough to know that Parker would like very much to climb to the top in the firm. For one thing, Parker has always tried to find out as much as he can about Jones's operation, and to ingratiate himself with Jones and his people.

Now Jones proceeds to make further preparations. He calls in his second in command, Harry Watson, and gives Watson a research assignment. Watson is to find out all he can in a number of specific areas about Mantee's recent sales history: who are its biggest customers, the state of customer relations, the ups and downs of customer service, and so on.

What, Jones asks himself, are the overall realities of the situation? For one thing, any settlement must not just bring one department or the other out on top. It must convince the president that it is the best possible solution in the light of the company's short- and long-range growth. Any other answer will make neither Jones nor Parker look good.

But the burden is on Jones to change things. The *status quo*—with the salesmen permitting customers to run the equipment at the higher rate—is satisfactory to Parker. It does not satisfy Jones. So he must change it.

When Watson has completed his research, Jones calls all of his key men together and goes over Watson's findings. They "brainstorm" the problem. Some of the suggestions are pretty wild, but Jones is beginning to formulate a plan. He roughs out the plan and then gets together with Watson for a head-to-head session. Watson is encouraged to play "devil's advocate"—to advance all the arguments that they both know Parker will advance.

Fortified with this preparation, Jones is ready to begin putting together a strategy. Certainly he is ready to consider the assumptions that will control the bargaining. •

Study Questions

1. Why should you "know thyself" to prepare for negotiations? What are some of the personal characteristics that a negotiator should examine in himself or herself? Which aspects of your personality and skills might help you to be effective in negotiations? Which aspects might hinder you in negotiations?

2. If "research supplies information to help anticipate the strategy of the impending negotiation," then how, where, and when should such research be done?

3. Define these terms and explain how they are used in preparation for negotiation: brainstorming; psychodrama (role playing); conferencing.

What If They Are More Powerful (Develop Your BATNA— Best Alternative To a Negotiated Agreement)

Roger Fisher
William Ury
Bruce Patton

Of what use is talking about interests, options, and standards if the other side has a stronger bargaining position? What do you do if the other side is richer or better connected, or if they have a larger staff or more powerful weapons?

No method can guarantee success if all the leverage lies on the other side. No book on gardening can teach you to grow lilies in a desert or cactus in a swamp. If you enter an antique store to buy a sterling silver George IV tea set worth thousands of dollars and all you have is one hundred-dollar bill, you should not expect skillful negotiation to overcome the difference. In any negotiation there exist realities that are hard to change. In response to power, the most any method of negotiation can do is to meet two objectives: *first,* to protect you against making an agreement you should reject and *second,* to help you make the most of the assets you do have so that any agreement you reach will satisfy your interests as well as possible. Let's take each objective in turn.

Protecting Yourself

When you are trying to catch an airplane your goal may seem tremendously important; looking back on it, you see you could have caught the next plane. Negotiation will often present you with a similar situation. You will worry, for instance, about failing to reach agreement on an important business deal in which you have invested a great deal of yourself. Under these conditions, a major danger is that you will be too accommodating to the views of the other side—too quick to go along. The siren song of "Let's all agree and put an end to this" becomes persuasive. You may end up with a deal you should have rejected.

The costs of using a bottom line. Negotiators commonly try to protect themselves against such an outcome by establishing in advance the worst acceptable outcome—their "bottom line." If you are buying, a bottom line is the highest price you would pay. If you are selling, a bottom line is the lowest amount you would accept. You and your spouse might, for example, ask $200,000 for your house and agree between yourselves to accept no offer below $160,000.

Having a bottom line makes it easier to resist pressure and temptations of the moment. In the house example, it might be impossible for a buyer to pay more than $144,000; everyone involved may know that you bought the house last year for only $135,000. In this situation, where you have the power to produce agreement and the buyer does not, the brokers and anyone else in the room may turn to you. Your predetermined bottom line may save you from making a decision you would later regret.

If there is more than one person on your side, jointly adopting a bottom line helps ensure that no one will indicate to the other side that you might settle for less. It limits the authority of a lawyer, broker, or other agent. "Get the best price you can, but you are not authorized to sell for less than $160,000," you might say. If your side is a loose coalition of newspaper unions negotiating with an association of publishers, agreement on a bottom line reduces the risk that one union will be split off by offers from the other side.

But the protection afforded by adopting a bottom line involves high costs. It limits your ability to benefit from what you learn during negotiation. By definition, a bottom line is a position that is not to be changed. To that extent you have shut your ears, deciding in advance that nothing the other party says could cause you to raise or lower that bottom line.

A bottom line also inhibits imagination. It reduces the incentive to invent a tailor-made solution which would reconcile differing interests in a way more advantageous for both you and them. Almost every negotiation involves more than one variable. Rather than simply selling your place for $160,000, you might serve your interests better by settling for $135,000 with a first refusal on resale, a delayed closing, the right to use the barn for storage for two years, and an option to buy back two acres of the pasture. If you insist on a bottom line, you are not likely to explore an imaginative solution like this. A bottom line—by its very nature rigid—is almost certain to be too rigid.

Moreover, a bottom line is likely to be set too high. Suppose you are sitting around the breakfast table with your family trying to decide the lowest price you should accept for your house. One family member suggests $100,000. Another replies, "We should get at least $140,000." A third chimes in, "$140,000 for our house? That would be a steal. It's worth at least $200,000." Who sitting at the table will object, knowing they will benefit from a higher price? Once decided upon, such a bottom line may be hard to change and may prevent your selling the house when you should. Under other circumstances a bottom line may be too low; rather than selling at such a figure, you would have been better off renting.

In short, while adopting a bottom line may protect you from accepting a very bad agreement, it may keep you both from inventing and from agreeing to a solution it would be wise to accept. An arbitrarily selected figure is no measure of what you should accept.

Is there an alternative to the bottom line? Is there a measure for agreements that will protect you against both accepting an agreement you should reject and rejecting an agreement you should accept? There is.

Know your BATNA. When a family is deciding on the minimum price for their house, the right question for them to ask is not what they "ought" to be able to get, but what they will do if by a certain time they have not sold the house. Will they keep it on the market indefinitely? Will they rent it, tear it down, turn the land into a parking lot, let someone else live in it rent-free on condition they paint it, or what? Which of those alternatives is most attractive,

all things considered? And how does that alternative compare with the best offer received for the house? It may be that one of those alternatives is more attractive than selling the house for $160,000. On the other hand, selling the house for as little as $124,000 may be better than holding on to it indefinitely. It is most unlikely that any arbitrarily selected bottom line truly reflects the family's interests.

The reason you negotiate is to produce something better than the results you can obtain without negotiating. What are those results? What is that alternative? What is your BATNA—your Best Alternative To a Negotiated Agreement? That is the standard against which any proposed agreement should be measured. That is the only standard which can protect you both from accepting terms that are too unfavorable and from rejecting terms it would be in your interest to accept.

Your BATNA not only is a better measure but also has the advantage of being flexible enough to permit the exploration of imaginative solutions. Instead of ruling out any solution which does not meet your bottom line, you can compare a proposal with your BATNA to see whether it better satisfies your interests.

The insecurity of an unknown BATNA. If you have not thought carefully about what you will do if you fail to reach an agreement, you are negotiating with your eyes closed. You may, for instance, be too optimistic and assume that you have many other choices: other houses for sale, other buyers for your secondhand car, other plumbers, other jobs available, other wholesalers, and so on. Even when your alternative is fixed, you may be taking too rosy a view of the consequences of not reaching agreement. You may not be appreciating the full agony of a lawsuit, a contested divorce, a strike, an arms race, or a war.

One frequent mistake is psychologically to see your alternatives in the aggregate. You may be telling yourself that if you do not reach agreement on a salary for this job, you could always go to California, or go South, or go back to school, or write, or work on a farm, or live in Paris, or do something else. In your mind you are likely to find the sum of these alternatives more attractive than working for a specific salary in a particular job. The difficulty is that you cannot have the sum total of all those other alternatives; if you fail to reach agreement, you will have to choose just one.

In most circumstances, however, the greater danger is that you are too committed to reaching agreement. Not having developed any alternative to a negotiated solution, you are unduly pessimistic about what would happen if negotiations broke off.

As valuable as knowing your BATNA may be, you may hesitate to explore alternatives. You hope this buyer or the next will make you an attractive offer for the house. You may avoid facing the question of what you will do if no agreement is reached. You may think to yourself, "Let's negotiate first and see what happens. If things don't work out, then I'll figure out what to do." But having at least a tentative answer to the question is absolutely essential if you are to conduct your negotiations wisely. Whether you should or should not agree on something in a negotiation depends entirely upon the attractiveness to you of the best available alternative.

Formulate a trip wire. Although your BATNA is the true measure by which you should judge any proposed agreement, you may want another test as well. In order to give you early warning that the content of a possible agreement is beginning to run the risk of being too unattractive, it is useful to identify one far from perfect agreement that is better than your BATNA. Before accepting any agreement worse than this trip-wire package, you should take a break and reexamine the situation. Like a bottom line, a trip wire can limit the authority of an agent. "Don't sell for less than $158,000, the price I paid plus interest, until you've talked to me."

A trip wire should provide you with some margin in reserve. If after reaching the standard reflected in your trip wire you decide to call in a mediator, you have left him with something on your side to work with. You still have some room to move.

Making the Most of Your Assets

Protecting yourself against a bad agreement is one thing. Making the most of the assets you have in order to produce a good agreement is

another. How do you do this? Again the answer lies in your BATNA.

The better your BATNA, the greater your power. People think of negotiating power as being determined by resources like wealth, political connections, physical strength, friends, and military might. In fact, the relative negotiating power of two parties depends primarily upon how attractive to each is the option of not reaching agreement.

Consider a wealthy tourist who wants to buy a small brass pot for a modest price from a vendor at the Bombay railroad station. The vendor may be poor, but he is likely to know the market. If he does not sell the pot to this tourist, he can sell it to another. From his experience he can estimate when and for how much he could sell it to someone else. The tourist may be wealthy and "powerful," but in this negotiation he will be weak indeed unless he knows approximately how much it would cost and how difficult it would be to find a comparable pot elsewhere. He is almost certain either to miss his chance to buy such a pot or to pay too high a price. The tourist's wealth in no way strengthens his negotiating power. If apparent, it weakens his ability to buy the pot at a low price. In order to convert that wealth into negotiating power, the tourist would have to apply it to learn about the price at which he could buy an equally or more attractive brass pot somewhere else.

Think for a moment about how you would feel walking into a job interview with no other job offers—only some uncertain leads. Think how the talk about salary would go. Now contrast that with how you would feel walking in with two other job offers. How would that salary negotiation proceed? The difference is power.

What is true for negotiations between individuals is equally true for negotiations between organizations. The relative negotiating power of a large industry and a small town trying to raise taxes on a factory is determined not by the relative size of their respective budgets, or their political clout, but by each side's best alternative. In one case, a small town negotiated a company with a factory just outside the town limits from a "goodwill" payment of

$300,000 a year to one of $2,300,000 a year. How?

The town knew exactly what it would do if no agreement was reached: It would expand the town limits to include the factory and then tax the factory the full residential rate of some $2,500,000 a year. The corporation had committed itself to keeping the factory; it had developed no alternative to reaching agreement. At first glance the corporation seemed to have a great deal of power. It provided most of the jobs in the town, which was suffering economically; a factory shutdown or relocation would devastate the town. And the taxes the corporation was already paying helped provide the salaries of the very town leaders who were demanding more. Yet all of these assets, because they were not converted into a good BATNA, proved of little use. Having an attractive BATNA, the small town had more ability to affect the outcome of the negotiation than did one of the world's largest corporations.

Develop your BATNA. Vigorous exploration of what you will do if you do not reach agreement can greatly strengthen your hand. Attractive alternatives are not just sitting there waiting for you; you usually have to develop them. Generating possible BATNAs requires three distinct operations: (1) inventing a list of actions you might conceivably take if no agreement is reached; (2) improving some of the more promising ideas and converting them into practical alternatives; and (3) selecting, tentatively, the one alternative that seems best.

The first operation is inventing. If, by the end of the month, Company X does not make you a satisfactory job offer, what are some things you might do? Take a job with Company Y? Look in another city? Start a business on your own? What else? For a labor union, alternatives to a negotiated agreement would presumably include calling a strike, working without a contract, giving a sixty-day notice of a strike, asking for a mediator, and calling on union members to "work to rule."

The second stage is to improve the best of your ideas and turn the most promising into real alternatives. If you are thinking about working in Chicago, try to turn that idea into at least one job offer there. With a Chicago job offer in hand (or even having discovered that you are unable to produce one) you are much better prepared to assess the merits of a New York offer. While a labor union is still negotiating, it should convert the ideas of calling in a mediator and of striking into drafts of specific operational decisions ready for execution. The union might, for instance, take a vote of its membership to authorize a strike if a settlement is not achieved by the time the contract expires.

The final step in developing a BATNA is selecting the best among the alternatives. If you do not reach agreement in the negotiations, which of your realistic alternatives do you now plan to pursue?

Having gone through this effort, you now have a BATNA. Judge every offer against it. The better your BATNA, the greater your ability to improve the terms of any negotiated agreement. Knowing what you are going to do if the negotiation does not lead to agreement will give you additional confidence in the negotiating process. It is easier to break off negotiations if you know where you're going. The greater your willingness to break off negotiations, the more forcefully you can present your interests and the basis on which you believe an agreement should be reached.

The desirability of disclosing your BATNA to the other side depends upon your assessment of the other side's thinking. If your BATNA is extremely attractive—if you have another customer waiting in the next room—it is in your interest to let the other side know. If they think you lack a good alternative when in fact you have one, then you should almost certainly let them know. However, if your best alternative to a negotiated agreement is worse for you than they think, disclosing it will weaken rather than strengthen your hand.

Consider the other side's BATNA. You should also think about the alternatives to a negotiated agreement available to the other side. They may be unduly optimistic about what they can do if no agreement is reached. Perhaps they have a vague notion that they have a great many alternatives and are under the influence of their cumulative total.

The more you can learn of their alternatives, the better prepared you are for negotiation. Knowing their alternatives, you can realistically estimate what you can expect from the negotiation. If they appear to overestimate their BATNA, you will want to lower their expectations.

Their BATNA may be better for them than any fair solution you can imagine. Suppose you are a community group concerned about the potential noxious gases to be emitted by a power plant now under construction. The power company's BATNA is either to ignore your protests altogether or to keep you talking while they finish building the plant. To get them to take your concerns seriously, you may have to file suit seeking to have their construction permit revoked. In other words, if their BATNA is so good they don't see any need to negotiate on the merits, consider what you can do to change it.

If both sides have attractive BATNAs, the best outcome of the negotiation—for both parties—may well be not to reach agreement. In such cases a successful negotiation is one in which you and they amicably and efficiently discover that the best way to advance your respective interests is for each of you to look elsewhere and not to try further to reach agreement.

When the Other Side is Powerful

If the other side has big guns, you do not want to turn a negotiation into a gunfight. The stronger they appear in terms of physical economic power, the more you benefit by negotiating on the merits. To the extent that they have muscle and you have principle, the larger a role you can establish for principle the better off you are.

Having a good BATNA can help you negotiate on the merits. You can convert such resources as you have into effective negotiating power by developing and improving your BATNA. Apply knowledge, time, money, people, connections, and wits into devising the best solution for you independent of the other side's assent. The more easily and happily you can walk away from a negotiation, the greater your capacity to affect its outcome.

Developing your BATNA thus not only enables you to determine what is a minimally acceptable agreement, it will probably raise that minimum. Developing your BATNA is perhaps the most effective course of action you can take in dealing with a seemingly more powerful negotiator. •

Study Questions

1. What are the advantages and disadvantages of the "bottom line" or resistance point?

2. What is a BATNA, how is it generated, and what purpose does it serve?

3. What are the benefits of a "trip wire?"

4. Should you disclose your BATNA to your opponent? Explain.

Preparing for Negotiations

Bill Scott

It is critically important, when one's strategy is towards cooperation to mutual advantage to build firm foundations at the start of the negotiation meeting. But before we can lay firm foundations, we must have a good job of preparing the ground.

Time after time, one finds negotiators having two cries. On the one hand, "We just have time to do our preparation properly before the meeting." On the other hand, after the meeting, "Well, that has certainly taught me that I ought to be more careful about the way I prepare."

There is no substitute for adequate preparation. We shall deal with the subject in this chapter, making three sets of assumptions:

1. That the negotiator will have done his homework on the content issues for negotiation. That is, the buyer will have researched all specifications, quantities, market competition, market prices, etc. The banker will be aware of the availability of funds, the appropriate rate of interest, the status of the client, etc.
2. That the negotiator is familiar with the rules governing the negotiating territory. The company rules for purchasing or for selling, the trade and/or international rules that apply, the essential legal matters.
3. We assume that the deal is one which can be settled within one or two meetings.

This chapter will give suggestions about:

- Conducting the preliminaries.
- A general approach to the planning of negotiations.
- The essence of the negotiating plan.
- Physical preparation.

Conducting the Preliminaries

Other Party comes to a meeting bringing with him not only knowledge of the basic facts. He brings also his own way of conducting negotiations, his expectations about the way that our Party will behave, and his counterintentions.

Whether he has done his preparations systematically or not at all, he will bring impressions and opinions which will influence his conduct.

To help him to bring the right attitudes and information, we need to have explored beforehand as far as possible the purpose of the meeting and the agenda of items which we will discuss. This may have been done through correspondence or by telephone or even, for major negotiations, through preliminary meetings between representatives.

A great deal of Other Party's basic values are deeply engrained. We cannot much influence them during the preliminaries, but we can and do influence his opinions of us and his expectations about the way we shall behave, which in turn influence the way he will prepare to behave with us.

In part his expectations will be based on factors outside our control, such as the stories he has heard about us, the sort of relationship he would expect with a different Party in our situation, and the experience he has had with other organizations in our own industry and culture.

He may have more direct evidence about us. Evidence from dealings which he or his colleagues have had with our organization, evidence of the manner in which we negotiate and of the effectiveness with which we have implemented previous deals.

There remain however the preliminaries through which we can ourselves influence him. The manner in which we communicate beforehand needs to reflect our interest in dealing with him; our integrity; our co-operativeness. To create the most positive expectations, we need to apply the basic ground rules for communication between people distant from one another: to be prompt and polite, clear, concise, and correct.

We need also to be sensitive in the volume of our preliminary work. Sometimes we have to deal with businesses which seem virtually to resist paperwork. Such organizations always appreciate some brief statement on paper, covering issues like purpose, time, and estimated duration; but with them, anything more than one sheet of paper is irritating and counterproductive.

For other organizations, where formality rules strongly, there is a need for meticulous detail in preliminary exchanges. Indeed, the preliminaries can escalate, almost to become the most important part of the negotiating process.

To summarize: it is important in the way we conduct the preliminaries to help the Other Party to prepare himself for the negotiations, and to ensure he enters the negotiating room looking forward to a desirable relationship.

General Approach to Planning

In principle, preparations for negotiation should lead to a plan which is simple and specific, yet flexible.

It must be sufficiently simple for the negotiator himself easily to carry the headlines in his own thinking. He must have these headlines, these principles of his plan, very clear in his mind; so clear, that he can handle the heavy on-going content of the negotiation with Other Party (making great demands on his conscious energy), yet at the same time subconsciously be able to relate to his plan.

Such simplicity is hard to achieve.

The plan must be specific: it cannot be simple without being very specific. No room for reservations or elaborations.

Yet it must be flexible. The negotiator must be able to listen effectively to Other Party; to see the relationship of Other Party's thinking to his own plans; and to adjust flexibly.

So the aim of our preparation is to produce a plan which is simple and specific, yet flexible.

That is the ideal, but the reality is usually very different. The negotiator hunts out the information, reads through the correspondence in the files, talks to half a dozen colleagues with interest in the negotiation—each putting a different picture—and is under pressure to be on his way to the motorway or the airport with very little time to form this ragged mass of impulses into any coherent pattern.

His need now is for a discipline; for a general approach which he can use quickly and which he can apply to many different types of negotiation.

The general approach we use is in three stages:

Ideas stage.
Thesis sentence.
Analysis stage.

The aim of the *ideas* stage is to make a quick review of the area for negotiation and at the same time to clear one's own mind. It corresponds to the brainstorming stage in preparation of information, but is now in two steps. Step one is quickly to jot down all one's jumbled ideas about the negotiation. . . . Step two is to jot down our thoughts about Other Party on another sheet of paper. What they do, where they are, what they look like, what we know of the individuals, what we know they want from the negotiation, what we guess they want, and what else we would like to know. Again, random thoughts (Figure 1).

This ideas stage has led us to the production of two sheets of paper. One with random ideas on the subject and one with random ideas on the Other Party. Having been filled in, having got our minds cleared, these sheets have already largely served their purpose. They should now be put away (not necessarily thrown away—they just might serve some useful purpose later in our preparations).

Our conscious energy is now free to prepare our plans, uncluttered by the jumble of thoughts that was previously there; and the first step in this *analytical stage* is to prepare a thesis sentence.

This thesis sentence is a statement in general terms of what we hope to achieve from the negotiation process. It is a statement for our own guidance, and may sometimes differ from the general purpose of the negotiation as defined to/agreed with Other Party.

The thesis sentence needs to be simple, so we should try to specify it within a maximum of 15 to 20 words. If it takes more, the negotiator has not sufficiently simplified his thinking about why he is entering the negotiating process.

Figure 1
Random Thoughts about Other Party

Jensen Electric Supply

30 years relationship

Annual golf match

Good customers

Tough but fair

Enjoy dealing

Probably see Alf

Hope not Doug

Are they in trouble?

Maybe need help

Maybe we need to protect

Is whole region in trouble?

Or just them?

Knows our processes

Keep it friendly

It is critical that his thinking should be so sharp. If he finds it difficult to state his Purpose within 20 words, then he needs to spend more time on clearing his mind, drafting his thoughts about the purpose of the meeting, then pruning and modifying until he gets inside the maximum of 20 words (Figure 2).

Continuing the analysis stage the second step is to develop a plan for handling the negotiation meeting.

The need now is to produce an ordered approach to the conduct of the negotiation, together with a statement of one's opening position.

The Essence of the Plan

The control of any meeting hinges on three of the "Four P's" . . .: the Purpose of the meeting, the Plan for the meeting, and the Pace of the meeting. (The Personalities element, the introduction of the people and their roles, should be a routine, not a part of the plan specific to any one meeting.) Our preparation must cover those 3 Ps.

Figure 2
Thesis Sentence

Jensen—General Contract

Thesis. To ensure goodwill,

Check their business strengths,

and

Get best compensation

The *Purpose* spelt out in one sentence which can be offered to Other Party as "our view of the purpose of this meeting." It should be "our declared view" of the purpose, not necessarily the same as the thesis sentence. The *Plan* or agenda must be kept simple. The human brain has the ability to keep clear image of only a few agenda topics throughout a negotiation meeting. About four main items. If in the preparation one tries to give equal significance to say seven or eight main points—then the brain is overstretched. It cannot later have a sharp recollection of so many main points. it cannot easily, during the negotiation, relate all that is going on to the prepared plan.

So at the analysis stage we are concerned to prepare our plans for the negotiation meeting under about four main headings.

The *Pace*—in terms of "how long"—should also be estimated.

The practical way to go about this preparation is—after going through the brainstorming stage and preparing the thesis sentence—to plan the agenda. Aim for the ideal of *four* main agenda points, subheading each if need be.

In negotiations "Towards Agreement," a sequence I regularly find useful is—"Ours—Theirs—Creative possibilities—Practical actions." "Ours" may, in one session, be "what we hope for from the negotiation," with the corresponding "theirs" being what they hope for; then the creative possibilities for the two of us working together; and finally—what we should do before we meet again.

In a later session, the same sequence might become—"our offer—their offer—overlaps and problem"—action needed to resolve problems.

And for the next meeting—"Where we'd got to and what we each had to do—our new position—

their new position—what is agreed and what remains to be done."

Having got the plan worked out, we should "top" it with a statement of Purpose (already considered when building our Thesis Sentence, though not necessarily to be repeated verbatim); and we should "tail" it with an estimate of the time we shall need (Figure 3).

Finally, the plan needs reducing to key words printed on a postcard.

The purpose of this final stage of planning is to provide a document which the negotiator can have in front of him in the negotiating room. He then needs the key statements prominent and visible at one glance of the eyes. He needs them as prompters for his subconscious, so that he can still control the negotiating process, even when his conscious energy is absorbed in the content of the negotiation (Figure 4).

In addition to this procedural preparation for a negotiation, there is another item to which we have already attached much importance. This is the Opening Statement to be made at the outset of the negotiating process.

Following this preliminary work the negotiator goes into the negotiating room properly prepared both to control the process of negotiating, and to present his own position.

What about the room he is going into?

Figure 3
Plan for meeting

Jensen—General Contract

Purpose	Agree settlement
Plan	Their reasons/our problems
	Any creative possibilities?
	How to settle?
	What settlement?
Pace	11:00–12:00

The Physical Preparation

In this section we shall look briefly at the negotiating room, the layout of the room and the need for services.

The negotiating room itself needs to have the obvious facilities—light, heating, air, noiseproofing.

More contentious are the furnishing and the layout of the room. Negotiators seem to need a table at which to be seated—they seem to feel defenseless without a table between them. But what sort of table? A rectangular table—or the typical businessman's desk—leads to parties being seated opposite to one another. This immediately creates a head-on physical confrontation.

Negotiators recognize that they feel differently on the rare occasions when they sit at round tables. In any poll of negotiators there will be a hefty majority who find it more comfortable and more constructive to use a round table than to use either a rectangular or a square one.

Should negotiators, whether at round or rectangular tables, split into their respective teams or should they intermix? It depends on the mood and style of the negotiations.

Where the parties are relaxed and collaborative, then the relaxation and collaboration is heightened by intermixing. At the extreme this would lead to each negotiator in a team being seated between two negotiators from the Other Party; but that would be contrived only by a formal approach to seating positions. Within an agreement-oriented group, the ice-breaking period leads to informality in the choice of seating positions. It is a purely random matter as to whether one walks up to the table with and sits beside a member of Own or of Other Party.

Figure 4
Prompter for Control of Negotiation

Generator Contract
To Agree Settlement

Reasons/Problems
Creative?
How Settle?
How Much?

11:00–12:00

Where the negotiation process is more conflicting, then it is natural that the parties will gather together, probably on opposite sides of the table. This is both for psychological and for practical reasons. Psychologically, the mood is of "all together against them." Practically, either Party may want to refer to papers which they want to keep obscured from Others (impracticable if others are neighbors) or they may want to sit together so that they can pass notes within their team.

Incidentally neither the regular reference to secret papers nor the passing of notes are symbols of good negotiators. Energy is needed for the exchanges with Other Party and not for private transactions. It is more skillful to take a recess, either to check on the private papers, or to handle private communication with colleagues.

It is not only the shape of table that is important—it is also size. There is a comfortable distance at which individuals or groups of individuals may sit from one another. If the parties are sitting a little closer, then the atmosphere becomes warmer. If they are sitting a lot closer then they become uncomfortable and heated. If the distance apart is, on the other hand, too much, then the parties become remote and the discussion becomes academic.

Apart from the question of the room and the furnishing, the host needs to make suitable provisions for sustenance and for the well-being of Other Party. A special courtesy is in providing Other Party with a room which they can use for recesses, together with such other facilities as typing, telex, and telephone.

Summary

1. The preparation for a negotiation meeting needs discipline. It needs time and the regular use of the same approach.
2. We suggest a disciplined approach of:
   a. Brainstorming.
   b. Thesis sentence.
   c. Planning.
3. The preparation needs to cover purpose, plan, and pace of the meeting.
4. The Opening Statement should be prepared equally carefully.
5. Physical arrangements influence the form of the subsequent negotiations. •

Study Questions

1. What is done during the "ideas" stage of negotiation, and how is it beneficial?

2. How many "main items" can be reasonably dealt with on a negotiation agenda?

Exercise: Preparation for an Upcoming Negotiation

Objective: Perhaps the best strategy to improve negotiated outcomes is to properly prepare for the negotiation encounter. The objective of this exercise is to help you understand the importance of preparation by developing a planning guide for an upcoming negotiation.

Assignment: Think of an upcoming negotiation for which you are still unprepared. If you can't think of one in particular, consider your "most likely" negotiation in the near future, e.g., purchasing a new car or home, deciding where to take the family on summer vacation, or simply, choosing where to go for dinner with your significant other. Your assignment is to choose one of these two negotiation situations, then write a planning guide to help you prepare for this most likely (or known) upcoming negotiation.

In developing the planning guide, consider and address the following:

issues at stake; your and the opponent's goals, priorities, BATNAs and/or resistance points; your image and behavioral expectations of the opponent (do an opponent analysis); your preferred and back-up negotiation strategies and tactics for reaching a settlement.

Strategies and Tactics of Distributive Bargaining

Richard E. Walton
Robert B. McKersie

Part 1: Manipulating Utility Parameters

A brief review of some propositions implicit in the model of distributive bargaining will suggest the various ways by which the negotiator can influence the outcome by directly influencing the other's perceptions of utilities (including values associated with the issue and strike action). We view these from the point of view of one negotiator, Party, whose general tactical assignment can be thought of as inducing Opponent to adopt a relatively lower (less ambitious) resistance point and to take explicit bargaining positions throughout negotiations consistent with the lower resistance point.

First, *Opponent's resistance point varies directly with the utilities he[1] attaches to possible outcomes.* Thus, Opponent's resistance point will be lower if he places a lower value on the conceivable outcomes, that is, if the whole or a major portion of his utility function is shifted appropriately. Party can manipulate Opponent's view of Opponent's utility function so that Opponent does not see as much advantage in maintaining his position. Opponent must be convinced that a proposal of his own is of less value to him than he originally thought or that a demand of Party is less unpleasant to him than he first thought.

According to our analysis of subjectively expected utilities (to which the resistance-point decision rule was coordinated), the resistance point also varies directly with subjective probabilities. Since the later value varies inversely with one's own strike costs, directly with the other's strike costs, and inversely with the other's utilities for the outcomes, we have the following additional derived propositions:

Second, *Opponent's resistance point varies inversely with his subjective strike costs.* Thus, Opponent's resistance point will be lower if he places a higher estimate on his own strike costs. Party can manipulate Opponent's view of his strike costs so that Opponent is somehow convinced that a strike would provoke a higher cost than he had originally assumed (either because of increased rate or increased duration).

Third, *Opponent's resistance point varies directly with Party's subjective costs of a strike.* Thus, Opponent's resistance point will be lower if he places a lower estimate on Party's strike costs. Party can convince Opponent that the former will experience a low rate of costs and perhaps that Party would derive some positive by-products from the strike which would tend to offset these costs.

Fourth, *Opponent's resistance point varies inversely with Party's utilities of possible outcomes.* Thus, Opponent's resistance point will be lower if he places a higher estimate on how much Party values the conceivable outcomes. Party can convince Opponent that Party attaches greater importance to issues than Opponent had earlier realized.

The explicit positions that Opponent takes at any time during negotiations, as well as his resistance point, are assumed to be subject to the influence of these basic parameters. Therefore, Party can influence the process and the outcome of bargaining by manipulating Opponent's subjective assessment of any or all of the four utility parameters.

Before discussing the specific tactical assignments implied by these propositions, it is necessary to deal with the matter of controlling information. The role of information or the lack of information is of such tactical importance in distributive bargaining that it needs to be handled at the outset. It affects all the other tactical operations.

The relative values of the four parameters change in response to the information generated and exchanged during bargaining. It is not necessary for the objective conditions to change; it is only necessary for the perceptions

Material taken from *A Behavioral Theory of Labor Negotiations* by Richard E. Walton and Robert B. McKersie. Used with permission of the publisher: ILR Press, School of Industrial and Labor Relations, Cornell University, Ithaca, New York 14853-3901. Copyright © 1991 by Cornell University.

of these conditions to change in order for a negotiator to alter his position. In contract negotiations objective knowledge virtually never becomes complete in the sense that the true nature of all factors is accurately understood by both sides. Thus, it is only necessary to change the other's perceptions in order to alter his bargaining position. This is not to say that parties do not influence each other through more basic changes in the conditions underlying utilities and probabilities. The point is that the purpose of changing the actual conditions will be to influence Opponent's perception. If the latter does not occur, then the tactical operation has not been successful. The following statements are suggestive of the attempts at manipulation and efforts of resistance that can take place at the *informational* level:

> I do not think that you really feel that strongly about the issues that you have introduced.
>
> I believe that the strike will cost you considerably more than you are willing to admit.
>
> I believe that a strike will cost me almost nothing in spite of your statements to the contrary.
>
> I feel very strongly about this issue regardless of what you say.

Part 1 will discuss four tactical assignments as follows: The first section treats a preliminary tactical requirement, namely, assessing Opponent's utilities. The second section treats the tactics which influence Opponent's perceptions of Party's utilities. The third section will discuss the tactics used by Party to manipulate Opponent's perceptions of his own utilities. In the second and third sections we shall be interested in both the content of communication and the techniques employed. The emphasis is primarily on attempts to influence perceptions of the utility parameters without changing objective conditions affecting the utilities themselves. Some tactics actually alter the objective costs of disagreement. This will be our subject in the fourth section.

Assessing Opponent's Utilities for Outcomes and Strike Costs

Party's first tactical assignment is to assess Opponent's utilities and strike costs and if possible ascertain his resistance point. Party may know that the parties hold differing objectives regarding the resolution of an agenda item; that is, he knows that he is dealing with a distributive issue. But what is not so obvious to Party is just how important the objective is to Opponent, particularly in terms of how much gain (loss) on the issue would be minimally acceptable to him. Moreover, while a negotiator usually knows whether a strike would be costly to the other party, he does not know *how* costly!

Knowledge about the relevant parameters is critical in deciding whether to maintain or abandon a position. Such knowledge enables Party to make in turn intelligent probability assessments. These assessments tell him how far he has to go in further manipulating the parameters in order to bring about movement on Opponent's part. They also tell him whether he had better consider altering his own position.

Party has two general ways in which he can gain knowledge about Opponent's resistance point. He can use an indirect route of assessing the factors which underlie each parameter, or he can attempt to obtain more direct clues regarding the resistance point which Opponent has at least tentatively set for himself. Much of the required information for both methods of assessment has to be obtained from Opponent himself. Other information is available through more public channels.

Indirect Assessment. Many factors affecting economic power, and in turn the resistance point, can be assessed by both parties: they include inventories, alternate production or warehousing facilities, market conditions, the percentage of the work force unionized, the size of the strike fund, the numbers involved in a strike vote, mutual assistance arrangements, etc. The "grapevines" supply this information to unions and management with varying degrees of accuracy.

More systematic research methods are often used. For instance, managements frequently hold prenegotiation conferences with their first-line supervisors to get their estimates of how strongly employees feel about certain issues and how willing they are to strike.

> Some companies have their foremen conduct informal meetings with employee groups. The purpose of this is to understand the needs and

problems faced by the employees. Foremen are in a good position to understand the strength of feeling about these matters and the willingness of the employees to strike.

One negotiator claimed that he could walk through the shop and by some kind of intuitive assessment of the atmosphere tell what was on the minds of the workers. As a negotiator he knew the range of issues, but by walking through the shop, he sought the intensity of feeling behind these issues and whether people were furious enough to force a showdown.

Managements sometimes have the industrial relations staff make an analysis of the content and patterns of the grievances processed to various stages of the machinery in order to discover any clues regarding the importance the employees and the union may attach to certain issues.

General Motors reportedly utilizes automatic data-processing equipment for this prenegotiating analysis. By tabulating the incidence of each issue persisting in upward movement through the grievance machinery, management is in a position to estimate the importance of most of the union's demands.

Managements occasionally ask their personnel research staff or some outside agency to administer opinion surveys to their employees to learn how employees feel about issues and striking.

Opinion polls taken before and during the early stages of the 1959 negotiations in the steel industry served this purpose for the steel companies. They indicated that the employees had been influenced by "inflation thinking" and did not feel strongly about a wage increase. The employees' feelings about the work-rule issue, whether tapped by this method or not, proved to be quite another matter.

If, with sufficient effort, some knowledge can be gained about issue utilities and strike costs, making the appropriate translations and then computing Opponent's resistance point is more difficult. Actually the problem is even more complicated—it is one of simulating how Opponent interprets these factors and how *he* computes his resistance point. After all, Party is interested in learning what Opponent's resistance point *is*, not what it should be. This being

so, it is often more rewarding for Party to try to induce Opponent to betray his own resistance point than it is to attempt to estimate it indirectly.

The validity of the inferences that Party makes about Opponent's position is enhanced, if the former has ever been in the latter's position. Members of management who have been employees or union officials can "put themselves in the shoes" of the union negotiators. Short of this, management can with a little empathy visualize the kinds of factors that would influence feeling in the union organization. Management can examine pattern settlements or precedent-setting circumstances in past settlements. Of course, the union engages in the same kind of vicarious thinking. It seeks to understand management's true position by examining such indicators as the profit and loss statement.

Tactics to Elicit Clues. When we turn to the problem of obtaining more direct clues about Opponent's resistance point, we must consider the ongoing negotiation process. Sometimes the efforts flow along ethically questionable channels and involve cloak-and-dagger operations, e.g., utilizing an informant from Opponent's headquarters or bugging Opponent's caucus room. The following incident is reported to have occurred during the 1959 negotiations between the International Union of Electrical Workers and the Gray Manufacturing Company, producers of electronic equipment:

The second incident which Mr. Hogan (IUE official) related to the case writer also occurred during the negotiations before the strike. The union committee was offered the use of Mr. Ditmar's (the company president's) office for their caucuses during one of the negotiating sessions. While the union committee was in caucus, one of the members discovered a microphone hidden under the radiator. A quick search revealed another microphone behind the wall clock. Hogan claimed that he "ripped them out of the wall." Mr. Bennett, federal mediator assigned to the negotiations, told the case writer that he went to the office to find Hogan standing with the two microphones in his hand and cursing them. The union moved its caucus to the union office which was near the plant.[2]

Informal conferences with negotiators of the other party are sometimes employed in order to sound them out regarding reactions to various types of proposals. Typically, however, reliance is placed on bargaining-table tactics. Some of these tactics are intended to elicit reactions that become data in estimating the resistance point. The most obvious way is to ask questions designed to clarify both the meaning of the proposal and its underlying rationale. Sometimes Party will direct such questions to some of the "less-coached" members of Opponent's team.

In reporting upon the practice of one company, a negotiator had this to say:

Before drafting any counterproposals, meetings are held with the union, and each of the union's proposals is discussed in detail in order to determine the precise intent of the union in each case. Since the atmosphere in these meetings is completely informal, it is possible for management, when necessary, to sow doubt in the union's mind about certain proposals, to recall operating requirements that may have been overlooked, and to test precisely how the union really feels about these issues.

By probing Opponent's team members regarding a specific proposal, Party can determine how well prepared they are, using this information as one basis for inferring how seriously they are advancing their proposal.

Tactics involving personal abuse may be introduced to induce or provoke Opponent into revealing more than he wishes. What we have in mind by "abuse" is well illustrated by an excerpt from a chemical company's negotiations:

Heath (U) And when you say you have discussed it, you are a damn liar. You can take that any way you want to take it, see. If you want to take it with coats off, we will take it with coats off as far as I am concerned; or if you want to select anybody on your side of the table to do it, I'll take my coat off.[3]

Ann Douglas describes how pressure and abuse can break an opponent down and force him to reveal his true position. She quotes a company negotiator who operated on this theory:

And I think a direct personal attack—a vicious personal attack on U2 would break him. Just—he'd just break under the thing.[4]

Tactics of exaggerated impatience which make it appear as if the negotiations were rushing headlong into their final stages may force the inexperienced negotiator into prematurely revealing the bargaining room he has allowed himself. That appears to have been the case in the Fanco Oil Company negotiations in which in the very first session the first two remarks below apparently induced the third:

Hayes (U) The morale of our men on the boats is very bad. More than 50% of the men are not paying dues, and I have instructed the delegates not to collect from them. We are not getting anywhere, so I think we may as well adjourn and let matters take their own course.
. . .

MacIntosh (U) No sense for further meetings, if we can't agree now on 7 and 7. . . .

Downs (M) If we add $25 monthly income to each man, you would be interested?

Black (U) It makes a lot of difference. . . .[5]

In one move Downs offered a monthly increase of $25, virtually everything the negotiating team had to bargain with. What frightened Downs, who was just gaining negotiating experience, was an implicit threat that the independent Fanco union would get discouraged and affiliate with the nearby International Longshoremen's Association. That threat was implicit in the apathy of workers mentioned by Hayes. Still the fact is that this was only the first negotiating session. Furthermore, regardless of how dreaded the consequences of the threat might have been, the threat itself actually was not very credible, because it is unlikely that the officials of the independent union actually had any serious intention of sacrificing an arrangement so beneficial to them.

The tactics discussed above—personal abuse and exaggerated impatience—are not without their risks. In his excitement the other negotiator may take a stronger position than he had originally planned and then become obliged to maintain that position.

Testing techniques are particularly useful for assessing Opponent's resistance point late in negotiations. Sometimes in order to test Opponent's position, Party will suggest calling in a mediator. If Opponent accepts the suggestion, this is taken as an indication that he sees the problem as one of exploring a way by which the positions of the parties can be brought together; he would presumably have some "give" left himself. If he rejects the bid, this may indicate that he has no room to move unless he had reason to believe that Opponent is just looking for an excuse to move all the way himself. Another tactic is for a union to bring the parties up to a strike deadline, arrange a last-minute postponement, and then bargain up to the new deadline in order to test and retest the company's limits.

Tactics to Record and Analyze Reactions. Even in the absence of "baiting" tactics, the verbal and nonverbal behaviors of members of Opponent's negotiating team are often rich with clues about the degree of interest they have in the items being discussed or passed over and about their expectations regarding these issues. The following is an excerpt from a conversation among members of one team as they process the clues available to them:

> . . . soon as he finishes I'll give ya a . . . full report on what took our discussion here and how I think the thing had to go. And it's going all right. *He showed disappointment. Now, a man that shows disappointment, his mind is open on that question.* What's *in* his mind or how far he'll go to buy that we have to find out. . . . But you're not gonna find out now, immediately.[6]

In a continuous relationship the negotiators learn in various subtle ways how to assess the position and intentions of the other person.

> When you have been negotiating with the union for as long and as often as I have this one, you get accustomed to the habits and ways of doing things. These may be famous last words, but I think I have Midge figured down to a "T."[7]

Several tactics are used to take full advantage of this source of data regarding Opponent's resistance point.

First, Party may have a man-to-man policy in composing his own negotiating team. Many managements find it useful to have one man-

agement committeeman for each union committeeman, so that the latter can be under constant observation during negotiation proceedings.

> One newspaper publisher told of a technique by which he organized his team on a two-platoon basis. By rotating committee members, he was able to keep them fresh and alert and in a position to constantly observe the reactions of the union committee. In addition, he assigned technical people who could understand the real meaning of the union's presentation on detailed subjects such as job evaluation.

Second, Party may be even more sophisticated in this practice by making a continually revised assessment about the influence of each member of Opponent's negotiating team. Since negotiations are not an isolated event but occur as part of a continuing labor-management relationship, most members of the negotiating committee are known to the opposite group. Respective individuals work together during contract administration, on problems and grievance handling. This type of familiarity enables each side to better assess the intentions of the other side. In his analysis of collective bargaining in the steel industry, Ulman notes the practice of analyzing the reactions of local union representatives.

> Nor is the sounding off by local union representatives mere sound, for, by carefully listening to the local people, the top negotiators can frequently obtain a truer ranking, in order of their significance to the membership, of the multitude of items included in the wage policy committee's shopping list.[8]

Modifying Opponent's Perceptions of Party's Utilities

This tactical assignment is to conceal or misrepresent the utilities for Party inherent in the agenda items. In a sense, this becomes the countermeasure to the first tactical assignment. If we assume that all of the verbal and nonverbal behaviors of Party are being scanned by Opponent for clues about Party's utilities, then Party has two responses. He can be inscrutable, that is, behave in a minimal or irrelevant way, or he can disguise his utilities by deliberately misrepresenting them. Of course, sometimes the best Party can hope to do is to accurately represent the importance of some particular demand, if, for example, Opponent is very likely to underestimate it.

Minimizing Clues. The earlier discussion of assessing Opponent's resistance point suggests certain tactical countermeasures which Party can take to minimize the number of revealing clues he admits. It is especially important for Party to minimize clues early in negotiations rather than fashion misleading ones, to the extent that he has not already developed clear notions about what his ultimate resistance point is in these negotiations. The point is that the negotiation process itself is a mechanism whereby Party gathers much of the information he needs to test the appropriateness of his own resistance point.

Perhaps a basic step in this direction is for Party to maintain a low rate of activity and interaction. He makes a deliberate effort to remain quiet, letting members from Opponent's committee do most of the talking. Another way in which Party sometimes ensures that minimum clues, or rather appropriate clues, will be produced is by using a single spokesman or a chairman who controls the participation of other members of his committee. The importance of such control can be illustrated by an instance in which it was not operating or at least could not cover the more subtle aspects of behavior at the bargaining table.

> The union negotiator, Watoski, had let it be known to management that the union placed considerable importance on the waiting-time issue. Employees were losing incentive pay, because in their opinion poor management practices resulted in excessive waiting time. After an initial proposal for a higher guaranteed rate for waiting time, the negotiators agreed that management should attempt to commit itself to remedial and preventive actions in a letter to the union. In the session in which management finally submitted its offer—the letter it had composed—the following took place:
>
> Scott, the management negotiator, passed out copies of the waiting-time letter to the union committee. At the suggestion of Watoski, Scott read the letter aloud point by point. After he had finished reading it, he waited for comment. One member of the union team, Jernas,

asked, "What color is this paper?" Everyone chuckled. Since the letter had been duplicated, the paper used was a special type that was light blue. After Jernas's comment, everyone on the union team except Watoski—who was carefully reading the letter—indulged in light conversation. After a few minutes, the union committee returned to the letter and asked several questions.

The point of the illustration is this: Jernas and then the committee by their lighthearted responses had revealed their general approval of the company's proposal. This was most clear when this particular response was contrasted with the more bitter and sometimes sullen way in which the committee had reacted on other occasions when they had not been happy with the company's position. In fact, in this instance the company had gone far in committing itself to action, but the tactical point is that only Watoski, the chief negotiator, appreciated that there were other items to be resolved and that it was too early to give the union's candid reaction to this aspect of the company's package.

Another tactic is for Party to compose the committee of people who obviously cannot reveal clues, because they themselves do not have significant knowledge of their party's resistance point. In fact, the chief negotiator may be such a person. This tactic of "calculated incompetence," as one union official has termed it, also can have other important tactical assignments which we shall note later. Consider an instance in which this tactic was used:

> The union negotiator had been demanding information from the company regarding its cost under the company's current insurance program. The union was urging a new insurance program from a different insurance firm and needed the current cost information to substantiate its arguments. The company had been adamant in its refusal, and the chief negotiator could effectively argue that neither he nor anyone else on the team had the information to give. In a surprise maneuver, the union negotiator brought in a representative from the insurance company whose program he was advocating. Both the union and company negotiators were interested in selling their respective proposals to the union committee. Therefore, the company negotiator's immedi-

ate reaction was to think of bringing in someone from the company's insurance firm or from the financial department. Later management decided against this because it would have exposed to the union negotiator a person who had the cost information being sought. The policy of calculated incompetence was observed.

Of course in some instances Party controls information about his own utilities by only appearing uninformed. At the base of the person's behavior is a rational and logical scheme, but on the surface he may appear completely ignorant about the important forces.

Party may make it difficult for Opponent to ascertain Party's true utilities by the tactic of submitting a large number of proposals. "Many demands cover up the hard core which one might accept as a settlement and mask the relative importance which the side making the demands ascribes to the various demands."[9]

The above are efforts to minimize the flow of information. Attempts to modify Opponent's perceptions of Party's utilities often involve some of the positive communication acts which we turn to now.

Conveying Deliberate Impressions. Party will attempt to communicate those facts which create the most advantageous impressions of his inherent demands and threats. When it is advantageous, he will provide Opponent with information which gives the latter a better appreciation of the basic importance of an issue. Party advances cogent reasoning and engages in emotional behavior in order to underscore the importance of a particular issue to him. For example, Party can convey the appropriate impression by informing Opponent of the costs that he faces. Several tactics have this as their purpose.

One tactic adopted by management with more frequency in recent years is to take the initiative by introducing positive demands of its own, and the function of these demands is to focus attention on difficulties encountered under the *status quo*. It allows management to focus attention on areas in which they can demonstrate basic costs or difficulties—areas which the union might not anticipate or fully consider. Even though these demands will relate to only a portion of the bargaining agenda,

the tactic tends to create the appropriate overall impression.

Another tactic for Party is to ensure himself that he has informed Opponent of all Party's costs associated with a given demand. Thus, it often takes the form of reporting: "Consequences for me of demand D include C_1, C_2, and C_3, whereas I have reason to believe that you were only aware of consequence C_1." The reporting can occur in relatively general terms.

> Management of Utility Mfg. Co. took pains to inform the union of the prospect of a drop-off in government contract business and of increasing competition from the entry of other producers into the market. It was equally conscientious about explaining the probable impact that these developments would have on the company's profit picture. Then it reported in frank terms the minimum profit expectations imposed by the parent company on the management of Utility, it being only one of many subsidiaries. Management had reason to believe the union had not fully appreciated that the "gravy train," which the company had enjoyed for the past three years, was about to come to an end, with important implications for management's inherent demands and threats. Management was, of course, selective in the facts that it reported.

The consequences of demands can also be discussed in somewhat more specific terms.

> In recent years many unions have asked for a voice in the investment of health and welfare funds. In some instances management has refused on the grounds of principle, e.g., management's rights. In other instances management has attempted to avoid the arrangement by asserting that the involvement of the union would probably result in higher-risk investments, that investments of this type would require the company to lay aside more money, and therefore that the union was asking for the company to contribute more money for the health and welfare funds.

The above statements by Party convince Opponent that Party perceives a real need to avoid the demand. Opponent does not need to accept the importance of costs from his own viewpoint, all that he needs to do is recognize that costs are something that motivate Party's behavior. In effect, Party is saying to Opponent, "if you were in my shoes, this demand would look like the following. A rational person in my shoes would resist such a demand because it has these contingent costs."

The use of specific cost information heretofore unknown or not even considered by Opponent sometimes involves precise disclosures.

> During the 1958 negotiations of an agricultural implement company a question developed regarding whether the company should share certain cost information. Line management advised against this action, arguing that issues should be settled on their "merits." Yet, to bring about a settlement, the chief negotiator believed that he needed to do this to convince the union that the company would move no further. Thus, he informed the union that the new administrative procedures covering piecework were costing the company a penny and a half. This apparently came as news to the union negotiators and gave them additional insight into the basis on which the company was opposing its requests.

The tactical use of economic cost information can get rather involved and contains liabilities. All the observer can be certain about is that *prior* to the signing of the settlement, the company is trying to convince the union that a given set of demands will cost too much, while the union is seeking to convince the company that the costs will not be as great.[10]

> In 1959 one company showed the union actual cost figures to demonstrate that it was spending 2 cents an hour more on certain health and welfare benefits than its competition was. Significantly, the additional costs did not result from higher benefits but rather from the fact that the company carried a higher share of the burden relative to the employees than, for example, its major competitor did.
>
> In 1961 the union brought into negotiations with the company estimates of what the pattern had cost its competitor. The company knew by comparison that its cost figures would indicate that the pattern would cost it less; not less in fact, in its opinion, but less in comparison with the union's figures, which the company believed were exaggerated for the occasion. Partly for this reason the company chose not to release cost figures.

When the importance of a demand is not merely underscored or slightly overstated but rather is grossly exaggerated, this tactic contains important risks. Peters quotes the observation of one seasoned negotiator:

> You've got to be careful how you handle some of these minor issues. You can be so anxious to sew them up, that you sound off too loud and too long about them. Then what happens? A slick management negotiator starts fighting back like they really were big issues. Then, before you know it, he surrenders with a big hullaballoo as if he were giving you the combination to the safe. Now he's jockeyed you into a weaker position when you get down to brass tacks on the major issues. . . .[11]

Clearly there are other risks in communicating misinformation. The point may come in distributive bargaining when Party would like to talk about his true feelings and his true perceptions as a way of closing a negative settlement gap. But it is very difficult to be oblique in one negotiation and accepted as a faithful reporter in the next negotiation. Moreover, unless one is consistent in the types of arguments he advances, his positions lose credibility. In certain situations one can influence perceptions by communicating cost information. Such information may give Opponent a better appreciation of the inherent importance of an issue. But if the use of cost information is turned on and off, then when it is not advanced, Opponent will assume that Party's position is weak and his arguments are designed to mislead.

Many other difficulties emerge from the tactical use of information. Opponent will be able to counter with tactics of his own. What then results is a buildup of misinformation on top of misinformation. Instead of negotiations progressing to more common perceptions, they may lead in the opposite direction. Such a spiraling of misinformation can lead to greater uncertainty and miscalculation.

Aside from the question of how communicating misinformation affects the distributive bargaining process, certain value judgments are involved. There is a fine line between misrepresentations which are viewed as "natural" and those which are viewed as "lies" and consequently provoke hostility. Since collective bargaining is a continuing relationship, abuses along these lines will eventually receive their due.

Modifying Opponent's Perceptions of His Own Utilities

The objective of this tactical assignment is to alter Opponent's subjective utility function either by changing his view of the value of his own demands to himself or by changing his view of the unpleasantness of Party's proposals. We see these efforts to revise Opponent's utilities as primarily consisting of bringing to bear the right information and arguments at the right point within Opponent's organization. We shall first discuss the substantive aspect of these tactics, i.e., the types of information and arguments employed, and then turn to the procedural aspects of these tactics, i.e., the problem of introducing these arguments into Opponent's decision-making apparatus.

Tactical Arguments. In the preceding tactical assignment Party attempted to selectively report the consequences of a certain demand for him. In the present tactical assignment Party is enlightening Opponent about the consequences Opponent will face if the latter should succeed in maintaining his position on a certain issue. The distinction can be characterized as follows: In the first instance Party was communicating, "Here is why I definitely can't concede this item to you in a settlement." In the second instance, the one we are concerned with here, Party is saying, "Even though I'm not saying whether you could have it or not, here is why for your own good you should not insist upon this item."

Generally, this maneuver takes the form of a union trying to convince the company that the union's demands are costless and the company trying to convince the union that the union's demands are valueless to the union. Stated in terms of a general example, the union would say something like this to the company, "Your proposal to cut crew size will not save you money; morale will suffer and overall output will drop significantly." Similarly, the company says something like this, "Your proposal for a change in the seniority system is really not going to be that valuable to you because of the repercussions that will take place in your own organization."

Negotiators use colloquial and colorful language in their effort to force the other person to reassess the cost and value of different issues. Such phrases as the following are frequently encountered: "it could backfire"; "it might come back to haunt you"; "you can't have your cake and eat it too"; "the cost of this proposal will eventually be shifted to you"; "increases in cost will hurt our ability to compete, meaning fewer jobs and less security for you"; and "don't kill the goose that lays the golden egg." But whatever the language, the intent is the same, namely, to force the other person to reappraise the utility of a given issue.

The disadvantages to Opponent of his position may be more or less immediate and may be more or less certain in their effect. Some undesirable consequences possibly not considered by Opponent may be shown to be "part and parcel" of his demand.

> During the 1958 negotiations, the union asked for an early retirement arrangement. The company said that it would be willing to grant this demand but that it would retire a number of people unilaterally. When the union realized that in asking for early retirement benefits they might be giving the company the right to weed out certain key people, they retracted the demand.

> During the 1961 negotiations the UAW asked for uniform salary continuation benefits. It desired to bring the lower benefit plants up to the higher plants. The company successfully squelched this demand by saying, "the Harmon plant, which had the highest salary continuation benefits, had to be closed."

One variant of this argument is the idea that "it could backfire" or that "it might come back to haunt you." An example showing how management used such an argument in negotiations is as follows:

> A 7-hour day would mean that we'd be cutting production back . . . it wouldn't mean any more employees. We don't have room for more equipment; we wouldn't wanta buy more equipment. We couldn't have a 1-hour or 1/2-hour shift to make up the difference; that wouldn't work. In the long run, it would mean that we'd give less service to our customers, we'd be producing less; and that, in turn, would prob'ly build up. We would gradually lose much of the special type of business we get now, which is based on service. On top of that, it would increase our costs tremendously in an area where . . . our prices are higher than

competition in many of our products. This would make the thing even worse. It would—it would hurt everybody.[12]

The content of the above tactics involves the sharing of information with Opponent. The same purpose, namely, influencing Opponent's estimate of the true value to him of a specific issue, may be accomplished by the selective *withholding* of information.

> In the Utility negotiations management withheld from the union officials information they had regarding future plans for technological changes which would result in layoffs, in which the effect of that knowledge would have been to cause the union to include in its minimum acceptable package some concrete language on separation pay and layoff procedures.

It should be noted that this tactic—enlightening the Opponent about certain costs he will face should he achieve a particular demand—runs the risk of patronizing. Presumably Opponent believes that he is capable of assessing the advantages and disadvantages of a particular demand; hence, one is usually cautious in telling him what is good for him.

> *Gambon* Look, Len, pardon me for sayin' this, but will you, for Christ's sake, let us start to worry how to—to portion this money out? Don't be tellin' us how to use it. . . . Let us try to determine what's needed here.[13]

In distributive bargaining each side is wary of the intentions of the other side. Consequently, it is difficult for Party to convince Opponent that the advice is being given solely for the latter's benefit. In distributive bargaining each correctly suspects the other side of having some ulterior motive or some personal gain at stake. Nevertheless, Party often succeeds in sowing sufficient doubt about the wisdom of the issue that Opponent will take a hard look at his position.

Procedural Tactics. The foregoing material dealt with the content of the arguments. How does Party introduce these arguments most effectively into Opponent's organization? There are several possibilities. First, Party may invite a higher official from Opponent's organization to participate in negotiations. Such officials may have wider experience in the industry, may better understand Party's language, may be better aware of the bigger picture; hence, if Party's logics are good, they may have more impact on the higher official. It is in this vein that the union often asks to speak to the company president or to a higher authority than that represented in the company's bargaining team. Management may seek to involve a representative of the international union for the same reason.

Second, Party may communicate directly with Opponent's principals. Employees, for instance, may be less familiar with the issues and hence more easily convinced by illogical but persuasive arguments, or the principals may be assumed to have some doubt about their bargaining agent or the importance of the union's bargaining positions and hence can be reached by arguments that are couched in terms of what is in the workers' best interest. Letters sent to employees' homes telling them about the "generous company offer" represent this kind of procedural approach.

Third, in situations which have features opposite to those above, it is sometimes tactical for management to try to deal strictly with local union officials. This is used when many of the union's demands are believed to have originated at higher levels of the organization and may contain mixed blessings for the local unit of the organization.

> In a negotiation between a teamster local and a large newspaper, the international representative made a demand that all route salesmen be provided with automobiles. The company negotiator countered this by calling on some individual members in the negotiating committee who were driver salesmen and asked them, "You know what we're doing?" By directing the question to people from the local organization, the company negotiator was able to get the union to admit that the company's compensation practices were not that inadequate.

Generally, the objective is to locate someone in Opponent's organization who will evaluate the issue in a way more favorable to Party. One union studied in a recent negotiation tried this technique rather successfully. They contacted company officials up and down the line until they found someone who was sympathetic to their position. This tactic is particularly effective when top management is strongly oriented toward maintaining principles and local management is strongly oriented toward administrative convenience. The union can obtain relief on issues by searching out the official who is not overly sensitive to the day-to-day costs inherent in the union's position.

Manipulating Strike Costs of Party and Opponent

In this section we consider two remaining tactical assignments which operate on strike costs: increasing Opponent's potential strike costs and minimizing Party's. They are considered together for reasons of convenience inasmuch as single tactics chosen by negotiators often operate simultaneously on both sides of the power equation. In the discussion of the distributive model we indicated that we would be limiting our treatment of the costs of disagreeing to that of strike costs. However, it should be understood that pressure can be inflicted in ways other than precipitating a strike. Consider the following interesting example:

> Instead of striking a restaurant, as a restaurant owner had expected and prepared for, a union arranged to have hundreds of the sympathizers enter the restaurant just before the noon rush hour, order a cup of coffee, and sit down. When the regular customers of the restaurant entered, they found all of the tables taken. As the coffee drinkers are strictly within their rights, the management could not eject them.[14]

In some negotiations, one side or the other will attempt to impose pressure by going to outsiders—the National Labor Relations Board, the courts, etc. This practice is more prevalent among white collar unions who are unable or unwilling to engage in strike action.

> Since the Association lacked strike power, its most dramatic weapon was the filing of an unfair labor charge with the NLRB, which brought publicity that the company might find distasteful or injurious in recruiting.

> While one cannot conclude that the Association deliberately filed unmeritorious charges for the sake of such publicity, it must be recognized that this was one of the strongest formal weapons at its disposal. Another publicity

device used by the Association was the issuance of bulletins during bargaining negotiations. Widely read within the management structure, the bulletin was credited by some Association leaders with winning influential members of management to the support of its position on occasion, with the result that the company's position was changed. Moreover, the bulletins provided a medium for shaping membership opinions on bargaining issues. The combination of membership meetings, informal group discussions, and bulletins permits the Association to use morale as a bargaining weapon in a way that would be impossible for unorganized professional employees.[15]

Sometimes the third party is the specter of a rival union. Independent unions may threaten to abandon their independent status, which the company typically values.

> In several negotiations in the oil industry the following sequence has taken place: the independent union drags its feet in bargaining, the membership believes that the delay is due to the company's failure to bargain, soon a militant union like the Teamsters or the Oil, Chemical, and Atomic Workers appears on the scene offering to represent the employees, and a certification election is held. The election is decided in favor of the independent union, but when negotiations resume, it turns out that the contract is quickly signed and the company makes additional concessions.

In most situations the company cannot go out of business, but sometimes there are steps that can be taken short of this.

> In an important negotiation between the musicians union and the Chicago Symphony Association over contract terms for a summer music festival, management announced that it was canceling the season's concerts when the union failed to accept its offer by a certain time. As it later turned out, the cancellation was only "on paper," and the concerts were held once an agreement was reached. However, cancellation of the season's concerts can be a very powerful form of economic pressure.

Since the total effect of a strike involves more than immediate economic losses, a party may try to enhance these collateral costs.

> In a long strike between the OCAW and the Shell Oil Company, the union made much of

the hard feelings that were developing between the foremen who were running the plant and the striking workers. The union knew management would be sensitive to the tenor of long-run relations between the foremen and the employees, since once the strike ended, these employees would have to return to the plant and work under the foremen who had been operating the plant. It was clear that the strike was not hurting the company in terms of economic losses, but the union was sure that it was hurting it in terms of foreman morale and management's concern about foreman-employee relations.

A frequently used device is to physically exhaust Opponent to the point at which his fatigue overwhelms his desire to attain his objective. This is often characteristic of the closing phases of negotiations. However, as the following two examples illustrate, it can be used throughout negotiations:

> A management person quite successful in the newspaper field told how he scheduled bargaining for the evening hours as a way of placing pressure on the union team. For one thing, they were tired after having worked a full day. In addition, the company was not paying them for the time spent in bargaining. He claimed that if the company could get away with it, it was the best way of putting pressure on the union bargaining team.

> In the public employment field, in which the economic strike is not a possibility, other forms of pressure have been developed. In one negotiation the employees just kept meeting, hoping to wear management down. The management officials, who were anxious to return to their desks, finally gave in on some issues, not because they felt that they should, but to end the time-consuming process of negotiations.

Many other examples could be given of the imaginative use of pressure tactics, particularly in situations in which the strike option is not meaningful. These include such devices as picketing in front of the president's home, appearing at stockholder meetings, adhering rigidly to safety rules, shifting tags of destination on luggage, boycotting a briefing session for insurance agents, etc. The techniques of labor protest are manifold. However, our discussion concentrates mainly on economic duress through the strike action.

In deciding how to place an opponent at a strike disadvantage, many structural and strategic questions are involved. In the short run it is difficult for a negotiator to manipulate the rate of cost that his opponent will experience should open conflict develop. However, in the long run many possibilities are available. Some of these are suggested by the factors outlined in the model chapter. For example, changes can be made in the structure of collective bargaining. Each side can attempt to alter the structure in a favorable direction. Companies may move toward industry-wide bargaining or move to strengthen one another's position through the development of mutual-aid arrangements. On the union side action may be taken toward the development of cooperating councils.

Either side also can alter the power equation by altering the location of the appropriate outer limit or reservation price. If the union enjoys great power because management has few other alternatives, management can take steps over the long run to lower its resistance point by constructing new plants, etc. Similarly, the union can do such things as improving the skill level of the workers, vesting pension rights, etc.—efforts designed to raise the lower limit and thereby increase the bargaining power of the workers.

Similarly, the effect of cyclical and seasonal factors can be handled by a skillful manipulation of the date of the contract expiration. The union prefers to have a contract expire when employees have more need for leisure time (for example, during hunting and fishing seasons or during the warm weather). The union would hesitate to have a contract expire near the Christmas season, when financial demands on employees are heavy. On the company's side they would prefer to have the contract expire during a slack period of the year.

Over the long run either party can maneuver the expiration date in its favor. However, it may be necessary to forego certain short-run gains in order to achieve a more favorable expiration. Obviously Party's objective is to have the contract expire when costs of conflict are greatest for Opponent and least for himself.

This was illustrated in the case of a skyscraper office building under construction in New York City some years ago. In New York City the renting season for office space almost invariably begins on May 1st and occupancy for tenants must then be available or they cannot move from their old locations. The union campaign was so timed, that cessation of work would make the completion of the building by May 1st impossible.[16]

In the absence of a favorable expiration date it is often possible, more for the union than for management, to continue working until the time is favorable for a showdown. The UAW adopted this strategy during the 1958 negotiations, when, at the contract expiration date there was an abnormally high inventory of cars available. As Leonard Woodcock expressed it, "We rocked and rolled through the summer." The UAW only became serious as the critical model changeover period approached.

Besides enabling the union to bide its time, the technique of working without a contract has another advantage. It forces management into an uncertain period which can have severe economic costs if as a result the company's customers regard it as a less reliable supplier and begin to divert orders to competitors.

Beyond manipulating the structural factors, many other steps can be taken by each side to gain the favorable side of the power equation. These tactics work on both the rate of strike cost and the amount of total resources available for withstanding a strike. A few of these tactics can be quickly summarized for the union and the company.

Union Tactics. First, the union can attempt to increase membership solidarity. The union can strive to bring all the employees within the bargaining unit, to quell factionalism, and to take other steps designed to create solid support for a strike.

Second, the union can increase the availability of other activities and benefits. Prior to the strike the union can survey the availability of alternate employment and make arrangements for various kinds of supplementary benefits. Over the long run the union can push for legislation that would provide state unemployment compensation to striking workers.

Third, the union can build strike funds and enter into mutual assistance pacts. Funds are usually collected and paid out by national headquarters. In preparing for the 1955 automobile negotiations, the UAW set the goal for their strike fund at $25 million. That would appear to be a large amount, but it would probably cover less than two weeks' normal earnings for striking General Motors employees.[17]

David Dubinsky reportedly had an imaginative technique for getting the most psychological impact out of the limited funds of the garment workers. He would open an organization campaign in a new area by depositing a substantial sum to the account of the union in a leading local bank. When local garment manufacturers learned of the deposit, they would assume that the union was able to finance a long strike and capitulate. Only later might they learn that the entire sum had been placed locally on the express condition that it be returned intact after serving its psychological purpose.[18]

Fourth, the union can encourage employees to increase their personal savings and place an upper limit on their fixed weekly financial commitments, such as regular payments for durable goods purchased on time. Both efforts limit the employees' dependence on continuous income.

The use of these and other tactics is revealed in a report in a union publication which summarizes the steps that can be taken by unions to prepare themselves for strike action.

Health, Welfare and Retirement Benefits—Unions have found it possible in many cases to work out arrangements for preserving the workers' stake in these funds and in some cases for continuing these benefits to union members during the strike. *Support of other unions*—Unions on strike have found it to their definite advantage to make certain that other interested unions in industrial areas are kept up to date regarding strike developments. *Support of local community*—In certain cases, unions have been able to win support for the strike (or at least neutralize the opposition) from certain enlightened elements in the business community. *Easing the financial burden of strikers*—Many unions have found it possible to make special arrangements with local merchants, banks, insurance companies, and credit agencies, under which striking union members would be given considerations in meeting with financial obligations. *Special assistance to strikers*—A variety of resources is often available to help individual strikers and their families suffering severe hardship during a strike.[19]

Company Tactics. First, the company may take steps to keep the plant open. It may go so far as to hire strikebreakers and proceed to replace the work force. Short of this the company can attempt to operate the plant with supervisors and regular employees who have been encouraged to return to work.

Second, the company can build inventories. The objective is to continue shipments during the course of the strike. Whether this can be done depends on the location of the firm's warehouses and the general questions of how easy and inexpensive it is to store materials. It also involves the question of who normally stores the inventories—customers or suppliers?

Third, the company can transfer production to alternate plants not represented by the union. If a plant is only one of several company plants which have similar production facilities, the company can reduce the cost of a strike by transferring production to other plants. The net cost of supplying customers from alternate production facilities will depend upon added transportation costs, amount of excess capacity available, how much adaptation of other production facilities is required, etc. Still an additional production capability may be achieved by subcontracting operations to another firm or otherwise arranging for them to supply customers.

Fourth, the company can secure financial resources in order to withstand a long strike. Many things can be done to avoid capitulation because of the lack of financial resources. Extra cash can be acquired. Resources from other parts of the company can be shifted into the plant.

Again, let management speak for itself. Consider the following analysis of an aircraft company official regarding the impact of strike action:

There are some points that should be made clear:

Only two major divisions are involved: Lockheed Missiles & Space Company, where the union has only 5,700 members out of a total work force of 31,200, and Lockheed-California Company, where the union has 11,600 members out of a total work force of 24,000.

We currently are in a good schedule position for deliveries of most of our important programs. Many are research, development, and engineering programs, which we can maintain with minimum delays. The effect on production programs would be more immediate and direct, but Lockheed intends to continue operations and will make every effort to minimize this effect.

Whether any of our programs would be moved away from Lockheed would, of course, be for the government to decide. Such action obviously would be as harmful to employees and to the community as to the company. In our opinion, there would be less added expense and schedule delay in leaving a project at Lockheed even during a strike than in moving the program to another plant and organization.

What we have been talking about are the steps that each side can take to influence the actual power equation. Of course it is also necessary to affect the other party's perceptions before these actual—changes can be made to influence him. •

Footnotes

[1] We are interested here in the magnitude of the utilities whether they be positive (value in obtaining his own demand) or negative (value in resisting Party's demands).

[2] Floyd Brandt, John Glover, and B. M. Selekman, "Gray Manufacturing Company ©," (Copyright by the President and Fellows of Harvard College, 1959). p. 10.

[3] B. M. Selekman, S. K. Selekman, and S. H. Fuller, *Problems in Labor Relations,* 2d ed., (New York: McGraw-Hill Book Company, 1958), p. 342.

[4] Ann Douglas, *Industrial Peacemaking* (New York: Columbia University Press, 1962), P. 26.

[5] Selekman, Selekman, and Fuller, 2d ed., *op. cit.,* pp. 568–569.

[6] Lloyd Ulman, *The Government of the Steel Workers' Union* (New York: John Wiley Sons, Inc., 1962), p. 66.

[7]J. T. Dunlop and J. J. Healy, *Collective Bargaining: Principles and Cases,* rev. ed. (Homewood, Ill.: Richard D. Irwin, Inc., 1953), p. 54.

[8]*After* the signing of the settlement the positions of the parties reverse for reasons that we shall explore later.

[9]Peters, *op. cit.*, pp. 169–170.

[10]Douglas, *op. cit.*, p. 477.

[11]*Ibid.*, p. 480.

[12]A. T. Jacobs, "Some Significant Factors Influencing the Range of Indeterminateness in Collective Bargaining Negotiations," unpublished Ph.D. thesis, Ann Arbor, Mich., University of Michigan, 1951, p. 296.

[13]Bernard Goldstein, "Unions for Technical Professionals: A Case Study, 1957," unpublished Ph.D. thesis, Dept. of Sociology, University of Chicago, August, 1957, P. 21.

[14]Jacobs, *op. cit.*, p. 296.

[15]Alfred Kuhn, *Labor Institutions and Economics* (New York: Holt, Rinehart and Winston, Inc., 1958), p. 183.

[16]*Ibid.*

[17]AFL-CIO Collective Bargaining Report, "Strikes," vol. 3 (November, 1958), p. 71.

[18]Douglas, *op. cit.*, p. 576.

[19]Edward Peters, *Strategy and Tactics in Labor Negotiations* (New London, Conn.: National Foremen's Institute, 1955), p. 17.

Study Questions

1. Why should we be concerned with the "utilities" (i.e., values) that our opponent attaches to possible outcomes of the negotiation?

2. What research and methods of assessment can we use to discover how our opponent values the potential outcomes of negotiation? How can we find out his or her perception of the costs of a failure to reach agreement (which the authors call "strike costs")?

3. What is meant by "modifying Opponent's Perceptions of Party's Utilities"? Put this phrase into your own words and give an example of how you've tried this in your own attempts to influence other people.

4. What is the purpose of telling your opponent things to get her or him to reassess the cost and value of different issues? What methods could you try to accomplish this goal?

5. In what way can it be said that the pressure tactics used in distributive bargaining are part of a psychological game?

Reaching Agreement: The Exchange Process

James P. Begin
Director, Institute of Management and
Labor Relations
Rutgers University

Edwin F. Beal
Professor Emeritus
University of Oregon

Once the collective bargaining relationship is established, the actors must negotiate an agreement and learn to live with it, or rather, learn to live with each other under its terms. This chapter deals with the preparations and procedures for negotiating. Chapter 9 analyzes the nature of the agreement in terms of the functions served by the substantive rules. Chapter 15 discusses the problems of living with the agreement and administering the rules.

Today most labor-management negotiations in the private sector are for the revision and renewal of existing agreements, which regularly expire at intervals usually ranging from one to three years, rather than for an initial agreement. Rare indeed is the agreement so carefully phrased and the labor-management relationship so nicely balanced that the parties renew it unchanged. One or the other, or both, almost always seek to adjust or improve it in response to feedback from the work place about needed changes (the feedback loop in our systems model in Chapter 1), and there was always the first time, when everything had to be considered. This chapter, therefore, treats negotiations as if they were for an initial agreement, though most of what is said applies to renewals as well. A strike can, of course, occur at any stage in a relationship if negotiations either for a new agreement or renewal of an old one break down. Chapter 8 will discuss strikes, their causes and resolution, as well as a variety of mechanisms available for improving union-management cooperation.

In negotiations the newly certified union and newly obligated management face the consequences and culmination of everything that has gone before: the organizing, the electioneering, the winning of recognition, the concentration of worker hopes and management fears. For the first time their representatives sit down face to face and formally engage in bargaining to set the conditions that will govern their day-to-day relations for the year, or two or three, ahead. Each set of subsequent negotiations sums up their experiences together over that year or two or three, and marks a new beginning. In the whole range of interaction that makes up a labor-management relationship, probably nothing is more concentrated and significant than negotiations.

Until recently, few scholars had closely examined what goes on around the conference table during negotiations, or how the participants prepare for that crucial test. Less vital aspects of collective bargaining have drawn greater attention. Arbitration, for example—an important, but still subsidiary activity, set in motion only if the negotiated agreement so specifies—has given rise to a vast amount of literature, with shelf after shelf of published awards and volumes of commentary and critique.

This neglect of negotiations is not as surprising as it might seem. Negotiations usually take place in private, and access to negotiations for research purposes is very limited until they crystallize in the final, formal agreement. Furthermore, negotiations remain fluid, tentative, usually informal and therefore difficult to recreate. Finally, once reached, the agreement captures attention and diverts interest from the preceding activity that produced it.

Academic examinations of labor-management relations have taken the form of case studies of actual negotiations, of laboratory experiments, and of model-building based on the findings of case studies and laboratory experiments reported in the literature. Ann Douglas, for example, in her book *Industrial Peacemaking,* works with records and with the participants in six sets of negotiations under mediation to make a psychological analysis of the interaction.[1] She admits it would be rash to generalize from so small a sample. Richard Walton and Robert McKersie in their book, *A Behavioral Theory of Labor Negotiations,* take an opposite approach. Without accumulating data from actual or experimental negotiations, they start from theory and build models for analysis.[2]

We first draw on the Walton and McKersie book to establish a theoretical model of the negotiations exchange process. The Walton and McKersie framework is used not because it has been thoroughly tested by researchers and found to be valid—because it has not—but because it is a useful teaching device for introducing students to the dynamics of the bargaining exchange process. Following the discussion of bargaining theory, we present a straightforward, practical description of the negotiating process, which includes an analysis of the environmental, organizational, and personality factors shaping its operation.

Negotiations in Theory

Negotiations take place whenever two social units (individuals, organizations, countries) that are dependent on each other are in conflict over one or more issues. The negotiations concern the division or exchange of resources and usually take the form of the presentation of demands and the evaluation of the demands, followed by counterproposals and concessions, and, ultimately agreement.

In a collective bargaining exchange process, the social units or actors are composed of union negotiators, the employees they represent, and the employers with whom they are negotiating. Government actors are not normally involved in the organizational or industry level bargaining exchange, although indirectly they are involved in setting boundaries to negotiating behaviors, and in the case of breakdowns in negotiations government agencies are sources of third-party mediators. It is the participation of the actors in the exchange process that gives a collective bargaining system its dynamic features, an important element which Dunlop omitted, as was discussed in Chapter 1. Incorporating an exchange process into our industrial relations system model provides a useful means for relating the input and output variables of a collective bargaining system so that we can understand more effectively how the parties to negotiations get from one point to another.

The following discussion will first sketch out a theoretical model of the bargaining *exchange* process. Then the negotiating process will be discussed in practical terms, including a coverage of the *inputs* affecting the operation of the bargaining exchange. In Chapter 9, an *output* model identifying the expected consequences of faculty bargaining will be presented. Chapters 10–15 will discuss aspects of the output model in greater detail. Figure 1 illustrates the relationships of the model components.

FIGURE 1
Collective Bargaining Systems Model

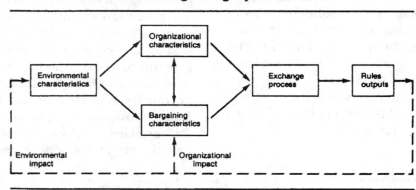

The Exchange Process

The following general description of Walton and McKersie's exchange framework is taken directly from their book.

Labor negotiations, as an instance of social negotiations, is comprised of four systems of activity, each with its own function for the interacting parties, its own internal logics, and its own identifiable set of instrumental acts or tactics.

We shall refer to each of the distinguishable systems of activities as a *subprocess*. The first subprocess is *distributive bargaining;* its function is to resolve pure conflicts of interest. The second, *integrative bargaining,* functions to find common or complementary interests and solve problems confronting both parties. The third subprocess is *attitudinal structuring,* and its functions are to influence the attitudes of the participants toward each other and to affect the basic bonds which relate the two parties they represent. A fourth subprocess, *intraorganizational bargaining,* has the function of achieving consensus within each of the interacting groups.

Distributive Bargaining. Distributive bargaining is a hypothetical construct referring to the complex system of activities instrumental to the attainment of one party's goals when they are in basic conflict with those of the other party. It is the type of activity most familiar to students of negotiations; in fact, it is "bargaining" in the strictest sense of the word. In social negotiations, the goal conflict can relate to several values; it can involve allocation of any resources, e.g., economic, power, or status symbols. What game theorists refer to as fixed-sum games are the situations we have in mind: one person's gain is a loss to the other. The specific points at which the negotiating objectives of the two parties come in contact define the issues. Formally, an *issue* will refer to an area of common concern in which the objectives of the two parties are assumed to be in conflict. As such, it is the subject of distributive bargaining.

Integrative Bargaining. Integrative bargaining refers to the system of activities which is instrumental to the attainment of objectives which are not in fundamental conflict with those of the other party and which therefore can be integrated to some degree. Such objectives are said to define an area of common concern, a *problem*. Integrative bargaining and distributive bargaining are both joint decision-making processes. However, these processes are quite dissimilar and yet are rational responses to different situations. Integrative potential exists when the nature of a problem permits solutions which benefit both parties, or at least when the gains of one party do not represent equal sacrifices by the other. This is closely related to what game theorists call the varying-sum game.

Attitudinal Structuring. Distributive and integrative bargaining pertain to economic issues and the rights and obligations of the parties, which are the generally recognized content of labor negotiations. However, we postulate that an additional major function of negotiations is influencing the relationships between parties, in particular such attitudes as friendliness-hostility, trust, respect, and the motivational orientation of competitiveness-cooperativeness. Although the existing relationship pattern is acknowledged to be influenced by many enduring forces (such as the technical and economic context, the basic personality dispositions of key participants, and the social belief systems which pervade the two parties), the negotiators can and do take advantage of the interaction system of negotiations to produce attitudinal change.

Attitudinal structuring is our term for the system of activities instrumental to the attainment of desired relationship patterns between the parties. Desired relationship patterns usually give content to this process in a way comparable to that of issues and problems in distributive and integrative processes. The distinction among the processes is that whereas the first two are joint decision-making processes, attitudinal structuring is a socioemotional interpersonal process designed to change attitudes and relationships.

Intraorganizational Bargaining. The three processes discussed thus far relate to the reconciliation process that takes place between the union and the company. During the course of negotiations another system of activities, designed to achieve consensus within the union and within the company, takes place. Intraorganizational bargaining refers to the system of activities which brings the expectations of principals into alignment with those of the chief negotiator.

The chief negotiators often play important but limited roles in formulating bargaining objectives. On the union side, the local membership exerts considerable influence in determining the nature and strength of aspirations, and the international union may dictate the inclusion of certain goals in the bargaining agenda. On the company side, top management and various staff groups exert their influence on bargaining objectives. In a sense the chief negotiator is the recipient of two sets of demands—one from across the table and one from his own organization. His dilemma stems from conflict at two levels: differing aspirations about issues and differing expectations about behavior.

Intraorganizational bargaining within the union is particularly interesting. While it is true that for both parties to labor negotiations many individuals not present in negotiations are vitally concerned about what transpires at the bargaining table, the union negotiator is probably subject to more organizational constraints than his company counterpart. The union is a political organization whose representatives are elected to office and in which contract terms must be ratified by an electorate.[3]

Figure 2 illustrates how the four subprocesses relate the union and management bargaining teams that are in conflict. The distributive bargaining, the integrative bargaining, and the attitudinal structuring subprocesses directly relate the union and management bargaining teams, while the intraorganizational bargaining subprocesses relate the bargaining teams to their respective constituencies.

The Relationship of the Subprocesses

The tactics peculiar to each subprocess are basic to the interaction of the four subprocesses. As will be seen, some of the tactics of the individual subprocesses facilitate the interaction of the subprocesses, while others create dilemmas for the bargaining teams.

Integrative and Distributive Subprocesses. In the distributive bargaining process in which fixed resources are being allocated, the basic tactic is to minimize the opponent's information about one's own bargaining position while maximizing one's information about the oppo-

FIGURE 2
The Exchange Model Subprocesses

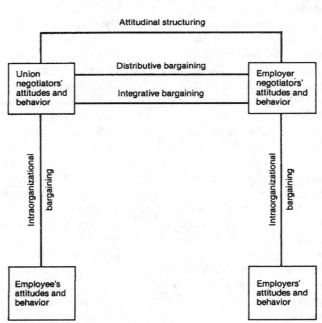

nent's position without making commitments. On the other hand, the integrative process is a problem-solving situation requiring relatively open communications as the parties identify alternative solutions to problems and then resolve them. To develop information for solving problems, subcommittees are often appointed, enhancing integrative bargaining. (The last part of Chapter 8 identifies additional nonadversarial problem-solving mechanisms.) However, if the negotiations have a largely distributive flavor, the parties may not want to indicate the degree of flexibility that the agreement to develop subcommittees conveys. Additionally, a high degree of trust is necessary for a problem-solving, integrative bargaining approach, whereas in distributive bargaining, trust exists "in more limited and subtle ways."[4] Since any bargaining situation involves both *issues* and *problems*, the name of the game is to combine the tactics in such a way as to attain agreement.

Attitudinal Structuring and Distributive Subprocesses.

The attitudinal structuring process involves the use of tactics aimed at maintaining or changing the nature of the bargaining relationship. The attitudinal structuring process and the distributive bargaining process are often mutually interfering processes:

> A tactic designed to promote a better relationship frequently entails a sacrifice of the substance of distributive bargaining; and conversely a tactic designed to achieve a distributive gain often adversely affects the relationship.[5]

Generally, attempts aimed at maintaining or improving a relationship interfere with the tactics of the distributive process. There are situations in which the tactics of the two subprocesses are mutually facilitating, but they tend to be extreme situations, e.g., developing minimum levels of trust and acceptance to prevent destructive outcomes.

Integrative and Attitudinal Structuring Subprocesses.

The tactics of the integrative and attitudinal structuring processes have few, if any, conflicts.

> Before integrative bargaining can take place, the two organizations need to develop a good measure of trust and friendliness. The activities of talking frankly about one's needs, shar-

ing information, jointly formulating solutions, etc. cannot be undertaken unless trust is present. The problem-solving activity serves to improve the relationship even further.[6]

Intraorganizational Bargaining and Distributive Subprocesses.

In intraorganizational bargaining the negotiating teams are responsible for bringing the expectations of their respective constituencies into line with the realities of bargaining. Keeping constituents from being committed or trying to reduce their commitment to certain preferred bargaining outcomes is a difficult task since the intraorganizational process is so closely linked with the other processes.

> Almost by definition the two processes of intraorganizational bargaining and distributive bargaining are in conflict. In distributive bargaining the negotiator attempts to modify the opponent's position toward the expectation of his principals. In internal bargaining the negotiator endeavors to bring the expectations of his principals into alignment with those of the opponent. In this sense, the purposes of these two activities are diametrically opposed. The two processes also frequently interfere with each other at the tactical level.
>
> Distributive bargaining involves tactical attempts to crystallize internal feeling and increase the willingness to fight. These and other steps are helpful in conveying strong commitment and increasing the power position of the party. All these activities conflict with intraorganizational bargaining, in which the negotiator reduces feeling, divests the membership of ambitious objectives, and generally strives to prevent the membership from developing too great an attachment to any particular proposal.
>
> A particularly important limitation is placed on effective distributive bargaining in which the negotiator is unsure of his ability to revise his own organization's position. He is foreclosed, for example, from making a timely concession—one which might lead to the best overall distributive results—when his own organization is not yet convinced of the need for a concession.[7]

However, the tactics used in the intraorganizational and distributive processes do not always conflict.

For example, by maintaining a firm position (distributive tactic), Opponent can help Party revise the position of his own organization. Similarly, by giving up on an issue very grudgingly and making a big issue over a small point (distributive tactic), Party can help Opponent distort the level of achievement as perceived by Party's organization. In both cases, the distributive tactics of one assisted the other in achieving internal consensus.[8]

Intraorganizational Bargaining and Attitudinal Structuring Subprocesses. The relationship between intraorganizational bargaining and attitudinal structuring processes is basic.

> The relationship between the two negotiators is sometimes a constraint on the behavior one negotiator might use to comply with the expectations of members of his own organization. At other times, the relationship bond actually enables the negotiator to be more effective in achieving internal consensus.[9]

In distributive bargaining particularly, attitudinal structuring plays an important part in accommodating intraorganizational needs to bargaining realities: ". . . many of the attitudinal tactics involved helping Opponent, sometimes in ways that strengthened his position internally."[10]

Intraorganizational Bargaining and Integrative Subprocesses. The intraorganizational bargaining and integrative bargaining processes can have positive or negative interactions.

> Very often integrative bargaining is impeded by intraorganizational pressures which require the negotiator to act in a specified way. His constituents may not tolerate off-the-record discussion, subcommittees, and the other tactics necessary for integrative bargaining. Nor may the constituents be satisfied with an agreement that had been reached via problem solving.[11]

On the other hand,

> Intraorganizational bargaining aims at developing flexibility in one's position. To the extent that the organization takes a more flexible position, the purposes of integrative bargaining can *also* be served.
>
> Consider the tactic of bringing the constituents face to face with the realities of the situation. Such a move can serve the purposes of intraorganizational bargaining by forcing the constituents to revise their aspirations and the purposes of integrative bargaining by making available more viewpoints and problem solvers (assuming that their energies are harnessed through subcommittees, etc.).
>
> Even the alternate tactic of isolating the membership serves the same double purpose. Such a move is functional for intraorganizational bargaining in that it prevents them from perceiving the actual level of achievement until it is too late; and it is functional for integrative bargaining in that it removes constraining influences from the bargaining room, thereby allowing the key participants to increase joint achievement through problem solving.[12]

Although this brief summary of Walton and McKersie's theory of social negotiations certainly does not do justice to the complex development given to it in their book, it serves as a useful base for exploring the factors that affect the exchange process, the focus of the following section.

Negotiations in Practice

We see labor-management negotiations, by analogy, as a kind of diplomacy, subject to possible war (strike action) and resulting eventually in a treaty (labor agreement). The terms of the treaty reflect the relative strength of the parties, or their bargaining power, and the persuasion skills of the actors carried out against that power background.

When managers and union representatives face each other across the bargaining table they approach the agreement they both want with separate and often conflicting objectives. Like diplomats, they generally behave courteously toward each other—at least at the start. They appeal to reason. They marshall facts and arguments (sometimes interspersed with emotional pleas) to promote their points of view. But each side brings to the encounter more than just a winning smile and a persuasive manner; they bring *power* to bear on the outcome. Behind the logic, the ritual, and the amenities, both sides are aware that the other has power, some of which is evident and easy to calculate, some hidden and hard to estimate. Each tries to gauge the other's relative strength, and willingness to use it. The ultimate test of strength—or in this context, of the use of power—is the union's ability to strike and the company's ability to take a strike. As we will see, the respective bargaining power of the parties to negotiation is shaped by characteristics of the environment, employer's organization, and union, including the personality characteristics of the negotiators.

Neither the union nor management makes power the only element in its calculations. The two normally have much more in common, a greater dependency, than an outsider would expect. Both stand to gain something, not lose everything, from the rules they establish for the workplace. They have always, inevitably, been interdependent, but the power latent in the work force side of their interdependency usually emerges only when the workers unionize and acquire the capability of taking concerted action. Bargaining power is basically standoff power; it is there in the background, looming over negotiations; but in the foreground, the actors engage in negotiations. They talk, they reason, and they try to persuade.

While bargaining power is usually in the background, it is fundamental to the conduct of any bargaining relationship, including a cooperative relationship which uses primarily integrative bargaining tactics. For even though the use of power is minimized in a cooperative relationship, a certain degree of power is necessary to establish the legitimacy of the parties to a cooperative relationship.

The law requires employers to recognize and bargain "in good faith" with certified unions, thus enhancing the power of the unions. But it does not force them to agree with the union. They are free to yield to the union's persuasions, but they do not have to be persuaded; providing, always, that they give the unions an opportunity—in good faith—to persuade them.

The union's task is to persuade the employer to accept policies and administrative procedures the union wants. If the union succeeds and the two parties reach agreement, then the law requires that, at the request of either party, they must reduce their agreement to writing. Since this requirement became a feature of the law, the universal practice has been to put the agreement in writing. The legal requirement to put agreements in writing is another example of how the government, in its rules for rule-making capacity, influences the balance of power in collective bargaining relationships.

This written document, signed by the employer and by union representatives, is commonly referred to as a contract, but as we shall see in Chapter 9, it is less a contract between union and company than an agreed-on code of rules that define the company's work contract with all—and each—of the employees in the bargaining unit. It specifies the conditions under which the employer offers work to the employees and it binds the company to abide by those conditions. It becomes, in effect, company policy and a pledge of company performance in all matters that it touches. If, for example, you were an assembly worker in a factory—or a toolmaker, or the operator of a fork-lift truck—you could find in the provisions of the labor agreement your appropriate range of pay, your seniority rights in relation to co-workers, your claim to paid vacation time or to various benefits, your right to present grievances and the procedure to go through, and so on. Just such items, and many more, become the issues to be settled in negotiations.

Labor and management work out the vast majority of collective bargaining agreements by what might be called peaceful diplomacy, with no resort to force or the overt use of power. Occasionally, agreement can be reached only by resort to force: a strike, or more rarely, a lockout. During a strike the face-to-face negotiations may temporarily break off, but a strike cannot be settled without negotiations. Although the threat of strike almost inevitably hovers over negotiations, it would be well to consider negotiations first, and then the strike.

Under the heading of negotiations one should first meet the actors, or the people who do the bargaining, then the preparations they make, then the actual conduct of negotiations. The always possible strike and strike settlement are discussed in Chapter 8.

The People Who Do the Bargaining

Preceding chapters have explored the various combinations of separate, and usually opposing, interests present in negotiations. But negotiating is an activity carried out by people who meet at a definite point in time and space.

These people stand in definite organizational relationships to the interests they represent and perform definite functions. They come from the ranks of unions, enterprises and, sometimes, from the government. Taken together, these people comprise the bargaining structure of a particular bargaining relationship.

Bargaining Structure. The bargaining structure determines the manner in which the parties relate to each other for bargaining purposes, and as discussed in Chapter 5, is generally a product of the interaction of government bargaining unit determination policy, the markets, and the organizational structure of the employer. Bargaining structure is important because it has a major effect on the bargaining power of the parties and on the type of bargaining relationship. If either party has difficulties in achieving internal consensus in the intraorganizational bargaining process, due to the bargaining structure, it will be more difficult for the negotiators to engage in strategies aimed at building a cooperative relationship (attitudinal structuring). Problems of achieving internal consensus for unions are created by bargaining structures with broad occupational and/or geographical dispersion. Generally, the more heterogeneous the bargaining unit, the more difficult it will be to achieve consensus within the union in respect to bargaining demands—intraorganizational bargaining will be more difficult. Difficulties between the craft and unskilled workers in UAW units over wage differentials are an example of intraorganizational problems created by occupational differences. The same problems are created for employers when the bargaining structure is complex. The instability of the various truckers' associations formed over the years to negotiate with the Teamsters Union is an example of the difficulties of achieving and maintaining consensus among employers with diverse goals.

Within the overall bargaining structure, the union and employer participants engage in a range of diverse roles.

The Union Negotiating Committee. There is no set rule about who is to negotiate with the company for the union. It may be the committee that drew up the demands and saw them through to ratification. It may be a standing committee, such as the union's executive board or, at the other extreme, a committee elected, and at-large from the whole membership, expressly for the occasion. It almost always includes, in any case, certain ex officio members such as the president, one or more vice presidents, the secretary, the chief steward. If the local has a business agent, he or she will certainly accompany the negotiators.

Also accompanying the negotiators in most cases will be someone who is not a member of the local union: the international representative.

The International Representative. On the union side in negotiations sits an "outsider," the international representative. Of all the participants, often this is the only one who does not make a living by working for the company. The international representative does not work for the local union as a paid officer or business agent does. The representative does act in behalf of a local union and is answerable to the executive board of the international union.

Status of the international representative. The representative is there in negotiations by request of the local union not only to guide and counsel, but usually to act as spokesperson, strategist, and tactician for the union side. The company cannot keep the representative out, despite an outsider status, for the law permits workers to be represented by "agents of their own choosing."

The international representative is a professional negotiator, perhaps the only professional in a group whose collective bargaining activities occur so rarely, and so incidentally to their own concerns, that in comparison they are amateurs. They meet each other to make an agreement no more often than once a year; the representative engages in like activity, with other groups as well as this, day after day. For everyone else present, the outcome of negotiations will be felt as dollars-and-cents additions to income, or added production costs; the representative loses not a cent nor, for that matter, stands to gain a penny by what transpires, though success will be its own reward.

The representative may enter the negotiations only when stepping in the door of the conference room but is more likely to work with the local through all stages or at least the later stages of preparations. The chances are that he or she will have shared in shaping the demands and putting them in draft-agreement form. It is through the representative that the research department of the international channels information to aid in the negotiations.

The role of international representatives. These outsiders to the groups that meet for negotiations are, in a sense, the only full-time "insiders" to the collective bargaining process: it is their life and living. They have no authority except the prestige of position, but they are key people in negotiations, and, as will be seen, are also key people in strikes. In single-employer bargaining (which accounts for most of industrial unionism) they have no regular counterpart on the employer side. In most negotiations they are the ones who call the signals and set the tone.

During discussions with the companies the international "reps" give tactical leadership to the union committee. Their role varies with the circumstances and each representative's talents and personality. Sometimes they spearhead the attack on the company, perhaps with the aim—and frequently with the effect—of making the local's committee of company employees look reasonable and moderate to their employer so that the company will offer concessions. Or, with a militant committee, they may seem moderate, receptive to "reasonable" offers of concessions, which they imply they will try to "sell" to the committee in the recess that they then call. Representatives often have to be actors, playing a role. Only after a number of encounters with a given management, getting to know them and to be known, can they drop into a consistent natural pattern of behavior. The representative will usually then be found to be a shrewd and sensible person with a good deal of personal integrity and pride—for it is a professional asset—on being "as good as my word."

Sometimes the international representative becomes almost a mediator between company and union, who soothes ruffled feelings, saves people's faces, and harmlessly grounds dangerous emotional charges that have built up in a labor relations situation. Sometimes one serves the useful function of scapegoat, again like a mediator, who assumes the "sins" of the community—both sides—and carries them away, to leave the local people cleansed and reconciled for the next period of the life they have to live together.

There are negotiations in which not one but two or several outside representatives participate, either alternately or together. One may deliberately build up tension, concentrating company hostility, so that a smiling colleague can walk in and, in the ensuing relief and atmosphere of cordiality, reach the settlement.

The Employer Representatives. Union agreements set or affect company policy. A line executive responsible for policy—president, vice president for industrial relations, or at the very least a works manager—sits in directly on this policy making process, or designates someone with authority to act.

Single-employer bargaining. In any single-company negotiations, the delegation of authority is a simple matter. The person exercising authority and speaking for the company is usually a production person and line executive, who has staff advisors such as the personnel director, and perhaps a public relations expert, and a company lawyer. Of all these, the lawyer has least to contribute, in most cases, to the actual progress of negotiations.

In contrast to the union representatives, the negotiators for the employer are usually armed with full authority to conclude an agreement, though in some cases the board of directors may have to ratify results. There is a simple reason for this: in the company, authority flows downward, in the union upward. At the policy-making level where negotiations take place, authority is already concentrated on the company side, while in the union there has to be specific act of delegation, and the delegation is not complete but only provisional and temporary. In terms of Walton and McKersie's framework, unions, at least in the private sector, have a much more difficult task of intraorganizational bargaining than management. This task is easier, however, in single-employer, single-plant bargaining, particularly where the occupational mix of the bargaining unit is homogeneous. In other words, the more homogeneous the negotiating unit, the easier it is for the union to achieve internal consensus through intraorganizational bargaining.

Multiemployer bargaining. Multiemployer bargaining, as has been noted, is more common in the trades, with craft unions, than in manufacturing. There are some notable exceptions—perhaps enough to constitute another rule, and not just exceptions.

In the garment industries, for instance, employer associations bargain as a group both with the Amalgamated Clothing and Textile Workers Union and with the International Ladies' Garment Workers' Union. These two well-known and well-organized industrial unions are the composite modern form of older separate craft unions. Some of these crafts were once truly skilled—cutters, for instance, who are direct descendants of custom tailors—while others formed satellite unions of the unskilled—floor boys, for example—and of the semi-skilled, as new machines created specialties. This situation is comparable in some ways to the construction unions, where skilled workers and their unskilled satellites form a complex of closely related unions under the Building Trades Council. The garment workers did not stay separate, they fused; and now they act together just as if they were a single union, though they are still enrolled in locals based on craft and occupations, not on workplace.

Garment-industry employers, faced with the problem of dealing with the huge, fused union, followed the lead of other similar employers throughout history and organized. The producing units of their industry are small and many; together in an association they are somewhat like a counterpart of the union with which they deal. Member firms promise to abide by bargains the association makes with the union.

The small size of the enterprise seems to be a factor in bringing employers together, but an equally compelling one seems to be competition; competition in both the product market and the labor market. Labor costs are so high a percentage of total costs that once the bulk of the industry was unionized the organized firms found themselves sharing the union's own interest in fighting cut-throat nonunion competition based on lower wages. In this, again, they are like the building trades or the trucking industry, which is also an area of small firms and big unions.

One exception to the small firm requirement of employer association bargaining is the steel industry, which is composed of large firms. However, the undifferentiated nature of the product made it advantageous for the employer to engage in industry-wide bargaining with the United Steelworkers in order to minimize the effects of the whipsawing, or the singling out of specific employers, usually the weakest ones, for job actions. For unions, multiemployer negotiations considerably complicate the task of achieving consensus through intraorganizational bargaining.

The employer association representative. This kind of multiemployer bargaining—of "employer unionization"—has brought forth a type of person who may fairly be called the equivalent of the international representative. That is the labor relations adviser and negotiator on the employer side. This type of negotiator is not universally present in multiemployer bargaining, for many associations speak through respected senior member-firm executives, but the neutral expert is coming to the fore.

This person's title is likely to be executive secretary or labor relations director of the association; duties are analogous to those of an international representative, and so is the function in negotiations. The employer association representative organizes—gets firms to join the association, helps draw up employer counterproposals to union demands, directs or arranges for research to back up the proposals, and negotiates. He or she also inspects the member firms' administration of the agreement, helps take care of grievances and arbitration, and polices the rules of the association. Wherever they are active, they, like the international representatives, are the key people.

(This is a field, incidentally, where the college graduate enamored of the labor relations "game" may find it possible to break in. The unions bring their representatives up from the ranks, while even in the medium-sized corporation it is a long way up from management trainee to industrial relations director. But the employer association often has room for a person from the outside who has had experience or training in labor relations work. Being from the outside is, in fact, an advantage. The future trend may be for more professionals on both sides of collective bargaining. Even the unions may have to turn to the colleges for representatives as the employers "wise up" and as the union old-timers die off).

The Government Representative. As long as labor and management obey the law, the government regards collective bargaining between them as a private matter.

But it is not a matter of indifference to the government, nor to the public which government represents, particularly if a strike seems a prospect. In order, therefore, to assist the bargainers to reach constructive results that are satisfactory to both, and compatible with the public interest, both state and federal governments provide *on a voluntary basis* the services of mediation and conciliation agencies. Skillful mediation can do a lot toward preventing strikes, or settling strikes effectively once they have broken out. In certain emergency strike situations, the government has procedures for intervening. In other situations in which the economic progress of the country may be affected by the outcome of the negotiations in major industries, for example, steel, the government has attempted to "jawbone" the parties to hold the line on wage increases. The next chapter will deal with these governmental roles in negotiations in more detail.

Preparation for Negotiations

The men and women who carry on labor-management negotiations shoulder a heavy responsibility. Their work sets policy. Its results are bound to affect the welfare, the earnings, the chances for promotion, the security, the job satisfaction of every member of the union, every employee of the company in the bargaining unit (and some outside it) for the length of the agreement. Equally affected are company profits, productivity, and competitive position, as well as prices and production available to the public.

Negotiating the agreement is the very heart of collective bargaining. Proper discharge of the bargainers' responsibilities calls for preparation.

The Union Initiative

Unions prepare more or less carefully for negotiations. Big national negotiations, such as those between the United Auto Workers and General Motors, have repercussions throughout the national economy and are carefully prepared for a year or more in advance, with full attention to public relations as well as to keeping the members informed. Many smaller local unions make little or no preparation other than to draw up demands.

Preparation for negotiations involves: (1) drawing up demands or formulating what the members want; (2) assembling information to support the demands; and (3) publicizing and explaining the demands. This last point usually means achieving consensus among the workers in the plant through intraorganizational bargaining. It often also requires spreading the information to the community at large.

Drawing Up Demands. The union ordinarily initiates negotiations. To the union member the most important thing is what she or he, personally, will get out of the agreement. Sometimes workers have specific wants; sometimes they only know that they want more than they have, but do not recognize it in concrete form until the union leaders formulate and explain it to them.

If they have had "nothing"—that is, if they have not worked under a union agreement before—then they want what workers in other shops and unions have already secured: such things as seniority, grievance procedure, a raise in wages, vacations with pay, and the like. If they are already working under a union agreement granting concessions of this sort, they want more of the same.

"New" demands. Sometimes union demands appear to be new, but almost invariably they turn out, upon examination, to be merely novel forms and extensions of older ideas. The 1955 demand for a guaranteed annual wage, which worked out in practice as the S.U.B. plan of Supplemental Unemployment Benefits was no more than a strengthening of the existing seniority system with increased pay (from private funds, to supplement public funds) for laid-off workers. The aim of the plan was to satisfy the workers' age-old demand for individual job

security. Its proponents also hoped that it would promote steadier employment in a cyclical industry and cushion the impact of automation. The demand for profit sharing aimed at increasing worker income by a supplement to wages was akin to many bonus schemes that preceded it. Ironically enough, the idea of giving workers a share in profits is one that had often been advanced by management as an antidote to unionism!

A new demand, once raised and won by a union in one enterprise, or the enterprises of one industry, gets copied by other unions. Thus after the auto workers pioneered the S.U.B. plan, the steelworkers took it up and secured even greater concessions based on the same idea. In neither case was the actual program a spontaneous creation. In both cases, sophisticated labor leaders formulated proposals that appealed to the members' human desire to be secure in what one has, and to have a little more, particularly considering the uncertainty inherent in industries with cyclical market demand.

Spread of a pattern. The leaders exercise their foresight and inventiveness to devise plans and formulate demands that the members will recognize as corresponding to their needs. Political, and even personal, inter-union rivalries spread first worker, and then company, acceptance of those demands that do successfully evoke worker response and support. The most recently organized local union therefore tends to adopt for its program of demands the schedule of gains registered, step by step, by others organized before it, just as a newly built factory gets the benefit of the latest technological progress.

There is no doubt that some union programs (S.U.B., for example) exert a far-reaching influence on the economy that may affect society in permanent and important ways, for good or ill. The workers and rank-and-file union members who think about this at all tends to minimize the question. In asking for a raise, the worker undoubtedly likes to believe that a pay increase will not send the national economy into an inflationary spiral—and union leaders gladly oblige with the necessary assurance. The question of whether there will be a raise in the next pay envelope is of more immediate interest to the worker, who tends to ignore the possible economic and social effects of an accumulation of separate union demands shaped to the same plan, paying attention chiefly to the special effects that flow from the local's direct action.

Restraints on the demands. Perhaps, in the back of the workers' minds, they look to the company to keep the situation from getting out of hand, just as they rely on the company to secure orders, maintain production, and pay wages. The workers regard the pressing of demands as a test of strength, and a necessary one, for it does not seem likely that they will get what they do not ask for, whereas they feel sure that the company will not give them more than what it can truly afford. They do not want their company to go out of business, costing them their jobs, but they are convinced that management will not let it happen. And so they draw up demands, or adapt the demands others like them have drawn up, and present them and, if need be, strike for them.

But if workers and their representatives may be reluctant to limit their demands, the reality of the economic situation places its own limits to negotiations. Some small companies and their unions, and some "sick" industries, have been forced to take a more careful look and act more cooperatively toward tempering union demands that would raise costs beyond the danger point. Higher wages and other concessions to the union in some situations could depress business and result in unemployment. Wage cuts, instead of wage raises, might even be in order, as was experienced during harsh economic times during the early 1980s.

Some problems. This question has many ramifications. Should a union subsidize inefficiency in a small or backward company by permitting low wages and substandard conditions? Or should it force the small-scale, low-pay producer out of business to make way for more progressive enterprises? Can the union help the company increase efficiency by boosting worker productivity? Should the union fight against technological improvements that would throw members out of work?

A consideration of these questions, and others equally pertinent, would lead away from the problem of *drawing up* demands into the *content* of the demands. Such questions might, in a given case, condition the nature of the demands, but the union negotiator is more likely to have to deal with them as management negotiators bring them up during the course of negotiations. In the early 1980s unions were confronted with numerous situations in which requests for give backs not only appeared during the negotiations for new contracts, but during the terms of the contract as well. Unions in the automobile, steel, rubber, newspaper, meat packing, farm implement, automobile supply, railroad, airline, smelting, and mining industries agreed to reopen contracts and accept reduced wages and benefits in response to management assertions that jobs, plants, companies and even industries were at stake. So the economic condition of companies in negotiations, and our country in general, places important boundaries on the bargaining power of the participants to the negotiations process and thus on the tactics and strategies available to them. It does the union little good to use distributive bargaining tactics during periods of economic duress if there are few resources to allocate. Needed instead are the problem-solving tactics of integrative bargaining, as illustrated by the willingness of unions, once they are convinced of the problems, to agree to concessions.

Assembling Information. A strike threat frequently hangs over negotiations from the start. When this is so, the negotiations are a test of strength, and the end result may register not so much the merits of the case on either side as the relative strength of the parties.

But the parties carry on negotiations by discussion: they talk, they use arguments, they reason and try to convince. In spite of, as well as because of, the strike threat that lurks in the background, in the foreground people sit around a table and try to persuade each other. They do persuade each other in many things. It is their function to reach an accommodation and reduce it to writing. Even when the general terms of their bargain reflect relative underlying strength rather than abstract objective judgment, these terms must at least be rationalized in wording acceptable to both sides. In order to reach common ground as well as to define their differences, the union and the company negotiators must exchange views and come to a meeting of the minds. Each side must show the logic of its position.

Both sides, therefore, build up information to support their arguments. The union negotiators want, basically, two kinds of information: (a) what might be called, by analogy with the military, "intelligence" that will help them gauge the company's strength and intentions, and (b) facts to back up arguments in favor of the union's specific demands. Under this heading would also come, of course, facts for rebuttal of possible company arguments.

"Intelligence." The union negotiators stand at a disadvantage unless they can find out something about matters on which the company already has a good deal of information: the state of the industry and the firm's position in the industry, competition, profits and sales, orders and prospects—in a word, economic and financial data. Some of these factors will indicate the company's ability to pay, others may give an inkling of the company's ability to withstand a strike, or willingness to make concessions. Such data remain confidential with the company, unless the company refuses union demands solely on the grounds of inability to pay. In such cases, the NLRB has ruled the company must open its books and show the union proof of its contention.

The international's research department provides most of the general economic information and financial data on the company. Experts and specialists employed by the international assemble and evaluate the information and make it available to the negotiators as part of the service provided to local unions by the international. Local information along the same lines and word of specific innercompany developments may leak to the union from friendly office workers or sources in the community. The reports of shop stewards keep the negotiators abreast on actions taken by management in the various departments. These and other scraps of isolated information, fitted together and evaluated, may give clues to the company's intentions.

Ordinarily the company may be expected to know more about economic and financial prospects than union intelligence can unearth and correctly put together, but unions have steadily gotten better at the game. Through its international, a local draws on the services of economists, lawyers, and accountants no less expert in their fields than the company's own specialists.

Facts for argument. Here again economic and financial data have a bearing, particularly when the costs of specific concessions are at issue, but a great deal of information comes from the shop itself. Experiences under the past agreement suggest changes in some of the provisions. The grievance records or other data drawn from practice provide facts for argument. The steward apparatus probably constitutes the main source of information in this category. Another important source of information is union contracts from similar types of companies.

On the company side the assembling of information for negotiations shows the same twofold nature: the need to try to gauge the union's strength and determination, and the need for facts and figures to counter union arguments and support the company's position. Sources of information for the company are analogous: employer associations, which correspond to the union international, and the company's own supervisory apparatus and personnel department.

Publicizing and explaining the demands. Both sides have a public to which they appeal for understanding and support, and the most important segment of that public is the working force of the enterprise.

The union keeps its members informed by means of meetings, printed or mimeographed bulletins of various kinds distributed at the plant gate or circulated by union stewards, and, on occasion, mass media such as radio or television. The union also—and most importantly—"talks up" its information through its steward system and circulates it by word of mouth. The department stewards are in daily personal contact with the entire body of employees. They are elected representatives who have the confidence of their constituents. The workers turn to them for facts, advice, and direction as the negotiations proceed.

The wider public which consists of the community does not usually hear much about specific demands under negotiation unless there is a strike. Then both sides take to the newspapers with their versions of the issue and wage a propaganda battle to win, or at least neutralize, public sentiment.

The Employer Defense and Counterinitiative

It still seems to be the practice of some employers to wait until the union has presented its demands before getting ready for negotiations. This is a purely defensive strategy. There is some justification for it in that decisions go by default to the employer unless the union requests a part in making them, and that most potential changes represent concessions by the employer to the union. Why give the union, as it were, things the union does not first ask for? Why not just sit back, see what they want, and say no?

Active Preparation for Negotiations. Nonetheless more and more employers are finding it wise to prepare more carefully and to anticipate union demands or deflect them with proposals of their own. Some of these counterproposals may actually be things the union has not asked for! Employer preparation for negotiations gives management an active, instead of a passive, function.

The farsighted employer or employer association calculates in advance the cost and relative desirability of various alternatives and meets the union with concrete proposals. Some employers have developed sophisticated computer programs to assist them in planning and conducting bargaining. Common ways for computing costs of agreements have included: (1) total annual cost of a given benefit, (2) cost per employee per year, (3) percent of payroll, or (4) cents per hour. However, relying solely on these static figures has been criticized because they do not take into account how an employer will adapt to the new agreement, they ignore the opportunity costs of the changes, and they ignore cash flow and time value of economic resources. These shortcomings could be eliminated if employers drew on the experience of the accounting community and developed discounted cash flow models to evaluate the costs associated with union proposals. A sophisticated model would include potential changes in prices, volume, and product mix. Despite the advantages of such an approach, relatively few firms appear to have adopted it.[13] The General Electric Company was an early leader of the trend toward detailed preparation. In its extreme form it came to be known as Boulewareism, after a former GE vice president who initiated it.[14] The appendix to this chapter contains a detailed list of preparation activities suggested by the Conference Board for employers. Obviously, many of the suggestions would be useful to unions as well.

Taking the initiative does not mean that the employer gives up the defensive position, which is a strong one despite some disadvantages. It means that the company plans its defense and supplements it with counteroffensive strategy that does not leave all the issues, or points of attack, entirely to the union.

The Law and the Scope of Negotiations

The area of company policy where employees usually desire changes are those defining the employees' individual work-contracts with the company. The standard phrase used to designate this area is "wages, hours, working conditions, and other conditions of employment." It does not by law normally include, for instance, company sales policy such as what colors the cars are to be painted and how many are to be painted each color; it does include such policies as layoff order, and practices that have to do with conveyor speeds or the way time studies are taken.

The legal duty to bargain in good faith both in initial contract negotiations and during the life of a contract is limited to mandatory subjects under section 8(a)(5) of the NLRA. Mandatory subjects are those items encompassed in the phrase "rates of pay, wages, hours of employment, or other conditions of employment." In respect to permissive areas of managerial authority, a union may not force an employer to impasse. Indeed, an employer may make unilateral changes in permissive subjects without bargaining. The benefits received by already retired employees, for example, are considered to be permissive subjects because retired employees are not within the NLRA

definition of "employee" and cannot be considered to be part of the unit. The law of the scope of bargaining negotiations issues is extensive and complex and will be discussed in Chapters 10–15 which deal in detail with the substance of negotiations. The point to be made here is that the government under its rules for rule-making power has placed important boundaries on the topics that unions can negotiate to impasse, and thus the problems they can resolve in negotiations.

Presenting the Demands

The union starts by drawing up its draft demands and presenting them to the company. The nature of this process varies between craft and industrial unions, and the demands themselves differ. What follows will describe the process in the typical industrial union situation of the single-union, single-employer pattern.

Procedure in the Local Union

At a meeting of the local industrial union the members charge a committee, or a group of officers, with the task of drafting proposals for negotiation. In due course this group reports back to the membership with the draft demands they have drawn up. These demands are in the form of a proposed agreement that sets forth the terms the union wants the company to incorporate in the individual work-contracts with each of its employees in the bargaining unit and to adopt as policy in its dealings with all of them.

The members of the local discuss the recommendations. They suggest additions, deletions, and improvements in the terms and wording. Following parliamentary procedure, they go over the document paragraph by paragraph and vote, first on its separate provisions, then on the document as a whole. When they are finished with this procedure they have ratified the demands. Once ratified, the draft agreement becomes the official union program of proposals for the forthcoming negotiations with the company, and the union's instructions to its negotiating committee.

In the case of a new union and an initial agreement, the draft demands usually take for their pattern a standard form recommended by the international union, or copy the model of some similar agreement known to the local union. The committee fills in specific items, such as wage rates or seniority rules, to make it applicable to local conditions.

In the case of an established union already working under an agreement, the deliberations center on proposed changes and improvements. Perhaps the history of grievance adjustment over the past year points out loopholes that need to be plugged, or too rigid wording that needs to be relaxed to give the union some leeway. Experience may suggest the addition of new clauses, the deletion of inoperative or undesirable ones. Words may be weighed, punctuation revised. Generally, the agreement grows at least a little every year. Clauses that have stood the test of time remain; new ones to cover previously unforeseen contingencies are added. Eventually, the draft demands are ratified and ready for negotiation. The union sends or presents them to the company as a basis for discussion.

The Act of Negotiation

The union presents its demands and asks for a meeting. The employer, ready or not with counterproposals, designates the company's representative and agrees on a date. The two sides meet and start negotiating. They continue to meet until they have achieved some result.

The Context of Negotiations

The union may be newly organized, seeking its first agreement. Negotiations then are new, exceptional to the experience of both management and labor, surrounded with uncertainty. Or, they may be routine renewal talks in an established and stable collective bargaining relationship. Whether the negotiations are for a first contract or for a renewal, however, the attitudinal orientation of the parties at the start of negotiations is a given context that drives the tactics and strategies of negotiations. By attitudinal orientation we mean the overall relationship pattern of the bargaining teams, as defined by Walton and McKersie. The parties may seek to maintain the existing pattern, or they may seek to change it, either for better or worse.

Table 1 identifies several categories of relationship patterns which have been identified, as well as the attitudinal dimensions that differentiate the patterns. On one end of the continuum is a conflict relationship which is characterized essentially as open warfare. Increasingly more cooperative relationship patterns are described as containment-aggression, accommodation, cooperation, and collusion. Collusion represents an illegal form of cooperation in which the negotiators arrive at self-serving agreements which often are not in the best interest of their constituencies.

The *determinants* of these relationship patterns are basically the inputs to our industrial relations system model discussed in detail in Chapter 1, that is, environmental characteristics such as product demand, organizational characteristics such as the size of the organization, characteristics of the bargaining process such as the type of union or bargaining structure, the personalities of the participants and, finally, the ideologies of the participants. The strong resistance of J. P. Stevens to unionization is an example of how anti-union ideology can condition the type of relationship patterns that develop. In a particular situation, the processes that produce a given type of relationship are extremely complex, and difficult to change once in place. But whatever the origins of a relationship type, its existence shapes the tactics and strategies of the parties in negotiations. For example, if the tradition of a relationship has been one of conflict, then it would be difficult for one side or the other to engage in integrative bargaining tactics which require open communications. Distributive bargaining tactics such as strike votes and strike threats would be more likely pre-bargaining behavior.

Summary

An exchange process is the means by which the parties to negotiations convert inputs into outputs. In collective bargaining, the parties or actors consist of the union negotiators and the workers they represent, and the employers. The government actors do not become directly involved in the exchange unless there is disagreement or conflict, in which case they provide

TABLE 1
Attitudinal Components of the Relationship Patterns

Attitudinal Dimensions	Pattern of relationship				
	Conflict	Containment Aggression	Accommodation	Cooperation	Collusion
Motivational orientation and action tendencies toward other	Competitive tendencies to destroy or weaken		Individualistic policy of hands off	Cooperative tendencies to assist or preserve	
Beliefs about legitimacy of other	Denial of legitimacy	Grudging acknowledgment	Acceptance of *status quo*	Complete Legitimacy	Not applicable
Level of trust in conducting affairs	Extreme distrust	Distrust	Limited trust	Extended trust	Trust based on mutual blackmail potential
Degree of friendliness	Hate	Antagonism	Neutralism-Courteousness	Friendliness	Intimacy— "Sweetheart relationship"

Source: Richard E. Walton and Robert B. McKersie, *A Behavioral Theory of Labor Negotiations* (New York: McGraw-Hill, 1965), p. 189. Reprinted with permission.

neutral hearing examiners and/or mediators. It is the participation of the actors in the exchange process that gives a collective bargaining system its dynamic features. In theory, the exchange process has been divided into four distinct, but related, subprocesses. *Distributive bargaining* deals with *issues* of resource allocation in a fixed-sum game. *Integrative bargaining* deals with *problems* for which there is potential for mutual gain. In *attitudinal structuring,* the parties engage in tactics and strategies aimed at affecting the nature of the *relationship*. In *intraorganizational bargaining,* the parties are involved with achieving internal *consensus* with their respective constituencies. The operation of these subprocesses is affected by inputs (economic conditions, bargaining structure, personalities) and results in outputs (the rules that comprise an agreement to guide the parties' relation during the term).

In practice, whatever the nature of environmental and organizational forces underlying the negotiations, it is usually more advantageous to focus on the *interests* underlying peoples' *positions* rather than the *positions* themselves. Proper preparation for negotiations helps both parties identify their interests more effectively and thus minimizes the chance that the ultimate power, the strike, will be employed. Chapter 8 discusses strikes and means for preventing them.

Appendix: Negotiations Preparation Check List, Manufacturing Firm

While preparation for negotiations will vary, the following preparation should be undertaken in most cases. The preparation should be started sufficiently before negotiations to allow careful and thorough work. Assign who is to be responsible for each item and the required date of completion.

I. Review of current status:

    A.   Items:

          1.   Contract language
          2.   Supplemental and side agreements
          3.   Grievances and arbitration
          4.   Existing practices
          5.   Operating problems

    B.   Review with:

          1.   Supervisors (may be combined with V, A-1 below)
          2.   Corporate employee relations staff
          3.   Top management

II. Back-up data:

    A.   Determine type needed

    B.   Pay and benefit surveys

          1.   National
          2.   Industry
          3.   Local
          4.   Competition
          5.   Union settlements
          6.   Cost-of-living data

    C.   Work Force Distribution by:

          1.   Seniority group
          2.   Age and sex
          3.   Labor grades
          4.   Job classification
          5.   Length of service
          6.   Minority groups
          7.   Shifts

    D.   Internal Economic Data

          1.   Average straight-time hourly rate
          2.   Cost of benefits in cents per hour
          3.   Participation in benefit plans
          4.   Average gross earnings
          5.   Average overtime earnings

E.   Changes in Legal Requirements

    1.   Pay
       a.   Maximum increase permitted
       b.   Minimum pay required
    2.   Benefits
       a.   Maximum increase permitted
       b.   Minimum benefits required
          (1)   Health and Welfare
          (2)   Holidays
          (3)   Vacations
          (4)   Life insurance
          (5)   Sick pay
          (6)   Termination pay
    3.   Practices
       a.   Promotion procedure
       b.   Seniority groupings
       c.   Leave practice
       d.   Job evaluations

F.   Union negotiation and ratification practices

    1.   Ratification pattern
       a.   When
       b.   Where
       c.   How
       d.   Who is present
    2.   Union negotiation practice
       a.   Pattern of movement
       b.   Method of signaling
       c.   Method of dropping demands
       d.   Any pattern of last-minute demands
       e.   Actual settlements compared to demands
       f.   How final agreement is made:
          (1)   When
          (2)   Who is present
          (3)   Mediation involved
       g.   Individual committee members' patterns of conduct

G.   Current business status and anticipated changes

H.   Costing

    1.   Notify accounting department of information needed
    2.   Present total cost (and average per employee) of:
       a.   Wages
          (1)   Straight time
          (2)   Premium (shift, overtime, other)
          (3)   Red-circle rates
       b.   Benefits
          (1)   Insurances

        (2) Paid time off
           (a) Vacation
           (b) Holiday
           (c) Jury
           (d) Funeral
           (e) Other
        (3) Pension
     c.   Legally Required Benefits
        (1) Unemployment compensation
        (2) Workers' compensation
        (3) Other
     d.   Union activity time
  3.   Future cost of each item for each 1¢ per hour increase in wages.

I.   Analyze back-up data

III. Identify anticipated union demands and their effect on (1) operating problems, and (2) cost:

  A.   Supervisor's input

  B.   Review of other settlements

  C.   Contact with union

IV. Select Company Negotiating Committee

  A.   Determine size and composition

  B.   Select members

     1.   Spokesperson
     2.   Others

  C.   Explain members' responsibilities to committee selected

V. Develop company negotiation objectives:

  A.   Determine contract changes necessary to correct current problems and meet future business needs from:

     1.   Supervisors
     2.   Top management
     3.   Employee relations staff

  B.   Write company proposals:

     1.   Review with and obtain approval of:
        a.   Company negotiating committee
        b.   Top management
        c.   Employee relations staff

VI. Prepare book containing back-up data necessary for use by company negotiating committee:

    A. Determine material to be included

    B. Review contents with company committee members

VII. Strike preparation for the facility:

    A. Develop strike committee responsibility

    B. Assign strike committee

    C. Policy questions—identify, recommend action, and approval on items such as:

        1. Plant remaining open
        2. Salaried employees performing production work
        3. Assuring ingress and egress
        4. Payment of benefits and last paycheck to striking employees
        5. Instructions to salaried employees and supervisors
        6. Strike replacements
        7. Publicity—who will handle and how much to release
        8. Picket line observation and control
        9. Availability and conduct of company guards and law enforcement officers

    D. Notice required to:

        1. Customers and vendors
        2. Government agencies
        3. Law enforcement agencies

    E. Maintenance and protection of:

        1. Plant facilities and equipment
        2. Food service

    F. Communications for:

        1. News media
        2. Employees
        3. Plant supervisors and management
        4. Management outside the plant
        5. Current strike status
        6. Resolving policy questions

    G. Legal action:

        1. Determine with the corporate employee relations counsel what possible legal remedies are available
        2. Arrange to obtain evidence of conduct on which any legal remedies may be sought
        3. Determine with the corporate employee relations counsel what arrangements for legal service need to be made

H.   Prepare a written guide for company use in the event of a strike

I.   Review strike preparations

VIII. Customer Contingency Plan—Strike Preparation:

A.   Assign a line manager this responsibility

B.   Establish a detailed plan to meet the customers' needs

IX. Negotiations communications program:

A.   Determine policy:

1.   Prenegotiation
2.   During negotiations
3.   After negotiations
4.   In event of a strike

B.   Assign responsibility

C.   Determine *what* to communicate, *when*—and *to whom*

1.   Supervisors
2.   Nonbargaining unit employees
3.   Bargaining unit employees
4.   News media

D.   Method of communication:

1.   Meetings
2.   Letters or memos
3.   Telephone
4.   Bulletin boards
5.   News media

X. Strategy:

A.   Determine company positions (and possible alternatives) on union demands and company proposals. Identify strike issues. Review and obtain needed approvals from:

1.   Company negotiating team
2.   Top management
3.   Corporate employee relations staff

B.   Review bargaining strategy with company negotiating team

C.   Obtain company end position from location general manager

1.   Position on company objectives should be cleared with appropriate management

D. Outline desired action plan for negotiation meetings

XI. Send formal notification of contract termination to:

A. Union

B. Mediation service (federal and state)

    1. If mediation is, or may be, used, establish personal contact with federal mediator prior to entering mediation sessions.

XII. Determine physical arrangements for negotiation meetings:

A. Place

B. Time

C. Pay for union negotiators for:

    1. Actual negotiations
       a. During normal working hours
       b. During overtime hours
    2. Subcommittee meetings
    3. Negotiation preparation

D. How is cost of negotiation facilities to be paid-company and/or union[15] •

*   *   *

Suggested Readings

Douglas, Ann. *Industrial Peacemaking.* New York: Columbia University Press, 1962.

Fisher, Roger, and William Ury. *Getting to Yes.* Boston: Houghton Mifflin, 1981.

Freedman, Audrey. *Managing Labor Relations.* New York: The Conference Board, 1979.

Granof, Michael H. *How to Cost Your Labor Contract.* Washington, D.C.: The Bureau of National Affairs, Inc., 1973.

Rubin, Jeffrey Z. and Bert R. Brown. *The Social Psychology of Bargaining and Negotiation.* New York: Academic Press, 1975.

Stevens, Carl M. *Strategy and Collective Bargaining Negotiations.* New York: McGraw-Hill, 1963.

Walton, Richard, and Robert McKersie. *A Behavioral Theory of Labor Negotiations.* New York: McGraw-Hill, 1965.

Footnotes

[1]Ann Douglas, *Industrial Peacemaking* (New York: Columbia University Press, 1962).

[2]Richard E. Walton, and Robert B. McKersie, *A Behavioral Theory of Labor Negotiations* (New York: McGraw Hill, 1965).

[3]Ibid, pp. 4–6. All material from Walton and McKersie has been reprinted by permission.

[4]Ibid, p. 182.

[5]Ibid, p. 270.

[6]Ibid, p. 279.

[7]Ibid, pp. 344–45.

[8]Ibid, p. 346.

[9]Ibid, p. 349.

[10]Ibid.

[11]Ibid, p. 350.

[12]Ibid, p. 351.

[13]This material on costing was drawn from Michael H. Granof, *How to Cost Your Labor Contract*

(Washington, D.C.: Bureau of National Affairs, Inc., 1973), pp. 5, 6.

[14]On October 28, 1969, the U.S. Circuit Court of Appeals in New York, acting in a legal process started in 1960, ruled that General Electric's "unbending patriarchal posture" violated the National Labor Relations Act. The company appealed the ruling to the U.S. Supreme Court, but lost. The Circuit Court's decision came one day after the IUE and 12 other unions struck in General Electric plants all over the country. In 1966 the company had refused to engage in coordinated bargaining with the IUE and seven other unions. This form of bargaining—one large firm with a number of different unions acting jointly, or as a coalition—was held to be proper in an NLRB decision of Oct. 24, 1968, when the board upheld a trial examiner's decision that GE had acted illegally in refusing to bargain.

[15]Audrey Freedman, *Managing Labor Relations* (New York: The Conference Board, 1979), Exhibit 3, pp. 19–23. Reprinted with permission.

Study Questions

1. Define and describe in your own words each of the four "subprocesses" of the bargaining "exchange process":

   a. Distributive bargaining;

   b. Integrative bargaining;

   c. Attitudinal structuring; and

   d. Intraorganizational bargaining.

2. Are there conflicts and contradictions between any two of these subprocesses, i. e, , between distributive bargaining and integrative bargaining, or between intraorganizational bargaining and distributive bargaining, etc.?

3. In what ways are labor-management negotiations analogous to diplomatic relations?

4. Why is the union-management contract considered a "code of rules"?

5. Who are the typical participants in the labor-management negotiation process?

6. What are the similarities and differences between the union's preparation for negotiations and the preparation of the employer's side?

7. What are the five patterns of labor-management relationships that the authors identify and what factors differentiate them?

8. How could the "negotiations preparation checklist" in the appendix be adapted for use in other negotiation contexts?

Negotiation Techniques

Charles B. Craver

Practicing lawyers negotiate constantly—with their partners, associates, legal assistants, and secretaries, with prospective clients and actual clients, and with opposing parties on behalf of clients. Although practitioners tend to use their negotiation skills more often than their other lawyering talents, few have had formal education about the negotiation process.

The process consists of three formal phases: the information phase, where each party endeavors to learn as much about the other side's circumstances and objectives as possible; the competitive phase, where negotiators try to obtain beneficial terms for their respective clients; and the cooperative phase, where if multiple-item transactions are involved, parties may often enhance their joint interests.

The Information Phase

The focus of this phase is always on the knowledge and desires of the opposing party. It is initially helpful to employ general, information-seeking questions instead of those that may be answered with a yes or no. Expansive interrogatories are likely to induce the other party to speak. The more that party talks, the more he is likely to divulge.

Where negotiators have effectively used open-ended questions to induce the other party to disclose its opening position and its general legal and factual assumptions, they should not hesitate to resort to specific inquiries to confirm suspected details. They can do this by asking the other side about each element of its perceived position. What exactly does that party hope to obtain, and why? What are the underlying motivational factors influencing that side's articulated demands?

Negotiators must try to learn as much as possible about the opposing side's range of potential and actual choices, its preferences and their intensity, its planned strategy, and its strengths and weaknesses. Bargainers need to be aware that the opponent's perception of a situation may be more favorable to their own than they anticipated. Even the most proficient negotiators tend to overstate their side's weaknesses and overestimate the opposing party's strengths. Only through patient probing of their adversary's circumstances can they hope to obtain an accurate assessment.

The order in which parties present their initial demands can be informative. Some negotiators begin with their most important topics in an effort to produce an expeditious resolution of those issues. They are anxiety-prone, risk-averse advocates who wish to diminish the tension associated with the uncertainty inherent in the negotiation process. They believe they can significantly decrease their fear of not being able to settle by achieving expeditious progress on their primary topics. Unfortunately they fail to appreciate that this approach may enhance the possibility of a counterproductive impasse. If their principal objectives correspond to those of their adversary, this presentation sequence is likely to cause an immediate clash of wills.

Other negotiators prefer to begin bargaining with their less significant subjects, hoping to make rapid progress on these items. This approach is likely to develop a cooperative atmosphere that will facilitate compromise when the more disputed subjects are explored.

Negotiators must decide ahead of time what information they are willing to disclose and what information they must disclose if the transaction is going to be fruitful. Critical information should not always be directly provided. If negotiators voluntarily apprise the other side of important circumstances, this may appear selfserving and be accorded little weight. If, however, they slowly disclose such information in response to opponent questions, what they divulge will usually be accorded greater credibility.

Where an adversary asks about sensitive matters, blocking techniques may be used to minimize unnecessary disclosure. Such techniques should be planned in advance and should be varied to keep the opposing party off balance. A participant who does not wish to answer a question might ignore it, and the other side might go on to some other area.

Where a compound question is asked, a negotiator may respond to the beneficial part of it. Skilled negotiators may misconstrue a delicate inquiry and then answer the misconstrued formulation; they may respond to a specific question with general information or to a general inquiry with a narrow response. On occasion, negotiators may handle a difficult question with a question of their own. For example, if one party asks whether the other is authorized to offer a certain sum, that side may ask about the first party's willingness to accept such a figure.

Many negotiators make the mistake of focusing entirely on their opponents' stated positions. They assume that such statements accurately reflect the desires of the other side. Making this assumption may preclude the exploration of options that might prove mutually beneficial. It helps to go behind stated positions to try to ascertain the underlying needs and interests generating these positions. If negotiators understand what the other party really wants to achieve, they can often suggest alternatives that can satisfy both sides sufficiently to produce an accord.

The Competitive Phase

Once the information phase ends, the focus usually changes from what the opposing party hopes to achieve to what each negotiator must get for his client. Negotiators no longer ask questions about each other's circumstances; they articulate their own side's demands.

"Principled" Offers and Concessions

Negotiators should develop a rational basis for each item included in their opening positions. This provides the other party with some understanding of the reasons underlying their demands, and it helps to provide the person making those demands with confidence in the positions. Successful negotiators establish high, but rational, objectives and explain their entitlement to these goals.

When negotiators need to change their position, they should use "principled" concessions.

They need to provide opponents with a rational explanation for modifications of their position.

For example, a lawyer demanding $100,000 for an injured plaintiff might indicate willingness to accept $90,000 by saying that there is a 10 per-cent chance that the plaintiff might lose at trial or a good probability that the jury in a comparative-negligence jurisdiction will find that the plaintiff was 10 percent negligent. This lets the other party know why the change is being made, and it helps to keep the person at the $90,000 level until he is ready to use a "principled" concession to further reduce the demand.

Argument

The power-bargaining tactic lawyers use most often involves legal and non-legal argument. Factual and legal arguments are advanced. Public policy may be invoked in appropriate situations. Emotional appeals may be effective in some circumstances. If an argument is to be persuasive, it must be presented objectively.

Effective arguments should be presented in a comprehensive, rather than a conclusionary, fashion. Factual and legal information should be disclosed with appropriate detail. Influential statements must be insightful and carefully articulated. They must not only be fully comprehended, but they must go beyond what is expected.

Contentions that do not surprise the receiving parties will rarely undermine their confidence in their preconceived position. But assertions that raise issues opponents have not previously considered will likely induce them to recognize the need to reassess their perceptions.

Threats and Promises

Almost all legal negotiations involve use of overt or at least implicit threats. Threats show recalcitrant parties that the cost of disagreeing with offers will transcend the cost of acquiescence. Some negotiators try to avoid use of formal "threats," preferring less-challenging "warnings." These negotiators simply caution opponents about the consequences of their unwillingness to accept a mutual resolution.

If threats are to be effective, they must be believable. A credible threat is one that is reasonably proportionate to the action it is intended to deter—seemingly insignificant threats tend to be ignored, while large ones tend to be dismissed. Negotiators should never issue threats unless they are prepared to carry them out, since their failure to do so will undermine their credibility.

Instead of using negative threats that indicate what consequences will result if the opposing party does not alter its position, negotiators should consider affirmative promises that indicate their willingness to change their position simultaneously with the other party. The classic affirmative promise—the "split-the-difference" approach—has been used by most negotiators to conclude a transaction. One side promises to move halfway if only the other side will do the same.

Affirmative promises are more effective than negative threats at inducing position changes, since the first indicates that the requested position change will be reciprocated. A negative threat merely suggests dire consequences if the other side does not alter its position. They are more of an affront to an opponent than affirmative promises, and, as a result, are more disruptive of the negotiation process.

Silence and Patience

Many negotiators fear silence, since they are afraid that they will lose control of the transaction if they stop talking. The more they talk, the more information they disclose and the more concessions they make. When their opponents remain silent, such negotiators often become even more talkative.

When negotiators have something important to say, they should say it and then keep quiet. A short comment accentuates the importance of what they are saying and provides the other party with the chance to absorb what was said. This rule is crucial when an offer or concession is being made. Once such information has been disclosed, it is time for the other side to respond.

Patience can be used effectively with silence. Where the other negotiator does not readily reply to critical representations, he should be given sufficient time to respond. If it

is his turn to speak, the first party should wait silently for him to comment. If the first party feels awkward, he should look at his notes. This behavior shows the silent party that a response will be required before further discussion.

Limited Authority

Many advocates like to indicate during the preliminary stages that they do not have final authority from their client about the matter in dispute. They use this technique to reserve the right to check with their client before any tentative agreement can bind their side.

The advantage of a limited-authority approach—whether actual or fabricated—is that it permits the party using it to obtain a psychological commitment to settlement from opponents authorized to make binding commitments. The unbound bargainers can then seek beneficial modifications of the negotiated terms based on "unexpected" client demands. Since their opponents do not want to let such seemingly insignificant items negate the success achieved during the prior negotiations, they often accept the alterations.

Bargainers who meet opponents who initially say they lack the authority to bind their clients may find it advantageous to say they also lack final authority. This will permit them to "check" with their own absent principal before making any final commitment.

A few unscrupulous negotiators will agree to a final accord with what appears to be complete authority. They later approach their opponent with apparent embarrassment and explain that they did not really have this authority. They say that their principal will require one or two modifications before accepting the other terms of the agreement. Since the unsuspecting opponent and his client are now committed to a final settlement, they agree to the concessions.

Negotiators who suspect that an adversary might use this technique may wish to select—at the apparent conclusion of their transaction—the one or two items they would most like to have modified in their favor. When their opponent requests changes, they can indicate how relieved they are about this, because their own client is dissatisfied. Then they can offer to exchange their items for those their adversary seeks. It is fascinating to see how quickly the opponent will now insist on honoring the initial accord.

The limited-authority situation must be distinguished from the one where an opponent begins a negotiation with no authority. This adversary hopes to get several concessions as a prerequisite to negotiations with a negotiator with real authority.

Negotiators should avoid dealing with a no-authority person, since he is trying to induce them to bargain with themselves. When they give their opening position, the no-authority negotiator will say that it is unacceptable. If they are careless, they will alter their stance to placate the no-authority participant. Before they realize what they have done, they will have made concessions before the other side has entered the process.

Anger

If negotiators become angry, they are likely to offend their opponent and may disclose information that they did not wish to divulge. Negotiators who encounter an adversary who has really lost his temper should look for inadvertent disclosures which that person's anger precipitates.

Negotiators often use feigned anger to convince an opponent of the seriousness of their position. This tactic should be used carefully, since it can offend adversaries and induce them to end the interaction.

Some negotiators may respond with their own retaliatory diatribe to convince their adversary that they cannot be intimidated by such tactics. A quid-pro-quo approach involves obvious risks, since a vituperative exchange may have a deleterious impact on the bargaining.

Negotiators may try to counter an angry outburst with the impression that they have been personally offended. They should say that they cannot understand how their reasonable approach has precipitated such an intemperate challenge. If they are successful, they may be able to make the attacking party feel guilty and embarrassed, shaming the person into a concession.

Aggressive Behavior

Such conduct is usually intended to have an impact similar to that associated with anger. It is supposed to convince an opponent of the seriousness of one's position. It can also be used to maintain control over the agenda.

Those who try to counter an aggressive bargainer with a quid-pro-quo response are likely to fail, due to their inability to be convincing in that role. Negotiators who encounter a particularly abrasive adversary can diminish the impact of his techniques through the use of short, carefully controlled interactions. Telephone discussions might be used to limit each exchange. Face-to-face meetings could be held to less than an hour. These short interactions may prevent the opponent from achieving aggressive momentum.

A few aggressive negotiators try to undermine their opponent's presentation through use of interruptions. Such behavior should not be tolerated. When negotiators are deliberately interrupted, they should either keep talking if they think this will discourage their opponent or they might say that they do not expect their opponent to speak while they are talking.

Uproar

A few negotiators try to obtain an advantage by threatening dire consequences if their opponent does not give them what they want. For example, a school board in negotiations with a teachers' union might say that it will have to lay off one third of the teachers due to financial constraints. It will then suggest that it could probably retain everyone if the union would accept a salary freeze.

Negotiators confronted with such predictions should ask themselves two crucial questions. What is the likelihood that the consequences will occur? and What would happen to the other party if the consequences actually occurred? In many cases, it will be obvious that the threatened results will not occur. In others, it will be clear that the consequences would be as bad or worse for the other side as for the threatened party.

Bargainers occasionally may have to call an opponent's bluff. If union negotiators were to indicate that they could accept the layoffs if the school board would only raise salaries of the remaining teachers by 30 percent, the board representatives would probably panic. They know the school system could not realistically function with such layoffs. They were merely hoping that the union would not come to the same realization.

Settlement Brochures and Video Presentations

Some lawyers, particularly in the personal injury field, try to enhance their bargaining posture through settlement brochures or video presentations. A brochure states the factual and legal bases for the claim being asserted and describes the full extent of the plaintiff's injuries. Video presentations depict the way in which the defendant's negligent behavior caused the severe injuries the plaintiff has suffered. Brochures are often accorded greater respect than verbal recitations, due to the aura of legitimacy generally granted to printed documents. Use of brochures may bolster the confidence of the plaintiff's lawyer and may enable him to seize control of the negotiating agenda at the outset. If the plaintiff's lawyer is fortunate, the opponent will begin by suggesting that the plaintiff is seeking too much for pain and suffering. This opening might implicitly concede liability, as well as responsibility for the property damage, medical expenses, and lost earnings requested.

Those presented with settlement brochures or video reenactments should not accord them more respect than they deserve. Lawyers should treat written factual and legal representations just as they would identical verbal assertions.

If lawyers are provided with settlement brochures before the first negotiating session, they should review them and prepare effective counterarguments, which they can state during settlement discussions. Lawyers should not allow their adversary to use a settlement brochure to seize control of the agenda. Where appropriate, they may wish to prepare their own brochure or video to graphically depict their view of the situation.

Boulwareism

This technique gets its name from Lemuel Boulware, former Vice President for Labor Relations at General Electric. Boulware was not enamored of traditional "auction" bargaining, which involves using extreme initial positions, making time consuming concessions, and achieving a final agreement like the one the parties knew from the outset they would reach. He decided to determine ahead of time what GE was willing to commit to wage and benefit increases and then formulate a complete "best-offer-first" package. He presented this to union negotiators on a "take-it-or-leave-it" basis unless the union could show that GE had made some miscalculation or that changed circumstances had intervened.

Boulwareism is now associated with best-offer-first or take-it-or-leave-it bargaining. Insurance company adjusters occasionally try to establish reputations as people who will make one firm, fair offer for each case. If plaintiff does not accept that proposal, they plan to go to trial.

Negotiators should be hesitant to adopt Boulwareism. The offeror effectively tells the other party that he knows what is best for both sides. Few lawyers are willing to accord such respect to the view of opposing counsel.

Boulwareism deprives the opponent of the opportunity to participate meaningfully in the negotiation process. A plaintiff who might have been willing to settle a dispute for $50,000 may not be willing to accept a take-it-or-leave-it first offer of $50,000. The plaintiff wants to explore the case through the information phase and to exhibit his negotiating skill during the competitive phase. When the process has been completed, he wants to feel that his ability influenced the final outcome.

Negotiators presented with take-it-or-leave-it offers should not automatically reject them simply because of the paternalistic way in which they have been extended. They must evaluate the amount being proposed. If it is reasonable, they should accept it. Lawyers should not permit their own negative reaction to an approach to preclude the consummation of a fair arrangement for their clients.

Br'er Rabbit

In *Uncle Remus, His Songs and His Sayings* (1880), Joel Chandler Harris created the unforgettable Br'er Rabbit. When the fox captured Br'er Rabbit, Br'er Rabbit used reverse psychology to escape. He begged the fox to do anything with him so long as he did not throw him in the brier patch. Since the fox wanted to punish the rabbit, he chose the one alternative the rabbit appeared to fear most and flung him in the brier patch. Br'er Rabbit was thus emancipated.

The Br'er Rabbit technique can occasionally be used against win/lose opponents who do not evaluate their results by how well they have done but by an assessment of how poorly their adversary has done. They are only satisfied if they think the other side has been forced to accept a terrible argument.

The Br'er Rabbit approach has risks. Although adroit negotiators may induce a careless, vindictive opponent to provide them with what is really desired, they must recognize that such a device will generally not work against a normal adversary. A typical win/win bargainer would probably accept their disingenuous representations and provide them with the unintended result they have professed to prefer over the alternative that has been renounced.

Mutt and Jeff

In the Mutt and Jeff routine, a seemingly reasonable negotiator professes sympathy toward the "generous" concessions made by the other, while his partner rejects each new offer as insufficient, castigating opponents for their parsimonious concessions. The reasonable partner will then suggest that some additional concessions will have to be made if there is to be any hope of satisfying his associate.

Single negotiators may even use this tactic. They can claim that their absent client suffers from delusions of grandeur, which must be satisfied if any agreement is to be consummated. Such bargainers repeatedly praise their opponent for the concessions being made, but insist that greater movement is necessary to satisfy the excessive aspirations of their "unreasonable" client when their client may actually be receptive to any fair resolution. The opponent

has no way of knowing about this and usually accepts such representations at their face value.

Negotiators who encounter these tactics should not directly challenge the scheme. It is possible that their opponents are not really engaged in a disingenuous exercise. One adversary may actually disagree with his partner's assessment. Little is to be gained from raising a Mutt and Jeff challenge. Allegations about the tactics being used by such negotiators will probably create an unproductive bargaining atmosphere—particularly in situations where the opponents have not deliberately adopted such a stratagem.

Those who interact with Mutt and Jeff negotiators tend to make the mistake of directing their arguments and offers to the unreasonable participant to obtain approval when it is often better to seek the acquiescence of the reasonable adversary before trying to satisfy the irrational one. In some instances, the more conciliatory opponent may actually agree to a proposal characterized as unacceptable by his associate. If the unified position of the opponents can be shattered, it may be possible to whipsaw the reasonable partner against the demanding one.

It is always important when dealing with unreasonable opponents to consider what might occur if no mutual accord is achieved. If the overall cost of surrendering to such an adversary's one-sided demands would clearly be greater than the cost associated with not settling, the interaction should not be continued.

Belly-Up

Some negotiators act like wolves in sheepskin. They initially say they lack negotiating ability and legal perspicuity in a disingenuous effort to evoke sympathy and to lure unsuspecting adversaries into a false sense of security. These negotiators "acknowledge" the superior competence of those with whom they interact and say that they will place themselves in the hands of their fair and proficient opponent.

Negotiators who encounter a belly-up bargainer tend to alter their initial position. Instead of opening with the tough "principled" offer they had planned to use, they modify it in favor of their pathetic adversary, who praises them for their reasonableness, but suggests that his client deserves additional assistance. They then endeavor to demonstrate their ability to satisfy those needs. The belly-up participant says the new offer is a substantial improvement, but suggests the need for further accommodation. By the time the transaction is finished, the belly-up bargainer has obtained everything he wants. Not only are his opponents virtually naked, but they feel gratified at having assisted such an inept bargainer.

Belly-up bargainers are the most difficult to deal with, since they effectively refuse to participate in the process. They ask their opponent to permit them to forgo traditional auction bargaining due to their professed inability to negotiate. They want their reasonable adversary to do all the work.

Negotiators who encounter them must force them to participate and never allow them to alter their planned strategy and concede everything in an effort to form a solution acceptable to such pathetic souls. When belly-up negotiators characterize initial offers as unacceptable, opponents should make them respond with definitive offers. True belly-up negotiators often find it very painful to state and defend the positions they espouse.

Passive-Aggressive Behavior

Instead of directly challenging opponents' proposals, passive-aggressive negotiators use oblique, but highly aggressive, forms of passive resistance. They show up late for a scheduled session and forget to bring important documents. When they agree to write up the agreed-upon terms, they fail to do so.

Those who deal with a passive-aggressive opponent must recognize the hostility represented by the behavior and try to seize control. They should get extra copies of important documents just in case their opponent forgets to bring them. They should always prepare a draft of any agreement. Once passive-aggressive negotiators are presented with such a fait accompli, they usually execute the proffered agreement.

The Cooperative Phase

Once the competitive phase has been completed, most parties consider the process complete. Although this conclusion might be warranted where neither party could possibly obtain more favorable results without a corresponding loss being imposed on the other party, this conclusion is not correct for multi-issue, nonconstant sum controversies.

During the competitive phase, participants rarely completely disclose underlying interests and objectives. Both sides are likely to use power-bargaining techniques aimed at achieving results favorable to their own circumstances.

Because of the anxiety created by such power-bargaining tactics, Pareto optimal arrangements—where neither party may improve its position without worsening the other side's—are usually not generated. The parties are more likely to achieve merely "acceptable" terms rather than Pareto optimal terms due to their lack of negotiation efficiency. If they were to conclude the process at this point, they might well leave a substantial amount of untapped joint satisfaction at the bargaining table.

Once a tentative accord has been achieved, it is generally advantageous for negotiators to explore alternative trade-offs that might simultaneously enhance the interest of both sides. After the competitive phase, one party should suggest transition into the cooperative phase. The parties can initial or even sign their current agreement, and then seek to improve their joint results.

Each should prepare alternative formulations by transferring certain terms from one side to the other while moving other items in the opposite direction. When these options are shown, each negotiator must candidly indicate whether any of the proposals are preferable to the accord already achieved.

Exploring alternatives need not consume much time. Negotiators may substantially increase their clients' satisfaction through this device, and the negotiators lose little if no mutual gains are achieved.

If the cooperative phase is to work effectively, candor is necessary. Each side must be willing to say whether alternatives are more or less beneficial for it.

On the other hand, this phase continues to be somewhat competitive. If one party offers the other an option much more satisfactory than what was agreed upon, he might merely indicate that the proposal is "a little better." Through this technique, he may be able to obtain more during the cooperative phase than would be objectively warranted.

Satisfying Clients

Lawyers who understand these common negotiating techniques can plan their strategies more effectively. They can enhance their skill in the information phase, increase the likelihood that they will achieve acceptable agreements during the competitive phase, and endeavor to maximize the gains obtained for their clients in the cooperative phase. •

Study Questions

1. With regard to perceived strengths and weaknesses of both parties, even the most proficient negotiators are often guilty of what?

2. How are anxiety-prone, risk averse advocates likely to order initial demands/issues? How is this problematic?

3. What strategy with regard to item ordering can develop a more cooperative atmosphere?

4. What happens when information disclosure is relatively slow in forthcoming? How can unnecessary disclosure be minimized?

5. What is the problem in assuming opponents' stated positions accurately reflect their desires?

6. What determines whether or not an offer/concession is "principled?"

7. Describe a good "argument."

8. When should threats be used? What characteristics should threats have? How is a negative threat less effective than an affirmative promise?

9. When should you speak (vs. not speak) in a negotiation? What are the advantages of silence?

10. What are the advantages of a limited-authority tactic? What can negotiators do if this is used? Should you bargain with a no-authority person?

11. How can individuals use anger to their advantage in negotiation?

12. How should you handle aggressiveness (including interruptions) during negotiation?

13. What is "boulwareism" in negotiation? What does its use say to the other party?

14. What is the problem with "belly-uppers?"

15. What are pareto optimal arrangements? Are they common? If not, what is possible during the cooperative phase with regard to trade-offs?

The Case Against Winning in Negotiations

Leonard Greenhalgh

If you pay close attention to the vocabulary people use when discussing negotiations, you'll note that "winning" occurs with striking frequency. People involved in management training offer to teach "winning negotiation tactics." Researchers who identified a paradox experienced by negotiators gave it the intriguing label, "the winner's curse." Other scholars have created their own unwitting paradox by characterizing mutual gain outcomes as "win-win" solutions.

Making a case against "winning" seems heretical, like attacking patriotic ideals or revered institutions. Nevertheless, my aim in this article is to point out that the metaphor of winning is not only inappropriate in most situations, but is actually dangerous when used to characterize negotiations. In a nutshell, winning implies losing, and this dichotomy is inherently zero-sum in nature. The metaphor of winning is appropriate for describing power struggles, but inappropriate for describing other means of resolving apparent conflicts, particularly cooperative solutions such as problem-solving or other forms of integrative bargaining.

Therefore I'd like to argue that scholars and practitioners should scrupulously question—and in most cases, avoid—the notion of winning when thinking about conflicts. Much more than a semantic debate is involved here. The notion of winning is a metaphor that has the power and potential to create tunnel vision, and lead people to visualize conflicts in counterproductive ways.

In the sections that follow, I'll talk about why people use metaphors, where the winning metaphor comes from and why it is so ubiquitous, the exact problems that result from a winning point of view, and the alternatives.

Importance of Metaphors

A metaphor is an image—often visual—that helps us think about and convey a complex or, unfamiliar phenomenon. For example, few people (if any) really understand what electricity is all about. So, most of us use a plumbing metaphor to help visualize and explain how it works. We talk about the "flow" of electricity as if it were water in a pipe, and even measure the "current." This use of metaphor makes an elusive phenomenon understandable, but it also limits our thinking. If we rely on the plumbing metaphor, how do we account for sparks, static electricity, transformation into heat, or microwave transmission? The adverse effects on our thinking may be worse than bafflement: We may become comfortable with a metaphor that offers only a partial (or even incorrect) understanding of the phenomenon, and never bother to seek a deeper understanding. In this sense, the metaphor encourages tunnel vision, and is distracting rather than enlightening.

At this point, it may occur to the reader that we're better off avoiding metaphors and using precise concepts and terminology to think about and discuss the phenomena that are important to us. Unfortunately, we don't have much choice. Scholars who have studied human understanding—from psychologists and linguists to philosophers agree that people invariably try to understand unknown phenomena by visualizing them in terms of familiar, well-understood phenomena. In other words, there's little choice about whether to use metaphors; the only choice is which metaphors to use. As the next section shows, negotiators—and the scholars who study them—have not been careful enough in their choice of metaphors.

Prevalence of Win-Lose Metaphors

Because of the prevalence of sports metaphors in the United States and in other Western cultures, winning comes up often as a theme in describing negotiations. Sports metaphors are somewhat interchangeable with military metaphors, as is evident from the prevalence of hybrid metaphors. We speak of war games, the

Leonard Greenhalgh, "The Case Against Winning in Negotiations," in *Negotiation Journal*, April 1987. Reprinted by permission of Plenum Publishing Corporation.

arms race, tennis volleys, shots on goal, knocking out a machine gun emplacement, and designation of players as lines, forwards, captains, guards, and so on. Thus it is not always possible to tell precisely when someone using win-lose metaphors is visualizing sports or war, and harder still to tell what imagery those metaphors evoke in the listener or reader. Either way, the win-lose metaphor is limiting when used uncritically to characterize negotiations.

Win-lose metaphors are pressed into service to characterize a wide variety of interaction situations, especially those in which there is some incompatibility of wills or interests. Sometimes win-lose metaphors are appropriate, such as when describing the relationship between two businesses attempting to gain sales among a limited set of customers. Indeed, it is difficult to avoid describing firms in such circumstances as "competing." However, more often than not, the application of the win-lose metaphor is inappropriate to describe the interaction situation.

An example of an obviously inappropriate sports metaphor occurs when teenage males characterize dates as opportunities to "score." In talking to other teenage males, they sometimes grossly elaborate the metaphor by boasting that they "got to second base." The manipulative behavior that is inspired by the use of a baseball metaphor in this context limits the possible outcomes. The relationship that results from this type of thinking is obviously likely to be unstable and unfulfilling.

Debates between presidential candidates (and more subtly, summit conferences between superpower leaders) provide another example of the imposition of a win-lose perspective on an event for which it is inappropriate. The idea of arranging for two presidential candidates to engage in a televised discussion of positions on vital issues, after which the press decides who "won," is ludicrous. The purpose of televising the candidates is, presumably, to provide samples of their thinking and presidential behavior, so that voters can make better-informed choices about who they want in the White House. It is not clear to me—and to most political scientists—that performance in a televised debate is a valid work sample for a U.S. president. More questionable still is the utility of having the press decide who "won," other than to satisfy a national obsession with contests at the expense of a thoughtful election process.

Winning as a Masculine Metaphor

Sports metaphors seem far more prevalent among males than among females. This can be traced to the fact that competitive games play a more prominent role in the early development and socialization of boys than they do in girls. More specifically, boys typically are taught to play games in which the objective is to defeat their playmates (now defined as opponents) and then gloat about the victory—or worse, ridicule the playmates who have lost the game. By contrast, girls tend to choose relationship-oriented games ("Barbie and Ken" doll games or "house"). When they do participate in competitive games, girls are taught to end the game or change the rules if it becomes apparent that the game has stopped being fun for their playmates who are not doing so well. In other words, girls are taught to play games that preserve and enhance the relationship, while boys are taught to preserve and enhance their feelings of self-worth at the expense of the relationship.

The vestiges of these childhood experiences are quite prominent in the thought patterns of adult negotiators. Men have a general tendency to think in terms of competing and therefore rely heavily on win-lose metaphors; women, on the other hand, have a general tendency to think in terms of preserving and enhancing relationships, and win-lose metaphors are less salient to them. These differences in general tendencies often parallel the differences in the way the two sexes approach negotiations. In particular, men tend to use negotiation tactics that are shaped by win-lose metaphors—tactics that tend to poison relationships preclude cooperative solutions to conflicts, and deny them the benefits of long-term reciprocal exchanges.

Pitfalls of Win-Lose Metaphors

The most obvious disadvantage of win-lose metaphors is their inherent zero-sum quality. Sports contests, like battles, are meant to be won. The common norm is for players to strive to the best of their ability, strength, and stamina to defeat the other player (or team). In fact, to do less is "unsportsmanlike"; nobody wants to beat or even be narrowly defeated by a player who wasn't trying very hard. Instead, the losing player is supposed to escalate the attack to make the other player's victory as difficult as possible. The emphasis on winning is so heavy that even a tie score is undesirable. In fact, many sports have rules that preclude ties or have mechanisms to eliminate them such as "sudden death overtime." As a result of these mechanisms, when the sports metaphor is applied to negotiation situations, there is little room for compromise, or even mercy.

Furthermore, the notion of a "win-win solution" in this context makes no sense. The metaphor cannot be stretched to accommodate a win-win outcome without violating the essence of sports contests or military engagements. It seems more advisable to abandon the inescapably zero-sum winning metaphor, therefore, when discussing nonzero-sum outcomes. It is better to talk about mutual advantage, because the focus is on the benefits of cooperation rather than on winning; the latter focus tends to portray the other negotiator as an opponent and implies that the benefit has to come at someone else's expense. Simply, the "win-win" notion, besides being illogical, conjures up all the wrong images.

The pervasiveness of the concept of win-win solutions—even among theorists who are wise enough to recognize the inherent paradox— probably reflects the prominence of game theory in scholars' thinking about conflict and its resolution. Game theory was inspired directly by military strategy metaphors, which share many of the shortcomings of sports metaphors.

Game theory provides many useful insights about conflicts, but would be much more useful if it came without its loaded metaphorical baggage. An abstract payoff matrix is rarely if ever understood in the abstract. Rather, people visualize outcomes by imposing imagery on the otherwise meaningless numbers. The average person's imagery is likely to involve battle or sports metaphors, because these tend to be evoked as a result of the tactical decision situations that inspired this way of structuring thinking about conflicts.

As a result of this "metaphorical baggage," when writers describe a positive sum outcome as "win-win," it suggests to me that they not only are using sports or military metaphors inappropriately, but are also inducing their audience to adopt the same potentially misleading interpretation.

Winning-oriented sports metaphors have several disadvantages beyond fostering a zero-sum perspective. One of these is the emphasis on rules rather than relationships. In sports contests, it is generally acceptable for players to stretch rules to the limit; the norms tolerate almost any tactic that can be used in pursuit of victory, so long as it doesn't violate explicit rules. Innovations within the rules that give the contestant an advantage make heroes of the rule-benders.

Knute Rockne, for instance, became a legend when he discovered that there was nothing in the rules of football that precluded a forward pass. This invention revolutionized football strategy. Similarly, race car designer Jim Hall discovered that the rules of road racing were silent on the topic of aerodynamic devices. So he added an "upside-down" wing to his Chapparal cars to force the tires against the pavement and thereby increase the grip necessary for high cornering speeds. This innovation, and the ground-effects cars he subsequently pioneered, changed the shape of automobiles. Other sports have seen analogous breakthroughs by people who violated the spirit of the rules. The important point here is that the "unfair advantage" they thereby gained was usually idealized rather than condemned.

Despite our admiration for those who sought the maximum advantage over competitors within the limits of the explicit rules of the game, we have to be critical of such behavior in negotiations. In fact, we need to examine carefully the effects of focusing on rules rather than relationships.

It appears, first of all, that a focus on rules easily can lead to attempts to exploit rather than negotiate fairly. The tactics of the sports-oriented negotiator are constrained by explicit rules rather than being motivated by the good of all the parties involved. In other words, rather than devise creative solutions to mutual problems, negotiators often spend valuable time and energy trying to figure out how much they can get away with. Even worse, ethical considerations tend to become subordinated to the rules applied to the situation; this has a profound impact on trust.

Consider, for instance, two close friends playing poker. In the game, they have no qualms about deceiving each other. In fact, the poker game would be no fun if both people were open and honest about the cards they held. Now, visualize the same two friends negotiating, with one trying to sell a major appliance to the other. Suppose the seller has found out that the manufacturer of the appliance is on the verge of going out of business, and, consequently, the value of the appliance will plummet because the guarantee will be worthless and spare parts will be difficult to obtain. The seller who defines this situation as a game might say nothing about the risks of buying the appliance. By contrast, the seller who focused on the relationship is more likely to make a full disclosure of information to the friend, or will sell the appliance to a stranger instead.

More subtle rules-oriented affects can occur in collective bargaining. The National Labor Relations Act specifies that the parties must "bargain in good faith." If management conceives of the interaction as a rules-bounded game, its tactics may be to cooperate as little as possible without violating "the letter of the law"; there will be little emphasis on mutual accommodation and the development of good-will. This situation actually happens with surprising frequency. Almost inevitably, management's relationship with the union suffers as a result of such treatment, and managers subsequently blame the union for not cooperating for the good of all, as if their own behavior had nothing to do with the outcome.

The emphasis on rules that arises from the sports metaphor may have an additional, perhaps even more subtle, negative effect: It may increase a disputant's tendency to litigate rather than mediate a dispute. This tendency occurs because, outside of sports situations, referees (or umpires) are poor models of conflict "resolvers."

Most of us do not immediately think of referees as conflict resolution professionals. If you want to be convinced, try playing a team sport in which there is high ego-involvement without a referee. The game will probably soon become interrupted as players argue over the application of rules, and you'll soon wish a referee were present to end the dispute summarily and let you get on with the game. Referees play an important role in settling conflicts over facts (e.g., who last touched the ball before it went out of bounds) or perhaps even the interpretation of rules (e.g., when is a trick keel on a 12-meter yacht illegal).

The reason why a referee is a poor model for a conflict resolver is that, unlike a mediator, a referee's role is to enforce rules narrowly. The analog in everyday life is the courtroom judge, whose job is usually remarkably similar to the referee's—to examine the available evidence, disregard inadmissible evidence (e.g., videotape replays), and decide in favor of one party or the other. Based on sports experiences, people seem more comfortable with the judge role than with the fuzzier role of the mediator, who does not observe strict rules of evidence and tries to avoid making decisions for the disputants.

Another disadvantage of having one's thinking shaped by sports metaphors is that they induce disputants to focus on the immediate conflict episode rather than take a longer-term perspective. Sports contests are discrete, independent events. Irrespective of who won or lost the last game, the scores are set at zero at the beginning of the next game. Furthermore, sports norms would not permit players to let one team win this week in exchange for reciprocal leniency by the other team the next week. Thus, the history and future of the ongoing relationship between contestants is irrelevant in sports.

When this same short-term perspective is applied to negotiation situations, the conflict becomes much more difficult to deal with than it would be otherwise. Negotiators with a short-term perspective can choose harsh or exploitive tactics without fear of repercussions, because they view any future interaction as "a new game." Likewise, there is nothing to gain in the future from being accommodating in the current interaction, since anything "given up" is perceived as forever lost. From this standpoint, intransigence—and even aggression—is rational.

For instance, imagine a salesman with a short-term perspective engaged in a dispute over the interpretation of ambiguous terms in a sales contract. Let's say, furthermore, that the purchasing agent is predisposed to avoid conflicts. The salesman acts on his belief that he can "win" the dispute by applying pressure: browbeating, ad hominem attacks, threats, withholding or distorting information, and other aggressive behaviors. This approach does indeed result in the predicted concessions from the purchasing agent. However, any winning in this scenario is likely to be a Pyrrhic victory: The purchasing agent will subsequently go to great lengths to avoid doing business with this abrasive salesman, and will no doubt tell other purchasing agents—and possibly the salesman's superior—about the experience. Thus the long-term cost in terms of relationships and reputation offsets the short-term gain.

A final disadvantage of the win-lose metaphor is that it induces negotiators to try to fractionate the other party. The rationale is that if the opposing group can be thrown into disarray, that group is easier to defeat. This strategy is the basis for propaganda campaigns against enemies. For example, after last fall's quasi-summit meeting in Iceland, Soviet General Secretary Mikhail Gorbachev began an energetic media campaign to encourage divisiveness within the U.S. and NATO over the Strategic Defense Initiative.

Fractionating the other party has the advantage of weakening coalitions; however, this practice also may subsequently make the conflict more difficult to resolve, simply because there is no clear leader or unified group that can agree to a comprehensive settlement. The Palestine Liberation Organization, the Organization of Petroleum Exporting Companies, and the Afghan resistance movement are familiar examples of parties to a conflict whose fractionation makes them difficult to negotiate with successfully. What happens is that some subgroups agree to a settlement, while others resist, engaging in passive resistance, subtle sabotage, wildcat strikes, outright defiance, or turning on the subgroups who have agreed.

A Better Metaphor?

What makes the win-lose metaphor particularly insidious in negotiations is its invisibility. It is so innocuous to most people that it goes unnoticed and, therefore, its usefulness and disadvantages are not evaluated. The metaphor is innocuous because it seems superficially compatible with the ways companies compete in the marketplace, but this apparent compatibility is actually spurious. Relationships between people are qualitatively different from relationships between organizations; therefore, people need to assess the metaphor's advantages and limitations for each application.

Sometimes a negotiator will encounter a zero-sum situation that is truly a single transaction unaffected by a past relationship or a potential future relationship. When this happens, a competitive approach is useful, and making sense of the situation in terms of winning and losing is appropriate. These situations, however, are rare.

The more typical situation involves an ongoing relationship and has some positive-sum possibilities. In these circumstances, awareness of how the win-lose metaphor can affect a person's thinking about a dispute and its settlement alerts the negotiator to be aware of the other party's frame of reference. When the other party is trying to "win" a negotiation, a negotiator might try to make the other party aware of the shortcomings of a win-lose approach. If such persuasion is to no avail, then the negotiator should also attempt to win, otherwise he or she is destined to lose.

Ideally, the negotiator would use win-lose metaphors only when absolutely necessary. This does not mean trying to engage in metaphor-free thinking, which would be almost impossible for most people. Rather, it means developing a set of alternative guiding metaphors that are appropriate when winning is inappropriate.

Metaphors are highly individualized because they must suit an individual's tastes and experiences; some themes, however, are likely to be more helpful than others. For example, synergy—or even symbiosis—is a better theme than competition for visualizing interdependent relationships. Singing a duet is a synergic metaphor: Simon and Garfunkel achieved musical heights neither could achieve alone.

Lovemaking is another: Romeo and Juliet gained such benefits from their relationship that neither wanted to live without it. Parenting is a third possible metaphor: Parents may experience considerable difference of opinion concerning how to raise the child, but both must settle on a joint course of action and then continually renegotiate agreements as new situations arise.

Perhaps no one metaphor is ideal for all situations, instead, people probably need to have a repertoire available. Whatever the choice, a scenario for negotiators to avoid is to have only win-lose metaphors available. •

Study Questions

1. Define a metaphor.

2. What is proposed to be the outcome of girls' vs. boys' play? How is this related to negotiation practices?

3. What are five disadvantages of the winning-oriented, sports metaphors in negotiation?

4. Is the win-lose orientation ever appropriate?

5. Explain optional non-competitive metaphors, and which is the "best."

How Can I Win If You Don't Lose? Games Where the Winner Doesn't Take All

Judith Knelman

In 1979, Robert Axelrod, Professor of Political Science at the University of Michigan, ran a tournament for computer programs addressing the Prisoner's Dilemma. The winning program was the shortest of all those submitted and based on the simple principle of tit for tat. Adopting the principle: Cooperate on the first move, and thereafter do exactly what the opposing player does, the program defeated all the complex strategies built into the other programs.

The results of this computer experiment have profound implications for our understanding of competition and collaboration, and the merits of collaboration in a competitive world. It shows that even in "zero-sum" situations, it is possible for everyone to win.

In the following paragraphs, Judith Knelman writes about her conversation with Anatol Rapoport, author of the winning program.

It's commonly believed so-called zero sum games like Monopoly, poker and bridge, in which what one player wins represents the loss to his opponents, are an imitation of life. Success means someone else's failure, a feast someone else's famine. Survival of the fittest means it's you or the other guy: to keep on top of the competition, you have to deprive others of what you all want.

Anatol Rapoport, professor emeritus at University of Toronto, director of the Institute for Advanced Studies in Vienna, demonstrates, among other things, the folly of this notion in a statistical analysis of how people tend to resolve conflict.

By means of a program of strategy he has worked out for a simple game called the Prisoner's Dilemma, which looks something like tic-tac-toe and takes even less time to play, he is able to show that life is not a zero-sum game at all. Not only is it not necessary for the winner to take all: it is impossible. The winner does best by sharing and never attempting to put one over on the opponent. To win, you quietly follow the other person's lead, never trying to out maneuver him except in immediate retaliation.

Life, says Rapoport, is a mixed-motive game in which the interests of people partly coincide and partly conflict. To get what they want, they have to co-operate. They must trust each other consistently and be prepared to share the rewards available.

The game, which was discovered and circulated in the early 1950s, has aroused a tremendous amount of interest in academic circles, he says, because it demonstrates an important moral lesson: that the meek shall inherit the earth. When it is played in a situation that simulates society or evolution—a tournament environment wherein every player uses his own peculiar strategy consistently against every other player and then against himself—those who co-operate do much better than those who try to trick their opponents.

"Think of two scorpions in a bottle," he suggests. "If neither attacks, both will survive. If one attacks, the other retaliates, and both die. An even worse situation for the scorpions develops when one has to plot its strategy for survival on the assumption that the other may attack at any time."

The game worked out to represent the prisoner's dilemma mathematically gives each prisoner two alternatives. Each is told that if both keep quiet they will both get a sentence of two years, but if one rats he will get off free while the accomplice will get five years. The catch is that if they rat on one another, both will get four years. If each is sure that the other will keep quiet as well, that is the best course for both. But can they trust each other?

The dilemma of the game is in the circumstance that it is in the best interest of each prisoner to implicate the other whether or not the other co-operates. If the other keeps quiet, he will still get a two-year sentence, while telling on the other gets him off free. As betrayal by both results in a four-year sentence, while keeping quiet could result a five-year sentence, it's best to rat no matter what the other does. However, if neither rats, both get only two years.

Robert Axelrod decided to extend this problem to a tournament using computers to find the best consistent strategy for this sort of dilemma, which regularly confronts individuals and governments, in the form of potential rewards rather than punishments. The goal is to do as well as possible in your dealings with others over the long term. Rapoport won over all the other experts with the shortest and simplest program submitted, TIT FOR TAT, which shows that you do not have to deprive others in order to succeed yourself. His strategy is to co-operate or defect according to the lead of the other player. Even the most successful of the rival programs came to grief when they had to play against themselves, but TIT FOR TAT did nothing to hurt itself. It demonstrates the golden rule, do unto others as you would have them do unto you.

You play the game over and over again with the same partner, so that what happens in one game influences what happens in the next. You also play it over and over again with other people, just as you interact more than once with a large group of people in your everyday life. The idea is to accumulate the highest overall score. It is not necessary to vanquish individual rivals in order to do this. . . .

The research has obvious implications in many areas from domestic to international. Rapoport uses it to plead publicly for nuclear disarmament. . . . He thinks that like two scorpions in a bottle we are doomed if we do not trust our rivals. And even if our trust is not justified, he points out—if the other side does not disarm and we do—we may actually be safer than if we remained armed, since once we are no longer a threat they would have no need to attack us.

"I have no use for either superpower," says Rapoport. "I very much admire the small democratic countries that are not powerful." Canada, he says, is "sensible." It has the advantages of the U.S. without succumbing to the excesses. . . . As in the game, the secret of success lies in the correct definition of the problem. "You make your choice by asking not 'How do I do better'," says Rapoport, "but 'How do we do better?' You have to trust each other to co-operate. Then the answer is obvious." •

References

Hofstadter, D.H.R. "Metamagical Themas." *Scientific American,* May 1983, 16–26.

Rapoport, Anatol. *Fights, Games and Debates.* Ann Arbor: University of Michigan Press, 1960.

Study Questions

1. Why is life a "mixed-motive game" and how is it "won?"

2. Explain the two scorpions in a bottle metaphor.

3. What is TIT FOR TAT, and how does the concepts inherent in this strategy apply to international nuclear disarmament?

Consider Both Relationships and Substance When Negotiating Strategically

Grant T. Savage
John D. Blair
Ritch L. Sorenson
Texas Tech University

When David Peterson, director of services for Dickerson Machinery, arrives at his office, he notes four appointments on his schedule. With his lengthy experience in negotiating important contracts for this large-equipment repair service, he does not take long to identify the agenda for each appointment.

A steering clutch disk salesman from Roadworks will arrive at 8:30 a.m. Peterson has relied for years on disks supplied by Caterpillar and knows those disks can provide the 8,000 hours of service Dickerson guarantees. Price is an issue in Peterson's selection of a supplier, but more important is a guarantee on the life span of the part.

A meeting is scheduled at 9:30 with a mechanic who has swapped a new company battery for a used battery from his own truck. This "trade" is, of course, against company policy, and the employee has been reprimanded and told his next paycheck will be docked. However, the mechanic wants to discuss the matter.

A representative for Tarco, a large roadbuilding contractor, is scheduled for 10:00 a.m. Peterson has been interested in this service contract for a couple of years. He believes that if he can secure a short-term service contract with Tarco, Dickerson's high-quality mechanical service and guarantees will result in a long-term service relationship with the contractor. The night before, Peterson had dinner with Tarco's representative, and this morning he will provide a tour of service facilities and discuss the short-term contract with him.

A meeting with management representatives for union negotiations is scheduled for 1:00 p.m. That meeting will probably last a couple of hours. Peterson is concerned because the company has lost money on the shop undergoing contract talks, and now the union is demanding higher wages and threatening to strike. The company cannot afford a prolonged strike, but it also cannot afford to increase pay at current service production rates. Negotiating a contract will not be easy.

Choosing Negotiation Strategies

Peterson's appointments are not unique. Researchers and scholars have examined similar situations. What strategic advice does the negotiation literature offer for handling these four situations?

One of the best developed approaches is *game theory,* which focuses on maximizing substantive outcomes in negotiations.[2] Peterson would probably do well by focusing on only the best possible outcome for Dickerson Machinery in his meetings with the salesman and the employee: He already has a good contract for a steering wheel clutch, but if the salesman can offer a better deal, Peterson will take it; and in the case of the employee, Peterson will hear him out but foresees no need to deviate from company policy.

In contrast, an exclusive focus on maximizing the company's substantive outcomes would probably not work in the other two situations: Tarco may continue being serviced elsewhere unless enticed to try Dickerson; and during the union negotiations, strategies to maximize outcomes for management only could force a strike.

Another well-developed strategic approach is *win-win problem solving.* It is designed to maximize outcomes for both parties and maintain positive relationships.[3] This approach could work in the union negotiation, but the outcome would probably be a compromise, not a true win-win solution.

Win-win negotiation probably is not the best strategy in the other three situations. Either Roadwork's salesman meets the guarantee and

From *Executive,* Volume III, Number 1, 1989, pp. 37–48. Copyright © 1989 by The Academy of Management *Executive.* Reprinted by permission.

beats current prices, or he does not; trying to find a win-win solution would probably be a waste of time. Similarly, because the meeting with the employee will occur after company rules have been applied, a win-win solution is probably not in the company's best interest. Lastly, an attempt to maximize the company's substantive outcomes in a short-term service contract with Tarco could hinder long-term contract prospects.

Any one approach to negotiation clearly will not work in all situations. Executives need a framework for determining what strategies are best in different situations. We believe the best strategy depends on desired outcomes. In this article, we characterize the two major outcomes at issue in the previous examples as *substantive* and *relationship* outcomes. Although both types of outcome have been discussed in the literature, relationship outcomes have received much less attention. Our contention is that a systematic model of strategic choice for negotiation must account for both substantive and relationship outcomes. In articulating such a model, we suggest that execu-

tives can approach negotiation strategically by assessing the negotiation context; considering unilateral negotiation strategies; transforming unilateral into interactive negotiation strategies; and monitoring tactics and reevaluating negotiation strategies.

Assessing the Negotiation Context

A crucial context for any negotiation is the manager's current and desired relationship with the other party. Unfortunately, in their rush to secure the best possible substantive outcome, managers often overlook the impact of the negotiation on their relationships. This oversight can hurt a manager's relationship with the other party, thus limiting his or her ability to obtain desired substantive outcomes now or in the future.

Each interaction with another negotiator constitutes an *episode* that draws from current and affects future relationships. Intertwined with pure concerns about relationships are concerns about substantive outcomes. Many times negotiators are motivated to establish or main-

Exhibit 1
Assessing The Negotiation Context

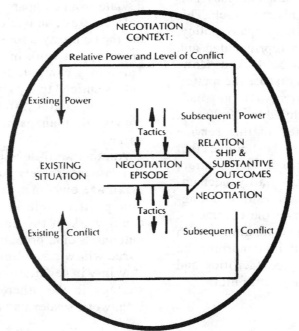

tain positive relationships and willingly "share the pie" through mutually beneficial collaboration. Other negotiations involve substantive outcomes that can benefit one negotiator only at the expense of the other (a fixed pie). These cases often motivate negotiators to discount the relationship and claim as much of the pie as possible.

Most negotiations, however, are neither clearly win-win nor win-lose situations, but combinations of both (an indeterminate pie). Such mixed-motive situations, in which both collaboration and competition may occur, are particularly difficult for managers to handle strategically.[4] The relationship that exists prior to the negotiation, the relationship that unfolds during negotiations, and the desired relationship often will determine whether either negotiator will be motivated to share the pie, grab it, or give it away.

In any case, managers should keep existing and desired relationships in mind as they bid for substantive outcomes. For example, when negotiators are on the losing end of a win-lose negotiation, they should examine the implications of taking a short-term loss. During his third appointment, Peterson's willingness to make only minimal gains in service contracts for the short term may create a positive relationship that will lead to a lucrative, long-term contract with Tarco. The relative importance of possible substantive and relationship outcomes should help executives decide whether and how to negotiate. To guide their decision process, managers should begin by assessing their relative power and the level of conflict between them and the other party. Both are key determinants of their current relationship with the other party.

Exhibit 1 illustrates the negotiation context, showing those aspects of the situation and negotiation episode that shape relationship and substantive outcomes. Existing levels of power and conflict influence (1) the relationship between the executive and the other party and (2) the negotiation strategies they choose. These strategies are implemented through appropriate tactics during a negotiation episode—a one-on-one encounter, a telephone call, or a meeting with multiple parties—and result in substantive and relationship outcomes.

The multiple arrows linking strategies, tactics, and the negotiation episode in Exhibit 1 show the monitoring process through which both the manager and the other party refine their strategies and tactics during an episode. A complex and lengthy negotiation, such as a union contract negotiation, may include many episodes; a simple negotiation may be completed within one episode. Each episode, nonetheless, influences future negotiations by changing the manager's and the other party's relative power, the level of conflict between them, and their relationship.

Relative Power

The relative power of the negotiators establishes an important aspect of their relationship: the extent of each party's dependence on the other. Researchers have found that individuals assess their power in a relationship and choose whether to compete, accommodate, collaborate, or withdraw when negotiating with others.[5] Managers can assess their power relative to the other party by comparing their respective abilities to induce compliance through the control of human and material resources. To what extent do they each control key material resources? To what extent do they each control the deployment, arrangement, and advancement of people within the organization?[6]

These questions will help managers determine whether their relationship with the other party is based on independence, dependence, or interdependence. Additionally, these questions should help executives consider how *and* whether their relationship with the other party should be strengthened or weakened. Often managers will find themselves or their organizations in interdependent relationships that have both beneficial and detrimental aspects. These relationships are called mixed-motive situations in the negotiation literature because they provide incentives for both competitive and cooperative actions.

In his relationship with the Roadwork salesman, Peterson has considerable power. He is satisfied with his current vendor and has other vendors wanting to sell him the same product. The numerous choices available allow him to make demands on the salesman. Similarly, Peterson has more relative power than the mechanic. On the other hand, he has relatively little power with Tarco, since the contractor can choose from a number of equipment-service shops. Moreover, Tarco's representative did not make the initial contact and has not actively sought Dickerson's services.

Level of Conflict

The level of conflict underlying a potential negotiation establishes how the negotiators perceive the affective dimension of their relationship—that is, its degree of supportiveness or hostility. Managers can assess the relationship's level of conflict by identifying the differences between each party's interests. On what issues do both parties agree? On what issues do they disagree? How intense and how ingrained are these differences?[7]

Answers to these questions will reveal whether negotiations will easily resolve differences and whether the relationship is perceived as supportive or hostile. These questions, like the questions about relative power, should also help executives consider how *and* whether the relationship should be strengthened or weakened. Very few negotiations begin with a neu-

tral relationship. Indeed, the affective state of the relationship may be a primary reason for negotiating with a powerful other party, especially if the relationship has deteriorated or been particularly supportive.

In Peterson's case, neutral to positive relationships exist with the Roadwork salesman and the Tarco representative. However, his relationships with the mechanic and the union are potentially hostile. For example, management and union representatives have already had confrontations. Their conflict may escalate if the relationship is not managed and both sides are not willing to make concessions.[8]

Considering a Unilateral Negotiation Strategy

Before selecting a strategy for negotiation, a manager should consider his or her interests and the interests of the organization. These interests will shape the answers to two basic questions: (1) Is the substantive outcome very important to the manager? and (2) Is the relationship outcome very important to the manager?

Exhibit 2
Considering a Unilateral Negotiation Strategy

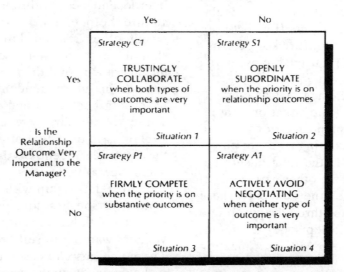

Four *unilateral* strategies (see Exhibit 2) emerge from the answers: *trusting collaboration, firm competition, open subordination*, and *active avoidance*.[9] We call these unilateral strategies because in using them, managers consider only their own interests or the interests of their organization, ignoring for the time being the interests of the other party.

The unilateral strategies presented in Exhibit 2 are similar to the conflict management styles suggested by the combined works of Blake and Mouton, Hall, and Kilmann and Thomas.[10] However, while we agree that personalities and conflict-management preferences influence a person's ability to negotiate, our selection of terms reflects our focus on strategies instead of styles. For example, Johnston uses the term "subordination" to refer to a strategy similar to the conflict-management style variously termed "accommodation" (Kilmann and Thomas), "smoothing" (Blake and Mouton), or "yield-lose" (Hall).[11] We, however, see using the openly subordinative strategy as more than simply "rolling over and playing dead" or "giving away the store." Rather, this strategy is designed to strengthen long-term relational ties, usually at the expense of short-term substantive outcomes. Our discussion below also goes beyond Johnston's conception, showing how a negotiator can focus the openly subordinative strategy according to his or her substantive goals.

Our view is consistent with research that suggests that individuals adopt different strategies in different relational contexts.[12] We anticipate that managers' success with these unilateral strategies depends on their ability to exhibit a variety of conflict styles. To highlight the role of relationship and substantive priorities, we describe these four unilateral strategies in their most extenuated, ideal form, and articulate their underlying assumptions. In many ways our descriptions are classic depictions of each type of strategy. Two of these strategies—competition and collaboration—are frequently discussed in the conflict and negotiation literature.

1. Trusting Collaboration (C1). In general, if both relationship and substantive outcomes are important to the organization, the manager should consider *trusting collaboration*. The hallmark of this strategy is openness on the part of both parties. By encouraging cooperation as positions are asserted, the executive should be able to achieve important relationship and substantive outcomes. The executive seeks a win-win outcome both to achieve substantive goals and maintain a positive relationship.

Trustingly collaborative strategies generally are easiest to use and most effective when the manager's organization and the other party are interdependent and mutually supportive. These circumstances normally create a trusting relationship in which negotiators reciprocally disclose their goals and needs. In this climate, an effective problem-solving process and a win-win settlement typically result.

2. Open Subordination (S1). If managers are more concerned with establishing a positive relationship with another party than obtaining substantive outcomes, they should openly subordinate. We use the term *subordination* instead of *accommodation* to differentiate this strategic choice from a conflict-management style. An openly subordinative strategy is a yield-win strategy that usually provides desired substantive outcomes to the other party but rarely to the manager. A subordinative strategy may be used regardless of whether the manager exercises more, less, or equal power relative to the other party. Our argument is that subordination can be an explicit strategic negotiation behavior—not simply a reflection of power. If the manager has little to lose by yielding to the substantive interests of the other party, open subordination can be a key way for him or her to dampen hostilities, increase support, and foster more interdependent relationships.

3. Firm Competition (P1). If substantive interests are important but the relationship is not, the manager should consider *firmly competing*. This situation often occurs when managers have little trust for the other party or the relationship is not good to begin with. In such situations, they may want to exert their power to gain substantive outcomes. To enact this competitive strategy, they may also become highly aggressive, bluffing, threatening the other party, or otherwise misrepresenting their intentions. Such tactics hide the manager's actual goals and needs, preventing the other party from using that knowledge to negotiate its own substantive outcomes. Not surprisingly, the credibility of the executive's aggressive tactics and, thus, the success of the firmly competitive strategy often rests on the organization's power vis-à-vis the other party. When following a firmly competitive strategy, the manager seeks a win-lose substantive outcome and is willing to accept a neutral or even a bad relationship.

4. Active Avoidance (A1). Managers should consider *actively avoiding negotiation* if neither the relationship nor the substantive outcomes are important to them or the organization. Simply refusing to negotiate is the most direct and active form of avoidance. Executives can simply tell the other party they are not interested in or willing to negotiate. Such an action, however, will usually have a negative impact on the organization's relationship with the other party. Moreover, managers must determine which issues are a waste of time to negotiate. We treat avoidance, like subordination, as an explicit, strategic behavior rather than as an option taken by default when the manager is uncertain about what to do.

However, we recognize that these unilateral strategies are most successful only in a limited set of situations. In the next section we include various interactive modifications that make these classic, unilateral strategies applicable to a wider set of negotiation situations.

Interactive Negotiation Strategies

Before using the unilateral strategies suggested by Exhibit 2, the executive should examine the negotiation from each party's perspective. The choice of a negotiation strategy should be based not only on the interests of the executive or organization, but also on the interests of the other party. The manager should anticipate the other party's substantive and relationship priorities, assessing how the negotiation is likely to progress when the parties interact. This step is crucial because the unilateral strategies described above could lead to grave problems if the other party's priorities differ. For example, when using either trusting collaboration or open subordination, the manager is vulnerable to exploitation if the other party is concerned

only about substantive outcomes. When anticipating the other party's substantive and relationship priorities, executives should consider the kinds of actions the other party might take. Are those actions likely to be supportive or hostile? Will they represent short-term reactions or long-term approaches to the substantive issues under negotiation? Are those actions likely to change the party's degree of dependence on, or interdependence with, the organization? The answers will depend on (1) the history of the executive's relations with the other party and (2) the influence of key individuals and groups on the manager and the other party.

In short, executives should take into account both their own and the other party's substantive and relationship priorities in choosing a negotiating strategy. Exhibit 3 is a decision tree designed to help managers decide which strategy to use. The left side represents, in a different form, the analysis in Exhibit 2; thus, Exhibit 3 also shows how the manager's substantive and relationship priorities lead to *unilateral strategies* based solely on the manager's position. The right side illustrates how these unilateral strategies may be continued, modified, or replaced after the manager considers the other party's potential or apparent priorities.[13]

Managers should examine the appropriateness of a unilateral negotiation strategy by accounting for the other party's priorities before they use it. Sometimes such scrutiny will simply justify its use. For example, when both substantive and relationship outcomes are important to an executive, the appropriate unilateral strategy is trusting collaboration. If the manager anticipates that the other party also values both substantive and relationship outcomes (see Exhibit 3, Situation 1), he or she would continue to favor this strategy. At other times, scrutiny of the other party's priorities may suggest some modifications. We discuss next each of the interactive variations of the classic, unilateral strategies.

1. Principled Collaboration (C2). The C1 collaborative strategy assumes that the other party will reciprocate whenever the executive discloses information. However, if the manager negotiates openly and the other party is not

Exhibit 3
Selecting an Interactive Strategy

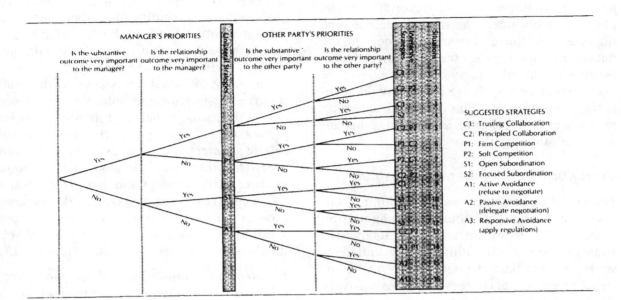

open or is competitive, the manager could be victimized. Under such circumstances, the manager should use the modified collaborative strategy of principled collaboration.[14] Rather than relying on only trust and reciprocity, the manager persuades the other party to conduct negotiations based on a set of mutually agreed upon principles that will benefit each negotiator.

2. Focused Subordination (S2). The openly subordinative strategy (S1) assumes that the substantive outcome is of little importance to the organization. Sometimes, however, an organization has both substantive and relationship interests, but the other party has little stake in either interest. By discovering and then acquiescing to those key needs that are of interest only to the other party, the manager can still gain some substantive outcomes for the organization while assuring a relatively positive relationship outcome. Here, managers both create substantive outcomes for the other party and achieve substantive outcomes for themselves or their organization.

3. Soft Competition (P2). Under some circumstances the directness of the firmly competitive strategy (PI) may need to be softened. For example, even though the manager may place little importance on the relationship outcome, this relationship may be very important to the other party. If the other party is powerful and potentially threatening, the manager would be wise to use a competitive strategy that maintains the relationship. Here the executive would avoid highly aggressive and other "dirty" tactics.

4. Passive Avoidance (A2). If the manager does not consider either the relationship or the substantive outcome important but the other party views the negotiation as important for a relationship outcome, the manager probably should *delegate* the negotiation. By passively avoiding the negotiation, the manager allows someone else within the organization to explore possible outcomes for the organization and keep the relationship from becoming hostile. Delegating ensures that possible opportunities are not ignored while freeing the executive from what appears to be a low-priority negotiation.

5. Responsive Avoidance (A3). By contrast, if the manager considers neither the relationship nor the substantive outcome important and the other party considers the substantive outcome important and the relationship unimportant, the manager should *regulate* the issue. Direct interaction with the other party is not necessary; the manager can be responsive but still avoid negotiating by either applying standard operating procedures or developing new policies that address the other party's concern.

Transforming Unilateral Strategies

The model of strategic choice in Exhibit 3 connects unilateral and interactive negotiation strategies. In many instances the interactive strategies are modifications of the unilateral strategies. We base the decision to modify or replace a unilateral strategy almost exclusively on the manager's and other party's differing outcome priorities. Three outcome conditions and three sets of assumptions influence the choice of interactive strategies.

1. Outcome Condition One: The manager may value the relationship, but the other party may not. For example, a manager who assumes that trust and cooperation will result in a fair outcome may be taken advantage of by another party who is concerned with only substantive outcomes.[15] Hence, we suggest either principled collaboration or soft competition for such cases to ensure that the other party does not take advantage of the manager (see Exhibit 3, Situation 2). On the other hand, the manager may simply want to create a long-term business relationship with someone who currently is interested in neither substantive nor relationship outcomes. In these cases the manager should choose to subordinate in a focused fashion—rather than to trustingly collaborate—to establish a relationship with the other party (see Exhibit 3, Situation 4).

2. Outcome Condition Two: The manager may not value the relationship, but the other party may. Given only their own substantive priorities, managers would firmly compete or actively avoid negotiation under these circum-

stances. However, if the other party is interested in the relationship, the manager may not have to compete firmly to obtain desired substantive outcomes. The manager may collaborate or softly compete and still gain substantive goals without alienating the other party (see Exhibit 3, Situations 5–8). Such strategies may also foster a long-term relationship with substantive dividends for the manager.

Similarly, in situations where neither substantive nor relationship outcomes are important to the manager but the relationship is important to the other party, the manager may choose an interactive strategy other than avoidance. The other party is in a position to choose a subordinative strategy and may offer substantive incentives to the manager. If the manager chooses principled collaboration or soft competition, he or she may gain some positive substantive outcomes (see Exhibit 3, Situation 13).

3. Outcome Condition Three. Both parties may value the relationship, but the manager may not value substantive outcomes. In these cases, whether or not the other party is interested in substantive outcomes, the manager may choose a trustingly collaborative strategy to maintain positive ties with the other party (see Exhibit 3, Situations 9 and 11).

4. Transformation Assumptions. Underlying these three outcome conditions are three sets of assumptions. First, we assume that most relationships will involve some mixture of dependence and interdependence as well as some degree of supportiveness and hostility. Second, we assume that most negotiators will view the relationship outcome as important under four separate conditions—high interdependence, high dependence, high supportiveness, or high hostility—or possible combinations of those conditions. Third, from a manager's perspective, each of the basic strategies has a different effect with regard to power and conflict: (1) collaborative strategies strengthen the interdependence of the manager and the other party while also enhancing feelings of supportiveness, (2) subordinative strategies increase the other party's dependence on the manager while also deemphasizing feelings of hostility, and (3) competitive strategies decrease the manager's dependence on the other party but may also escalate feelings of hostility.

Thus many of the interactive negotiation strategies in Exhibit 3 seek to enhance interdependent relationships or favorably shift the balance of dependence within a relationship. These same strategies also attempt to dampen feelings of hostility or heighten feelings of supportiveness.

Illustrations of Negotiation-Strategy Transformations

To demonstrate more concretely how Exhibit 3 works, we will examine how Dickerson's Peterson might act if he were to follow the decision tree to choose his negotiation strategies.

1. From Avoidance to Collaboration or Competition. In planning to meet with the steering clutch salesman, Peterson first considers whether the substantive outcome is very important to Dickerson Machinery. Because the company already has a satisfactory source for clutch disks, the substantive outcome is not very important. Second, Peterson considers the importance of the relationship outcome. Given that Dickerson Machinery currently has no ties with Roadworks and Peterson foresees no need to establish a long-term relationship, the relationship outcome is not very important either. Based on Peterson's priorities only, unilateral avoidance strategy (A1) seems appropriate.

However, Peterson now considers the salesman's priorities. First, is the substantive outcome important to the salesman? Obviously, it is—Roadworks is a struggling, new company and needs new clients. Second, is the relationship outcome important to Roadworks? Because the salesman works on a commission with residuals, he probably desires a long-term sales contract, so the relationship outcome is important. The salesman's priorities suggest that he would probably collaborate trustingly (C1).

After answering the questions forming the decision tree in Exhibit 3 (see Situation 13), Peterson has two options for an interactive strategy. Since he is in a position of power, he does not need to make concessions. Moreover, the salesman may have products worthy of consideration. Thus, Peterson can engage in principled collaboration (C2) or softly compete (P2). In other words, he can collaborate based on principles, taking a strong stand on what he expects in a sales contract; or he can softly compete by making product demands that do not offend the salesman.

2. From Collaboration to Subordination. For the situation with the contractor, the relationship outcome is very important to Dickerson Machinery but the immediate, substantive outcome is not. Peterson realizes that Dickerson needs Tarco's business for long-term stability but does not need to make a profit in the short term. Therefore, his unilateral strategy would be to subordinate openly (S1). He decides to change his strategy from the trustingly collaborative (C1) approach he has used in past dealings with Tarco.

As Peterson considers the contractor's priorities, he anticipates that the substantive outcome is important to Tarco but the relationship outcome is not. Tarco's representative has made clear the need for reliable service at the lowest possible price; conversely, Tarco has not responded to Peterson's bids to provide service for more than two years. Peterson recognizes, based on Exhibit 2, that Tarco can compete firmly (P1). After assessing both parties' priorities using the decision tree (see Exhibit 3, Situation 10), he decides he should continue with an interactive strategy of open subordination (S1). Such a strategy is more likely to induce Tarco's representative to offer a contract than the trustingly collaborative strategy he has used previously. For example, he is prepared to subordinate by offering a "winter special" to reduce labor costs by 10%, cutting competitive parts costs by 15%, and providing a new paint job at 50% the normal costs or providing a 6-month deferment on payment, all in addition to paying for the trip to the plant.

3. From Competition to Collaboration. Peterson's analysis of the negotiation with the labor union includes an assessment of the recent history of and level of conflict between the union and the company. Previous episodes in this contract negotiation have led both the union and Dickerson Machinery to change their priorities. During the first few episodes, both parties focused on only substantive outcomes and ignored relationship outcomes, using firmly competitive strategies. Also, during these earlier episodes, both sides' demands hardened to the point where the union threatened to strike and management threatened to give no increases in wages or benefits.

Now, however, Peterson believes that both substantive and relationship outcomes are important to Dickerson. The company wants to find a way to increase productivity without giving much of an increase in pay and benefits. It also does not want to lose good mechanics or stimulate a strike. Dickerson's unilateral strategy under these new conditions should be trustingly collaborative (C1).

From analyzing the union's position, Peterson realizes that both the substantive and relationship outcomes should be important to the union. His informal discussions with union representatives have assured him that both sides are now concerned about maintaining the relationship. Nonetheless, the union clearly wants an increase in pay and benefits even though it also does not want a strike. In short, the union now is likely to trustingly collaborate but could easily shift its priorities and choose to firmly compete.

As he enters the negotiation strategy session this afternoon, Peterson plans to recommend to the management negotiation team the use of a principled collaborative (C2) strategy (see Exhibit 3, Situation 2). Because of the current instability in the relationship, he does not want to provide the union with any opportunity to exploit a perceived weakness that a more trustingly collaborative strategy might create.

Monitoring and Reevaluating Strategies

After implementing their interactive strategy, managers should monitor the other party's tactics. How the other party acts will signal its strategy. Based on the other party's tactics, executives can (1) determine if their assumptions and expectations about the other party's strategy are accurate and (2) modify, if needed, their strategies during this and subsequent negotiation episodes. Exhibit 1 provides an overview of this process. The arrows linking strategies to tactics and the negotiation episode represent how tactics (1) are used to implement a strategy (first arrow), (2) provide information to each party (second, reversed arrow), and (3) may affect the choice of alternative strategies during a negotiation episode (third arrow).

Monitoring Tactics

More specifically, we view tactics in two ways: (1) as clusters of specific actions associated with the implementation of one strategy or another, and (2) as actions that derive their strategic impact from the particular phase of the negotiation in which they are used. In Exhibit 4, we combine these two perspectives to provide executives with descriptions of competitive, collaborative, and subordinative tactics across various phases of negotiation. We suggest that most negotiations go through four phases: (1) the search for an arena and agenda formulation, (2) the stating of demands and offers, (3) a narrowing of differences, and (4) final bargaining.[16] Not every negotiation will involve all of these phases. Rather, these phases characterize typical negotiations in mixed-motive situations. Hence, a specific phase may be skipped or never attained.[17]

For example, the search for an arena in which to carry out discussions may be unnecessary for some ongoing negotiations; however, most negotiations will initially involve some Phase 1 interaction about the items to be discussed. During the second phase, both the manager and the other party express their preferences and establish their commitments to specific issues and outcomes. The third phase may be skipped, although it usually occurs if the manager and the other party are far apart in their preferences and commitments. Both sides may add or delete bargaining items or shift preferences to avoid an impasse. The fourth phase completes the negotiation: The manager and the other party reduce their alternatives, making joint decisions about each item until a final agreement is reached.

Exhibit 4 should help managers recognize (1) how using certain tactics during various phases of a negotiation is essential to implementing their strategy and (2) how the tactics of the other party reflect a particular strategic intent. An unanticipated strategy implemented by the other party may indicate that the execu-

Exhibit 4
Using Tactics Across Negotiation Phases

Negotiation Phases	*Negotiation Tactics*		
	COMPETITIVE	COLLABORATIVE	SUBORDINATIVE
The Search for an Arena and Agenda Formulation	• Seek to conduct negotiations on manager's home ground	• Seek to conduct negotiations on neutral ground	• Seek to conduct negotiations on the other part's ground
	• Demand discussion of manager's agenda items; curtail discussion of other party's items	• Elicit the other party's agenda items and assert manager's items: incorporate both	• Elicit the other party's agenda items and subvert manager's items
	• Ignore or discount the other party's demands and requests	• Consider other part's demands and requests	• Concede to the other party's demands and requests
The Stating of Demands and Offers	• Insist other party make initial offers or demands on all times	• Alternate initial offers and demands on items with other party	• Make initial offers or demands on all other party-relevant items
	• Respond with very low offers or very high demands	• Respond with moderate offers or moderate demands	• Make high offers or low demands
	• Commit to each item; exaggerate manager's position and discredit other party's	• Indicate reasons for manager's commitment to item outcomes; probe the other party's reasons	• Accept the other part's commitment to items; explain manager's commitments
A Narrowing of Differences	• Demand that other party make concessions; back up demand with threats	• Seek equitable exchange of concessions with the other party	• Concede to the other party's demands
	• Delete, add, or yield only on low manager-interest items	• Delete, add, or yield items if mutual interests converge	• Delete, add, or yield to any party-relevant item
	• Magnify degree of manager's concessions; downplay other party's	• Honestly assess manager's and other party's concessions	• Acknowledge the other party's concessions; downplay manger's concessions
Final Bargaining	• Seek large concessions from the other party	• Seek equitable exchange of concessions from the other party	• Yield to the other party's relevant preferences by accepting low offers and making low demands
	• Concede only minimally on high manager-interest times	• Seek mutually beneficial outcomes when conceding or accepting concessions on items	
	• Use concession on low manager-interest items as bargaining chips		

tive inaccurately assessed the negotiation context or under- or over-estimated the strength of the other party's priorities. Hence, once the manager recognizes the other party's actual strategy, he or she should reassess the negotiation, repeating the process discussed in previous sections to check the appropriateness of his or her strategies.

Sometimes, however, the other party's use of an unanticipated strategy does not mean the executive's assessment of the negotiation context was inaccurate. In Exhibit 3, some combinations of the manager's and other party's pri-

orities result in the listing of two interactive strategies. Managers should normally use the first (left-hand) strategies in these listings. The secondary (right-hand) strategies are suggested as countermoves the executive should use if the other party uses a strategy different from the one expected, but the executive remains convinced that his or her diagnosis is accurate.

Reevaluating Negotiation Strategies

Take, for example, Peterson's appointment with the mechanic who had swapped a battery from a company truck with his own used battery. Going into the negotiation, Peterson decides that his unilateral strategy should be trusting collaboration: The mechanic is highly skilled and would be hard to replace, yet the infraction is a serious matter. He also anticipates that the employee will be interested primarily in retaining a good relationship with Dickerson's management. Hence, Peterson decides to stick with trusting collaboration as his interactive strategy (see Exhibit 3, Situation 3).

However, during the first five minutes of the meeting, Peterson's efforts to discuss returning the battery to the company and removing the infraction from the mechanic's personnel record are repeatedly rebuffed by the employee. Instead, the mechanic threatens to retire early from Dickerson and collect the benefits due him unless Peterson transfers him. Peterson recognizes that the mechanic is employing competitive tactics to set the agenda, which reflects an interest in substantive outcomes but little concern for relationship outcomes.

As the negotiation enters the next phase, Peterson considers the mechanic's apparent priorities and reevaluates his own priorities. Now neither the substantive nor the relationship outcomes are very important to him. He knows that Dickerson has no opening for the mechanic at any other shop; moreover, if the employee wants to leave, the relationship is of little value. Based on this reassessment (see Exhibit 3, Situation 14), Peterson sees that he has two interactive strategic options: He can regulate the matter (A3) by pressing criminal charges or compete firmly (P1) with the employee.

Rather than withdraw from the interaction, Peterson decides to compete firmly and tells the mechanic that unless the battery is returned, he will do everything he can legally do to prevent the mechanic from receiving optimal severance benefits. If the employee refuses to return the battery, Peterson can still request Dickerson's legal department to file criminal charges against him (A3) as a way to publicize and enforce a legitimate regulatory approach designed to help the company avoid this kind of negotiation.

Discussion

Most of the negotiation literature focuses on substantive outcomes without systematically considering the ways negotiations affect relationships. The approach we have taken underscores how negotiation strategies should address both parties' substantive and relationship priorities. Further, we encourage executives proactively to view negotiation as an indeterminate, reiterative, and often confusing process. It requires them to anticipate and monitor the other party's actions. The other party's tactics will inform managers as to whether their assumptions about the other party's priorities and strategy are correct. Based on this assessment, managers can modify their negotiation strategies as needed during current or future episodes.

Managers should heed, however, a few caveats about our advice:

1. Underlying the strategic choice model in Exhibit 3 is the assumption that most negotiations are of the mixed-motive sort; that is, the manager and other party usually negotiate over several substantive items. Some items have potential outcomes that can benefit both negotiators; others have potential outcomes that can benefit only one negotiator. Under these conditions, collaborative, competitive, and subordinative strategies may all come into play as the negotiators seek either win-win, win-lose, or yield-win substantive outcomes. Our emphasis in the model is on win-win substantive outcomes brought about through collaborative strategies (C1 and C2).

2. We assume that most relationships will involve some mixture of dependence and interdependence. Furthermore, we posit that most negotiators will view the relationship outcome as important when it is characterized by either high interdependence or high dependence. Collaborative strategies will strengthen the interdependence of the organization and the other party, subordinative strategies will increase the other party's dependence on the organization, and competitive strategies will decrease the organization's dependence on the other party. Our advice about negotiation strategies is directed particularly toward managers who want to enhance relationships of interdependence or

favorably shift the balance of dependence within a relationship.

3. We also recognize that the history and level of conflict between an organization and another party strongly influence each negotiator's attitude toward the existing relationship. Feelings of hostility, we assume, will be escalated by a competitive strategy; in contrast, feelings of hostility will be deemphasized by a subordinative strategy. Following this same logic, feelings of supportiveness will be enhanced by a collaborative strategy. Several of the strategies suggested in Figure 3—trusting collaboration, soft competition, open subordination, and passive and responsive avoidance—attempt to dampen hostilities and increase supportiveness between the manager and the other party.

4. Our advice to executives is simultaneously well-supported and speculative. On one hand, the classic (unilateral) strategies suggested in Exhibit 3 are fairly well supported within the negotiation literature; the link between these strategies and both relationship and substantive outcomes is the special focus of our approach. On the other hand, the effectiveness of the interactive strategies suggested in Exhibit 3 remains open to continuing empirical investigation. We have developed this interactive model of strategic choice by linking our concerns about relationship outcomes with what is currently known about the basic strategies of negotiation.

Although the three sets of assumptions we make about relationships are usually warranted in most organization-related negotiations, executives should carefully consider whether their situations fit with these constraints before using our strategic choice model (Exhibit 3). However, regardless of the situation, we believe that managers will generally be more effective negotiators when they carefully assess both (1) the relationship and the substantive aspects of any potential negotiation and (2) what is important to the other party and what is important to them. •

Footnotes

The authors wish to think the three anonymous Editorial Review Board members who reviewed an earlier draft of this article for their developmental critiques and constructive suggestions for improving the manuscript.

[1]The incidents reported in this vignette and throughout the article are based on actual experiences in a multi-state machinery servicing company.

[2]See H. Raiffa's *The Art and Science of Negotiation* (Cambridge, MA: Harvard University Press, 1982) for a discussion of how game theory can help negotiators maximize their substantive outcomes under a diverse set of situations.

[3]Both R. Fisher and W. Ury's *Getting to Yes: Negotiating Agreements Without Giving In* (Boston: Houghton-Mifflin, 1981) and A. C. Filley's "Some Normative Issues in Conflict Management" *(California Management Review,* 1978, 21(2), 61–65) treat win-win problem solving as a principled, collaborative process.

[4]See S. Bacharach and E. J. Lawler's *Power and Politics in Organizations: The Social Psychology of Conflict, Coalitions, and Bargaining* (San Francisco, CA: Jossey-Bass, 1980) for a recent discussion of mixed-motive negotiation situations.

[5]See L. Putnam and C. E. Wilson's "Communicative Strategies in Organizational Conflicts: Reliability and Validity of a Measurement Scale," in M. Burgoon's (Ed.) *Communication Yearbook 6* (Newbury Park, CA: Sage Publications, 1982) 629–652. See also R. A. Cosier and T. L. Ruble, "Research on Conflict-Handling Behavior: An Experimental Approach," *Academy of Management Journal,* 1981, 24, 816–831.

[6]Power as the ability to induce compliance is discussed in J. March and H. Simon's *Organizations* (New York: Wiley, 1958) and in P. Blau's *Exchange and Power in Social Life* (New York: Wiley, 1964). Two recent books discussing power from a material-resource perspective are H. Mintzberg's *Power In and Around Organizations* (Englewood Cliffs, NJ: Prentice-Hall, 1983), and J. Pfeffer's *Power in Organizations* (Marshfield, MA: Pitman, 1981). A. Giddens' *The Constitution of Society: Outline of the Theory of Structuration* (Berkeley: University of California Press, 1984) discusses power from a critical-theory perspective within the field of sociology, emphasizing how power involves control over human resources.

[7]For discussions of conflict intensity and durability, see I.R. Andrews and D. Tjosvold, "Conflict Management under Different Levels of Conflict Intensity," *Journal of Occupational Behavior,* 1983, 4, 223–228 and C. T. Brown, P. Yelsma, and P. W. Keller, "Communication-Conflict Predisposition:

Development of a Theory and an Instrument," *Human Relations,* 1981, 34, 1103–1117.

[8]See M. Deutsch's *The Resolution of Conflict* (New Haven: Yale University Press, 1973) for a discussion of how spiraling conflicts can be both inflamed and controlled.

[9]For further discussions of these basic strategies, see C. B. Derr's "Managing Organizational Conflict: Collaboration, Bargaining, and Power Approaches," *California Management Review,* 1978, 21, 76–82; Filley, Endnote 3; Fisher and Ury, Endnote 3; R. Johnston's "Negotiation Strategies: Different Strokes for Different Folks," in R. Lewicki and J. Litterer (Eds.), *Negotiation: Readings, Exercises, and Cases* (Homewood, IL: Richard D. Irwin, 1985) pp. 156–164; D. A. Lax and J. K. Sebenius, *The Manager as Negotiator: Bargaining for Cooperation and Competitive Gain* (New York: The Free Press, 1986); and D. G. Pruitt's "Strategic Choice in Negotiation," *American Behavioral Scientist,* 1983, 27, 167–194.

[10]For an overview of the contributions by these and other conflict-management researchers, see the special issue on "Communication and Conflict Styles in Organizations," L. L. Putnam (Ed.), *Management Communication Quarterly,* 1988, 1(3), 291–445. See also R. Blake and J. Mouton's "The Fifth Achievement," *Journal of Applied Behavioral Scientist,* 1970, 6 413–426; J. Hall's *Conflict Management Survey: A Survey of One's Characteristic Reaction to and Handling of Conflicts Between Himself and Others* (Conroe, TX: Teleometrics, 1986); and R. H. Kilmann and K. W. Thomas' "Interpersonal Conflict-Handling Behavior as Reflections of Jungian Personality Dimensions," *Psychological Reports,* 1975, 37, 971–980 and "Developing a Forced-Choice Measure of Conflict-Handling Behavior: The 'Mode' Instrument," *Educational & Psychological Measurement,* 1977, 37, 309–325.

[11]See Endnote 10 above; especially see Johnston.

[12]M.L.Knapp, L.L. Putnam, and L.J. Davis, "Measuring Interpersonal Conflict in Organizations: Where Do We Go From Here?" *Management Communication Quarterly,* 1988, 1, 414–429; Putnam and Wilson, Endnote 5; and J. Sullivan. R. B. Peterson, N. Kameda, and Shimada, "The Relationship Between Conflict Resolution Approaches and Trust—A Cross Cultural Study," *Academy of Management Journal,* 1981, 24, 803–815.

[13]We call these strategies interactive because they take into account the interactive effect of the manager's and the other party's anticipated or actual priorities concerning substantive and relationship outcomes. Interactive strategies based on anticipating the other party's priorities, as we later discuss in some length, may be changed to reflect more closely

the actual priorities of the other party, as revealed through the interaction during a negotiation episode.

[14]See Fisher and Ury, Endnote 3.

[15]See, for example, L. L. Cummings, D. L. Harnett, and O. J. Stevens, "Risk, Fate, Conciliation and Trust: An International Study of Attitudinal Differences Among Executives," *Academy of Management Journal,* 1971, 14, 285–304.

[16]Different researchers offer varying descriptions of negotiation phases. See L. Putnam's "Bargaining as Organizational Communication," in R. D. McPhee and P. K. Tompkins'(Eds.) *Organizational Communication: Traditional Themes and New Directions* (Beverly Hills, CA: Sage Publications, 1985) for a summary of this research. Ann Douglas proposed the first three-step model in "The Peaceful Settlement of Industrial and Intergroup Disputes," *Journal of Conflict Resolution,* 1957, 1, 69–81. However, this model and subsequent three-stage models do not consider the search for the arena as a component phase of a negotiation. P. Gulliver's *Disputes and Negotiations: A Cross-Cultural Perspective* (New York: Academic Press, 1979) proposes an eight-stage model of negotiation, remedying that oversight. Our proposed four-phase model condenses and draws extensively from Gulliver's work.

[17]Additionally, we view the phases of negotiation as conceptually separate from our notion of negotiation episodes (see Exhibit 1). All four phases may take place during one episode, particularly if the negotiation involves a single issue of low concern to one or another negotiator. On the other hand, during very complex negotiations stretching over a period of months, numerous episodes may constitute each phase.

*   *   *

Grant T. Savage (Ph.D., Ohio State University) is an assistant professor of management in the College of Business Administration at Texas Tech University and an assistant professor of health organization management in the Texas Tech School of Medicine. He began his research on negotiation while working as a third-party facilitator for the Quality of Work Life Program in the City of Columbus, Ohio. With additional research interests in health-care management, interpersonal and organizational communication, and leadership and small-group behavior, he has published articles in *Communication Monographs, Health Care Management Review, Hospital & Health Services Administration,* and the *International Journal of Small Group Research.* He is currently coauthoring, with David A. Bednar, a book on managerial communication for Praeger Publishers. He has also provided training and consultation for the New York City Cooperative Labor-Management Program, the U.S. Air Force's Civilian Comptroller Career Management Program, and the Center for Professional Development at Texas Tech University.

John D. Blair is a professor of management in the College of Business Administration at Texas Tech University and the associate chairman of the Department of Health Organization Management in the Texas Tech School of Medicine. His current research interests are in the turbulent environment facing health-care organizations and appropriate responses, including a strategic approach to negotiation. He has also written about the sociology of management as a scientific discipline. He is the coauthor of two books and author of numerous articles on the military organization. His latest book, with Myron Fottler, is *Stakeholder Management for Health Care Organizations* (Jossey-Bass). His most recent research appears in *Hospital & Health Services Administration*, *Health Care Management Review*, the *Journal of Management*, and the *National Journal of Sociology*. He was associate editor of the *Journal of Management* (1983–86) and founding coeditor of the *Yearly Review of Management* (1985–87).

Ritch L. Sorenson (Ph.D., Purdue University) is an associate professor of management in the College of Business Administration at Texas Tech University. His research interests include conflict management, leadership, and organizational communication. In addition to research on conflict management and negotiation, he is currently examining the relationship of individual leadership prototypes to organizational effectiveness and the relationship of situational variables and communication to leadership. He has published articles in *Human Communication Research*, *Communication Education*, and *Communication Quarterly*. An active trainer in management development, conflict management, managerial communication, and human relations, he has provided consultation to such organizations as Rockwell International, Preferred Risk Insurance Company, the U.S. Air Force's Civilian Comptroller Career Management Program, and the Center for Professional Development at Texas Tech University.

Study Questions

1. The authors advocate an approach to negotiation that takes into account the importance of developing or maintaining a future relationship with the other negotiator. What factors might make it difficult to accurately assess whether one will be interdependent with the other negotiator in the future?

2. How could you discover an opposing negotiator's priorities? What information or cues might you use to do so?

3. Exhibit 4 outlines negotiation phases and negotiation tactics. Is it possible to change negotiation tactics as you go from one negotiation phase to another? What factors might make it difficult to change tactics?

Exercise: El-Tek, Inc.

© 1994 M. Bazerman and J. Breet, Northwestern University

Materials to be obtained from your professor.

SECTION 5

Getting What You Want in Negotiations: Using Influence Tactics

Being influential is neither genetic nor a matter of luck. Rather, choosing appropriate tactics will increase the odds of being successful. Too often many of us are in the habit of using a limited range of tactics. With planning and increasing our repertoire of influence tactics, we can be more successful in negotiations than we imagined. However, becoming influential is a double-edged sword. We can readily satisfy our needs and desires by using influence tactics. Yet, being knowledgeable about influence technology presents us with ethical dilemmas. Thus, we need to consider emerging ethical issues while practicing our enhanced influence skills.

In their article about becoming an influential manager, "**How to Become an Influential Manager**," Keys and Case present us with a detailed and attractive perspective on using tactics other than direct authority or intimidation. The same tactic may have a different effect depending on who and where it is used. They present the steps necessary to develop and maintain influence at work.

In "**An Influence Perspective on Bargaining Within Organizations**," Kipnis and Schmidt describe the language of influence which includes the strategies and styles of influence that people use at work. They also describe the most frequently used influence strategies up, down, and around organizations. Finally, the authors identify the factors affecting the choice of influence strategies.

Jones ("**Flattery Will Get You Somewhere: Styles and Uses of Ingratiation**") shows us the forms of ingratiation and its uses. We learn that ingratiation tactics include other-enhancement, conformity, and self-presentation. The author describes how these tactics are used and their effects.

In her article "**But I'm Not a Funny Person: The Role of Humor in Dispute Resolution**," King reminds us that having a sense of humor may be an effective tactic. Breaking the tension of a conflict with humor can start successful dispute resolution.

Ethics of organizational life become a pressing issue because organizational politics are a natural part of our work lives. As such, we need ethical guidance in playing the organizational games. Cavanagh, Moberg, and Velasquez, in "**The Ethics of Organizational Politics**," propose a decision tree to evaluate the ethics of political behavior in organizations. They base their work on the ethical theories of utilitarianism, moral rights, and justice.

In "**When is it Legal to Lie in Negotiations?**" Shell outlines the elements of legal fraud. The difference between illegal and unethical may not be a meaningful distinction. Increasingly, the law is expanding to penalize unethical negotiating behavior.

With respect to the role of ethics in negotiation classes, Bulkeley ("**To Some at Harvard Telling Lies Becomes a Matter of Course**") describes how a Harvard Business School class simulates real world business negotiations. The article suggests that students may experience the efficacy of both honesty and lying in negotiation courses.

*　　*　　*

How To Become An Influential Manager

Bernard Keys
Thomas Case

Because of the increasing diversity of the goals and values of employees and their increasing interdependence, the effectiveness of formal authority is diminishing. It must be replaced with influence. In this article, we have summarized our research and that of others which have focused on managerial influence behaviors. Those tactics which are used most frequently and those which are most effective in having an impact on superiors, subordinates, and peers are discussed. Five steps which must be taken to develop and maintain managerial influence are outlined.

A hospital department head attempted in vain to persuade physicians working in a large metropolitan hospital to bring patient medical records up to date. Although doctors consider this an abhorrent chore, hospitals cannot begin the billing process until each record is completed and signed by the physician. After many frustrating attempts, the department head describes how he proved equal to the challenge.

Every month we served the doctors breakfast and lunch and organized games that would allow them to win prizes. Sometimes we would place balloons on a bulletin board and let them throw darts at the balloons. At other times we would do something ridiculously childlike such as hosting a watermelon seed spitting contest or playing pin the tail on the donkey. The sessions worked beautifully because the doctors knew that when they came in someone would be there to help them and they would even have a little fun. Once when we were really desperate we hired a popular entertainer. The room was full that day and we completed over 1,000 charts.

Influence is simply the process by which people successfully persuade others to follow their advice, suggestion, or order. It can be contrasted with power which is a personal or positional attribute that enables one to influence others and which can be thought of as "continuing or sustained" influence.[1] A number of popular books have suggested that influence must replace the use of formal authority in relationships with subordinates peers, outside contacts, and others on whom the job makes one dependent.[2] The writers of these books attribute the need for greater influence to the rapidity of change in organizations, the diversity of people, goals and values, increasing interdependence, and the diminishing acceptability of formal authority. Bennis and Nanus have suggested that leaders must empower themselves by empowering their subordinates. Kouzes and Posner agree with this conclusion, explaining that the more people believe they can influence and control the organization, the greater will be the effectiveness of the organization. Tichy and Devanna extend this thought even further by suggesting that today we need transformational leaders who will allow networks that funnel diverse views upward from the lower level of the organization where a need for change is often first detected. Similarly, John Kotter observes that the increasing diversity and interdependence of organizational role players is creating a "power gap" for managers who often have knowledge and good ideas for organizations but who have inadequate authority to implement their ideas.

For example, effectiveness with subordinates has been found to depend heavily on the ability to develop upward influence with superiors.[4] Influence with the boss often depends on the ability to accomplish things through one's subordinates.[5] Laterally, managers must spend time in group meetings, interorganizational negotiations, and in bids for departmental resources.[6] This is a role replete with power gaps. Most assuredly lateral relationships require the ability to influence without formal authority representatives with unions, customers, and government, or highly autonomous professionals such as the physicians in our introductory example.[7]

Reprinted from *Academy of Management Executive*, (No. 4, 1990), by permission of Academy of Management Publications, Ohio Northern University. All rights reserved.

Recently managers have begun to view leadership as the orchestration of relationships between several different interest groups—superiors, peers, and outsiders, as well as subordinates.[3] Effectiveness at leadership requires balance in terms of efforts spent in building relationships in these four directions. Good relationships in one direction can often be leveraged to obtain influence in another.

The concept of "linking groups" seems to drive the middle manager's work while both middle management and executive levels are heavily engaged in "coordinating" independent groups. In this latter role, they must persuade other organizational groups to provide information, products, resources needed, and negotiate working agreements with other groups. Additionally, executive levels of management must frequently maintain relationships with management-level vendors, consultants, and other boundary-spanning agents through outside meetings. Recent research suggests that the "ambassador role" of "representing one's staff" is vitally important to all levels of management. It consists of developing relationships with other work groups and negotiating for information and resources on behalf of the manager's own group.[8]

Building on the previous thoughts and the research of others, we conducted field studies to collect incidents, similar to the one describing the hospital department head, and used these to analyze how managers build and sustain influence. This article explains our research findings and those of related studies for managers who wish to become more influential with subordinates, superiors, peers, and other target groups.

Influence Tactic Research

Only a few writers have identified influence tactics from research investigations.[9] David Kipnis and his colleagues asked evening graduate students to describe an incident in which they actually succeeded in getting either their boss, a coworker, or a subordinate to do something they wanted. Their analysis revealed that the tactics of ingratiation (making the supervi-

sor feel important) and developing rational plans were the most frequently used methods to influence superiors. When attempting to influence subordinates, respondents most often used formal authority, training, and explanations. Only one tactic, that of requesting help, was frequently associated with influencing coworkers.

Our studies were aimed at strengthening the previous research. Since the studies cited above utilized categories of influence tactics derived from research with MBA students, we developed categories from influence incidents collected from practicing managers. Our three studies used trained students from several universities and structured interview forms to collect a wide geographic dispersion of responses.

Attempts were made to collect one successful incident and one unsuccessful incident from managers in a wide variety of both large and small businesses. One study focused on lateral influence processes, another on upward influence processes, and a third study examined downward influence. The primary question asked of each manager was, "Please think of a time when you successfully/unsuccessfully tried to influence a (superior, peer, or subordinate) toward the attainment of a personal, group, or organizational goal . . . Please tell exactly what happened."

Exhibit 1 presents the summary of findings from these studies.[10]

The numbers to the right of each tactic portray the rank order of the frequency with which influence tactics were reported for each target group.

Influencing Superiors

In influence attempts with superiors and peers, rational explanations were the most frequently used tactic. Often these techniques included the presentation of a complete plan, a comparative or quantitative analysis, or documentation of an idea or plan by way of survey, incidents, or interviews. In a few isolated cases, subordinates challenged their superiors' power, tried to manipulate them, bargained for influence, or threatened to quit. When these more assertive techniques were used, the subordinate was successful about 50 percent of the time—not very good odds for the risks which they were taking.

Exhibit 1
Rank of Frequency with Which Each Influence Tactic was Reported By Target Groups

	Boss	Peers	Subordinates
Presenting a rational explanation	1	1	3
Telling, arguing, or talking without support	2	0	0
Presenting a complete plan	3	0	0
Using persistence or repetition	4	0	0
Developing and showing support of others (employees, outsiders, etc.)	5	2	12
Using others as a platform to present ideas	6	0	0
Presenting an example of a parallel situation	7	3	5
Threatening	8	4	10
Offering to trade favors or concessions	9	5	0
Using manipulative techniques	10	6	7
Calling on formal authority and policies	0	8	6
Showing confidence and support	0	0	1
Delegating duties, guidelines, or goals	0	0	2
Listening, counseling, or soliciting ideas	0	0	4
Questioning, reviewing, or evaluating	0	0	9
Rewarding with status or salary	0	0	7
Developing friendship or trust	0	7	11

In most narratives we found that the subordinate using these methods had discovered a powerless boss, or had developed an unusual position of power themselves by becoming indispensable. In a few cases they had simply become frustrated and thrown caution to the wind.

Upward influence tactics were characterized by numerous supporting tactics such as mustering the support of a variety of other persons (both internal and external to the organization) or by choosing appropriate timing to approach the boss. Only two tactics appeared with significant enough frequency differential to be clearly distinguished as a successful or unsuc-cessful tactic. Subordinates using the tactic of "talking to or arguing with the boss without support" were more likely to fail. On the other hand, those who continued persistently or repeated an influence attempt continuously were likely to succeed. Caution is in order, however, in interpreting the use of persistence and repetition; this was usually a secondary tactic used in combination with others such as presenting facts and rational plans.

The rational persuasion technique was used by a plant manager to prevent a cutback in his work force when the army phased out one of its tanks.

First the plant manager sold a new product line to divisional staff who reported to his boss. In the meantime he developed a presentation in the form of a comparative analysis showing the pros and cons of taking on the new product line. Ideas presented included such things as the reduced burden on other products, risk reward factors, and good community relations from the layoff avoided. The presentation was polished, written on viewgraphs, and presented in person. The plant manager made certain that his technical staff would be at the meeting ready to answer any questions that might damage the strength of the presentation.

Not only did the plant manager succeed with this influence attempt, he felt that his boss and peers were easier to convince on subsequent attempts.

Influencing Subordinates

When dealing with subordinates, of course, the manager may simply tell an employee to do something. But our research suggests that managers who rely on formal authority alone are greatly limiting their options. The power gap noted earlier exists with subordinates as well as with other groups. Today more than ever, it must be filled with methods of influence other than authority. The following incident presents an interesting view of a furniture manufacturer trying to persuade his upholstery foreman to accept the position of plant superintendent.

The manager met with foreman Z in the foreman's office for short periods to talk about the promotion. Anticipating resistance, he covered small increments of the superintendent's responsibilities and allowed the foreman time to think about each session. The manager made sure that each session ended on a positive note. He pointed out that many tasks and skills required of the superintendent's job were already inherent in the foreman position. He downplayed the more complex responsibilities, relying on his commitment to future training to resolve these. Several such meetings took place in a five-day period. On one occasion the foreman alluded to resentment from fellow foremen. This prompted the manager to enlist the help of the other foremen— several hunting buddies, to talk favorably about Z taking the position. In the last meeting the manager outlined the responsibilities and cited the salary and prestige which accompanied the position.

As expected, managers often use the tactic of explaining (policies, tasks, benefits) or delegating assignments when attempting to influence subordinates. Frequently they showed confidence, encouragement, or support when trying to win subordinates over. The use of reason or facts often came in the form of a suggestion of a superior procedure or an example. Managers often counseled with subordinates or solicited their ideas to influence them.

The senior manager in this incident later commented that he had always had success at using this technique—that is, breaking down a complex influence task into incremental steps and attacking each step separately. While there is some merit to this process, most readers would agree that the major reason for success in this case was the persistence exerted by the senior manager to win in his influence attempt. The mild deception in over-simplifying the open position could merit criticism but must be moderated by the manager's willingness to train and support the foreman. In this case, the influence tactic had positive long-term consequences; the foreman became a very successful plant superintendent and later trained his own successor.

Frequently, subordinates were questioned, reviewed, evaluated, threatened, warned, reprimanded, or embarrassed to change their minds or to solicit compliance with plans of the superior. These more threatening and negative techniques were more frequently associated with failure than success. Occasionally subordinates were transferred or relocated to influence them, but usually with little success. The more assertive tactics were typically used in cases where subordinates were initially reluctant to comply with reasonable requests or had violated policies or procedures.

Influencing Peers

Only one tactic from our lateral influence study was noted significantly more often in successful influence attempts with peers—that of "developing and showing support of others." This tactic was most often used along with others and therefore represented a part of a multiple influence tactic. Often a peer in a staff department or a subordinate is used to support a proposal, as in the influence attempt described by a zone manager with a large tire and rubber company.

During this time I was managing 25 company-owned stores in which I initiated an effective program to control the handling of defective merchandise. I wanted to see the method utilized by the other store managers throughout the country who were supervised by other zone managers, but I felt that they would consider me to be intruding if I approached them directly. Therefore, I asked my store managers to tell the store managers in other zones about the sizeable savings to be had from the use of the method. The other store managers told their zone managers and soon they came to me for information about my program. The new program saved the company $90,000 per year, which increased our pay in bonuses at the end of the year.

When dealing with peers, managers made extensive use of rational facts or ideas. They often presented an example of another organization using their idea or proposal. Demonstrating that they had the support of others was a frequently used managerial influence tactic. Occasionally they threatened to go to higher level management or called on formal authority or policies to support their case. Assertive and manipulative tactics were used more often when attempting to influence the boss or subordinates, but less frequently with peers.

Influence Tactic Effectiveness

Our research on individual influence attempts somewhat simplifies the area of influence effectiveness. In the first place, the methods listed in Exhibit I are the ones that are most frequently used and not necessarily the ones which are most successful. In all three studies we found that techniques that succeed in some instances fail in others. The few exceptions to this finding are noted in Exhibit I when the ranks of tactics are underlined. These represent tactics that were reported significantly more often, for either successful or unsuccessful influence attempts. For example, unsuccessful influence attempts with the boss often consisted of simply telling the boss something, arguing, or presenting an idea or suggestion without support. While this technique occasionally succeeded, it was more likely to be

associated with unsuccessful episodes. Similarly, the use of persistence or repetition was reported more often in successful influence attempts with the boss than with unsuccessful ones.

Judging from the incidents collected, subordinate influence tactics of "threatening or questioning, reviewing, or evaluating" are significantly more likely to lead to failure than to success. Consider the experience of a plant operations manager attempting to introduce quality circles in an area to improve productivity.

The operations manager requested the assistance of the manager of organizational development, who warned that such implementation would take time, patience and the building of trust among his employees. Turnover in the operations area was high and negative attitudes tended to prevail. The operations manager became impatient, viewing QC as a quick fix for morale problems. The OD manager made available several persons who had worked successfully with a QC implementation, but after conversing with them the operations manager elected not to listen. He chose two subordinates to be trained as QC facilitators and immediately upon the completion of their training, began to implement QC. The operations manager and facilitators subtly coerced employees to join the circles and directed them toward the projects that management wanted attacked. After several months employee interest fell sharply and several complaints were filed with employee relations leading to abandonment of the project.

Contrast this occurrence with a less threatening attempt reported by a manufacturing manager in another part of the country:

The manager first read numerous articles about QC programs and learned the pitfalls to avoid. QC information handouts were given to the supervisors over a period of a couple of months. The supervisors were never pressured and gradually they approached their manager, asking how they could get quality circles started in their departments. The program was then implemented using recognized procedures and is still operating successfully several years later.

The analysis of influence attempts such as the quality circles incidents demonstrates the need for careful implementation of management processes.

Steps in Becoming an Influential Manager

Power, or sustained influence, may be accumulated and stored by a manager for future use. This allows one to call on existing strength to bolster influence tactics and often affects the future choice of influence tactic. Power may also be provided by the strategic position that one occupies in an organization, but position is often beyond the control of the incumbent. Fortunately, power may also be acquired through the development and exercise of certain skills by the manager within the organization. It is this skill-based power that we discuss throughout the rest of this article.[11]

Our research, and that of other writers reviewed in this article, indicates that there are five key steps to establishing sustained managerial influence.

- Develop a reputation as a knowledgeable person or an expert.
- Balance the time spent in each critical relationship according to the needs of the work rather than on the basis of habit or social preference.
- Develop a network of resource persons who can be called upon for assistance.
- Choose the correct combination of influence tactics for the objective and for the target to be influenced.
- Implement influence tactics with sensitivity, flexibility, and adequate levels of communication.

These steps in developing influence might be compared to the development of a "web of influence" (no negative implication intended). Unlike the web of a spider, the manager's web of influence can be mutually advantageous to all who interact within it. The web is anchored by a bridgeline of knowledge and expertise. The structure of the web is extended when invested time is converted into a network of resource persons who may be called upon for information and special assistance or support with an influence attempt. These persons—superiors, peers, subordinates, outside contacts, and others—might be thought of as spokes in the web. Establishing the web, however, does not insure influence attempts will be successful. An effective combination of influence tactics must be selected for each influence target and influence objective sought. Finally, the tactics chosen must be communicated well within the sector of the web targeted.

Our research suggests that the web of influence is continually in a state of construction. It is often broken or weakened by an ill-chosen influence attempt requiring patch-up work for a portion of the web. Some webs are constructed poorly, haphazardly or incompletely, like the tangled web of a common house spider, while others are constructed with a beautiful symmetrical pattern like the one of the orb weaver.

Develop a Reputation as an Expert

Of all the influence tactics mentioned by respondents in our interviews, the use of rational facts and explanations was the most commonly reported—although in isolation this method succeeded no more often than it failed. Managers who possess expert knowledge in a field and who continually build that knowledge base are in a position to convert successful attempts into sustained power. In the early stages of a career (or shortly after a move) power from expertise is usually tentative and fragile like the first strands of a web. Hampton and colleagues explain how expertise is extended to become sustained influence with the following example of Bill, a young staff specialist, hired to provide expertise to a number of production managers:

Initially, the only influence process available to the specialist is persuasion—gaining the rational agreement of the managers. To be effective he prepares elaborate, clear presentations (even rehearsing with a colleague to anticipate any questions). By data, logic, and argument, he attempts to gain the agreement of his superiors. After a year of this kind of relationship, he goes one day to talk with Barbara, one of the managers. An hour has been reserved for the presentation. He arrives and begins his pitch. After a couple of minutes, however, the busy manager interrupts: "I'm just too busy to go over this. We'll do whatever you want to do."[12]

But enhancing expert-based power involves publicizing one's expertise as well as acquiring it. For example, Kotter contrasts two 35-year-old vice presidents in a large research and development organization, who are considered equally bright and technically competent.

Close friends and associates claim the reason that Randley is so much more powerful is related to a number of tactics that he has used more than Kline has. Randley has published more scientific papers and managerial articles than Kline. Randley has been more selective in the assignments he has worked on, choosing those that are visible and that require his strong suits. He has given more speeches and presentations on projects that are his own achievements. And in meetings in general, he is allegedly forceful in areas where he has expertise and silent in those where he does not.[13]

Balance Time With Each Critical Relationship

Managers who desire to become influential must strike a reasonable balance in the investment of their time. In another study using a questionnaire, we surveyed managers from the United States, Korea, Hong Kong, and the Philippines to learn how they spent their time. These managers say that they spend about 10 percent of their time interacting with the boss, approximately 30 percent interacting with subordinates, and about 20 percent interacting with peers. As one might expect, the pattern of outside relations varies with the job (i.e., sales, engineering, etc.), but the managers report, on the average, spending from 15–20 percent of their time with external contacts. Time spent alone varies from 15–28 percent.[14] Although we cannot argue that this pattern is descriptive of all managers, it is similar to the pattern of communication distribution discovered from a sample of United States managers by Luthans and Larson.[15]

Some popular writers are calling for a heavy rescheduling of time and communications efforts.[16] Peters argues that 75 percent of a middle manager's time must be spent on horizontal relationships to speed up cross-functional communications in the middle of organizations. Johnson and Frostman see this kind of communication as being so critical that it must be mandated by upper level management. Peters emphasizes the argument that upper level managers spend too little time visiting with customers or in face-to-face relationships with subordinates (management by walking around). The

bottom line is that time should be spent where influence is most needed to accomplish organizational goals.[17]

During our seminars on influence over the years, managers have often told us that they failed to spend enough time with the boss or with peers, or in simply keeping up with organizational happenings. This may be due to the fact that many managers are uncomfortable spending time with those who have more formal power than they (superiors), or with those with whom they must compete (peers). Sayles believes that managers' uneasiness with peers grows out of the organizational difference in values across departments and work groups, the ambiguities which exist in cross-organizational relationships, and the conflict often generated in lateral relationships.[18] Other things being equal, realigning from a narrow focus on subordinates to a bigger picture which includes lateral and upward relationships can often yield a stronger web of sustained influence and should provide the supporting spokes needed to launch influence tactics.

A strong web of influence may even be quite desirable from the boss's viewpoint. Schilit found that managers who had been working for the same upper manager for a long period of time were quite capable of influencing that manager even on strategic issues facing the company. He concludes that: "[Managers] should be encouraged to be assertive in presenting their strategic thoughts because widespread strategic thinking may have a positive impact on their division or organization."[19]

Develop a Network of Resource Persons

Although managers do not use other people in most influence attempts, the more important attempts invariably involve others. For example, in the incident cited earlier about the furniture manufacturer who wanted a foreman to accept the plant manager's job, the assistance of other foremen (fishing buddies) was solicited. Similarly, in the case of the plant manager who tried to avoid a cutback in his work force after the phaseout of a military contract, the manager sold his idea to division staff and ensured that his own technical staff would be in attendance at the meeting in which he was making a presentation to the boss. The ability to establish and exploit a network is clearly demonstrated by a branch manager of a bank who used the following tactic with his superior, a vice president, when he found his operation in need of additional space.

My strategy was to convince my immediate superior that the current facilities were too small to not only handle the current volume of business, but too small to allow us to increase our share of the market in a rapidly growing area. First, I persuaded my superior to visit the branch more often, especially at times when the branch was particularly busy. I also solicited accounting's help to provide statistical reports on a regular basis that communicated the amount of overall growth in the area as well as the growth of our competitors. These reports showed that our market share was increasing. I then asked my superior to visit with me as I called on several customers and prospects in the area to let him know the type of potential business in the area. During this period of time, I kept pushing to increase all levels of business at the branch. Finally, I encouraged key customers in the bank to say favorable things about my branch when they visited with my senior managers. Eventually my superior got behind my proposal and we were able to build an addition to the building which allowed me to add several new employees.

Such influence attempts clearly illustrate the fact that many managers do not assume that achievement in traditional areas of management—selling, organizing, promoting customers—will inspire sufficient confidence by others. Rather than waiting for good publicity and resources to come to them, they seek them out through influence approaches built on carefully planned networks and persistent effort. The findings of our influence studies are supported by the observations of Luthans and his colleagues who concluded that managers who are both effective (have satisfied and committed subordinates and high performance in their units) and successful (receive relatively rapid promotions) strike a balanced approach between networking, human resource management communications, and traditional management activities.[20]

To some extent, networking activities may affect the positional strength of managers. The more contacts a manager has with others and the more independent the position relative to others, the more control the manager has over the flow of information. Positions that involve interaction with more influential managers of the organization or control information on which they rely, will typically be ones of power.[21]

Kaplan compares the strengthening of lateral relationships in the organization to the establishment of trade routes in international trade. According to this writer, managers, unlike countries which trade products, often trade power and the ability to get things done. Their goal is to build strong reciprocal relationships with other departments so that when the manager has immediate needs sufficient obligation exists to ensure fast cooperation. Often positions on the boundary of an organization can be especially influential. Consider the example referred to by Kaplan when describing a newly appointed manager of corporate employee relations. "I wanted a base that was different from what the groups reporting to me had and also from what my superiors had, so I established a series of contacts in other American industries until I knew on a first-name basis my counterpart at IBM, TRW, Proctor & Gamble, DuPont, and General Electric, and I could get their input—input which the people in my organization didn't have."[22] Kaplan suggests that networks of trading partners can be built by rotating jobs frequently, establishing strong friendships (and maintaining them), and seeking commonality with other managers, such as a shared work history.

Choose the Correct Combination of Influence Tactics

Influence tactics are the threads that complete a web, hold the spokes of the webbed network in place, and in turn are supported by the network. They must be chosen carefully on the basis of influence targets chosen and objectives sought.[23] One of the studies by Kipnis and colleagues found, as did we, that considerably more approaches were used to influence subordinates than were used to influence superiors or peers. Incidents in our studies suggested that most first influence attempts by managers involved soft approaches such as requests or reason, but later attempts included stronger tactics when the target of influence was reluctant to comply. This notion was confirmed statistically in the Kipnis study. Both superior and subordinate target groups in the Kipnis sample tended to use reason to sell ideas and friendliness to obtain favors. These authors also emphasize that influence tactics must vary with the target and objective of influence attempts: "only the most inflexible of managers can be expected to rely rigidly on a single strategy, say assertiveness, to achieve both personal and organizational objectives. It may be appropriate to 'insist' that one's boss pay more attention to cost overruns; it is less appropriate to 'insist' on time off for a game of golf."[24]

Taking a cue from the fact that few tactics were found to be associated more frequently with success than failure in any of our studies, we began to examine combinations of influence tactics. In each of the three influence studies (upward, downward, and lateral), managers who used a combination of approaches tended more often to be successful than managers who relied on a single tactic.

We noted that in many incidents short term success seemed to lead to enhanced influence in the long term, therefore, we sought ways to measure sustained influence over time. Consequently, in our downward influence study, we asked managers about the nature of the subordinate-superior relationship that occurred two months following an influence attempt. As we expected, successful influence attempts led the managers to perceive that their relationships had improved and to believe they had expanded their potential for future influence. For example, the bank branch manager, who was able to enlarge his building reported that because of his success with the influence attempt his profile at the bank was raised, that he was given a promotion and a raise, and that he was transferred to the main office.

Although we cannot be certain that the managers experiencing short-term influence success derived power with their boss from these episodes, the fact that managers believed this to be so caused them, in most cases, to plan additional influence attempts. These findings are supported by a study by Kipnis and his colleagues which found that managers who perceive that they have power are more likely to select assertive influ-

Complex and vital influence attempts, such as those required for major strategies or new projects, always require multiple influence tactics. A successful attempt is likely to begin with homework to gather facts, a citation of parallel examples (who is doing this?), a marshalling of support of others (perhaps insured by an effective web of influence), precise timing and packaging of a presentation, and, in the case of initial resistance, persistence and repetition over weeks or even months. Less frequently, but sometimes successfully, managers may resort to manipulation, threats, or pulling rank.[25]

ence tactics.[26] Failures at influence attempts may cause managers to plan fewer future attempts and to experience a period of weakened relationships with the boss. Frequently when a subordinate attempts to influence upper level management in a manner where his or her intention is clearly for the advantage of the organization, failure is not damaging to future influence. When the purpose of an influence attempt is clearly seen as a personal goal, failure may be more serious. Such a case was reported by a supervisor of security services dealing with a vice president of operations:

I wanted an assistant so that I could have some help in managing my department and would not have to handle petty problems of my employees. I tried to convince my boss that I was overworked since my staff has almost doubled and I was having a lot of people problems. I failed because I was just trying to make it easier on myself and wanted an assistant to do the job that I was supposed to be doing. I was also asking to increase the payroll of the company with no plans to increase revenue or profits. After my boss turned me down, I pouted for a few weeks and later learned that my boss thought I was immature. I then decided to forget about past disappointments and only worry about the future.

Communicate Influence Tactics Effectively

It is very difficult to separate influence tactic choice with the communications process itself. Cohen and Bradford stress the importance of knowing the world of potential allies—the needs, values, and organizational forces working on them. For example, they suggest that setting the stage for an influence attempt by wining and dining influence targets at a fancy restaurant may work well for a public relations director, but may appear to be a buy-out attempt when directed toward the head of engineering.[27]

Many of our research participants mentioned the importance of their presentation or their manner of approaching the target. Managers who choose rational ideas based on the needs of the target, wrap them with a blanket of humor or anecdotes, and cast them in the language of the person to be influenced, are much more likely to see their influence objective achieved.

Effective communications become interwoven coils of silk in the web of influence that help ensure the success of tactics. Consider for example the combination of influence tactics and communication used by Iococca in his turnaround strategy of Chrysler. Kotter capsules these as follows: "He developed a bold new vision of what Chrysler should be . . . he [then] attracted, held onto, and elicited cooperation and teamwork from a large network . . . labor leaders, a whole new management team, dealers, suppliers, some key government officials and many others. He did so by articulating his agenda in emotionally powerful ways ('Remember, folks, we have a responsibility to save 600,000 jobs'), by using the credibility and relationships he had developed after a long and highly successful career in the automotive business, by communicating the new strategies in an intellectually, powerful manner and in still other ways."[28]

Upward and lateral communications require more listening and more appreciation of the ideas and thoughts of others than dictated by subordinate relationships. Laborde suggests that a person who would master the communicator part of influence must see more and hear more than most people and must remain flexible to vary their behavior in response to what they see and hear.[29] Kaplan strongly emphasizes the importance of variation in the arsenal of communications skills—knowing when to meet with a person face-to-face, when to call group meetings, and when to use memos.[30]

Implications of Influence Research For Managers

No research is subtle enough to capture all of the relationships present between managers as they work together as peers, subordinates, and superiors. While incident- or questionnaire-type research may be subject to some self-report bias (if possible managers try to make themselves look rational to the researcher), observers, even if they could remain long enough in an area, could never capture and connect all of the thoughts necessary to precisely determine motives, processes, and outcomes of managers attempting to develop long-term influence relationships. We have attempted to capture some of the pieces, reviewed the best of what other experts have said about the subject, and tried to establish some connections. While recognizing these limitations, our influence research over the past ten years leads us to the following conclusions.

- Managers are continually in a state of building and extending webs of influence and repairing damaged threads. With every career change new webs must be built. In the early part of a career or after a career move, a manager must establish a web of influence by developing a reputation as an expert, balancing this with key influence targets, networking to establish resources, and selecting and communicating appropriate influence tactics.
- No one influence tactic can be isolated as being superior to others. Tactics must be chosen on the basis of the influence target and objective sought. For more important influence objectives, a combination of influence tactics will be necessary.
- Frequency of reported tactic usage suggests that most contemporary managers initially try positive techniques with targets, but will quickly resort to threats or manipulation if necessary, especially if the target is a subordinate.
- The variety of approaches used to influence subordinates is wider than suggested by the traditional leadership models and wider than the variety used in upward and lateral influence attempts.[31] This appears to be due not only to the additional power bases available

when dealing with subordinates, but also to the growing difficulty of obtaining subordinate compliance through traditional means.

- Contrary to traditional views that networking outside the hierarchy is disruptive, today's leaders must recognize the value of reciprocal influence relationships and must encourage them as long as they can be fruitfully directed toward organizational goals. Webs of influence may provide advantages for all involved.

- For these reasons, we are quite convinced that influential managers are ones who have developed and maintained a balanced web of relationships with the boss, subordinates, peers, and other key players; influence in each of these directions is banked for leverage to accomplish goals in the other directions. If knowledge alone and positional authority alone will not accomplish the manager's job, those who would be influential must fill power gaps with webs of influence. •

Notes

The authors appreciate the helpful suggestions to an earlier draft of this manuscript by W.J. Heisler, manager, Management Development and Salaried Employee Training, Newport News Shipbuilding, and Fred Luthans, George Holmes Professor of Management, University of Nebraska. We especially appreciate the work of the anonymous reviewers who assisted us with the paper. Thanks also to the professors who participated in original research studies: Robert Bell, Tennessee Tech University; Lloyd Dosier and Gene Murkinson of Georgia Southern University; Tom Miller and Coy Jones, Memphis State University; Kent Curran, University of North Carolina, Charlotte; and Alfred Edge, University of Hawaii.

[1]These definitions follow those of D.R. Hampton, C.E. Summer, and R.A. Webber, Chapter 3, *Organizational Behavior and the Practice of Management,* (Glenview, Illinois: Scott, Foresman, 1987), Fifth Edition.

[2]See Chapter 1 of A.R. Cohen and D.L. Bradford, *Influence Without Authority,* (New York: John Wiley, 1990). For a review of these thoughts, see W. Bennis and B. Nanus, *Leaders: The Strategies for Taking Charge,* (New York: Harper and Row, 1985) and J.M. Kouzes and B.Z. Posner, *The Leadership Challenge,* (San Francisco: Jossey-Bass, 1988). For a book that relates leadership influence to the way

in which change is implemented in the American economy, see N.M. Tichy and M.A. Devanna, *The Transformational Leader,* (New York: John Wiley & Sons, 1986). See also Chapter 2 of J.P. Kotter, *Power and Influence—Beyond Formal Authority,* (New York: The Free Press, 1985).

[3]For the review of literature and our conceptualization of an influence model, see J.B. Keys and R. Bell. "The Four Faces of the Fully Functioning Middle Manager." *California Management Review,* 24 (4), Summer 1982, 59–66; a condensed version of this article can be found in *World Executive's Digest,* 4 (7), 1983, 25–31.

[4]For the original research on the importance of upward influence to supervisory success, see D.C. Pelz, "Influence: Keys to Effective Leadership in the First Level Supervisor," *Personnel,* 29, 1959, 209–217. For a later discussion with case illustrations, see F. Bartolome and A. Laurent, "The Manager: Master and Servant of Power," *Harvard Business Review,* 64 (6), Nov/Dec. 1986, 77–81. The ways in which managers, especially middle managers, acquire and sustain upward influence are outlined in D.H. Kreger, "Functions and Problems of Middle Management," *Personnel Journal,* 49 (11), November 1970, 935; P.D. Couch, "Learning to Be a Middle Manager," *Business Horizons,* 22 (1), February 1979, 33–41; R.A. Webber, "Career Problems of Young Managers," *California Management Review,* 18 (4), Summer 1976, 19–33; H.E.R. Uyterhoeven, "General Managers in the Middle," *Harvard Business Review,* 50 (2), March–April 1972, 75–85. For an article that has become a best selling classic on the subject, see J.J. Gabarro and J.P. Kotter, "Managing Your Boss," *Harvard Business Review,* 58 (1), January–February, 1980, 92–100. For a recent article on maintaining loyalty and developing an initial relationship with the boss, see R. Vecchio, "Are You In or Out With The Boss," *Business Horizons,* 29 (6), November–December 1986, 76–78.

[5]For the review of the way in which managers create influence downward, see Uyterhoeven Endnote 4 and S.H. Ruello, "Transferring Managerial Concepts and Techniques to Operating Management," *Advanced Management Journal,* 38 (3), July 1973, 42–48. For a discussion of the importance of defending and supporting subordinates, see Bartolome and Laurent, Endnote 4.

[6]For a discussion of how managers develop political skills, see Ruello, Endnote 5 and Uyterhoeven, Endnote 4. To review the integrative role of middle managers, see J.L. Hall and J.K. Leidecker, "Lateral Relations: The Impact on the Modern Managerial Role," *Industrial Management,* June 1974, 3.

[7]For a discussion of external relationships, see D.W. Organ, "Linking Pins Between Organizations and Environment," *Business Horizons,* 14 (6). December 1971, 73–80.

[8]A.I. Kraut, P.R. Pedigo, D.D. McKenna, and M.D. Dunnette, "The Role of the Manager: What's Really Important in Different Management Jobs," *The Academy of Management Executive,* 3 (4), 286–293.

[9]For other studies on influence tactics see: D. Kipnis, S.M. Schmidt and I. Wilkinson, "Interorganizational Influence Tactics: Explorations in Getting One's Way," *Journal of Applied Psychology,* 65 (4), August 1980, 440–452. This study differed from our field study in that it surveyed evening MBA students and allowed them to describe any successful influence episode in which they had been involved. W.K. Schilit and E.A. Locke, "A Study of Upward Influence in Organizations," *Administrative Science Quarterly,* 1982, 27 (2), 304–316 found that Kipnis and Schmidt's fourteen tactic categories were not sufficient to categorize upward influence incident accounts collected from undergraduate and graduate business students and full-time employees or supervisors. They found evidence supporting the use of 20 types of upward influence tactics. Because these previous investigations relied so heavily on unchallenged global categories derived from a relatively small sample of evening MBA students which might not be representative of managers, we began our studies from scratch and collected narrative accounts of incidents from practicing managers. Each study focused on only one type of target and at least 250 influence tactics were collected. Flanagan's critical incident method was used to develop categories and to content analyze the responses. J.C. Flanagan, "Defining the Requirements of the Executive's Job," *Personnel,* 28, July, 1951, 28–35. Our findings for upward influence were more similar to those of Schilit and Locke than to those of Kipnis et al. Over 46 distinct tactics were observed across the three types of targets. Of course, tactics used to influence some targets are rarely, if ever, used to influence other types of targets. The description of managerial influence tactics which emerges from our three studies is much more detailed and therefore more suited to management applications than that provided by the previous investigations. Of equal importance, unlike the previous studies, our investigations also addressed the use of combinations of tactics vis a vis single tactics, and the long-term consequences of the influence attempt for the initiator and the organization.

[10]For a more complete description of the research methods and statistical findings of the three studies reported here, see J.B. Keys, T. Miller, T. Case, K. Cunan, and C. Jones, "Lateral Influence Tactics," *International Journal of Management,* 4 (3), 1987, 425–431; L. Dosier, T. Case, J.B. Keys, G. Murkinson, "Upward Influence Tactics," *Leadership and Organizational Development Journal,* 9 (4), 1988, 25–31; T. Case, J.B. Keys, and L. Dosier, "How Managers Influence Subordinates: A Study of Downward Influence Tactics," *Leadership and Organizational Development Journal,* 9 (5), 1988, 22–28.

[11]For an interesting theoretical discussion of these and other power producing factors see D. Mechanic, "Source of Power on Lower Participants in Complex Organizations," *Administrative Science Quarterly,* 7 (3), 1962, 349–364. For an excellent case study of how a middle manager combines expertise, networking and the other techniques noted see D. Izraeli, "The Middle Manager and the Tactics of Power Expansion: A Case Study." *Sloan Management Review*, 16 (2), 1975, 57–69.

[12]See Endnote 1, p. 35

[13]See Kotter in Endnote 2, p. 35.

[14]B. Keys, T. Case, and A. Edge, "A Cross-National Study of Differences Between Leadership Relationships of Managers in Hong Kong with those in the Philippines, Korea, and the United States," *International Journal of Management,* 6 (4), 1989, 390–404.

[15]For a look at the pattern of managerial communications and time investment see F. Luthans and J.K. Larson, "How Managers Really Communicate," *Human Relations,* 39 (2), 1986, 161–178.

[16]For a discussion of the need for middle managers to spend time in lateral and external relationships, see also T. Peters, *Thriving on Chaos: Handbook for a Management Revolution,* (New York: Harper & Row, 1987); T. Peters and N. Austin, *Passion for Excellence,* (New York: Random House, 1985); and L. Johnson and A.L. Frohman, "Identifying and Closing the Gap in the Middle of Organizations," *The Academy of Management Executive,* 3(2), 107–114.

[17]R.E. Kaplan, "Trade Routes: The Manager's Network of Relationships," *Organizational Dynamics,* 12 (4), 1984, 37–52 and J. Kotter, *The General Managers,* (New York: The Free Press, 1983).

[18]For an excellent guide to handling lateral relations complete with case illustrations, see Chapter 5 of L. Sayles, *Leadership: Managing in Real Organizations,* (New York: McGraw Hill), Second Edition.

[19]For a discussion of why managers should encourage their subordinates to influence them, see W.K. Schilit, "An Examination of Individual Differences as Moderators of Upward Influence Activity in Strategic Decisions," *Human Relations*, 30 (10), 1986, 948. The author's findings from this empirical

study lend support to the suggestions about transformational leaders by Tichy and Devanc and Kotter in Endnote 2.

[20]For a further discussion of the activities of successful and effective managers, see F. Luthans, R.M. Hodgetts, and S.A. Rosenkrantz, *Real Managers,* (Cambridge: Ballenger Publishing Company, 1988).

[21]For a review of network theory, see J. Blau and R. Alba, "Empowering Nets of Participation," *Administrative Science Quarterly,* 27, 1982, 363–379. See also Endnote 18.

[22]See Kaplan, Endnote 17 above.

[23]For an excellent treatment of the objectives and targets of influence, see D. Kipnis, S. Schmidt, C. Swaffin-Smith, and I. Wilkinson, "Patterns of Managerial Influence: Shotgun Managers, Tacticians, and By Standers," *Organizational Dynamics,* 12 (3), 1984, 58–67 and Kipnis, et al., 1980, Endnote 9 above. These studies and the Erez et al. study noted below also used a common questionnaire and a similar factor analysis to find broader categories of influence in which individual influence tactics (similar to those in exhibit 1) fall. The categories derived include: Reason: The use of facts & data to support logical arguments; Manipulation: The use of impression management, flattery, or ingratiation; Coalitions: Obtaining the support of other people in the organization; Bargaining: The use of negotiation and exchange of benefits or favors; Assertiveness: Demanding or acting in a forceful manner; Upward Appeal: Making an appeal to higher levels of management in the organization to back up requests; Sanctions: Threatening to withhold pay, advancement or to impose organizational discipline. M. Erez, R. Rim and I. Keider, "The Two Sides of the Tactics of Influence: Agent vs Target," *Journal of Occupational Psychology,* 59, 1986, 25–39.

[24]See D. Kipnis, et al, Endnote 23 above, p. 32.

[25]For a discussion of the use of manipulation as an influence, and/or managerial approach, see Erez, Endnote 23 above and A. Zalesnik, "The Leadership Gap," *The Academy of Management Executive*, 4 (1), 1990, 7–22.

[26]See D. Kipnis, et al, in Endnote 23, p. 32.

[27]A.R. Cohen and D.L. Bradford, "Influence Without Authority: The Use of Alliances, Reciprocity, and Exchange to Accomplish Work," *Organizational Dynamics* 24, 17 (3), 1989 5–17.

[28]J. P. Kotter, *The Leadership Factor,* (New York: The Free Press, 1988), 18.

[29]G. Laborde, *Influencing Integrity: Management Skills for Communication and Negotiation,* (Palo Alto: Syntony Publishing, 1987).

[30]See Endnote 17, above, p. 32.

[31]For a discussion of power and influence as a leadership approach, see G. Yukl, "Managerial Leadership: A Review of Theory and Research," *Journal of Management*, 15 (2), 1989, 251–289.

* * *

J. Bernard Keys is Callaway professor of business at Georgia Southern University and directs the Center for Business Simulation. His Ph.D. in Management is from the University of Oklahoma. He is the North American Editor of the **Journal of Management Development** and Co-Editor of **Executive Development**. In addition to his research on influence methods, he conducts research and serves as a consultant throughout the world in the design of customized executive development programs utilizing simulations. He is the author of six books including three business simulations. He is past chair of the Management Education and Development Division of the Academy of Management and vice president of Southern Management Association.

Thomas L. Case is currently an associate professor and acting head of the Department of Management at Georgia Southern University. He obtained a Ph.D. in social psychology at the University of Georgia and has attended both the basic and advanced MIS Faculty Development Institutes sponsored by the AACSB. In addition to managerial influence tactics, his main research and publications have been in the areas of organization development, R & D information systems, and program evaluation for supported employment and other services for developmentally disabled workers. He has been a member of the Academy of Management and Southern Management Association since 1982. He has been proceedings editor and is currently treasurer for the International Academy for Information Management (IAIM).

Study Questions

1. Define influence. How is it different from power?

2. What is the reasoning behind increased use of influence (vs. authority) in the workplace? Give examples.

3. What is the role/view of persistence with regard to upward and downward influence?

4. List the five key steps to establishing sustained managerial influence.

5. Explain the "web of influence" metaphor. What characterizes a strong web (network)?

6. What is the "bottom line" on how communication should be pursued in the organization? What percentage of time is spent NOT communicating with others? Describe who effective/successful managers are and what they do.

7. How are managers like international traders?

8. What communication skills are particularly critical when influencing others?

9. Review conclusions.

An Influence Perspective On Bargaining Within Organizations

David Kipnis
Stuart M. Schmidt

Empirical studies of bargaining typically focus on outcomes. This research tradition has usually examined the connection between bargaining contexts and the nature of outcomes, to the exclusion of the actual bargaining process. Yet as Kochan (1980) points out, there is a need to examine the behavioral process of bargaining rather than treating it as a "black box." The purpose of this chapter is to describe what happens inside this black box of the bargaining process. The specific focus is on the interpersonal tactical actions taken by managers when influencing superiors and subordinates.

While not necessarily labeled bargaining, these tactical actions, or influence attempts, occur on a daily basis. Whenever people seek to influence each other at work, there occurs, implicitly or explicitly, a process of negotiation. The process remains implicit if both parties agree with each other. However, this negotiating process becomes explicit when disagreement occurs.

Influence is exercised for a variety of reasons. Sometimes it is used to satisfy personal objectives such as securing benefits or better work assignments. Other times it is used reactively to prevent interference with one's own activities. Most often influence is used to pursue organizational objectives, as, for example, to encourage others to perform effectively, to promote new ideas, or to introduce new work procedures (Schmidt & Kipnis, 1982). Frequently, a combination of these personal and organizational reasons underlies the use of influence in organizations.

Within organizations, influence may be exercised in a variety of ways. These attempts include changes in the target's work environment (Kipnis & Cosentino, 1969), the use of

nonverbal behavior and symbols (Pfeffer, 1981), of behavior modification (Babb & Knopp, 1978), and direct verbal influence. This chapter focuses on three interrelated aspects of direct verbal influence among organizational participants. These are the range of influence strategies used by managers to influence both their superiors and subordinates, the parameters governing the use of the strategies, and the effects of using various strategies on subsequent interpersonal relations among the persons involved.

Previous Descriptions of Influence

Social scientists have been interested in developing a parsimonious system for classifying the various ways by which people attempt to influence others. The reason for this interest is that if we are to understand how influence is exercised and the consequences associated with its use, it is necessary to be able to classify forms of influence into meaningful categories. However, despite the many years of research on social influence, we know very little about how people actually exercise influence. Our most prevalent ideas about compliance-gaining behavior are based on armchair speculations that have been organized into rational classification schemes. Examples of such schemes include those based on the nature of controls (Etzioni, 1961), the amount of control and manipulation (Tedeschi, Schlenker, & Bonoma, 1973), or the bases of power (French & Raven, 1959), to name a few of the many current deductively derived classification schemes.

A number of problems with these deductive classification schemes have been noted. One problem, as Raven (1974) has observed, is not only that they overlap each other, but also that each has a different number of dimensions specified. For example, if influence tactics are derived from the French and Raven (1959) bases of power, five influence strategies will emerge: rewards, coercion, expertise, legitimacy, and charisma. Alternatively, if influence tactics are derived from Kelman's (1958) scheme, three influence strategies will result

Reprinted, by publisher's permission, from *Negotiating in Organizations* by M. Bazerman and R. Lewicki (Eds.). Copyright © 1983, Sage Publications, Inc., Newbury Park, CA.

based on the use of sanctions, personal charm, and credibility.

Another problem with many of the existing classification schemes is that they blur the distinction between "resources controlled," which provides the potential for exercising influence, and the actual influence tactics used. Due to the many problems with deductive classification schemes, recent studies of influence have adopted the methodology of first asking people in a given setting to describe the actual tactics that they use. With few exceptions (e.g., Cartwright, 1965; Dahl, 1957), the distinction between resources and influence strategies has not been made explicit. As a result, an assumption has developed that when the bases of power are known, the influence tactics are also known (see, for example, Tedeschi et al., 1973). It is assumed that threats are used when the base of power is coercive and that promises are used when the base of power is reward. This assumption may be incorrect. It may be that there is little relationship between the nature of the resources controlled and the tactics used. One possibility is that control of practically any resource needed by a target person provides an influencer with many options for behavior. Not only may users of sanctions promise and threaten, but they may also coax, hint, and argue as well. Perhaps control over many resources expands the range of influence tactics powerholders use, rather than simply dictates which tactics will be chosen.

Yet another problem with deductive classification schemes is that they are both deficient and excessive. When influence tactics are actually studied, it is found that people do not use all of the tactics described by the classification schemes. Not only that, but people use influence tactics not even mentioned in these schemes. This point was first revealed in a study by Goodchild, Quadrado, and Raven (1975), in which college students wrote brief essays on the topic, "How I got my way." Many of the influence tactics described by these students could not be easily classified into preexisting categories. Indeed, several influence tactics, such as the use of expert power, were not even mentioned.

Inductive Studies of Influence

These descriptions are then used to construct questionnaires that contain the influence tactics described by respondents. Factor analysis and other multidimensional analyses of these questionnaire data have found underlying structures that could not be deduced from existing classification schemes. In studies of interpersonal influence in nonorganizational settings, two or three dimensions of influence tend to emerge (Cody & McLaughlin, 1980; Falbo, 1977; Falbo & Peplau, 1980; Kipnis & Cohn, 1979). These dimensions involve using assertive tactics, rational tactics, and nondirective or manipulative tactics. Clearly, these dimensions differ from those that have been derived from deductive classifications of power (Student, 1968; Perreault & Miles, 1978).

The above methodology was also used by Kipnis, Schmidt, and Wilkinson (1980) to study managerial use of influence within organizations. In that study, managers described actual incidents in which they attempted to change the behavior of subordinates, peers, and superiors. Based on these descriptions, a questionnaire was constructed containing 58 influence tactics. Then, new groups of managers used the questionnaire to describe how frequently they used each tactic when attempting to influence their superiors, peers, or subordinates. Up to seven dimensions of influence were found, depending on the target of influence. Combining the results from the three target groups, seven influence strategies were isolated as shown in Table 1. A new scale, the Profile of Organizational Influence Strategies (POIS), was developed to measure these seven influence strategies (Kipnis & Schmidt, 1982).

Again it is apparent that the dimensions, or strategies of influence, in Table 1 differ from any that could be derived from existing classifications. As previously mentioned, for instance, influence tactics deduced from French and Raven's (1959) classification would use rewards, punishment, expertise, legitimacy, and charisma. Such a set of influence tactics would be both redundant in terms of the underlying factor structure, and deficient, because it would not contain strategies of coalitions, ingratiation, or appeals to higher authority.

In order to explore patterns of influence usage in organizations, a three-nation study of managerial influence was conducted. The POIS was administered to first- and second-line managers in England (N = 121), Australia (N = 126), and the United States (N = 113). In each country, two versions of the POIS scale allowed managers to indicate how frequently they used each of seven strategies to influence subordinates and superiors. Additionally respondents completed a supplemental questionnaire describing their work and attitudes toward their work situations.

TABLE 1
Strategies of Organizational Influence

Strategy	Behavior
Reason	This strategy involves the use of facts and data to support the development of a logical argument. Sample tactic: "I explained the reasons for my request."
Coalition	This strategy involves the mobilization of other people in the organization. Sample tactic: "I obtained the support of coworkers to back up my request."
Ingratiation	This strategy involves the use of impression management, flattery, and the creation of goodwill. Sample tactic: "I acted very humbly while making my request."
Bargaining	This strategy involves the use of negotiation through the exchange of benefits or favors. Sample tactic: "I offered an exchange (if you do this for me, I will do something for you)."
Assertiveness	This strategy involves the use of a direct and forceful approach. Sample tactic: "I demanded that he or she do what I requested."
Higher Authority	This strategy involves gaining the support of higher levels in the organization to back up requests. Sample tactic: "I obtained the informal support of higher-ups."
Sanctions	This strategy involves the use of organizationally derived rewards and punishments. Sample tactic: "I threatened to give him or her an unsatisfactory performance evaluation."

Most Frequently Used Strategies

It is reassuring to find great similarities among Australian, U.S. and English managers in how they exercise influence. Furthermore, in all three countries the frequency of using the influence strategies was virtually identical. When seeking to influence their superiors, managers reported that they relied most often on reason followed by coalition and then ingratiation. Going over the "boss's head" or resorting to higher authority was used least often to influence superiors.

The rank order of preferred strategies was somewhat different when influencing subordinates. Once again managers reported that the most frequently used strategy was reason. What was of interest however was that the second most popular strategy was assertiveness. While perhaps not surprising it confirms the common belief that managers can aggressively demand compliance from their subordinates but not from their superiors. These findings are shown in Table 2.

Factors Affecting the Choice of Influence Strategies

Having identified seven influence strategies the next question concerned the factors that affected their use. Why do managers demand compliance in one instance, plead in another and rationally argue in a third? Available research on this topic suggests that a complex of personal organizational and situational factors may determine which strategy is used. These factors include a manager's relative power, objectives for wanting to use influence and expectations of the willingness of targets to comply.

Power

Power enters into the selection of influence strategies in two ways. First, managers who control resources that are valued by others or who are perceived to be in positions of dominance use a greater variety of influence strategies than do those with less power. Second, managers with power use assertiveness with greater frequency than do those with less power.

1. **Variety of influence strategies.** Perhaps the most striking illustration of the variety of influ-

ence strategies used by managers with power can be found by examining how they influence superiors and subordinates. In all countries, managers use the following four strategies more frequently to influence subordinates than to influence superiors: assertiveness, ingratiation, bargaining, and higher authority. Only reason was used more frequently to influence superiors. While perhaps not too surprising, this finding indicates that managers apply substantial pressure on subordinates to comply because they potentially have a larger range of strategies available. Thus if one strategy does not gain compliance, pressure is maintained on subordinates through the use of an alternative strategy.

TABLE 2
Most to Least Popular Strategies Used in All Countries

	When Managers Influenced Superiors*	When Managers Influenced Subordinates
MOST POPULAR	Reason	Reason
	Coalition	Assertiveness
	Ingratiation	Ingratiation
	Bargaining	Coalition
	Assertivess	Bargaining
	Higher Authority	Higher Authority
LEAST POPULAR		Sanctions

*The strategy of sanctions is omitted in the scale that measures upward influence

---

Another example of this relationship between power and variety of influence strategies is found by comparing the approaches of managers who direct units of varying technological complexity. Hickson, Hinings, Lee, Scheneck, & Pennings (1971) and Perrow (1967) have pointed out that managers who supervise nonroutine technology are relatively powerful because other units depend on their expertise to solve important organizational problems. In comparison, managers who direct routine kinds

of work are generally taken for granted because the contributions of their units tend to be of less consequence. Consistent with this reasoning, we found that managers who directed nonroutine technologies used a greater variety of strategies when attempting to influence their superiors. In particular, they frequently used reason, assertiveness, and higher authority. It may be that managers of nonroutine technologies use reason because their work generates information and ideas that must be communicated, assertiveness because their control of uncertainty provides them with a base of power, and higher authority because they are less concerned with retaliation from their superiors.

2. **Assertiveness.** In addition to using a greater variety of influence strategies, managers who have power are more likely to invoke assertive and directive strategies. While the relationship between power and assertive tactics is hardly surprising, it is found with unceasing regularity within both organizations and general social relations. For example, it is reported in studies among children attempting to influence younger children, peers, and adults (Goldstein, Miller, Griffin, & Hasher, 1981), among lovers attempting to influence each other (Kipnis & Cohn, 1979), and among business organizations (Wilkinson & Kipnis, 1978). In all instances, those with more power (or resources) are likely to use directive tactics to influence others. We speculate that there is an "iron law of power" such that the greater the discrepancy in power between influencer and target, the greater the probability that more directive influence strategies will be used.

This does not necessarily mean that powerful managers use assertiveness as their first strategy. Given a choice, most managers initially seek to exert influence through simple requests and reason. Assertiveness is used when the target of influence refuses or appears reluctant to comply with a request. When such resistance is encountered, managers with power tend to use more directive strategies. Typically they shift from using simple requests to insisting that their demands be met. In contrast, managers without power are more likely to stop trying to influence when they encounter resistance or shift to other influence strategies such as coalition or ingratiation. This is because they feel the costs associated with assertiveness are unacceptable. For example, they may be unwilling to provoke the ill will of the target.

Objectives

Our findings clearly indicate that managers also vary their strategies in relation to their objectives. When managers seek benefits from a superior, they often use "soft" words, impression management, and the promotion of pleasant relationships—tactics measured by the strategy of ingratiation. In comparison, managers attempting to persuade their superiors to accept new ideas usually rely on the use of data, explanations, and logical arguments, that is, tactics measured by the strategy of reason. In addition, they are likely to use assertiveness to obtain organizational objectives but not personal objectives.

Similarly, this matching of strategies to objectives holds true when managers influence their subordinates. For example, reason is used to sell ideas to subordinates and ingratiation is used to obtain favors. As a general rule, the more reasons managers have for exercising influence, the greater will be the variety of strategies that they will use.

Expectations of Compliance

Managers also vary their strategies according to how successful they expect to be in influencing their target. Where past experience indicates a higher probability of success, managers use simple requests to gain compliance. In contrast, when success is less predictable, managers are increasingly tempted to use assertiveness and sanctions to achieve their objectives.

Lowered expectations for successful influence frequently are based on a realistic appraisal by managers of the targets' potential resistance. In other instances, however, managers' expectations are not based on reality. Thus, for example, the social psychological literature consistently reports that as individuals become increasingly dissimilar in terms of attitudes, race, sex, and social orientations, they expect that others will be less cooperative (Byrne & Griffitt, 1973). Given these lowered expecta-

tions, it is understandable that there are frequent complaints that managers use more assertiveness and sanctions with minority employees. This behavior may be attributed to managers' mistaken notion that reason will not yield compliance. Hence they feel that it is necessary to use more directive tactics.

Other personal variables that can distort expectations for successful influence include the degree of liking the target (Wartman & Linsenmeier, 1977), trusting the target (Deutsch & Krauss, 1962), and lacking self-confidence (Kipnis & Lane, 1962; Mowday, 1978). In all instances, these lowered expectations increase the probability that managers will shift from reason to assertiveness and sanctions in attempting to influence targets who they do not expect to be compliant.

Summary of Factors Affecting Choice of Influence

Integrating the findings presented in the preceding sections, we hypothesize that managers will use *assertiveness* when they have a predominance of power, their objectives are organizational (rather than personal), and their expectations about their ability to influence the target are low. Managers will use reason when the target and the manager approach equality in power, organizational objectives are sought, and they have high expectations about their abilities to exercise influence. Finally, ingratiation is most likely to be used when managers have less power than the target of influence, personal objectives are sought, and expectations of successful influence are low.

Combinations of Influence Strategies

Managers were found to vary the combination of influence strategies that they typically use. Cluster analyses of data from the Profile of Organizational Influence Strategies instrument indicated that managers in England, Australia, and the United States fall into the following three clusters of influence usage: *shotgun* managers, *tactician* managers, and *bystander* managers.

Shotgun Managers

This group of managers had higher scores on all seven influence strategies than did tactician or bystander managers. Shotgun managers, then, attempt to get their way by using the full range of influence strategies. One possible explanation for this behavior is that they want much from others and as a result have to try out different strategies.

To test this possibility, discriminant analysis was used to analyze the questionnaire data of all managers. This analysis indicated that shotgun managers reported having significantly more unfulfilled objectives in terms of ability to sell their ideas, obtain personal benefits, or get others to work more effectively. In addition, they are the ones in each country with the least organizational experience. In summary, shotgun managers are inexperienced, probably ambitious, and want much. To this end, they openly attempt to obtain what they want through the indiscriminant use of influence strategies.

Tactician Managers

This group of managers relied heavily on reason to influence others, though they had at least average scores on the remaining strategies. That is, tactician scores on the use of reason were as high as shotgun managers'. Their remaining strategy scores, however, were lower than shotgun managers but higher than bystanders. Tacticians, then, get their way primarily by using facts in logical arguments. The image portrayed here is that of rational organizational managers exercising organizational influence in a deliberate manner.

Discriminant analysis indicated several organizational and personal characteristics that distinguish tacticians from other managers. Perhaps most important is that they have power in their organizations. This was shown in several ways. First, tacticians manage work units that do technologically complex work. Their employees are skilled, and the work requires considerable planning before it can be carried out. As noted earlier, managers of "high tech" units should have power in their organizations. Our data confirmed this. Tacticians stated that they have considerable influence over such

matters as selling budgets, influencing company policy, and dealing with personnel matters. In general, they expressed satisfaction with their ability to perform their work.

In sum, it seems that tacticians are flexible in their use of influence, find their organizational objectives generally met, and rate themselves effective in carrying out their tasks. At the same time, they occupy positions of power based on their skills and knowledge, which allows them to influence others by relying mainly on the strategy of reason.

Bystander Managers

This group had the lowest scores on all seven influence strategies. They exercise little influence in their organizations, despite the fact that they occupy managerial positions. There are two alternative explanations for their inactivity. One alternative is that bystanders occupy such powerful positions in their organizations that others continually anticipate their needs. Hence, they do not have to exercise influence, because they get their way without effort. The other alternative explanation for their inactivity is that they lack power in their organizations. Therefore, bystanders feel it is futile even to try to influence them.

The results of the discriminant analysis support the second explanation. Bystanders are managers who direct organizational units that do mostly routine work. They also supervise the greatest number of subordinates, which is another indication of routinization. Given this kind of work, it is not surprising that they rate themselves as having little organizational power. They are unable to influence decisions about budget, personnel, and company policy. Further, in each country, the managers in this group are those who have been in the same job the longest.

In sum, our impression is that bystanders are managers who are marking time in mundane jobs and who see themselves as helpless, because they have little or no organizational impact. This interpretation is consistent with Seligman's (1975) description of "learned helplessness." This condition is produced by having little personal control over important life events. The result of this loss of control is that individuals stop wanting and stop trying.

Such inactivity was also shown by bystander managers. They no longer attempt to influence others in their organizations, either to obtain personal benefits or to achieve organizational objectives. Not surprisingly, as a group they express the least satisfaction with their abilities to work effectively.

Differential Consequences of Influence Strategies

The choice of strategies used in the influence process affects the influencer's perceptions of the target in predictable ways. Successful use of strategies such as sanctions or assertiveness increases an influencer's perception of control over the target. In such cases, compliance is attributed by influencers to their own demands and orders rather than to the free choice of the target. For instance, if a manager said to a subordinate, "I insist that you do what I say," and the subordinate subsequently complied, a reasonable inference by the manager is that the order caused compliance. Such an inference is less likely to be made if a manager said (and meant), "Here's what I would like you to do, but you decide for yourself." Compliance subsequent to this second tactic is more likely to be attributed by the manager to the subordinate's own decision to comply. In terms of attribution theory (Kelley, 1967), one consequence of using assertiveness and sanctions is that the target's behavior is perceived as externally rather than internally controlled. The use of reason and ingratiation are less likely to produce such attributions (Kipnis, 1976) because they allow target persons freedom to decide for themselves whether or not to comply. Another consequence of successfully using assertiveness and sanctions is that the target is less favorably evaluated. This is because the target is seen as externally controlled. To illustrate, in a recent experimental simulation of an organizational work experience (Kipnis, Schmidt, Price, & Stitt, 1981), subjects were appointed as leaders of small work groups and instructed to act as either authoritarian or democratic leaders. Authoritarian leaders were instructed to use assertive and directive tactics in which all decisions were made by themselves. Democratic leaders used reason and nondirective tactics. They also delegated deci-sion-making power to group members. At the end of the work session, autocratic leaders perceived group members as externally controlled. That is, they were less likely than democratic leaders to attribute group members' performance to "group members' own motivation to perform well." Further, authoritarian leaders evaluated the task performance of group members less favorably than democratic leaders did.

The apparent explanation for these less favorable evaluations is that the behavior of the target (workers), no matter how excellent, is seen as guided by the leader's orders rather than by the target's abilities and motivation. Hence the target is not given full credit for his or her performance. Evidence supporting this negative relationship between beliefs about control of the target's behavior and evaluations of the target are found consistently in field studies among dating and married couples (Kipnis, Castell, Gergen, & Mauch, 1976; Kipnis & Cohn, 1979) and in experimental studies of work groups (Kipnis, 1972; Kipnis et al., 1981). In all instances, the more a person perceived unilateral control over another, the greater the devaluation of the other.

Implications for Bargaining

The literature concerned with bargaining generally focuses on the outcomes of bargaining, the resources of the contending parties, and the social-psychological context in which bargaining occurs. Actual strategies of influence used in bargaining have, for the most part, been neglected. Emerging research suggests that this is an important omission, because tactical action is at the heart of bargaining (Bacharach & Lawler, 1981). Influence in bargaining is not limited to offers, threats, and inducements as is so often portrayed in the gaming literature (Chertkoff & Esser, 1976). At a methodological and substantive level, knowledge of the bargaining process would be strengthened by empirical studies of the variety of influence tactics that are actually used, as well as by analyses of their underlying structure (see Wall and Schiller, this volume).

In general, recent research (Kipnis et al., 1980; Mowday, 1978; Tedeschi et al., 1973) suggests that the choice of tactics will vary according to the objectives involved, the relative power of the contending parties, and their general expectations of the willingness of each other to comply. Other chapters in this book have also provided information about one or another of these variables. What we would like to stress is that these social psychological variables not only serve to guide the choice of tactics initially, but also guide subsequent forms of influence if the contending parties do not reach an immediate settlement. That is, there appear to be predictable shifts in the use of tactics that require study. Such shifts do not simply involve escalation, but also the use of coalitions, ingratiation and other strategies.

We also suggest that there may be important individual differences in styles of bargaining. Some negotiators may attempt to overwhelm their opponents by using all available influence strategies as was true of shotgun managers. Still others may rely mainly on reason. Still others may do very little (for instance, bystander managers). The implication of these variations in negotiating style for the bargaining process needs to be explored.

Finally, we suggest that the choice of influence strategies has predictable consequences for the process of bargaining over time. The use of assertive and directive strategies may cause long-term disruptions in social relations through their effects on a negotiator's attributions of control. In a general way, Deutsch (1969) spoke of these long-term effects in his discussions of destructive and productive conflicts. However, his work had not examined the long-range effects that are actually caused by the choice of influence strategies. An understanding of this contingency appears to depend on the development of a general taxonomy of influence strategies within the bargaining paradigm. •

References

Babb, H.W., & Knopp, D.G. Application of behavior modification in organizations: A review and critique. *Academy of Management Review,* 1978, 3, 281–292.

Bacharach, S. & Lawler, E.J. *Bargaining.* San Francisco: Jossey-Bass, 1981.

Byrne, D., & Griffitt, W. Interpersonal attraction. *Annual Review of Psychology,* 1973. 24, 317–336.

Cartwright, D. Influence, leadership, control. In J. March (Ed.), *Handbook of Organizations,* Chicago: Rand McNally, 1965.

Chertkoff, J.M. & Esser, J.K. A review of experiments in explicit bargaining. *Journal of Experimental Social Psychology,* 1976, 12, 464–486.

Cody, M.J. & McLaughlin, M.L. A multi-dimensional scaling of three sets of compliance-gaining strategies. *Communication Quarterly,* 1980, 1, 34–36.

Dahl, R. A. The concept of power. *Behavioral Science,* 1957, 2, 201–215.

Deutsch, M. Conflicts: Productive and destructive. *Journal of Social Issues,* 1969, 25, 7–41.

Deutsch, M. & Krauss, R. M. Studies of Interpersonal bargaining, *Journal of Conflict Resolution,* 1962, 6, 52–76.

Etzioni, A. *A comparative analysis of complex organizations.* New York: Free Press, 1961.

Falbo, T. Multidimensional scaling of power strategies. *Journal of Personality and Social Psychology,* 1977, 35, 537–547.

Falbo, T., & Peplau, L.A. Power strategies in intimate relations. *Journal of Personality and Social Psychology,* 1980, 38, 618–628.

French, J.R. P., Jr., & Raven, B. The bases of social power. In D.Cartwright (Ed.), *Studies in social power.* Ann Arbor: Institute for Social Research, University of Michigan, 1959.

Goldstein, D., Miller, K., Griffin, M., & Hasher, L. *Patterns of gesture and verbal communication in a tutorial task.* Unpublished manuscript, Department of Psychology, Temple University, 1981.

Goodchilds, J. D., Quadrado, C., & Raven, B. H. Paper presented at the meeting of the Western Psychological Association, Sacramento, California, 1974.

Hickson, D. J., Hinings, C. R., Lee, C. A., Scheneck, R. H., & Pennings, J. M. A strategic contingencies' theory of intraorganizational power. *Administrative Science Quarterly,* 1971, 16, 216–129.

Kelley, H. H. Attribution theory in social psychology. In D. Levine (Ed.), *Nebraska symposium on motivation.* Lincoln: University of Nebraska Press, 1967.

Kelman, H. C. Compliance, identification and internalization: Three processes of opinion change. *Journal of Conflict Resolution,* 1958, 2, 51 :60.

Kipnis, D. Does power corrupt? *Journal of Personality and Social Psychology,* 1972, 24, 33–41.

Kipnis, D. *The powerholders.* Chicago: University of Chicago Press, 1976.

Kipnis, D., Castell, P., Gergen, M., & Mauch, D., Metamorphic effects of power. *Journal of Applied Psychology,* 1976, 61, 127–135.

Kipnis, D. & Cohn, E.S. *Power and affection.* Paper presented at the meetings of the Eastern Psychological Association, Philadelphia, 1979.

Kipnis, D., & Cosentino, J. Use of leadership in industry. *Journal of Applied Psychology,* 1969, 53, 460–466.

Kipnis, D., & Lane, W.P. Self-confidence and leadership. *Journal of Applied Psychology,* 1962, 46, 291–295.

Kipnis, D., & Schmidt, S. M. *Profile of organizational influence strategies.* San Diego: University Associates, 1982.

Kipnis, D., Schmidt, S., Price, K., & Stitt, C. Why do I like thee: Is it your performance or my orders? *Journal of Applied Psychology,* 1981, 66. 324–328.

Kipnis, D., Schmidt, S. M., & Wilkinson, I. Intraorganizational influence tactics: Explorations in getting one's way. *Journal of Applied Psychology,* 1980, 65, 440–452.

Kochan, T. A. *Collective bargaining and industrial relations.* Homewood, IL: Irwin, 1980

Mowday, R. T. The exercise of upward influence in organizations. *Administrative Science Quarterly: 1978,* 23, 135–156.

Perreault, W. D. & Miles, R.H. Influence strategy mixes in complex organizations. *Administrative Science Quarterly,* 1978, 23, 86–98.

Perrow, C. A. A framework for the comparative analysis of organizations. *American Sociological Review,* 1967, 32, 194–204.

Pfeffer, J. *Power in organizations,* Boston: Pitman, 1981.

Raven, B.H. The comparative analysis of power and influence. In J. T. Tedeschi (Ed.), *Perspectives on social power.* Chicago: Aldine, 1974.

Schmidt, S. M., & Kipnis, D. *Managers' pursuit of individual and organizational goals.* Paper presented at the American Psychological Association National Meetings, Washington, 1982.

Seligman, M.E. *Helplessness.* San Francisco: Freeman, 1975.

Student, K. R. Supervisory Influence and workgroup performance. *Journal of Applied Psychology,* 1968, 52, 188–194.

Tedeschi, J. T., Schlenker, B.R., & Bonoma, T.V. *Conflict, power and games.* Chicago: Aldine, 1973.

Wilkinson, I., & Kipnis, D. Interfirm use of power. *Journal of Applied Psychology,* 1978, 63, 315–320.

Wortman, C.B. & Linsenmeier, J. A. Interpersonal attraction and techniques of ingratiation in organizational settings. In B. Staw & G. Salancik (Eds.), *New directions in organizational behavior.* Chicago: St. Clair Press, 1977.

Study Questions

1. For what purposes do we exercise influence?

2. Besides direct verbal influence, what other influence modes can be used?

3. How are control of resources and use of influence tactics potentially linked?

4. What are the first and second most used strategies when dealing with subordinates. Is this pattern consistent with English and Australian managers?

5. What tactic is least used in influencing superiors?

6. How are power and influence behaviors related?

7. Why do managers of nonroutine technology use more influence tactics?

8. What is the "iron law of power?"

9. What do managers without power often do when encountering resistance to influence? Why?

10. How are your objectives related to your influence behavior? What is the general rule of this relationship?

11. If my success at influencing is less predictable (from past experiences), which tactics are likely to be used?

12. Personal variables such as low degrees of similarity, liking, trusting, and self-confidence lead individuals to what type of influence strategies? Workplace implications?

13. Note the three hypotheses summarizing factors affecting influence choice.

14. Contrast characteristics and practices of shotgun, tactician, and bystander managers.

15. What perception of employees often follows compliance with assertive- (vs. reason-) based tactics? Implications?

Flattery Will Get You Somewhere

Styles and Uses of Ingratiation

Edward E. Jones

Dale Carnegie, author of *How to Win Friends and Influence People* was enraged at the implication that he would advocate using compliments just to get something out of people: "Great God Almighty!!! If we are so contemptibly selfish that we can't radiate a little happiness and pass on a bit of honest appreciation without trying to screw something out of the other person in return—if our souls are no bigger than sour crab apples, we shall meet with the failure we so richly deserve." The chapter containing this observation (entitled "How to Make People Like You Instantly") is composed of anecdotes describing precisely how complimenters *do* gain advantages. The message is clearly stated in other chapters as well: success in one's chosen line of work may be dramatically furthered by practicing the arts of ingratiation along the way.

Carnegie is not the only advocate of "applied human relations" who has had trouble distinguishing between the legitimate and illegitimate in social behavior. In certain business and political circles, for example, "sincere" is used as a synonym for agreeable. Self-serving flattery is usually deplored—but when does "honest appreciation" become flattery? Everyone likes a cooperative, agreeable attitude, but where is the line between manipulative conformity and self-effacing compromise? Many see great evil in ingratiation; Milton considered it hypocrisy, which he called "the only evil that walks invisible, except to God alone." Norman Vincent Peale, on the other hand, is much more tolerant; he considers pleasantness a mark of Christian virtue, from which peace of mind and prosperity flow naturally—and rightly.

Between these two extremes we find the charmingly honest Lord Chesterfield:

Vanity . . . is, perhaps, the most universal principle of human actions . . . if a man has a mind to be thought wiser, and a woman handsomer than they really are, their error is a comfortable one for themselves, and an innocent one with regard to other people; and I would rather make them my friends, by indulging them, than my enemies by endeavoring (in that to no purpose) to undeceive them.

Adlai Stevenson was also willing to counsel moderation with the remark, after being given a glowing introduction, "I have sometimes said that flattery is all right if you don't inhale."

What is custom and what is manipulation depends on time, place, the society, and often the individual. In those cultures where fulsome compliments are the norm, like the more traditional groups in Japan, anything less may be considered insulting. On the other hand, in many masculine circles in our own society praise is considered an affectation—a man who pays compliments easily will be thought untrustworthy or effeminate.

Most theories of social structure make the strong assumption that persons adjust their actions to what is generally accepted and expected. Ingratiation can be defined as impression-management which stretches or exploits these expectations or norms. Acts of ingratiation are designed to increase an individual's attractiveness beyond the value of what he really can offer to his target. Ingratiation is the illegitimate—the seamy—side of interpersonal communication.

Breaking the Social Contract

But how do we determine when behavior is "legitimate"? Relationships and associations involve, in normal circumstances, an unstated contract between the actors. Different authorities describe this contract in different ways. Sociologist Erving Goffman, in his book *The Presentation of Self in Everyday Life* emphasizes what he calls "ritual elements" in social interaction. Goffman believes that not only does communication take place in its usual sense but the communicators also engage in a "performance"—each transmits and receives clues about his definition of the situation, his view of himself, and his evaluation of the other. Mutual adjustment occurs. *Perhaps most important, the actors enter into a silent compact to help each other save face.* Each becomes involved in "facework"—give-and-take actions that smooth over potentially embarrassing threats, lend mutual support, and make for coherent and consistent performances. Each person has a "defensive orientation toward saving his own face and a protective orientation toward saving the other's face."

Within this frame of reference, the ingratiator may be seen as exploiting this contract while seeming to support it. He neither violates the contract openly, nor merely fulfills it. Rather, he keeps sending out reassuring signals that he accepts the terms of the contract: but all the while he is actually working toward other goals.

To put it in slightly different terms: while relying on his target to stick to the rule that each should get out of a relationship what he brings to it, the ingratiator deliberately violates the rule himself in hopes of gaining a one-sided advantage. By definition, ingratiation occurs when a person cannot or does not want to offer as much as he hopes to get from the other, so he tries to make his "offer" appear more valuable by fancy packaging, misrepresenting how much he brings to the relationship, or advertising the effort or cost involved in his contribution. For instance, the worker may apply himself with greatest industry when he expects the supervisor to appear momentarily, he may try to convince others that his job is more difficult than it really is, or attempt to convince his boss that it requires considerable experience or specialized education.

While the dependent member of a relationship has more to gain from successful ingratiation than the more powerful member, the latter may be also quite concerned about his image. It has often been noted that men rising in organizations tend to lose the spontaneity of old relationships and certainty about the loyalty and reliability of old colleagues. In spite of their increasing power, they are dependent on subordinates for signs of their own effectiveness and—perhaps as a way of hedging their bets—they will use ingratiating tactics to increase morale and performance.

Ingratiation raises important problems in human relations and self-knowledge. Much of our understanding of the world around us, and of ourselves, comes to us indirectly through the impressions we get from others. In particular, self-evaluation is to a large extent determined by how others judge us—personal qualities like friendliness, respectability, or moral worth can only be assessed by social means or mirrored in the reactions of others. Since ingratiation subverts this response, it is a threat to normal interaction and to reliable information. Like the traditional Hollywood producer and his yes-men, the executive surrounded by ingratiators may find himself adrift in a sea of uncertainties in which the only markers are the selfish interests of his advisers.

Ingratiation takes three general tactical forms.

Other-Enhancement. The ingratiator may try to elicit favorable reactions to himself by building up his target. At the extreme this involves obvious flattery, but there are also more subtle and indirect ways. The ingratiator may, for instance, concentrate on playing up the real strong points of the target, passing over or playing down the weak ones.

The ultimate design is to convince the target that the ingratiator thinks highly of him. We tend to like those who like us. Sometimes, however, the tactics are not simple or direct. The higher the target's regard for himself, the less he needs the ingratiator's praise, and the more he accepts it as obvious and routine. Targets may prefer praise, as Lord Chesterfield puts it, "upon those points where they wish to excel, and yet are doubtful whether they do or not . . . The late Sir Robert Walpole, who was certainly an able man, was little open to flattery upon that head . . . but his prevailing weakness was to be thought to have a polite and happy turn of gallantry of which he had undoubtedly less than any man living . . . (and) those who had any penetration—applied to it with success."

Conformity. People tend to like those whose values and beliefs appear similar to their own. Again, however, the relationship is not always direct. The ingratiator must seem sincere. His agreement must seem to be arrived at independently, for no ulterior purpose. The tactical conformer might be wise to disagree on non-essentials in order to underline the "independence" and value of his agreement on essentials. Agreement may be more valued if it seems to result from a change in opinion, made at some psychological cost, seeming to reflect a sincere change of conviction.

Self-Presentation is the explicit description or presentation of oneself in such a way as to become attractive to the target. This includes avoiding those characteristics the target might consider unpleasant, and subtly emphasizing those he might approve. The ingratiator walks a tightrope: he must boast without seeming to, since open boasting is frowned on in our society; he must "be" those things his target considers ideal for his situation, and yet appear sincere; he must seem admirable to the target and yet not a threat. He may have to ride a paradox—to be both self-enhancing and self-deprecating at the same time. This may not be difficult for someone with strong and obvious credentials—someone widely acknowledged to be the best in his field may gain by not mentioning it, and instead acknowledging his all-too-human failings. But those with dubious credentials must be more blatant in advertising their strengths.

In sum, in each of these classes the main problem of the ingratiator is to seem sincere and yet impressive and engaging. It is also better if his tactics and stated opinions support some pet but not universally admired or accepted ideas of the target.

Little research has been done on ingratiation. To carry the inspection of the subject beyond anecdote and intuition, we conducted a number of experiments in which college student subjects were given strong or weak incentives to make themselves attractive to a particular target. Sometimes targets knew that the ingratiators were dependent on them for benefits and therefore had selfish reasons to be attractive; sometimes they did not know. In other experiments, subjects were exposed to ingratiating overtures by others and their impressions of these others were assessed.

One experiment, designed to test ingratiation tactics in an organizational hierarchy, used as subjects seventy-nine male volunteers from the Naval ROTC unit at Duke University. Pairs of freshmen (low-status) and pairs of upperclassmen (high-status) were brought together in units of four. Each subject in the experimental condition (designed to promote ingratiation) was told that the purpose of the study was to find out if "compatible groups provide a better setting in which to test leadership potential than do incompatible groups." The experimenter's instructions continued: "For this reason I hope that you will make a special effort to gain (the other's) liking and respect, always remembering your position as commander (or subordinate)." With the remaining subjects, in the control condition, emphasis was on the importance of obtaining valid information: "We are not especially concerned with whether you end up liking each other or not. . . . We are interested only in how well you can do in reaching a clear impression of the other person."

Another experiment used fifty male volunteers from the introductory psychology course at the University of North Carolina in what was supposed to be a game designed to simulate a business situation. An experimental accomplice, presented as a graduate student from the School of Business Administration, was introduced as the "supervisor," conducting and scoring the games. Actually, the "business games" were used to discover and measure ingratiation tactics which might be used to gain advantage in comparable professional or business contexts.

From the results of the experiments thus far completed *there is no doubt that the average undergraduate behaves differently when he wants to be liked than when he wants only to be accurate in presenting himself socially.*

Specifically, let us break down the results in terms of the three major types of ingratiation tactics.

Self-Presentation. Generally, when instructed to try to make a good impression, our subjects played up their strong points and played down their weaknesses. (These varied according to the situation.) However, there were a few significant exceptions:

- In a status hierarchy, tactics vary according to the ingratiator's position. In the ROTC experiment, the lower-classmen usually inflated only those qualities they considered unimportant. Apparently they felt that to inflate the important qualities might make them seem pushy, and perhaps even threatening. Upper-classmen became more modest about all qualities. They felt secure, and their high status was obvious because of age and rank—therefore they did not feel it necessary to assert superiority. Modesty, we infer, helped them build up the impression of friendliness toward the lower ranks, which they considered desirable.

- Who and what the target is influences how the ingratiator describes himself. In the business games, those trying to impress the supervisor favorably emphasized their competence and respectability rather than their geniality. "Attractiveness" can, therefore, be sought by emphasizing what is more desired in a given situation—perhaps efficiency, perhaps compatibility, perhaps trustworthiness or integrity. If the ingratiator knows that the target is aware of his dependence, his tactics are apt to be subtle or devious. He may very well deprecate himself in those areas he does not consider important in order to build up his credibility in areas he does consider important. If, however, the ingratiator believes the target is innocent enough to accept him at face value, he will be tempted to pull out all stops.

Conformity. Perhaps the clearest research finding was that, to be successful, ingratiation must result in greater public agreement with the target's stated opinions. (Hamlet asked Polonius, "Do you see yonder cloud that's almost in the shape of a camel?" "By the mass, and 'tis like a camel, indeed." "Methinks it is like a weasel." "It is backed like a weasel." "Or like a whale?" "Very like a whale.")

Such conformity was true of both high-status and low-status students—with some significant differences. The low status freshmen conformed more on relevant than irrelevant items. Upper-classmen conformed more on the irrelevant than the relevant—presumably they were eager to appear good fellows, but not at the price of compromising any essential source of power or responsibility.

Further, as the business games showed, an ingratiator will cut the cloth of his agreement to fit the back of what is important to his target. If the target clearly values tact, cooperation, and getting along with others, the ingratiator will understand that the strategic use of agreement will probably result in personal advantage. Subjects were quick to reach this conclusion and to act on it, in contrast to their show of independence when the target appeared to be austerely concerned with the productivity of subordinates rather than the congeniality of their views.

When the ingratiator happens to agree closely with the target anyway, there is some evidence that too much agreement is deliberately avoided. Actually, agreement is almost never total. In most of the experimental cases of conformity, the ingratiator's final stated view was a compromise between his original opinion and that of his target. He might be described as avoiding extreme disagreement rather than seeking close agreement; nevertheless, the evidence is clear that expressed opinions are influenced by a desire to create a good impression.

Other-Enhancement. In this tactical area the results were quite inconclusive. There was some evidence that low-status subjects, after being instructed concerning the importance of compatibility with their superiors, were more complimentary than when operating under instructions to be accurate. High-status subjects did not show this same tendency to flatter more under conditions stressing compatibility. On the other hand, they were more inclined to view the low status complimenter as insincere in a final private judgment, when the instructions stressed compatibility. The low status subjects showed no such suspicions of their superiors.

The Bounds of vanity

Our experiments have answered a few questions and posed many more which may be profitably studied. Among the more important questions raised:

- Given the ethical barriers to deceit and social manipulation, what *are* the modes of rationalization or self-justification in ingratiation? How does the ingratiator keep his self-respect? Though our data consistently revealed differences between experimental (compatibility) and control (accuracy) conditions, we were unable to detect any intent to win favor, or the *conscious* adoption of attraction-gaining strategies.

- How are power differences affected by ingratiation tactics? Does ingratiation by the follower subvert or augment the power of the leader?
- How precisely do the distortions of ingratiation affect our perceptions of ourselves and others?
- What of the psychology of favor-giving as part of ingratiation? When does it help and when does it hurt the ingratiator? Is it possible that sometimes targets will like us more if we let *them* do favors for *us?* Why might this be so?

There remains the problem of defining ingratiation. Microscopic examination of ingratiating behavior keeps revealing an evanescent "something" that in any given case can be identified under more familiar headings such as: social conformity, deference to status, establishing credibility. It is my contention, however, that the concept of ingratiation links together various kinds of communicative acts that would otherwise be separately viewed and studied. By recognizing that there is a strategic side to social interaction, we open to examination the forms in which one person presents his "face" to another, when that other occupies an important position in his scheme of things.

Perhaps by acknowledging that ingratiation is part of the human condition, we may bring its facets into the light of day. As psychologists, if not as moralists, we may in this vein, admire Lord Chesterfield's candor:

Vanity is, perhaps, the most universal principle of human actions. . . . If my insatiable thirst for popularity, applause, and admiration made me do some silly things on the one hand, it made me, on the other hand, do almost all the right things that I did. . . . With the men I was a Proteus, and assumed every shape to please them all: among the gay, I was the gayest; among the grave, the gravest; and I never omitted the least attention to good breeding, to the least offices of friendship, that could either please or attach them to me. . . . •

Edward E. Jones is professor of psychology at Princeton University. This article was developed from Professor Jones' book, *Ingratiation*, published by Appleton-Century-Crofts.

Study Questions

1. Contrast ingratiation practices of businessmen in the U.S. and Japan (as noted in the article).

2. Explain the differences in the use of ingratiation by more and less powerful organizational members.

3. Describe the three general forms of ingratiation.

4. What was the "bottom line" finding of ingratiation studies?

But I'm Not a Funny Person . . .

The Use of Humor in Dispute Resolution

Karen N. King

One could argue that, with a serious situation like dispute resolution, one should always be serious. However, in the words of George Bernard Shaw, "Life does not cease to be funny when people die any more than it ceases to be serious when people laugh."

The use of humor during dispute resolution, whether the topic is family mediation, labor arbitration, public policy dispute settlements, or whatever can reduce tension, as well as create social cohesion among the parties. It can also encourage creativity, thereby resulting in other positive effects on the progress and outcome of the session. Learning to utilize humor as a positive strategy during dispute resolution will help the practitioner become a more skilled negotiator and, at the same time, enjoy the process more. Let's examine the functions that humor can serve in dispute resolution.

It is a generally held belief that humor is an excellent strategy for coping with stressful situations. In fact, having a good sense of humor is considered by many to be necessary for optimal mental health. Those individuals who are in stressful professions, such as a hospital's emergency room staff, or those who deal daily with tension producing situations (for instance, an alcoholic spouse), know the value of a good laugh or an amused chuckle. For example, "Stubs," a professional clown, is a member of the staff in the Big Apple Circus/Clown Care Unit at New York's Babies Hospital, where he uses humor to help young children cope with the stress related to chronic illness (Long, 1987).

The level of tension in a dispute resolution situation is typically high for both disputants and those committed to helping them bring about resolution to the conflict. This is espe-cially true when one or both sides appear to have taken a position from which they will not deviate. Using humor appropriately during a dispute resolution session can reduce the tension level of everyone involved and increase the possibility of a successful outcome.

I was mediating a consumer fraud case recently in which the plaintiff claimed that the defendant, a retail shop owner, had cheated him by charging $88 to repair a video camera while it was still on warranty. The retailer explained that the cost of repairing the machine was covered by the warranty, but that the fee for opening the machine to determine the problem was $88. Both sides were committed to their positions.

To encourage some forward movement, I asked if the vendor could think of any exceptions to this standard rule. He thought briefly and then told of a young mother who had brought her malfunctioning video camera in to be fixed and, when the salesman picked up the machine, out fell half a dozen marbles! I immediately asked, "What is the charge for shaking out marbles?" We all chuckled when the salesman responded, "No charge for shaking out marbles." This bit of light humor released a great deal of tension, and made the rest of the mediation run smoothly.

Another recognized function of humor is that of building social relationships. When one person shares a humorous observation with another, a feeling of closeness is created that tends to reduce the divisions that separate them.

As a mediator in a neighborhood dispute involving a barking dog, I listened as the two women disputants recounted the difficulties in being homeowners, family members, and employees. When I pointed out that they both shared the same concerns, one woman told a funny story concerning one of her children that made us all laugh. From that point on, the disputants shared humorous incidents about family matters, and the issue of the barking dog was resolved almost as an afterthought.

Humor that bonds individuals together in a dispute resolution setting increases the likelihood of a positive outcome. Bonding humor may occur between any of the participants or include the whole group. The negative aspect of this dynamic is that humor that creates bonds between several individuals can, in some situations, backfire. Everyone has been on the outside of an "inside joke" that presumes special knowledge or experience among those who share it and, deliberately or not, excludes others. Humor that includes some participants in the dispute resolution but excludes others is a negative influence.

Humor can also increase creativity. Psychologist Alice Isen proposes this function of humor in an intriguing study (Russo, 1987). She gave two similar volunteer groups the same problem to solve. Before they began, she showed one group a film on mathematics and the other one on TV bloopers. The results of the study indicated that 75% of those shown the funny film solved the problem, but only 20% of those who had viewed the math film came up with the correct answer. The outcome of this experiment suggests that humor that brings unrelated things together in surprising ways may help disputants and negotiators alike explore a variety of alternatives as they seek to develop an acceptable resolution.

Creating an agreement in a dispute situation that satisfies all parties demands a great deal of creativity on the part of everyone involved in a dispute resolution process. The greater the number of options offered, the greater the likelihood of a successful resolution. One of the most unusual solutions that I had a part in was one in which the plaintiff, who claimed that her neighbor's dog frightened her with his ferocious behavior, agreed to "meet" with the defendant's dog on a weekly basis so that they could "get to know each other." This solution was offered in a lighthearted manner but it became part of the final agreement because it met the needs of both of the parties involved by allowing the defendant to keep his dog and, at the same time, relieving the plaintiff of the anxiety she felt when the dog was around.

When humor is used to exert social control, it can be termed wit or sarcasm. The distinction between humor and wit is that humor is basically good-natured and directed toward oneself but wit is aggressive and almost always directed toward others (Nilsen, 1983). Wit may be considered the universal corrective for deviancy in the social order. Instead of using force to bring about acceptable behavior, wit communicates disapproval but, at the same time, allows people to save face and remain friends.

For example, women use wit to control the sexual behavior of their peers for the purpose, presumably, of protecting their own marriages and families. For one woman to label the clothing or behavior of a friend as being too "sexy" might jeopardize the friendship and invite greater deviation from the accepted norm. However, she might react to a friend who is wearing a skirt that is considered too short by saying "cute top." This witticism suggests disapproval but it also encourages conformity and maintains the friendship.

Any participant in a dispute resolution can employ wit to control the behavior of other participants. In a positive sense, the use of wit by a negotiator could encourage the appropriate use of the dispute resolution process while discouraging behavior that impedes it. Using the familiar "time out" hand signal when the situation has gotten out of hand is an excellent way to control behavior without appearing to be condemning.

One does not need to be a funny person or the "class clown" to utilize humor to aid the process of dispute resolution. The effective use of humor is a communication skill that can be learned like many others, such as active listening and artful questioning.

I call an approach I have designed for developing humor as a positive strategy during dispute resolution the "WRAP System." This model consists of four sequential steps: watch, risk, analyze, and persevere. By following these guidelines, I believe practitioners can develop a high degree of skill and, at the same time, learn to appreciate and share humor more.

The first step of the WRAP System is to watch for humor as it occurs naturally in social interaction situations, and observe the impact it has on others. After all, humor is all around us and to raise our awareness of it is to open a whole new world of observation. Ask yourself what kinds of humor elicit the most positive responses. In what kind of situations are people most receptive to humor? How do you know that people are sharing a humorous moment? What kills humor?

To become more aware of your style of humor, keep a file of cartoons and jokes that tickle your funny bone. What you select to include in your "humor book" tells a lot about you. In addition, you can thumb through your humor book when you are feeling discouraged or depressed and know you will find something that will lift your spirits.

Sitting in on dispute resolution sessions for the purpose of observing the role humor plays is an excellent way to increase your sensitivity to the ways humor can enhance, or retard, the process. Ask fellow negotiators to share how and when they use humor during dispute resolution.

Once you have an understanding of how humor functions in social situations, risk using it yourself, the second step of the WRAP System. How and when you will use it depends on the observations you have already made. Although using humor is always a risk because you do not know ahead of time how people will react, your chance of success will be greater if you have already "researched" it.

When you have had a success using humor, write the incident down and add it to your humor book. Tell someone else about your skillful use of humor during dispute resolution. And remember to reinforce others' use of humor.

When you have consciously made an attempt to use humor in dispute resolution sessions, ask yourself if you were successful. How did you know? If you felt that your attempt at humor was not well received, how did you know that? Was the timing wrong? The content? How would you do it differently if you could do it all over again? Ask a trusted and knowledgeable fellow negotiator to critique your use of humor.

Finally, keep on trying to improve your understanding and skillful use of humor. In other words, persevere. Each time you risk using humor and analyze its impact, you have increased your ability to use it for positive ends in a wide variety of social situations. Give yourself credit for expanding your repertoire of communication skills.

The WRAP System is a process to assist you in becoming more effective in using humor to enhance social interaction, specifically during dispute resolution, not to help you become a stand-up comic or the life of the party. Watching, risking, analyzing, and persevering are guidelines for developing the skillful use of humor. The what, when, and how of humor are a reflection of the user's unique way of looking at life and the world.

Is the use of humor always a suitable strategy for advancing the dispute resolution process? Of course not. When the level of hostility is high, the tension-reducing capability of humor disappears and its use will only increase anger.

The use of wit or sarcastic humor by one person to control the behavior of another may have a negative impact on the resolution and may, in fact, make a successful agreement impossible.

The skilled negotiator needs to recognize when humor is being misused and make efforts to control it. In some situations, ignoring the sarcastic remark and moving on to another topic is enough to demonstrate to the speaker the unsuitability of his or her use of humor. At other times, confronting the participant directly by saying something such as, "Your comment is inappropriate and interferes with the progress of this negotiation" maybe necessary. One experienced mediator I know has been known to cry "Foul" in a jocular tone when humor has gotten out of hand.

In conclusion, it is good to remember that humor is an important part of our lives: It makes the rough spots a bit smoother and adds zest to the joyful ones. Used wisely, it can enhance most social interchanges, including dispute resolution. Well known for his use of humor, President John F. Kennedy often gave silver mugs to special friends with these words engraved on them:

There are three things which are real:
God, human folly, and laughter.

The first two are beyond our comprehension
So we must do what we can with the third. •

References

Long, P. (1987). "Laugh and be well?" *Psychology Today* 21:28, 29.

Nilsen A. (1983). "Wit: an alternative to force." *Et Cetera* 40: 445–450.

Russo, C. (1987). "Laughter: a creative muse?" *Psychology Today 2:21.*

Study Questions

1. Is humor appropriate in dispute resolution? What are some advantageous functions of humor?

2. Contrast wit and humor.

3. What is a good way to use wit in negotiations?

4. Explain (briefly) the "WRAP" system.

5. When should humor NOT be used in dispute resolution?

Profiles of Organizational Influence Instrument

Influence Scale

Directions

1. There are twenty-seven statements in this scale. Each describes a different tactic that can be used to influence a manager.

2. For each tactic, describe how frequently you use the tactic as a FIRST attempt to influence your manager. Circle this answer. (see example below).

SAMPLE

Influence Tactics	How frequently do you use this tactic to influence your manager?				
	When you first try to influence your manager				
	Almost Always	Frequently	Occasionally	Seldom	Never
1. I point out to my manager the benefits of doing what I want.	5	4	3	(2*)	1

*This example indicates that the respondent seldom uses this tactic in an initial attempt to influence a manager (the number 2 corresponds to "seldom").

*   *   *

Survey Starts on the Next Page

Influence Tactics	How frequently do you use this tactic to influence your manager?				
	When you first try to influence your manager				
	Almost Always	Frequently	Occasionally	Seldom	Never
1. I obtain the support of my coworkers in persuading my manager to act on my request.	5	4	3	(2)	1
2. I make my manager feel important by noting that only he or she has the brains, talent, and experience to do what I want.	5	4	(3)	2	1
3. I write a detailed action plan for my manager to justify the ideas that I want to implement.	5	(4)	3	2	1
4. I set a date or time deadline for my manager to do what I want.	5	(4)	3	2	1
5. I offer an exchange in which I will do something that my manager wants if he or she will do what 1 want.	5	4	(3)	2	1
6. I act very humble and polite when making my request.	5	(4)	3	2	1
7. I appeal to higher management to put pressure on my manager.	5	4	3	2	(1)
8. I become a nuisance by continually bothering my manager in order to get what I want.	5	4	3	2	(1)
9. I remind my manager of how I have helped him or her in the past and imply that now I expect compliance with my request.	5	4	3	2	(1)
10. I file a report with higher management as a means of pressuring my manager to do what I want.	5	4	3	2	(1)
11. I go out of my way to make my manager feel good about me before asking him or her to do what I want.	5	4	(3)	2	1

Influence Tactics	Almost Always	Frequently	Occasionally	Seldom	Never
	How frequently do you use this tactic to influence your manager?				
	When you first try to influence your manager				
12. I request that my manager go to higher management to let it deal with the problem.	5	4	3	(2)	1
13. I sympathize with my manager about the added problems that my request could cause.	5	(4)	3	2	1
14. I repeatedly remind my manager of what I want.	5	4	3	(2)	1
15. I use logical arguments in order to convince my manager.	(5)	4	3	2	1
16. I provide my manager with a job-related exchange for his or doing what I want.	5	4	(3)	2	1
17. I wait until my manager appears to be in a receptive mood before asking him or her to do what I want.	5	(4)	3	2	1
18. I have a face-to-face confrontation with my manager in which I forcefully state what I want.	5	4	(3)	2	1
19. I act in a friendly manner toward my manager before making my request.	5	(4)	3	2	1
20. I present facts, figures and other information to my manager in support of my position.	(5)	4	3	2	1
21. I obtain the support and cooperation of my subordinates to back up my request.	5	4	3	(2)	1
22. I obtain the informal support of higher management to back me up.	5	4	3	(2)	1
23. I offer to make a personal sacrifice such as giving up my free time if my manager will do what I want.	5	(4)	3	2	1

Influence Tactics	How frequently do you use this tactic to influence your manager?				
	When you first try to influence your manager				
	Almost Always	Frequently	Occasionally	Seldom	Never
24. I point out to my manager that organizational rules require that he or she comply with my request.	5	4	3	2	(1)
25. I offer to help with my manager's work if he or she will do what I want.	5	(4)	3	2	1
26. I very carefully explain to my manager the reasons for my request.	(5)	4	3	2	1
27. I verbally express my anger to my manager in order to get what I want.	5	4	3	2	(1)

* * **E N D** * *

	HIGH	MED	LOW
FRIENDLINESS			
BARGAINING			
REASON			
ASSERTIVENESS			
HIGHER AUTHORITY			
COALITION			
(SANCTIONS)			

Scoring Key
Attempt to influence

The numbers that you have circled are to be transferred to the scoring key.

Do this by writing the numbers that you circled in the corresponding boxes on this page, i.e., place your answer (number) for item I in box 1. Next, place your answer for item 2 in box 2. Continue this procedure until all the numbers that you circled are entered on this page.

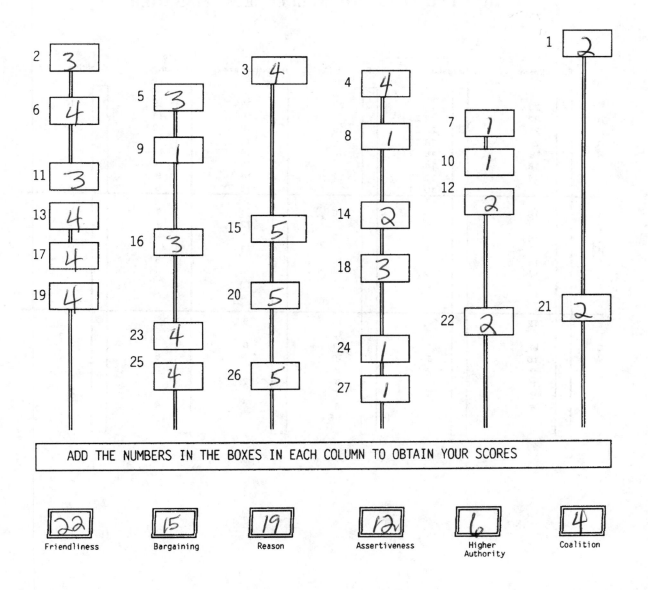

ADD THE NUMBERS IN THE BOXES IN EACH COLUMN TO OBTAIN YOUR SCORES

Friendliness	Bargaining	Reason	Assertiveness	Higher Authority	Coalition
22	15	19	12	6	4

Influencing Your Manager
Profile Sheet

Scores

Your column scores describe how you typically attempt to influence your manager.

This profile allows you to compare your scores to the scores of others who already have completed the **Influencing Your Manager** profile. A high score means that you use the strategy more frequently than 70 percent of those who were surveyed previously. A low score means that you use the strategy *less* frequently than 30 percent of those who were surveyed.

To obtain your profile: Fill in each column up to the level of your score as it appears on the Scoring Key.

HOW I FIRST TRY TO INFLUENCE MY MANAGER

	Friendliness	Bargaining	Reason	Assertiveness	Higher Authority	Coalition
H I G H	23 + 22 21 20 19 18 17	22-23 + 20-21 18-19 16-17 14-15 12-13 10-11	20 19 18 17	20 + 19 18 17 16 15 14 13	15 + 14 13 12 11 10 9 8	10 9 8 7 6
A V E R A G E	16 15 14	9 8 7	16 15 14	12 11 10	7 6	5 4
L O W	12 11 10 9 8 7 6	6 5	13 12 11 10 9 8 7 6 4-5	9 8 7 6	5 4	3 2

Interpretation of Influence Strategy Scores

Friendliness

Friendliness is the strategy of attempting to influence your manager by causing him or her to think well of you. There are a number of tactics that you use to accomplish this, such as "acting friendly" and "sensing your manager's mood before making a request." This strategy is designed to create a favorable impression of you so that your manager will be more inclined to do what you want. Your use of this influence strategy is based on your own personality, your interpersonal skills, and your sensitivity to the moods and attitudes of your manager.

A *high score* indicates that you use the creation of favorable impressions as a means to obtain what you want.

A *low score* indicates that you place little emphasis on trying to make your manager like you in order to influence him or her.

Uses: Friendliness is used most frequently as a strategy when you want personal favors from your manager, you want assistance from your manager with your work, or your power base is weak but you must convince your manager. However, overuse of this strategy could lead your manager to suspect your motives and your work competence.

Bargaining

Bargaining is attempting to influence your manager by means of negotiation and the exchange of benefits or favors. The tactics are based on the social norms of obligation and reciprocity. You remind your manager of past favors that you have done and/or you offer to make additional concessions in order to obtain what you want. In short, you rely on a trade. What you have to trade with your manager comes from two sources: your own time, effort, and skills and the organizational resources that you control.

A *high score* indicates that you attempt to get your way by offering to do something in exchange if your manager will do what you want. You remind your manager of past obligations and offer an exchange or tradeoff.

A *low score* indicates that you do not attempt to influence your manager by reminding him or her of past favors that you have done or by offering an exchange.

Uses: Bargaining involves making concessions in exchange for getting what you want. This strategy is used most frequently when you seek personal benefits from your manager. A drawback of this strategy is that you create obligations that you must fulfill in the future. What you trade might not be worth what you receive in exchange.

Reason

Reason is the strategy of attempting to influence your manager by relying on data and information to support your requests. It involves planning, preparation, and expertise on your part. It does not involve "shooting from the hip." Facts and logical arguments are used to convince your manager. Reason is the most popular strategy used in organizations to convince managers. The base of power here is your own knowledge and your ability to communicate this information to your manager.

A *high score* indicates that you try to persuade your manager on the basis of the objective merits of what you want. Additionally, a high score indicates that you avoid emotion and rely on reason.

A *low score* indicates that you rely less on logical arguments to convince your manager to do what you want. You tend not to use facts and figures or to explain to your manager the reasoning behind your requests.

Uses: Reason is used most frequently when you are selling ideas. If your job requires expertise, you most likely will find this strategy to be advantageous and effective. Its use is associated with acceptance of your objectives. One possible problem in using this strategy could be a failure to develop your ideas adequately and to organize your information logically. The use of reason requires preparation time, thought, and communication skills.

Assertiveness

Assertiveness as a strategy is an attempt to influence your manager by means of your forceful manner. It involves the use of demands, the setting of deadlines, and the expression of strong emotion. Assertiveness gives the impression that you are "in charge" and that you expect compliance with your wishes. At times, emotional displays of temper accompany this strategy.

A *high score* indicates that you use demands and direct requests. These may be accompanied by displays of anger and refusal to take "no" for an answer.

A *low score* indicates that you avoid tactics that your manager might view as insistent and demanding. You tend not to be forceful with your manager.

Uses: Assertiveness is a two-edged sword. It is useful when you know that you are right and you wish to improve organizational effectiveness. When used effectively, assertiveness may overcome your manager's resistance. However, when used ineffectively, it can create ill will. This strategy often is used as a backup strategy when your manager is reluctant to accept your ideas. Assertiveness can be used in combination with other influence strategies such as reason. It frequently is used when your duties require that you convince your manager of some course of action.

Higher Authority

Higher authority as a strategy of influence relies on the chain of command—people higher up in the organization who have power over your manager. This is an indirect means of influence; people other than yourself are used to influence your manager. This strategy is used in two ways. One is to appeal formally to the chain of command. The second is to ask higher management informally to deal with your request or to speak to your manager on your behalf.

A *high score* indicates that you call on higher management to help you handle your problems with your manager.

A *low score* indicates that you tend to avoid calling the attention of higher management to problems that you have in influencing your manager.

Uses: Higher authority is a backup strategy to be used when you know from experience that your manager will not agree to your request. This strategy is used for many different reasons. The problem that results from frequent reliance on this strategy is that it could undermine your relationship with your manager.

Coalition

Coalition is the strategy of mobilizing other people in the organization to assist you in influencing your manager. You operate on the basis that there is "power in numbers." If many people make the same request that you make, or argue for you, your manager is more likely to grant your request. Your power in using this strategy is based on your alliances with your coworkers and others in the organization. This is a complex strategy that requires substantial skill and effort to be effective.

A *high score* indicates that you use social pressure to gain compliance from your manager, i.e., you enlist the aid of others to help persuade your manager.

A *low score* indicates that you do not often attempt to form coaliations or alliances with others in order to back up your requests.

Uses: Coalitions frequently are used for both personal and organizational reasons. Coalitions can be used to obtain benefits and assistance with your job from your manager. The strategy also is useful in selling ideas to your manager. This can be a powerful strategy but it is not without danger. Overuse of coalition could create the impression that you are conspiring against your manager. •

Coalition Bargaining

Developed by Roy J. Lewicki

PURPOSE:

(1) To understand the different sources of power, or "leverage," that groups have in multiparty decision making.

(2) To observe the types of power and influence that are actually used, and their impact on others.

(3) To explore the dynamics of trust and cooperation in a strongly competitive situation.

ADVANCE PREPARATION:

None.

GROUP SIZE: Three teams of 3 to 10 members, approximately the same number of members on each team. Other class members may be used as observers.

TIME REQUIRED: 1-1/2 hours; may be divided into two class periods if necessary (see Instructor's Manual).

SPECIAL MATERIALS: None, unless real money is used.

SPECIAL PHYSICAL REQUIREMENTS: One or two other rooms, near the classroom, are useful for a "caucus" room for the team not directly involved in negotiations. Hallways may be used if necessary.

RELATED TOPICS: Negotiation and conflict, Managers as leaders, Organizational communication, Group decision making and problem solving, Organizational realities.

INTRODUCTION

A coalition may be loosely defined as a group of individuals, or subgroups, that assembles together to exert influence on one another. In an environment where there are many individuals, there are often many different points of view. Each individual views things differently, and each individual would like to have the "system" represent his views. In a dictatorship, the system usually represents the views of the dictator, but in a democratic environment, the views that are represented are usually those of a subgroup who have agreed to "work together" and collectively support one another's views in exchange for having a stronger impact on the system than each individual could have by himself.

Many of us are familiar with the work of coalitions. The patterns of influence in national politics and government provide us with some excellent examples. Whether it be the "coalitions" that are formed along traditional party lines—Democrats or Republicans—or along the concerns of special interest groups—Common Cause, Moral Majority, The Sierra Club, AFL-CIO, National Rifle Association, National Organization for Women, or hundreds of others—each group is attempting to influence the direction of the larger system by effectively pooling its resources, working together as a team, and persuading those who have control of the current system.

Coalitions are a common phenomenon in organizations as well. Most organizations are composed of a variety of different groups—Production, Sales, Research and Development, Accounting, and so on—who have different perspectives on the functioning of the organization, different views on the major problems and challenges to the organization, and hence different priorities on the policies and practices that the organization needs to adopt and follow. But these are not the only groups who exert pressure; other groups in the environment also make demands on organizations—employees, shareholders, customers, suppliers, and governmental agencies. Hence organizations are a complex

---

web of pressures among various subgroups, each one striving to have its own priorities adopted as the primary goals of the total organization.

This activity will help you understand, by either participating or observing negotiations between groups, how coalitions form and how they can exert influence. You will also observe what type of rewards various coalitions feel they deserve if they are successful at influence attempts.

PROCEDURE

Step 1: 5 Minutes

Form three teams with approximately an equal number of members on each team. Your group leader may assign you to a team, or this may be done randomly. Designate teams *A, B,* and *C*.

Each member should contribute $1.00 to the "stake" or "prize" for the game. (You may want to use "points" rather than real money. The group leader will announce this.)

Step 2: 10 Minutes

Read the following rules:

RULES OF THE GAME

Objective
To form a coalition with another team, in order to divide the stake. The coalition must also decide on a way of dividing the stake so as to satisfy both parties.

The Stake
Each team has *unequal* resources. In spite of the fact that you each contributed $1.00, you will receive a different stake, depending on the coalition you form. The following table should be filled in with information provided by the group leader (the individual payoffs are determined by the number of participants in the activity):

AB coalition will receive a stake of $_____
AC coalition will receive a stake of $_____
BC coalition will receive a stake of $_____

The Strategy
Each team will meet separately to develop a strategy before the negotiations. You should also select a negotiator.

Rules for Negotiation
1. All members on a team may be present for negotiations; however, only the negotiator may speak.
2. Notes may be passed to negotiators if desired.
3. A team may change its negotiator between conversations.
4. At the termination of the game, the stake will be allocated only if a coalition has been formed.
5. Only one formal coalition is permitted.
6. If no coalition is reached, no funds are allocated.
7. Negotiations will be conducted in the following fixed order, and for the following *fixed* periods of time:

Order of Negotiation	Time for First Round of Negotiation	Time for Second and Third Rounds of Negotiation
Team *A* and *B*	5 min.	3 min.
Team *A* and *C*	5 min.	3 min.
Team *B* and *C*	5 min.	3 min.

8. The team *not* in negotiations—that is, while the other two teams are negotiating—must leave the negotiation room.

Valid Coalitions
1. A coalition will be recognized by the group leader only if (a) no two teams are permitted to receive the same amount of money, and (b) neither team in the coalition is allowed to receive zero.

2. After negotiations, all three teams are given the opportunity to submit a written statement in the following form: "Team *X* has a coalition with Team *Y*, whereby Team *X* gets $9.00 and *Y* gets $3.00." When written statements meeting the above requirements from any two teams agree, a valid coalition has been formed.

Step 3: 10 Minutes

Meet in a separate area with your team to plan your strategy. During the strategy session, you will want to decide which team you might want to coalesce with, how you will want to decide which team you might want to coalesce with, how you might want to divide resources, what kind of offers the other team might make, and so on. You must also select a negotiator.

Step 4: 15 Minutes

Each pair of teams will report to the "negotiation area" for *five* minutes to conduct its discussions. Only the negotiators will speak, but other team members can be present and pass notes. At the end of each 5-minute block, the group leader will stop the negotiations and move to the next pair. The team *not* in negotiations on a particular round *must leave the negotiating room.*

Step 5: 20 Minutes

Each pair of teams reports to the negotiating area for 3-minute discussions for the *second* and *third* rounds (in the same sequence as above).

Step 6: 5 Minutes

The group leader will ask each team to meet separately, and to submit a ballot stating the coalition that they believe was formed. The ballot should be in the following format: "Team _____ has a coalition with Team _____, whereby Team _____ receives _____ (dollars or points) and Team _____ receives _____ (dollars or points)." Put your own team number on the ballot.

Each team brings its written statement to the negotiating room. The group leader will announce whether a valid coalition has been formed (two ballots agree); the money is then distributed as specified on the ballots. If a coalition has not been formed, or if the coalition that has formed does not use up all of the initial stake, a problem will arise as to what to do with the funds.

Step 7: 30 Minutes, Discussion

1. What was the initial strategy that each team decided on?
2. How were strategies influenced by the resources (dollars or points) that each team could contribute to a coalition?
3. How did the sequence of conversations between teams influence strategy?
4. How did the prior "reputation" of people on your own team, or the other team, affect your strategy?
5. Was your strategy modified after you had talked to the other teams? How?
6. How were strategic decisions made within your team?

7. How was the negotiator chosen? In looking back on the negotiations, did you make the right choice? Why or why not?
8. What did the negotiators do that encouraged or hurt the development of trust between teams?
9. Were negotiators ever changed? If so, for what reason?
10. What factors most influenced the ultimate settlement between teams? Do you think you could have predicted this earlier? Why?

GENERALIZATIONS AND CONCLUSIONS

In this activity, you observed how two important factors—the amount of "worth" to the final settlement, and the relative position in the order of negotiations—directly affected the view that each group took toward the division of the stake. In addition, you observed how the personal reputations, trustworthiness, and credibility of various group members affected the willingness of others to make deals with them. In organizations, the amount of power and influence that a particular subgroup or constituency may have on overall goals and policy will also be determined by these same three factors. First, the relative "resource power" that the group possesses (e.g., how much the group contributes to the organization's final product) will affect its amount of influence. Second, the "strategic position" that a group occupies (e.g., whether it has final veto power or whether it can disrupt others from accomplishing goals) will determine whether a group uses its power to enhance its own goals, or to impede others from achieving their goals. Finally, individuals within an organization clearly differ in their personal reputations and in their ability to influence others toward their point of view; the better the reputation and the skills, the more likely it will be that these individuals will be successful in achieving their objectives.

Participant's Reactions

READINGS AND REFERENCES

Caplow, T., *Two Against One* (Englewood Cliffs, NJ.: Prentice Hall, 1968).
Cyert, R. M., and J. G. March, *A Behavioral Theory of the Firm* (Englewood Cliffs, NJ.: Prentice Hall, 1963).
Pfeffer, Jeffrey, and Salancik, G. E., "Organization Design: The Case for a Coalitional Model of Organizations," *Organizational Dynamics,* Autumn (1977), 15–29,
Weick, K., "Educational Organizations as Loosely Coupled Systems," *Administrative Science Quarterly,* March (1976), 1–19.

The Ethics of Organizational Politics

Gerald F. Cavanagh
Dennis J. Moberg
Manuel Velasquez

Political uses of power demand explicit consideration of ethical restraints, in part because current management theory focuses on the value of outcomes rather than on the value of the means chosen. We have developed a normative model of ethical analysis that can be helpful in determining what these restraints are. The model integrates three kinds of ethical theories: utilitarianism, theories of moral rights, and theories of justice.

Power is the cornerstone of both management theory and management practice. Few concepts are more fundamental to the study of organizations, and power is a vital and ubiquitous reality in organizational life [Dahl, 1957; Zald, 1970; Zalesnik, 1970]. Our primary purpose here is to develop a framework for evaluating the ethical quality of certain uses of power within organizations. We will first distinguish political from nonpolitical uses of power and then canvass the literature of normative ethics in order to construct a model of ethical analysis that can be applied to political uses of power in organizations.

Organizational Politics

The contemporary view of power in organizations is that it is the ability to mobilize resources, energy, and information on behalf of a preferred goal or strategy [Tushman, 1977]. Thus, power is assumed to exist only when there is conflict over means or ends [Drake, 1979; Pfeffer, 1977]. More specifically, this view of power is based on two fundamental propositions:

1. Organizations are composed of individuals and coalitions that compete over resources, energy, information, and influence [Hickson, Hinings, Lee, Schneck, & Pennings, 1971; Thompson, 1967].

2. Individuals and coalitions seek to protect their interests through means that are unobtrusive when compared to existing controls, norms, and sanctions [Allen, Madison, Porter, Renwick, & Mayes, 1979; Pfeffer & Salancik, 1974].

This perspective has led some authors to distinguish between political and nonpolitical uses of power [Gandz & Murray, 1980]. For example, Mayes and Allen [1977] draw the distinction in terms of organizational sanctions: nonpolitical uses of power are those that involve sanctioned means for sanctioned ends, and political uses involve unsanctioned means, or sanctioned means for unsanctioned ends. That is, when individuals and coalitions choose to move outside of their formal authority, established policies and procedures, or job descriptions in their use of power, that use is political. When they use power within these sanctions for ends that are not formally sanctioned through goal statements, this too is a political use of power, according to the Mayes and Allen definition.

Unlike more encompassing conceptualizations that equate politics with *any* use of power [e.g., Martin & Sims, 1956], *the Mayes and Allen definition underlines the discretionary nature of organizational politics*. In spite of formal systems designed to control the use of power, organizational members can and do exercise political power to influence their subordinates, peers, superiors, and others [Schein, 1977]. And coalitions may employ politics in their reaction to policy changes that threaten their own interests [Crozier, 1964; Pettigrew, 1973].

When individuals and coalitions move outside normal sanctions, the traditional authority/responsibility linkage is broken, and important ethical issues emerge. However, current treatments of organizational politics either beg the ethical issues entirely [e.g., Kotter, 1977] or offer simplistic ethical criteria. For example, Miles asserts that "it is . . . important to

Reprinted from *Academy of Management Review,* No. 3, 1981, by permission of Academy of Management Publications, Ohio Northern University. All rights reserved.

recognize that politics need not be bad, though common parlance uses the term in a pejorative sense. The survival of an organization may depend on the success of a unit or coalition in overturning a traditional but outdated formal organization objective or policy" [1980, p. 155]. However, there are a host of political actions that may be justified in the name of organizational survival that many would find morally repugnant. Among these are such Machiavellian techniques as "situational manipulation," "dirty tricks," and "backstabbing."

There is, then, a clear need for a normative theory of organizational politics that addresses ethical issues directly and from the standpoint of the exercise of discretion. Unfortunately, the business and society literature, where one might expect to find such issues discussed, offers little guidance in this regard. The emphasis in this literature is on institutional interactions (e.g., government regulations) and on broad human resource policy issues (e.g. affirmative action), and not on the day-to-day political decisions made in the organization.

Discussions of political tactics in the management literature also offer little guidance. The literature is, of course, rich with political guidelines: there are leadership theories, lateral relations prescriptions, notions about how to design and implement reward and control systems, conflict resolution strategies, and the like, all of which provide fodder for the development of political behavior alternatives (hereinafter PBA). However, the form of these theoretical notions tends to reduce decisions to *calculations based on effect*—that is, they provide the manager with an understanding and predication of what PBAs are likely to evoke in terms of an outcome or set of outcomes. Armed with contemporary leadership theories, for example, managers can presumably determine the type of face-to-face direction that will result in the desired level of performance and satisfaction. This calculative emphasis defines theoretical debate over ethics in terms of the desirability of outcomes and tends to ignore the value of the activities, processes, and behaviors involved, independent of the outcomes achieved. What a manager should do is thus determined by the desirability of the outcomes

and not by the quality of the behaviors themselves. Such an emphasis inevitably leads to a kind of ends-justify-the-means logic that fails to provide guidance for managers beyond linking alternatives to outcomes. Consider the following case.

Lorna is the production manager of a noncohesive work group responsible for meeting a deadline that will require coordinated effort among her subordinates. Believing that the members of the work group will pull together and meet the deadline if they have a little competition, Lorna decides in favor of a PBA. She tries to create the impression among her subordinates that members of the sales department want her group to fail to meet the deadline so that sales can gain an edge over production in upcoming budgetary negotiations.

How might we evaluate this PBA? Management theory tends to focus our attention on consequences. One might argue that if it works and Lorna's group pulls together and meets the deadline, it's okay. Or, a more critical observer might argue that even if the objective is accomplished, an important side effect could be the loss of a cooperative relationship between the sales and production departments. What we tend to lose sight of, though, is that "creating an impression" is a euphemism for lying, and lying may not be ethically acceptable in this situation.

This example illustrates what may be termed the teleological or goal-oriented form of management theory [Keeley, 1979; Krupp, 1961; Pfeffer, 1978]. This leads managers and management scholars alike to restrict normative judgments about organizational behavior to outcomes (e.g., performance, satisfaction, system effectiveness) rather than consider the ethical quality of the means employed.

In contrast, the field of normative ethics provides fertile ground on which to develop a normative theory of organizational politics. We will therefore turn to the literature of this field in order to draw out a set of principles that can provide the basis for a normative analysis of organizational politics that may reduce the ethical uncertainty surrounding the political use of power.

Ethical Criteria Relevant to Political Behavior Decisions

Work in the field of normative ethics during this century has evolved from three basic kinds of moral theories: utilitarian theories (which evaluate behavior in terms of its social consequences), theories of rights (which emphasize the entitlements of individuals), and theories of justice (which focus on the distributional effects of actions or policies). Each of these has a venerable heritage. Utilitarian theory was precisely formulated in the eighteenth century [Bentham, 1789; Mill, 1863; Sidgwick, 1874]. Formulations of rights theories appeared in the seventeenth century [Hobbes, 1651; Locke, 1690; Kant, 1785]. Aristotle and Plato first formulated theories of justice in the fifth century B.C. This past decade has seen a continuing discussion of a subtle and powerful variant of utilitarianism called "rule utilitarianism" [Brandt, 1979; Sobel, 1970], an elaboration of several rights theories [Dworkin, 1978; Nozick, 1974], and the publication of sophisticated treatments of justice [Bowie, 1971; Rawls, 1971].

Utilitarian Theory

Utilitarianism holds that actions and plans should be judged by their consequences [Sidgwick, 1874; Smart, 1973]. In its classical formulation, utilitarianism claims that behaviors that are moral produce the greatest good for the greatest number [Mills]. Decision makers are required to estimate the effect of each alternative on all the parties concerned and to select the one that optimizes the satisfactions of the greatest number.

What can be said about the ethical quality of PBAs from a utilitarian standpoint? In its present form, utilitarianism requires a decision maker to select the PBA that will result in the greatest good for the greatest number. This implies not only considering the interests of all the individuals and groups that are affected by each PBA, but also selecting the PBA that optimizes the satisfactions of these constituencies. Obviously, this can amount to a calculative nightmare.

Accordingly, there are several shortcuts that may be used to reduce the complexity of utili-

tarian calculations. Each of these involves a sacrifice of elegance for calculative ease. *First*, a decision maker can adopt some ideological system that reduces elaborate calculations of interests to a series of utilitarian rules. For example, some religious ideologies specify rules of behavior that, if followed, are supposed to result in an improved human condition (e.g., the Golden Rule). Certain organizational ideologies, like professionalism, allow complex utilitarian calculations to be reduced to a focus on critical constituencies [Schein, 19661. *Second,* a decision maker can adopt a simplified frame of reference of affected parties. For example, an economic frame of reference presupposes that alternatives are best evaluated in terms of dollar costs and dollar benefits. In this way, utilitarian calculations can be quantified. And *third*, a decision maker can place boundaries on utilitarian calculation. For example, a decision maker can consider only the interests of those directly affected by a decision and thus exclude from analysis all indirect or secondary effects. Similarly, a decision maker can assume that by giving allegiance to a particular organizational coalition or set of goals (e.g., "official goals"), everyone's utilities will be optimized.

Calculative shortcuts like these do not automatically free decision makers from moral responsibility for their actions. Normative ethicians typically suggest that decision makers should periodically assess these simplifying strategies to assure themselves that certain interests are not being ignored or that decision rules do not lead to suboptimal outcomes [e.g., Bok, 1980].

Whatever form of utilitarianism is employed, two types of PBAs are typically judged unethical: (1) those that are consistent with the attainment of some goals (e.g., personal goals) at the expense of those that encompass broader constituencies (e.g., societal goals), and (2) those that constitute comparatively inefficient means to desired ends. Take the case of an employee of a company who uses personal power to persuade policy makers to grant unusually high levels of organizational resources to a project by systematically excluding important information about the progress of the project. This PBA is unethical if other resource allocation schemes would better satisfy a greater number of individuals or if persuasion of this kind is less efficient than being more open about how the project is progressing.

Theory of Rights

A theory of moral rights asserts that human beings have certain fundamental rights that should be respected in all decisions. Several fundamental rights have been incorporated into the American legal system in the form of the Constitutional Bill of Rights. In light of these Constitutional guarantees, advocates of moral rights have suggested the following:

1. *The right of free consent.* Individuals within an organization have the right to be treated only as they knowingly and freely consent to be treated [Bennis & Slater, 1968; Hart, 1955].

2. *The right to privacy.* Individuals have the right to do whatever they choose to do outside working hours and to control information about their private life, including information not intended to be made public [Miller, 1971; Mironi, 1974; Wasserstrom, 1978].

3. *The right to freedom of conscience.* Individuals have the right to refrain from carrying out any order that violates moral or religious norms to which they adhere [Ewing, 1977; Walzer, 19671.

4. *The right of free speech.* Individuals have the right to criticize conscientiously and truthfully the ethics or legality of the actions of others so long as the criticism does not violate the rights of other individuals [Bok, 1980; Eells, 1962; Walters, 1975].

5. *The right to due process.* Individuals have the right to a fair and impartial hearing when they believe their rights are being violated [Ewing, 1977, 1981; Evan, 1975].

Making decisions based on a theory of rights is much simpler than with utilitarian theory. One need only avoid interfering with others who might be affected by the decision. This can be complicated, of course, but generally a theory of rights does not involve the decision complexities that utilitarianism requires.

Theory of Justice

A theory of justice requires decision makers to be guided by equity, fairness, and impartiality. Canons of justice may specify three types of moral prescriptions: distributive rules, principles of administering rules, and compensation norms.

Distributive Rules. The basic rule of distributive justice is that differentiated treatment of individuals should not be based on arbitrary characteristics: individuals who are similar in the relevant respects should be treated similarly, and individuals who differ in a relevant respect should be treated differently in proportion to the differences between them [Perelman, 1963]. This rule is the basis for contentions that certain resource allocations are "fair." When applied to salary administration, for example, it would lead to a distribution of rewards such that those whose jobs are equal in terms of importance, difficulty, or some other criterion receive equal rewards.

A second distributive rule is that the attributes and positions that command differential treatment should have a clear and defensible relationship to goals and tasks [Daniels, 1978]. Clearly, it is unjust to distribute rewards according to differences unrelated to the situation at hand.

Principles of Administering Rules. Justice requires that rules should be administered fairly [Feinberg, 1973; Fuller, 1964]. Rules should be clearly stated and expressly promulgated. They should be consistently and impartially enforced. They should excuse individuals who act in ignorance, under duress, or involuntarily [Rawls, 1971].

Compensation Norms. A theory of justice also delineates guidelines regarding the responsibility for injuries [Brandt, 1959]. First, individuals should not be held responsible for matters over which they have no control. Second, individuals should be compensated for the cost of their injuries by the party responsible for those injuries.

While a theory of justice does not require the complicated calculations demanded by utilitarian theory, it is by no means easy to apply. There is the problem of determining the attrib-

Table 1: Ethical Theories Relevant To Judging Political Behavior Decisions

Theory	Strengths as an Ethical Guide		Weaknesses as an Ethical Guide	
Utilitarianism (Bentham, Ricardo, Smith)	1.	Facilitates calculative shortcuts (e.g., owing loyalty to an individual, coalition, or organization	1.	Virtually impossible to assess the effects of a PBA on the satisfaction of all affected parties.
	2.	Promotes the view that the interests accounted for should not be solely particularistic except under unusual circumstances (e.g., perfect competition)	2.	Can result in an unjust allocation of resources, particularly when some individuals or groups lack representation or "voice."
	3.	Can encourage entrepreneurship, innovation and productivity.	3.	Can result in abridging some persons' rights to accommodate utilitarian outcomes.
Theory of Rights (Kant, Locke)	1.	Specifies minimal levels of satisfaction for all individuals.	1.	Can encourage individualistic, selfish behavior—which, taken to an extreme may result in anarchy.
	2.	Establishes standards of social behavior that are independent of outcomes.	2.	Reduces political prerogatives that may be necessary to bring about just or utilitarian outcomes.
Theory of Justice (Aristotle, Rawls)	1.	Ensures that allocations of resources are determined fairly	1.	Can encourage a sense of entitlement that reduces entrepreneurship, innovation, and productivity.
	2.	Protects the interests of those who may be underrepresented in organizations beyond according them minimal rights.	2.	Can result in abridging some persons' rights to accommodate the canons of justice.

utes on which differential treatment is to be based. There are fact-finding challenges associated with administering rules. And there is the thorny problem of establishing responsibility for mistakes and injuries.

However, as applied to political behavior decisions, these canons of justice are useful in clarifying some ethical issues. First, PBAs for the purpose of acquiring an advantageous position in the distribution of resources are ethically questionable if there is no legitimate basis for the advantage. Second, PBAs based on an exchange of rule leniency for other favors are patently unethical unless everyone qualifies for the same level of leniency. Finally, political

advantage should not be based on favorable attributions of responsibility or the compensation for injury [Allen et al., 1979]. In short, a theory of justice demands that inequality or advantage be determined fairly.

An Analytical Structure for Evaluating Political Behavior Decisions

Each of the three kinds of ethical theories has strong and weak points, as depicted in Table 1. Most important for our purposes, each can be shown to be inadequate in accounting for issues accounted for by another. Utilitarian theory cannot adequately account for rights and claims of justice [Lyons, 1965]. Rights theories proved deficient in dealing with social welfare issues [Singer, 1978]. And theories of justice have been criticized for both violating rights [Nozick, 1974] and diminishing incentives to produce goods and services [Okum, 1975]. One solution to the problem of theoretical inadequacy is to combine these three theories into a coherent whole.

To that end, we have incorporated all three normative theories in a decision tree, diagrammed in Figure 1. The three categories of ethical criteria that bear on a political behavior decision are arbitrarily arranged in the diagram. In addition to incorporating all three theories, the decision tree accounts for overwhelming factors that preclude the application of any of these criteria. These overwhelming factors will be specified after two cases illustrating the use of the decision tree have been presented.

Illustrative Cases

Sam and Bob are highly motivated research scientists who work in the new-product development lab at General Rubber. Sam is by far the most technically competent scientist in the lab, and he has been responsible for several patents that have netted the company nearly six million dollars in the past decade. He is quiet, serious, and socially reserved. In contrast, Bob is outgoing and demonstrative. While Bob lacks the technical track record Sam has, his work has been solid though unimaginative. Rumor has it that Bob will be moved into an administrative position in the lab in the next few years.

According to lab policy, a $300,000 fund is available every year for the best new-product development idea proposed by a lab scientist in the form of a competitive bid. Accordingly, Sam and Bob both prepare proposals. Each proposal is carefully constructed to detail the benefits to the company and to society if the proposal is accepted, and it is the consensus of other scientists from blind reviews that both proposals are equally meritorious. Both proposals require the entire $300,000 to realize any significant results. Moreover, the proposed line of research in each requires significant

mastery of the technical issues involved and minimal need to supervise the work of others.

After submitting his proposal, Sam takes no further action aside from periodically inquiring about the outcome of the bidding process. In contrast, Bob begins to wage what might be termed an open campaign in support of his proposal. After freely admitting his intentions to Sam and others, Bob seizes every opportunity he can to point out the relative advantages of his proposal to individuals who might have some influence over the decision. So effective is this open campaign that considerable informal pressure is placed on those authorized to make the decision on behalf of Bob's proposal. Bob's proposal is funded and Sam's is not.

An ethical analysis of Bob's action in this case could begin by using the decision tree shown in Figure 1. The first question in the sequence requires a utilitarian analysis. Clearly, Bob's interests are better served than Sam's. However, the nature of the two proposals seems to require one of the two to be disappointed. Moreover, the outcome in terms of broader interests (i.e., company, society) appears not to be suboptimal, since both proposals were judged equivalent in the blind reviews. Consequently, it is appropriate to answer the first question affirmatively.

The second question inquires into the rights respected by Bob's behavior. Here again, the evidence seems persuasive that no one's rights were violated. Sam did not have (did not create) the same opportunity to point out the advantages of his proposal to those at whom Bob directed his lobbying campaign, but Bob's open campaign involved no deceit, and Sam's inaction may be taken as implied consent.

It is in light of the third question that Bob's actions are most suspect. Justice would have best been served in this case if there had been a clear situation-relevant difference between the two proposals. The blind reviews found them equivalent, so some other basis for differentiating between the proposals presumably had to be found. Bob's efforts served to create irrelevant differences between them. If anything, Sam's superior technical track record would have been a more relevant factor than Bob's initiative and social skills in determining who should be favored to perform a technical

Figure 1: A Decision Tree for Incorporating Ethics into Political Behavior Decisions

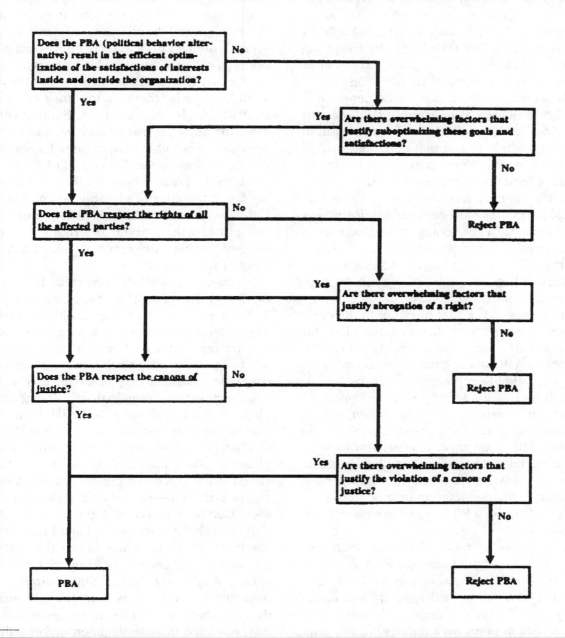

task. Bob's actions in this regard were therefore unjust. Interestingly, had the proposals required supervision of others or the ability to persuade others, Bob's approach would have been justified.

Let us examine another case. Lee, 61, has been Director of Engineering for American Semiconductor for 14 years. He is very bright

and a fine supervisor but he has not kept abreast of new developments in technology.

American Semiconductor's manufacturing process creates substantial quantities of toxic materials. Lee's rather casual attitude toward the disposal of these chemicals has resulted in a number of environmental citations. The firm is now tied up in court on two cases and will probably be forced to pay a considerable amount in damages. Yet, Lee still does not perceive the disposal problem as urgent. For three years, Charlie, the executive vice president, has tried to persuade Lee to make this a priority issue but has failed. Charlie has reluctantly concluded that Lee must be taken out of his position as Director of Engineering.

Charlie recognizes that it would demoralize the other managers if he were to fire Lee outright. So, Charlie decides that he will begin to tell selected individuals that he is dissatisfied with Lee's work. When there is open support for Lee, Charlie quietly sides with Lee's opposition. He casually lets Lee's peers know that he thinks Lee may have outlived his usefulness to the firm. He even exaggerates Lee's deficiencies and failures when speaking to Lee's coworkers. Discouraged by the waning support from his colleagues, Lee decides to take an early retirement.

In response to the first question in the decision tree, we can conclude that getting Lee out of his position may indeed bring about the "greatest good for the greatest number," presuming a suitable replacement can be found. Not only is Lee hindering the achievement of the apparent goals of the organization, but he is also causing external diseconomies in the disposal of the toxic wastes. Both of these problems, especially when taken together, bring us to the conclusion that Lee is hurting both American Semiconductor and many other people. Thus, Charlie's PBA seems to pass utilitarian criteria.

On the issue of rights, however, there are some difficulties with Charlie's PBA. Namely, Lee's right of free consent was violated. Lee has the right to be treated honestly and forthrightly and Charlie's attempt to destroy Lee's reputation behind his back failed to respect this right.

Overwhelming Factors

A still-unexplained qualification in the decision tree we have described is the concept of an "overwhelming factor"—i.e., a situational factor that may, in a given case, justify overriding one of the three ethical criteria: utilitarian outcomes, individual rights, or distributive justice. What counts as an overwhelming factor?

Conflicts between Criteria. As we have suggested, the three criteria are intended to systematically focus our attention on three kinds of decision factors: (1) the congruence between the decision and the efficient satisfaction of the greatest number of people, (2) the effect of the decision on individuals who have rights, and (3) the distributional consequences of the decision. Obviously, these factors may come into conflict. As in the American Semiconductor case, the decision maker may be faced with a situation in which a choice must be made between, on the one hand, a course of action that achieves the greatest good for the greatest number but at the price of violating an individual's rights, and, on the other hand, a course of action that protects the individual's rights but at the price of a substantial reduction in the achievement of the greatest good.

There are no well-defined rules for solving the moral dilemmas that these conflicts pose. The dilemmas can be resolved only by making a considered judgment concerning which of the conflicting criteria should be accorded the most weight in the given situation. In some cases the judgment may be easier than in others. Suppose, for example that violating an employee's right to privacy on the job is the only way to stopping continuing thefts that deprive thousands of customers from getting quality pharmaceutical products. Then the utilitarian criterion may be given greater weight than the rights criterion—employee's rights must be sacrificed for "the greatest good."

Although there are no hard and fast rules for resolving moral dilemmas of this sort, there is a systematic procedure for handling them—the *principle of double effect.* Stated simply, this principle holds that it is acceptable to make a decision that has two effects, one good and one bad, provided that the decision maker's dominant motivation is to achieve the good effect and provided that the good effect is important enough to permit the bad effect [Grisez, 1970].

Conflicts within Criteria. Not only may the three criteria conflict with each other, but each may conflict with itself as well. *First,* there may be conflict between the utilitarian consequences of those involved or with the means chosen to accomplish the appropriate goals. This is probably typical in organizations that have coalitions with conflicting goals or where there is conflict among coalitions about the appropriate means to consensual goals. *Second,* there may be conflict between the rights of competing individuals. The decision maker may be forced to choose between permitting one person to preserve the right to privacy and allowing another person to exercise the right of free speech. *Third,* there may be a conflict between different canons of justice. Administering a rule with literal consistency, for example, may conflict with the principle that individuals who differ in relevant ways should be treated differently. Or there may be a conflict between individuals. A situation may, for example, call for hard choices between using seniority or using merit as the basis for deciding who is to be given preference.

As with conflicts between ethical criteria, there are no well-defined rules for resolving the dilemmas within ethical criteria. Again, the decision maker is forced to employ a weighting procedure. For example, when rights come into conflict, the decision maker must make a conscientious judgment concerning the relative importance of the interests protected by one right as compared to the interests protected by the conflicting right. Although sometimes easy and obvious, such judgments can also be exceedingly difficult to make.

Lack of Capacity to Employ the Criteria. Three kinds of factors might legitimately relieve the decision maker of the responsibility of adhering to the ethical criteria relevant to a certain decision. All three of these factors relate to the decision maker's personal incapacity to adhere to the relevant criteria.

First, the decision maker may legitimately lay aside a certain ethical criterion if there is no freedom to use it. For example, a manager may be so pressured by others that ethical criteria cannot be brought to bear on the decision. Or a decision maker may be only in partial control of a certain decision and thus unable to use a specific ethical criterion.

Second, the decision maker might legitimately fail to employ a certain ethical criterion owing to a lack of adequate information for using that criterion. As we have seen, this is more often the case with the utilitarian and justice criteria than with the rights criterion.

Third, the decision maker who has strong and reasonable doubts about the legitimacy of an ethical criterion can legitimately be excused from adhering to that criterion. There is nothing sacred about the specific ethical criteria proposed in this article. They represent a consensus among normative ethicians, but that does not preclude other, more or less constraining norms being employed, as long as they are arrived at conscientiously.

Faced with any of these three kinds of incapacitating factors, the decision maker may legitimately accord a lesser weight to one criterion. The underlying rationale for such systematic devaluation of ethical criteria is simple. Persons cannot be held responsible for matters they cannot control or for matters about which they are ignorant or sincerely in doubt. However, determining whether a decision maker's lack of freedom, lack of information, or lack of certitude is sufficient to abrogate ethical responsibility requires one to make some exceedingly difficult judgments.

Implications

An important implication of any research on ethics lies in the area of education and development. This is particularly true regarding the subject of organizational politics. Presented in an ethically bland fashion, theories of organizational politics tend to evoke an unfortunate combination of cynicism, defeatism, and paranoia. Without ethical paradigms, individuals too often infer that success is controlled by others or attained only by those who engage in unproductive behavior. In contrast, confronting the ethical issues in organizational politics leads individuals to assume responsibility for their political behavior decisions. It is unlikely that such an approach will enable individuals to solve all the ethical dilemmas they will face in their careers, but it may stimulate "moral" development [Kohlberg, 1973].

Several lines of research are also suggested by the foregoing analysis. First, there would be some value in further developing ethical paradigms for other areas of discretion faced by organizational members. For example, the areas of obedience, whistle blowing, self-promotion, and bottom-up social intervention all cry out for ethical guidance. Second, there is a need to conduct empirical research regarding what rights, canons of justice, and utilitarian rules are commonly accepted in general and in specific dilemmas. Third, the *process* of ethical judgment about politics and other issues needs empirical work. For example, what antecedent conditions are associated with ethical actions? Similarly, how do ethical codes formalized in an organization influence political behavior decisions?

Concluding Remarks

As should be clear from this discussion, reducing the ethical uncertainty surrounding political behavior decisions places significant cognitive burdens on the decision maker [Simon, 1976]. Judging the normative equality of PBAs can involve confronting complicated ethical dilemmas. Yet, there seems to be no satisfactory substitute for individual discretion that addresses these complexities directly and to the limits of one's cognitive capabilities.

As we have seen, management theory offers little guidance in this regard. Its calculative form influences us to be ethically myopic when we evaluate political behavior. Instead of determining whether human rights or standards of justice are violated, we are often content to judge political behavior according to its outcomes. This orientation invites cynicism about what are termed the political realities of organizational life [Nord, 1978]. For example, in describing a patently unethical political act, one writer asserted "many people think it is wrong to try to influence others in this way, even people who, without consciously recognizing it, use this technique themselves" [Kotter, 1977], as if to justify the action. We do not intend to replace cynicism of this kind with Polyanna assertions that ethical managers (politicians) will be more successful than unethical ones. They may or may not be, but that is really not the point. Ethics involves standards of conduct, not guidelines for personal gain. When it comes to the ethics of organizational politics, respect for justice and human rights should prevail for its own sake. •

References

Allen, R. W.; Makison, D. L.; Porter, L. W.; Renwick, P. A.; & Mayes, B. T. Organizational politics: Tactics and characteristics of its actors. *California Management Review* 1979, 22(4), 77–83.

Aristotle. *The Nicomachean ethics* (J.A.K. Thomson, trans.). London: Allen & Unwin, 1953. (330 B.C.)

Bennis, W.; & Slater, P. *The temporary society*. New York: Harper & Row, 1968.

Bentham, J. *An introduction to the principles of morals and legislation*. New York: Hafner, 1948. (1789).

Bok, S. Whistleblowing and professional responsibilities. In D. Callahan & S. Bok (Eds.), *Ethics teaching in higher education*. New York: Plenum, 1980.

Bowie, N . E. *Toward a new theory of distributive justice*. Amherst: University of Massachusetts Press, 1971.

Brandt, R. B. *A Theory of the good and the right*. New York: Oxford University Press, 1979.

Crozier, M. *The bureaucratic phenomena*. Chicago: University of Chicago Press, 1964.

Dahl, R. A. The concept of power. *Behavioral Science*, 1957, 2, 201–205

Daniels, N. Merit and meritocracy. *Philosophy & Public Affairs*, 1978, 7, 206–223.

Drake, B. *Normative constraints on power in organizational decision making*. Unpublished manuscript, School of Business Administration, Wayne State University, Detroit, 1979.

Dworkin, R. *Taking rights seriously*. Cambridge: Harvard University Press, 1978.

Eells, R. *The government of corporations*. New York: Free Press, 1962.

Evan, W. M. Power, conflict, and constitutionism in organizations. *Social Science Information* 1975, 14, 53–80.

Ewing, D. W. *Freedom inside the organization*. New York: McGraw-Hill, 1977.

Feinberg, J. *Social philosophy*. Englewood Cliffs, N.J.: Prentice-Hall, 1973.

Fuller, L. *The morality of law*. New Haven: Yale University Press, 1964.

Gandz, J. & Murray, V. V. The experience of work place politics. *Academy of Management Journal* 1980, 23, 237–251.

Grisez, G. *Abortion: The myths, the realities and the arguments*. New York: Corpus Book, 1970.

Hart, H. L. A. Are there any natural rights? *Philosophical Review* 1955, 64, 175 191.

Hickson, D. J.; Hinings, C. R.; Lee, C. A.; Schneck, R.E.; & Pennings, J. M. A strategic contingencies theory of intraorganizational power. *Administrative Science Quarterly*, 1971, 19, 216–229.

Hobbes, T. *The leviathan,* New York: Bobbs-Merrill, 1958. (1651)

Kant, I. *The metaphysical elements of justice* (J. Ladd, trans.). New York: Library of Liberal Arts, 1965. (1797)

Keeley, M. *Justice versus effectiveness in organizational evaluation.* Paper presented at the annual meeting of the Academy of Management, Atlanta, 1979.

Kohlberg, L. *Collected papers on moral development and moral education.* Cambridge: Center for Moral Education, Harvard University, 1973.

Kotter, J. P. Power, dependence, and effective management. *Harvard Business Review* 1977, 53(3), 125–136.

Krupp, S. *Patterns of organization analysis.* New York: Holt, Rinehart & Winston, 1961.

Locke, J. *The second treatise of government.* New York: Liberal Arts Press, 1952. (1690)

Lyons, D. *The forms and limits of utilitarianism.* Oxford: Clarendon Press, 1965.

Martin, N. H.; & Sims, J. H. Power tactics. *Harvard Business Review* 1956, 34(3), 25–36.

Mayes, B. T.; & Allen, R. W. Toward a definition of organizational politics. *Academy of Management Review* 1977, 2, 672–678.

Mill, J. S. *Utilitarianism.* Indianapolis: Bobbs-Merrill, 1957. (1863)

Miller, A. R. *The assault on privacy.* Ann Arbor: University of Michigan Press, 1971.

Mironi, M. The confidentiality of personal records: A legal and ethical view. *Labor Law Journal* 1974, 25, 270–292.

Nord, W. R. Dreams of humanization and the realities of power. *Academy of Management Review,* 1978, 3. 674–679.

Nozick, R. *Anarchy, state and utopia.* New York: Basic Books, 1974.

Okum, A. M. *Equality and efficiency: The big trade-off.* Washington: Brookings Institution, 1975.

Perelman, C. *The idea of justice and the problem of argument.* New York: Humanities Press, 1963.

Pettigrew, A. M. *The politics of organizational decision making.* London: Tavistock, 1973.

Pfeffer, J. Power and resource allocation in organizations. In B. Staw & G. Salancik (Eds.), *New directions in organizational behavior.* Chicago: St. Clair Press, 1977, pp. 235–266.

Pfeffer, J. The micropolitics of organizations. In M. W. Meyer and associates (Eds.), *Environments and organizations.* San Francisco: Jossey-Bass, 1978, pp. 29–50.

Pfeffer, J.; & Salancik, G. Organizational decision making as a political process. *Administrative Science Quarterly* 1974, 18, 135–151.

Rawls, J. *A Theory of Justice,* Cambridge, Mass.: Belknap Press, 1971.

Schein, E. G. The problem of moral education for the business manager. *Industrial Management Review* 1966, 7, 3–11.

Schein, V. E. Individual power and political behaviors in organizations: An inadequately explored reality. *Academy of Management Review* 1977, 2, 64–72.

Sidgwick, H. *The methods of ethics.* New York: Dover, 1966. (1874)

Simon, H. A. *Administrative behavior* (3rd ed.). New York: Free Press, 1976.

Singer, P. Rights and the market. In J. Arthur & W. Shaw (Eds.), *Justice and economic distribution.* Englewood Cliffs, N.J.: Prentice-Hall, 1978, pp. 207–221.

Smart J. J. C. An outline of a system of utilitarian ethics. In J. C. C. Smart & B. Williams (Eds.), *Utilitarianism for and against.* New York: Cambridge University Press, 1973, 3–74.

Sobel, J. H. Utilitarianism: Simple and general. *Inquiry* 1970, 13, 394–449.

Thompson, J. D. *Organizations in action.* New York: McGraw-Hill, 1967.

Tushman, M. T. A political approach to organization review and rationale. *Academy of Management Review* 1977, 2, 206–216.

Walters, K. D. Your employee's right to blow the whistle. *Harvard Business Review* 1975, 53(4), 26–34.

Walzer, M. The obligation to disobey. *Ethics* 1967 77(3), 163–175.

Wasserstrom, R. Privacy and the law. In R. Bronaugh (Ed.), *Philosophical law.* Westport, Conn.: Greenwood Press, 1978.

Zald, M. N. (Ed.). *Power in organizations.* Nashville: Vanderbilt University Press, 1970.

Zalesnik, A. Power and politics in organizational life. *Harvard Business Review* 1970, 48(2), 47–60.

*   *   *

Study Questions

1. Contrast political and nonpolitical uses of power with regard to organizational sanctioning.

2. What is the focus of teleological, or goal-oriented forms of management?

3. Explain briefly the three basic kinds of moral/ethical theories. What are the "roots" of each?

4. How can utilitarians avoid complicated calculations (i.e., use shortcuts) in determining a course of action for the greatest good?

5. According to utilitarianism, what two political behavior options would be unethical?

6. Moral rights advocates identify five fundamental rights. Explain each.

7. Explain the three basic rules associated with the theory of justice.

8. Be familiar with the strengths and weaknesses of the three theories with regard to serving as a guide for ethical behavior.

9. Be generally familiar with the Decision Tree.

10. Explain the "overwhelming factor" in the decision tree. How should these moral dilemmas be resolved?

11. Explain the principle of double effect.

12. What three factors may legitimately relieve the decision maker of the responsibility of adhering to relevant ethical criteria?

13. What is the value of confronting ethical issues associated with political behavior?

When Is It Legal to Lie in Negotiations?

G. Richard Shell

If you are negotiating to sell your business and you lie about its debts, that's illegal, right? But what if you begin negotiations with everything squarely on the table. The new quarterly reports come in and they're not as rosy as the previous ones. You don't disclose them to the prospective buyer. Illegal or just unethical? Surprisingly, as this article reports, business negotiations law is increasingly infused with ethical considerations. Shell outlines the basic elements of legal fraud, illustrating the evolving concepts with numerous cases in which negotiators have been penalized for what some consider merely unethical behavior. He argues that when entering into negotiations, your conscience may be your best guide.

Commercial negotiations seem to require a talent for deception. In simple, distributive bargaining, when someone asks, "What is your bottom line?" few negotiators tell the truth. They dodge, they change the subject, or they lie.[1] In more complex, multi-issue negotiations, even relatively cooperative bargainers often inject straw issues or exaggerate the importance of minor problems in order to gain concessions on what *really* matters.[2] In nearly all bargaining encounters, a key skill is the ability to communicate that you are relatively firm on positions when you are, in fact, flexible—in short, to bluff about your intentions.

The apparent necessity for misleading conduct in a process based on cooperation and coordination makes bargaining deception a prime target for ethical theorizing and empirical investigation. Given the high degree of academic interest, one would think that the investigation of deception would have included by now a detailed look at what one of our most powerful social institutions—the law—has to

say on the subject. Curiously, academic students of negotiation have essentially ignored the law. Ethical discussions of deception either overlook it completely or assume that it proscribes only the most clear-cut types of fraud, leaving moralists to distinguish, and in some instances, justify the finer points of deceptive conduct.[3] Behavioral studies of bargaining deception, meanwhile, usually take place in academic laboratories where the problems are not subject, as are actual transactions, to legal limits or consequences.[4]

This article fills the existing gap in the bargaining literature. As the recent legal cases discussed here will demonstrate, what moralists would often consider merely "unethical" behavior in negotiations turns out to be precisely what the courts consider *illegal* behavior.[5] In light of the rather broad legal standards that are beginning to govern bargaining, behavioral investigators should consider research on how legal incentives affect negotiator conduct. Business negotiators and teachers of negotiation skills in business schools and executive training programs need to be aware of the legal consequences of deceptive bargaining tactics.

Legal Fraud: The Basics

American law disclaims any general duty of "good faith" in the negotiation of commercial agreements.[6] As the United States Court of Appeals for the Seventh Circuit recently stated:

In a business transaction both sides presumably try to get the best deal. That is the essence of bargaining and the free market. . . . [N]o legal rule bounds the run of business interest. So one cannot characterize self-interest as bad faith. No particular demand in negotiations could be termed dishonest, even if it seemed outrageous to the other party. The proper recourse is to walk away from the bargaining table, not sue for "bad faith" in negotiations.[7]

This general rule assumes, however, that no one has committed fraud. As we shall see, fraud law reaches deep into the complexities of negotiation behavior.

The elements of common law fraud are deceptively simple. A statement is fraudulent when the speaker makes a knowing misrepresentation of a material fact on which the victim reasonably relies and which causes damages.[8] A car dealer commits fraud when he resets an odometer and sells one of his "company" cars as brand new. The dealer knows the car is not new; he misrepresents its condition to the buyer; the condition of the car is a fact that is important, or "material" to the transaction; the buyer is acting reasonably in relying on the dealer's assertions that the car is new; and damages result. Similarly, a person selling her business commits fraud when she lies about the number and kind of debts owed by the business.

Lies about important facts are not unknown in business negotiations, but most negotiators know to avoid them. The interesting questions about lying come up on the margins of fraud law. What if the dealer says you had better buy the car today because he has another buyer ready to snatch it away tomorrow? That is a statement of fact. Is it fraudulent if it is a lie? What if the person selling her business says that a large account debt might be renegotiated if you buy the business? That is not really a statement of fact; it is an opinion. Could it nevertheless be deemed so misleading as to be fraudulent when she knows that the creditor would not consider renegotiation? Below, I address these and other questions by exploring in depth each element in the legal definition of fraud with reference to recent cases that have extended the boundaries of the law.

Knowing

The common law definition of fraud requires that the speaker have a particular state of mind with respect to the fact he misrepresents: the statement must be made "knowingly." This generally means that the speaker knows what he says is false. One way of getting around fraud, therefore, might be for the speaker to avoid contact with information that would lead to a "knowing" state of mind. For example, a company president might suspect that his company is in poor financial health, but he does not yet "know" it because he has not seen the latest quarterly reports. When his advisers ask to set up a meeting to discuss these reports, he tells them to hold off. He is about to go into negotiations with an important supplier and would like to be able to say, honestly, that so far as he knows the company is paying its bills. Does this get the president off the hook? No. The courts have stretched the definition of knowing to include statements that are "reckless" that is, those made with a conscious disregard for their truth. Thus, when the information that will give the speaker the truth is close at hand and he deliberately turns away in order to maintain a convenient state of ignorance, the law will treat him as if he spoke with full knowledge that his statements were false. A recent case applied this concept, complete with a punitive damage award, against a company that negotiated a sale of computer and other equipment based on reckless assertions of performance capability.[9]

Nor is reckless disregard for truth the limit of the law. Victims of misstatements that were made *negligently* or even innocently may obtain relief in the proper circumstances. These kinds of misstatements are not deemed fraudulent, however. Rather, they are a way of recognizing that a deal was based on a mistake. If someone sells land relying, either carelessly or without any fault whatsoever, on a deed that contains incorrect notations of the land's proper boundaries, the buyer may be able to have the sale rescinded or the boundaries reformed. But if the seller knows that the deed is incorrect and does not tell the buyer, she has committed fraud.

Misrepresentation

In general, the law requires the speaker to make a positive misstatement before it will attach liability for fraud. Thus, a basic rule for commercial negotiators is to "be silent and be safe." As a practical matter, of course, silence is difficult to maintain if one's bargaining opponent is an astute questioner. In the face of inconvenient questions, negotiators are often forced to resort to verbal feints and dodges such as, "I don't know about that," or, when pressed, "That is not a subject I am at liberty to discuss."

There are circumstances when such dodges will not do, and it may be fraudulent to keep your peace about an issue. When does a negotiator have a duty to frankly disclose matters that may hurt his bargaining position? Under recent cases, the law imposes affirmative disclosure duties in the following four circumstances:

1. *When the nondisclosing party makes a partial disclosure that is or becomes misleading in light of all the facts.* If you say your company is profitable, you may have a duty to disclose whether you used questionable accounting techniques to arrive at that statement. If you show a loss in the next quarter and negotiations are still ongoing, you may be required to disclose the loss. One way to avoid this is to make no statements on delicate subjects in the first place. Then you have no duty to correct or update yourself.

2. *When the parties stand in a fiduciary relationship to one another.* In negotiations involving trustees and beneficiaries, parties must be completely frank and cannot rely on the "be silent and be safe" rubric. Note, however, that courts have recently broadened the notion of a "fiduciary" to include banks, franchisors, and other commercial players who deal with business partners on a somewhat-less-than-arm's-length basis. In short, it is becoming increasingly risky to withhold important information in negotiations with parties who depend on you for their commercial well-being.

3. *When the nondisclosing party has "superior information" vital to the transaction that is not accessible to the other side.* This is a slippery exception, but the best test is one of conscience. Indeed, courts often state that the legal test of disclosure is whether "equity or good conscience" requires that the fact be revealed.[10] Would you feel cheated if the other side didn't tell you about the hidden fact? Or would you secretly kick yourself for not having found it out yourself? If the former, you should consult an attorney. A recent case applying this exception held that an employer owed a duty to a prospective employee to disclose contingency plans for shutting down the project for which the employee was hired.[11] In general, sellers have a greater duty than buyers to disclose things they know about their own property. Thus, a home seller must disclose termite infestation in her home.[12] But an oil company need not disclose the existence of oil on a farmer's land when negotiating a purchase.[13]

4. *When special transactions are at issue, such as insurance contracts.* Insurers must fully disclose the scope of coverage, and insurers must fully disclose their insurance risk. If you apply for a life insurance policy and do not disclose your heart condition, you have committed fraud.

If none of these four exceptions applies, you are not likely to be found liable for common law fraud based on a nondisclosure. Beware of special statutory modifications of the common law rules, however. For example, if the sale of your company involves a purchase or sale of securities, state and federal antifraud rules may impose a stiffer duty of disclosure than may apply under the common law. Companies repurchasing stock from employee shareholders in anticipation of a lucrative merger, for example, have been held liable for failing to disclose the existence of the merger negotiations to their employees.[14] And companies selling their securities are required to disclose important adverse facts about their business to prospective buyers.

Material

Most people lie about something during negotiations. Often they seek to deceive others by making initial demands that far exceed their true needs or desires. Sometimes they mislead others about their reservation price or "bottom line." Of course, demands and reservation prices may not be "facts." One may have only a vague idea of what one really wants or is willing to pay for something. Hence, a statement that an asking price is too high may not be a true misrepresentation as much as a statement of preference. Suppose, however, that a negotiator has been given authority by a seller to peddle an item for any price greater than $10,000. Is it fraud for the negotiator to reject an offer of $12,000 and state that the deal cannot be closed at that price? In fact, the deal could be closed for that price so there has been a knowing misrepresentation of fact. The question is whether this fact is material in a legal sense. It is not.

Lies about reservation price are so prevalent in bargaining that many professional negotiators do not consider such misstatements to be lies.[15] Indeed, some social science researchers, noticing that exaggerated demands and misstatements about reservation price seem to be the norm across cultures, have hypothesized that they serve a ritual function in negotiation. Lies about initial demands enable the parties to assert the legitimacy of their preferences and set the boundaries of the bargaining range without risk of loss.[16] Misleading statements about reservation prices enable parties to test the other side's commitment to their expressed preferences. The U.S. legal profession has gone so far as to enshrine this practice in its Model Rules of Professional Conduct. These rules provide that "estimates of price or value placed on the subject of a transaction and a party's intention as to an acceptable settlement of a claim" are not material facts for purposes of the rule prohibiting lawyers from making false statements to a third person.[17]

There are thus no legal problems with lying about how much you might be willing to pay or which of several issues in a negotiation you value more highly. Demands and reservation prices are not, as a matter of law, material to a deal.

Some experienced negotiators may be surprised to learn, however, that there are legal problems when negotiators try to embellish their refusals to accept a particular price with supporting lies. Lies about "other offers" are classic problem cases of this sort. For example, take the following relatively older but still leading case from Massachusetts.[18] A commercial landlord bought a building and proceeded to negotiate a new lease with a toy shop tenant when the tenant's lease expired. The proprietor of the toy shop bargained hard and refused to pay the landlord's demand for a $10,000 increase in rent. The landlord then told the shop owner that he had another tenant willing to pay the amount and threatened the current tenant with immediate eviction if he did not promptly agree to the new rate. The tenant paid, but learned several years later that the threat had been a bluff, there was no other tenant. The tenant sued successfully for fraud. In a more recent case, this time from Oklahoma, a real estate agent was held liable for fraud, including *punitive* damages, when she pressured a buyer into closing on a home with a story that a rival

buyer (the contractor who built the house) was willing to pay the asking price and would do so later that same day.[19] In these cases, the made-up offer was a lie; it concerned an objective fact (either someone had made an offer or they had not), and the courts ruled that the lie could be material given all the circumstances. Note that such lies are not always illegal. Rather, the law is content to leave the ultimate question of liability to a jury, with all the expense and risk of a full trial. Of course, victims of such conduct may decide that litigation is not worth the trouble.

Fact

On the surface of the legal doctrine, it appears that only misstatements of objective fact are illegal. Negotiators seeking to walk close to the legal line are therefore careful to couch their "sales talk" in negotiation as opinions, predictions, and statements of intention, not statements of fact. Moreover, the law views a good deal of exaggeration or "puffing" about product attributes and likely performance as "part of the game." Buyers and sellers cannot take everything said to them at face value.

The surface of the law can be misleading, however. Courts have found occasions to punish statements of intention and opinion as fraudulent when faced with particularly egregious cases. The touchstone of fraud law is not whether the statement at issue was one of pure fact, but whether the statement was designed to conceal a set of facts detrimental to the negotiator's position.

Is it fraud if you misstate an intention—state that you are going to spend a loan on new equipment if you are really going to pay off an old debt? Yes. In the memorable words of a famous English judge, "The state of a man's mind is as much a fact as the state of his digestion."[20] Lies regarding intention even have a special name in the law, promissory fraud. All but a handful of states judicially recognize the tort of promissory fraud.[21] The key element in such a case is proof that the speaker knew he would not live up to his promise at the *time the promise was made,* that is, that he made the promise with his fingers crossed behind his back. Strict proof requirements would make this claim a legal rarity, because subjective intent can rarely, if ever, be conclusively proven. But the courts have not been uniformly strict in the proof required to show an intent not to keep a promise. Fraudulent intent cannot be inferred solely from nonperformance of the promise,[22] but circumstantial evidence such as "sharp" dealing throughout the transaction[23] or a refusal to acknowledge that a contract was made[24] is enough to get to the jury.

A particularly vivid example of this sort of conduct was litigated in *Markov v. ABC Transfer & Storage Co.*[25] A commercial tenant entered into negotiations to renew its lease on a warehouse and railroad yard. The warehouse was vital to the tenant's continued business relationship with its main client, the Scott Paper Company, because Scott used the warehouse as a regional product distribution facility. At a meeting during contract renewal negotiations, the landlord assured all parties, including Scott, that the tenant's lease would be renewed for a three-year term.

Unbeknownst to the tenant, the landlord was secretly negotiating to sell the property to the Boeing Company at the same time it was negotiating the lease renewal. The sale went through, and the landlord notified the tenant that it would have to vacate within twenty days. As a result, the tenant lost the Scott Paper contract and incurred extraordinary relocation expenses. The court found that the landlord's promise regarding the lease renewal was fraudulent, essentially made to string the tenant along in case the sale did not go through. It awarded damages for the tenant's lost profits from the Scott Paper contract and required the defendant to pay the tenant's extra moving expenses.

What about statements of opinion? Self-serving statements about the value of your goods or the qualifications of your product or company are standard fare at the negotiating table. However, when negotiators offer opinions that are flatly contradicted by facts known to them about the subject of the transaction, they may be liable for fraud. In one recent New York case, for example, the seller of a machine shop business opined to a prospective buyer that the buyer would have no trouble securing work from his largest customer.[26] In fact, the seller was in debt to his customer, intended to pay off the debt from the sale's proceeds, and had virtually no work there due to his reputation for poor workmanship. The buyer was able to prove that the sale was induced by the seller's fraudulent statement of opinion.

In summary, the seemingly strict requirement that fraud be based on statements of fact is, in reality, a flexible concept informed by a notion that parties must take responsibility for the impression they create by the words they use. What is important is not whether some verifiable object exists that corresponds to the speaker's statement. What matters is whether a statement so conceals the true nature of the negotiation proposal that a bargaining opponent cannot accurately assess an appropriate range of values or risks to price the transaction.

Reliance and Causation

Negotiators who lie sometimes defend themselves by saying, in effect, "Only a fool could have believed what I said. He had no business relying on me to tell him the truth!" The standard elements of fraud give some support to such defenses. The burden of proof is on the fraud victim and, among other things, the victim is supposed to prove she relied on the misstatement that caused damages. Surprisingly, however, most courts do not inquire too deeply into the reasonableness of the victim's reliance when the defendant is shown to have made a positive misrepresentation of fact. Courts have trouble swallowing the idea that overt fraud should go unpunished just because victims are lazy or fools. Where statements of opinion or mere nondisclosures are concerned, however, courts are more sympathetic to defendants. When the facts were obvious or the truth was accessible to the complaining party, courts will reject their claims of fraud.

Finally, in cases of promissory fraud, victims of false promises have particular trouble proving reasonable reliance when the speaker can show that the final written contract language flatly contradicts his earlier statements. So long as the contract document accurately corrects the representation alleged to be fraudulent, negotiators may escape liability.[27] If the misstatements are quite specific, however, and the contract terms negating them are only general, vague disclaimers, the negotiator may be in trouble. Two examples will help illustrate the legal limits on fraud in these circumstances. A seller named Turner negotiated the sale of his company's principle asset, an electronic thermometer, to Johnson & Johnson. The detailed contract included, as part of the purchase price, a promise of future royalties from thermometer sales.[28] During the negotiations, Johnson & Johnson assured Turner that it would aggressively market the thermometer. The contract as signed, however, specifically stated that Johnson & Johnson had the legal right to shelve the product if it wished. Johnson & Johnson elected to stop marketing the product soon after the sale in favor of another thermometer it had acquired, and Turner sued for fraud. The court held that, even if Johnson & Johnson made its promise without intent to keep it, the plaintiffs were not entitled to rely on it after seeing that the final written contract negated the promise. "If a jury is allowed to ignore contract provisions directly at odds with oral representations allegedly made during negotiations," the court said, "the language of a contract simply would not matter anymore. . . . And the give and take of negotiations would become meaningless if, after making concessions in order to obtain other contractual protections, a knowledgeable party is later able to reclaim what it had given away by alleging that it had, in fact, relied not on the writing but on the prior oral statements."[29]

By contrast, when the contract says only that the subject of the transaction is being sold "as is," such language does not provide ironclad protection to a seller for exaggerated or false negotiation claims about the condition of the property.[30] As one federal appeals court explained, "When a contract contains an 'as is' clause or other ambiguous language, the agreement is to some extent left undefined, and the plaintiff's understanding of the agreement logically may be colored by the defendant's prior statements, fraudulent or otherwise. Moreover, there is nothing on the face of the contract to trigger alarm."[31] Courts have similarly held that fraud victims may sue even if the contract contains language integrating all pre-contract representations into the final written document.[32] The lessons of these cases are twofold. First, *read contracts carefully before you sign*

and do not accept assurances that changed contract language is "just a technicality" or is "required by the lawyers." Second, if you have made some bold assurances in negotiations that you cannot live up to, *make sure the final contract document negates them specifically*. A general disclaimer may not protect you from fraud liability.

The Boundaries of Bad Faith: Implied Fraud

Although U.S. law disclaims a general duty of good faith in negotiations, it will nevertheless stretch to punish clear instances of bad faith. In such cases even though the strict legal elements of fraud are missing, the courts will "imply" a promise or misrepresentation and will bend the usual rules to achieve a desired result.

For example, buyers usually have no duty to disclose the value of the object a seller is selling. Misrepresentations of value are considered nothing to get excited about because they are neither facts nor material to the seller's estimate of what the transaction is worth. However, if an elderly widow is selling an old painting that is, unknown to her, a museum piece, and a professional art dealer assures her that he is buying the work "primarily for the frame" he may run afoul of fraud law.[33] Misrepresentations of value may conceal an important fact to a relatively helpless seller, and the law is flexible enough to respond to such abuses in extreme cases.

Occasionally, negotiators use the bargaining process itself to get what they want, then walk away from the table. The law has a variety of ways of penalizing such bad faith conduct. In *Skycom Corp. v. Telstar Corp.*, for example, a company negotiating a sale of all its assets agreed, as part of preliminary negotiations, to let the prospective buyer take over ongoing negotiations with a third party for a valuable license.[34] The prospective buyer succeeded in getting the license but ultimately refused to go forward with the asset purchase. The disappointed seller sued. The court held that the parties' "letter of intent" left too many issues open to be construed as a completed contract, but it let the seller sue for the value of the lost license. The court said the buyer "may have induced [the seller] to turn over the negotiations and that [the seller] may have relied in a commercially reasonable way on representations made to him."

Courts have similarly ruled in favor of inventors and others who have disclosed trade secrets in the course of negotiations to sell their discoveries.[35] The prospective buyers in these cases have, in effect, attempted to use the negotiation process to get something for nothing, and the law is not sympathetic to such breaches of common good faith and trust. In essence, the courts have held that the buyer assumes an implied duty of confidentiality when it undertakes to review ideas or inventions. It can be fraudulent to breach this duty by trying to misappropriate the inventor's property during negotiations.

Conclusion: Business Ethics and the Law

When business theorists ask if lying in business negotiations is "ethical," they assume that deceptive conduct is often legal and argue that ethical sensibilities should govern one's negotiating behavior. As it turns out, this perspective on law and ethics is distorted. As this review of cases has shown, business negotiation law is infused with the norms of ethical business conduct. Indeed, the leading legal treatise writers on fraud candidly admit that "a new standard of business ethics" has resulted in complete shifts of legal doctrine in the past fifty years.[36] Unethical bargaining practices are, as often as not, illegal or become so after they are brought to light. The law simply expands to include them, definitions notwithstanding. However, when ethically acceptable conduct such as lying about reservation price appears to run foul of legal definitions, the law adjusts and refuses to penalize it. Thus, an ethical sensibility, far from being a "luxury" in business negotiations, may be a negotiator's best counselor.

In commenting on Michael Milken's recent guilty plea to securities law violations, financier H. Ross Perot gave this advice to young business people: "Don't govern your life by what's legal or illegal, govern it by what's right or wrong." It turns out this is good legal as well as business advice, at least insofar as negotiation is concerned. In negotiation, people who

rely on the letter of legal rules as a strategy for plotting unethical conduct are very likely to get into deep trouble. But people who rely on a cultivated sense of right and wrong to guide them in legal matters are likely to do well. •

Footnotes

[1]Professor Robert H. Frank summed this up best when he wrote, "The art of bargaining, as most of us eventually learn, is in large part the art of sending misleading messages about [reservation prices]." See R. H. Frank, *Passions within Reason* (New York: Norton, 1988), p. 165.

[2]Bargaining situations are often characterized as either distributive (zero-sum negotiations) or integrative (non-zero-sum negotiations). Distributive negotiations typically involve a single, divisible issue such as money. Integrative bargaining involves many issues that differ in importance to the parties, making possible mutual gains from trade across issues. See R.E. Walton and R.B. McKersie, *A Behavioral Theory of Labor Negotiations* (New York: McGraw-Hill, 1965). Both distributive and integrative bargaining situations, however, are "mixed motive" in character and contain within them incentives to lie or at least mislead. See: D. A. Lax and J. K. Sebenius, *The Manager as Negotiator* (New York: The Free Press, 1986), pp. 30–35.

[3]The most famous recent treatment of the ethics of lying is Sissela Bok's book *Lying: Moral Choice in Public and Private Life* (New York Vintage, 1978). Other influential articles include A.Z. Carr, "Is Business Bluffing Ethical?" *Harvard Business Review,* January–February 1968, pp. 143–150; and R.E. Wokutch and T. L. Carson, "The Ethics and Profitability of Bluffing in Business" in *Ethical Issues in Business,* 3rd ed., eds. T. Donaldson and P.H. Werhane (Englewood Cliffs, New Jersey: Prentice Hall, 1988), pp. 77–83. None of these works focuses on legality of lying and some, such as Carr's piece, explicitly assume that the law's reach extends only to the most blatant forms of fraud.

[4]I have conducted an extensive search of the social scientific literature on bargaining deception and have found none that examine the effects of legal rules on bargaining behavior.

[5]This trend extends to other areas of law as well. See: G. R. Shell, "Substituting Ethical Standards for Common Law Rules in Commercial Cases: An Emerging Statutory Trend, *Northwestern University Law Review* 82 (1988): 1198–1254.

[6]The Uniform Commercial Code states that the UCC's general duty of good faith applies only to the

performance and enforcement of agreements, not their negotiation. *Uniform Commercial Code* 1-203. See also: *Restatement (Second) of Contracts* 205 (1981) comment c ("Bad faith in negotiation" is not "within the scope of this Section." Id. 205 comment c.

[7]Feldman v. Allegheny International, Inc., 850 F.2d 1217,1223 (7th Cir. 1988).

[8]W.P Keeton, D.B. Dobbs, R.E. Keeton, and D.G. Owen, *Prosser and Keeton on the Law of Torts,* St. Paul, Minnesota: West, 1984), p. 728.

[9]Computer Systems Engineering, Inc. v. Qantel Corp., 740 F2d 59 (1st Cir. 1984).

[10]Eckley v. Colorado Real Estate Commission, 752 P.2d 68 (Colo. 1988).

[11]See Berger v. Security Pacific Information Systems, Inc., No. 88CA0822 (Colo. App. April 5, 1990); and "Companies Must Disclose Shaky Finances to Some Applicants, a Colorado Court Rules," *Wall Street Journal,* 20 April 1990, p. B12. Award of $250,000 in actual and punitive damages against employer.

[12]Miles v. McSwegin, 388 N.E.2d 1367 (Ohio 1979).

[13]Zaschak v. Traverse Corp., 333 NW.2d 191 (Mich. App. 1983).

[14]Jordon v. Duff & Phelps, Inc., 815 F 2d 429 (7th Cir. 1987).

[15]Rather, they refer to them as "puffery" or "feints." See P. Freund, *The Acquisition Mating Dance* (Clifton, New Jersey: Prentice Hall, 1987), p. 164; and G. Nierenberg, *Fundamentals of Negotiating* (New York: Hawthorn/Dutton, 1973), p. 159.

[16]See J. G. Gross, *The Economics of Bargaining* (New York: Basic Books, 1969), pp. 166–179; and P.H. Gulliver, *Disputes and Negotiation: A Cross-Cultural Perspective* (New York: Academic Press, 1979), pp. 135–141.

[17]American Bar Association, *Model Rules of Professional Conduct* Rule 4.1(a) official comment (1983).

[18]Kabatchnick v. Hanover-Elm Building Corp., 103 N.E.2d 692 (Mass. 1982).

[19]Beavers v. Lamplighters Realty, Inc., SS6 P.2d 1328 (Okla. App. 1976).

[20]Edgington v. Fitzmaurice, L.R. 29 Ch. Div 3S9 (1885).

[21]Indiana courts have rejected the doctrine. Illinois courts require that the plaintiff prove a "scheme" to defraud in addition to other promissory fraud elements. Tennessee courts have explicitly reserved judgment on the existence of the tort. States such as New York, California, and Texas approve the doctrine.

[22]Britt v. Britt, 3S9 S.E.2d 467, 471 (N.C. 1987); and Hodges v. Pittman, 530 So.2d 817, 818 (Ala. 1988).

[23]Hanover Modular Homes v. Scottish Inns, 443 F. supp. 888 891–92 (W.D La. 1978); and Brier v. Koncen Meat Co., 762 S.W.2d 499, S00 (Mo. App 1988).

[24]New Process Steel Corp. v. Steel Corp.,703 S.W.2d 209,214 (Tex. App. 1985).

[25]457 P2d S3S (Wash. 1969). See also Gibraltar Savings v. LDBrinkman Corp., 860 F 2d 127 S (5th Cir. 1988). Debtor promised creditor to keep holding company solvent when plans were under way to dissolve holding company. This was deemed fraudulent, resulting in a $6 million verdict.

[26]Alio v. Saponaro, S20 N.Y.S.2d 245 (A.D 1987).

[27]The statement in the text does not extend to "consumer" cases. See, for example Boykin v. Hermitage Realty, 360 S.E.2d 177(Va. 1987). Condominium owners claimed fraud based on assurances by a realtor that the lot behind their units would remain undeveloped even though readily available public records showed that it was the site of a future playground.

[28]Turner v. Johnson & Johnson, 809 F.2d 90 (1st Cir. 1986).

[29]Turner v. Johnson & Johnson, 809 F.2d at 96.

[30]See V.H.S. Realty, Inc. v. Texaco, Inc., 757 F.2d 411, 418 (1st Cir. 1985).

[31]Turner v Johnson & Johnson, 809 F.2d at 96.

[32]Turner v. Johnson & Johnson, 809 F.2d at 95 (citing cases). But see Grumman Allied Industries, Inc. v. Rohr Industries, Inc., 748 F.2d 729 (2d Cir. 1984). Contractual language stipulating that a buyer of company assets has not relied on any warranties or representations regarding design of new bus precludes claim based on failure to disclose poor "stress test" results on bus prototype.

[33]Zimpel v. Trawick, 679 F Supp. 1502 (W.D Ark. 1988). An elderly, sick widow was defrauded when a professional land speculator bought her land without telling her that oil and gas had been discovered on it.

[34]813 F.2d 810 (7th Cir. 1987).

[35]See Smith v. Snap-On Tools Corp., 833 F.2d 578 (5th Cir. 1988). No liability was found when the inventor made a gift of invention to the company. See also Smith v. Dravo Corp., 203 F.2d 369 (7th Cir. 1953). Liability was found when the inventor intended negotiations to lead to sale of a trade secret.

[36]Keeton et al. (1984), pp 739, 751–52. In the past half century, nondisclosure law has evolved to a "standard requiring conformity to what the ordinary ethical person would have disclosed," and the "new

standard of business ethics" has "led to an almost complete shift" in law regarding reasonable reliance.

G. Richard Shell is Pfizer Foundation Term Assistant Professor of Legal Studies at the Wharton School, University of Pennsylvania, where he teaches negotiation and business law.

* * *

Study Questions

1. Is protecting your interests in negotiation a violation of "good faith?" Explain.

2. Define fraudulent statements.

3. What are "reckless" statements?

4. Are misstatements made negligently, or even innocently, fraud? What can they lead to for the victims as far as awards?

5. In what circumstances are you required to disclose information to an opponent in negotiation?

6. What is the legal test for disclosure? Who has a greater duty here—buyers or sellers?

7. Are there legal problems in lying about target and resistance points? What about lies of "other offers?" Is that fraud?

8. Because lies of fact are always illegal, what tactics do some negotiators use? Are these tactics ever found fraudulent?

9. What is "promissory fraud?"

10. When are opinions considered potentially fraudulent?

11. What is the "flexible" concept of fraud?

12. When are courts more sympathetic to defendants in fraud cases?

13. What about written contracts that contradict spoken assurances?, i.e., what lessons should we learn?

To Some at Harvard, Telling Lies Becomes A Matter of Course

Untruths Can improve Grade in Business-School Class; Peer Pressure and Ethics

William M. Bulkeley

Gerald M. Thomchick got the highest grade in part of his Competitive Decision Making course at Harvard Business School because "I was willing to lie to get a better score."

That's fine with Prof. Howard R. Raiffa, whose course is designed to teach budding businessmen to negotiate in the real world. Like it or not, Prof. Raiffa says, lying—or "strategic misrepresentation," as he calls it—is sometimes resorted to in business negotiations.

Each week, Prof. Raiffa and his students play a game. He pairs them off and assigns them roles in a negotiation. One week a big-city mayor and a police-union leader bargain over a contract. Another week, a plaintiff and an insurance company try to reach a settlement. Next time, one executive tries to buy a company from another. The students negotiate outside the classroom during the week, then report the results.

The results determine the grade. The mayor who held the police union to the smallest wage-and-benefit package gets the best grade among the mayors; the police-union chief who negotiated with him gets the worst grade among the union leaders.

"Naive When They Start"

Students find that hiding certain facts, bluffing or outright lying often gets them a better deal. But the idea isn't necessarily to teach them to lie. Rather, Prof. Raiffa says, it is to teach them they may be lied to. "I think they become much more aware," he says. "They're very naive when they start."

One-third of the course grade is based on success in the negotiating games. For ambitious, aggressive students, the pressure to win is intense, and the course evokes strong reactions. During one class discussion of a game, a woman burst into tears. She had discovered that the man she negotiated with, who repeatedly assured her he opposed any misrepresentation, had in fact lied blatantly. Another student, James N. Beers, who has worked for Arabian American Oil Co. in Saudi Arabia negotiating construction contracts, said he found the students here less reasonable than the people he dealt with in the business world.

It's a safe bet that students in the course will eventually get to practice what they learn. According to surveys by the school, 14% of its alumni are presidents or chief executives of their firms, and 19% of the top three officers of all Fortune 500 companies are Harvard Business School graduates.

The school regards ethics as a "critically important" part of business education, according to Dean W. Currie, assistant dean for educational affairs. But business school teachers don't tell students that certain actions are right or wrong; they just try to make sure that the students realize that the ethical questions are there. "It's part of the pedagogy," Dean Currie says. "We don't have a 'teacher tell' attitude on anything, even dividend policy."

Learning From Experience

Prof. Raiffa doesn't tell his students how to negotiate in any particular game. The students develop their own strategies and methods as they go along. Part of the course is theoretical—students learn how to analyze competitive situations. But to the baldish, voluble Prof. Raiffa and most of his students, the actual negotiations are the heart of the course.

"You learn a lot about negotiating and a lot about yourself," says Dale M. Nicholls, a lawyer who put in a year as counsel to a congressional subcommittee before taking the course.

Letters to the Editor: *'Strategic Misrepresentation' at Harvard B-School*

Howard Raiffa

Your January 15 page-one article about my course in Competitive Decision Making at the Harvard Business School left the impression that I condone lying—or, as I euphemistically say, strategic misrepresentation. In strategic negotiations (buying a house, selling a firm, negotiating a labor contract or an international treaty) it is unfortunately not always true that completely unadorned, open honesty is the best policy. We don't always want to be represented by negotiators who will truthfully disclose our vulnerabilities, our rock-bottom walkaway prices, our very tradeoffs between conflicting objectives. Neither do we want to be represented by schemers who poison the atmosphere and make reasonable joint compromises impossible.

Because I am deeply concerned, personally and professionally, as a teacher and researcher, about ethical choices in decision making, a good many of the games I use are designed to force students to grapple with the ethical considerations inherent in the problems.

My course deals with real-world problems, among them lying for advantage. Not to consider strategies in negotiations in which lying may be used to try to maximize a position is to pretend we live in an ideal world. The object of the course is not to condone lying as a defensible means to a profitable end, but to confront it in a context which also reckons with the moral values of integrity and trust. The very real dilemma in, as well as outside, the classroom is: How do you do what is ethically right when it sometimes conflicts with what may be economically or strategically beneficial?

Here is an example. Mrs. B has been seriously injured in an automobile accident caused by driver Q's negligence. She is suing Q. When the attorney for Q's insurance company approaches Mrs. B's Attorney and says, "Tell me your client's honest, rockbottom figure for settling out of court, and we'll see if we can meet it." Mrs. B's lawyer does not quote $25,000 (the sum he knows she would accept). He feels that a jury would probably award her $100,000 or more in damages, and he believes the insurance company knows this, too. So he replies, "My client won't take a penny less than $100,000."

What a whopping lie, or what a sizable strategic misrepresentation, if you will! Is it inappropriate for a course in Competitive Decision Making to address such misrepresentations? As future business persons, students must realize that occasions will arise when they will be particularly vulnerable if they honestly reveal information that could be exploited by less scrupulous adversaries. It is important that they learn how to protect themselves—not necessarily by lying in turn, but by proposing ways of competing, negotiating, trading, and so on that do not punish them for disclosing honest values.

In the case of Mrs. B, her lawyer might respond, "It is not in my client's interest to tell you her rock-bottom price unless you are willing to reveal your company's absolute maximum offer." Now who do you suppose will speak first in that situation?

For the last class of my course, students were asked to complete a questionnaire on ethical values. Your readers would be pleasantly surprised, I think, at their moral responses. After distributing and discussing their answers, I expressed my hope that they would set higher ethical standards for themselves than for others, and that they would be happier for it.

Howard Raiffa is the Frank Plumpton Ramsey Professor of Managerial Economics at Harvard Graduate School of Business.

Prof. Raiffa says he structures the negotiations so that in some of the early games, "the truth teller is at an extreme disadvantage against someone who lies or bluffs. In later games, liars may lose a chance to reach a profitable settlement because their opponent is outraged and becomes more stubborn. People have to learn to understand the nature of the game," Prof. Raiffa says, "and understand how they are vulnerable."

Many students are surprised at the amount of lying. "Some people never misrepresent their position; others do it pathologically," Mr. Nicholls says. Another student, Priscilla R. Paff, an academic research assistant at Harvard before coming to the business school, says that attitudes toward lying changed during the semester. "There was a period when it seemed as if everyone was lying. It wasn't bluffing; it was outright lying," she says. "I did it too."

Miss Paff says the experience taught her that peer pressure can overcome personal ethics. Since she doesn't want to lie, she plans to avoid fields where she thinks dishonesty is commonplace.

Mary K. Knowles, who worked for the National Park Service before entering the business school, says she preserved her ethical standards but lost in several negotiations to people who lied. Deeply disturbed, she went to Prof. Raiffa to discuss the course and her future in business. "I concluded there are businesses I'd better not go into," she says. "I'm unwilling to compromise my principles to the point of baldfaced lying."

Inside and Outside

Some students say that lying in the course is acceptable but that lying outside isn't. Most students, however, feel that the way they play the game does indicate what techniques they'll be using in their careers. "I think what you do here matters very much," Mrs. Knowles says. "If you'd do it in a game, you'd do it in real life."

Mr. Thomchick, the class's most successful negotiator, and one of only 20% of the Harvard Business School students to come to the school directly without work experience, says the morality question is irrelevant. "Too much of an issue was made of ethics," he says. "I'm sorry if it made people uncomfortable, but that's the way the world is. I guess that sounds hardnosed. But if it was better for me, I did it. Most people did."

Henry E. Jusciewicz, a plastics engineer who worked for General Motors, recalls two early negotiations in which he and his opponent both disclosed their true situations completely. In each case, Mr. Jusciewicz's bargaining position was substantially weaker, "so I got my clock cleaned twice."

Changed Tactics

After that, he says, he remembered something he had learned in a labor-relations course: If the facts aren't in your favor, use emotion. From then on, he avoided disclosing facts, and, he says, so did the people he negotiated with: "There's an implicit understanding," he says, "that when you don't use a hard fact, you're misrepresenting."

In the later stages of the course, lying is a more risky strategy because the games become more complicated. "Unless you're very sophisticated and have spent a great deal of time analyzing the situation," says Mark Cancian, a U.S. Marine Corps captain studying at the business school, "you're as likely to hurt as help yourself."

The semester-long course lacks one bargaining alternative that perhaps promotes honesty in the business world. "In the classroom, it isn't an option not to play," says David F. Feeny, an Englishman who worked in industrial sales for 14 years before studying at Harvard Business. "I suspect in the real world, people get a reputation for dishonest bargaining. In the real world you can decide against doing business with them." •

William M. Bulkeley is a Staff Reporter of *The Wall Street Journal.*

Study Questions

1. What is another term for lying?

2. What was the purpose of Prof. Raiffa's exercises with regard to lying?

3. What is your opinion about lying in negotiation?

CASE: Heaven Help Her

Alexander D. Hill
Associate Professor of Law and Ethics,
Seattle Pacific University

Topic: Negotiations
Characters: Mary, Broker for a firm which buys and sells businesses
             Rev. Smith, a retired minister now managing a nonprofit organization
             George, Mary's supervisor

Mary, a recent college graduate, works for a company which represents clients who are interested in either buying or selling businesses. As a "business broker," her job is to arrange such sales.

Rev. Smith, a retired minister, contacts Mary's company to arrange for the purchase of a small manufacturing plant just outside of town. He has recently formed a nonprofit corporation to aid troubled youths and wants to convert the building into a recreation center. He desires to work with Mary because she formerly attended his church and he trusts her implicitly.

Mary's supervisor, George, has assigned her the task of negotiating a deal for Rev. Smith's organization. Some of the machines at the manufacturing plant are in poor condition and would require $100,000 to repair. Rev. Smith intends to remove them in any event.

The seller is asking for a $250,000 down payment on a $1,000,000 sale. Rev. Smith's organization can only raise $150,000. After studying the situation, George is convinced that if the seller can be led to believe that repairing the machines is important to Rev. Smith, the down payment request would be reduced to $150,000 and the asking price to $950,000.

George therefore instructs Mary to mislead the seller. She is told to insist—with a straight face—that either the seller repair the machines or drop the down payment and asking price. Mary is uncomfortable with this strategy, both for the sake of honesty and because Rev. Smith has not approved it. Yet, as a new employee, she wants to please her supervisor.

Study Questions

1. To whom, the company or Rev. Smith, does the agent Mary owe the higher duty? What does each of these parties have a right to expect?

2. Is telling untruths an acceptable part of Mary's job?

3. What could Mary do to provide the greatest benefit to the greatest number and how would the costs and benefits be measured?

4. What constraints on ethical behavior exist in this case?

SECTION 6

Communication Issues in Negotiation

Ultimately, negotiations are people talking to each other trying to solve problems. This section presents three types of communication skills that are relevant to fruitful negotiation. These are: (1) viewing effective communications between negotiators as a problem-solving process; (2) possessing effective interpersonal skills; and, (3) being aware of crucial cultural differences in communicating across nationalities.

In their article about communication as a problem-solving processing, **"Communication: The Problem-Solving Process,"** Strauss and Sayles emphasize the process of active listening as a cornerstone to problem solving. Active listening in negotiation is essential to understanding the agendas of other negotiators. Strauss and Sayles describe the techniques that enhance our ability to be active listeners.

Fisher and Davis, in **"Six Basic Interpersonal Skills for a Negotiator's Repertoire,"** prescribe six techniques for improving emotional communication in tense situations. With these techniques, negotiators can improve their relationship and engage in problem solving rather than dysfunctional fighting.

Copeland and Griggs (**"Communication: How Do I Talk to These People?"**) discuss communicating with people from different cultures. The authors describe some of the language and thinking barriers that occur in international business negotiation. Getting and giving good information is usually more difficult than it may seem. The authors provide us with rules for improving our communication with negotiators from different nationalities.

*   *   *

Communications: The Problem-Solving Process

G. Strauss
L. Sayles

"My boss doesn't give a hoot about me. As far as he is concerned I am another piece of machinery."

"I'll say this about my boss: no matter what your problem, she'll hear you through."

Effective communication requires effort both by the sender of the message and the receiver. In this chapter we shall deal with the specifics of the receiving or listening process. Listening is one of the most important of all management tools. Yet, though people learn to listen before they learn to talk, relatively few listen well.

Listening is sometimes viewed as interviewing, and in this chapter we use the two terms, listening and interviewing, interchangeably. This may cause some confusion, since most people think of interviewing in the sense of formal interviews connected with getting a job. By *interviewing* we mean much more than this: we mean deliberate, active listening whose purpose is to draw other people out, to discover what they really want to say, to give them a chance to express themselves fully, and to assist in the solution of mutual problems.

The following interchange illustrates dangers that arise when managers fail to listen.

Jane: *Bill, I think the time has come for us to investigate new office copying equipment.*
Bill: *No. Our budget won't stand it. We invested too much when we decided to buy rather than rent Brand X equipment three years ago.*
Jane: *But we can rent this time, and we'll have equipment available when we need it. The cost won't be much more than our present repair bills and we'll save on clerical time. Furthermore . . .*

Bill (interrupting): *No. This isn't the year. We don't have the budget. You'll have to do a better job with what you've got.*
Jane: *If you only knew how badly off we are now . . .*
Bill: *No.*

Of course, Bill may be right but he hasn't listened to Jane. He has cut her down, injured her self-esteem and cast doubt as to her ability to handle her job. The next stage may be escalation:

Jane: *You're just being pig-headed because it wasn't your idea.*

Whether Jane says this or not, she feels it. What could have been an objective discussion leading to cost-benefit analysis has degenerated into a personal flareup. Note how differently the scenario might have been:

Jane: *Bill, I think the time has come for us to investigate new office copying equipment.*
Bill: *Tell me more what you have in mind, Jane.*

Bill doesn't have to agree with Jane after the discussion is over but her feelings about him and the job will be very different if he hears her out.

Historical Background

Management first became aware of the value of listening in industrial relations during the 1930s as a consequence of studies conducted at the Hawthorne plant of the Western Electric Company. These studies were primarily concerned with the determinants of morale and productivity. Attempting to uncover basic feelings, however, the researchers found that questioning subjects about specific aspects of their jobs resulted in superficial lifeless answers. Even worse—or so it seemed at the time—instead of giving straightforward responses interviewees tended to talk about what interested them most at the moment.

Following this clue the interviewers tried a radically new experiment. They sat back and let the interviewees direct the interviews. Now they discovered that people began to express their feelings. Employees launched into long tirades (to which the interviewers patiently listened) revealing attitudes that might otherwise have been kept carefully-guarded. In fact, some employees expressed attitudes that they had not been consciously aware of themselves. As a consequence, the interviewers discovered surprising relationships about which they would never have learned by asking direct questions.

More important: the employees benefited greatly. Just by talking freely in the presence of a sympathetic listener they got their problems off their chests and felt better. They experienced what psychologists call *catharsis* (from the Greek: to make pure). In addition, merely by talking things over, the employees began to gain insights into the nature of their own problems. Once they had relieved their feelings by speaking openly in a receptive environment, they were able to look at their problems more objectively. And their clearer understandings, supplemented by further discussion, often enabled them to work out solutions (at least to those problems that they were in a position to solve themselves).

Impressed by the value of the Hawthorne experience, Western Electric instituted a program of formal counseling. Specially chosen counselors were trained in the use of *nondirective* interviews. (By nondirective interviews we mean—as we shall explain later—a type of interview in which the interviewer encourages the interviewee to express his own thoughts with considerable freedom—as contrasted to directive interviewing, in which the interviewer asks direct questions and tries to keep the discussion within predetermined limits.)

These "free-floating" counselors were given no regular supervisory duties. Their function was merely to listen to employees' problems without giving advice. Other companies rapidly followed Western Electric's example. Particularly during World War II, counseling was very popular, especially to help women workers.

The counselors faced a tough ethical problem of what to do with the information they received. If they repeated to management what they had been told, the workers would no longer trust them. On the other hand, if they could use their information in a discreet manner, they might be able to eliminate the causes of trouble. Often the counselors compromised by giving management general reports without revealing details that might identify individuals.

In recent years, the use of such counselors as a personnel tool has declined. It was discovered that this technique has many drawbacks, including the following:

- Although counseling might help an individual make a better adjustment to a poor environment (say to an inept supervisor), it did not improve the environment itself. Employees often began to feel that they were wasting their time talking to a counselor who could do little for them, and they ended up almost as frustrated as before.
- Counseling is directed almost entirely toward changing *individual* attitudes and behavior, in spite of evidence that group attitudes are often more important than individual attitudes.
- The counseling system gave subordinates a chance to bypass and tattle on their supervisors. Naturally, the supervisors objected.
- The counselors discovered that they were spending most of their time with a few disturbed individuals who really needed deep psychotherapy rather than counseling.

The basic trouble with free-floating counseling was its separation from line management. Line management emphasized downward communication; counseling provided upward communication. But the two forms of communication went along different channels.

Management began to learn that effective communications must go both ways. Upward communication and downward communication, listening and order-giving, are both more effective if done by the same person. Furthermore, if they are merged into the same process, something new and better emerges. Thus, there has come the realization that interviewing or active listening is not a special technique for use by personnel experts only, but a vital aspect of good management generally.

Listening As A Management Tool

To enumerate the uses of listening would be almost to itemize the functions of management itself. Listening is useful for bosses dealing with subordinates, for subordinates dealing with their bosses, for staff people dealing with line people (and vice versa) and for colleagues at the same level dealing with one another. Listening is obviously well suited to formal interviews, such as those used for hiring, exit, and requests for transfer. But it is also appropriate for other purposes, such as the following:

Low morale: finding out the cause of employee dissatisfaction, turnover, or absenteeism.

Discipline: discovering why employees are performing unsatisfactorily and helping them to evolve means of correcting themselves.

Order-giving: getting reaction to and acceptance of orders, to see that the person who receives the order really understands it.

Resistance to change: gaining acceptance of new techniques, tools, procedures.

Merit rating and evaluation: helping an employee correct his weaknesses.

Grievance-handling: finding out the real causes of a union grievance and getting the union officers to agree to a constructive solution.

Settling Disputes: finding out the causes of the disputes between employees and getting them to agree to settlement.

The listening approach is not something to be applied only when dealing with specific problems. It is a general attitude which the manager can apply day in and day out in dealings with fellow supervisors, subordinates, and the boss. In a nutshell, it is a matter of always being ready to listen to the other person's point of view and trying to take it into account before taking action oneself.

Establishing Confidence

Managers must take the initiative in encouraging subordinates to come to them with their problems. They must show that they are willing to hear them out. Otherwise, minor irritations may grow to tremendous proportions, even before the manager has become aware of the danger. If the initial discussion is a pleasant experience, the subordinate will come back more freely and more regularly when new problems arise. If it has been an unpleasant experience and if he feels he has been put on the spot, he will be reluctant to reveal what is on his mind

in the future. The manager should be aware that some of the people who report to him will be easier to get to know than others. Some will talk quite freely and easily. Others will hold back because of fear or natural timidity. Managers must be careful not to spend all their time with those to whom it is easy to talk.

To avoid the charge of favoritism, and to insure that he is able to deal with the problems of all his employees, the manager must go out of his way to make contact with employees who are reluctant to come to him. The manager must recognize that there is an invisible barrier which separates him from his subordinates. For some, this status difference is of little importance, but for many, it makes effective upward communication much harder.

Finally, listening takes time. The manager should make time available for his subordinates to talk to him. But if he doesn't have time at the moment, it is far better to postpone the discussion to some specific hour than to rush through a discussion in an abrupt distracted manner.

Initiating Action

Nondirective listening is useful not just when someone initiates action for you (as Jane tried to do with Bill in the case that begins this chapter), but also when you try to initiate action yourself, that is, when you try to get your boss, your subordinate, or someone at your own level to accept your ideas.

Suppose you are the division manager, and you want to introduce a new system of quality control. Although you have not yet consulted the production supervisor, you have heard through the grapevine that she has strong objections to the new system. Yet, her cooperation is essential if the system is to succeed.

You feel fairly certain that your plan is good and that the production supervisor's objections are not well grounded. You are the boss, of course, and you could give her a direct order to put the plan into effect. (Question: How would the supervisor react to this order? How loyally would she carry it out?)

Instead, you decide to listen to her point of view. In spite of the grapevine, you can't be sure you know what her objections are until she has spoken to you, personally. (Question: What would happen it you had already made up your mind and just went through the formalities of listening?)

So you call her into your office, explain to her that you would like her reactions to the proposed plan, and briefly explain what is involved (assuming she is not aware of this already). You emphasize that you still have an open mind as to whether to adopt the plan at all and that within limits (which you are careful to explain) the details of the plan are subject to modification.

You then ask for her comments. You listen carefully and encourage her to express herself more fully. As she speaks, she relaxes and explains her point of view with less restraint than she would if she felt she were on the defensive. Instead of trying to answer her arguments, you encourage her to tell you everything she thinks and feels about the change. When she finishes, you briefly summarize what she has said, to make sure you understand—and also to indicate to her that you understand.

After speaking her piece, she feels free to listen to your point of view, which may have changed since you heard her comments. You fill in some of the areas where you feel she was misinformed and indicate the points on which you have changed your own thinking. You agree that many of the problems she raises are real ones and ask for her suggestions in dealing with them. You make concessions yourself. Eventually, you work out a detailed program which includes as much of her input as seems feasible (subject, of course, to similar consultation with other affected managers).

At the end, even if the supervisor is not fully convinced of the wisdom of the modified plan, she agrees to carry it out and probably feels pleased that you consulted her.

The above example illustrates the flexibility of the listening technique as a means of initiating action (though we must emphasize that the results are frequently not as good as we have pictured). Note the steps you went through in the above example.

1. Stating the nature of your proposal, indicating that it was tentative.
2. Listening carefully to the supervisor's reactions.

3. Summarizing these to indicate that you understood them.
4. Seeking her cooperation in working out a solution, carefully indicating the framework within which the solution must be made.
5. Modifying your original proposal in the light of her suggestions.
6. Making a joint commitment to carry out the agreed upon action.

Managers sometimes use listening techniques to help employees solve personal off-the-job problems. Normally stable individuals have unexpected trouble and try to use their boss as a wailing wall. However, the bosses should be careful not to run their subordinates' personal lives.

The manager should be particularly cautious when sensitive areas are reached in the course of a discussion. What most people want is a sympathetic, understanding listener rather than an adviser. They may ask for advice, but actually they want only a chance to talk. Even when advice-giving is successful, there is the danger that the employee may become over-dependent on his boss and run to him whenever he has a minor problem.

The manager should be still more careful when deep-seated personality problems are involved. In such a case it is wise to refer the person to a professionally trained specialist rather than to play amateur psychologist. The average manager is not equipped to do counseling, nor is this part of his job. The patient-psychiatrist or client-counselor relationship is just not consistent with that of subordinate and boss. And the nondirective technique may trick subordinates into blurting out confidences they will later regret.

The Use of the Nondirective Approach

In understanding how the nondirective approach should be used, it is helpful to think of the interview as running through three stages: feelings, facts, solutions.

1. **Feelings.** The interviewee is encouraged to release his feelings; the interviewer is concerned with helping the interviewee express himself. This stage is the most purely nondirective, for the interviewer still has little idea where the discussion will go.

2. **Facts.** Having blown off steam, the interviewee is now ready to look at the facts rationally. In this stage, the interviewer can be more directive and may even use "probes" (to be discussed later) to bring out information that the interviewee has not already volunteered. In fact, the interviewer may contribute additional information on his own.

3. **Solutions.** Once the facts have been assembled, the interviewee is in a position to weigh alternate solutions and pick the best one. As we have mentioned frequently, it is preferable to help the interviewee work out his own solution; however, the supervisor may have to be rather strongly directive to make sure that the solution is consistent with the needs of the organization.

These, then, are the three major stages of the listening process, although it may switch back and forth from one stage to another as different problems are considered. Still, on a given problem, the interviewer should stick to the order indicated: feelings, facts, solutions. Certainly one should avoid the common human tendency to jump to a solution before getting all the facts.

Equally important, he should not waste his time trying to isolate the facts before the interviewee has had a chance to express his feelings, to blow off steam. Why? Because feelings color facts, and as long as someone is emotionally excited, he is unlikely to approach problems rationally. Furthermore—and the point is subtle—the feelings of the people concerned in the situation are themselves facts that must be considered. For instance, the office manager has been having trouble getting Bill to do a full day's work. The most important fact in this solution may be the manager's intense dislike of Bill as a person. Until the manager's feeling is recognized as a complicating element, "facts" he presents will be distorted by his antagonism toward Bill.

Does this mean that the interviewer should never express himself—that he should never try to correct the other person if he is wrong nor try to change his opinion? Of course not. It may be enough for the psychiatrist or the professional counselor merely to listen. The manager must also take action. But in most cases, before he takes action he should wait until he has heard the employee's whole story.

The nondirective approach is not a magic solution to all human-relations problems, of course. There are times when a supervisor may have to be quite firm and directive in the solution stage of the discussion to make sure that the solution is consistent with the needs of the organization. For instance, the supervisor may listen patiently to the subordinate's objections to a new system; the subordinate may persist in his resistance; and the supervisor may still have to overrule him, explaining why, and insist that the system be used. However, the subordinate will have had the satisfaction of being consulted, of knowing that he had his day in court to present his side of the story.

Listening Techniques

Skillful listening is an art, and like all arts it requires training and experience. It can be learned better by practice than by reading a book, especially when the practice is supervised by an experienced instructor. Fortunately, one can gain unsupervised practice every day of the year.

Each manager must develop a system that is comfortable for him and that fits his personality, but he should avoid using the same technique with all people and for all purposes. An interview held for disciplinary reasons will naturally be different from an interview held for the purpose of order-giving.

Regardless of the form of the interview, here are a few hints that may prove useful.

Encouraging the other person to talk. Your primary objective is to get the other person to talk freely, not to talk yourself: The best way to find out what the other person wants to say is to listen, and the best interview is usually the one in which the interviewer talks least.

But listening is not easy, for our natural impulse is to talk. This is particularly true when we feel threatened by what is being said to us—for instance, when we are being criticized. Under these circumstances our normal impulse is to defend ourselves rather than to listen.

Listening is more than just not talking, however. It requires an active effort to convey that you understand and are interested in what the other person is saying—almost that you are helping him say it. A friendly facial expression and an attentive but relaxed attitude are important. A good listener also makes use of door-opening comments such as "uh-huh," "I understand," "That explains it," "Could you tell me more?" or "I'd be interested in your point of view."

Even silence can be used to keep a person talking. When he pauses in his discourse, he is either being polite and giving you a chance to talk, or he wants you to comment, to evaluate what he is saying. Merely by not taking his challenge, perhaps by a nod, by waiting through his pause, you indicate that you have nothing to say at the moment, that you want him to continue talking.

Reflective Summary. One of the most effective ways to encourage the other person to talk is the reflective summary, in which you try to sum up the feelings the other person has expressed, disregarding the factual details and incidents. For example: "The reason I want to quit is that the so-and-so boss keeps pestering me. He won't give me a chance!" Then he (or she) stops, wondering whether he has gotten himself into trouble by saying too much. Your response, "He won't give you a chance?" encourages him to tell the rest of his story, but it does not commit you in any sense. Such a summary serves a number of purposes:

1. It shows the other person that you are giving his ideas careful consideration and that you understand him—in other words, that you are being fair.
2. It gives him a chance to restate and elaborate his attitudes if he feels that you haven't quite grasped his point.
3. It serves to highlight what he has really been saying. Often people are surprised to learn what their words have meant to someone else, and are rewarded with deeper insight into their own attitudes.

The reflective summary is particularly effective if you reflect not only what the other person has actually said, but can somehow put into words what he has tried, unsuccessfully, to express. Be careful, however, not to hear more in his words than he intends to put into them. For if he finds you reading things into his words that he did not mean to be there, he will be doubly careful to watch what he says.

Your summary should indicate neither approval nor disapproval of what the interviewee is saying. It should simply indicate that you are listening attentively. For instance, he says, "It's got to the point where I may lose my temper and take a poke at the boss." If you were to say, "Well, that's quite understandable," you would almost be inviting him to carry out his threat! A more satisfactory response would be "You are sore at him because. . . ."

There are limits, however, to the extent to which reflective summaries are appropriate. It sounds patronizing and manipulative to parrot the interviewee's phrases without any indication that you are responding to their meaning. For example:

Employee: *"So I want to find out exactly what I'm expected to do. How many units am I expected to do a day? It seems I'm getting a run around."*

Boss: *"You want to know exactly what you are expected to do. You want to know how many units a day you are supposed to do? You feel you are getting a run around."*

The boss has heard the employee's words but has failed either to hear the fact-related question or to respond to the employee's feelings. Possibly the boss might have responded as follows:

Boss: *"Perhaps we can do something to make your work assignment clearer, but I'm concerned about your feeling that you've been given a run around."*

Listening Empathetically.[1] Active listening requires that you put yourself in the other person's shoes. Only if you can understand the message sender's own frame of reference and his world of reality, can you really grasp the real meaning of his or her message. Though few of us can qualify as psychiatrists, we can learn to listen with a "third ear" by asking ourselves such questions as: "What did Joe really mean when he told me he was 'fed up'? Was it his assignment? His family? His chances for promotion? Me, as his boss? Why did he remain silent when I asked him for details?"

There is a hidden content in many communications that can only be inferred by the listener. (This underlying element is frequently referred to as the latent content as distinct from the manifest content.) Although the listener should keep his imagination in check, he should try to go beyond the logical verbal meaning where there is some evidence that emotional feeling is involved. Most communications are, in fact, a combination of fact and feeling.

A good example of this hidden content is provided by the word *communications* itself. An office manager complains to the personnel director that all her human-relations problems stem from "poor communications." If the personnel director wants to be of assistance, he will try to get behind the manager's use of the word *communications*. The manager might mean that there are divisive cliques that tend to distort her orders or that she, the boss, never hears the "real truth" about what is going on in the office. She might be using the word *communications* to mean that cooperative teamwork is lacking, or to mean many other things. The point is that the words used by a speaker may not be very informative until we have an opportunity to question him on what he really means in terms of actual observable behavior. The listener must try to get back to the *referents* of the speaker and to avoid the easy assumption that both people are attaching the same meaning to abstract terms like your communication.

Empathetic interviewing means also that you respond to the other person's comments as a person, yourself, not as a machine. To the best of your ability, you show sincere concern (insincere concern is easily discerned and is worse than nothing). There is nothing wrong in demonstrating emotion yourself; on the other hand, there is no need to match the other person's display, emotion by emotion. But it helps to be spontaneous, *yourself,* which means that none of the suggestions made in this chapter should be made mechanically. Unless you are straightforward and honest, you are unlikely to receive honesty in return.[2]

Probes. The "free-floating" counselor is interested primarily in getting at underlying feelings. And as a manager you, too, are interested in the feelings of your subordinates. But if you know that you must *act* on the basis of what you learn in the discussion, you will also want to get all the facts, the whole story.[3] This means that after the feeling stage has passed, you

should to some extent direct the interview. Tactfully and calmly, you should steer the conversation, but without forcing the interviewee into an area he does not want to enter, and with no hint that you have already made up your mind.

One way to direct the interview is to build on what the interviewee has already said. By repeating certain words selected from what he has said, you can indicate that you would like him to talk more about this particular area. This device is called a "probe." For example, in explaining how a fight started between himself and another employee, Bill says, "Joe was always riding me. When he picked up my lunch bucket, that was the last straw." Now if the supervisor wants to find out more about what Joe has done to arouse Bill, he has a good chance to insert a probe: "You say Joe was always riding you?" Then he stops and waits for Bill to go on. Notice that the interviewer does not say: "What did Joe do to make you so sore?" Rather, he simply repeats the employee's own words.

Weighing Alternatives. Sometimes it is enough if the interview helps you find out how the other person feels about the situation and what the essential facts are as he or she sees them. In other instances, however, you may wish to help him devise a solution. How can you do this without seeming to impose your own ideas on him? The following approach may be useful.

Let us assume one of your managers wishes to discipline severely an employee who has been a troublemaker. The manager's first suggestion may be to fire the troublemaker immediately. If you keep asking for additional suggestions, she may suggest lesser penalties. Finally, she may even come around to suggesting certain changes in her own behavior.

Now, after the manager has offered all these suggestions, you would attempt to get her to examine each one: What would its probable effect be? How would the other employees react? How would it help her solve her problem? By helping the interviewee think through her problem, you may succeed in having her come to a conclusion that is hers, not yours. And if it is hers, she will be much more likely to act on it with enthusiasm.

Things to Avoid

Too Much Warm-up. Many people feel that before getting down to the subject of an interview, particularly if it is an unpleasant one, they should try to place the interviewee at ease by discussing some irrelevant topic—baseball, traffic jams, the weather. This approach may relieve the supervisor's anxiety, but it intensifies that of the worker, particularly if he has some idea of why he has been called in. While he is on the "hot seat," he may be thinking, "Why doesn't this character get down to business? Why does he have to play cat-and-mouse? What's this building up to?" Such "warming-up" is useful at times; however, the interviewer should be careful to use it only when it actually reduces anxiety.

Premature Judgment. The listener should avoid giving any indication of pleasure or displeasure at what the subordinate says. Judgment must be suspended until all the facts are in. This restraint is extremely important, because subordinates look for verbal or facial cues that will tip them off to what the superior wants or does not want to hear. (Of course, unconsciously, we are always forming impressions, even on the most meager facts. However, supervisors should be aware of their predispositions and try to keep them from warping their judgment or communication.)

Criticizing or moralizing puts the other person on the defensive. Even if he does not argue back, he will begin to edit what he says in order to win the interviewer's approval. He will concentrate on proving that he is right rather than on giving an honest explanation. Certainly, putting someone on the defensive makes it harder to find out what that person really thinks.

Even praise or sympathy should be avoided until the end of the discussion, for it makes the interviewee think his present approach is correct and encourages him to avoid the hard work of thinking the problem through.

Direct Questions. One of the most frequent errors made by inexperienced interviewers is transforming the interview into a game of "twenty questions." Bill has fallen into the habit of coming to work late and his supervisor is anxious to straighten him out before discipline becomes necessary. Having had some training in human relations, the manager suspects that a home problem is involved. His end of the conversation may run something like this:

"Do you have trouble starting your car?" "Is there any trouble at home?" "Does your alarm clock go off on time?" "Did you have a drink too many last night?"

To each question Bill replies, "No, it isn't that." And to himself he says, "That's none of his business." And then another question is shot at him.

Here the manager, not Bill, is directing the interview. Note that every one of these questions is phrased in such a manner as to put Bill immediately on the defensive and make him overcautious in what he says. Some of the questions, such as, "Did you have a drink too many last night?" are downright insulting.

The listener rarely knows the right questions to ask; if he did, he would probably know the answers as well. The other person's problem is usually more complex than it seems at first glance, and direct questions tend to narrow it down too quickly.

To complicate matters, most subordinates try to say what they think will please their supervisor. Direct questions often imply the kind of answer the supervisor wants, or at least give the subordinate an "out." For instance, the question "Did you have trouble starting your car?" provides a ready excuse for a tardy worker.

If the supervisor wants to find out what the subordinate really has on his mind, he should leave the situation as free as possible to permit the subordinate to emphasize the things that are important to him.

If possible, the interviewer should avoid questions that can be answered with a simple yes or no. "Well, do you like your job?" "Do you think the tools are in bad shape?" Questions of this sort shut off discussion because they can be answered by a relatively meaningless, "Oh, I guess so," or "I suppose you might say that."

Arguing. Little is gained from argument, particularly in the early stage of the interview. Yet everyone has a strong human tendency to correct the other person when he says something that is obviously wrong. Especially, if the interviewer himself is attacked personally, he must exercise tremendous restraint not to answer back.

For example, an employee says he is having trouble doing the work because the stock has been changed. "The company must be buying cheaper material these days." Now if you know that there has been no change whatsoever in the materials, you will be strongly tempted to "set the employee straight" on this point, although his complaint may be a symptom of something much more basic. If you give way to this temptation, you may simply transform the interview into a fruitless argument.

Hard as it may be, you should avoid being defensive, even when criticized. This is difficult, because often even your unconscious feelings are revealed through facial expressions.

Advice-Giving. When you finally get the complete picture as the employee sees it, you may be able to provide advice or information that has not previously been available. But again it is often better to help him work through his own problems. In any event, you should hold off giving advice until after the interviewee has told his entire story—until you have all the facts.

Active Listening at the Wrong Time. Nondirective listening is not the solution to every problem. When someone is legitimately asking for information, for a helping hand, or for some resource you can provide him, he may have no need to talk things out. Sometimes managers abuse the nondirective technique by shifting the discussion from the technical aspects of the question at hand to the subordinate's motives in dealing with it. Such abuse occurs most commonly when the manager has a psychology or social work background. For example, a subordinate may have a sound practical objection to something the boss may want to do. Instead of listening to the objections themselves, the excessively psychologically-oriented boss may look upon the subordinate's attitude as an example of hostility and may seek its emotional basis. Such an approach often adds to the hostility it is designed to alleviate.

Masterminding. Many people go through the motions of the nondirective interview but violate its spirit. They hope, by asking shrewd questions, to manipulate the interviewee into believing that he is thinking through his problem by himself, though the way questions are worded inevitably forces the interviewee to arrive at the interviewer's own predetermined conclusion.

Masterminding is used with various degrees of sophistication. One of the less subtle forms makes constant use of the leading question, the "don't you feel . . .?" approach: "Don't you feel it would be better for the company and your own future if you came to work on time?" Questions like this usually permit only one answer. They are thinly veiled forms of advice, judgment, or just plain bawling out.

The basic purpose of nondirective listening is to enable the listener to find out how the individual sees the problem or situation at issue, and then to help him think and, above all, *feel* his way through to a solution. The goal of this whole philosophy is for the supervisor to be perceived as a source of help—as a person who can assist the subordinate to develop and do a better job. •

Footnotes

[1] Empathetic listening does not necessarily mean that you agree with the other person's message, only that you are trying to understand it. Some authorities argue that the interviewer should accept the interviewee's feelings. We disagree. Perhaps acceptance is required for psychotherapy. But if an employee says, "I think Race X is inferior, and I'll be damned if I work with one or them," the boss may perhaps try to understand this feeling but has no obligation to accept it.

[2] For a good discussion, see Jack Gibe, "Defensive Communication," in Harold Leavitt and Louis Pondy, *Readings in Management Psychology,* 2nd ed. (Chicago: Univ. of Chicago Press, 1973).

[3] In other words, your interviewing is "organization centered," not "client centered."

* * *

Study Questions

1. How do they define "interviewing?"

2. What did the Hawthorne Study researchers discover about interviewing techniques meant to bring out attitudes and opinions? What was their eventual style of interviewing called? How different is this from other types of interviewing?

3. What were eventual problems with constant use of "catharsis" interviewing sessions?

4. Why should managers try to facilitate both upward as well as downward communication?

5. What really matters when adopting a "listening approach?"

6. Should managers try to help employees with personal matters during interview/listening sessions?

7. What can reflective summaries do?

8. How is active listening empathetic?

9. Explain the "probe."

10. What should be avoided during interviewing?

11. What follows when managers criticize and/or moralize too early in an interview? What about early praise or sympathy?

12. Explain "masterminding" an interview.

13. How are nondirective interviewing techniques applicable to the negotiation process?

Six Basic interpersonal Skills for a Negotiator's Repertoire

Roger Fisher
Wayne H. Davis

A well-rounded person has a large repertoire of interpersonal skills, and exercises them appropriately depending upon the circumstances. All of us, however, find ourselves stronger in some skills than in others. We naturally tend to use those skills in which we feel more adept and to avoid those in which we feel less comfortable or less competent.

A skilled negotiator not only has a broad repertoire of interpersonal skills, but also uses those most appropriate to the circumstances of a particular situation. He or she recognizes that one's effectiveness within a given negotiation is likely to be enhanced by being able to change pace and approach.

There is an infinite range and variety in interpersonal skills. Many of these skills can be seen as attractive opposites, such as being independent and being cooperative, or being pragmatic and being imaginative, or being controlled and being expressive. We would like to be good at both but tend to be stronger in one than the other.

These desirable qualities can be visualized as lying on the circumference of a circle, so that becoming more skillful is seen as extending our skills in all directions. Improving our skills can then be recognized not only as correcting a fault (such as "I am too flexible"), but rather as becoming more skillful at its attractive opposite (e.g., "I want to become better at being firm when that is appropriate").

To broaden one's repertoire, it may help to think of these qualities as falling into six basic categories of interpersonal skills in which each effective negotiator enjoys some competence and confidence. We have tentatively identified these as follows:

- expressing strong feelings appropriately;
- remaining rational in the face of strong feelings;
- being assertive within a negotiation without damaging the relationship;
- improving a relationship without damage to a particular negotiation;
- speaking clearly in ways that promote listening; and
- inquiring and listening effectively.

In use, these skills are often closely associated with each other, but in developing the skills and in practicing them it helps to focus on them one at a time. The following checklist can be used as a guide for negotiators who wish to develop a strong, well-balanced repertoire.

Expressing Strong Feelings Appropriately

Disliked Symptoms. Many negotiations take place as if the only effective mode of influence is the kind of rational dialogue that might take place between two computers. We may suppress or ignore flesh and blood feelings. In other negotiations, we may find our rational arguments overwhelmed by emotions such as anger, fear, insecurity, or hatred.

Possible Diagnoses. Many of us learn as children that it is naughty to be angry. We may treat feelings as private problems best dealt with by suppressing them, or by denying their existence. Sometimes we may regard feelings as having less merit than reasoned argument—as something to be ashamed of.

At other times, we may contain feelings because we see no way to express them other than by losing our temper—a performance that our rational selves tell us is likely to appear ridiculous, damage our credibility, and at best prove ineffective.

General Prescriptive Approach:

Recognize feelings. A negotiator needs to recognize that feelings are a natural human phenomenon. They exist. There is nothing wrong with having emotions, although expressing them in particular ways may be costly or counter-productive.

Be aware. It is a wise practice to become aware of the emotions—both our own and those of the other side—that are involved in any given negotiation. It appears to be true that if we suppress or deny our own feelings, we are likely to be unaware of the feelings of those with whom we are dealing. Before we can safely and appropriately express our feelings, we need to become aware of them, and to acknowledge them consciously.

In general, when some feeling inside seems to be growing larger and out of control, naming or identifying that feeling internally will, by itself, tend to reduce the feeling, make it more life-size, and help bring it under control.

Develop a range of expression. When it comes to communicating feelings to someone else, it is well to recognize that there is a spectrum of ways to do so, ranging from talking rationally about them, through increasing the emotional content of verbal and nonverbal communication, to letting the emotions take charge.

Because of inhibitions, we often err on the side of insufficiently communicating our emotions. It is good to find a safe environment within which to experiment and practice. It is often useful to explore a range of possible expressions of emotion by deliberately overshooting. When we fear going too far we are unlikely to learn how far we can, in fact, safely go.

Relate tone to substance. Too often we fail to relate the emotional content of a communication to the substantive issue being discussed. It is far easier to be assertive—and certainly more effective—if we have something sensible to assert. Key to an effective communication of feeling is likely to be some well-prepared substantive content that identifies the purpose of the communication, justifies the feeling, and enlists its expression in the furtherance of that purpose.

Remaining Rational in the Face of Strong Feelings

Disliked Symptoms. When others display strong emotions—particularly those hostile to us—we are likely to react and let emotions overwhelm our rationality. The cycle of emotional action and reaction is likely to preclude rational negotiation.

Possible Diagnosis. We get caught up in the fray. We react to the last thing the other side said, and lose sight of the original purposes of talking. We may mistake their expression of strong feelings as a personal attack on us, so we feel obliged to respond in self-defense. If neither side acknowledges the existence or validity of the other's feelings, both may amplify their expression of feelings so that the underlying "message" will be heard. We may try to silence each other's expression of feelings, which compounds the frustration and felt need to be heard.

General prescriptive approach. There are several different ways to deal effectively with displays of strong emotion in negotiation. Depending on the circumstances, any one of the following suggestions should prove useful:

Acknowledge their feelings. When others begin to heighten the emotive content of their speech, they may not be fully aware of the feelings growing inside them. If we acknowledge that they may (don't attribute!) be feeling a certain way, that will usually help them to become more aware and in control of their feelings, and give us enough distance so that we don't react.

Step above the fray. When the discussion turns so emotional that rational discussion seems pointless, we might withdraw from the discussion long enough for us and others to regain some composure. State frankly our reasons for withdrawing, and couple that with a commitment to return.

Step aside; let their emotions hit the problem. If they're expressing an emotion, encourage them to express it fully and completely—so they can feel that they've "got it all out."

Separate the causes of their feelings from the substantive problem, and deal with them in parallel. Once feelings have been fully expressed and acknowledged, it may be appropriate to analyze what engendered the feelings and take steps to alleviate those causes.

Be purposive. At the outset, consciously consider and decide on the purpose of the negotiation. Then, when emotions run too strong, we can ask the parties to question whether or not the direction of the discussion serves the agreed-upon purposes of the meeting.

Being Assertive Without Damaging the Relationship

Disliked Symptoms. Often in a negotiation, we may refrain from being assertive (we fail to speak with conviction or tenaciously pursue a particular point) for fear that assertiveness will damage either the immediate or the long-term relationship. We may acquiesce when it ill serves our interests to do so.

Possible Diagnoses. When a relationship seems to be more important than any one substantive issue, some people tend to give in as soon as the other party's preference becomes clear. But giving in does not help the relationship. It may reward bad behavior or be mistaken for a lack of conviction or spinelessness—undesirable qualities for a partner in most relationships.

General prescriptive approach. With or without increasing the emotional content of our expressions, it is possible to be assertive without damage to a relationship. The suggested general strategy is:

Disentangle relationship issues from substantive ones and work on them in parallel. Although substantive disagreements can make a working relationship more difficult, and although a good working relationship can make it easier to reach agreement, the process of dealing with differences is usefully treated as a subject quite distinct and separate from the content and extent of those differences.

Be "soft on the people." Avoid personal judgments. Acknowledge some merit in what the other side has said or done. Be open, polite, courteous, and considerate.

Have something to assert. Know the purpose of the session in terms of some product that it is reasonable to expect. Focus on one or two points that we would like to communicate forcefully, such as: the strength of our BATNA (Best Alternative to a Negotiated Agreement); the necessity of meeting some interest of ours; or our adherence to a particular standard of legitimacy unless and until we are convinced that some other standard is at least equally fair.

Be firm and open. Be prepared to remain firm as long as that appears to us to make sense on the substance of the negotiation. At the same time, be open—both in words and thought—to alternative views that are truly persuasive.

Improving a Relationship Without Damage to a Particular Negotiation

Disliked Symptoms. We often hesitate to be open and warm with people on the other side of a negotiation for fear that it will prejudice the outcome. We hesitate to acknowledge merit in what they say for fear that it will undercut what we say.

Possible Diagnoses. We may operate under a zero-sum assumption about ideas and arguments: To the extent that someone with whom we disagree is right, then we must be wrong. This assumption may stem from childhood fears of being pushed around, from formal high school or college debates, or from the general adversary nature of so much of our society. Some of us may assume that to develop a relationship in a negotiation, we must buy it with substantive concessions.

General Approach:

Good relations help reach good outcomes. It is important to recognize that relationship-building moves tend to strengthen rather than weaken our chances for achieving a good agreement.

Acknowledge merit in something they have done. It is almost always possible to find something meritorious that the other side has done—perhaps in an area apart from what is being negotiated. By acknowledging that, we can communicate that we recognize and respect their worth as people.

Acknowledge a need on our part. Relationships tend to be stronger when there is some interdependence: both sides feel and recognize their need or reliance on the other side in order to achieve mutually desired ends.

Take steps outside the negotiation to improve the relationship. We can concentrate our relationship-building actions in temporally-discrete segments of the negotiation, or when we are physically away from the table.

Speaking Clearly in Ways That Promote Listening

Disliked Symptoms. They don't seem to be paying much attention to what we say.

Possible Diagnoses. We may be including in what we say things that they know or believe to be mistaken. We often do so when we attribute particular intentions or motives to those on the other side. In the course of rejecting what they know to be wrong they are likely to reject a lot of other ideas that are closely associated with them. Or something we say early in a long statement raises a red flag for them; they then tune out because they're busy thinking of a retort. Or we may be making unwarranted assumptions about what they know, when in fact they lack certain information needed to make our statements comprehensible.

General prescriptive approach:

Speak for yourself. Phrase statements about their behavior, motives, statements, etc. in first-person terms of our perceptions and feelings. They may deny the accusation, "You're a bigot!" They can't deny the statement, "I'm feeling discriminated against."

Avoid attribution and check assumptions. Recognize when we make assumptions about their thoughts, feelings, motives, and so on, and try to verify those assumptions with the other side before acting on them. Inquire about their understanding of the background issues or information.

Use short clear statements. The longer any statement we make, the more they will edit it so they can respond. The more important our message is, the more succinct it should be. If the message is complex, break it down into small parts and confirm their understanding of each segment.

Ask them to repeat back what we've said. In effect, encourage them to be active listeners by asking them to confirm in their own words what they've heard us say.

Actively Inquiring and Listening

Disliked Symptoms. We don't learn as much as we should about the other side's interests and perceptions and the resources they could bring to bear on our joint problem. We may miss options and ideas that could lead to good solutions for us.

Possible Diagnosis. We are often so concerned with our own interests that we ignore those of the other side. We are often bored or tired. When they say something that surprises or angers us, we may ignore the rest of what they have to say while we ready our response. We may fear that if we understand them, our resolve will weaken; or that if we show we've heard and understood, they will mistake that for acquiescence or agreement.

General prescriptive approach:

Explicitly allocate time to listen and understand the other side. Set portions of the agenda for them to explain their interests and ideas. That helps to put us into a "listening mode." An added benefit of this practice is that it establishes a precedent for reciprocal treatment of us by them.

Separate understanding their arguments from judging and responding to them. Make sure that their full argument has been stated, and that we understand it before trying to respond.

Repeat back their statements in our own words.

Inquire actively about the reasoning behind their statements. Even if we repeat back what they said, often they haven't said all they were thinking. There will be some implicit reasoning or logic underlying their statements. It's helpful to ask them to make that reasoning explicit, and then to repeat back their explanation. •

Note

Many of the ideas in this article were developed in collaboration with Richard Chasin, M.D. and Richard Lee, Ph.D.

Roger Fisher is Williston Professor of Law at Harvard Law School and Director of the Negotiation Project. He is coauthor (with William Ury) of *Getting to YES: Negotiating Agreement Without Giving In* (Boston: Houghton Mifflin, 1991). **Wayne H. Davis** is an associate of the Harvard Negotiation Project and is a negotiation consultant with Conflict Management Inc., Cambridge, MA.

Study Questions

1. Identify the basic categories of interpersonal skills for negotiators.

2. What is the "prescribed" way to deal with feelings, in general?

3. What can be done to reduce and control a "growing" feeling?

4. What is meant by "relate tone to substance?"

5. Be aware of the suggestions for dealing with an opponent's strong feelings.

6. What can contribute to opponents being inattentive to our comments?

7. How do they suggest we make listening a more effective and strategic endeavor?

How Do I Talk With These People?

Lennie Copeland
Lewis Griggs

International business requires communication between people from different cultures. Whatever the assignment, whether consulting, teaching, selling, buying, supervising, preaching or representing a government, the job will require ability to get across information and ideas to employees, suppliers, customers, students, the media, and government officials. The American way of "telling it like it is" is often the wrong approach abroad. The job is also likely to require the skillful acquisition of information. In international business, very crucial information is lodged in foreign subsidiaries, joint ventures or customer companies. It can be difficult to extract unless you know how people provide information in those countries. In most places you can't just ask questions to get what you want. You have to have a strategy for how to extricate information, and that strategy must vary from country to country.

Most Executives Agree That the Single Biggest Problem For the Foreign Business Traveler is Language.

Every time language barriers must be crossed, important nuances are lost and potential misunderstandings jeopardize business. International travelers agree that it is always easier and less treacherous to do business when there is no language gap. Even with an interpreter, much is missed.

"They Speak English, Don't They?" Less Than You Think.

It is simply not true that most people around the world speak English. Outside the major cities and in most of the new construction projects or field offices, the average worker, engineer or official does not speak English. Gregory Zaretsky, president of The Corporate Word, a Pittsburgh-based translation service, says that American executives often talk with a foreign buyer who speaks perfect English, not realizing that their proposal will be passed along to be reviewed by others in the company who do not speak English. In such instances, the others are likely to pass over the proposal in favor of a rival's proposal in their own language. A Bechtel executive stationed in Hitachi village, outside Tokyo, says the American perception that all Japanese speak English is entirely wrong. In Hitachi, most of the people can read and write English as they were taught in school, but they cannot speak it or understand an American talking to them.

Many foreigners complicate the situation by not admitting when they don't understand you. Or they may speak your language, but have great difficulty understanding what you are saying because you speak too fast, unclearly, in an accent they haven't heard, and use too many idioms. Walter Hayes, vice chairman of Ford-Europe, says: "The American executive makes a big mistake thinking that people who speak English will understand what you are saying. Comprehension can be fairly superficial."

A growing number of foreign nations are now insisting that government contracts and negotiations be conducted solely in the local language. Defense ministries in West Germany, Belgium, Spain and Thailand, among many others, insist that their contracts be written only in the national language. India, Pakistan and Sri Lanka, too, are moving in this direction. Once there was a great incentive for people to learn English; they needed it in order to read most technical and medical journals and to watch TV and American movies. Now more and more media are in the local languages as well as English. If anything, English is becoming less of an international language.

Increasingly, the international business traveler is likely to have to deal with a medley of languages. Assembly-line workers at the Ford plant in Cologne speak Turkish and Spanish as well as German. In Malaysia, Indonesia and

Thailand, many of the buyers and traders are Chinese. In Belgium, French and Flemish are spoken, and the visitor should be careful *not* to speak French to the Flemish-speaking crowd or vice versa. French, not Arabic, is the respected commercial language in some Arabic-speaking countries, such as Tunisia and Lebanon, and not all Arabs speak the same Arabic. Algerian, Egyptian, Syrian and Kuwaiti Arabic are all very different. In India there are fourteen official languages and considerably more unofficial ones. Some eight hundred languages are spoken on the African continent.

Language Failures Can Be Extremely Costly.

When *Shogun* was being filmed in Nagashima, one of the scenes called for Blackthorn (Richard Chamberlain) and Lord Toranaga to blast their way through the evil Lord Ishido's ships at the mouth of a harbor. By prior arrangement, the samurai were to start firing when Chamberlain yelled "Now!" The director was on edge: he was desperate to get the scene before sunrise. Finally everything was set and the ships were moving into position when Chamberlain realized that the director hadn't told him when to start firing. He yelled over, "Jerry, when do you want me to say 'now'?" Of course, the Samurai heard "now" and began firing away, long before the boats were in position or the cameras ready to roll. By sunrise, the ammunition was gone. If the director had taken the time to learn just one Japanese word, a lot of money would have been saved.

Ignorance of a language can be embarrassing too. President Reagan tells a story about a speech he made in Mexico City. After his speech, he says, "I sat down to a rather unenthusiastic and not very impressive applause, and I was a little embarrassed. It was worse when a gentleman followed me and started speaking in Spanish, which I didn't understand, but he was being applauded about every paragraph. So, to hide my embarrassment, I started clapping before everyone else until our ambassador leaned over to me and said, 'I wouldn't do that if I were you. He's interpreting your speech.'"

Mistakes abound even when contact is by mail. A European or Canadian customer ex-pecting shipment or other action by January 6, 1986, written 6.1.86 in Europe and Canada but 1/6/86 in the United States, will be irritated (at least) when action is delayed six months because of the reversal of numbers. Newcomers to the British, Australian or Canadian business scene should talk to others in their line of work to uncover possible communication pitfalls. A Mobil Oil executive says: "In a way, the worst language difficulty we have is in the U.K. or Australia, because you feel like a fool asking people to repeat themselves." When you don't understand something, you should admit your confusion.

The Hardest Time to Get Information is When You Really Need It.

Faced with a problem, an American manager likes to call a crony into the office and say, "Hey, what's going on here?" We get information, then we go out and fix the problem, often by confronting an individual who appears to be at fault. While this may be natural in the United States (even more so in Australia), it would be asking for trouble in most other parts of the world. The manager would find blank stares, deep hostility, or in the extreme, could provoke sabotage.

So how *do you* get information when no one is speaking up? There are a number of ground rules, but the overriding principle is this: Wherever you go, you must watch how the local people who are respected get information from one another and how they try to get it from you. Watch how subordinates, supervisors and colleagues give and get information; the approach may vary with an individual's status or relationship. Wherever you are, you can use the cultural patterns to your advantage if you know what they are. It is easier to sail in the direction the wind blows. Likewise, it is easier to communicate with foreigners by doing it their way.

How to Give and Get Good information.

Rule 1: Know where information flows.

In America, information is usually generated outside and flows in to a manager. The system works because responsibility is delegated and

The English don't speak American.

The British don't have occasion to use the word "billion" very often, because it means a million million (1,000,000,000,000). In the United States and Canada a billion is only a thousand million (1,000,000,000). In England, to "table" a subject means to put it on the table for present discussion. In the United States, "tabling" means postponing discussion of a subject, perhaps indefinitely. Nuances can be confusing too, as when the British say something is "quite good," an indication that something is really less than good or somewhat surprisingly better than expected.

initiative is valued. Personnel move toward the managerial hub. In cultures where authority is centralized, such as Europe and South America, the reverse is true. The manager must take the initiative to seek out information, and personnel take less responsibility to keep managers informed. In countries where many people are involved in a decision, there are customary patterns for information flow that might leave out the foreigner who doesn't know the dynamic.

Aside from the formal communication routes, every culture has its informal information channels, variations on the Old Boy network or the executive washroom. In Japan it is standard procedure to go out drinking after work. This is where the problems of the day and personal feelings can be safely aired over a bottle of sake. If you disdain the nightly drinking scene, you isolate yourself from a fundamental fact of life in Japanese business, as important as any staff meeting. In some lines of business this kind of involvement may not be needed, but a newcomer is advised to join in a number of times to be sure.

Rule 2: There is No Point in Getting Straight to the Point.

Getting straight to the point is a uniquely Western virtue. In the West we try to get a deal; others try to know us. We like facts, while others like suggestions. We specify, while others imply.

Cross-cultural consultant George Renwick says: "If we want to communicate with people, we have to understand the patterns of their thinking, and we can get glimpses of that by looking at how they talk." When Americans talk, they take the most direct route, one step at a time in a straight line to the finish. Not so the Arabs. They talk about other things before business. Then after they have talked about business for a while, they will loop off to talk about more social things, and eventually loop back to the business at hand. They will continue in this manner forever, and if forced by an impatient American to stay on what the American insists is the subject at hand, will become very frustrated. Renwick says forcing our linear thinking on Arabs only "cuts off their loops," causing resentment and ultimately loss of productivity.

Europeans don't go straight to the point either. An American who wants to talk business with a Frenchman over dinner will find that his French colleague wants to enjoy his meal. He may venture a few business remarks but is unlikely to entertain a business proposition at the dinner table. You need to build up slowly to new proposals, allowing time for the French to digest information and ideas. Indirectly, you can work into any conversation the background or credibility that must be established. French written communication will also be tentative and cumulative. An American will write a detailed letter with all the facts and plans and a sense of completion or finality. The Frenchman will write quite a different letter. It will be the first in a series, full of subtleties that will be elaborated upon in future correspondence. Both will be confused and each will try to second guess what the other is really trying to say.

Africans, too, are suspicious of American directness. Nigerians complain that Americans have an "espionage mentality," asking for detailed information. Africans also feel that Americans talk too much, especially in public places. Many Africans consider it foolish to talk too much because "people may work against you if they know your plans."

As a general rule, business travelers and expatriates need to learn to slow down and sneak up on information, asking questions indirectly or obliquely, as a courtroom lawyer might. In most places it is best to get information conversationally or "educationally" by asking broader (even hypothetical) nonspecific questions and circling in gently on what is wanted. As anthropologist Tom Rohlen says, you have to learn to "mine for information." In other places, such as China, building a good rapport may be the only way to get people to give you information. Certainly, the direct question will be appropriate in some places; but most often you will need to learn how to beat around the bush.

Rule 3: Speak Simple But Not Simple-Minded English to a Foreigner.

When speaking English to your foreign counterpart, speak slowly and avoid cumbersome words. Don't be condescending, but say "letter" instead of "communication," "pay" instead of "compensation," and "soon" rather than "momentarily." Avoid slang and jargon such as "blue chip" or "profit maximization." Become familiar with the metric system and convert dollar figures into the local currency. Don't pack too much into one sentence, and pause between sentences. Enunciate clearly and remember not to raise your voice.

In their exuberance to be friendly, many garrulous travelers add extra banter to their communications with foreigners. Asking a Chinese waiter, "Hey, hate to trouble you, but would you mind going along to get me some ice? I'd sure appreciate it," will have the poor fellow thoroughly confused. Better to say "Ice, please."

Throughout any conversation with someone who speaks English as a second language, try to ascertain how well you have been understood by asking questions, but avoid "yes" or "no" questions.

Rule 4. Don't Mistake a Courteous Answer for the Truth.

Americans think "telling the truth" is especially important—honesty is the best policy. We respect candor, "telling it like it is," straight talk. Other cultures are no less honest or dishonest; they simply draw the line in different places and have their own ways of communicating real meaning.

Naked candor in many places is not as high a priority as other values such as courtesy, sensitivity to feelings, loyalty to family, and "face." Asians, for example, are more concerned with the emotional quality of an interaction than with the meaning of words or sentences. Form is more important than the actual communication, and social harmony is the primary function of speech. Leonard Woodcock, former ambassador to China, recounts the story of a group of Americans on an agricultural tour of China. The Chinese asked the Americans for their criticisms. After the third pig farm on the tour the Americans, who knew about pig farming, gave their honest and no doubt well-intentioned comments. Woodcock says, "They never saw another pig in China."

"Yes" does not always mean "yes." There is a saying in embassies around the world that "when a diplomat says yes, he means maybe. If he says maybe, he means no. If he says no, he's no diplomat." Probably the worst thing you can ask an Asian is "Give me a simple yes or no." In America the statement is mildly confrontational, but in most of Asia it would be out of step with the whole communication system. Asians rarely say no—there is, for example, no word for it in Thailand. To save face for you and themselves, they will answer in the affirmative. "Yes" can mean "Yes, I have heard you," not "Yes, I agree with you," and not necessarily "Yes, I understand." In Japan there are some sixteen ways to avoid saying no. A banker in Tokyo told us that one of his employees asked him: "What does 'maybe' mean in English? I know what it means in Japanese, it means no, but what does it mean in English?"

"No" does not always mean "no" either. Just as many Asian peoples use affirmatives in the extreme, Americans are often astonished by the negativism of many Europeans. When San Francisco attorney Lewis Burleigh worked on behalf of the General Counsel of the U.S. Air Force, negotiating NATO contracts in Germany a few years ago, he learned that when the Germans said with finality, "This is false, this

Koreans take considerable care not to disturb one's *kibun,* the sense of harmony, or "wellness," in a person. They will hold back or delay or "adjust" bad news to avoid upsetting a person's *kibun.* This is not considered dishonest; the *kibun* takes priority over accuracy. It is rare for anyone to give bad news in the morning. No matter how urgent the matter may appear, the news is likely to be given in the afternoon so the recipient can recover his *kibun* at home.

---

is wrong, unacceptable!" they were not the stonewalls that they appeared. Very often minor cosmetic editing of the legal language was all that was needed. The French too often say "no" when they actually mean "maybe" or know they will come around to saying "yes."

Everywhere you go, except in Europe and Australia, people will tell you what they think you want to hear. If you ask a Mexican, Lebanese or Japanese for directions and he doesn't know the way, he will give you directions anyway to make you happy. In any country, from Pakistan to Paraguay, if you ask how far some place is, the answer will be "Not far." Experienced travelers say the only solution is to ask questions in such a way that the foreigner can't figure out what you want to hear. Better yet, don't ask questions but engage the foreigner conversationally in such a way that the information you need will "fall out." When you hear the words "No problem," don't stop worrying.

Some people may give us more than we asked for. At the other extreme from Asian solicitousness, Australians and often the British are so direct that their statements can be quite cutting to an American. An American is flabbergasted and feels attacked when the Briton says "Rubbish" or the Australian says, "You don't know what you're talking about." An Australian executive says the correct response to that is, "I'm sorry, but it's you who don't know." You must forge on! In Australia and France, people sometimes find Americans bland because we tend to seek approval and run from a good argument. You are likely to be better respected in those countries if you can be a good sparring partner.

Rule 5: You Need to Know the Context to Know the Meaning.

Overseas Americans constantly struggle with ambiguity. Even when we get a correct answer, it is not always what we consider a full answer. We get only information that we specifically request, not more, no matter how relevant (to us) the additional information would be.

Some languages are inherently vague, so that even the well-educated have difficulty communicating clearly among themselves. A Tokyo professor specializing in communications estimates that the Japanese are able to fully understand each other only about 85 percent of the time. The language is so vague that in many ordinary conversations people frequently have to stop and trace ideograms in the air or on a surface in order to illustrate their meaning.

Uncompleteness is exacerbated by indirection. "Perhaps," "Maybe" and "We'll consider it" are Chinese stock in trade. When something is "inconvenient" it is most likely downright impossible. "Maybe it is time to go" means "It is time to go." When asked something that seems odd, the Chinese will reply to a question that perhaps should have been asked, giving an answer that may have no relation to the actual question. As a result, the Chinese can be entirely unhelpful even if their intentions are good.

Incomplete information is costly.

During a negotiation some Americans asked the Chinese, "Do you have access to a small computer?" They meant and should have said, "Do you have a computer in your facility so that you can do this software development?" The Chinese answered "yes," but in fact the nearest computer to which they had "access" was over fifty miles away. It was entirely unfeasible for them to develop the software, yet the contract was signed, In the end the American company had to give them $30,000 worth of computer hardware and software for free.

Arabs are equally inexact and confusing to us. With the Arabs, however, we struggle not with lack of information but with overexpression. Arabic is a poetic language conducive to exaggeration, fantastic metaphors, strings of adjectives, and repetitions which enhance the significance of what is said. In the Middle East what one has to say is often outweighed by how one says it. Arab rhetoric makes it hard to interpret precisely what is going on in the Middle East, not only for us but for other Arabs as well. The language allows for people to say things they don't mean, often with terrible results when what they say is taken seriously. During the Arab-Israeli skirmishes just before the Six-Day War, the Arab media threatened Israel with "We are going to burn your homes, rape your women and drive you into the sea." The Arabs were astonished when Israel took this literally as a declaration of war and retaliated accordingly.

In Asia, the Middle East or Africa, Americans need to read between the lines. We need to know the *context* of a communication to understand it, because that's where much of the information is. The anthropologist Edward T. Hall calls these cultures "high context." The opposite are "low context" cultures, such as Switzerland, Germany and Scandinavia, where information is explicit and words have specific meanings.

Rule 6: Make Sure Your Personal Style of Expression Does Not Communicate Things You Do Not Mean to Say.

In America, children are taught, "Sticks and stones may break my bones, but words will never hurt me." The Arabs say the opposite: "A sharp tongue cuts deeper than the sword." Thus they attach great importance to compliments, insults or indifference. Jerry Kenefick, an American executive with Whittaker Corporation in Saudi Arabia, found that affectionate mimicking of a favorite Saudi tennis instructor's efforts to say "Smash it," which came out "Smotch it," backfired. The Arab could not be convinced that he was not being ridiculed and was deeply hurt. Americans must be careful with teasing, for the foreigner is not likely to understand ordinary American kidding. Ethnic jokes are almost guaranteed to offend.

A German automobile engineering company contracted with an American supplier to develop a component for a new car. At one point during the project the Americans went to see the company in Germany and tested the component. It wasn't quite right—they would need to work out one small snag. One of the Americans came out with the familiar American quip: "Oh well, back to the old drawing board!" The Germans, assuming more was wrong with the component than was the case, cancelled the contract. The message: Watch what you say and don't make light of serious business—people may not understand you.

The words we choose give different impressions in different areas of the world. To some, Americans seem too literal-minded. Latins delight in verbal play. Double entendres, turns of phrase, or quotations, expressed at the right moment in an otherwise ordinary conversation, are an important part of daily speech. In both the Arab world and South America, speaking is like singing—allowances should be made for extravagance of expression and emotion.

Other cultures prefer more restrained use of language. Nigerians, for example, prefer a quiet, clear, simple form of expression. Germans are typically direct and understated, using simple terms and avoiding hype. The German who speaks softly is the one to listen to in a meeting, not the one who makes the most noise. Germans complain that Americans blow things out of proportion and get attention by hyperbole, especially in our advertising.

Many peoples find us obsessed with competition, statistics and measurements of excellence. We abuse superlatives: most, best, biggest. Americans also are self-referenced, using "I" and "my" often. The French seldom put themselves forward in conversations, saying instead, "It is said that" (*On dir que*). When they do say "I," they may add, "I do not want to boast but . . ." A Chinese, too, will avoid the implicit arrogance of the word "I" and refer to "we" even when speaking of himself.

Chinese polite evasiveness can be frustrating, but sometimes charming and effective in assuaging feelings, as in the following rejection slip from a Beijing paper to a British journalist: "We have read your manuscript with boundless delight. If we were to publish your paper, it would be impossible for us to publish any work of a lower standard. And as it is unthinkable that, in the next thousand years, we shall see its equal, we are, to our regret, compelled to return your divine composition, and beg you a thousand times to overlook our short sight and timidity."

The traveler should not be so careful to avoid offense as to become insipid. The French may shun boasting, and the Arabs may resent teasing, but neither are timid about disagreements. Where an American might be embarrassed by a heated discussion or made uncomfortable by conflict, French or Arab men (not women) will find an argument stimulating.

Be careful how you express emotion. Forms of emotional expression vary around the world. The kiss, for example, is not always associated with romance or love. Some people see kissing as unsanitary and crude, or certainly not something to be done in public. Americans might suspect marital discord if a couple did not kiss or hug at the airport, for example. In Japan you would seem odd if you did embrace when getting off a plane because men and women do not touch in public. While the British and Scandinavians are quite cool in demonstrating affection, the French or Brazilians kiss enthusiastically in public.

Asians describe Americans as hot-blooded, impulsive and emotionally wild. Latin Americans describe us as cold and controlled *hombres de hielo* (men of ice), not in touch with the feelings of the heart. Europeans find us noisy in our enthusiasm and nosy in our questions. We may find the British aloof and the French condescending. The point is that our habits of emotional expression have an impact on how others perceive us and on how effective we are working with them. Nor should we come to wrong conclusions when others display emotion differently. In the Arab world, people are encouraged to express their feelings without inhibition. Men are free to weep, shout and gesture wildly.

In discussions among equals, Arab men can attain decibel levels that are obnoxious by American standards. To the Arab, loudness is a sign of strength and sincerity, while soft tones

imply weakness or even deviousness. Less expressive cultures are not necessarily unfeeling. Asians are apt to giggle or smile when embarrassed or when told bad news. An expatriate in Hong Kong told us that when her car rolled into a ditch, Chinese bystanders giggled; they also laugh at the sad parts in movies. It is useful to learn to tell the difference between a smile of pleasure and a courtesy smile meant to suppress emotion—often the eyes will tell you.

In most foreign countries, expressions of anger are unacceptable; in some places, public anger is taboo. Even where anger is displayed openly, an American's anger directed at a local will be met with outstanding resentment.

Rule 7: Silence is a Form of Speech. Don't Interrupt It.

Americans rush to fill silences. We talk when we should wait patiently. We tend to crowd our foreign colleagues, preventing them from getting their message across. This hurts our ability to gather information, evaluate a situation and develop the relationships so important in international business.

Many people are put off by our haste to talk. Scandinavians, for example, are flustered by the American tendency to interrupt or finish sentences. Swedes enjoy silence and use it to formulate their next move. Africans are offended by our tendency to talk at them and to interrupt, even when we agree with them. Saying "I know, I know" is taken as a putdown. It is much better to listen quietly and listen a lot.

We need to give the foreigner more air, more time. When the foreigner seems to be struggling with how to say something, be patient, and be careful not to put words into anyone's mouth. If you do, you will surely become more confused because politeness may require the foreigner to agree with your suggestions, no matter how wrong. Klaus Schmidt, director of the Center for World Business at San Francisco State University, says the typical American must learn to treat silences as "communication spaces" and not interrupt them. "Hold on to your chair until you get white knuckles, but don't talk!"

Rule 8: Learn To Speak Body Language.

Westerners assume that most of our meaning can be put into words, so we are more careful about what we say than about our body language. However, about 60 to 70 percent of what we communicate has nothing to do with words; abroad, it may be closer to 90 percent. More important than speaking the language is what you communicate without words.

Many travelers trust that if they don't speak the language, there are a hundred gestures to get across almost any meaning. But gestures have quite different meanings in different parts of the world; body language is not universal. Subtleties are noticed, like the length of time you hold on while shaking hands. On a very unconscious level many of us abroad can turn people off even when we are on good behavior. Thumbs up is considered vulgar in Iran and Ghana, equivalent to raising the middle finger in the United States. Touching a person's head, including children's, should be avoided in Singapore or Thailand. In Yugoslavia, people shake their heads for yes—appearing to us to be saying no.

In general, avoid gesturing with the hand. Many people take offense at being beckoned this way, or pointed at, even if only conversationally. In parts of Asia, gestures and even slight movements can make people nervous. If you jab your finger in the air or on a table to make a point, you might find that your movements have been so distracting that you have not made your point at all. Unintentionally, Americans come across as aggressive and pushy. Yet, in other parts of the world, particularly in Latin America or Italy, gesturing is important for self-expression, and the person who does not move a lot while talking comes across as bland or uninteresting. As always, watch what local people do. Or ask. While in England we once asked, "How do you point out someone without pointing?" Our companion dropped a shoulder, raised his eyebrows and jerked his head to the side, as though tossing it in the direction he meant to point. Clear as day, he pointed without pointing.

Body language is more than gestures. You communicate by the way you stand, sit, tense facial muscles, tap fingers, and so on. Unfortunately, these subtler body messages are hard to read across cultures; mannerisms don't translate. We recently saw an American teacher scolding a young Vietnamese boy. Exasperated by his apparent lack of respect, she barked, "Don't stand there sulking; stand up straight and look at me." Standing with arms folded, head down, staring at the ground, the poor boy was showing her the greatest respect, Vietnamese style. An American in the exact same stance would be obviously arrogant, defiant and hostile. To the Asian, it meant only humility.

In many parts of the world, looking someone in the eye is disrespectful. We are more likely to trust and like someone who looks us straight in the eye than someone who looks away. In Japan a person who looks a subordinate in the eye is felt to be judgmental and punitive, while someone who looks his superior in the eye is assumed to be hostile or slightly insane. The Arabs like eye contact ("The eyes are the windows to the soul") but theirs seem to dart about much more than Americans'. We don't trust "shifty-eyed" people.

Subtle differences in eye contact between the British and North Americans can be confusing. According to Edward T. Hall, proper English *listening* behavior includes immobilization of the eyes at a social focal distance, so that either eye gives the appearance of looking straight at the speaker. On the other hand, an American listener will stare at the speaker's eyes, first one, then the other, relieved by frequent glances over the speaker's shoulder. A British anthropologist points out that eye contact during *speaking* differs too. Americans keep your attention by boring into you with eyes and words, while the British keep your attention by looking away while they talk. When their eyes return to yours, it signals they have finished speaking and it is your turn to talk. It seems you can't interrupt people when they are not looking at you. These almost imperceptible differences in eye contact interfere with rapport building and trust.

You can tell a lot about people by the way they walk or sit. In America we tend to relax

An American petrochemical company won eight major contracts with the Saudi government, but a Japanese firm won the design and construction part of the project. When the American and Saudi managers went to Japan to meet with the Japanese engineers, the cross-cultural problems between the Saudis and Japanese were instant, dramatic, and chronic. The Saudis stood too close, made intense eye contact and touched the Japanese. On top of that, the Saudis were enjoying Tokyo's sights. Their leisurely approach clashed with the Japanese work ethic; the Japanese concluded they weren't serious about the project. The tension escalated until Americans became the buffers between the Saudis and Japanese. For once, the Americans were not the bad guys.

SOURCE: Moran, Stahl & Boyer, New York

in business settings. We often slouch almost to a reclining position, and this has the effect of creating an atmosphere of comfortable rapport. Do this in northern Europe, however, and you reveal that your parents didn't teach you proper posture. In Asia it also means that you haven't achieved the proper physical balance that enhances the spiritual. To make a good impression in Japan or Korea, for example, you must sit with your feet squarely placed on the ground. Your shoulders may be relaxed and your stomach may even hang out a bit. You must talk in a slow, measured pace, showing the body and spirit in balance. All this gives an indication of good breeding, maturity and reliability. After work hours, in a bar or home, you can relax, but never to the degree customary among Americans.

Rule 9: Don't Trust People Just Because They Speak English

A common mistake we make is to affiliate with personnel or business contacts because they speak English. Do not assume that speaking your language is any indication of intelligence, business know-how or local competence. Fluency in our language is only an indication of language skills, nothing more. Needless to say,

the reverse is also true. Do not assume that non-English speakers are unintelligent or incompetent. It is hard to estimate people's intelligence when they are struggling with broken English. We habitually gauge intelligence by what is said and tend to discount people who can't communicate. Get some other measure, such as field data of competence or the judgment of an appropriate business colleague.

Rule 10: Learn the Language

If you are going to spend a year or more in a country—definitely, absolutely, do your utmost to learn the language. It will make a tremendous difference to your state of mind. Ability to understand the local language seems to play a major role in adjustment to culture shock and personal success in a foreign world, not to mention enjoyment.

It is not clear why speaking the language makes such a big difference, but it does. Obviously it makes getting around a lot easier. In hundreds of moments of struggling to get something done, from shopping to household repairs to getting directions, just knowing some of the language removes huge portions of aggravation and helps you gain a sense of safety and self-assurance. When people around you are babbling away in a foreign language, you become vaguely insecure and feel isolated. Knowing the language gives you a sense of mastery in situations where you may feel vulnerable.

The mere process of learning the language gets you more in tune with the culture and breaks the ice, putting you in the right frame of mind to adjust. In some places, speaking a second language is important to enhance your image as a well-bred, educated person—you may be somewhat better off even if the language you learn is not the language spoken in the country. One expatriate said he studied the language because he couldn't stand feeling inferior to his colleagues who had learned it.

The frequent traveler should think about learning languages too, of course, depending on the amount of travel and bilingualism of the business community. Speaking a language fluently can permit you to attain levels of relationship and business advantage unattainable by someone who doesn't. In China one might hear,

"She's no foreigner, she speaks Chinese." According to the bureau chief of a U.S. news agency: "Foreigners who cannot understand are spoon-fed what their hosts wish to spoon-feed them . . . Many American executives become showroom managers, sitting in well-decorated offices with a staff of secretaries but having little control over operations. Business goes on around them and decisions are made without them."

Fluency in the language will allow the traveler into otherwise exclusive realms of local business. The process of negotiation often depends on behind-the-scenes information flow; the American team left out of these information streams can only operate in the dark. Unison Corporation, in San Francisco, has been tremendously successful in helping American companies get an entree into China because the company has been accepted by the Chinese in a way that no other American company has. The president, C. B. Sung, is an American, but he is so established in China that he is privy to exclusive information about upcoming projects. During negotiations he gets late-night calls from the other side saying in effect, "Look, here's what's really going on."

Learning the language is no substitute for learning the culture and appropriate behavior. People who are fluent in a language but not sensitive to the culture can make worse mistakes, perhaps because the locals expect more of them. And there are dangers in speaking a language if you are not competent in it. Not knowing the nuances of words or being careless with intonations, you might say things you don't mean. In most languages, some common words have extremely vulgar meanings if pronounced incorrectly. Or you may hear unintended meanings, as when American negotiators become ruffled with the French *nous demandons*, which does not mean "we demand" but, less combatively, "we request." The French call these similar-sounding words *faux amis*, false friends, because they can get you into trouble. You may also be confused by foreign words that have become part of our language; for example, the "entree" here is the main course, but in France it is the appetizer. Try to find out what common mistakes you should try to avoid.

If you don't speak the language well, it is best to reveal that you have made the effort to learn—but then rely on English or an interpreter. Experts advise that it is generally best to speak the language for socializing and daily activities, but not when transacting business. As a rule of thumb, if you are not fluent and your foreign counterpart does not speak fluent English, always transact business with an interpreter. Traders who meet frequently with foreigners say that while English is the business language around the world, buyers are far more comfortable talking in their native language, and even if they can speak English, it is often better to have an interpreter. They don't have to struggle so hard, and it puts them at ease.

Rule 11: Put Your Money Where Your Mouth Is—Get Good Interpreters and Translators.

It is a mistake to assume that anyone who can speak two languages fluently can function as an interpreter. It is even worse to expect that someone on your team who speaks both languages fluently can fulfill that special and demanding function in addition to the job. An employee used as an interpreter may seem to have been demoted in the eyes of some foreigners.

Interpreting involves much more than speaking a language well. It is much easier to speak your own mind in a foreign language than it is to interpret the words of someone else, getting across precise ideas, nuances and connotations. A good interpreter is trained to adjust to the cultural context, turning American idiom into a foreign version with the same message, deleting expletives, correcting for ignorance of terminology (such as Republic of China instead of People's Republic of China), and so on. An interpreter will let you know that a joke has been made, as did Honey, the interpreter in a Doonesbury cartoon, when she told the audience, "The joke has been made. He will be expecting you to laugh at it. Go wild."'

You should always make sure your interpreter is thoroughly briefed and understands your requirements. In some countries, interpreters normally play the role of liaison, asserting themselves to assist you or the other party. This may range from answering the foreigner's questions directly rather than telling you the question and having you provide the answer, all the way to interfering with the elements of a deal. You may notice that some of your one-word answers become long speeches in translation, or vice versa, your long speeches are summed up in a word. Sometimes this is a function of the two languages, but sometimes it is an indication that the interpreter is overstepping bounds. Keep clarifying the role if you think it is being misused or get a new interpreter.

Good interpreters must be comfortable speaking in front of audiences large and small, and with dignitaries and people of low rank. They must be able to submerge their own egos and take on the personalities of their speakers, like good actors, without overdoing it and becoming too much the ham. When your foreign host provides an interpreter, yours should sit quietly by your side, responsible only for whispering to you modifications on what the other interpreter says.

You must help your interpreter get your message across. You reduce the risk of being misunderstood if you make your interpreter's job easier. A few tips: Before any meeting, explain to your interpreter the gist of the agenda and what you will be saying. If you are in an esoteric field or one filled with its own terminology, give the interpreter a list of words and a chance to prepare. Be as visual as you can be, using charts and graphics more than you normally might. Avoid slang and figures of speech that are difficult to translate and impossible to look up in a reference book. Speak slowly and stop frequently. Don't expect your interpreter to retain long paragraphs of information; if the message is complex, break it down into smaller parts. If you are very concerned about the particular nuance you want to get across, discuss it with the interpreter. During long sessions it may be prudent to have two interpreters so that one is always fresh; interpreting is extremely strenuous.

Don't lose it in the translation. The perplexing problem of translation can be assuaged by taking a few simple steps each time a transla-

tion is necessary. It helps to start with materials that are not highly idiomatic in the first place, and the multinational advertising agency, public relations office, training department and others should keep future translations in mind when writing copy. Colloquialisms will very likely cause translation problems.

Choose a translator with care. If your business is specialized (for instance, medical, legal, scientific or technical), you should get a translator who is particularly well versed in your field. You should also be able to find someone with the right writing style for your needs. Use only a translator who is a native of the country and who lives in that country or travels there frequently, keeping in touch with locals.

Once you have found a translator, make sure your preferences in style and vocabulary are understood. Explain your audience and your message, particularly any ambiguous words. Point out trade names or other words that must remain in the original language. Make notes as to places where you want the actual words translated and where you want simply the idea or mood translated. Also explain the pace of the writing wanted: relaxed or breathless, flowing or staccato. American ads are usually hard-sell; your translator should be asked for more soft-sell language, as appropriate to the culture.

Experienced international business people often involve two writers in the translation process, one for literal and technical accuracy of translation, one for the creative aspects of the writing. There is also security in "back-translation": by having another translator turn the translation back to English, you get a good idea of what mutations might have occurred in the first translation. Finally, allow plenty of time for proofreading, and make sure your proofreader understands your editing remarks. Judy Esterquest of Booz Allen & Hamilton says: "When our U.S. people get into report production in Europe, there are always problems of proofreading symbols not being international." When companies are rushing to meet report-presentation deadlines, it is easy to make mistakes that in a foreign language are not noticed easily.

Rule 12: Your Dog-and-Pony Show May Turn into a Circus If You Don't Adjust Your Presentation to the Foreign Audience.

By now it should be no surprise that the American style of speechmaking and demonstration may leave the foreigner cold, confused or offended. Time after time an American team comes home complaining its presentation fell on deaf ears, not realizing that the speakers came across as ill-prepared, insincere and rude.

As a general rule, any presentation to a foreign audience should be more formal, orderly and restrained than at home. We may take pride in appearances of spontaneity and "thinking on our feet." We like to sound naturally articulate, not rehearsed. For special effect we mark up our flip charts and transparencies, often with dramatic flair. Many foreign audiences, from Germany to Japan, consider this type of presentation unprofessional. They may feel slighted when they see that the speaker has not made the effort beforehand to rehearse and to complete the visual aids—in their language, of course. Prior preparation and formality are a matter of respect, the more the better.

Presentations must be simple, noncolloquial and presented slowly enough to be translated and absorbed. It helps to stand on the right side of any props in countries where people read from right to left—in the West we stand on the left side so that the eyes come back to the speaker after reading the screen or chart. Visual aids must be simple too. In many places (such as the Arab world), colorful media presentations may come across as entertainment and the message be lost.

Remember that the pacing of business varies around the world, and this will affect the flow of your presentation. Don't launch abruptly into your show in Latin America, Africa, Asia or the Middle East—plan for extended courtesies. Where you must expect many interruptions, notably in Saudi Arabia and the Gulf countries, prepare a presentation which can be delivered in small segments.

In some places you may want to make sure that the people you send are the same age as your audience, or you will face a credibility or protocol problem. People can rise at meteoric rates in American companies, and the young are permitted to do business with their elders; but this is not true everywhere. In some places it would be inappropriate to send a thirty-five-year-old "youngster" to deal with a sixty-year-old executive. Find out if age will be a problem before you go.

Summary

The biggest problem for the traveler is language. They speak less English than you think. The English don't speak American. The hardest time to get information is when you really need it.

How to Give and Get Good Information:

RULE 1: Know where information flows.

RULE 2: There is no point in getting straight to the point.

RULE 3: Speak simple but not simple-minded English to a foreigner.

RULE 4: Don't mistake a courteous answer for the truth—"yes" does not always mean "yes" and "no" may not mean "no."

RULE 5: You need to know the context to know the meaning.

RULE 6: Make sure your personal style of expression does not communicate things you do not mean to say.

RULE 7: Silence is a form of speech. Don't interrupt it.

RULE 8: Learn to speak body language.

RULE 9: Don't trust people just because they speak English.

RULE 10: Learn the language.

RULE 11: Put your money where your mouth is—get good interpreters—and translators.

RULE 12: Your dog-and-pony show may turn into a circus if you don't adjust your presentation to the foreign audience. ●

Study Questions

1. What is the problem with the assumption that most foreign executives speak/accept English for business transactions?

2. What is the overriding principle for getting information in foreign countries?

3. If a British negotiator wants an issue "tabled," what is requested?

4. How can Americans modify (or compensate for) their linear, straight-forward style of thinking and speaking?

5. Is honest, straight talk a priority value in all cultures? Explain.

6. What is unique to Asian culture regarding the meaning of "yes" and "no?"

7. Which cultures are least likely to tell you what they think you want to hear?

8. Describe the Arabic language, in general.

9. Contrast a high vs. low context culture with regard to communication.

10. What should Americans do when their foreign opponents are silent?

11. What percentage of meaning/communication is nonverbal? Is "body language" universal or cultural? Explain.

12. How does a Brit keep your attention (and prevent interruption) while speaking?

13. Why are two interpreters often used in the translation process? With writing documents?

14. What presentation style is most appropriate for the foreign audience? Why?

Exercise: The Power of Four-Letter Words.

A. Hochner, Temple University

Materials to be obtained from your professor.

Study Questions

1. What accounts for the discrepancies between the groups' choices?

2. What other words that we use to describe others have a great impact on our thinking about them and behavior toward them? Discuss the role of frameworks and stereotypes in judging others.

3. Why are first impressions we make and that others make on us so important?

4. What advice would you give negotiators to more realistically assess the characteristics and abilities of their counterparts?

Two Person Bargaining: The Ugli Orange Case

Originally developed by Robert J. House. Adapted by D. T. Hall and R. J. Lewicki, with suggested modification by H. Kolodny and T. Ruble

---

PURPOSE:
1. To explore the dynamics of two-person bargaining.
2. To experiment with creative problem solving.

ADVANCE PREPARATION:
None.

GROUP SIZE: Subgroups of two or three. Total group can be any size.
TIME REQUIRED: 30 minutes.
SPECIAL MATERIALS: None.
SPECIAL PHYSICAL REQUIREMENTS: None.
RELATED TOPICS: Group decision making and problem solving, Interpersonal communication.

INTRODUCTION

In many work settings it is not possible for people to work independently as they pursue their work goals. Often we find ourselves in situations where we must obtain the cooperation of other people, even though the other people's ultimate objectives may be different from our own. This will be your task in the present exercise.

PROCEDURE

OPTION ONE

Step 1: 5 Minutes

Count off the class in groups of two. In each group of two, one person will play the role of "Dr. Roland," one will play "Dr. Jones."

The person playing Dr. Jones should read the role description for Dr. Jones only, and the person playing the role of Dr. Roland should read the role description for Dr. Roland only. (Role descriptions can be found at the back of the volume in the Appendix.)

OPTION TWO

Step 1: 5 Minutes

Count off the class in groups of three. In each group of three, one person will play the role of "Dr. Roland," one will play "Dr. Jones," and one will be an observer.

The person playing Dr. Jones should read the role description for Dr. Jones only, and the person playing the role of Dr. Roland should read the role description for Dr. Roland only. The observer should read both role descriptions. (Role descriptions can be found at the back of this volume in the Appendix.)

BOTH OPTIONS

Step 2: 10 Minutes, Negotiation

At this point the group leader will read the following statement: "I am Mr. Cardoza, the owner of the remaining Ugli oranges. My fruit-exporting firm is based in South America. My country does not have diplomatic relations with your country, although we do have strong trade relations.

"After you have read about your roles, spend about 10 minutes meeting with the other firm's representative and decide on a course of action. Then pick a spokesperson who will tell me: (1) What do you plan to do? (2) If you want to buy the oranges, what price will you offer? (3)To whom and how will the oranges be delivered?

"After you have done this, you may negotiate with the other firm's representative."

Step 3: 15 Minutes

Following the negotiation, the spokesperson and the observer will report on the solution reached in each group and the process by which agreement was reached.

DISCUSSION QUESTIONS

1. Was there full disclosure by both sides in each group? How much information was shared? What is the relationship between trust and full disclosure?

2. How do assumptions about the nature of the conflict (i.e., distributive vs. intergrative) affect the nature of communication between the parties?

3. What advice can you give negotiators to enable them to communicate so they can avoid obstacles as well as avoid giving away too many of their own secrets?

Additional Question for Option 2

4. What was the impact of having an audience or constituency on the behavior of the negotiators? Did it make the problem harder or easier to solve?

GENERALIZATIONS AND CONCLUSIONS

Concluding Points

1. What is the relationship between trust and disclosure of information?

2. In a bargaining situation such as this, before competing or collaborating with the other person, what should you do first?

3. How does mistrust affect the creativity or complexity of bargaining agreements?

4. Do audiences to a negotiation increase competitiveness or cooperativeness? Why?

Participant's Reactions

READINGS AND REFERENCES

Filley, Alan, *Interpersonal Conflict Resolution* (Glenview, Ill.: Scott Foresman, 1975).

Thomas, Kenneth, "Conflict and Conflict Management," in M. Dunnette, *Handbook* of *Industrial and Organizational Psychology* (Chicago: Rand McNally, 1976).

SECTION 7

Third Party Intervention

Third parties generally get involved in helping to settle disputes when the first two parties either feel they need help or when they cannot resolve things themselves. The most common methods are mediation and arbitration. Whereas the arbitrator makes a decision for the parties, the mediator helps the parties make a resolution themselves. Where arbitration focuses on the end point of the negotiation, mediation is a method that facilitates the negotiation process. The two readings in this section give detailed explications of this process, in intellectual and pragmatic terms.

Moore ("**How Mediation Works**") discusses the history and varieties of mediation, from labor-management relations to community relations, civil rights, schools, criminal justice, family disputes, environmental and public policy issues, to international disputes, among others. He takes us step by step through the stages of the mediation process. In many ways, mediation is an adaptation of cooperative strategies of negotiation, differing, however, in that a third party is striving to steer the warring parties in a more integrative direction.

Tom Colosi ("**The Role of the Mediator**"), a mediator with a national reputation, explains the subtle skills at the heart of the mediator's art. Effective mediators need to both gain the trust of the parties and build trust between them. They also need to understand the parties' positions so well that one can shake up their thinking (i.e., raise and maintain doubts about their entrenched positions) in order to promote better solutions.

*　　*　　*

How Mediation Works

Christopher W. Moore

Although mediation is widely practiced in interpersonal, organizational, community, and international disputes, and techniques have been documented in particular applications or cases, there has been little systematic study or description of specific strategies and tactics used by mediators. What analysis and description have been conducted either have been presented on the most general level or are so specific as to limit their broad application.

A Definition of Mediation

When a mediator from the United Nations enters an international dispute, a labor mediator is engaged in negotiations prior to a strike, or a family mediator assists a couple in reaching a divorce settlement, what activities are they performing? What is their relationship to the parties? What are the objectives of the mediators?

Mediation is the intervention into a dispute or negotiation by an acceptable, impartial, and neutral third party who has no authoritative decision-making power to assist disputing parties in voluntarily reaching their own mutually acceptable settlement of issues in dispute. I will examine several components of the definition.

For mediation to occur, the parties must begin negotiating. Labor and management must be willing to hold a bargaining session, governments and public interest groups must create forums for dialogue, and families must be willing to come together for mediation to begin. *Mediation is essentially negotiation* that includes a third party who is knowledgeable in effective negotiation procedures, and can help people in conflict to coordinate their activities and to be more effective in their bargaining. Mediation is an extension of the negotiation process in that it involves extending the bargaining into a new format and using a mediator who contributes new variables and dynamics to the interaction of the disputants. Without negotiation, however, there can be no mediation.

Intervention means "to enter into an ongoing system of relationships, to come between or among persons, groups, or objects for the purpose of helping them. There is an important implicit assumption in the definition that should be made explicit: the system exists independently of the intervenor" (Argyris, 1970, p. 15). The assumption behind an outsider's intervention is that a third party will be able to alter the power and social dynamics of the conflict relationship by influencing the beliefs or behaviors of individual parties, by providing knowledge or information, or by using a more effective negotiation process and thereby helping the participants to settle contested issues. Rubin and Brown (1975) have argued that the mere presence of a party who is independent of the disputants may be a highly significant factor in the resolution of a dispute.

The third aspect of this definition is *acceptability,* the willingness of disputants to allow a third party to enter a dispute and assist them in reaching a resolution. Acceptability does not mean that disputants necessarily welcome a mediator and are willing to do exactly as he or she says. It does mean that the parties approve of the mediator's presence and are willing to listen to and seriously consider the intervenor's suggestions.

Impartiality and neutrality are critical to the process of mediation (Young, 1972). *Impartiality* refers to the attitude of the intervenor and is an unbiased opinion or lack of preference in favor of one or more negotiators. *Neutrality,* on the other hand, refers to the behavior or relationship between the intervenor and the disputants. Mediators often either have not had a previous relationship with disputing parties or have not had a relationship in which they have directly influenced the rewards or benefits for one of the parties to the detriment of the other. Neutrality also means that the mediator does not expect to directly gain benefits or special payments from one of the parties as compensation for favors in conducting the mediation.

People seek a mediator's assistance because they want procedural help in negotiations. They do not want an intervenor who is biased or who will initiate actions that are detrimental to their interests.

The need for impartiality and neutrality does not mean that a mediator may not have personal opinions about a dispute's outcome. No one can be entirely impartial. What impartiality and neutrality do signify is that the mediator can separate his or her opinions about the outcome of the dispute from the desires of the disputants and focus on ways to help the parties make their own decisions without unduly favoring one of them. The final test of the impartiality and neutrality of the mediator ultimately rests with the parties. They must perceive that the intervenor is not overtly partial or unneutral in order to accept his or her assistance.

Kraybill (1979) and Wheeler (1982) address the tensions between impartiality and neutrality and the personal biases of mediators by distinguishing between the substantive and procedural interests. Wheeler argues that mediators generally distance themselves from commitments to specific substantive outcomes—the amount of money in a settlement, the exact time of performance, and so forth—but have commitments to such procedural standards as open communication, equity and fair exchange, durability of a settlement over time, and enforceability. Mediators are advocates for a fair process and not for a particular settlement.

Conflicts involve struggles between two or more people over values, or competition for status power and scarce resources (Coser, 1967). Mediators enter a variety of levels of conflicts—latent, emerging, and manifest—according to their degree of organization and intensity. Latent conflicts are characterized by underlying tensions that have not fully developed and have not escalated into a highly polarized conflict. Often, one or more parties may not even be aware that a conflict or the potential for one even exists (Curle, 1971). Changes in personal relationships in which one party is not aware of how serious a breach has occurred, future staff cutbacks, unannounced plans for the siting of a potentially controversial facility such as a mine or waste disposal site, or poten-

tial unpopular changes in public policy are examples of latent conflicts.

Mediators (or facilitators) working with people involved in the resolution of latent disputes help participants to identify people who will be affected by a change or those who may be concerned about the future problem, assist them in developing a mutual education process about the issues and interests involved, and work with participants to design and possibly implement a problem-solving process.

Emerging conflicts are disputes in which the parties are identified, they acknowledge that there is a dispute, and most issues are clear, but no workable negotiation or problem-solving process has developed. Emerging conflicts have a potential for escalation if a resolution procedure is not implemented. Many disputes between coworkers, businesses, and governments illustrate this type of conflict. Both parties recognize that there is a dispute, and there may have been a harsh verbal exchange, but neither knows how to handle the problem. In this case the mediator helps establish the negotiation process and helps the parties begin to communicate and bargain.

Manifest conflicts are those in which parties are engaged in an ongoing dispute, may have started to negotiate, and may have reached an impasse. Mediator involvement in manifest conflicts often involves changing the negotiation procedure or intervention to break a specific deadlock. Labor mediators who intervene in negotiations before a strike deadline are working to resolve manifest conflicts. Child custody and divorce mediators also usually intervene in fully manifest disputes.

A mediator has no authoritative decision-making power. This characteristic distinguishes the mediator from the judge or arbiter, who is designated by law or contract to make a decision for the parties based on societal norms, laws, or contracts rather than the specific interests or personal concepts of justice held by the parties. The goal of the judicial decision is not reconciliation but a decision concerning which of the parties is right.

The judge examines the past and evaluates "agreements that the parties have entered into, violations which one has inflicted on the other," and "the norms concerning acquisition of rights, responsibilities, etc. which are connected with these events. When he has taken his standpoint on this basis, his task is finished" (Eckhoff, 1966–67, p. 161).

The mediator, on the other hand, works to reconcile the competing interests of the two parties. The mediator's goal is to assist the parties in examining the future and their interests or needs, and negotiating an exchange of promises and relationships that will be mutually satisfactory and meet their standards of fairness. The mediator does not have decision-making authority, and parties in dispute therefore often seek the services of a mediator because they can retain ultimate decision-making power.

If the mediator does not have authority to decide, does he or she have any influence at all? The mediator's authority, such as it is, resides in his or her ability to appeal to the parties to reach an agreement based on their own interests or the past performance or reputation of the mediator as a useful resource. Authority, or recognition of a right to influence the outcome of the dispute, is granted by the parties themselves rather than by an external law, contract, or agency.

So far I have identified that a mediator is a third party who is impartial in attitude and neutral in relationship toward disputing parties. I will now describe the mediator's functions. The definition states that a mediator assists disputing parties. Assistance can refer to very general or to highly specific activities. I will examine here some of the more general roles and functions of the mediator, and will discuss specifics later when analyzing intervention moves made during particular phases of negotiation.

The mediator may assume a variety of roles and functions to assist parties in resolving disputes (American Arbitration Association, n.d.):

- The *opener of communications channels* who initiates communication or facilitates better communication if the parties are already talking.
- The *legitimizer* who helps all parties recognize the right of others to be involved in negotiations.

- The *process facilitator* who provides a procedure and often formally chairs the negotiation session.
- The *trainer* who educates novice, unskilled, or unprepared negotiators in the bargaining process.
- The *resource expander* who provides procedural assistance to the parties and links them to outside experts and resources, such as lawyers, technical experts, decision makers, or additional goods for exchange, that may enable them to enlarge acceptable settlement options.
- The *problem explorer* who enables people in dispute to examine a problem from a variety of viewpoints, assists in defining basic issues and interests, and looks for mutually satisfactory options.
- The *agent of reality* who helps build a reasonable and implementable settlement and questions and challenges parties who have extreme and unrealistic goals.
- The *scapegoat* who may take some of the responsibility or blame for an unpopular decision that the parties are nevertheless willing to accept. This enables them to maintain their integrity and, when appropriate, gain the support of their constituents.
- The *leader* who takes the initiative to move the negotiations forward by procedural, or on occasion, substantive suggestions.

The last component of the definition refers to mediation as a voluntary process. *Voluntary* refers to freely chosen participation and freely chosen settlement. Parties are not forced to negotiate, mediate, or settle by either an internal or external party to a dispute. Stulberg (1981b, pp. 88–89) notes that "there is no legal liability to any party refusing to participate in a mediation process. . . . Since a mediator has no authority unilaterally to impose a decision on the parties, he cannot threaten the recalcitrant party with a judgment."

Voluntary participation does not, however, mean that there may not be pressure to try mediation. Other disputants or external forces, such as judges or constituents, may put significant pressure on a party to try negotiation and mediation. Some courts in family and civil cases have even gone so far as to order that parties try mediation as a means of resolving their dispute before the court hears the case. Attempting mediation does not, however, mean that the participants are forced to settle.

Arenas of mediation

Mediation has a long history. The Bible refers to Jesus as a mediator between God and man:

"For there is one God, and one mediator between God and man, the man Christ Jesus; who gave himself as ransom for all, to be testified in due time" (I Timothy 2:5–6). Churches and clergy have often been mediators between their members or other disputants. Until the Renaissance, the Catholic church in Western Europe was probably the central mediation and conflict management organization in Western society. Clergy mediated family disputes, criminal cases, and diplomatic disputes among the nobility. Bianchi (1978), in describing one mediated case in the Middle Ages, details how the church and the clergy provided the sanctuary where the offender stayed during dispute resolution and served as intermediary between two families in a case involving rape. The families agreed to settle with monetary restitution to the woman's family and promises to help her find a husband.

Jewish rabbinical courts and rabbis in Europe were vital in mediating or adjudicating disputes among members of that faith. These courts were crucial to the protection of cultural identity and ensured that Jews had a formalized means of dispute resolution. In many locales they were barred from other means of dispute settlement because of their religion.

With the rise of nation-states, mediators took on new roles as formal secular diplomatic intermediaries. Diplomats such as ambassadors and envoys acted to "raise and clarify social issues and problems, to modify conflicting interests, and to transmit information of mutual concern to parties" (Werner, 1974, p. 95).

The practice of mediation is not confined to Western culture. In fact, mediation has probably been more widely practiced in China and Japan, where religion and philosophy place a strong emphasis on social consensus, moral persuasion, and striking a balance or harmony in human relations (Brown, 1982). Mediation is currently widely practiced in the People's Republic of China through People's Conciliation Committees (Ginsberg, 1978; Li, 1978).

Latin America and other Hispanic cultures also have a history of mediated dispute settlement. Nader (1969) reports on the dispute resolution process in the Mexican village of Ralu'a, where a judge assists the parties in making consensual decisions. Lederach (1984) describes other mediation models in Hispanic culture such as the *Tribunal de las Aguas* (water courts) in Spain.

Mediation is also utilized in Africa where the *moot court* is a common means for neighbors to resolve disputes (Gulliver, 1971). Mediated settlement is also practiced in some Arab villages in Jordan (Antoun, 1972).

In Melanesia, the Tolai villages in New Britain each have a counselor and committee that meet regularly to hear disputes (Epstein, 1971). The role of the counselor and committee is to "maintain conditions for orderly debate and freedom of argument by the disputants and anyone else who wishes to express opinion" (Gulliver. 1979, p. 27). The process is both a "mode of adjudication" and a "settlement by consensus" of the parties (Epstein, 1971, p. 168).

Mediation also has a long history in the American colonies and the United States. Auerbach's *Justice Without Law* (1983) is an excellent history that describes the dispute resolution mechanisms of the Puritans, Quakers, and other religious sects; procedures of Chinese and Jewish ethnic groups; and informal alternative dispute resolution efforts.

For the most part, mediation historically and in other cultures has been performed by people with informal training, and the intervenor's role has usually occurred within the context of other functions or duties. Only since the turn of the twentieth century has mediation become formally institutionalized and developed into a recognized profession.

The first arena in which mediation was formally institutionalized in the United States was in labor-management relations (Simkin, 1971). In 1913 the U.S. Department of Labor was established, and a panel, the "commissioners of conciliation," was appointed to handle conflicts between labor and management. This panel subsequently became the United States Conciliation Service, and in 1947 was reconstituted as the Federal Mediation and Conciliation Service. The rationale for initiating mediation procedures in the industrial sector was to promote a "sound and stable industrial peace" and "the settlement of issues between employer and employees through collective bargaining" (Labor-Management Relations Act, 1947). It was expected that mediated settlements would prevent costly strikes or lockouts for workers and employers alike and that the safety, welfare, and wealth of Americans would be improved.

Federal use of mediation in labor disputes has provided a model for many states. Numerous states have passed laws, developed regulations, and trained a cadre of mediators to handle intrastate labor conflicts. The private sector has also initiated labor-management and commercial relations mediation. The American Arbitration Association was founded in 1926 to encourage the use of arbitration and other techniques of voluntary dispute settlement.

Mediation sponsored by government agencies has not been confined to labor-management issues. The U.S. Congress passed the Civil Rights Act of 1964 and created the Community Relations Service (CRS) of the U. S. Department of Justice. This agency was mandated to help "communities and persons therein in resolving disputes, disagreements, or difficulties relating to discriminatory practices based on race, color, or national origin" (Title X, Civil Rights Act, 1964). The agency assists people in resolving disputes through negotiation and mediation rather than having them utilize the streets or the judicial system. CRS works throughout the country on such issues as school desegregation and public-accommodation cases. In 1978, a team from CRS mediated the dispute that erupted when a neo-Nazi political group announced its intention to demonstrate in Skokie, a predominantly Jewish suburb of Chicago (Salem, 1984).

Diverse state agencies, civil rights commissions, and private agencies also use mediation to handle charges of sex, race, and ethnic discrimination conflicts (Chalmers and Cormick, 1971; Kwartler, 1980; "Municipal Human Relations Commissions . . .," 1966).

Since the mid-1960s, mediation has grown significantly as a formal and widely practiced approach to dispute resolution. In the commu-

nity sector, the federal government funds Neighborhood Justice Centers (NJCs) that provide free or low-cost mediation services to the public to resolve disputes efficiently, inexpensively, and informally. Many of these NJCs are institutionalized and have become part of city, court, district attorney programs for alternative dispute resolution. Some community programs are independent of governmental agencies and offer a grass roots independent dispute resolution service in which community members sit on mediation or conciliation panels and help neighbors resolve their disputes (Shonholtz, 1984).

Mediation is also practiced in schools and institutions of higher education. In this setting, disputes are mediated among students, such as the potentially violent interracial conflict handled by Lincoln (1976); between students and faculty; between faculty members; or between faculty and administration (McCarthy, 1980; McCarthy and others, 1984).

The criminal justice system also utilizes mediation to resolve criminal complaints (Felsteiner and Williams, 1978) and disputes in correctional facilities (Reynolds and Tonry, 1981). Mediation in the latter arena takes the form of both crisis intervention in case of prison riots or hostage negotiations and institutionalized grievance procedures.

Perhaps the fastest-growing arena in which mediation is practiced is in family disputes. Court systems and private practitioners provide mediation to families in child custody and divorce proceedings (Coogler, 1978; Haynes, 1981; Irving, 1980; Saposnek, 1983; Moore, forthcoming); disputes between parents and children (Shaw, 1982; Wixted, 1982), conflicts involving adoption and the termination of parental rights (Mayer, 1985), and spousal disputes in which there is domestic violence (Bethel and Singer, 1982; Orenstein, 1982; Wildau, 1984). In family disputes, mediated and consensual settlements are often more appropriate and satisfying than litigated or imposed outcomes. Models of practice in this area include mandatory court-connected programs in which disputants must try mediation before a judge will hear the case; voluntary court programs; and forms of private practice such as sole practitioners, partnerships, and private nonprofit agencies.

Mediation is also used within and between organizations to handle interpersonal and institutional disputes. The scope of mediation application ranges from mediating one-on-one personnel disputes, managing problems between partners (such as in law or medical practices), interdepartmental conflicts, and altercations between companies (Biddle and others, 1982; Blake and Mouton, 1984; Brett and Goldberg, 1983; Brown, 1983).

Mediation is also applied to a variety of larger disputes over environmental and public policy issues (Talbot, 1983; Bingham, 1984; Carpenter and Kennedy, 1977; Cormick, 1976; Lake, 1980; and Mernitz, 1980). Disputes over power plant siting, dam construction, and land use have all been successfully mediated. Government agencies are experimenting with negotiated rule making in public policy issues (Bingham, 1981; Harter, 1984). The Negotiated Investment Strategy, a mediated procedure initiated by the Kettering Foundation, enables local, state, and federal agencies to coordinate their decisions on program funding (Shanahan and others, 1982).

Mediation is also being applied in landlord-tenant conflicts (Cook, Rochl, and Shepard, 1980), personal injury cases ("AAA Designs . . .", 1984), police work (Folberg and Taylor, 1984), disputes between elderly residents and nursing homeowners, and consumer disputes (Ray and Smolover, 1983). The arenas in which mediation is being applied are very broad. If trends continue, the process will be used to resolve a variety of disputes in arenas not conceived of today.

Negotiation is composed of a series of complex activities or "moves" people initiate to resolve their differences and bring the conflict to termination (Goffman, 1969, p. 90). Each move or action a negotiator conducts involves rational decision making in which outcomes of alternative actions are assessed according to their relationships to the following factors: the moves of the other parties, their standards of behavior, their styles, their perceptiveness and skill, their needs and preferences, their determination, how much information the negotiator has about the conflict, his or her personal attributes, and resources available.

Mediators, like negotiators, also initiate moves. A *move* for a mediator is a specific act of intervention or "influence technique" focused on the people in the dispute that encourages the selection of positive actions and inhibits the selection of negative actions relative to the issues in conflict (Galtung, 1975b). The mediator, a specialized negotiator, does not *directly* effect changes in the disputants by initiating moves; he or she is more of a catalyst. Changes are the result of a combination of the intervenor's moves with the moves of the negotiators (Bonner, 1959).

In negotiations, people in conflict are faced with a variety of procedural or psychological problems or "critical situations" (Cohen and Smith, 1972) that they must solve or overcome if they are to reach a settlement. All problem-solving groups face these situations, which can be categorized according to size, type, time, and frequency. The largest categories and most frequent problems are hereafter referred to as *stages* because they constitute major steps that parties must take to reach agreement. There are stages for both negotiation and mediation, which, for the most part, directly correspond to each other.

Mediators make two types of interventions in response to critical situations: *general* or *noncontingent* and *specific* or *contingent* moves (Kochan and Jick, 1978).

Noncontingent moves are general interventions that a mediator initiates in all disputes. These moves are responses to the broadest categories of critical situations and correspond to the stages of mediation. They are linked to the overall pattern of conflict development and resolution. Noncontingent moves enable the mediator to:

1. Gain entry to the dispute,
2. Assist the parties in selecting the appropriate conflict resolution approach and arena,
3. Collect data and analyze the conflict,
4. Design a mediation plan,
5. Practice conciliation,
6. Assist the parties in beginning productive negotiations,
7. Identify important issues and build an agenda,

8. Identify interests,

9. Aid the parties in developing settlement options,

10. Assist in assessing the options,

11. Promote final bargaining, and

12. Aid in developing an implementation and monitoring plan.

I will examine these moves and stages in more detail later in this chapter.

Smaller noncontingent moves are initiated by mediators within each stage. Examples of this level of moves include activities to build credibility for the process, promote rapport between the parties and the mediator, and frame issues into a more manageable form, as well as develop procedures to conduct cost-benefit evaluations on settlement options.

Contingent moves are responses to special or idiosyncratic problems that occur in some negotiations. Interventions to manage intense anger, bluffing, bargaining in bad faith, mistrust, or miscommunication are all in this category of specific interventions. While some contingent moves, such as the caucus—private meetings between the parties and the mediators—are quite common, they are still in the contingent category because they do not happen in all negotiations.

Hypothesis Building and Mediation Interventions

For a mediator to be effective, he or she needs to be able to analyze and assess critical situations and design effective interventions to counteract the causes of the conflict. Conflicts, however, do not come in neat packages with their causes and component parts labeled so that the parties, or the intervenor, know how to creatively respond to them. The causes are often obscured and clouded by the dynamics of the interaction.

To work effectively on conflicts, the intervenor needs a conceptual road map or "conflict map" of the dispute (Wehr, 1979) that should detail why a conflict is occurring, should identify barriers to settlement, and should indicate procedures to manage or resolve the dispute.

Most conflicts have multiple causes; usually it is a combination of problems in the relations of the disputants that leads to a dispute. The principal tasks of the mediator and the parties are to identify central causes of the conflict and take action to alleviate them. The mediator and participants in a dispute accomplish this by trial-and-error experimentation in which they generate and test hypotheses about the conflict.

First, the parties and the mediator observe the aspects of the dispute. They examine attitudinal or behavioral problems in the interactions of the disputants, disagreements over "facts," compatible and competing interests, interaction dynamics, power relations, and value similarities and differences. From the observations, the mediator tries to identify the central critical situations or causes of the dispute. He or she often uses a framework of explanatory causes and suggested interventions such as those identified in Figure 1. Once the mediator believes that a central cause has been identified, he or she builds a hypothesis. "This conflict is caused by a, and if b is changed, the parties will be able to move toward agreement." The hypothesis must then be tested.

Testing hypotheses about conflicts involves designing interventions that challenge or modify the attitudes, behaviors, or structural relationship of the disputants. These interventions are often grounded in a theory that identifies a particular cause for the conflict and suggests prescriptive actions. For example, one theory about the cause of conflict has communication as its base. Most communication theories propose that conflict is the result of poor communication in either quality, quantity, or form. The theory postulates that if the *quality* of the information exchanged can be improved, the right *quantity* of communication can be attained, and if these data are put into the *correct form,* the causes of the dispute will be addressed and the participants will move toward resolution.

A mediator following the communications theory of conflict might begin by observing disputants communicating very poorly: One can hardly speak without the other interrupting, they have difficulty focusing on present issues and constantly digress to arguments over past wrongs that tend to escalate the conflict, and the dispute develops into a shouting match. The mediator observes the interaction, hypothesizes that one cause of the dispute is the inability of the disputants to talk with each other in

Figure 1
Sphere of Conflict
Causes and Intervention

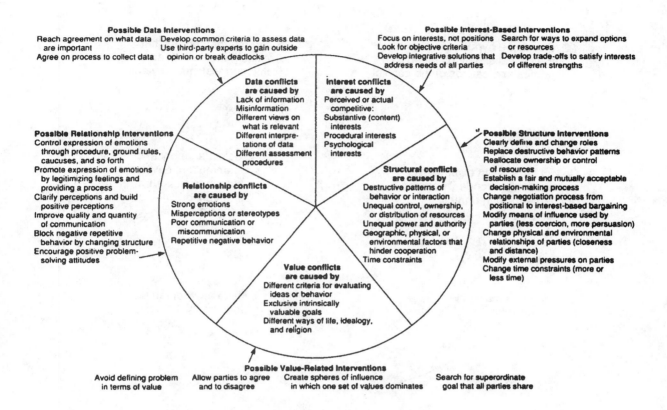

a constructive and restrained manner, and proceeds to experiment with modifications of their communication patterns (quality, quantity, and form) to see if he or she can change the conflict dynamics. The mediator may suggest that they discuss one topic at a time, may obtain their permission to monitor them, may establish ground rules about insults, or may even separate them so that they can communicate only through the mediator.

Each intervention is a test of the theory and a hypothesis that part of the dispute is caused by communication problems, and that if these difficulties can be lessened or eliminated, the parties will have a better chance of reaching settlement. If the desired effect is not achieved, the intervenor may reject the specific move as ineffective and try another. If several interventions based on one theory do not work, the intervenor may shift to another theory and begin trial-and-error testing again. The cycle of hypothesis building and testing is the basic process of intervention and conflict resolution (see Figure 2).

The Stages of Mediation

One of the broadest spheres of mediator hypothesis building occurs in the process of conceptualizing the stages of mediation and designing appropriate interventions based on the stage of development that a particular dispute has reached.

The stages of mediation are often difficult to identify. Mediator and negotiator moves seem

Figure 2
Mediator Process of Building and Testing a Hypothesis

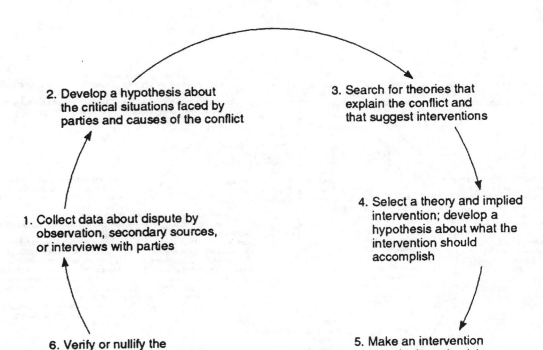

2. Develop a hypothesis about the critical situations faced by parties and causes of the conflict

3. Search for theories that explain the conflict and that suggest interventions

4. Select a theory and implied intervention; develop a hypothesis about what the intervention should accomplish

1. Collect data about dispute by observation, secondary sources, or interviews with parties

6. Verify or nullify the hypothesis

5. Make an intervention (test the hypothesis)

to blend together into an undifferentiated continuum of interaction. Only through careful observation of negotiations and mediated interventions can distinct stages composed of general moves be identified and hypotheses generated about the critical situations that the disputants will experience.

The stages of mediation intervention fall into roughly two broad categories: work that the mediator performs before joining the parties in joint session and moves made once the mediator has entered into formal negotiations. Five stages occur in the pre-negotiation work of the mediator, and seven stages occur after the mediator begins to work jointly with the disputants (see Figure 3).

In each of the twelve stages the mediator will design hypotheses and appropriate strategies and will execute specific moves. These moves are both sequential and developmental and are designed to assist disputing parties in accom-

plishing specific tasks at particular times in the negotiation process. If a task has not been completed either by the negotiators alone or with the assistance of a mediator, the parties generally encounter great difficulties in moving on to the next stage of negotiation.

Regardless of when a mediator enters negotiations—at the beginning, middle, or end—he or she will usually perform all the general or noncontingent moves. Naturally, the amount of time spent in each stage and the emphasis on each set of moves will vary considerably according to variables that will be discussed in the remaining section of this chapter—level of conflict development, timing of entry, productive conflict resolution capabilities of the disputants, power and influence relations of the parties, negotiation procedures being used, complexity of the issues, and definition of the mediator's task.

Variables That Influence Mediation Strategies and Moves

Although mediators make a variety of interventions to help parties move through the negotiation and mediation stages, their moves are not perfectly identical from case to case. While there are general patterns of moves, each mediator will have to modify his or her activities according to variables present in the case. The most critical variables that influence interventions are:

1. The level of conflict development and the timing of a mediator's entry.
2. The capability of negotiators to resolve their own dispute.
3. The power equality of the disputants and the mediator's role as a power balancer and agent of empowerment.
4. The negotiation procedures used by the parties.
5. The complexity of the issues negotiated.
6. The role and tasks of the mediator as mutually defined by the parties and the intervenor.

I will examine each of these variables and how they affect the role of the mediator and his or her application of general and specific strategies.

Conflict Development and Timing of Entry. The stage of conflict development and the degree of emotional intensity of the parties influence the tasks that negotiators have to perform. If a mediator enters a dispute in its early stages before extreme issue polarization or the development of intense emotions, he or she will use a different strategy and set of moves to assist the parties than if he or she arrives at a later stage when the parties have been negotiating and have reached a substantive impasse. In viewing mediation as a general process, however, the change in strategy and moves is primarily one of emphasis rather than a specific change in the type of move. Conciliation, for example, generally must occur more at the beginning of negotiations rather than later. If, however, a mediator enters in the later phases of a negotiation, after impasse, for example, he or she will probably still have to conciliate. The mediator will generally have to complete this phase prior to pursuing developmental moves more appropriate to the stage in which the parties have reached impasse.

Figure 3
Twelve Stages of Mediator Moves and Critical Situations to Be Handled

Stage 1: Initial Contacts with the Disputing Parties

- Making initial contacts with the parties
- Building credibility
- Promoting rapport
- Educating the parties about the process
- Increasing commitment to the procedure

Stage 2: Selecting a Strategy to Guide Mediation

- Assisting the patties to moss various approaches to conflict management and resolution
- Assisting the parties to select an approach
- Coordinating the approaches of the parties

Stage 3: Collecting and Analyzing Background Information

- Collecting and analyzing relevant data about the people, dynamics, and substance of a conflict
- Verifying accuracy of data
- Minimizing the impact of inaccurate or unavailable data

Stage 4: A Detailed Plan for Mediation

- Identifying strategies and consequent noncontingent moves that will enable the parties to move toward agreement
- Identifying contingent moves to respond to situations peculiar to the specific conflict

Stage 5: Building Trust and Cooperation

- Preparing disputants psychologically to participate in negotiations on substantive issues
- Handling strong emotions
- Checking perceptions and minimizing effects of stereotypes
- Building recognition of the legitimacy of the parties and issues
- Building trust
- Clarifying communications

Stage 6: Beginning the Mediation Session

- Opening negotiation between the parties
- Establishing an open and positive tone
- Establishing ground rules and behavioral guidelines
- Assisting the parties in venting emotions
- Delimiting topic areas and issues for discussion

Capability of Disputants to Resolve Their Own Disputes. Whether the disputants are capable of resolving their own dispute also strongly affects the mediator's intervention strategies. Parties who are able to negotiate rationally, who are aware of problem-solving procedures, and who appear to be progressing toward a settlement will require little assistance from a mediator. In this situation, the

Figure 3
Twelve Stages of Mediator Moves and Critical Situations to Be Handled
(Continued)

Stage 7: Defining Issues and Setting an Agenda

- Indentifying broad topic areas of concern to the parties
- Obtaining agreement on the issues to be discussed
- Determining the sequence for handling the issues

Stage 8: Uncovering Hidden Interests of the Disputing Parties

- Identifying the substantive, procedural, and psychological interests of the parties
- Educating the parties about each other's interests

Stage 9: Generating Options for Settlement

- Developing an awareness among the parties of the need for options
- Lowering commitment to positions or sole alternatives
- Generating options using either positional or interest-based bargaining

Stage 10: Assessing Options for Settlement

- Reviewing the interests of the parties
- Assessing how interests can be met by available options
- Assessing the costs and benefits of selecting options

Stage 11: Final Bargaining

- Reaching agreement through either incremental convergence of positions, final leaps to package settlements, development of a consensual formula, or establishment of a procedural means to reach a substantive agreemet

Stage 12: Achieving Formal Settlement

- Identifying procedural steps to operationalize the agreement
- Establishing an evaluation and monitoring procedure
- Formalizing the settlement and creating an enforcement and commitment mechanism

mediator may lend support to the work of the parties merely by his or her presence or by minimal support of the principal negotiators (Perez, 1959; Kolb, 1983). On the other hand, if parties are in the grip of intense emotions, do not have skills or expertise in negotiations or problem-solving procedures, or have reached an impasse on substantive issues, the mediator will probably be more active and more visible in the negotiations. He or she may assist the parties in productively venting strong emotions, narrowing the bargaining range, creating agendas, generating and assessing options, and initiating a variety of other procedures or moves that assist the parties in reaching a settlement.

Power Equality between Disputants. In order to derive mutually satisfactory and acceptable decisions from negotiations, all parties must have some means of influence, either positive or negative, on other disputants at the table. This is a prerequisite for a settlement that recognizes mutual needs (Lovell, 1952). If the power or influence potentials of the parties are well developed, fairly equal in strength, and recognized by all disputants, the mediator's job will be to assist parties in using their influence effectively while producing mutually satisfactory results. If, however, influence on each other is not equal and one party has the ability to impose an unsatisfactory settlement on another, an agreement that will not hold over time, or a resolution that will result in renewed conflict later, the mediator will have to decide whether and how to assist the weaker party.

Assistance or possible empowerment of the weaker party by the mediator requires very specific intervention moves—activities that shift the mediator's function dangerously close to advocacy. This problem in mediation has been debated among mediators (Bernard, Folger, Weingarten, and Zumeta, 1984). One argument states that a mediator has an obligation to create just settlements and must therefore help empower the underdog to reach equitable and fair agreements (Laue and Cormick, 1978; Suskind, 1981; Haynes, 1981). Another school argues that mediators should not do anything to influence the power relations of disputing parties because it taints the intervenor's impartiality (Bellman, 1982; Stulberg, 1981b).

In examining this question and how it affects the mediator's choice of intervention moves, it is important to distinguish between a mediator assisting in recognizing, organizing, and marshaling existing power of a disputant and a mediator becoming an advocate and assisting in generating new power and influence. The latter strategy clearly shifts the mediator out of his or her impartial position, while the former keeps the mediator within the power boundaries established by the parties. There is no easy answer to this strategic and ethical problem, but it does have an important impact on the types of moves a mediator initiates.

Negotiation Procedures. Negotiation is a form of joint problem solving. The topical problems that negotiators focus on are often called *issues*. An issue exists because the parties do not agree on a particular topic and because they have perceived or actual exclusive needs or interests.

* * *

Parties to a conflict select one of two major negotiation procedures to handle issues in dispute: *positional bargaining or interest-based bargaining* (Fisher and Ury, 1981). Positional bargaining usually occurs when a negotiator perceives that contested resources are limited and a distributive solution, one that allocates shares of gains and losses to each party, is the only possible outcome (Walton and McKersie, 1965). Interest-based bargaining, on the other hand, occurs when negotiators seek integrative solutions that meet as many of the needs of both parties as possible (Walton and McKersie, 1965). Generally, interest-based bargaining occurs when parties do not see resources as limited and solutions can be found in which all parties can have at least some of their needs met.

Positional bargaining derives its name from the practice of selecting a series of positions—particular settlement options that meet a party's interests—and presenting these to an opponent as the solution to the issue in question. A party's position may or may not be responsive to the needs or interests of other negotiators. Positions are generally ordered sequentially so that the first position is a large demand and represents a negotiator's maximum expectation of gain should his or her opponent acquiesce. Each subsequent position demands less of an opponent and results in fewer benefits for the initiating party. Characteristically, positional bargaining often commits parties early in negotiations to very specific solutions to issues in dispute and often reduces flexibility to generate other equally acceptable options.

* * *

Disputants often adopt positional bargaining when:

- The stakes for winning are high.
- The resources (time, money, psychological benefits, and so forth) are perceived to be limited.
- A win for one side will mean a loss for another.
- Interests of the parties are not interdependent or are contradictory.
- Future relationships have a lower priority than immediate substantive gain.
- All major parties have enough power to damage the others if an impasse in the negotiations occurs (Moore, 1982b).

Interest-based bargaining, in contrast to positional bargaining, is based on different assumptions about the substantive issues to be negotiated, the content of an acceptable solution, and the process by which an agreement is to be reached.

In interest-based bargaining, the negotiators do not necessarily assume that the substantive resource in question—money, time, behavior, and so forth—is necessarily limited. They do not assume that the resource must be divided into shares in which one bargainer is a winner and the other a loser. The attitude of the interest-based bargainer is that of a problem solver. The goal of negotiation is to find a solution that is mutually satisfactory and results in a win-win outcome.

Interest-based bargainers believe that settlements in negotiations are reached because a party has succeeded in having his or her interests satisfied. *Interests* are specific conditions (or gains) that a party must obtain for an acceptable settlement to occur. Interests are of three broad types: substantive, procedural, and psychological. *Substantive interests* refer to the needs that an individual has for particular tangible objects such as money and time. Substantive interests are usually the central needs on which negotiations focus.

Procedural interests refer to the preferences that a negotiator has for the *way* that the parties discuss their differences and the *manner* in which the bargaining outcome is implemented. Possible procedural interests may be that each person have the opportunity to speak his or her mind, that negotiations occur in an orderly and timely manner, that the parties avoid derogatory verbal attacks, that the plan for implementing the agreement be worked out in detail prior to final settlement, and that a written document or contract should result from bargaining.

Psychological interests refer to the emotional and relationship needs that a negotiator has both during and as a result of negotiations. Negotiators want to have high self-esteem, want to be respected by their opponent, and do not want to be degraded in negotiations. If the relationship is to be ongoing, the negotiators may want to have ongoing positive regard from the other party for their openness to future communication.

* * *

Interest-based bargaining begins with an understanding of each of the interests of the two parties, not statements of positions. Often the parties identify their interests and those of other disputants in private and then hold a joint meeting to share their results. Parties discuss and modify their interests based on these early discussions. Once the interests have been revealed, explored, and accepted at least in principle, the parties can begin a mutual search for solutions that will meet their needs. Reaching an agreement requires negotiators to develop settlement options that meet at least some of the combination of substantive, procedural, and psychological needs of all parties.

Interest-based bargaining focuses on the satisfaction of particular interests rather than advocacy of a particular position that may or may not meet the needs of the individuals, as is the case in positional bargaining. The procedure in interest-based bargaining is one of mutual problem solving, similar to the process involved in putting together a puzzle. The parties sit side by side and attempt to develop a mutually acceptable settlement.

Mediators can help parties conduct either positional or interest-based bargaining more efficiently and effectively. Since the goal of mediation is to help parties reach a mutually acceptable settlement, mediators generally have a bias toward interest-based and integrative solutions. Often parties are engaged in a positional process that is destructive to their relationships, is not generating creative options, and is not resulting in wise decisions. One of the mediator's major contributions to the dispute resolution process is assisting the negotiators in making the transition from positional to interest-based bargaining.

Complexity of the Case and Issues Negotiated. Disputes come in a variety of levels of complexity. The simple-issue landlord-tenant case in which two parties argue over a security deposit is very different from the complexity of a child custody and divorce dispute that involves multiple issues and very complex psychodynamics between the disputants. The latter case may in its own right be very uncomplicated when compared to a multiparty case that involves American Telephone and Telegraph, a local Bell company, multiple independent phone companies, the Public Utilities Commission, and numerous consumer or public interest groups, and that centers around multiple and complex technical issues.

Mediators entering disputes must design intervention strategies that respond to the complexity of a specific dispute. In one case, detailed data collection procedures may be required to understand the causes and dynamics of the conflict, while in another case a simple intake interview at the first joint session with the parties is sufficient. In some cases the mediator must break a particularly difficult impasse, and, when successful, may withdraw and return the parties to negotiations on their own. In other cases, the mediator may play an active role throughout negotiations and provide the major procedural framework for negotiations. In exploring the stages of mediation in later chapters, it is important to consider the complexity of the dispute to determine the amount of detail required in the intervention.

Definition of the Mediator's Role and Types of Interventions. The final variable that affects the noncontingent and contingent moves of a mediator is the definition of the tasks and role that the mediator is to perform in the negotiations. Mediators differ significantly when deciding their role and involvement in promoting successful negotiations. The division usually occurs when determining how much the mediator should focus on process and substance.

One school argues that mediators should focus primarily on the process of negotiations and leave decisions about the substantive content as the exclusive domain of the parties (Stulberg, 1981b). Procedurally oriented mediators define their role this way for a variety of reasons. First, mediators often believe that the parties are better informed about the substantive issues in dispute than any third party could ever be. These intervenors believe that the best quality decision is that determined by the parties. Second, mediators from this school believe that what the parties need is procedural help, not a substantive suggestion or decision. Third, these intervenors believe that the parties' commitment to implement and adhere to a settlement will be enhanced if they make the substantive decisions themselves, as opposed to having the deal decided or forged by the intervenor. Finally, the mediators of this school believe that a focus on the process and an impartial stance toward substance builds trust between the intervenor and disputants, decreases the risk to the parties of involving another party in the dispute, and makes them more open to procedural assistance.

Many labor-management mediators, especially intervenors from the Federal Mediation and Conciliation Service, subscribe to this role for the mediator (Kolb, 1983). They see themselves as "orchestrators" of a process that enables the parties to make their own substantive decisions.

Some environmental mediators also follow this procedurally oriented definition of the mediator's role. Bellman (1982) generally does not try to influence the substantive outcome of a dispute even if he ethically disagrees with the outcome, considers the settlement environmentally unsound, or believes that it is based on inaccurate or inadequate information. He sees himself purely as a process consultant.

Some family mediators also adhere to the procedurally oriented approach to intervention. They argue that in a divorce, for example, the parents generally know what is best for both the children and the family system as a whole (Phear, 1984; Saposnek, 1985). The parents do not need a substantive expert to tell them what

to do. What they need is procedural help to assist them in problem solving.

The other school of thought argues that although the mediator is impartial and neutral, this does not mean that he or she should not work with the parties directly on substantive matters to develop a fair and just decision according to the intervenor's values. Suskind (1981, pp. 46–47), an environmental mediator, argues that intervenors should be involved in substantive decisions when (1) "the impacts of negotiated agreement will affect underrepresented or unrepresented groups," (2) there is "the possibility that joint net gains have not been maximized," (3) the parties are not aware of the "long-term spill-over effects of the settlements," and (4) the precedents that they set "may be detrimental to the parties or the broader public." Suskind further notes that "although such intervention may make it difficult to retain the appearance of neutrality and the trust of the active parties, environmental mediators cannot fulfill their responsibilities to the community-at-large if they remain passive" (p. 47). Some labor-management mediators also belong to this school. These "deal-makers" intervene substantively when the parties are uninformed, ill-prepared to negotiate, or unaware of mutually acceptable substantive settlements (Kolb, 1983).

Child custody and divorce mediators also have advocates in the second school. Saposnek (1983) argues that the mediator should advocate the unrepresented interests of the children in negotiations between the parents and believes that the mediator should intervene and influence the substantive outcome if those interests are violated and not taken into consideration. Coogler (1978) also urges the mediator to engage in substantive negotiations and advocates that the intervenor write a letter of nonconcurrence that is sent to the court if the mediator seriously disagrees with the settlement.

Haynes (1981), another family mediator, believes that the intervenor should be active in power balancing help to define the terms of the substantive decision. Haynes, Coogler, and Saposnek directly disregard the concept of substantive impartiality as a critical component of the mediator's role.

There is a spectrum along which mediators place themselves in defining their degree of involvement in the procedure and substance of negotiations. On one side are those who advocate mostly procedural interventions; on the other side are advocates of substantive involvement by the mediator that may include actually forging the decision. Between them are mediators who pursue a role with mixed involvement in process and substance.

I lean strongly toward the process end of the spectrum because I believe that the parties should have the primary responsibility for self-determination. On rare occasions, however, the mediator has an ethical responsibility to raise critical questions about substantive options under consideration by the parties. These situations include cases where the agreement appears to be extremely inequitable to one or more of the parties, does not look as if it will hold over time, seems likely to result in renewed conflict at a later date, or where the terms of settlement are so loose (or confining) that implementation is not feasible. I believe the mediator should also intervene in cases involving the potential for violence or actual violence to one or more parties, either primary or secondary.

Depending on the role that the mediator or the mediator and the parties assign the intervenor, he or she will have to decide which types of interventions he or she will perform. In defining interventions, the mediator must decide on (1) the level of intervention, (2) the target of intervention, (3) the focus of intervention, and (4) the intensity of intervention.

The *level of intervention* refers to how much the mediator concentrates on helping negotiators move through the general critical situation, for example, the stages of bargaining, versus a focus on particular idiosyncratic problems that are pushing the parties toward impasse. In some disputes the parties may need assistance to break a particular deadlock, while others will need mediator assistance throughout the bargaining process.

The *target of intervention* refers to the person or people to whom the mediator directs or her moves. Should moves be directed to all parties, to a relationship within the group such as a subgroup or team, or to a particular person? In a postmarital dispute, for example, should the mediator focus on changing the ex-wife's move, the ex-husband's, or both, or should he or she focus on the entire family system, including children, ex-spouses, stepparents, and grandparents? In a community dispute, should the mediator focus on the spokespeople, specific team members, the team as a whole, or the constituents of the parties?

The *focus of intervention* refers to the particular critical situations at which the mediator directs his or her moves. The mediator may focus his or her energies on changing the *psychological relationship* of parties to each other. This is often referred to as a conciliation. He or she may aim at creating the psychological conditions that are necessary for productive negotiations. The mediator may also focus on changing the *negotiation process* or the procedure that is being used by one or more people to solve the dispute. The focus may be on the process for moving through the stages of solving a specific problem, such as how to help a party make a proposal that will be acceptable to the other side.

The focus may also be on changing the *substance* or *content* of the dispute. The mediator may look for ways to explore data, to expand the number of acceptable options on the negotiation table, to narrow the choices when the parties are overwhelmed with possibilities, or to integrate proposals made by the disputants.

Finally, the intervenor may focus on changing the relationship *structure* among the parties. This may mean influencing their personal or interactive relationship in regard to such factors as power, communication patterns, face-to-face versus private negotiations, team structure, or a party's relationship to its constituents. •

Study Questions

1. Define mediation.

2. In what way is mediation "facilitated" negotiation?

3. Define intervention, and explain the relevant assumptions within this definition.

4. What makes a mediator "acceptable?"

5. How are impartiality and neutrality related?

6. Why do people seek a mediator's assistance?

7. Explain the levels of conflict and give examples of each.

8. How is a mediator different from a judge or arbiter? How are they potentially more advantageous to negotiators?

9. Explain who gives authority to mediators.

10. List the roles/functions of a mediator.

11. Historically, what were the qualifications/characteristics of mediators?

12. Briefly recount the history of the Federal Mediation and Conciliation Service. Its purpose?

13. In what area of dispute resolution is mediation growing the fastest? Why is this method of alternative dispute resolution (ADR) seen as most appropriate and satisfying for this issue?

14. What is a mediation "move?"

15. How do mediators address "critical situations?"

16. What determines a mediator's effectiveness?

17. What is the basic process of intervention and conflict resolution?

18. Using the six critical variables affecting intervention tactics as a base, explain when a mediator is most involved in conflict resolution.

19. What dilemma exists with unequally powered disputants and the mediator's role?

20. What is an issue?

21. How does positional bargaining get its name?

22. When are disputants most likely to adopt positional bargaining?

23. Explain the three types of "interests" integrative bargainers have.

24. What reasons do procedurally-oriented mediators give for staying out of directing substantive issues/content?

25. What rationale is used when mediators decide to make substantive interventions?

The Role of the Mediator

T. Colosi

Because the essence of negotiations is to provide an opportunity for parties or disputants to exchange promises and thus resolve their differences, some measure of trust between the parties is critical. While some students of negotiation contend that trust is irrelevant to negotiations, it is hard to see how a serious exchange of promises can occur without trust. Each side must have some confidence that the other will keep its word once a promise is given (whether the promises involve benefits or threats). Trust need not be blind, of course. It may be supported by information that is uncovered and processed in the course of negotiation; it may rest on relationships that have strengthened in the course of negotiation; ultimately it may emerge even from the shared experience of coming to understand the negotiation process.

Parties can reach an impasse in negotiations, where no further discussion is possible because either their trust has run out or there was too little trust in the first place. Indeed, in the absence of trust, negotiations might never even begin. Parties with no trust between them can be said to be in a trust vacuum. This underlies their fears of each other. Moreover, it interferes with the very communication that might dispel such fears. Without open lines of productive communication, very little education can take place.

The necessary trust between the parties may be developed in three steps. First, a mediator must work to win the trust of the parties. Next, the mediator educates the parties about the negotiation process (not the mediation process) and works to encourage them to transfer their trust from him to it. Finally, the mediator persuades the parties to begin trusting each other, again using the negotiation process as a vehicle to demonstrate that trust.

The Evolution of Trust

Trust In The Outside Third-Party Mediator

The mediator gains the trust of the parties principally by demonstrating that he or she is truly neutral. The capacity of a mediator to win trust may be at its highest if intervention occurs when the situation is particularly polarized and trust between the parties is at its lowest.

Others contend that a mediator should intervene before the parties are frozen into positions, but the particular mediator (and mediation in general) may very well be rejected early in the dispute. At best, the mediator may be underutilized or "bargained with" by parties, both of which make it difficult for him to determine their true objectives.

Just as nature abhors a vacuum, the negotiation process abhors the absence of trust. When parties are polarized, they also have a better idea of what they want the mediator to do. The issues and alternatives are better defined and, as a result, the disputants will be more likely to understand that it is they (and not the mediator) who must assume responsibility for the outcome of negotiations. This is, after all, a fundamental objective of the mediator. In addition, the more time the mediator is involved in the dispute, the less he or she will appear neutral to everyone involved. This perception, of course, can sabotage the mediator's effectiveness.

Mediators may use a number of techniques to demonstrate their neutrality and win the parties' trust. Mediators must learn, for example, how to listen and not say much; likewise, they cannot reveal their emotions and attitudes. Taking care to express only positive or neutral opinions of the groups involved in the dispute is one important approach. Mediators should listen to people's ideas with an open mind, not only to obtain a comprehensive view of the problem but to set an example by showing that there is little risk in entertaining other points of view. Mediators should emphasize that they are only there to help the parties, and have absolutely no decision-making authority regarding the substance or the issues. Mediators must also assure the parties that all conversations will be held in strict confidence. Additionally, a hard-won reputation for helping people in other cases obviously provides a solid foundation for winning the parties' trust.

A mediator may also be able to use other processes for gaining trust. For example, parties who shy away from mediation nevertheless may be willing to engage in fact-finding. Viewed narrowly, fact-finding is a process of gathering information, understanding and organizing the issues in a dispute, and giving advice about a possible settlement; the parties are not bound by the fact-finder's recommendations. Sophisticated mediators, however, see broader potential in fact-finding: It can serve as a first step in negotiations, the mechanism by which the mediator gets to meet with all the parties and begins to win their trust.

The process of enhancing trust in the mediator is not without risk. Inexperienced mediators frequently feel empowered by the confidence and acceptance that the disputants may quickly show toward them. Mediators must keep in mind, however, that their perception of power comes from the parties' need to fill the trust vacuum. Furthermore, their perceived power is only an early stage in a developmental process that ideally should lead to the empowering of the negotiators themselves through the help of the mediator.

Trust in the Process

Having obtained the parties' trust, the mediator must next work to transfer it from himself to the negotiation process. The parties must be shown that the negotiation process is the way through their problem. They must become comfortable with the negotiation process, experiment with it, and use it to achieve success. In the early stages of a dispute, the best kind of intervenor often will avoid substantive issues and concentrate instead on procedural matters in order to educate the parties about negotiation and mediation. The parties should know that mediation is available if they want it, but they should not move into mediation until they really need it.

Because negotiating skills are not taught in our society to any great extent, there is very poor understanding about how the negotiation process works. People tend to concentrate on whether or not another *party* should be trusted,

rather than on trusting the process itself. Learning to trust negotiations is a useful interim step between no trust and trust in another party. Disputants who do not take the interim step usually end up using alternative dispute resolution processes. In some cases, the alternative may be litigation; in others, a strike or a riot. The role of the mediator is to call attention to the need for establishing an understanding of, and confidence in, the negotiation process before trust in the other parties is sought.

Trust Among the Parties

Once the interim steps have been taken and trust in both the mediator and in the negotiation process is established, the professional mediator must work hard to transfer that trust to the parties themselves. This can occur in two ways. First, the mediator acts as a role model: demonstrating good listening skills; showing respect for other people's opinions and constraints; and creating an atmosphere of trust by encouraging the negotiators to develop a statement of common goals. Second, trust is established among the parties though practice. The preliminary stages of negotiation involve some cooperation among the parties in relatively simple process decisions. These may involve minor procedural matters—"housekeeping issues" if you will—yet over time they provide a shared experience that allows the parties slowly to develop a more trusting relationship), one that is essential when more fundamental, high stakes issues are tackled.

The case that follows illustrates how these trust-building steps are implemented in practice.

Building Trust: An Example In Community Multilateral Negotiations

In 1973 a riot in a Rochester, New York, high school sent 16 students and teachers (8 blacks and 8 whites) to the hospital. I was one of two intervenors from the American Arbitration Association's National Center for Dispute Resolution in Washington, D.C., who entered the dispute as fact-finders. In truth, we borrowed from the public sector labor-management model to characterize our roles, using the Newman model of "mediators wearing fact-finders' hats." The particular intervenors were teamed because one is white and the other black.

About 18 different organizations, representing students, specific racial and ethnic groups, teachers, parents, and local citizens, were identified by the school board and one another as interested parties. They were invited by the American Arbitration Association to meet each other and the fact-finders. The purpose of the meeting was to determine what had caused the riot and to try to set up a process for avoiding future disruption. Once this group was assembled, one of the first questions that had to be answered was whether still other parties and organizations should be involved. Some groups already present voiced objections about inviting certain others, contending that they would ruin the process. Nevertheless, as mediator/fact-finders, we encouraged those who were involved to invite the threatening groups to participate on the ground that any outsiders who had enough power to stymie the process would likely be important to implementing any agreement. Ultimately, the original participants did decide who would be at the table and added several parties. In effect, the negotiators defined themselves.

Once the group's composition was established, the parties had to determine how decisions would be made. Two competing models of decision-making were offered: majority vote and full consensus. Some conservative groups supported the majority vote, while the minority organizations felt better protected by full consensus; indeed, they threatened to leave the table over this issue. The intervenors kept the parties together by observing that an effective solution to the high school problem would be possible only if all the groups present were involved in the negotiations. The intervenors pointed out that a settlement unanimously endorsed by a group as broadly based as those convened would carry a great deal of clout with the school board and the public. The parties remained at the table because they had begun to believe that some common goals and solutions were possible, even though these had yet to take concrete form.

Each group's attitude on the decision-making issue was affected, in part, by its own internal structure and experience. Some groups that were accustomed to operating under an authoritarian model assumed that the mediator/fact-finders would make the decisions. Others thought that committees would be formed to discuss the issues and be given delegated powers. Majority rule, with and without minority opinion reports, were other suggestions. Before long, participants came to see how differently they all made decisions, and began to educate one another about the relative merits of each process.

The intervenors had to conduct side-bar meetings (caucuses with groups in isolation from other groups) because of one minority group's flat refusal to participate under any process except full consensus. The mediator/fact-finders created doubts in the conservative camp as to the viability of the majority rule process by asking its members if they realized how much power was available to them through the full consensus process. The intervenors pointed out that a simple veto could be exercised by any group to prevent proposals and directions that were perceived to be inappropriate or undesirable from being adopted. After many internal discussions with the conservative group, full consensus decision-making was accepted.

Continuing the process discussions, we next suggested to the group that they begin their negotiations by agreeing upon a common goal. The initial proposals were sweeping and often contradictory. Some said that the goal should be to stop busing. Others said that desegregation should be eliminated. One proposal was to abolish the school board. Even amendments to the U.S. Constitution were put forth. It was clear that the parties were still a long way from reaching a mutually acceptable goal.

We worked patiently in a variety of process configurations and settings to try to close the many gaps. Talks took place chiefly in informal meetings. Internal discussions took place within some of the parties; there was also direct talk between the parties, both with and without the mediators. In the course of these discussions, the mediators came to realize that despite the parties' obvious differences, they shared a common attitude: fear. They feared each other, but beyond that they feared what might happen in the schools and in the community if accommodation could not be achieved. Still, they were not ready to trust each other to be reasonable or to deliver on promises.

The parties met over a six-month period with the mediators and a local coordinator. A church basement was used as the formal meeting area. There was near-perfect attendance at all the weekly and biweekly meetings; no group pulled out of the process. Ultimately, the groups agreed on a common goal: to have safe schools. In retrospect, the goal may seem obvious, yet the fact that it eluded the parties for so long shows that polarization and lack of trust can keep disputants from recognizing their shared interests that, under other circumstances, might be easily perceived. Once the common goal was articulated, the parties tried to formulate an overall strategy for achieving it. Their initial strategy was to continue negotiations. Trust in the negotiation process and in each other was beginning to be established, and as the parties assumed greater responsibility for tasks, the mediators of course did less.

The outside neutrals entered this polarized situation as fact-finders, forced to establish trust—first in themselves and then in the negotiation process—by showing the parties how mediation could help them. By encouraging the parties to work together on small, seemingly procedural issues, the intervenors demonstrated how people with different priorities and outlooks could work cooperatively.

Once trust is established in the negotiation process and in each other, the negotiators will find that they no longer need a mediator. When this happens, the mediator should begin to leave the dispute, as his job may essentially be over. The mediator may make himself available for other process-management tasks, of course, or to resume mediation if the trust relationship breaks down for any reason.

The Mediator's Capacity to Raise and Maintain Doubts

Effective mediators create and maintain doubts by raising questions about alternatives and implications that the negotiators may not have considered or fully appreciated. Like any good negotiator, the mediator avoids flat statements. If, for instance, a mediator wants a negotiator to think about the reaction of the negotiator's superiors to a certain proposal, the mediator is better off asking, "What would your boss say?" rather than declaring, "Your boss may not support you

on that." The same axiom would apply in a situation in which a mediator and a negotiator are discussing a negotiator's decision to leave the bargaining table. Assuming that the negotiators are using full consensus in their decision-making process, the mediator might privately say to the reluctant negotiator, "The other parties might come to some decision in your absence. Have you considered the implications of your not being present to veto decisions that would hurt your side?" The use of questions rather than statements gives negotiators more room to respond and more freedom to consider what the mediator is saying. It also allows the mediator to play a more neutral, laissez-faire role as declarations tend to be more leading and value-loaded than questions. The negotiators are thus subtly encouraged to take maximum responsibility in the negotiation process.

As noted earlier, most important negotiating takes place in the internal team caucuses. As a consequence, this usually is where the mediator is most active as well. Private meetings are normally the best forum for the mediator to raise doubts.

During horizontal (across-the-table) negotiations, each team tries to educate the other about its position. The negotiators try to raise new doubts in the minds of their counterparts. As a result, a new set of assumptions and proposals may become plausible, and new issues and problems may arise as well. In this phase of negotiation, the stabilizers and nonstabilizers tend to open up to each other in the caucuses when these new concerns are discussed. If the quasi-mediator is unable to create doubts in the nonstabilizer's mind, an outside, neutral mediator may be enlisted before the team resorts to autocratic decision-making, or internal disciplinary measures to bring the dissenter along. Committed to stability, the mediator concentrates on internal team bargaining and similarly tries to raise doubts about the viability of nonsettlement in the mind of the nonstabilizer. Sometimes the emphasis is less on outcomes and more on process. If the nonstabilizer does not trust the negotiation process because of preconceived notions, the mediator must raise doubts about the competing process alternatives. By contrast, of course, effective mediators would not work to create doubt in the minds of the stabilizers, since this group wants settlement.

Parties Who Will Not Settle

The mediator's function is thus to create and maintain doubts in the minds of individual negotiators who oppose settlement. What can a mediator do if an entire team is composed of nonstabilizers?

Some negotiators enter the process quite committed to talking but not to settling. For them negotiation may only be a device to stall for time. They may be waiting for the other side to exhaust its strike fund or other resources. They may have calculated that in time public opinion will shift in their favor. Time may be needed to prepare a lawsuit, launch a media campaign, or use some other external pressure on the other side. It may simply be that these "negotiators" prefer the status quo to any foreseeable alternative.

When one team is negotiating just to buy time, the situation between the contending parties is similar in many respects to the internal process that occurs within a team between stabilizers and nonstabilizers. The nonstabilizers are the ones who must be convinced by the quasi-mediator (and the stabilizers) to remain at the table, to listen to the other teams, to consider their arguments, and, ideally, to revise their positions to enable their negotiating team to offer deliverable proposals. The quasi-mediator first tries to raise doubts in the mind of the uncooperative teammates about the consequences of nonsettlement. (What losses would have to be incurred: a strike, litigation, violence; can the group afford such losses?)

A team dedicated to nonsettlement occupies the same position in horizontal negotiations as does the nonstabilizer within his team. It, too, is uninterested in settlement. In this instance, however, it is the mediator rather than the quasi-mediator who steps in. Although the person is different, the role is much the same. The mediator relies on the same basic technique of raising doubts about the team's decision to stall, probing to see if all the implications of nonsettlement have been evaluated.

In any case when it becomes obvious that a party has carefully considered its position and has determined that settlement is not in its interest, then, after appropriate probing, the mediator ultimately must accept the party's own judgment. When a party believes that it is better to stall than to settle, the mediator might reasonably continue with the process if the other party accedes.

Negotiation and Litigation

Deadlines are important monitors of the parties' success at reaching an agreement. Timing is a critical factor in a mediator's assessment of a party's willingness to settle. When there is no court-imposed or other "natural" deadline (for example, the expiration of a labor contract), the mediator can help the parties set the clock. He can warn the parties that if settlement is not reached by a certain time, then the parties may have to proceed without him. Mediators have to take care in using this tactic. The deadline should not be artificial; disputes are not poker games for bluffing. Instead, the mediator should use his general experience, combined with his knowledge of the specific dispute, to determine at what future point a failure to agree would show that his time was spent inefficiently.

The difficulty a mediator may have in getting negotiators to settle within a time limit gives much support to arguments that favor the deadlines imposed by the litigation process. In litigation, deadlines are perceived to be firmer and more believable. Disputes therefore can be settled within a set period of time. Although some proponents of negotiation extol it as an alternative to the courts, nothing settles a dispute better than the combined force of the strong arm of the court (or an arbitrator) and active negotiation.

Negotiation is often called an "alternative" dispute resolution process, a characterization that implicitly regards the judicial system as dominant. This view also seems predicated on a belief that negotiation and litigation represented entirely divergent paths, yet practice often reveals that the two can be inextricably bound.

This point is illustrated by a heated land use dispute in New York State in which negotiation and litigation occurred in tandem. A group of Mohawk Indians occupied some open land, and town officials moved to have them evicted. Before the state police were deployed, however, help was sought from the National Center for

Dispute Settlement. The center (a division of the American Arbitration Association) was contacted to serve as "Rumor Control Experts." (This term was carefully chosen to help the intervenors win the trust of all the parties, as rumors were potentially harmful to everyone.) Under that authority, representatives of the center began the delicate process of building trust. In time, the process came to be directed explicitly at negotiation. Prosecutorial actions were held in abeyance. Nevertheless, the specter of a court-imposed resolution kept the process on track. The mediators assured the parties that no action would be taken by the court so long as the negotiation process was reported as being fruitful. Neither side was confident what the judge would order if negotiation broke down.

In disputes that erupt spontaneously (such as the one just described), parties often find themselves simultaneously involved in lawsuits and negotiations. Usually their lawyers are likewise involved in both processes. But is a lawyer the best representative for a party in a negotiation process? Certainly, lawyers are assumed to be good negotiators. Yet the parties themselves may be just as good if they are educated properly about the process. Moreover, many lawyers are biased in favor of the judicial process and act with little enthusiasm for negotiation. Sophisticated clients could become knowledgeable about the negotiation process (using the mediator as a mentor, if necessary) and employ lawyers for advice on how the negotiations could influence the simultaneous litigation. In such a case, the lawyers should not take over the negotiation process, though their advice could be useful. The mediator, in turn, could help the negotiator and the lawyers coordinate their respective responsibilities. In a sense, this is just another example of building team cohesion: It is similar to the work a mediator does to produce greater harmony among the stabilizers and nonstabilizers. •

Study Questions

1. How do mediators gain trust from their parties?

2. List the techniques mediators use to demonstrate neutrality and win trust.

3. What is fact finding?

4. After mediators have the parties' trust, on what other areas of trust should they concentrate?

5. How can mediators help parties trust each other?

6. What common attitude among disputants became clear in the Rochester, NY case? What ultimately was identified as a common goal?

7. What is an unfortunate consequence of polarization and lack of trust with regard to collaborative negotiation?

8. What primary strategy is effective for mediators who want to raise and maintain doubts in parties? Where should most of these interactions take place? Would stabilizers or nonstabilizers be the target of these techniques?

9. How should mediators handle use of deadlines?

10. Can negotiation and litigation work together? Explain.

How the Oslo Connection Led to the Mideast Pact

Clyde Haberman
Special to The New York Times

The Secret Peace

Jerusalem, Sept. 4—At the time, in April 1992, the somewhat gray and academic meeting in Tel Aviv hardly seemed a place where dreams might be built. But if the tentative and potentially momentous new agreement reached by Israel and the P.L.O. could be said to have a birthplace, it was the gathering in Tel Aviv.

There, Yossi Beilin, then an opposition Labor member of Parliament, got to know Terje Rod Larsen, head of a Norwegian institute researching conditions in the Israeli-occupied territories. If Mr. Beilin wished, Mr. Larsen said, he could put him in touch with senior Palestinian officials.

The Israeli did not leap at the opportunity, in part because he had more pressing matters on his mind, like the approaching national election in June. But he was interested enough to ask a university professor friend to keep in touch with the man from Oslo.

Norway Takes Secret Role

By mid-July, the Labor Party was voted into power, Mr. Beilin was Israel's new Deputy Foreign Minister, and Mr. Larsen was back in Jerusalem, renewing his offer. What in April had been an uneventful meeting of policy researchers led directly in September to another gathering in Tel Aviv, where this time a senior Norwegian diplomat proposed to Mr. Beilin that Norway become the secret passage for direct talks between Israel and the Palestine Liberation Organization leadership, which is based in Tunis.

That was the start of the Oslo Connection.

A Variety of Sites

In the months to follow, on elegant country estates and in ordinary hotel rooms, representatives of Israel and the P.L.O., enemies to the death for three decades, met secretly and stitched together a set of principles that is supposed to lead them out of their long struggle. The core of their plan has been known for the last week:

Assuming the two sides can get past difficulties that have popped up in the last few days, they will soon formally recognize each other—something that seemed almost impossible two weeks ago—and set in motion a shift of authority in the territories from Israel to Palestinians, starting in the Gaza Strip and the West Bank City of Jericho.

As radical a change as this is, its thunder built gradually. Officials and others interviewed in Israel, Norway and the United States—knowledgeable P.L.O. officials were not available—say there was no single turning point, no startling pronouncement that suddenly made it happen.

Rather than high drama in Norway, participants say, there was a more subtle combination of relaxed settings, home-cooked meals, mutual esteem, a knack for telling the right joke to ease a tense situation and more important, an ability to keep secrets. "That was the difficult part—keeping our mouths shut," said Professor Yair Hirschfield of Haifa University, Mr. Beilin's academic friend and a key go-between from the start.

No more than a dozen people knew exactly what was going on at all times, participants say. The regular delegations to the Middle East peace talks were kept in the dark. So were local Palestinian leaders and Israeli Cabinet ministers.

While the Norwegians kept the United States informed almost from the start, the Americans were never actively involved, sticking instead both to the episodic talks in Washington and to their policy of not dealing with the P.L.O. or its chairman, Yasir Arafat.

In Washington, senior Clinton Administration officials said the United States would be ready to resume its dialogue with the P.L.O. when it met Israel's terms of renouncing terrorism and unequivocally recognizing Israel's right to exist.

Administration officials said that on Tuesday they will begin sounding out lawmakers about removing the legal barriers to the dialogue, which was broken off in 1990 after a P.L.O. faction's abortive raid on an Israeli beach.

Perhaps even more critical than tight lips and country homes was the fact that Israel and the P.L.O. both badly wanted their meetings to succeed, each for its own reasons.

The P.L.O. was in disarray. Mr. Arafat was scrambling to hold onto power, the organization's once-fat bank accounts were drying up, in large measure because of its own political miscalculations, and its loyalists were losing ground fast in the occupied territories to Islamic militants gathered under the banner of Hamas. Mr. Arafat needed a deal that would leave no doubt he was still on top.

The Israelis were also eager. They had lost faith in the negotiations stumbling along in Washington with Palestinians from the territories who, it became painfully clear, could not deliver the goods. Knowing he would ultimately be judged on whether he fulfilled his campaign promise to come to terms quickly with the Palestinians, Prime Minister Yitzhak Rabin endorsed the secret contacts, even if he was not persuaded they would work and even though, as he said the other day, it meant dealing with enemies he detests.

In suspending his skepticism, he worked in tandem with Foreign Minister Shimon Peres, who had become involved in the Norwegian dialogue in early spring and then guided it along until he himself met secretly with a senior P.L.O. official in Norway, capping the talks with a draft agreement initialed on Aug. 20.

Throughout their political lives, Mr. Rabin and Mr. Peres have fought nasty battles for Labor Party supremacy. It is axiomatic among Israelis that anything one of them does is intended at least in part to undercut the other.

But starting in spring, the two politicians worked closely together, cementing an odd symbiosis that they had formed through the years of rivalry. Mr. Peres, a man with grand

ideas but also fragile public support, and Mr. Rabin, more of a nuts-and-bolts analyst but also a tough ex-general who can persuade Israelis that he will not sell them out to the Arabs, found that they could not succeed without each other. This time, jealousies shriveled before their task.

"Look, we're grown-up people," Mr. Peres said this week. "We're not searching anymore for power. We're leading the nation toward the future, to save ourselves from being Balkanized in Israel and the territories, to spare us a Yugoslavia-like situation."

The Beginning
From Tel Aviv to London to Oslo

None of this seemed dimly on the horizon when Mr. Beilin and Mr. Larsen shook hands in Tel Aviv and discussed daily life in Gaza and the West Bank.

Mr. Larsen is director general of FAFO, the Norwegian Institute for Applied Social Science, which was preparing a report on living conditions in the territories and was looking for Israeli cooperation both in and out of Government. Mr. Beilin, a close Peres associate, was interested in the project but otherwise engaged. He put the Norwegian in touch with Yair Hirschfield, who teaches Middle East history at Haifa University.

Right after the elections, Mr. Larsen came back. His focus now, officials say, was not research so much as an attempt to put the new left-leaning Israeli Government in direct touch with senior Palestinians who might be able to reach an agreement that had eluded official delegates in Washington. Again, the Israeli said the Haifa professor was the best contact.

But he clearly was interested in exploring new possibilities.

On Sept. 10, 1992, Mr. Larsen returned once more, bringing with him Norway's No. 2 diplomat, State Secretary Jan Egeland. They sat down with Mr. Beilin and Professor Hirschfield at the Tel Aviv Hilton. Mr. Egeland's offer was straightforward:

Norway could be a bridge between Israel and the P.L.O., not as a mediator but as an expediter, one graced with diplomatic sophistication, familiarity with the key figures and distance from the region and prying cameras.

Not that Norway's relations with Israel had always been smooth. They were especially strained after an Israeli hit squad gunned down a Moroccan waiter in Lillehammer, Norway, in July 1973. They thought he was an agent of the Arab guerrilla group that killed 11 Israeli athletes at the 1972 Summer Olympics in Munich. They shot the wrong man.

As an additional sign that the Norwegians meant business, Johan Jorgen Holst, the Defense Minister and seven months later Foreign Minister, supported the idea. By no coincidence, his wife, Marianne Heiberg, was the author of the FAFO study that got these negotiations started.

Yes, he was intrigued, Mr. Beilin said. Actually, he later told associates, he had no solid reason to believe that this effort could produce anything—a doubt that would persist for months. And he wanted to be personally removed; it would be politically damaging if word leaked out that he was secretly meeting officials of the outlawed P.L.O. Once again, his point man was Professor Hirschfield.

On a December morning, the 49-year-old professor walked into the Gallery Lounge of the modern Forte Crest St. James's hotel central London. He was to have breakfast with Mr. Larsen.

But after a brief conversation, the Norwegian slid out of his seat and left the room. In his place sat Ahmed Suleiman Khoury, a senior P.L.O. official in charge of finances and better known by the nickname Abu Alaa.

Abu Alaa, a highly educated businessman in his 60's, belonged to Mr. Arafat's Fatah group—"brilliant and tremendously tough, elegant and polished," as Mr. Larsen described him. To the Israelis, he was an acceptable partner, high-ranking but with "no blood on his hand" as an active participant in anti-Israel terrorism.

From the first talk, Professor Hirschfield said, "it was very clear that the P.L.O. felt it had to make moves now, that Hamas was getting stronger in the territories and that the 'outside' people in Tunis felt they had to bring about successful negotiations."

But he added: "It was an exercise to see if an agreement was possible. It wasn't a negotia-

tion. And they felt the same way on the other side."

Technically, Professor Hirschfield was committing a crime at the London hotel. Israeli law prohibited such private contacts with declared terrorist groups, including the P.L.O. But the law was repealed a month later, and officials say that gave extra impetus to the secret discussions.

On Jan. 20 the Haifa professor and the P.L.O. finance chief moved their talks to Norway, the first of 14 sessions in that country. At the start, Abu Alaa had only an assistant or two. Professor Hirschfield was accompanied by a colleague, Professor Ron Pundak of Tel Aviv University, who shared the tasks of taking notes, typing papers and making plane reservations because secrecy requirements ruled out secretaries.

The first talks were near the town of Sarpsborg, 60 miles east of Oslo, where the Borregard paper company owns a mansion that during the Middle Ages was the summer residence of Norwegian kings. It is a grand estate surrounded by acres of fields and forest—the perfect place, the Norwegians thought, for the Israelis and Palestinians to take off their jackets and ties, sit in front of the fire and get to know one another.

And no one else.

"We told the staff that it was a meeting of eccentric professors who would talk all hours and order up sandwiches at three o'clock in the morning because they were working on a book," Mr. Larsen said. Private cars were used instead of official black limousines to bring them from hotels in Oslo. And Foreign Minister Holst was present, not actively joining the discussions but standing by to lend a hand when snags developed.

Progress
From Setbacks to Living Together

They indeed did develop, sometimes in relation to outside events, most times not.

After Israel had expelled 415 accused extremists to southern Lebanon in mid-December as a response to a series of killings by Hamas, the Washington talks broke down, not to resume for four months. But the Oslo Connection held.

In March, however, another wave of killings in Israel led to a sealing-off of the territories, and the grim atmosphere spread to Norway. "There was a feeling that we were somewhat lost and couldn't get ahead," Professor Hirschfield said. But the crisis passed, he added, in part because the United States officials who were aware of the contacts since early November had encouraged them to continue.

At the point, neither Mr. Peres no Mr. Rabin reportedly was in the picture.

Yet Abu Alaa and Professor Hirschfield—as early as their second Norway session in February—had already drawn up a draft agreement, what would prove to be the first of many.

By this point, the concept of linking Gaza and Jericho had been introduced.

Transferring a limited form of self-rule to Palestinians in Gaza first was no problem for the Israelis. Increasingly, they viewed the overcrowded coastal strip as nothing but a political and financial headache, a seething source of terrorism and a death trap for Israeli soldiers forced to patrol its towns and refugee camps. Give it up, a large majority of Israelis said.

But to whom?

For Mr. Arafat, Gaza alone was no prize. If he were to agree to Israel's demand that for now he put aside discussion of Jerusalem's future and the final status of the territories, he wanted more: a foothold in the West Bank to underline the point that the territories are a single unit forming his hoped-for Palestinian state.

Small and sleepy Jericho seemed the right place, but it was hardly without problems. For one thing, the Israelis insisted that during an interim self-rule period they remain in control of the bridge links to Jordan. For another, they rejected Palestinian demands for a "corridor" of their own across Israel to connect Gaza and Jericho. Arguments on these and other points would consume another half-year.

Still, there was a piece of paper, and that was something. "We had mapped out the geography of the Rubicon," Professor Hirschfield said.

In March, Mr. Beilin, who himself never went to Norway, decided that he had to take what he knew to Mr. Peres. According to knowledgeable officials, the Foreign Minister expressed interest but was far from overwhelmed. He took several weeks to read the draft.

It proved to be an important period for Mr. Peres. He has an active mind, and was known to be frustrated by Mr. Rabin's tight personal hold on responsibility for the direct negotiations between Israel and the Palestinians and neighboring Arab nations. If he were to supervise the back-channel talks in Norway and not tell the Prime Minister, it would look to many like another attempt at an end run in the eternal Rabin-Peres rivalry.

Besides, Mr. Rabin would know something was up from intelligence reports. "Yitzhak is informed twice about every one of Peres' actions," an unidentified Government official told the newspaper Yediot Ahronot this week. "Once, Peres tells him about it, and a little earlier he learns about it from the security services."

In April, having read the Abu Alaa-Hirschfield draft, Mr. Peres went to the Prime Minister. Officials say they coordinated their efforts from then on. If anything, they say, Mr. Rabin was more skeptical than the Foreign Minister. Nevertheless, losing patience with the regular Washington channel, he decided the secret talks were worth a try, regardless of his personal feelings about the P.L.O.

"I am ready for painful compromises," he said this week. "In general, peace is not made with friends. Peace is made with enemies, some of whom—and I won't name names—I loathe very much."

It was also decided in April that the Norway talks had to be raised to an official level. Abu Alaa reportedly had begun to insist on dealing directly with a Government official as a test that Jerusalem meant business and was not engaged merely in an academic exercise.

The designated official was Uri Savir, recently installed as Foreign Ministry director general, a senior job rarely given to someone so young, only 40. "He's a brilliant diplomat, very charming and also deeply committed to the cause of peace," said Professor Hirschfield, who remained on the Israeli team throughout.

Another important addition was Yoel Zinger, an Israeli lawyer who had moved to Washington to join a law firm there. Mr. Zinger was an expert on international law and had drafted agreements that ended Israel's invasion of Lebanon a decade ago. Perhaps as significant, he was an army reserve officer who had Mr. Rabin's respect and trust. Indeed, a knowledgeable official says, it was Mr. Zinger who ultimately persuaded the Prime Minister in early summer "that this was a serious arrangement, that if the other side knew Israel was serious, it could lead to vital concessions."

From the end of April when Mr. Savir took charge to late August, there were 11 meetings in Norway, with Abu Alaa joined by a P.L.O. legal adviser, Taher Shash.

These sessions moved from place to place: another country estate, in Grinsheim, near Lillehammer; a labor union hall north of Oslo; several hotels in downtown Oslo, and Foreign Minister Holst's roomy house in Hoff, on the outskirts of the capital.

In each location, participants say, the key was a relaxed atmosphere. Israelis and Palestinians lived together in the same house for days at a stretch, taking all meals together, drinking and chatting well into the night. At the Holst home, Mrs. Heiberg, the Foreign Minister's wife, served home-cooked meals and Chilean wines.

"We had to take dietary rules into account," Mr. Holst said, "and we ate a lot of lamb."

And there were the jokes passed back and forth.

"They shared a sense of humor," Mr. Larsen said of Abu Alaa and Mr. Savir. "Each time tension rose, it was broken off by some joke or by a cryptic reference to a joke they all understood."

"It was an informal relationship—intense, complex, characterized by passionate and silent poetry," he said.

During the discussions, a form of verbal shorthand developed in which people like Mr. Peres and Mr. Holst were called the fathers, top leaders like Mr. Rabin and Mr. Arafat became the godfathers, and officials at Mr. Beilin's level were the sons.

"Has the father talked to the godfather about this?" one would ask.

"Yes," came the reply. "He told the son yesterday that he would like to have another meeting."

"We had hundreds of such calls," Mr. Egeland said.

Final Issues
The Agreement is Concluded

But jokes and shared meals, officials say, did not camouflage the fundamental difficulties involved in hammering out an agreement between two peoples whose mutual suspicions and hatreds had not miraculously disappeared by a Norwegian fireside.

"All of us were skeptical throughout," Professor Hirschfield said. "The potential for failure lasted throughout, and there were lots of ups and downs in July."

He declined to say what they were. But officials say problems remained over control of the Allenby Bridge crossing into Jordan, the "corridor" issue and a persistent resurfacing of Jerusalem's status, an issue that the Israelis insisted was absolutely not negotiable at this stage.

During the summer, another issue arose: mutual recognition by Israel and the P.L.O., on condition that the Palestinian group abandon terrorism as a tactic and drop sections of its covenant calling for Israel's destruction.

With Israeli recognition, the United States is considered likely to resume its talks with the P.L.O. This central issue is apparently one reason that the expected P.L.O. approval of the draft agreement has slowed down in the last few days.

As the Israeli officials in Norway fielded each of these new problems, they asked for guidance from Jerusalem, where Mr. Rabin and Mr. Peres reportedly put together the replies in secrecy. But there was also a perceived need here for "reality checks."

One such check was a trip to Cairo in June by Nimrod Novick, a close Peres associate. There, he learned of Mr. Arafat's favorable response to the Gaza-Jericho plan through Osama al-Baz, foreign affairs adviser to President Hosni Mubarek of Egypt.

Another check was a meeting in Cairo in late July between Environment Minister Yossi Sarid and Nabil Shaath, a senior P.L.O. figure. The same month, yet another session was held in Jerusalem by Health Minister Haim Ramon and Dr. Ahmed Tibi, an Israeli Arab who is close to Mr. Arafat.

None of these contacts altered the fact that the real channel was in Norway.

In August, Mr. Savir told Mr. Peres that a deal was at hand. Gaza-Jericho and mutual recognition were in the plan, as were Israeli control of the borders and an outline for economic cooperation. Gone were the Jerusalem question for now, the Gaza-Jericho corridor and the Allenby Bridge dispute.

On Aug. 19, Mr. Peres flew to Oslo, ostensibly as part of a routine trip to Scandinavia. Late that night, after all the dinner guests had gone, he climbed the stairs of the government guest house. Waiting for him in a large room was Abu Alaa. The two men shook hands as they met for the first time.

Officials say the actual initialing of the agreement was done by Abu Alaa and by Mr. Savir. Mr. Peres could not act since his fellow Cabinet ministers had not given their formal approval. But the Foreign Minister's presence there in the early hours of Aug. 20 affirmed that it had the blessing of the Israeli Government at the highest levels. Early that morning, the newspaper *Maariv* reported, Mr. Peres phoned Mr. Rabin at home, awakening him.

"We signed," he said.

"Mazel tov," the Prime Minister reportedly replied. "Good work."

There was still much to be done. The Washington-oriented Mr. Rabin sent his Foreign Minister to California last week to show the agreement in secret to the vacationing Secretary of State, Warren Christopher. Israel also wanted the Americans to overstate the role they had played in the negotiations, on the theory that Israelis might be persuaded to accept the plan more easily if they viewed it as something Washington really wanted. But the Americans balked at the idea.

Now, the formal signing of the accord has been delayed by disputes within the P.L.O. But the man who was there from the beginning, Yair Hirschfield, is convinced that it is only a matter of time.

He has already crossed his Rubicon, he said: "If I understand anything about politics, we reached the point of no return." •

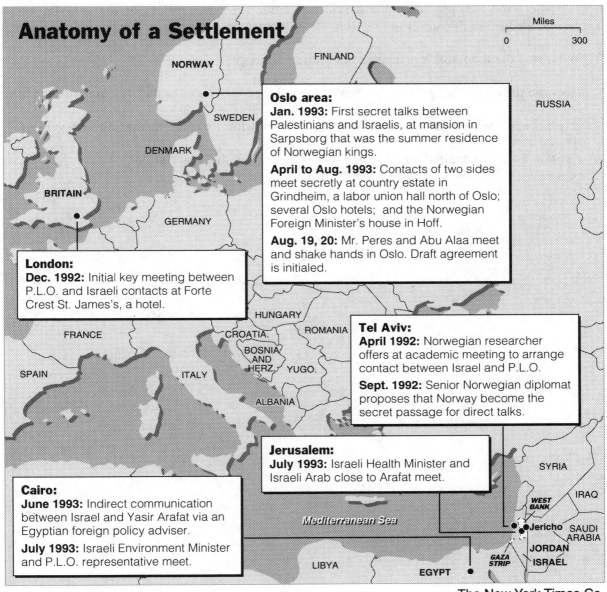

Anatomy of a Settlement

Miles
0   300

Oslo area:

Jan. 1993: First secret talks between Palestinians and Israelis, at mansion in Sarpsborg that was the summer residence of Norwegian kings.

April to Aug. 1993: Contacts of two sides meet secretly at country estate in Grindheim, a labor union hall north of Oslo; several Oslo hotels; and the Norwegian Foreign Minister's house in Hoff.

Aug. 19, 20: Mr. Peres and Abu Alaa meet and shake hands in Oslo. Draft agreement is initialed.

London:

Dec. 1992: Initial key meeting between P.L.O. and Israeli contacts at Forte Crest St. James's, a hotel.

Tel Aviv:

April 1992: Norwegian researcher offers at academic meeting to arrange contact between Israel and P.L.O.

Sept. 1992: Senior Norwegian diplomat proposes that Norway become the secret passage for direct talks.

Jerusalem:

July 1993: Israeli Health Minister and Israeli Arab close to Arafat meet.

Cairo:

June 1993: Indirect communication between Israel and Yasir Arafat via an Egyptian foreign policy adviser.

July 1993: Israeli Environment Minister and P.L.O. representative meet.

The New York Times Co.

Study Questions

The article describes a conflict relationship which resulted in a negotiated agreement through mediation. The mediation process is applicable to a variety of relationships characterized by little trust, conflict, and meager faith in achieving an agreement. Regardless of the specific context dispute, the mediation dynamics are similar across situations.

1. What was the mediator's primary intervention strategy?

2. How did the mediators gain the parties' trust and then facilitate the parties' trust in each other?

3. Explain the changes in the negotiation process resulting from the mediation intervention.

4. Explain how "attitudinal structuring" was important in the negotiations.